THE POLEMICS OF POSSESSION
IN SPANISH AMERICAN NARRATIVE

ROLENA ADORNO

The Polemics of Possession in Spanish American Narrative

YALE UNIVERSITY PRESS   NEW HAVEN & LONDON

Published with assistance from the foundation established in memory of Philip Hamilton McMillan of the Class of 1894, Yale College.

Set in Scala Roman and Scala Sans by Keystone Typesetting, Inc.
Printed in the United States of America.

Library of Congress Cataloging-in-Publication Data

Adorno, Rolena.
The polemics of possession in Spanish American narrative / Rolena Adorno.
p. cm.
Includes bibliographical references and index.
ISBN-13: 978-0-300-12020-2 (hardback)
ISBN-10: 978-0-300-21476-5 (paperback)

1. Spanish American fiction—To 1800—History and criticism. 2. Latin America—Civilization—16th century. 3. Latin America—Civilization—17th century. 4. Spain—In literature. 5. Imperialism in literature. 6. Colonies in literature. I. Title.
PQ7082.N7A256 2007
863'.30998—dc22

2007015551

A catalogue record for this book is available from the British Library.

The paper in this book meets the guidelines for permanence and durability of the Committee on Production Guidelines for Book Longevity of the Council on Library Resources.

CONTENTS

The Polemics of Possession is the culmination of three decades of research and reflection about colonial texts and their legacies. The etymological resonances of *polemics* and *possession* are intentional, if only metaphorical. *Polemical* as *warlike* harks back to the ancient Greeks, even though the term as we know it has its sixteenth- and seventeenth-century origins in the field of theological disputation and its Enlightenment-era plenitude in many other types of disputation and controversy. My choice of the term derives from this later, broader usage, even though its referential echoes of war and religion are central to my inquiry. *Possession,* too, has many resonances. I use it first and foremost here in its meaning as a concept of law, as it relates to physical control and implies ownership, actual or asserted, or occupancy and actual control without ownership, and the ownership or control, for example, of war captives as slaves. "Poseer" and "posesión" were used in Castilian at the time in this legal sense, as evidenced by Bartolomé de las Casas's use of the term in the expression "to have and to possess," referring nonredundantly to Amerindian societies' actual and legal (de facto and de jure) possession over their "princedoms, kingdoms, states, high offices, territorial jurisdictions, and domains." I also use *possession* in its broader sense, as defined by Sebastián de Covarrubias's Castilian dictionary of 1611 and exemplified in the *Oxford English Dictionary* as "holding or having something (material or immaterial) as one's own or in one's control." Thus I expand its use beyond concepts of sovereignty and the ownership of lands to include those of the practice of governance and self-governance, the enjoyment of the full exercise of human intellect and reason, and the actual or perceived holding of authority, be it political, historical, or literary.

In the territorial sense, *possession* cannot do without the preparation of, or recourse to, a map or chart. The reader will find many maps in this volume, one of the earliest being a fragment of a world map, dated 1527 and attributed to Hernando Colón, and the latest, the maps that Patrick Pautz and I created in 1999 for our study of Álvar Núñez Cabeza de Vaca's La Florida account and his other continent-spanning endeavors. But there is one map that until recently had been missing, and it is the earliest of all those that are relevant. To my great dismay, when I was preparing to show this unusual map to my graduate seminar at Yale's Beinecke Rare Book and Manuscript Library in the fall of 2006, I learned that this map, the first published European representation of a New World city, had disappeared. The Beinecke publicly announced that it had gone missing from its collections in June 2005. The map comes from *Praeclara de Nova Maris oceani Hyspania narratio* (1524), the Latin edition of Hernán Cortés's second and third letters, the Spanish-language original of the second having been signed by him on October 30, 1520, and published in Seville in 1522 (fig. 1). The famous second letter is the most spectacular of Cortés's five letters to his emperor, Charles V, because it describes events that include the decision to conquer Mexico, the Spanish march to the Mexica (Aztec) capital of México-Tenochtitlán, Cortés's brilliant description of the city, his reception by the Mexica lord Moctezuma, the imprisonment and death of Moctezuma, and the Spaniards' retreat on the fateful night of June 30, 1520 ("la Noche Triste").

The consummate mastery of Cortés's narration is matched by the powerful graphic rendering of the city. It is accompanied by a map of the Gulf of Mexico that had been the object of my close attention in my coauthored 1999 study of Cabeza de Vaca, but for my 2006 graduate seminar I wanted my students to examine the map, part cosmological, part historical, of México-Tenochtitlán. Here the island city floats in its own lagoon, and, with its neatly arranged buildings and towers, evokes Venice more than the Indies. All similarity ends there, however, for at the center of the map a headless idol in human form is depicted with racks of

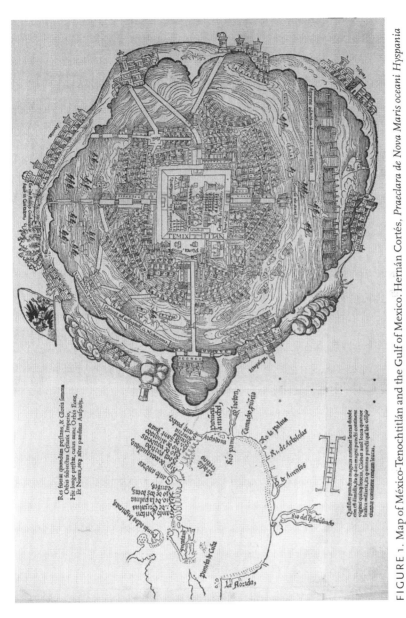

FIGURE 1. Map of México-Tenochtitlán and the Gulf of Mexico. Hernán Cortés, *Praeclara de Nova Maris oceani Hyspania narratio*. Nuremberg: F. Peypus, 1524. Beinecke Rare Book and Manuscript Library, Yale University.

skulls beneath its feet, thus displaying the unspeakable horror of human sacrifice described in Cortés's account. Charles V's imperial banner flies triumphantly on the mainland shore: civilization confronts barbarity. When Cortés completed his second letter in 1520, it was not certain that victory in Mexico would fall to the Spanish. By the publication of the *Praeclara de Nova Maris oceani Hyspania narratio* volume in 1524, however, the Aztec confederation had collapsed, having succumbed three years earlier to Cortés, his men, and their armies of Mexican allies. The map of México-Tenochtitlán celebrates the conquered city's splendor. The hand coloring of the woodcut in the edition owned by the Newberry Library, Chicago, with its jewel-like tones of emerald and turquoise and touches of primary red and yellow, makes the map shine like a war trophy.

The 1524 map evokes the themes of this study. It has its Inca empire counterpart in a graphic representation that combines Andean cosmology and European pictorial conventions to represent the viceroyalty of Peru, founded a few years after that of New Spain (see fig. 11). The Peruvian *mapamundi* of Felipe Guaman Poma de Ayala is not a woodcut but a pen-and-ink drawing. Together, these two depictions symbolize the introduction of European culture into the sites, México-Tenochtitlán and Cuzco, of the highest levels of pre-Columbian civilization of their day. Both maps aspire to, or anticipate, a new social-political-religious regime superimposed on the foundations of an autochthonous American order.

These maps are portraits, but they are portraits that tend to idealize. They reflect the imposition of a new order and the attempt to portray that new order. To impose, and then to portray, are the sequential, founding procedures of colonialism. But in these sixteenth- and seventeenth-century maps evoking ancient Mexico and Peru, the imposition of foreign rule has already taken place. The events are past, the historical referents are long gone; all that remains are the real consequences of those acts of imposition and the writings that describe, interpret, and justify or condemn them. These are the works, some created by writers who were European and others by writers who belonged to Amerindian traditions, that I discuss here. But these works were scattered in location, and they differed in culture and learning; academically, they had been absorbed into various national literatures or excluded from them. It seemed to me there must be a link among them, and I found such a link in the voluminous writings of Bartolomé de las Casas and the brief works of Juan

Ginés de Sepúlveda, whose respective *Brevísima relación de la destrucción de las Indias* and *Demócrates Segundo* might both be called the tail that wagged the dog, that is, the minor work that had a major impact. After reading the unique and now ubiquitous *El primer nueva corónica y buen gobierno* by Guaman Poma I had many questions about the controversies produced by colonialism. Guaman Poma led me to Las Casas, and Las Casas led me to Sepúlveda; soon I found that all the writers who are commonly read in the colonial canon could be inserted into the Las Casas–Sepúlveda matrix. In relation to one another and in various direct and indirect ways they inevitably took positions on the fate of the American lands, their resources, and, most of all, their peoples.

This book is thus my attempt to offer a sustained argument about the centrality of the "polemics of possession" in Spanish American literature that follows the topic through the early "historical" writings and ends with reflections provided by contemporary fiction. I have eschewed comprehensive coverage, and I focus instead on a few writers whose works I have considered in depth and in relation to one another. The chapter-by-chapter organization traces the elaboration and persistence of colonial debates cast in narrative form, posits the importance of literary authority over historical testimony, and ends by exploring their literary legacy today.

Chapter 1 lays out the problems and principles I have discovered in these early texts. Chapter 2 examines the historical personage of Guaman Poma and his chronicle, in particular with regard to his reading of Las Casas. Because my readings of the *Nueva corónica y buen gobierno* motivated the questions about conquest polemics and literary authority I address in this book, this chapter provides their first exposition. Chapter 3 is devoted to Las Casas; here, too, I focus briefly on his life and lay out his writings on the grid of his reformist career. This is not a chapter of textual analysis as such, but it is essential to a minimal understanding of Las Casas, one of the most controversial figures in the Spain of his day (and in Europe and Latin America for centuries afterward). Chapter 4 takes up the major writings and positions in the Spanish debates on the rights to conquest. Las Casas, seen alone in chapter 3, is here positioned in counterpoint to his major interlocutors, Juan Ginés de Sepúlveda, and also Francisco de Vitoria. Chapter 5 turns from arguments advocating the establishment of royal policy to the writing of history, and now Sepúlveda has moved from one chamber, that of court councilor, to another, that of historian. He is appropriately accompanied by like-minded historians such as Francisco López de Gómara and by an heir of the Mexican House of Texcoco, Fernando de Alva Ixtlilxochitl, who takes another view. Ixtlilxochitl's perspective may be oppositional in intent, but it is complementary in realization, insofar as the colonized cannot easily afford to take a radically oppositional stance. Chapters 6 and 7 take up the retelling of history from the perspective of the nonelite, that is, the eyewitness foot soldier. At midpoint in this book and occupying two chapters, Bernal Díaz del Castillo plays a pivotal, Janus-like role, looking back to the debates on royal policy (in which he participated) and forward to the establishment of his own literary authority.

Chapter 8 lies squarely in the domain of representation (to the European reader) of the never before seen. Here, the issue is not the representation of the magnificence of the city of México-Tenochtitlán but rather the magnificence and strangeness of American civilizations, their gods, their customs, and their heroes, as portrayed in works that are variously historical, ethnographic, and poetic. The remarkable map of México-Tenochtitlán pulsates here; attraction and repulsion in equal measure produce a riveting fascination and also provoke the exercise of censorship. Chapters 9 and 10 are opposite sides of the same coin: the Spanish mariner/conquistador "gone native." Gonzalo Guerrero is all but a literary invention; Cabeza de Vaca is a historical figure so real that invention of some of his attributes has been the only recourse of an ongoing, ever-evolving cultural tradition. Both Gonzalo and Cabeza de Vaca have generated enduring myths about the first Europeans marooned and held captive in America. Chapter 11 moves from the work of Cabeza de Vaca to that of El Inca Garcilaso de la Vega, as I continue my argument about how, to assert their own historical authority, writers take up earlier writers (El Inca Garcilaso reading Cabeza de Vaca) in order to establish a credibility that claims to be historical but is in fact literary. As Garcilaso looks back to Cabeza de Vaca, he anticipates, in the Borgesian sense of a precursor, the writings of twentieth-century novelists (Juan Rulfo, Gabriel García Márquez) with respect to the literary creation of place. Chapter 12 takes up the re-creation of historical figures (Las Casas, Christopher Columbus) in the novels of Reinaldo Arenas and Alejo Carpentier. Taken together, chapters 11 and 12 demonstrate how literary tradition critically reincorporates historical antecedents into its themes and, therefore, how old books and (seemingly) outdated ideas do, in fact, matter.

I present my arguments in the conviction, based on many years of study, that Latin American literature today, or at least Latin American literature through the period of the literary Boom in the 1960s and 1970s, cannot be read without (or, rather, is best read with) its antecedents from the Spanish colonial era. Just as the Renaissance was in part defined and enriched by the rediscovery of Greek and Latin classical literature, I believe that the Boom was partially defined and definitely enriched by the rediscovery of the writings of the Spanish conquest and colonial era.

But what of the missing map, newly recovered, and the book from which it had been (criminally, as we learned recently) removed? Because of federal and state law enforcement and insurance investigations the book was inaccessible for almost two years; now that those investigations have been completed, the book and its map have become available for public, scholarly use once more. (In other words, possession, as physical control and as legal ownership, has been restored.)

Books have long been sequestered. In the Spanish colonial era, sequestration was mandated if not accomplished by ecclesiastical and civil authorities to prevent the dissemination of ideas; now, in the twenty-first century, it is more often undertaken by state and federal agencies of law enforcement, as in the recent case mentioned here, to catch and convict a thief. In the first chapter of this book, I describe the history of Spain's America as the story of a paradise lost. Lost to us, nowadays, are many of the maps and charts that, in the fifteenth and sixteenth centuries, were guarded as state secrets; their absence today represents the loss of universal cultural patrimony. Depictions of faraway or unknown places, in words or graphic images, are intriguing, mysterious, interpretation-heavy, and interpretively insufficient. The objective of this book, imagined as a hypothetical map of Spanish American colonial letters, is to survey and describe its familiar and unfamiliar regions, some of them already exploited but not cultivated and therefore still rightfully designated as terra incognita.

I have incorporated in this book many illustrations for whose reproduction I am grateful to the lending institutions cited; the reader will find references to these figures in the index. As evidence for my arguments, I provide quotations from many sixteenth- and seventeenth-century Spanish-language works as well as their English translations. Unless otherwise credited, the translations into English are my own. Much of my previous work has been crucial to the creation of this book, and I gratefully acknowledge the prior publication of articles and book chapters that are listed under my name in the bibliography and cited in the endnotes where appropriate. Here they have been recast and transformed into arguments aimed at showing how the narrative web created by writers in sixteenth- and early seventeenth-century Spain and America constitutes the living core of the Spanish American literary tradition.

ACKNOWLEDGMENTS

Because this book has been a long time in the making, the debts of gratitude I owe go back many years. Ever the student, I have always desired to present any newly finished work to my teachers. Four of mine are not here to receive this book, and they departed in the following order: Irving A. Leonard (1896–1996), whose *Books of the Brave* inspired me in the 1970s, and whose collaborator I became in the 1992 edition of that work and, most recently, in the posthumous, commemorative edition of 2006 published by the Fondo de Cultura Económica, Mexico City. If longevity was ever accompanied by grace and good wit, it was personified in Professor Leonard, whose ninety-ninth and last birthday my husband, David, and I shared. David S. Adorno (1927–2003) is the gravest of these four losses; our life's loving companionship, his devotion to my work, from the moment he said to me, on New Year's Eve in 1970, "I think you should go to graduate school," through the days just after New Year's in 2003, when his mortal struggle prevented him from reading the words I was writing, his support has been the major fact of my life. The next of these teachers was the inimitable Lascasista, the independent scholar Helen Rand Parish (1912–2005). Helen's scholarly pursuit of the life and writings of Bartolomé de las Casas, from the Vatican Library in Rome to the Bancroft Library in Berkeley, will always be remembered. Finally, John V. Murra (1916–2006), who breathed his last during the very days when I was writing these words, was the greatest of teachers, for the example of his single-minded devotion to the pursuit of knowledge about the ancient Andes, his intellectual generosity, and his help in teaching me how to write. Our collaboration in studying and editing the chronicle of Guaman Poma, which lasted from the typewriter age to the era of the Internet, stands as a testament to what I owe him.

In the category of teacher *and* colleague, Roberto González Echevarría occupies a unique place. His days as one of my Cornell professors in the early 1970s turn out to have been a mere preamble to the cordial and stimulating friendship I enjoy with him as his colleague at Yale, where our ongoing exchange of ideas has become a congenial habit. His encouragement and support for this book have accompanied me every step of the way, and his confidence in my work has strengthened my own. In the disorienting days (years) that followed the loss of my husband, David, Roberto made sure I did not lose sight of my work or where it was headed.

Family members, too, have been important in more ways than they know. My daughters, Pamela Fitch, Patricia Madden, Margaret Adorno, and Penny Towery, predated, tolerated, and continue to witness my life in scholarship, aiding and abetting it in numerous and loving ways. My niece, Kim Klahn Pearson, has taken a special interest in my work for many years, occasionally providing me with an out-of-print book germane to whatever topic I was pursuing, and, when visiting, sitting side by side with me at the computer or cheerfully enduring the hours when I sat there alone. My brother and sister-in-law, Delmar and Beverly Klahn, spent the penultimate days of work on this project with me, adding a welcome and intimate experience to our long life together. From my upstairs study window, as I watched my brother transform my garden, ridding it of wild overgrowth and dead branches, I hoped I was making equivalent progress in readying this book for readers. Ours has been an inspiring comradeship. One of my deepest inspirations comes from the memory of our parents, LeRoy Klahn and Hilda Lage Klahn, who taught me that a thinking life, accompanied by industriousness, is a worthy goal.

My friends on Blake Road deserve special mention. Serendipitous geographic proximity gave me, a decade ago, neighbors who have become treasured friends. Ellen and Leonard Milstone and Ann and Sidney Altman, each in his and her unique and special manner, have surrounded me with a fortress of friendship and supported me in ways too numerous to mention, including many timely suppers and much dinner table companionship. Ann Altman sat with me for hours and days, helping me complete and check this book's bibliography and editing some of my prose. She has shared with me each historic moment of this book's near completion and completion. Also to be recognized are Stuart Gardner and Renée Chotiner, Michael Vollmar and Paulette Rosen, and Lincoln Caplan and Susan Carney; their caring concern and lighted windows in predawn mornings and long late evenings are welcome daily companions.

And then there are the students who have become friends and colleagues in this vocation or other professions, and who, while I thought I was teaching them, have taught me. From Syracuse University to the University of Michigan, from Princeton University to Yale, and including the University of Salta, Argentina, they are Susana Jákfalvi-Leiva, Cynthia Leigh Stone, Osvaldo Fabián Pardo, Eyda M. Merediz, José Antonio Mazzotti, Andrew M. Shapiro, Paul Swigart, Cristián Roa-de-la-Carrera, Beatriz de Alba-Koch, Victoria Campos, María de Jesús Cordero, Elena M. Altuna, José Antonio Rodríguez Garrido, John Charles, Fernanda Macchi, Jonathan Carlyon, Patricio Boyer, and José Cárdenas Bunsen. The fact that each one is part of my life today reveals to me the permanence of the pleasures generated by our shared humanistic pursuits.

Patrick Charles Pautz is part of the above group but stands out from it at the same time, as my coauthor on *Álvar Núñez Cabeza de Vaca: His Account, His Life, and the Expedition of Pánfilo de Narváez*. As I turned to our book countless times in the course of completing *The Polemics of Possession*, I appreciated again and again the fruits of our decade-long collaboration and the enduring quality of our friendship.

Ivan Boserup, Keeper of Manuscripts and Rare Books at the Royal Library, Copenhagen, also deserves my thanks. Ivan has taught me a great deal about the codicological study of manuscripts, from our examination of the Guaman Poma manuscript in 2001–2002 through our continuing comparison of the manuscripts of Guaman Poma and Fray Martín de Murúa. His learning as a classical philologist has enhanced our common work, and as an interlocutor he has been deferential but also demanding. His stewardship of the manuscript catalogued as Copenhagen, Royal Library, GkS, 2232, 4to (the autograph manuscript of Guaman Poma) merits the gratitude of scholars worldwide in all fields of Hispanic, Latin American, and colonial studies. Also in Copenhagen, Marianne Alenius, Director of the Museum Tusculanum Press, has my grateful appreciation for the publication of *Guaman Poma and His Illustrated Chronicle* and for the inimitable Scandinavian hospitality with which she and Ivan have generously opened their home to David and me, and then to me. The Director of the Royal Library of Denmark, Erland Kolding Nielsen, has provided the executive vision and collegial support essential for the successful pursuit of scholarship.

Raquel Chang-Rodríguez, colleague and friend, exemplifies a deep conviction about the value of literary and historical colonial studies on Latin America. Her personal commitment, realized in the conceptualization, foundation, general editorship (1992–2003), and ongoing stewardship of the *Colonial Latin American Review,* has provided a needed forum in colonial studies across the disciplines. Her support of my work and her steadfast friendship, from our first meeting in Pittsburgh in 1979 and especially through the dark days after the loss of David, are hereby gratefully acknowledged. Other longtime friends in the profession, Regina Harrison, Maureen Ahern, Verónica Salles-Reese, and Birgit Scharlau, are also fondly remembered.

In addition to Roberto González Echevarría, other friends at Yale, whose daily departmental life I've shared, cannot be overlooked: Josefina Ludmer, María Rosa Menocal, and Noël Valis have provided good cheer and comradery of a very special kind in the Yale fraternity of which we are sisters. Sandra Guardo's deep literary culture and tireless devotion to our department have been a source of ongoing support to me, not only in my role as department chair, but also as teacher and scholar. The cordial support of Emily P. Bakemeier, Associate Provost, has helped me to manage this triad of complex academic and administrative responsibilities.

Three friends, far away but always in mind, must be recognized: Kenneth J. Andrien, historian of colonial Latin America; Susan M. Hartmann, historian of the contemporary United States; and James Axtell, historian of colonial North America. Ken has been my coeditor on *Transatlantic Encounters: Europeans and Andeans in the Sixteenth Century,* a colleague on the editorial board of *Colonial Latin American Review,* and a stimulating interlocutor since our days together on the faculty at the Ohio State University. With Susan, also an Ohio State colleague and my running partner in Columbus and sometimes Ann Arbor and Princeton (we take walks in New Haven and Hamden), I have shared much conversation about our intellectual and professional lives, as well as many revitalizing visits in Columbus and Hamden. Jim's has been the one voice, heard if not heeded over many, many years, urging me to write this book. I now complete it and put it in his hands, if for no other reason than to silence, with gratitude, his gentle but insistent nudging.

First and last, however, are the librarians and curators. First, because with their help the work of scholarship begins; last, because the final words written tend to include (have included, in my case) the insertion of forgotten bibliographic entries and the incorporation of graphic illustrations. Carrying out these last tasks, in their myriad details, has triggered my recollections of the exhilaration I have always felt when crossing the thresholds of the research libraries where my study of old books and manuscripts has been conducted. I recognize, with gratitude and respect, Norman Fiering, Director and Librarian Emeritus, Susan Danforth, Assistant Librarian for Library Operations and Curator of Maps and Prints, and Richard Hurley, truly a photographer extraordinaire, all of the John Carter Brown Library, Providence, Rhode Island; Richard A. Ryan, former Curator of Books, and David Bosse, former Curator of Maps, at the William L. Clements Library, Ann Arbor, Michigan; Richard H. Brown, former Academic Vice President, Paul F. Gehl, Custodian of the John M. Wing Foundation on the History of Printing, Robert W. Karrow, Jr., Curator of Special Collections and Curator of Maps, and John S. Aubrey, Ayer Librarian, at the Newberry Library, Chicago, Illinois. At Yale, César Rodríguez, Curator of the Latin American Collection, Sterling Memorial Library, and George A. Miles, Curator of the Western Americana Collection, Beinecke Rare Book and Manuscript Library, are treasured colleagues who over the years have provided needed information and access to rare materials, many times on short notice and always with consummate expertise. Frank M. Turner, Director of the Beinecke Library and Associate University Librarian, and Alice Prochaska, University Librarian, have provided friendship and inspiration through the values that we deeply share.

At Yale University Press I have benefited greatly from the keen discernment and deft editorial guidance of Lawrence Kenney, Senior Manuscript Editor.

To each and every one of the aforementioned persons, I give my heartfelt thanks.

I gratefully and lovingly dedicate this book to the memory of David Samuel Adorno, mathematician and lifelong humanist.

CHAPTER 1

Overview

THE POLEMICS OF POSSESSION IN
SPANISH AMERICAN NARRATIVE

COLONIAL SPANISH AMERICAN LETTERS OCCUPY a central place in the tradition of Latin American literature and the cultural history of the hemisphere. The greatest Latin American writers of our times confirm it; the earliest writers of North America could not have founded the national literature of the United States without it. The life of Christopher Columbus provided the theme for the great, final work of one of Latin America's preeminent novelists in the twentieth century, and it was the topic of the first important historical study undertaken in the United States in the early decades of the nineteenth.[1] This interest is not confined to our hemisphere. Spain's cultural commerce in this domain is marked by the continual publication of the colonial era's firsthand accounts, chronicles, and histories, beginning in earnest in the nineteenth century after their eighteenth-century "rediscovery."[2] Footnotes to this history of publication and reading are the statues occasionally erected to conquest-era figures: Álvar Núñez Cabeza de Vaca in Jerez de la Frontera, Andalusia; Francisco Pizarro in Trujillo, Extremadura; Gonzalo Guerrero in Mérida, Yucatán; the viceroy Francisco de Toledo in Salta, Argentina; Felipe Guaman Poma de Ayala in Sondondo, Peru. In short, the publication, study, and fictionalization of colonial Spanish American writing on three continents, plus the sculpted commemoration of some of its key figures, attest to how the polemics of literal and symbolic possession link the cultural histories of now-disparate national literary traditions to one another and to their common past.

Early writings about Latin America have endured over the centuries and across cultures because of the story they tell: it is the tale of the arrival in Paradise, the expulsion from it, and resettlement in a world that was not, in any case, new.[3] This sounds like the Europeans' story, but it is not only theirs. The precious legacy of indigenous Americans' interpretive testimonies, although limited in number, reveals that it is also their story, told from another angle. Paradise existed in the hopes of the Europeans and colored their expeditionary expectations; the paradise of the Amerindians, living within their own domains, was also governed by hopes and dreams. It was not without its wars and conflicts, but it was theirs. The natural expanse, bounty, and beauty of the Antilles, Mexico, Central America, and the Andes provided opportunity for the Europeans to name the newly found places and their flora and fauna, but they could not have done so without the naming already done by the Taínos of the Antilles, the Nahuas of the central valley of Mexico, and the Quechua speakers of the former Inca empire of Tawantinsuyu. The names they have left us—such as, from Taíno, hammock, hurricane, canoe, cacique—are their (and our) enduring legacy.

Events soon overcame expectations—the Europeans', of the natives' peaceful submission and conversion to Christianity, the Amerindians', of hospitality peacefully offered and graciously received—and all were expelled from their respective paradises. Here the polemics of possession begins. Resettlement and reconfiguration follow, occupying the longest part of the tale: the new settlement of Europeans in America, the Amerindians' forced resettlement when being removed from their traditional home areas to locations where their labor was demanded. The reconfigurations were of blood, producing "the greatest racial mixing that has ever been contemplated" and resulting in extraordinary symbioses of "cultures, beliefs, and popular arts."[4] These stories, told over and over again during the period of Spain's dominion in the Americas, were in one way exceptional and in another universal. That is, the "New" World was defined as such by Europeans, but the notion of a paradise, by whatever name in whatever European or Amerindian language, was a common human aspiration. These simultaneously exceptional and universal dimensions account for the fascination with the Spanish colonial literary

tradition by its far-flung readerships, its reformulations in literature today, and its reinterpretations in literary criticism and scholarship.

The recovery and study of this long literary tradition began in Latin
America when the first histories of the national literatures were written in
the nineteenth century, but systematic treatment began in the 1940s. On
the brink of World War II and throughout the war years, Latin American
intellectuals and critics teaching and lecturing in the United States consolidated for themselves and their English-speaking audiences new visions of Latin American literary experience.[5] The writings of the colonial
era were the rock on which they founded their formulations, and they
conceptualized continuities and transformations of themes that led from
the late fifteenth century to the twentieth.[6] Colonial Spanish American
writing became the sine qua non for explaining the literary life of Latin
America. The most potent development, however, was not explanatory
and scholarly but literary and creative. The sixteenth-century accounts of
encounter, conflict, and destruction have kindled the imaginations of
Latin America's novelists from the post–World War II years to the present. The best of Latin America's writers renewed these narratives and
transformed them, making them vital and pertinent, that is, making them
our stories, too.[7]

Also in the 1940s, pioneering Hispanist scholars of Anglo-American
tradition, in dialogue with their Latin American peers, brought the study
of colonial Spanish America squarely into the U.S. academy.[8] The development of these lines of research accelerated in the 1960s, when the
U.S. government and North American universities began to invest in
Latin American studies in the wake of the Cuban Revolution. Latin Americanist studies in the humanities were further developed in the 1970s,
which was when I began my own scholarly work in Spanish and Spanish
American colonial literature. Interest in the colonial field continued into
the 1990s, when a burst of new interest was spurred by the Columbian
Quincentenary.[9]

The latest development in U.S. universities has been the comparative
studies taking place between the fields of Anglo-American and Latin
American literatures. These exchanges take up and transform the dialogue among peers that occurred when the founders of the U.S. national
literary tradition looked to the south, and therefore also to Spain, to find
their hemispheric origins.[10] Now, with new players and new interests,

these interactions reformulate the major literary critical events of the 1940s, when Latin American and Anglo-American literary scholars met for the first time on U.S. soil. In short, the writings of colonial Spanish America are emerging once again, now in concert with colonial North American studies, as the common coin of scholarly Americanist interests.

PRINCIPLES AND PRACTICES OF WRITINGS ON THE INDIES

This study poses two main questions: What did the writers of the sixteenth century have to say on the subject of the polemics of Spanish territorial possession of the Indies? and Does it matter today? The answer to the first of these questions is complicated and lengthy, the answer to the second is simply yes. My central argument is that the incandescent core of the Spanish American literary tradition is constituted by the writings that debated the right of Spanish conquest in the Americas and the treatment of their native inhabitants. I examine this narrative domain at the point of its sixteenth- and early seventeenth-century origin and apogee, and I conclude by locating its literary legacy in writings of our era that take up that early tradition.

In assessing the writings of the early Spanish colonial period, I have made assertions that have been borne out by the passage of time and my experience as a reader. The first is that the writings produced were "not merely reflective of social and political practices but were in fact constitutive of them."[11] These works do not describe events; they *are* events, and they transcend self-reference to refer to the world outside themselves. This referentiality, however, is not historical, as in the historical truth whose referent is a past event. It is instead rhetorical and polemical, with the objective of influencing readers' perceptions, royal policies, and social practices.

My view of colonial writing as a social practice, rather than merely a reflection of it, accounts for my formulation of the polemics of possession as central to the Latin American literary tradition. I include in that tradition works in a variety of genres (chronicle, *relación* [teleological narration], Socratic-style dialogue, epic poem) and a range of modes (narrative, argumentative, descriptive, and speculative). I take up authors of European birth or ancestry, but also Amerindian writers who took up the pen in a tradition that was not, by heritage, their own.

A second principle of which I have long been convinced is that "the native—colonized or indomitable—stands always at the heart of colonial writings, even when not explicitly mentioned."[12] Whether as the object of debates about royal policy or as the fallen hero of literary epics, the figure of the Amerindian is the common element among all these writings. This presence—ghostly or bloody, idealized or denigrated, and quite often enslaved—draws into a body the works generated in and about the Spanish Indies, and it constitutes the essence of what makes them colonial, with respect to the time period of their production, and colonialist, with regard to the outlooks, pro and contra, expressed in them.

Otherness, with respect to the Amerindian, does not exist. Alterity in its modern philosophical sense was an impossibility in the theological world of sixteenth-century Spain. The theorist of just war in the Indies, Juan Ginés de Sepúlveda, proposed differences between Spaniard and Indian, pagan and Christian that were, even to him as a proconquest partisan, in Aristotelian terms, accidental, not essential. His foil in his dialogue on "the just causes by which to make war against the Indians," entitled *Demócrates Segundo*, is the Lutheran-leaning Leopoldo, who asserts that "the pagans have nothing in common with us." To this, Sepúlveda's hero, the advocate of conversion by force and colonialist Demócrates, replies, "It is not true, as you assert, that there is nothing in common between us and the pagans; rather, we have very much in common, because they are, and they are called, our brothers, our fellow creatures and sheep of the same shepherd, although not of the same flock."[13] In the present context, the other means simply "not us." It does not carry any notion of radical difference.

A third principle is that "behind the label of 'otherness' stand real people in their lived experience."[14] My interest extends beyond the contours of the writing subject to include those elements of the "real people" that make it possible to avoid committing interpretative errors. To know, for example, that Bernal Díaz del Castillo defended, at a royally authorized junta at court in Spain in 1550, his prerogative to enjoy in perpetuity certain privileges over the native peoples in his charge helps immeasurably to focus one's attention on what he narrates and how he does so; ultimately, it helps one understand why, in his *Historia verdadera de la conquista de la Nueva España,* he so vividly recreates the events that took place at Cholula and attacks Bartolomé de las Casas for having condemned them.[15] Knowing the historical circumstances of the writers and the debates in which they were engaged is central to understanding their writings as they understood them. These factors make it possible to approach, however imperfectly, the interactive and dialogic relationships that prevailed between generative circumstance and finished work. The consideration of "lived experience" also involves the moral imperative attendant in these writings. Even the occasional expression of humor is the quiet laughter, or sometimes the bitter chuckle, needed to leaven the solemnity of the matters treated.

What makes the works studied here part of a corpus is the web of connections among them. In the broadest sense, this relationship is thematic, and it refers to the absent historical referent, that is, the events of the invasions, conquests, and colonization by the Spanish in the Americas. Just as these works are connected to a common theme, so they are also connected to one another. The mutual responsiveness and the polemic—the polemic that the Russian formalist V. N. Vološinov identified as hidden or the overt, self-identified one—can be documented and traced, as I have done here.[16] Even when implicit, that polemic always centered on the rights of conquest and the treatment of the Amerindians.

Too often the chronicles of the Indies are read as though they were textual configurations positivistic in conception and unmediated in execution. Such assertions are both imperious and misguided. To distort these works by treating them as though they were transparent historical sources is a dangerous procedure. The prescriptive and descriptive works of literary and historical theory of the sixteenth and seventeenth centuries, such as Las Casas's remarkable prologue of 1552 to his *Historia de las Indias,* as well as the works of preceptists such as Alonso López Pinciano (1596) and Luis Cabrera de Córdoba (1611), reveal that nothing was less transparent or more complex than the writing of history in that era.[17] This is why Bernal Díaz had to work so hard to establish his authority in the *Historia verdadera.* He learned that being an eyewitness participant in the events he narrated was helpful but insufficient in establishing his historiographic authority.[18]

The juridical institutions of the Castilian monarchy that ascertained the actions of expeditions and assessed the services of their members underscore the point: the certified accounts (*probanzas, informes*) that testified to events and their protagonists were necessarily collective, calling upon numerous witnesses, and they took priority over the individually written accounts of merits and deeds (*relaciones de méritos y servicios*).[19] When in the late 1540s the historian of the Indies Gonzalo Fernández de Oviedo y Valdés compared the collective and individual accounts of the Pánfilo de Narváez expedition to La Florida, he declared in his *Historia general y natural de las Indias* that he preferred the collective, certified report (the now-lost joint report) given in 1536 by Andrés Dorantes, Alonso del Castillo Maldonado, and Álvar Núñez Cabeza de Vaca, the expedition's three Castilian survivors, over Cabeza de Vaca's highly personalized rendition (the published *Relación* of 1542, known from its 1555 edition onward as *Naufragios*). In doing so, Oviedo signaled the historian's confidence in collective testimony and his distrust of the individual's as bona fide sources for writing history.[20]

The retrospective character of conquest writings is called to mind by the six-year gap between the preparation of the Narváez survivors' joint report and the writing of Cabeza de Vaca's *Relación*. One of the romantic fictions regarding the accounts of conquests in the Indies is that they were written at night in military encampments by soldier-hidalgos who, with quill in hand, bravely ignored the intimidating sounds of enemy war cries and drums. Hernán Cortés and Alonso de Ercilla y Zúñiga are among the authors who create this familiar impression, even though Cortés's famous second letter (*segunda carta de relación*), which narrates the events from August 1519 through July 1520, beginning with the journey from the coast of the Gulf of Mexico to México-Tenochtitlán and the company's eventual expulsion from the city ("la Noche Triste"), was written in the autumn months that followed his army's retreat to Segura de la Frontera (Tepeaca, Puebla) and dated October 30, 1520.[21] Ercilla's epic saga of the interminable war of conquest against the Araucanians of Chile was written in the decades following his return to Spain.[22] This retrospective quality applies also to the works of Bernal Díaz, Las Casas, Cabeza de Vaca, and El Inca Garcilaso de la Vega as well as to the debates about the conquests themselves: Sepúlveda was commissioned to write his *Demócrates Segundo* in the mid-1540s, well after the occurrence of the most significant and dramatic mainland conquests in Mexico and Peru, that is, more than two decades after the fall of México-Tenochtitlán and almost a decade and a half after that of the Inca state. The famous debates between Las Casas and Sepúlveda in Valladolid, on the topic of whether the evangelization of the natives should be carried out through force of arms, were not convened by the emperor Charles V (he was also Charles I of Spain) until 1550.[23]

Narrative is the essential mode at the core of all the writings on the Indies, even those that are presented as scholarly and Scholastic-style disputations or deliberative rhetorical presentations made before policy-making bodies at the royal court. This is most evident in Las Casas's *Brevísima relación de la destrucción de las Indias,* which is overtly a narration of events, a *relación,* yet whose primary purpose is deliberative and persuasive. Another of the striking cases is Sepúlveda's *Demócrates Segundo,* in which the author narrates events of the conquest of Mexico as evidence for his polemical, theoretical justification of the conquests. In both the *Brevísima relación* and the *Demócrates Segundo,* the narration of events plays a role subservient to other ends, but it is the fundamental means used to achieve them.

The permanence and malleability of narrative in Spanish colonial writings are most dramatically illustrated by Sepúlveda's works. Here one of the principles of colonialist writing, mentioned above, reappears: the fulcrum of the argument is the ever-present and variously portrayed Amerindian. On different occasions for different purposes and writing in Latin, Sepúlveda narrated and interpreted events of the conquest of Mexico in diametrically opposed ways. In the *Demócrates Segundo,* in order to defend the Spanish rights of conquest, he denigrated the Aztecs in war as cowardly and described them in battle as fleeing like women. Yet when celebrating the deeds of Cortés and his army in his history of the Mexican conquest in *De Orbe Novo,* he praised the Aztecs for their wartime valor. Sepúlveda's example is the strongest case I can make for how the writings of the Indies, even those that presumably narrated historical events, are better characterized as polemical or moralistic narratives than as objective history, and also for how they are best studied by examining the persuasive features of their representation, not by attempting to confirm or accepting their claims to the truthfulness of the events narrated.

The triumph of narrative authority over historical authority is brought into focus most sharply in El Inca Garcilaso's *La Florida del Inca.* Here my argument is that Garcilaso's endeavor to write an account of the Hernando de Soto expedition to La Florida (1539–1542) sought its referent not in the historical deeds it recounted, but rather in the oral and written narrative reports that consecrated them.[24] This practice pertains not only to Garcilaso in his *Comentarios reales de los Incas* as well as in *La Florida,* but also to Bernal Díaz's *Historia verdadera* and to every work that cited at length (complementing or refuting or both) the works that went before it. Forty years ago Francisco Esteve Barba characterized seventeenth-century writings on the Indies as reworkings, even plagiarisms, of previous chronicles or oblique remembrances of deeds long past.[25] The pertinent point, however, is not that those later writings were failed histories but rather that they played a role in the development of a narrative tradition that carried with it and transformed its own carefully chosen antecedents. This tradition is narcissistic, polemical, and weighty (that is, it is baroque), and it antedates the seventeenth century. It begins soon after the collective eyewitness testimonies of Spanish conquest have been certified; it commences when the mariner or soldier, finding himself no longer aboard ship or on the battlefield and relying to a greater or lesser extent on earlier accounts, quietly sits down with pen in hand to tell the tale, persuasively, in his own way.[26]

If the absence of the historical referent effectively generates the Spanish American narrative tradition as it emerges post-1492, this greatest of all generative absences is not the sole one to characterize Spanish colonial writing. The revealing absences or, perhaps better said, the pregnant, permanent pauses and silences speak loudly to the reader. The phenomenon of that which is not said perpetuates the interest of successive generations of readers in these narratives that always seem to proclaim, "Let me tell you what really happened" or "Let me tell you how the other fellow got it wrong; I'll tell you the true story, the *historia verdadera,*" and always, "I'll tell you what happened to me."

Ironically, if convinced by the writer's claims, it is our supposition as readers about the existence of an external, historical referent that makes these narrations elliptical. With regard to the events narrated, it is often the case that the more we are told, the greater our awareness of what has been left unsaid. Cabeza de Vaca's account of his long North American captivity and survival invites the reader to ask about the elements he left out of the narrative account of his ten-year odyssey (1527–1537). As readers, we seek the evidence of the narrative logic that gives us the expectation of a fully coherent sequence of events, even if that sequence is not fully described, much less explained. As readers of narrative, not history, we ask not for verity but for verisimilitude, that is, consistency and completeness within the narrative system itself, not correspondence to the irretrievable events that stand outside it.

The same may be said regarding our expectations of the writing subject. We have long recognized the centrality of the eyewitness narrator in early Spanish American writings, and it is precisely the role of the writing-subject-as-narrative-protagonist that makes the reader wonder about the character of the individual who created the writing subject: blustery old braggart; tiresome, pedantic preacher; sharp military strategist and capable diplomat; earnest sojourner trekking among the Indians of North America; or shipwrecked Spaniard-turned-Maya warrior chief. These figures, like Don Quijote, step out of the pages of the books that portray them, and the fuller their profiles emerge, the more questions we raise about what we see, and do not see, of them. This principle applies not only to the author-protagonists, but also to the protagonists who, in third person, walk in silence through their scenes or have their speech reported indirectly by others: Doña Marina (La Malinche), Jerónimo de Aguilar, Estevan (Estevanico), and, most notable of all, the fabled and fabulous Gonzalo Guerrero (who is given voice, in direct speech, by Bernal Díaz).[27] The power of this narrative tradition lies in the fact that these stories of exploration, conquest, and colonization are ones that we in the Americas, the Caribbean, and Spain all know, even if we have never read them. In this regard, it is the already known as well as the never said that captures readers' interest and makes these old books attractive and their stories readable and even familiar.

With respect to the agents of the polemics of possession, one of the most salient features of the colonial writing subject is the multiplicity of positions the speaking subject takes. In his *Historia eclesiástica de nuestros tiempos* (1611), the Dominican historian Alonso Fernández makes the point in his encomium to Las Casas: "When the emperor came from Germany, Las Casas presented his cause with much erudition and prudence, speaking like a saint, informing like a jurist, giving judgments like a theologian, and testifying as an eyewitness."[28] Simultaneously representing various social roles and disciplinary perspectives, the writing subject occupies a position that is complex, and it is further compounded by the passage of time and the retrospective nature of the writings.

This characteristically retrospective dimension of Indies writings, whether narrative, argumentative, or speculative, had a significant impact on the writing subject, increasing the complexity of its simultaneous and multiple positions by adding the dimension of change over time. If Bernal Díaz had written his *Historia verdadera* immediately after the conquest of Mexico, or even subsequent to his participation in Cortés's expedition to Hibueras (Honduras), it would have been a different work: he would have been a young conquest veteran, not, as he is when at last we meet him, an old *encomendero* (Spanish trustee to whom native labor and tribute were rendered) desperately seeking his place in history and struggling against the shifting political winds at court to maintain for himself and his heirs the privilege of receiving the land's bounty and the services of its native laborers (*encomienda*). If in the early 1550s in Seville Las Casas had not learned about the origins of the Portuguese slave trade in the published works of Portuguese maritime history, it would not have been revealed to him that the natives of western Africa sold as slaves had not been prisoners, as was generally supposed, taken in the war against Islam (considered by Christendom to be just), but rather that they had been captured while "living peacefully and safe in their homes," committing no offense to anyone and being thus unjustly enslaved.[29] In the *Historia de las Indias* Las Casas was able to disclose the error he and his generation committed because he wrote it long after his early encouragement of bringing slaves to the Antilles. Ironically, his retrospective discovery and disclosure served only to brand him, wrongly, as the author of black African slavery in the Americas.[30]

Overall, Las Casas is the best example of the principle of retrospection and sequence at work in the colonial-era corpus. Over the course of fifty years his colonialist activism, evidenced through the reams of works he wrote on how to serve the Christian mission and achieve colonial reform, underwent a radical transformation. He moved from a position of fomenting Spanish settlement and regulating and punishing its excesses to one of advocating that the Castilian monarchy abandon its sovereignty over the Indies altogether. Thus temporality and sequence orient and define the cases of all the writers studied here as well as Spanish colonial-era writings in general.

AUTHORS AND ISSUES

Ideas are not always developed in a straight line, but chapters in a book must be. The series of propositions, arguments, themes, historical personalities, and literary protagonists presented here did not occur to me in chronological succession but rather in a logical sequence. That sequence sometimes demanded moving forward in time, and sometimes back. That is, the questions generated by a chronologically later topic often required me to look back in time to earlier writings to find the answers. Sometimes those answers generated further questions that seemed to point neither forward nor back, but sideways. As a result, I have arranged the contents of the following chapters in a sequence that reflects the course in which the topics, or rather the questions that generated the topics, appeared. The relatedness they bear to one another makes it necessary to move forward a considerable distance in time and then travel back again (as in chapters 2 and 3, respectively).

The metaphor of travel is an apt one because questions of geographical location play a large role in my study of Spanish-language writings on the Indies. In some cases, the locations are geographically literal. With Cabeza de Vaca and his sojourn in the wilderness of North America, we always must start with a map. In other cases, such as that of El Inca Garcilaso's Floridian Guancane, the sites described do not exist on a map, contemporary or historical. But for all that they are no less real. Place and space are imbued with meaning only by their inhabitants and invaders. The maps that illustrate this volume underscore the point.

The polemics of possession starts with the possession of place: who possessed the land? Whose sovereignty was at stake? The great debates of the sixteenth century that inspired and animated the early writings on the Spanish Indies (half of today's Latin America and the Caribbean) really started there. Some, jurists, humanists, theologians, debated it; others, historians, conquistadores, conquistador-chroniclers, assumed they knew the answers or that the answers were self-evident, not open to scrutiny. Who owned the lands opened out to the question of who had the right to rule them. Who had the right to rule was answered, for some, by who was fit to rule. Here the question devolved onto that of the possession of virtues needed for self-governance: the exercise of prudence over oneself, one's household, the wider social and political order, that is, the categories defined by sixteenth-century interpretations of the political philosophy of Aristotle. And who, first and also last, had the right and authority to speak? Who had the right and prerogative to presume to write history, and by what authority? Needless to say, these questions were intimately entangled with one another, and each comes up in combination with the others in the course of the chapters that follow.

If *possession* fans out to cover a variety of topics, from the possession of the traits of sociability and solidarity (*humanitas*) and therefore civil conduct to the possession of the rights of the victor and the rights to govern others or to self-govern, *polemics* is an equally multifaceted and perhaps more subtle category. Sometimes polemic is open and formal, as in the debates carried out by Las Casas and Sepúlveda before a distinguished panel of fourteen judges at the court in Valladolid in the sweltering summer of 1550 and April 1551. Sometimes it is concealed, and, when concealed, it is often masked as something else, such as the supposedly expository narration of history or the anecdotal content of a sermon, a moralizing parable or tale, or an epic poem. Polemics is the abiding trait of all Spanish-colonial-era writings, and it was because of polemics and ongoing controversies that the Council of Castile and the Council of the Indies, under the leadership of Philip II, saw fit to monitor and control the publication and dissemination of writings about the Indies, especially from 1556 onward.[31] Polemics invite censorship, and so it was the case in the Indies in the second half of the sixteenth century. Censorship is not a main topic in these pages, but its occasional appearance underscores the weight and influence that works in manuscript or print circulation were perceived to possess by the officials who sought to stifle controversy through their attempted suppression.

The cast of characters presenting themselves before the royal councils in Castile, or the Audiencias in America, that is, the high courts of civil and criminal jurisdiction in the viceroyalties, in Santo Domingo, México-Tenochtitlán, Lima, and so forth, is necessarily large. Each of the major figures treated here spent time—in some cases, weeks, in others, years—before the officials of such governing bodies. No doubt they spent most of their time waiting, shuffling from one foot to the other and reviewing the documents they wished to present to the authorities. We will not wait that long for them to appear here. There are five historical figures, five pillars that support the archways that the following pages are intended to construct. They may seem at first like a motley crew, utterly, anecdotally disconnected from one another. Yet they shared the same interests, the polemics of possession—of lands, sovereignty, the right to rule, the right to speak (and write) with authority, the right to be heard—albeit from different and often opposing perspectives.

One, Felipe Guaman Poma de Ayala (1530s–c. 1616), from Hua-manga (today's Ayacucho) in early colonial Peru, was an Andean of dynas-tic tradition, reviled by his enemies as an imposter. Another, Fray Bar-tolomé de las Casas (1484–1566), trained in canon law, ordained into the priesthood, and admitted to the Dominican order, was beloved by his allies and supporters but despised by his detractors, not only during his lifetime but long afterward and to the present day. The third, Bernal Díaz del Castillo (c. 1495–1584), an aging ex-conquistador of Mexico and an encomendero in Guatemala from Medina del Campo in Castile, spent more than the final third of his long life writing a narrative account of his participation in the conquest of Mexico. Hoping for a hero's welcome at court in Madrid, he was met with the snarls of a conciliar official who challenged him, "Who gave you the right to conquer?" The fourth, Álvar Núñez Cabeza de Vaca (1485–1492 to c. 1559), was a caballero (untitled nobility) from Jerez de la Frontera, Andalusia, who spent years marooned on the east Texas coast and, after decades of royal service on three conti-nents, ended up being brought back to Spain from his governorship in Río de la Plata in chains. The fifth, El Inca Garcilaso de la Vega (1539–1616), who was born in the ancient Inca capital of Cuzco, where he was raised, and spent his adult life in Córdoba and Montilla, Andalusia, im-mortalized the attempted conquest of La Florida by one of his father's colleagues in the conquest of Peru, Hernando de Soto.

Despite their diverse backgrounds and experiences, Guaman Poma, Bernal Díaz, Cabeza de Vaca, and El Inca Garcilaso had one thing in com-mon: An engagement with the fiery Dominican friar Las Casas. The An-dean, Guaman Poma, knew him by his works, some forty to fifty years after Las Casas died; Bernal Díaz knew him personally, criticized him roundly, and wrote him letters asking him to use his influence on his behalf; Cabeza de Vaca may have met Las Casas in the capital of New Spain, but Las Casas knew and cited with admiration Cabeza de Vaca's North American account in support of the positions he took in the polemics of his day on the question of Amerindian aptitudes and accomplishments; El Inca Garcilaso met Las Casas personally on the streets of Seville, but their commitment to common (and other, opposing) causes preceded and followed their encounter.

There are other historical figures, no less important, who interact through their writings with the aforementioned authors. Notable among them are Juan Ginés de Sepúlveda, humanist translator of Aristotle and chronicler at the court of the emperor Charles V, and Gonzalo Fernández de Oviedo, administrator (*alcalde*) of the fortress of Santo Domingo and the author of the *Historia general y natural de las Indies*. The reader will meet here Francisco López de Gómara, historian of the conquest of Mexico and friend of Sepúlveda and of the marquis del Valle himself, Hernán Cortés. Included as well are the works of the great missionary clergy, the Franciscan friar Bernardino de Sahagún, whose lifework provided an unparalleled ethnographic record of Nahua civilization, and the Jesuit José de Acosta, who also wrote about the Indies and its peoples but from a philosophical point of view. Each of the figures who appear in these pages knew Las Casas by his deeds or his writings.

Las Casas is the point of convergence for these writers' many exchanges and efforts to make sense of and give meaning to the history of Spain in the Indies and, at the same time, to orient it toward its future. It is Las Casas whose figure and conscience hover over the entire proceedings. His shadow lingers in the pages that close this book, in the remarkable reflections on his legacy to Latin America and to the world that his real-life admirer Fray Servando Teresa de Mier y Noriega (1763–1827), now fictionalized, evokes in the novel by Reinaldo Arenas and that Alejo Carpentier's Cristóbal Colón (Christopher Columbus) must face, fictionally, at his real-life, nineteenth-century canonization tribunal.

When the national literatures of Latin America were established and consolidated in the nineteenth century, and when the authors of these respective, now nationalized works were canonized—not into sainthood but into the literary canon of today's Latin American, North American, European, and also Asian programs of study—the linkages among these figures, the larger and the lesser of them, came to be forgotten. My goal here, therefore, is to speak to their connectedness.

In arguing my case for the existence and importance of the polemics of possession in Spanish American narrative, my objective is to confirm my assertion that the writers represented played a founding role in the literary tradition of Latin America. Their literary and personal relationships to one another constitute the means I have employed to make the argument persuasive. In other words, by "founding role" I do not mean only those, such as Las Casas, whose works influenced others, but also those, such as Guaman Poma, in whose works such influence is registered. Influence does not really exist without the confirmation of one influenced; it is, as always, a relational matter. The pertinent criterion is not statistical evidence regarding the publication of works but rather the literary evidence of their circulation, in print or in manuscript. It is not the impact of book sales but rather the influence of ideas that is measured here.

Theirs was not a period in which literary self-identifications were self-effacing, much less erased. On the contrary, their works were crafted with great care and most often with theoretical juridical criteria in mind. The literary persona conveyed by the writer putting quill to paper mattered, be it the aggrieved native lord who claimed that his only goal was to represent the interests of the members of his race, the curmudgeonly old conquistador in the shadow of Cortés, the noble servant of his monarch come home from the Indies bringing only information and strategic intelligence, the heir to the Incas proclaiming the military values of both the conqueror and the conquered, and, finally, the now-elderly Dominican who spent fifty years toiling over affairs in the Indies. What is special, if not unique, about these colonial-era writers is that they do not lend themselves to approaches in which considerations of life and limb are understood to muddy the issues raised in the work. In the act of writing, these writers insisted that there was motive and meaning in their works precisely because the welfare of lives *and* limbs, in fact, hung in the balance.

DOES IT MATTER?

The sixteenth- and early seventeenth-century accounts of conquests and controversy may strike us as interesting, but so what?[32] They are lost in time and confined to centuries-old books and manuscripts. Yet some of these figures and the ideas they espoused *have* stepped out of the pages they authored and into the present. This is true of the literary persona of Guaman Poma and also that of El Inca Garcilaso, which have proven to be so powerful, so attractive, and so ubiquitous that one trend in pseudoacademic gossip has been to deny them their due and their greatness, in effect promoting the demise of the historical figures' literary achievements.

I believe that the reasons these writings hold interest for a wider audience than those of us who are specialists fall into three categories: surprise, currency, and mystery.[33] First of all, we come to these old chronicles with a poorly understood set of expectations: if published in their own day, they seem to us overlong and probably boring; if in manuscript form, they look impossible to read; if written by authors of ethnic American tradition, they seem exotic, and we expect them to be primitive. Our surprise is generated by the sophistication they reveal upon close examination. We share with those writers the desire to be known and recognized, but recognized as we would represent ourselves, not as we are seen from the outside. We recognize our own complexity, and we do not claim any cultural or ethnic "purity." Likewise, with regard to authors of indigenous American background, we can (and must) recognize that no self-representation can lay claim to an ethnic or cultural purity that is untainted and uncontaminated by outside influences. The Guaman Pomas and the Alva Ixtlilxochitls of the generation that saw the Spanish conquest or were born shortly after it could not go back to any pristine, pre-Columbian state of mind.

The element of surprise comes when we see these authors, of whatever cultural background and experience, in their complexity and when we examine the fruits of their intellectual efforts to make sense of their respective old worlds and new circumstances. In this process of discovery, we are surprised, shamed, and delighted. Once we have understood that these literary monuments and artifacts of other peoples in other times are not simple objects of curiosity, irrelevant to our own, we face the next challenge: to avoid treating them anachronistically. The moment we recognize something that seems to look like ourselves, that is, like our own human impulses, we discover our common humanity, and we can appreciate the currency of their struggles and their values today. But once we become comfortable with this, our expectations adjust accordingly, and we may expect them to exhibit an impossible consistency and to have all their conflicts and self-contradictions resolved; in short, we all too easily transfer to them the illusions we harbor about ourselves. Once again, they confound our expectations.

In this regard, one of the joys and privileges that we who are teachers have is returning to some of our own approximations, our own innocent first readings, through the eyes and minds of our students, who sometimes predictably follow our earlier paths of first encounters (and sometimes, also predictably, leap right past them to get to our thinking as it is in the present or beyond it). At this point, in recognizing the shared humanity between ourselves and those whose long-ago words we study, the principle of a false currency appears, and we are again required to take stock: we are required to understand that we do not—and cannot—fully understand their lost experiences. We cannot step into their shoes. If we're reflective enough, we understand that this awareness of our inadequacy matters, and that it matters very much. In our studies or even in trying to render such texts in translation, we can never claim, naively, to have captured the spirit of the original. There are indeed areas of impenetrability, and these blind spots in our understanding are important to keep in mind, too.

In short, the exhilaration of surprise, the pleasure of the sense of shared human experience, and the puzzlement at the conundrums that remain in our exploration of these artifacts provide us with the aesthetic and intellectual pleasures of looking at them, even as they challenge us to look at ourselves, *our* primitive assumptions about their cultures, *our* naïve expectations about the simplicity and crudeness of their meanings, and, hence, the folly of *our* illusions about ourselves. I have long considered Guaman Poma one of my best teachers. What I mean is that his twelve-hundred-page manuscript helped me to generate, for myself, the questions about it—the conditions of its emergence, the meanings of its contents, and its situation within a larger forum—that demanded answers. The hallmark of every good teacher is to help lead the student in the process of self-discovery, which consists not first and foremost of finding answers but of learning to ask new and appropriate questions.

Over the past four centuries Las Casas has been everywhere present. The ubiquitous Dominican seemed never to flag in his campaign for colonial reform, and the immortality (his detractors, then and now, would say immorality) achieved by his polemical *Brevísima relación de la destrucción de las Indias* (1552) makes it one of the best-known works in the Spanish language, along with *El ingenioso hidalgo Don Quijote de la Mancha* (1605, 1615) and *Cien años de soledad* (1967). In the literary and cultural traditions anchored in the Spanish language, Las Casas's name may be eclipsed only by those of Miguel de Cervantes, Gabriel García Márquez, and Jorge Luis Borges.

Starting from a dozen years after the Dominican's death, the *Breví-*

sima relación was published outside Spain in an increasing variety of languages, and it would be difficult if not impossible to tally the number of editions—"*numerosísimas*"—that are in print in many languages today. Its currency should be self-evident. In our day the program to democratize the globe is as zealously advocated and defended as was the desire to Christianize it in the sixteenth century. The notion that some peoples and nations today need tutelage in perfecting their civil orders replays the arguments and efforts made in the sixteenth century to tutor those peoples in the Western hemisphere who, it was supposed, would thereby achieve a civil order for the first time. Insofar as the meanings of sovereignty, the struggle for justice, the human and civil rights of peoples, and the desire to interpret and understand them are constants of our world today, their rehearsal in the realm that the court councilor to Ferdinand and Isabel, Pietro Martire d'Anghiera, called a New World provides the first theater of such intercontinental military and political operations in the early modern period.

The figures that fill these pages, however, lifted not the sword but the pen, and the quiet hours they spent reading and writing (not in the din of battle but rather with the cacophony of conciliar debates ringing in their ears) draw our attention here. This absorption with reading is the note on which I would like to close this introductory chapter, because I find in the following poetic anecdote the essence of the discursive engagements I have examined. It comes in a poem that presents a tableau of a reader reading, and its narrative is about the exchange between reader and book. It is Wallace Stevens's "The House Was Quiet and the World Was Calm."[34]

The poet presents the picture of a quiet house on a still summer night; the scene is of a reader, leaning over a book. The familiar physical attitude of bodily inclination expresses succinctly the reader's intellectual and affective engagement with the work he is reading: "the reader became the book" (311). At the same time, the reader desires to become "the scholar to whom his book is true" (311). Thus, while the reader gives himself over to the book, he asks, at the same time, something from it: that the book be, or become, true to the scholar that the reader desires to be. For the book to be true to its reader, it must render up the full humanity of the experience it describes. The reader hopes to become the scholar in order to apprehend the truths of human experience contained in the book, and for the book to be true to him, it will thus necessarily be peopled by deceptions and falsehoods and contradictions and failures and out-rages against humanity, all of which have been perceived, expressed, and communicated by other scholar-readers.

The image of the reader bent over his reading table in stillness (a quiet house, a calm world) distills an image in the centuries-long tradition of reading and interpretation that is my focus here. I have attempted to capture some of those long-ago but ever-present moments in which the quiet of reading and the silence of writing prevailed, if only briefly, over the distractions of a house—palace, convent, or borrowed lodging—that was never quiet, and a world—Spain's America—that was never calm.

CHAPTER 2

Felipe Guaman Poma de Ayala and the Polemics of Possession

MY ACCOUNT OF THE POLEMICS of possession in the narrative tradition of Latin America must begin with the work that initially stimulated this inquiry: *El primer nueva corónica y buen gobierno* (1615) by Felipe Guaman Poma de Ayala (fig. 2). The manuscript came to international attention a century ago, in 1908, when the director of the library of the University of Göttingen, Richard Pietschmann, came upon it in the Royal Library of Denmark in Copenhagen. It had been part of the Danish royal collection since the early 1660s, a gift, probably, to his king from a Danish diplomat, in grateful acknowledgment for the title of nobility just received.[1] With its elaborately calligraphic headings and 399 full-page line drawings, the 1,190-page manuscript graphically provided a bold and scathing look at Spain's actions in "The Indies of Peru," not unlike the one provided by the copper engravings in Theodor de Bry's Latin translation of Fray Bartolomé de las Casas's *Brevísima relación de la destrucción de las Indias* (Frankfurt, 1598) (see chapter 3 and figure 16). The comparison of Guaman Poma's work with those of Las Casas is not gratuitous. My most arresting discovery about the *Nueva corónica* has been that a half century after Las Casas's death in 1566, it adapted and incorporated Las Casas's theories about the sovereignty of the native peoples of the Americas. Guaman Poma did not merely echo ideas that can be called vaguely Lascasian; instead, he cited directly from one of Las Casas's final and most

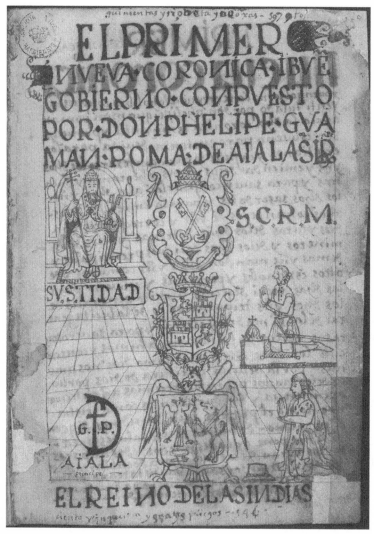

FIGURE 2. Frontispiece, Felipe Guaman Poma de Ayala, *El primer nueva corónica y buen gobierno*. Copenhagen, Royal Library, GkS 2232, 4°. Courtesy of The Royal Library, Copenhagen, Denmark.

provocative works, which in 1564 proposed that Spain abandon altogether its rule over the Indies.

The present chapter functions as a first step in the elaboration of a larger argument about the polemics of possession which honors two goals, the first being to lay claim to rights and prerogatives in the world *outside* the book, and the second (and enduring one), to lay claim to authority that comes precisely (if not exclusively) from the world *of* the book. Because of the importance of Guaman Poma's work to the task I have set for myself here, I probe deeply the experiences that preceded and led to his writing of the work that he called "the first of the new chronicles" [*El primer nueva corónica*]. Guaman Poma's chronicle reveals that the struggle over rights to lands and debates about the governance of peoples included not only contentions over places marked on maps, but also the creation of new maps, new imaginings, that floated free of considerations of topography. The final chapters in this inquiry into the polemics of possession speak to such places—imagined yet real—in writings that will take us from Bartolomé de las Casas and Álvar Núñez Cabeza de Vaca to El Inca Garcilaso de la Vega, Alejo Carpentier, Reinaldo Arenas, Juan Rulfo, and Gabriel García Márquez.

THE *INDIO LADINO* IN THE CONTACT ZONE

Guaman Poma's discussions of his own experience and that of others in the *Nueva corónica y buen gobierno* elucidate the challenges and dilemmas faced by native interpreters who occupied a "contact zone," or rather, "zona de contacto," as I called it in my Spanish-language introduction to the 1987 Murra-Adorno-Urioste edition of Guaman Poma's work. By using the term, I attempted to evoke the notion of a colonial society in which the simple line between Spaniard and Andean that defined native experience at the moment of conquest no longer existed with such clarity: "It is precisely this difference which makes the work of Guaman Poma an almost unique point of departure by which to reconstruct the experience of the *indio ladino*—the indigenous subject who knew Spanish and lived in the contact zone between early Spanish colonial society and the native one—during the first century of colonialism in Spanish America."[2] Well past the decade of those first intercultural, European/Andean contacts when he came to adulthood, Guaman Poma was born after the Spanish invasion of Peru and the fall of the Inca state, probably in the later 1530s or 1540s. This is a "zona de contacto" not only in a synchronic dimension but also on a temporally organized cross-cultural grid: Guaman Poma's life experience pertains to a period of time in which he and his peers could claim that the generation of their parents had served both the Inca lords of Tawantinsuyu and the faraway king of Castile. Those who labored in the contact zones between Spanish colonial and native Andean society fell into two large groups of individuals, who, because of at least nominal skills in Castilian, were referred to as "ladino." There were those who worked in the domestic service of the colonizers as slaves or servants—black Africans, native Andeans, women as well as men—and those, like Guaman Poma, who performed the role of interpreter (*lengua*) in the negotiations between the colonizer and the colonized.

The term *ladino* was used from the very beginning of Spanish colonial times in Hispaniola, Mexico and Peru, and it had been imported from Spain in one of its standard usages.[3] Although *ladino* as a noun came to be used to refer to the language of the Sephardim, its use in reference to Castilian did not disappear. On the contrary, in the sixteenth and seventeenth centuries, the adjective *ladino* continued to carry one of its original meanings in reference to Latin—that of linguistic purity—now applied to proper pronunciation, usage, and cultivated speech in Castilian; this is the meaning captured in phrases like "ladino español" and "ladino castellano." Inasmuch as the term implied skill in the use of Castilian on the part of those who possessed it, it was logically applied as well to any foreigner who spoke it; one could be described, for example, as "muy ladino" or "no muy ladino."[4] Such was the usage in which it spread to Spanish America to apply to nonnative speakers of Castilian.

Although the term referred specifically to language use, the descriptions presented by early chroniclers of the Indies suggest as well the meaning of acculturation to Spanish ways. If in the sixteenth century today's concepts of cultural transformation or hybridization did not exist, the intimate connections between language and customs were well understood. Hence we find Gonzalo Fernández de Oviedo's vivid description of the cacique Enriquillo of Hispaniola: "Among these modern and most recent lords of this island Hispaniola, there is one who is called Don Enrique, who is a baptized Christian and knows how to read and write and is very ladino and speaks the Castilian language very well." Another sixteenth-century chronicler of the Indies, Fray Pedro de Aguado, used the phrase "ladino o españolado" to refer to Hispanicized Indians.[5] Language proficiency, literacy, Christianity, and custom all converged in the concept ladino.

But these are positive meanings. If at one extreme it connoted the qualities of prudence and sagacity, at the other it signified cunning and craftiness. At the opposite pole of the positive values of linguistic expertise and practice of Christian customs, it could refer to the "big talker" and the charlatan. Guaman Poma, who felt the sting of its negative as well as its positive sign as applied to himself, remarked that those called "indios ladinos" were often scorned as "bachilleres," in the sense of great and impertinent talkers, and as zealous converts and busybodies, that is, as objects of suspicion and mistrust: "The indio ladino is cast out and cruelly punished, being called 'ladino jerk' [*ladinejo*]"; "all their efforts upset the priests, and the parish priests who punish them, calling them 'holy little ladino jerk'" [Y todo lo dicho estorua los padres y curas de las dotrinas y castiga, deciéndole: "santico ladinejo"].[6] The examples provided by Guaman Poma suggest the conflictive nature of the sign ladino as used in America, where its application always implicitly carried, even at its neutral best, the notion of the outsider to full participation in Castilian society. At its worst, it painted its object as suspect or guilty of insubordination after submission. Ironically, those who were called indios ladinos, ever present in the documentary record of colonialism as interpreters, translators, and scribes, most easily remain hidden within it.[7]

The importance of native interpreters is evident in the range of functions they fulfilled, extending from the time of the Spanish conquests and long into the colonial period; they were guides in exploration, intermediaries in conquest negotiations, and, later, official translators in the investigations of the conduct of civil officers (*residencias*) as well as interpreters and witnesses on tours of civil and ecclesiastical inspection (*visitas*), and in the courts of civil and criminal justice (*audiencias*). While some of these first American natives were captured and taken to Europe ("Don Diego Colón," captured by Columbus on his first voyage; "Don Martín de Pizarro," taken to Spain by Pizarro in 1528) or captured and imprisoned in America so that they could learn Spanish,[8] the later generations of indios ladinos who worked as *lenguas* seem to have been recruited voluntarily. Such was the common experience of Guaman Poma's generation.

GUAMAN POMA, *LENGUA*, AND LITIGANT

Taught Christian doctrine and reading and writing, Guaman Poma worked in the service of Spanish colonial institutions while remaining grounded in the languages and traditions of his own culture. The complexity of such a subject's social identity, in which background and behavior were easily at odds with one another, meant that the binary model of Andean versus Spaniard or Spaniard versus Andean was no longer capable of providing a protocol of social conduct. In order to survive in a colonial society, the Guaman Pomas did not have the luxury of rejecting or accepting exclusively Andean or Spanish ways. They could not have done so in a colonial situation in which their best friend and ally, or their worst enemy, might well have been a Spanish friar or a priest of mixed Andean/European parentage (*mestizo*), a Spanish judge and administrator of a municipal Indian district (*corregidor*), or a local Andean authority of inherited (or colonially appointed) rank (*kuraka*). Acculturated Andeans such as Guaman Poma had affiliations to diverse and often conflicting groups, and their experience was nothing if not complex and often contradictory.

Guaman Poma's youthful participation in the missionary church's campaigns to root out native Andean religions was a defining feature of his life experience. He writes of having served the ecclesiastical inspector (*visitador*) Cristóbal de Albornoz in the identification and punishment of practitioners of traditional Andean religion in the earliest campaigns to extirpate, literally, to root out idolatry in early colonial Peru (fig. 3). Albornoz's extirpation of idolatries campaigns probably provided Guaman Poma's earliest significant experience with the policies and practices of the missionary church in native Andean communities. It is likely that Guaman Poma was recruited in Huamanga for Albornoz's campaign to the provinces of Lucanas Andamarca, Lucanas Laramati, and Soras in 1568–1570 (figs. 4, 5). In the *Nueva corónica y buen gobierno* Guaman Poma mentions the names of inspection team personnel who appear in Albornoz's official reports from this specific tour as well as the names of local Andeans who were punished for their adherence to traditional practices.[9]

Guaman Poma expressed approval of the work carried out by Albornoz, and he pointed out that Albornoz punished the practitioners of Taki Unquy, a radical nativist movement that preached the triumph of Andean gods over the Christian god, advocated rejection of all that was European, and coincided with the threat of armed aggression against the Spaniards from the neo-Inca stronghold at Vilcabamba, where the last Inca princes still reigned (see fig. 4). Guaman Poma referred to the practitioners of Taki Unquy as "false shamans" [hechiceros falsos], meaning that he interpreted their behavior as exploitation, for their own personal and political gain, of the traditional rituals that in Inca times had been mounted to expel illnesses.

FIGURE 3. Cristóbal de Albornoz, church inspector (*visitador*) and Guaman Poma's employer. Guaman Poma, *Nueva corónica*, 689. Courtesy of The Royal Library, Copenhagen, Denmark.

Guaman Poma also reveals his familiarity with the provincial church councils held in Lima in 1567 and 1582–1583 to establish and refine policies for evangelizing the Andean peoples. His enthusiastic support of their decrees on a broad range of issues suggests that he viewed rigorous and thorough evangelization as a pressing need in Andean society. In addition to his knowledge of church council edicts, Guaman Poma's mention of some of the churchmen who participated in the important Third

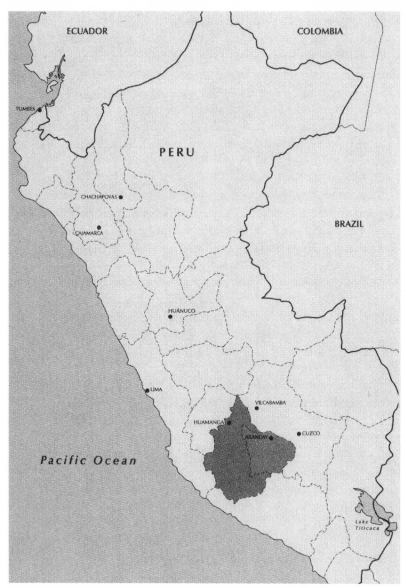

FIGURE 4. Map of Peru, drawn by Henrik Maribo, in Rolena Adorno, *Guaman Poma and His Illustrated Chronicle from Colonial Peru/Guaman Poma y su crónica ilustrada del Perú colonial*. Copenhagen: Museum Tusculanum Press, 2001, 10. Reproduced by courtesy of Museum Tusculanum Press, University of Copenhagen.

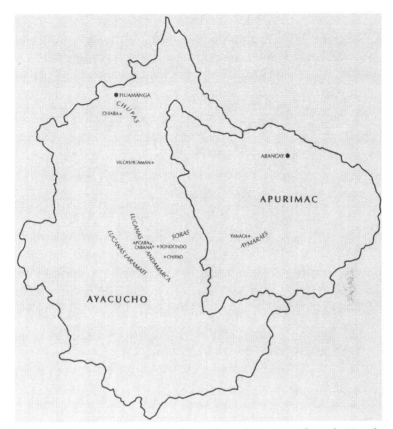

FIGURE 5. Map of the Departments of Ayacucho and Apurimac, drawn by Henrik
Maribo, in Rolena Adorno, *Guaman Poma and His Illustrated Chronicle from Colonial
Peru/Guaman Poma y su crónica ilustrada del Perú colonial*. Copenhagen: Museum
Tusculanum Press, 2001, 11. Reproduced by courtesy of Museum Tusculanum Press,
University of Copenhagen.

Church Council, convened in Lima in 1582–1583, suggests that he had
served as an interpreter there. Yet his references to one of the council's
principal theologians, the Jesuit author José de Acosta, as well as to the
Franciscan friar Luis Jerónimo de Oré and the secular priest Miguel Ca-
bello Balboa evoke them not as personages whom he had met or worked
for, but rather as authors of the books whose titles he cited.[10] Despite his
praise of the Jesuits, Guaman Poma mentions only two Jesuits by name in
the course of his entire work, which indicates that he probably knew few
of them personally. In general, the priests who populate Guaman Poma's

chronicle are overwhelmingly those who served in local Andean parishes in the provinces of Lucanas Andamarca, Lucanas Laramati, Soras, and Aymaraes in the southern Peruvian Andes.

The portion of Guaman Poma's life best known from sources external to his work is the six-year period from 1594 to 1600. During this time Guaman Poma served as an interpreter and witness in proceedings in Huamanga that confirmed land titles and implemented the policies resulting from the viceroy Francisco de Toledo's forced resettlements (*reducciones*) of Andean communities in locations where a colonial labor force was needed.[11] At the same time, Guaman Poma was defending his and his kin's land interests, as we have learned from a series of legal petitions and transactions known as the Expediente Prado Tello.[12] The map he created and introduced as part of his suit is considered to be the very first known cartographic representation of any area that falls within today's Department of Ayacucho (fig. 6).[13] It reveals Guaman Poma's detailed geographical knowledge of the area as well as his understanding of the importance of such written and graphic representations in supporting claims in the Spanish viceregal legal system.

In the decade of the 1590s Guaman Poma petitioned for the return of rights to lands outside Huamanga (today's Ayacucho) in Peru's south central Andes in the valley of Chupas (found near the top of Guaman Poma's map [p. 33], at the convergence of seven waterways). He traveled twice from Huamanga to present his case before the Audiencia Real in Lima, and both times, in September 1597 and March 1599, his claims were upheld. But upon returning to Huamanga with the confirming documents in hand, he was accused by his enemies (the Chachapoyas, members of an ethnic group emigrated from the northern Andes to the Huamanga area, who lost the suit) of being an imposter. A compendium of legal petitions and decrees thirty-two folios in length and known as the Compulsa Ayacucho, documents the fateful charges and the outcome. In 1600, Guaman Poma was tried and convicted for falsely representing himself as a lord of inherited rank, or *kuraka* (the commonly used Taíno term *cacique* appears in the court's documentation), and he was sentenced to two hundred lashes and a two-year exile from Huamanga and its environs.

Acknowledging his loss in these legal battles only allusively in the *Nueva corónica y buen gobierno*, Guaman Poma nevertheless lets slip the observation, in discussing the pretensions and criminal activities of "common Indians," that he first became aware of the high level of social disintegration—Andean society being turned "upside-down"—when he began his travels "in the year that we left, of 160[0] and afterward," that is, after his legal defeat.[14] Guaman Poma (411, 918) punningly expressed his frustration at this outcome by sarcastically remarking that to file legal petitions was to render losses (the play on words is "peticiones," or petitions, and "perdiciones," or losses), that the legal representation by licentiates (*licenciados*) was so poor that they should be called "licentiate-asses" ["lecenciasnos"; "asno," or ass], and that court advocates (*procuradores*) did not seek justice, but rather personal gain ["proculadrones"; "ladrón," or thief].

Guaman Poma's experience between 1600 and 1615 is richly represented in his manuscript work, and it is mostly limited, not surprisingly, given his criminal sentence, to the Lucanas region. The province of Lucanas is the site of the twenty-odd settlements, and the home of the majority of local colonial officials, that he names in his chronicle; the *Buen gobierno* is suffused with such references. Local events mentioned span the years from 1608 to 1615, and the years 1611, 1612, and 1613 are frequently cited with regard to noteworthy occurrences.

On February 14, 1615, Guaman Poma wrote a letter to King Philip III, dispatched from Santiago de Chipao in the province of Lucanas (the document was discovered decades ago by Guillermo Lohmann Villena in the Archivo General de Indias in Seville). In the letter Guaman Poma informed the monarch that he had just completed a "chronicle or general history" of Peru and that he would be glad to send it to the king upon request: "I beg Your Majesty to be served by requesting that the viceroy who governs these kingdoms receive it and send it, well guarded, to Your Majesty, since I am ready to deliver it to him as soon as he requests it of me" [Suplico a Vuestra Majestad siendo servido se lo mande al virrey que gobernare este reino que lo reciba y envíe a buen recaudo a Vuestra Majestad, que yo estoy presto de se lo entregar luego que me lo pidiere]. Guaman Poma addressed his work to King Philip III, twice urging that the monarch have it published so that it could be of use to all the officials and citizens of "the Indies of Peru."[15]

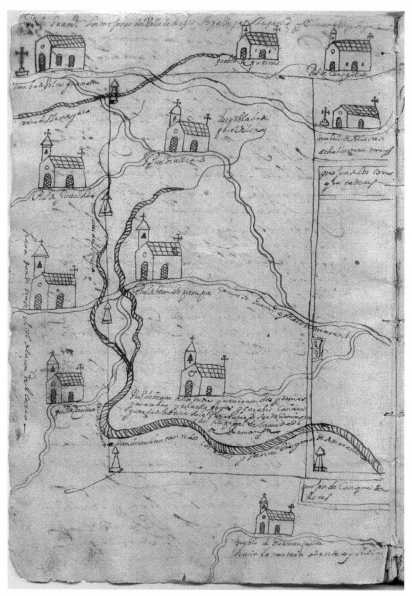

FIGURE 6. Map of Huamanga, drawn by Guaman Poma. Expediente Prado Tello.
Courtesy of Dr. Alfredo Prado Prado, Presidente, Centro de Investigación y Promoción
Amazónica, Lima, Peru.

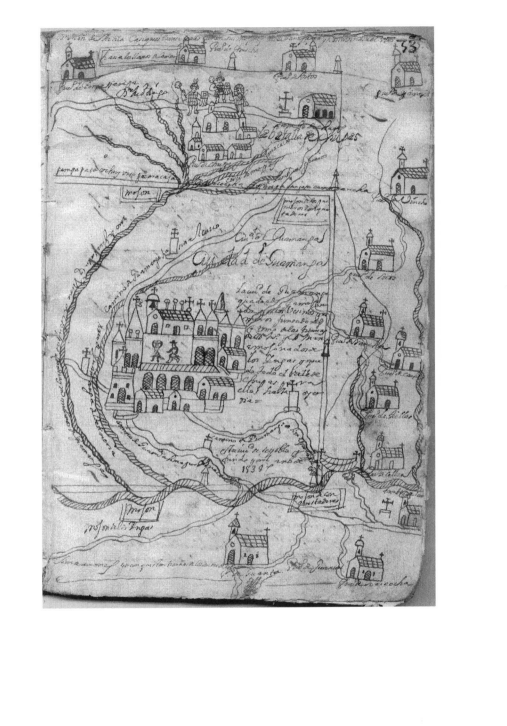

GUAMAN POMA, ARTIST

The temporal gap between the document recording the criminal sentence against Guaman Poma in 1600 and his 1615 letter to the king announcing the completion of his chronicle has been illuminated recently by the publication of the manuscript book, written by the Mercedarian friar Martín de Murúa, which dates from after 1600. This is the first of two extant manuscript versions of Murúa's history of the Incas, and it is entitled *Historia del origen y genealogía real de los reyes ingas del Pirú*.[16] Although it carries on its frontispiece the date of 1590, it was illustrated by Guaman Poma with ninety-nine water-colored line drawings in a period that, thanks to textual references to events outside the work, can have begun no earlier than 1596 and necessarily extends beyond 1600.[17] Given Guaman Poma's relocation south to Lucanas after 1600, Guaman Poma must have illustrated Murúa's manuscript during the latter's tenure as parish priest (*cura*) and prefect or magistrate (*comendador*) in the province of Aymaraes, between 1604 and 1606 (see fig. 5).[18]

The Murúa/Guaman Poma collaboration has been a subject of speculation for more than half a century, ever since a scantly illustrated edition of Murúa's first manuscript, the *Historia del origen,* was published in 1946. This edition was based not on the original manuscript, then lost, but on a copy of it that had been made at Loyola in 1890. Murúa's second manuscript, the *Historia general del Perú,* was rediscovered in London in 1951 and published in Madrid in 1962–1964. With the evidence of both Murúa manuscripts in hand, the first of the two Murúa manuscripts offers insight into how the Mercedarian's and the Andean's collaboration worked.[19]

Guaman Poma illustrated Murúa's *Historia del origen* manuscript after Murúa had finished its prose text, which had been clean-copied by a single scribe and was subsequently augmented and corrected by the author's own hand. A first, unknown artist prepared two series of portraits (the Incas, followed by their royal consorts, or *coyas*) as well as three other drawings. Then Guaman Poma came on the scene, his task being to create frontispieces (on the verso of every sheet) to accompany the chapter that occupied the recto on the facing page. Because Murúa occasionally had written additional passages after the scribe finished his work, and because authorial additions took up space on the versos, with the result that Guaman Poma sometimes could create no drawing at all, sometimes only half-page or even smaller ones, squeezing them into the remaining blank spaces of the sheet. He apparently worked with little consultation with Murúa, illustrating chapters according to his own lights. This accounts for the indirect relationship between Murúa's prose texts and Guaman Poma's respective frontispieces, which sometimes led Murúa to write short explanations (or to cancel those of Guaman Poma) on the pictorial field. The evidence presented by the finished manuscript reveals that they worked not side by side, as has often been hypothesized, but successively, one following the other and perhaps with only minimum prior consultation.[20]

On one occasion, where one would expect to find the coat of arms of Peru, Guaman Poma created instead a magnificent heraldic device. But he put his own self-designed "coat of arms," which he reproduced later on the frontispiece of the *Nueva corónica,* into the shield's privileged upper-left-hand quadrant (fig. 7; see fig. 2). Beneath the shield he wrote a lengthy description that proclaimed one of his forebears, Guaman Chaua, as the first great lord of Peru.[21] Along with three other illustrated folios, Murúa later removed the folio containing this splendid coat of arms from his earlier, *Historia del origen* manuscript and placed it in the second (*Historia general*), under a new title. Murúa canceled Guaman Poma's brief captions above the shield and penned "The arms of Peru" [Las armas del Pirú] as the new title of the drawing. Even though he did not subscribe to Guaman Poma's Yarovilca version of pre-Incaic history that celebrated his ancestor, Murúa did not cancel Guaman Poma's caption but rather let it stand, preferring not to mar or disfigure it by attempts to correct it.

The evidence of the Murúa/Guaman Poma working relationship testifies to the difficulty, if not the impossibility, of establishing, at that moment and in those circumstances, a dialogue and collaboration of the type that would be gratifying to imagine. Whereas at the Colegio de Santa Cruz de Tlaltelolco in Mexico Fray Bernardino de Sahagún named and praised four of his most accomplished native collaborators, Murúa did not mention Guaman Poma's name once. Guaman Poma subsequently broke with Murúa, and each then wrote independently his own work: Murúa's *Historia general del Perú,* now housed at the J. Paul Getty Museum in Los Angeles (MS Ludwig XIII 16), and Guaman Poma's *El primer nueva corónica y buen gobierno* (*Nueva corónica y buen gobierno*), conserved at the Royal Library in Copenhagen (GkS 2232, 4°). As in his earlier (*Historia del origen*) manuscript, Murúa secured an artist who took up the task of

FIGURE 7. Coat of arms of Peru, drawn for Fray Martín de Murúa's history of the Incas by Felipe Guaman Poma de Ayala. MS Ludwig XIII 16, fol. 307 r. The J. Paul Getty Museum, Los Angeles.

creating for the *Historia general del Perú* a traditional series of portraits of Incas, *coyas*, and military captains, plus a coat of arms. This unknown artist abandoned his work after creating portraits of the eleventh Inca and the eleventh *coya*, but this time there was no one to carry on the project, as Guaman Poma had done in Murúa's earlier manuscript. In order to complete the series of twelve Incas and twelve *coyas*, Murúa now cut out and pasted three of the drawings from the first manuscript (two of which had been created by Guaman Poma) into the second one.[22] Murúa also pasted the sheet containing Guaman Poma's drawing of the coat of arms, mentioned above, into the later manuscript.[23]

Guaman Poma's other known (and famous) artistic achievement as illustrator consists of the 399 full-page line drawings (they are not water-colored) that he created for his *El primer nueva corónica y buen gobierno*. Transforming the concept of the introductory frontispiece, Guaman Poma created detailed drawings that constitute the primary exposition of his work. This contrasts sharply with the illustration program he carried out in Murúa's *Historia del origen*, in which the drawings were added after the prose texts were transcribed, with the result that the drawings were sometimes only loosely related to the written text they accompanied. In the *Nueva corónica y buen gobierno*, pictorial and prose expositions are intimately related, even when they occasionally present opposite interpretations of the same subject. With regard to content, Guaman Poma expanded the repertoire of images of ritual and daily life during Inca times that he drew for Murúa to create a wide-ranging pictorial record (better said: exposé) of the actions of every social category of every ethnic group and every institution in the Peruvian viceroyalty, focusing on violence, corruption, and the colonial exploitation of Andean society. With regard to their aesthetic values, Guaman Poma's drawings, as can be appreciated in the ones reproduced here, are consistently narrative in mode, variously devout, didactic, satirical, or polemical in interpretation, abundant in detail, and unfailingly dynamic in their expression.

Guaman Poma was not shy about criticizing Murúa's historical work in his own. He (1090) complained that Murúa had written nothing about the provenance or legitimacy of the Incas or about the ancient dynasties that had preceded them; he lamented that Murúa had devoted himself instead to telling a tale of the Incas' menacing intimidation and conquest of other peoples, forcing them into idolatry, just as the Romans, wrote Guaman Poma, had conquered and imposed their gods on the ancient peoples of Spain.

"DON FELIPE DE AYALA, AUTOR"

"Don Felipe de Ayala, autor" was the signature Guaman Poma used in signing his dedicatory epistles to the pope and the king. His title, *El primer nueva corónica y buen gobierno*, captured the main thrusts of his work: his interpretation of the Andean past and his program of recommendations for its future. Calling his work the first of the "new chronicles" and a treatise on "good government" or governmental reform, Guaman Poma set forth his account of Andean history as new because he presented a version of pre-Columbian and Spanish conquest history unfamiliar to readers of the Spanish-authored histories of Peru then in print. That is, Guaman Poma did not present the Incas as a society rising from barbarity to civilize the Andes with their solar religion, which he described as idolatrous. Instead, he created an elaborate and complex cosmology that wove the dynasties of the Andean past (pre-Inca and Inca) into a Christian (Augustinian) model of universal history. Furthermore, he made the Incas not the first and only great Andean dynasty, but the last one, succeeding, among others, the dynasty of the Yarovilcas of Allauca Huánuco, featured in the coat of arms he created for Murúa's work (see fig. 7).

With respect to the theme of good government, Guaman Poma wanted to convince the king to take action to combat the dire situation he described in these terms: the traditional Andean social hierarchies were being dismantled. The native Andeans were being exploited in the countryside and in the mines, and they were fleeing to the cities, where they engaged in lives of dissipation as rogues and prostitutes. The mestizo population was increasing because of miscegenation and intermarriage, and the ethnic Andean population was declining dangerously because of colonial violence and exploitation, disease, and the race mixing of *mestizaje*. Remedial action needed to be taken immediately, in Guaman Poma's view, and his sense of urgency and despair seems to have increased during the years of the preparation of his work. He warned that the Andean race would perish and Peru be destroyed if appropriate measures were not taken.[24] Such warnings are the first clue that he followed Las Casas's lines of argumentation.

When Guaman Poma set about to write his own chronicle, he had many models from which to choose, and he employed nearly all of them. He modeled his prose at various moments on the published histories of the conquest of Peru, on the didactic, moralistic works of Christian religious devotion, and even (and especially) on the mundane documents of colonial administration. His prose reveals his book learning and the impressive range of genres with which he was familiar, from the sermon and devotional literature to historical narration and the biographies of kings, including his use of literary preliminaries, notably his exuberant use of the prologue.[25] Like his graphic representations, his prose is variously didactic, satirical, polemical, and devout. His mastery of verbal expression came not only from an ear that was attuned to the rhetorical rhythms of the sermons to which he listened and those he read in the publications of the Third Church Council and the works of Fray Luis de Granada, but also from his appreciation of the firebrand harangues and history-dramatized-as-argument that he knew from the writings of Las Casas.

The less bookish dimension of Guaman Poma's engagement with the written word comes from his familiarity with the mundane documents of civil and ecclesiastical administration. In addition to his enumeration of legal ordinances, the information gathered from various types of inspection tours, such as those that monitored parish priests and their congregations as well as those that took head counts for the purpose of assigning tribute quotas, permeates every part of his work.[26] In its entirety, the *Buen gobierno* (occupying two-thirds of his manuscript book) is presented as a *visita* report in which the colonizers are grouped according to occupation (from Spanish miners to African slaves) and the Andeans are presented in categories defined by their inherited social rank and traditional or colonial administrative offices. Insofar as the twin pillars of any *visita* report were review and reform, that is, the description of the current situation in its particulars and recommendations for the resolution of problems cited, Guaman Poma's emphasis on correction and reform is everywhere evident.[27] His final chapter, "Camina el autor," frames for the last time the itinerant inspection tour, as he narrates his journey from site to site and details, settlement by settlement in the area of Huarochirí, the havoc wreaked by the most recent campaigns to extirpate idolatry.[28]

THE POLEMICS OF POSSESSION

Guaman Poma was well aware of the polemics that in his own day continued to orient discussions of the origin of the peoples of America and the rights of Spanish conquest over them. He takes up the first of these issues in his account of pre-Inca history. He (60–61) pointed out that "some say that the Indians came from the caste of the Jews; but they would look like them and wear beards, being 'blue-eyed and blond like Spaniards,' and have the law of Moses and letters, knowing how to read and write and [perform their] ceremonies. And if they were of the caste of Turks or Moors, they would also be bearded and possess the law of Mohammed. And others say that the Indians are savage animals; but if so, they would not have the law or spirituality or costume of Adam, and they would be like horses and beasts, and they would not know the Creator nor would they cultivate fields nor have houses and arms, fortresses and laws and ordinances and the knowledge of God and His holy presence."[29] Thus he dispatches such theories, and, as indicated in this passage, he attributes to the ancient, pre-Inca generations of Indians the knowledge of the Christian god, attributing to them "a shadow and the light of the knowledge of the Creator and Maker of heaven and earth and everything that is in it" [una sonbrilla y lus de conosemiento del Criador y Hazedor del cielo y de la tierra y todo lo que ay en ella].[30]

While this is standard Scholastic thinking, Guaman Poma's next, related claim is controversial and daring. He asserts that the Indians became Christian long before the arrival of the Spaniards.[31] In doing so, he sets the stage for denying the Spanish encomenderos their supposedly legitimate overlordship of the Indians of Peru.[32] This is a first step in his argumentation regarding the polemical issues of the rights to Spanish conquest and the imposition of its colonial institutions, which he handles in a much more complex manner (see below).

The Nueva corónica and the Buen gobierno, as formally discrete segments of his work, are, in fact, deeply integrated. The entity that draws them together is the section of the work devoted to the conquest era, entitled "Conquista." Not named in the work's title except implicitly (a new and different chronicle of conquest history), "Conquista" is the site, the "zona de contacto" (see endnote 2) internal to the work, where the reelaboration of ancient Inca and Spanish conquest history and the formulation of the project Guaman Poma proposes for the Andean future come together. It is the place where Guaman Poma works out and dramatizes ideas as events in a historical narrative that will allow him, in the chapter in which he created a "dialogue with the king," to propose the full restoration of Andean sovereignty over the Andes. Central to his formulations are his reworkings of the principles and propositions he gleaned from the writings of Las Casas.

LAS CASAS'S *TWELVE DOUBTS* IN GUAMAN POMA'S *BUEN GOBIERNO*

In 1977, I discovered that Guaman Poma quoted and paraphrased one of Las Casas's formal treatises in the field of political polemics, the *Tratado de las doce dudas* (1564), in his important chapter on moral and spiritual considerations in the *Nueva corónica y buen gobierno* (fig. 8). The *Doce dudas* circulated among the Dominicans in the Peruvian viceroyalty, and it is likely that the Andean author became acquainted with it through the local clergy in Huamanga. At the time of my discovery, however, I did not understand that Guaman Poma's proposal for a universal empire of autonomous kingdoms follows directly from Las Casas's *Doce dudas*.[33]

The principles of Las Casas's proposal can be summed up as follows: By natural, divine, and human law, the native inhabitants of the Americas, who never harmed or had been subject to any Christian prince, are free and sovereign in their own lands; the papal bulls of donation gave the church the right to evangelize but not to dispossess the native peoples of their lands or to abrogate their right to rule them. Spain's invasion and rule of the Indies is illegitimate and tyrannical; the only means by which Spain can rule legitimately is at the invitation and with the free and willing consent of the native peoples of the Indies.[34] The logical conclusion, in Las Casas's own words, was the restoration of sovereignty to the native lords of Peru: they were to recognize "His Majesty and his successors, the kings of Castile and León, as supreme lords or protectors, but retaining in all else their complete liberty and hence the peaceful possession of those kingdoms" [Harán ciertos actos jurídicos por los cuales protesten recibir a Su Majestad por superior monarca o protector, y a los sucesores de Castilla y León, quedando ellos en lo demás en su entera libertad, y de aquello le den pacífica posesión en aquellos reinos].[35] Las Casas wrote the *Doce dudas* while the last Inca princes, Titu Cussi Yupanqui and Tupac Amaru, were alive, so his proposal for the Inca restoration, though visionary and quixotic, was not illogical.

By the time Guaman Poma wrote his work after the turn of the seventeenth century, it was another era altogether. Titu Cussi and Tupac Amaru had been gone for more than forty years; Titu Cussi was deceased in 1571, and Tupac Amaru was executed by the viceroy Francisco de Toledo in 1572. Guaman Poma nevertheless reiterated Las Casas's propositions, adapting them in a chapter that emulates the style and content of moralis-

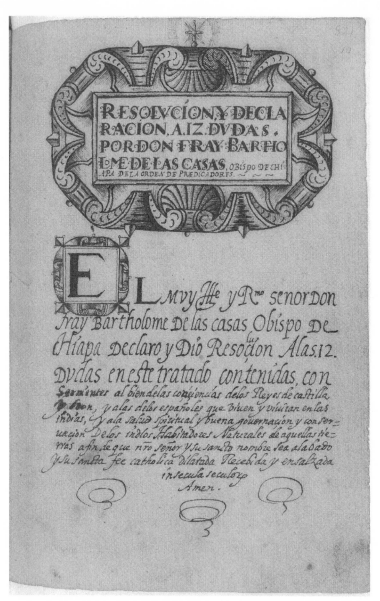

FIGURE 8. Frontispiece of the presentation manuscript of Fray Bartolomé de las Casas's *Tratado de las doce dudas*, 1564. The John Carter Brown Library at Brown University.

tic reflections, or "considerations." Guaman Poma's text can be taken apart, statement by statement, to show that the *Doce dudas* is its source: Addressing himself to his princely reader, Guaman Poma (929) writes, "You must consider that all the world is God's, and thus Castile belongs to the Spaniards and the Indies belongs to the Indians, and Guinea, to the blacks. . . . each one of these is a legitimate proprietor, not only according to the law, as St. Paul, who for ten years resided [in Rome] and called himself a Roman, wrote" [Que aués de conzedearar que todo el mundo es de Dios y ancí Castilla es de los españoles y las Yndias es de los yndios y Guenea es de los negros. Que cada déstos son lexítimos propetarios, no tan solamente por la ley, como lo escriuió San Pablo, que de dies años estaua de posición y se llamaua romano].

This passage refers to the first principle (Principio I) of Las Casas's (486) treatise: All pagans have sovereign jurisdiction over their own territories and possessions; this right to jurisdiction is mandated not only by human legislation (Guaman Poma's "no tan solamente por la ley"), but also by natural and divine law. Las Casas cites St. Augustine's reference to Paul's epistle to the Romans (Rom. 13:1), in which the apostle insists that the Christian community obey the monarch under whose jurisdiction that community lives, even though the ruler be a pagan. Thus, says Guaman Poma, Saint Paul "called himself a Roman" [se llamaua rromano]. In the same manner, Guaman Poma implies, the Spaniards and all other foreigners should obey the Andean authorities while in the sovereign kingdom of Peru.

In the passage that follows, Guaman Poma (929) points out that natives of Castile, whether Jews or Muslims, are subject to the laws of that land. Analogously, those Spaniards living in Peru are considered foreigners or outsiders (in Quechua, *mitmaq*); that is, they are persons sent out from their own homeland to attend to interests abroad (this was the Inca-era meaning of the term *mitmaq*). As foreigners living in a sovereign Andean land, the Spaniards are duty bound to obey Andean, not Spanish, law.[36] In this instance, Guaman Poma is reiterating Las Casas's (487–88) second principle (Principio II), in which the Dominican refers to the four classes of non-Christians and their respective rights and jurisdictions. The first class consists of those, among whom he names the Jews and Muslims, who, by living in Castile, are subject to the rule of the Christian king by right and in deed ("de jure y de facto") and are thus obligated to obey the just laws of the Spanish realm. Guaman Poma relates this concept to that of the mitmaq of the Inca era, who were sent out to reside in newly conquered lands but were bound to obey the laws and customs of those lands, even though settled there for the purpose of teaching the Incas' language and religion.

Guaman Poma concludes his argument as follows, again relying on Las Casas's Principio II:

> Each one in his own kingdom is a legitimate proprietor, owner, not because of the king but by God and through God's justice: He made the world and the earth and established in them every foundation, the Spaniard in Castile, the Indian in the Indies, the black in Guinea. . . . And thus, although [the Spanish king] grants a favor to the priest or to the Spaniard in the lands that are settled under the king's authority, they are not landowners. And thus there must be obedience to the principal lords and magistrates, the legitimate owners of the land, whether they be male or female [Cada uno en su rreyno son propetarios lexítimos, poseedores, no por el rrey cino por Dios y por justicia de Dios: Hizo el mundo y la tierra y plantó en ellas cada cimiente, el español en Castilla, el yndio en las Yndias, el negro en Guynea. . . . Y ancí, aunque (el rey español) le haga merced al padre, al español en las tierras que se componga con el rrey, no es propetario. Y ací a de tener obedencia al señor [sic] principales y justicias, propetarios legítimos de las tierras, que sea señor o señora (929)].

Here Guaman Poma classifies the Andeans as belonging to the fourth category of nonbelievers, that is, those who have never been and are not at present subject to a Christian ruler, either by right or by deed.

The reasons he gives are those that Las Casas (489) articulated: namely, that the Andeans had neither usurped Christian lands nor done Christians any harm nor intended to do so; they had never been subjugated by any Christian prince or any member-state of the church. By emphasizing the rights of the legitimate possessors and declaring that such rights are mandated by God, not by the king, Guaman Poma appeals to one of the basic precepts of natural law, the Scholastic concept of the right of all peoples to jurisdiction over their own lands, followed since Thomas Aquinas[37] and made explicit by Las Casas in Principio II:

> All these [nations] have their kingdoms, their dominions, their kings, their jurisdictions high and low, their judges and magistrates and their territories, within which they exercise legitimately, and can use freely, their power, and within them, it is not lawful for any king in the world, without breaking natural law, to enter without the permission of their kings or their republics, and much less that they should use or exercise any authority or power whatsoever [Tienen todas éstas (repúblicas) sus reinos, sus señoríos, sus reyes, sus jurisdicciones, altas y bajas, sus jueces y magistrados y sus territorios, dentro de los cuales usan legítimamente y pueden libremente usar de su potestad, y dentro dellos a ningún rey del mundo, sin quebrantar el Derecho natural, es lícito sin licencia de sus reyes o de sus repúblicas entrar, y menos usar ni ejercitar jurisdicción ni potestad alguna (489)].

Furthermore, Guaman Poma's reference to the first chapter of the book of Genesis ("Dios hizo el mundo y la tierra y plantó en ellas cada cimiente") reiterates Las Casas's (486) own citation of Genesis 1, which he offers in Principio I as proof of all people's rights to sovereignty in their own lands under the precepts of natural law.

In addition to Guaman Poma's reelaboration of Las Casas's arguments favoring the rights of all peoples to their own sovereignty (Principles I and II), the remaining six principles in the *Doce dudas* presented two additional clusters of ideas of great importance in Guaman Poma's thinking about Andean affairs. First, the only right granted to the Catholic kings by the pope had been to evangelize, not to conquer, subdue, or rule the native populations. Second, the conquests had been illegal.[38] They had not conformed to generally accepted principles of just war, namely, the right of a sovereign realm to defend its sovereignty when threatened, to recover that which had been unjustly taken, and to punish an enemy for harm received.[39] For Las Casas there existed no just title of war in the Indies according to the above criteria, but by the same criteria he did recognize as legitimate and just the war of Spain (and Europe) against the

Ottoman Turk.[40] Through these eight principles, Las Casas argued in the *Doce dudas* that the only way by which the king could save his soul was to make restitution to the Incas and their descendants and to restore the Incas as legitimate lords in their own lands.[41]

Guaman Poma follows up, arguing not that the conquest of Peru had been illegal, but that it simply had not occurred: there had been no war of conquest because the Inca's ambassadors (in Guaman Poma's account, his own forebears) had accepted Spanish rule peacefully, and later attempts at Inca resistance had been quelled by miraculous visions of Santiago (Saint James the Major) and Saint Mary (figs. 9, 10). Briefly, the major claims he makes on the basis of the history he narrates are as follows: first, that the encomienda system was illegal because Tawantinsuyu had not been conquered in a just war: "there was no conquest" [no ubo conquista] is Guaman Poma's (564) way of putting it; second, because the gratuitous aggression of the foreign invasion had violated natural, divine, and human law, the Spanish were bound by their religion to make restitution for lands and wealth taken and dominion exercised (572, 573, 741); third and finally, the king of Spain would preside ceremonially over all the world, which would be divided into four great autonomous monarchies, representing Europe, Africa, the world of the Ottoman Turk ["el Gran Turco"], and the Indies (the latter of which would be headed by Guaman Poma's princely son) (963). Furthermore, each crowned head would be a sovereign lord: Philip III would occupy the role of universal monarch ["monarca del mundo"], whose prerogatives would be restricted to serving as protector of the faith (over the Christian kingdoms) but without political jurisdiction over the duly sovereign realms.[42]

OLD MODELS AND NEW MONARCHIES

In his formulation, Guaman Poma combined fundamental elements of Andean cosmology, in which perfect order is created by a quadripartite division of space organized around a center.[43] His global design of four imperial divisions headed by a universal monarch represented the placement of European and other non-Andean elements in an Andean scheme. However, inasmuch as Guaman Poma illustrated the Andean paradigm (the four realms of Chinchaysuyu, Antisuyu, Collasuyu, and Condesuyu, with the Inca at center) in a map he called "mapamundi y reino de las Indias," it is clear that his conceptualization was already a synthetic one (fig. 11).

FIGURE 9. "Don Martín de Ayala, the first ambassador of Huascar Inca, to Francisco Pizarro, ambassador of the emperor Charles V." Guaman Poma, *Nueva corónica*, 377. Courtesy of The Royal Library, Copenhagen, Denmark.

FIGURE 10. "Miracle of Saint James the Major, apostle of Jesus Christ, in Cuzco."
Guaman Poma, *Nueva corónica*, 406. Courtesy of The Royal Library, Copenhagen,
Denmark.

FIGURE 11. Guaman Poma's "Mapamundi of the kingdom of the Indies." Guaman Poma, *Nueva corónica*, 1001–02. Courtesy of The Royal Library, Copenhagen, Denmark.

The quadripartite division of the world was an honored tradition in medieval European cosmography, as it was in the Andes. In maps of 1110 onward, Jerusalem occupied the center, the "umbilicus mundi," of this sacred geography. An explicitly quadripartite division is found in the thirteenth-century Ebstorf (Germany) map, in which the inhabited world is inscribed on the crucified and resurrected body of Christ: the head, feet, and hands occupy the four cardinal directions, and the navel of Christ is the center of the world.[44] Such notions were not definitively discarded until the discoveries of the second half of the fifteenth century. However, myths of a New Jerusalem and of a center (geographical, spiritual, political, and mythic), tied to notions of the chosen people and the chosen monarch, continued to be important through the seventeenth century.[45] Guaman Poma's sources were not only iconographic. His proposal for the reorganization of the world is his variant of Las Casas's 1560s proposal, and he places it on the grid of his own "mapamundi."

Guaman Poma's offer of his son as "king of the Indies" is in effect the repetition, but with a twist, of Las Casas's bid for the Inca restoration presented a half century earlier in the *Treatise of the Twelve Doubts*. First, Guaman Poma's presentation of a new candidate effectively replaces the departed Inca princes, the last of whom had been executed in 1572 by the viceroy Toledo. Second, this new prince, as described by Guaman Poma, represents both the Inca dynasty and a more ancient one insofar as he identifies his son as a great-grandson of Tupac Inca Yupanqui and also as an heir to the Yarovilca dynasty of Allauca Huánuco. While the self-serving character of this nomination has caused it to be dispatched with a scoffing dismissal, what is more pertinent is its articulation of a proposal that takes into account events in Peru of the preceding half century and combines initiatives made decades earlier on behalf of the Inca and non-Inca Andean leaderships, respectively. Guaman Poma presents the only reasonable alternative to prior proposals: a replacement for Las Casas's last Incas and one who fulfills the viceroy Toledo's criteria for ancient, legitimate rule in the Andes.

To understand this convergence of factors, we must turn to events of a half century earlier. In the mid-1550s the Spanish encomenderos of Peru (including the captain Garcilaso de la Vega, El Inca Garcilaso de la Vega's father; see the section entitled "Las Casas and the Encomenderos of Peru" in chapter 3) offered to purchase from Philip II all rights in perpetuity to their encomiendas, that is, to the landed labors of Peru's native inhabitants. In 1555, nearly a decade before writing the *Doce dudas,* Las Casas had written urgently to the royal confessor, the Dominican friar Bartolomé Carranza de Miranda, who was with Prince Philip in London.[46] Rejecting the proposition that the encomenderos of Peru had the right to purchase their grants to encomiendas in perpetuity, Las Casas argued that the natives of the Americas should be removed from the control of private citizens, in fact, that the king should "cancel all the encomiendas, returning the Indians to their original liberty and restoring the native rulers." These restored leaders would need only give the Spanish monarch a token tribute for overseeing the propagation and maintenence of the Christian faith.[47]

In 1560, in response to the encomenderos' offer, Las Casas and his Dominican colleagues in Peru, notably Domingo de Santo Tomás, the author of the first grammar and dictionary of the Quechua language,[48] presented Philip with a counteroffer on behalf of the native lords of Peru designed to best the offer of the encomenderos. In the end, neither the encomenderos' offer to purchase their rights in perpetuity nor the kurakas' offer to buy their own freedom was accepted. Subsequently, in January 1562, hundreds of Andean lords met outside Lima to grant powers of attorney to the archbishop of Lima, the Franciscan friar Jerónimo de Loaysa, and to the Dominicans Las Casas and Santo Tomás, among other trusted persons, to advocate for the restitution of all the lands, properties, and possessions which had been taken from the Andean lords by the Spaniards.[49] In October and November 1562, the kurakas of Chucuito and Arequipa, again with the help of Domingo de Santo Tomás, demanded an end to encomienda, the full restitution of lands and properties usurped by the Spaniards, and the payment of rewards and liberties for services they had rendered to the king.[50] Las Casas presented his proposal for the full Inca restoration in 1564. His death in 1566 seemingly ended the agitation on behalf of restoring Andean sovereignty. Guaman Poma surely knew about these events.

When Francisco de Toledo arrived in Lima on November 30, 1569, to assume the position of viceroy of Peru, he soon discovered that the arguments in favor of returning to Inca rule were still alive and potent. Toledo realized that such demands could not be countered by trying once again to prove the Spanish right to rule; the only effective argument was to

prove the illegitimacy of the rule of the Incas.[51] Through a series of inquiries of the non-Inca native leadership, Toledo collected a preponder-
ance of testimony in 1570–1572 that indicated (not surprisingly) that the
Incas had been Johnny-come-latelies and were not considered by contemporary native witnesses to have been legitimate rulers.[52] Therefore, the
threat to Spanish rule posed by the surviving members of the Inca dynasty
was diminished.[53]

Yet Las Casas's influence was still keenly felt, as the viceroy himself
acknowledged. Toledo's urgency to prove the illegitimacy of Inca rule
stemmed from what he saw as the dangerous influence of Las Casas's
followers, Dominicans and others, for whom Las Casas's ideas and books
were "the heart of most of the friars of Peru" [los de Chiapa era el coraçón
de los más frailes de este reino].[54] Toledo therefore ordered that Las Casas's printed pamphlets of 1552–1553 be suppressed in line with a royal
mandate that all books that had been published without royal sanction
were to be withdrawn from circulation.[55] Philip was willing to have ex-
communicated anyone who owned Las Casas's books, and Toledo wanted
special punishments for those who were guilty of possessing them because he considered the ordinary sanctions to be insufficient.[56] Toledo
definitively solved the problem of a potential Inca restoration when he
executed the fifteen-year-old prince Tupac Amaru on September 24, 1572.

Guaman Poma was intimately familiar with most of these events,
according to his remarks in the *Nueva corónica y buen gobierno,* and he
knew the viceroy Toledo's tenure of 1569–1581 well. Circumstantial and
textual evidence suggests that he formed part of the entourage that accompanied the viceroy's personal inspection tour of Huamanga. His precise recollection of the names of the officials who had been in charge forty
years earlier, as well as his account of the inspection tour, lends credibility
to his claims.[57] Guaman Poma's description of Toledo's arrival in Cuzco,
his intimate knowledge of and praise for many of the laws promulgated
by Toledo, his condemnation of the execution of Tupac Amaru, and his
criticism of the forced resettlements carried out by Toledo all signal his
vivid recollection of Toledo's times.[58]

Guaman Poma's grand scheme of 1615 for the creation of the universal monarchy, with the Spanish king reigning over the sovereign and
autonomous kingdoms of the "four parts of the world" and with the
Indies being ruled by a prince who combined both Inca and non-Inca

lineages, thus updates the earlier proposal by Las Casas. Though not restored to power, Guaman Poma knew that the Inca descendants of his own generation, such as Don Melchor Carlos Inca (1571–1610) (fig. 12), who was sent to Spain (exiled, says Guaman Poma), were honored by the Spanish monarch (753).[59] So Guaman Poma (754) claimed to be the grandson of Tupac Inca Yupanqui as much as he harked back to the prestige of his Yarovilca heritage. He argued that in this new universal order the "monarca del mundo," the Spanish king, unlike regular kings and emperors, would have no specific jurisdiction. Rather, he would have beneath him "crowned kings, who would be salaried" in his court "for the grandeur of the universal world of all the nations and types of persons: Indians, blacks and Spanish Christians, Turks, Jews, the Moors of the world: consider this for the greatness of His Majesty the king" (963). In his appeal to Philip III, who was the son of the monarch who had received from Las Casas a similar plan, Guaman Poma brings up anew the notion of an Andean restoration and a new, universal commonwealth of nations. Because the era of Toledo with its attacks on Inca legitimacy was long gone, and the last direct descendants of the Inca Huayna Capac had since perished, the presentation of a candidate who could be seen either as an Inca descendant or as the heir of an older, presumably legitimate dynasty was logical, making up in boldness what it suffered in impracticality.

Other World Monarchies

Were there precedents for Guaman Poma's grand scheme? Designs for a world monarchy had medieval origins, Dante being the thinker who went farther than anyone else in his time in "breaking with the old ideal of a unified Christian commonwealth controlled in both its branches by a revealed tradition of thought and action," for the purpose of extending to an absolute degree "the principle of the autonomy of the State, already partially admitted by Christian Aristoteleans like St. Thomas."[60] Thinkers from the thirteenth century through the early sixteenth helped bring to an end "the distinctive political role which Western Europe had conceded to the Church . . . since the conversion of Constantine."[61] By the middle of the sixteenth century, the basic medieval political idea of a Christian commonwealth with coordinated secular and religious branches had fallen away.[62]

In America, however, the notion of a universal empire had appeared in

FIGURE 12. Don Melchor Carlos Inca, Knight of the Order of Santiago. Guaman Poma, *Nueva corónica*, 753. Courtesy of The Royal Library, Copenhagen, Denmark.

the fourth and fifth letters (*cartas de relación*), of 1524 and 1526, respectively, of Hernán Cortés to the emperor Charles V. Speaking of conquests carried out and those yet to come, such as the conquest of the Chichimecas to the north of New Spain, Cortés opined that there would remain no area "superfluous" in the world, and that Charles would be "monarca del mundo."[63] Taken together, the Franciscan vision of the conversion of all peoples worldwide, as well as Erasmian and imperialist dreams of a universal empire along with Cortés's own dreams of the conquest of Cathay ("an empire which he himself would help to found by pressing on from Mexico, across the Pacific to the East"), furnished Cortés with a vision of a "world empire subject to a Charles V, who would become 'monarch of the universe.' "[64] Distinct from such freshly minted ideas about universal monarchies, which had been inspired by the discovery of the Americas, the European model of Guaman Poma had its origin, as we have seen, in Las Casas's *Doce dudas*. More like Dante, insofar as his idea of a commonwealth of nations left implicit the possibility of non-Christian members,[65] and quite unlike Cortés, for whom a universal Spanish monarchy implied conquests and Christianization everywhere, Las Casas's idea as developed by Guaman Poma specifically made room for the non-Christian world. Guaman Poma's emphasis on other cultural and religious traditions ("Moors, Turks, Jews") corresponded to a larger, legal and ethical view of the world taken from (and extending) Las Casas's most advanced arguments on the topic. In this vision of the world, Christian Europe loses its preeminence, and even the Spanish "monarca del mundo" plays a symbolic rather than a jurisdictional role.

The modernity of Guaman Poma's formulation is underscored not only by its contrast to Cortés's views in decades past but also to works exactly contemporaneous with Guaman Poma's. A Franciscan friar, Juan de Silva, published works in Madrid in 1613 and 1621 that gave a role to Philip III not unlike the one Guaman Poma suggested for him. Silva's *Advertencias importantes acerca del buen gobierno y administración de las Indias, assí en lo espiritual como en lo temporal* integrated the earlier advocacy of the peaceful conversion of the Indians by the missionary friars, specifically Las Casas, with official Spanish messianism.[66] Advocating the peaceful conversion of the natives and inveighing against their exploitation through forced labor, Silva insisted that the peaceful conversion of the peoples of the "southern continent" was far more important than the

recovery of Jerusalem. However, the Franciscan's project of universal conversion had no place in Guaman Poma's (963) vision of "the grandeur of
the universal world of all the nations and types of persons: Indians, blacks
and Spanish Christians, Turks, Jews, the Moors of the world."

WHOSE WAR WAS JUST?

Guaman Poma's argument for the full restitution of "life, honor, and
wealth" to the Andeans and the restoration of Andean autonomy was
based on his denial of the Spanish right to currently held encomiendas,
which was grounded in turn on arguments about the peaceful and voluntary acceptance of Spanish rule by the Andeans. Here again, Guaman
Poma gives a startling twist to Las Casas's arguments of the same type.
Las Casas had argued that the conquests had been illegal (the general
argument of Las Casas's "Avisos y reglas para confesores" and of Principles VII and VIII of his *Doce dudas;* see chapter 3) and that the only
hypothetical alternative to a justified Spanish rule would have been the
peaceful and voluntary submission of the natives. As noted briefly in the
section above entitled "The Polemics of Possession," Guaman Poma
turns the two around, arguing that his father, along with the three other
lords of the four divisions of the empire (*suyus*), had welcomed the arrival
of the Spanish emissaries of Charles V (the Pizarro invading party).
Therefore, there had been no war, just or unjust, and the imposition of the
encomienda system had been entirely without justification.[67] By making
his first claim, he dispensed with the need to argue the other two.

Guaman Poma's dramatization of events to effectively deny the violent military conquest of Peru was not wishful, retrospective thinking on
his part; in this case, he was following what was generally known and
commonly published about the Spanish conquest of Peru at the time. The
full extent of Inca aggression against the Spanish invasion has been revealed relatively recently.[68] The impression given by Guaman Poma
squares with the accounts published at the time. Many of the early published accounts of the war conveyed the idea that the Incas had succumbed without a struggle. The eyewitness reports of Francisco de Xerez
and Cristóbal de Mena estimated the Andean death toll on that first encounter (massacre) at Cajamarca to have been between six and eight
thousand persons (Hemming, *Conquest,* 551).[69] Las Casas, most likely on
the basis of these sources, offers the same numbers in the *Doce dudas.*

Guaman Poma's (388) account of the massacre declares that the Spanish soldiers killed the Andeans "like ants . . . so many Indian people died it was impossible to count them" [como hormiga . . . murieron mucha gente de yndios que no se puede contar].

Upon returning to Spain in 1535, other veterans of and writers about the military encounters in Cajamarca, Jauja, and Cuzco ended their narratives with the fall of Cuzco; Juan Ruiz de Arce, Pedro Sancho, Diego de Trujillo, and Miguel de Estete belong to this group. As Hemming observes, all the eyewitnesses who left a substantive record of the first years of the conquest terminated their narratives in 1535, with the result that the "history of the Conquest suffers seriously from the resulting hiatus."[70] All in all, these early published reports conveyed the notion of a swift and complete conquest, before the Quito campaign and the siege of Cuzco led by Manco Inca and before the Incas' ability to hold out for so long (until 1572) at Vilcabamba could have been imagined. From the sixteenth-century historiographic perspective, the notion that Peru was conquered without a great military conquest, conveyed by the early chroniclers and repeated by Las Casas in his *Doce dudas* and Guaman Poma in his *Nueva corónica*,[71] was neither novel nor surprising.

Guaman Poma effectively ended the conquest where some of the earlier chroniclers did, with the first shipment of gold to Castile after Atahualpa paid his ransom and was executed at Cajamarca (393). He described the remainder of the violence in the "Conquista" segment of his work as the simple lawlessness of armed and unruly men and the Spaniards' rebellion against their own king.[72] According to Guaman Poma, the first Spaniards conquered Peru with these words: " 'Have no fear: I am the Inca.' They said this shouting to the Indians, who fled with fear. Thus, they did not conquer with arms or the spilling of blood or great labor" [*Ama mancha. Noca Ynga*, que no tenga miedo que él era Ynga. Decía a boses a los yndios y se huyan de ellos por temor. Y no conquistó con armas ni derramamiento de sangre ni trabajo (397)].

On the other hand, Guaman Poma does grant that a just war occurred in Peru in the 1530s. It was the one waged by the last regularly reigning Inca, Huayna Capac's fourth son, Manco Inca (c. 1516–1545), against the Spaniards. Taking over the role of monarch, Guaman Poma (401) writes, Manco Inca waged a just war of self-defense, laying siege to Cuzco for the offenses suffered at the hands of the Spaniards. His account has a familiar ring, and it corresponds to Las Casas's rendering in *Doce dudas* of how the Spaniards had usurped control of Cuzco when the Incas had justly defended themselves; the Spaniards' actions constituted wanton rapine and plundering, not a just war, for they had taken everything by force and against the will of the owners in their very presence. Henceforth until the day of judgment, Las Casas declared, the Inca kings and commoners, too, had every right to make war against the Spanish for injuries suffered.[73] It is this right of just war that Guaman Poma attributed to Manco Inca.

Guaman Poma portrayed the actions of Manco Inca and, after him, Quis Quis Inca, as legitimate acts of self-defense that occurred after the peaceful Inca submission to Spanish rule (401, 408). Defeated not by arms but by a miraculous vision of a mounted Santiago, Guaman Poma asserts, Manco Inca retired to Vilcabamba, leaving "the kingdom and crown and royal fringe [*masca paycha*] and weapons to the lord king and emperor, our lord Don Carlos of glorious memory, who is in heaven, and his son, Don Felipe II, who is in heaven and his son Don Felipe III, our lord and king" (408). Guaman Poma's principal arguments about there having been no just Spanish war of conquest was based not on one historical episode but two:[74] the diplomatic submission of the four *suyus* at Tumbes and Manco Inca's relinquishment of royal command as he fled to Vilcabamba. Both events are important, for they make the executions of Atahualpa and Manco Inca's son, Tupac Amaru, illegal in exactly the same manner, that is, as gratuitous crimes committed against the already acquiescent and submissive Andeans. According to Guaman Poma's argument, the peaceful submission at Tumbes in 1532 and its reiteration by Manco Inca in 1539 leave open to the Spanish king no course other than that of accepting the restoration of Andean sovereignty to Andeans. With these assertions, Guaman Poma's recommendations for a universal monarchy and the creation or recognition of four princely, autonomous realms are fully rationalized.

Although the viceroy Toledo had appreciated Philip II's warning about the need to keep an eye on friars who thought they could intervene in affairs of state,[75] and although Toledo suggested that special punishments were required to deter friars from reading Las Casas's works, it was demonstrably impossible for Toledo or his successors to control the circulation and suppress the promulgation of ideas whose goal was the return of Andean sovereignty over Peru. The strenuous battle Toledo waged against the ideas of the potential Inca restoration is a testimony to the vitality of those ideas, not only as presented by Las Casas but as advocated by his colleagues and followers in the 1570s in Peru. Guaman Poma's writing to Philip III in 1615 to suggest a new version of the ideas Philip II had rejected reveals that Toledo's vehemence against Las Casas's recommendations for colonial reform in the decade immediately following the Dominican's death had been well placed. Guaman Poma's work stands as testimony to the fact that the powerful ideas of reform could not be easily destroyed. Decades earlier, two Castilian visionaries, Cortés, in the flush of victory over the conquest of Mexico, and, somewhat later, Las Casas, in despair over matters in the Indies, had imagined variations on a universal temporal and symbolic order. Guaman Poma's vision came later, and although it was in its moment hopelessly quixotic, it expressed the endurance of ideas that not long ago had lost their currency.

"FOR THE RECORD"

Did Guaman Poma truly have hope for an Andean restoration with his own son as its anointed and crowned Andean prince? I think not. Guaman Poma's despairing lament about the hopelessness of the Andean situation, to the effect that "there is no hope or recourse in this world" [y no ay rremedio en este mundo], overwhelms the reader with each iteration as it must have overwhelmed its author, more directly, upon each utterance. Did, then, Guaman Poma write his work to argue for colonial reform? or did he write it "for the record"? I believe that in the course of his writing, the latter impulse emerged and overtook his earlier, hopeful aims.

I take the hint of this from Las Casas's decisions in the last years of his life. He requested that a young novice at the Dominican convent of San Gregorio at Valladolid, where his works were housed, be selected to catalogue all the accounts directed to Las Casas that had poured in from every part of the Indies. His hope was that they could stand as testimony and proof of the "truth that he always and for many years defended, thanks to God's mercy, of the injustices, injuries, and violence, oppressions, calamities, and deaths" that the Indians had received at the hands of the Spanish. If, he concluded, God should see fit to destroy Spain, those testimonies would give account of its causes.[76]

Writing "for the record" was clearly Guaman Poma's aim, too, when he asked that his chronicle be preserved "in the archive of heaven as in that of earth," that is, in eternity, and in Rome and in Castile. It was to stand as testimony and record ("para memoria") and to serve the cause of justice, both in this life and the next ("en el archibo del mundo como del cielo . . . para uer la justicia").[77] Guaman Poma wrote his program for the future on the basis of previous events *and* their canonization in writing. He wrote his history of the conquest of Peru, concluding it with the payment of Atahualpa's ransom and his execution, on the basis of events *and* the published accounts of the early histories of the conquest of Peru. He portrayed the aggression of Manco Inca against the Spanish as a just war waged by the Inca prince, on the basis of the *Tratado de las doce dudas* as antecedent. In other words, the work of Guaman Poma serves as a first clue to suggest that when historical veracity is propounded its illusion is created not by fidelity to historical events but by the ability to generate authority on the basis of that of others and that the pursuit of historical credibility is often in consonance with a set of goals that has less to do with the past than with the future.

The polemics of possession is very much about the possession of authority based more on literary antecedents than on historical events. The case of Bernal Díaz will reveal how literary authority overrides even eyewitness testimony, which proves insufficient in the face of the works that had found their way into the written record, either in manuscript or in print (see chapters 6 and 7). Guaman Poma was aware that his eyewitness testimony of life in the colonized viceroyalty was inadequate for the task at hand, and so he relied on, modified, and transformed the ideas of renowned authorities. The fact that he did not name the most important of them—Las Casas—serves to underscore the Dominican's significance to his work. Guaman Poma's example, half a century after the death of Las Casas, provides the theoretical justification to pursue the role of conquest polemics in the historical and fictional writings of the period and to pose the question about their potential resonance in the writings of today.

CHAPTER 3

Fray Bartolomé de las Casas, Polemicist and Author

FRAY BARTOLOMÉ DE LAS CASAS (1484–1566) occupies a prominent place in this inquiry, not only because his writings were read by others, but also because he was a reader, reading. His high-decibel, high-impact image, the legacy of which we know through his writings (as he remarked, more than two thousand folios in the course of his half-century-long public life), is not that of someone sitting quietly and reading. Even the famous engraving by Tomás López Enguídanos, which shows him in a contemplative pose, pictures him poised to write (fig. 13).[1] Yet Las Casas sat and read, mightily. For our purposes, his most pertinent readings were, for his *Historia de las Indias,* those of Portuguese maritime history and the four expeditions of Christopher Columbus; for the *Apologética historia sumaria,* they were the reports of the Indies experience of others, such as Álvar Núñez Cabeza de Vaca's *Relación,* or *Naufragios* (1542), the account of his sojourn in La Florida in 1527–1536.[2] Las Casas studied the work of Gomes Eanes de Zurara, the historian of Prince Henry the Navigator of Portugal, and also that of João de Barros, and he relied a great deal on the documentary trove of writings by and about Columbus. Las Casas gave Cabeza de Vaca's *Relación* a high-profile role in the work that was aimed at demonstrating the creation of civil order and the readiness for religious conversion by the native inhabitants of the Americas, a topic that must have impressed its urgency upon Las Casas after his debates before

FIGURE 13. Portrait engraving of Fray Bartolomé de las Casas, by Tomás López Enguídanos, *Retratos de los españoles ilustres*. Madrid: Imprenta Real, 1791, portrait no. 82. Reprinted from Pérez Fernández, *Inventario documentado*, 4.

a royally appointed commission in Valladolid in 1550–1551. There, his opponent, the venerable Juan Ginés de Sepúlveda, moved away from the announced (and royally mandated) topic of "exploring the manner in which the conquests in the Indies can be carried out justly and in good conscience" toward that of the nature, that is, the native capabilities, of the peoples who were to be (in fact, had been) conquered. Although generously cribbed by Fray Jerónimo Román y Zamora in his *Repúblicas del mundo* (1575, 1595), the *Apologética historia sumaria* was not published in Las Casas's lifetime, and its first appearance in the nineteenth century was only a partial edition.[3] Nevertheless, the *Apologética* reveals how readers and writers, taking highly visible positions in the sixteenth-century polemics of possession, engaged one another's work.

BIOGRAPHICAL NOTES, BRIEFLY

Bartolomé de las Casas was born in Seville on November 11, 1484.[4] He went to the Antilles in 1502, when he joined his merchant father's provisions business on the island of Hispaniola, and he also managed there the *encomienda* that had been granted by Columbus to Las Casas's father, who had accompanied the Admiral on his second voyage in 1493. Las Casas returned to Spain and became a deacon in Seville in 1506; he was ordained a priest in Rome on March 3, 1507, in his twenty-third year. Upon his return to America, and while serving as chaplain to Pánfilo de Narváez in the conquest of Cuba in 1514, he witnessed (at the age of thirty) an unprovoked massacre of Taíno Indians. The incident was, by his own account, the source of his conversion to the cause of protecting the natives of America from wanton destruction.[5]

Las Casas's reformist career began immediately thereafter. In the autumn of the following year (1515) he visited the aged and ailing King Ferdinand at court in Plasencia, taking with him "a written memorandum describing some of the cruelties that had been done [to the natives] on the island of Cuba in his presence"; similar denunciations followed in 1516 to Charles's ambassador, the rector of the University of Louvain, Adrian Florenz, known as Adrian of Utrecht, who effectively served as coregent with the cardinal of Spain, Fray Francisco Jiménez de Cisneros. To Adrian in Latin and to Cisneros in Castilian, Las Casas denounced the treatment of the Indians in a battery of memoranda throughout 1516.[6]

The reformist career of Las Casas should be seen as an evolution from his initial attempts in 1516 to protect the Indians while at the same time ensuring the economic prosperity of the crown to his ultimate recommendation, made forty-eight years later, that Spain abandon its rule in the Indies. Three key moments define this arc: (1) the recommendation in 1516 to alleviate the burden on the Indians by increasing the number of slaves imported from Africa and granting licenses to do so to Castilian settlers, and his first attempts, in 1518, to challenge the Indians' subjection to slavery and the encomienda system; (2) his proposal in 1542 to abolish Indian slavery and the encomienda system (which resulted in the passage of the New Laws in Spain, ultimately rejected by governmental and private interests in America); and (3) his recommendations in 1562 and 1564 that Spanish rule in the Americas cease and that sovereignty over all lands, possessions, and persons be returned to the native peoples.[7] This sequence of reformist activity was broken for some eight years, from the time Las Casas entered the Dominican order in September 1522 through the end of 1530, after which a letter he wrote to the Council of the Indies evidenced his return to the cause of seeking justice for the Indians.[8]

In his last will and testament, written two years before his death, Las Casas bequeathed his voluminous papers as well as the "multitude of letters and accounts" he had received from all parts of the Indies to the Colegio de San Gregorio de Valladolid.[9] Las Casas died in his eighty-second year on July 18, 1566, in the Dominican convent of Nuestra Señora de Atocha in Madrid.

LAS CASAS ON AFRICAN SLAVERY

The erroneous portrayal of Las Casas as the instigator of African slavery in the Americas has been a theme coloring the evaluation of his life and work since the eighteenth century. Contrary to popular opinion, Las Casas was not the originator of African slavery in the Indies. It had begun within the first decade of Columbus's arrival in America. Slave traffic was already under way when King Ferdinand issued royal instructions on September 16, 1501, to the newly appointed governor of Hispaniola, Nicolás de Ovando, on whose expedition the eighteen-year-old Las Casas made his first voyage to the Indies in 1502. These instructions set forth provisions for the governance of the "islands and mainland of the Ocean Sea" that included the importation of black slaves from Africa, as long as they had been born "under the tutelage of Christians": "You are not to consent or allow to go [to the Indies] Muslims, Jews, heretics, former apostates reconciled to the church, or those persons who are newly converted to Our Faith, except for those who are black or other slaves, born under the tutelage of Christians, our subjects and native peoples" [Non consentyreis nin dareis logar que allá vayan moros nin xudíos, nin erexes nin rreconcyliados, nin personas nuevamente convertidas a Nuestra Fée, salvo si fueren esclavos negros u otros esclavos que fayan nascido en poder de cristhianos, nuestros súbditos e naturales (CDI 31:23)]. The royal instructions suggest that members of the aforementioned groups had already found their way to the Indies, and hence Ovando as new governor was charged with stemming the tide of this undesirable migration, carefully excepting slaves, black Africans, or others who had been born under the jurisdiction of Christians, which likely would have meant in Seville and its environs, where black African slaves, imported by the Portuguese, were common. In 1503, Ovando requested the king to halt the flow of black slaves to Hispaniola because "they fled into the Indian communities, taught the natives bad ways, and could never be recaptured."[10] Ovando's complaint about the impossibility of controlling the African slaves suggests that their numbers were considerable in the Antilles by the time Las Casas arrived in Hispaniola with Ovando, which was more than a decade before Las Casas recommended increasing their numbers.

In 1516, Las Casas recommended that additional slaves, black and white (that is, fair-skinned Berbers), from the North African coast, who had been acquired in a just war, be imported for specific purposes (mining) and in limited numbers.[11] He did so both to protect the declining Indian population and to increase the crown's coffers. At that early juncture, he questioned not Castile's right to rule in the Indies, but only the policies that had led to the exploitation of the natives. When he learned about the historical circumstances that had given rise to African slavery, Las Casas, regretting his earlier recommendation, became one of the few Europeans in the sixteenth century to speak out against it.[12]

In the sixteenth century, two types of slavery were generally condoned. One was the legal slavery of captives taken in a just war; this was called civil slavery. The other was natural slavery, a doctrine which postulated that the governance of certain peoples by others was justifiable insofar as one group could be considered inferior in some way to the other (see chapter 4, "Councilors Warring at the Royal Court"). Hardly any sixteenth-century European thinker opposed civil slavery; Las Casas, like everyone else, condoned the taking of slaves in a just war, and this meant, in the Christian world, the war against Islam. Las Casas argued that there were only three just causes for war: (1) to defend the Christian nation against those, such as the Turks and Muslims of the Mediterranean and North Africa, who invade and make war against it; this, he says, is not called war but rather a natural and legitimate defense ("legítima defensión y natural"); (2) to defend the nation against those that seek to impede or destroy Christianity and spread their own creed in its place; and (3) to oppose those who have wronged the republic and refuse to make restitution. These reasons were commonly accepted at the time; in his *Demócrates Segundo*, Sepúlveda summed them up as: (1) the right to repel force with force; (2) the right to recover possessions and properties unjustly usurped; and (3) the prerogative to punish those who committed such offenses.[13] In Las Casas's view, peoples who had neither invaded nor attacked a Christian principality gave no just cause to make war against them. He applied this principle to the Indians of the New World and, when he learned about the origins of the international slave trade, to the Africans as well.

Who were these slaves, where did they come from, and why was their enslavement generally condoned? They were presumed to be from North Africa and enslaved in a just and defensive war of several decades' duration in which the Ottoman empire was making war on Europe, planning to conquer it. The Muslim dynasties across Africa threatened Mediterranean commerce by means of corsairs such as Barbarrosa, who sailed under Turkish auspices, attacking ships and taking captives for ransom. All of Europe—all of Christendom—was engaged in a defensive war against Islam. The Turks reached Vienna, overran parts of Italy, and did not receive their first serious blow from Christian Europe until their naval defeat at the battle of Lepanto in 1571 (four years after Las Casas's death).

The tradition of taking Muslim prisoners of war was a long-standing one in Spain and Portugal. Thus, according to William D. Philips, when Portugal purchased or kidnapped Africans to sell them as slaves in the fifteenth century, it seemed to be a continuation of the ways in which "Iberians held slaves or traded them in the Middle Ages." In fact, as Philips shows, in "the first two centuries of the Atlantic slave trade, blacks were confined almost exclusively to the same European areas that they had been in the Middle Ages, and within those areas they were most numerous in Portugal and Spain."[14]

Upon reading the Portuguese histories of Eanes de Zurara (1453) and Barros (1553) in the 1550s, Las Casas learned that the slaves sold by the Portuguese had not been obtained in a just war, but rather had been captured under papal licenses granted to Portugal in the mid–fifteenth century. Three papal bulls, issued in 1452, 1455, and 1456 by Pope Nicholas V and Pope Calixtus III, had granted Portugal the exclusive right to navigation, conquest, and settlement in all newly discovered regions of the world. The privilege pertained to the territories of the entire northern coast of Africa, as far south as, and including, Guinea, a general term for the west coast of Africa that later became known as the slave coast. The papal bulls extended the crusade against the Muslims to include all pagan peoples and accordingly authorized their enslavement. In 1493 the Spanish pope Alexander VI reaffirmed this exclusive privilege to the Portuguese in the Bulls of Donation that divided the unknown world between them and the Spanish. Portuguese coastal explorations and slaving expeditions extended down the entire west coast of Africa. By 1487 Bartolomé Díaz rounded the Cape of Good Hope, and in 1497–1498 Vasco da Gama navigated around it to India.

When Las Casas learned about this papally sanctioned enslavement of the non-Muslim peoples of Africa, he opposed it vehemently. In his *History of the Indies* he recalls his earlier misunderstanding and subsequent revelation: "When the cleric Las Casas first gave that advice—to grant the license to bring black slaves to the islands—he was not aware of the unjust ways in which the Portuguese captured and made slaves of them. But after he found out, he would not have proposed it for all the world, because from the beginning the black people of Africa were enslaved unjustly and tyrannically, exactly as had happened to the Indians."[15] He doubted, he said, that being in a state of ignorance about the falsity of the premises on which his recommendation had been based, would be sufficient to excuse him from the wrath of divine judgment:

> Of this advice that the cleric gave, he soon afterward repented,
> judging himself guilty through ignorance because, as he later
> saw and came to understand that, as will be shown, the captivity

of the blacks was as unjust as that of the Indians. The remedy he proposed, that blacks be brought in order to free the Indians, was not an appropriate one. Even though he had supposed that they had been taken captive justly, he was not sure that his ignorance in this matter and his good intentions would excuse him at the time of divine judgment [my translation].

[Deste aviso que dió el clérigo, no poco después se halló arrepiso, juzgándose culpado por inadvertente, porque como después vido y averiguó, según parecerá, ser tan injusto el cautiverio de los negros como el de los indios, no fue discreto remedio el que aconsejó que trujesen negros para que se libertasen los indios, aunque él suponía que eran justamente captivos, aunque no estuvo cierto que la ignorancia que en esto tuvo y buena voluntad lo excusase delante el juicio divino. (*Historia* 3:275 [bk. 3, chap. 129])]

Having a new understanding of the origins of African slavery, Las Casas wrote a critical history of Portuguese coastal exploration and slaving down the west coast of Africa, and he placed it at the beginning of book 1 (chapters 17 through 27) of the *Historia de las Indias*. Although this account was apparently a late addition to his history, Portuguese exploration and slaving in the Canaries and Africa must have represented, in Las Casas's modern view, the beginning of the era of European expansion into the Atlantic world. As a result, the Portuguese slave trade occupies the essential early chapters of Las Casas's study of European overseas expansion. His recognition of the injustice of the African slave trade, which "tear[s] people out of the peace of their homes" as opposed to conquering them in the war against Islam, harks back to his legal conception of secular dominion and rejects the papal sanctions that had permitted the capture and enslavement of people from the northwestern and western coasts of Africa since the middle of the fifteenth century.

The idea of Las Casas as the author of African slavery in America seems to have begun with Enlightenment thinkers of the eighteenth century, specifically the works of the French Jesuit Pierre-François-Xavier de Charlevoix (1730–1731), the Dutch cleric Cornelius de Pauw (1768–1769), and Guillaume-Thomas, the abbé de Raynal (1770), which interpreted wrongly a passage in Antonio de Herrera y Tordesillas's *Historia general de los hechos de los castellanos en las islas y tierra firme del Mar Océano* (*General History of the Deeds of the Castilians in the Islands and Mainland of the Ocean Sea*) (1601–1615).[16] The notion became solidified in the English-language tradition when the Scottish historian William Robertson wrote, in his classic *History of America* (1776), "Las Casas proposed to purchase a sufficient number of negroes from the Portuguese settlements on the coast of Africa, and to transport them to America, in order that they might be employed as slaves in working the mines and cultivating the ground. . . . While he contended earnestly for the liberty of the people born in one quarter of the globe, he laboured to enslave the inhabitants of another region; and in the warmth of his zeal to save the Americans from the yoke, pronounced it to be lawful and expedient to impose one still heavier upon the Africans."[17]

If this attribution to Las Casas of the introduction of African slavery to the Spanish Indies was made in the eighteenth century by readers of Herrera, twentieth-century readers have had at their disposal Las Casas's own statements on the subject. Published for the first time in 1875–1876 but more widely available after the editions of 1951 and 1957, Las Casas's *Historia de las Indias* contains his expressions of regret, cited above, at having proposed selling licenses to Castilian settlers in the Indies for the purchase of African slaves, innocent victims of assault and capture, plucked from their homes: "The princes ordered those whom they typically sent forth, to assault and rob those who lived in their homes peacefully and securely" [mandaban los infantes a los que solían enviar a saltear y robar los que vivían en sus casas pacíficos y seguros].[18]

LAS CASAS, *LICENCIADO*

Las Casas's work, whether as activist reformer, missionary, historian, or theorist of culture and ethnographer, was grounded in the authority of textual traditions: Greco-Roman, biblical, patristic, theological, philosophical, and juridical, that is, civil and particularly canon law. These constituted his library and the laboratory of his thought. He famously remarked in a letter written to his Dominican brethren, circa 1563, that he had been studying the law and trying to draw sound conclusions about justice for forty-eight years, and, if he was not mistaken, he had finally penetrated its basic principles. He added that many of his writings in Latin and Castilian (by his calculation two thousand folios in all, as men-

tioned earlier) had been read by learned theologians, by the great professors of the universities of Salamanca and Alcalá de Henares, and by the
members of the Dominican house of San Gregorio in Valladolid.[19] His
contemporaries, whether friends, admirers, or enemies, referred to him
as "licenciado" or "licenciado en leyes" [licentiate in law], and he himself
did not reject the title but repeated it when citing others' references to
him. Although positive evidence of any formal degrees has not been
brought forward, Las Casas's considerable knowledge of the law, and of
canon law in particular, is increasingly well attested by modern scholars
who have documented its use in his works.[20]

One of Las Casas's most ardent critics of his influence in persuading
the emperor and his councils that the Incas had been legitimate rulers of
their vast empire was the *licenciado* Juan Polo de Ondegardo. Polo had
remarked scornfully about Las Casas that "before he joined the religious
order, he was a cleric licensed in law" [Este fraile, antes que fuera re-
ligioso, era un clérigo licenciado en leyes].[21] Insofar as useful and reliable
information often comes from a hostile witness, Polo's attempts to dis-
credit Las Casas as a voice of Christian moral authority result in his
corroboration of Las Casas's principal expertise as a jurist. In a letter Polo
wrote on March 16, 1571, from Yucay, he stated three objectives: to tell how
the error of calling the Incas "legitimate lords" had come about, to detail
the great damage this had caused, and to argue that the only true and
legitimate dominion over the Andes resided with the Spanish king. He
attributed to Las Casas alone the blame for impressing the views of Inca
legitimacy on the emperor and his ministers. More important, in the
course of his defense of Spanish jurisdiction in the Andes, Polo revealed
that Las Casas's arguments had been based on legal grounds (rather than
on moral issues) inasmuch as he, Polo, refuted them by resorting to the
same juridical principles.[22]

Two of Polo's arguments reveal his attempt to rebut Las Casas's legal-
istic arguments: one asserts that there existed in pre-Columbian Peru no
civil order but only the domestic order of house and lineage; another, that
the principle of voluntary submission and acceptance of a new ruler could
not be applied to the spread of Inca rule in the Andes.[23] The latter principle was, as we shall see, one of the fundamental tenets of canon law on
which Las Casas grounded his work; Polo's rebuttal of it met Las Casas on
his own turf. Polo's letter was written five years after Las Casas's death and

well into the reign of Philip II, who did not ponder the legitimacy of Spain's claims to the Indies, as had his father, Charles V. The field of law on which Polo debated these ideas confirms its centrality to Las Casas's work and views.

Lewis Hanke had long held (although he did not demonstrate) that Las Casas was knowledgeable in the area of canon law. Hanke remarked that "this thorough knowledge of the law which Las Casas came to acquire must help to explain the fact that few of his contemporary opponents chose to meet him on the field of theory."[24] On the field of legal theory, that is. Las Casas's most celebrated opponent, Sepúlveda, went to the field of philosophy, not the law, to debate him. Aristotelian social philosophy and anthropology were the métier of Sepúlveda. Sepúlveda and Las Casas debated one another on the basis of entirely different disciplines.

While Las Casas is commonly considered to be Thomistic in his thought, following the Aristotelian-Thomist school of neo-Scholastic philosophy, particularly regarding natural law, it is also true, as Kenneth J. Pennington (151) observed, that "Las Casas was a jurist whose ideas were based on medieval juridical theory; . . . he developed a central tradition of medieval legal thought in original and interesting ways." Not unusual in this respect, Las Casas was "part of a general movement of adapting ecclesiological and canon law concepts to political theory": "The basic premise in Las Casas's position on the rights of the Indians is that legitimate secular power does exist outside the church. Las Casas insisted throughout his life that the Indians' *dominium* was legitimate and just, and that the Spaniards did not have the right to usurp the Indians' just title. From this basic principle sprang all the rest of Las Casas's ideas."[25]

Las Casas followed juridical tradition and augmented it with theological sources, but theology was not his field of primary expertise, and theology was not as clear-cut on the principle of *dominium* as was canon law.[26] The basic canon law tenet employed by Las Casas was the principle of *Quod omnes tangit debet ab omnibus approbari*, "what touches all must be approved by all" (157). Developed to regulate the affairs of a bishopric, the principle was applied by Las Casas to a wholly new situation. As it would be dangerous to assign a prince or a bishop to an unwilling people, so too a foreign king should not be imposed on a free people; as a consequence, Las Casas concluded, the pope could not impose a foreign king, on Christians or non-Christians, without their will and consent (157). Applying this definition of *dominium,* Las Casas was able to conceptualize the rights of the Indians to sovereignty in their own lands on the authority and logic of the law.

Las Casas had applied the canon law principle of a community's free election of, or consent to, its rulers in 1518, that is, prior to the conquest of Mexico; he gave it its culminating and final form after that of Peru. This juridical foundation allowed Las Casas to conceptualize history and his ethnological theory on a basis other than the passions revealed by his most strident rhetoric, such as is found, for example, in the *Brevísima relación de la destrucción de las Indias* (1552). On the contrary, his intellectual training provided a disciplinary basis for his humanitarian approach to the resolution of problems of justice. Canon law theory was central to his major initiatives for legislation, to his conflict with Sepúlveda vis-à-vis the Inquisition, and to his boldness in arguing that the king of Spain had no right to dominion in the Indies (a charge that was interpretable as high treason).

Fifty years after Las Casas's death, reference to his legal background would still be made, as when, for example, El Inca Garcilaso de la Vega referred to him by the title "licenciado" and derisively called him the official solicitor of the New Laws (Garcilaso, *Comentarios reales* 3:225 [pt. 2, bk. 4, chap. 3]). Such dismissals become for us an interpretive key of considerable value in probing the character and unifying principles of Las Casas's writings, be they on politics, history, or ethnology.

THE COMMUNITY SCHEME OF 1518

To return to Las Casas's earliest efforts at colonial reform, I want to examine the other dimension of the first landmark in his trajectory, the so-called community scheme, which is found in his "Memorial de remedios para las Indias" of 1518. Here he proposes remedies for the islands of Hispaniola, Cuba, Puerto Rico, and Jamaica and Tierra Firme:[27] The Indians should be removed from the control of private citizens ("que salgan del poder de los cristianos, porque de otra manera hanlos de matar como hasta aquí y acabar de destruir la tierra a vuestra alteza") (34); the enslaved Indians imported from the northern coast of South America (Tierra Firme) to the Caribbean islands, as well as those who had been taken to Spain, should be freed and returned to their homelands (36); and the inhabitants of both the islands and Tierra Firme should be informed by peaceful means that they had a new king and be allowed to live in their own settlements and homes. Thus, although Las Casas proposed that the Indians move closer to the mines and ports to be nearer to the gold and "the things of Castile" (33, 36) and continue to be obligated to pay tribute to the king as his free vassals (32, 33, 37), these early recommendations anticipate the principles of the abolition of encomienda and Indian slavery and the restoration of autonomy to the Indian settlements under the new Castilian king.

Las Casas also inaugurates at this time his developing campaign for the restoration of the land, hereby urging the king to reinvest a fifth (and if this is not sufficient, a third) of the wealth gained in the Indies into recovering and restoring to the Indians the lands that his Spanish vassals had ruined (33). Las Casas's proposed obligation on the king in 1518, to restore to the Indians of the islands and Tierra Firme the prosperity of their lands destroyed by Spanish conquistadores and settlers, will eventually become his proposals of the 1550s and 1560s for full restoration and the withdrawal of Castilian political sovereignty over the Indies.

LAS CASAS ON PAPAL DOMINION AND EVANGELIZATION

The question of papal power and authority was a complex one, and the meaning of the papal bulls of 1493 was vigorously debated after their promulgation. Las Casas argued that they did not constitute a legitimate claim for Castile to rule the Indies, but only a general permission to preach the gospel there. In other words, he denied the temporal power of the pope over the Indies; thus, in Las Casas's view, Columbus had carried on his second expedition not a title of donation for the Indies but merely a letter of papal emissary such as that carried by Marco Polo to China. However, in the first half of the sixteenth century, the weight of opinion augmented the traditional prerogative of the papacy to authorize missions to the heathen and allot to Christian communities—be they kingdoms or religious orders—the exclusive right and duty to proselytize in a particular pagan area, extending it by arguing that the pope, in order to support missionary endeavor, might lawfully allot to Christian princes the lands and temporal possessions of pagan rulers.[28] This doctrine, commonly associated with Henry of Susa, the archbishop of Ostia (named 1261 or 1262), known as Hostiensis, was rejected by Las Casas.

For Las Casas, even the papal invitation to evangelize without force of arms had strict limitations. His position on this matter came from the Christian gospel itself, and it appears at the beginning of part one of *De unico vocationis modo omnium gentium ad veram religionem* [*Del único modo de atraer a todos los pueblos a la verdadera religión*].[29] One might call it the doctrine of "shake the dust from your feet," and it appears in the books of Matthew, Mark, and Luke. Jesus gives instructions to his disciples as to the manner in which they are to go from town to town preaching (their prerogatives are decidedly limited): "Whatever town or village you go into, ask for someone trustworthy and stay with him until you leave. As you enter his house, salute it, and if the house deserves it, let your peace descend upon it; if it does not, let your peace come back to you. And if anyone does not welcome you or listen to what you have to say, as you walk out of the house or town, shake the dust from your feet."[30] "Shake the dust from your feet" implies that in the foreign land the Christian is guest, not lord; the Christian priest abroad, likewise, is only an outsider. The Christian prince is similarly limited. According to the principle of "Quod omnes tangit," the Christian prince abroad cannot impose a new ruler on a people without their free and voluntary consent. Although Las Casas's authorities were scriptural and medieval, he elaborated on their basis a modern view of Europe in the Atlantic world.

LAS CASAS, THE NEW LAWS, AND THE BLACK LEGEND

The second landmark in the evolution of Las Casas's political thought is the period of the New Laws and his interventions at the Castilian court in the 1540s. Las Casas returned to Spain from Mexico in 1540 to plead the case at court for the enactment of new legislation to regulate and limit Spanish intervention in the Indies. His first objective was the abolition of encomienda and Indian slavery by taking control over the Indians out of the hands of private citizens. In 1542 he read before the Council of Castile two texts; one was a set of legislative proposals and the other was an exposé and harangue designed to encourage their enactment. Thus, Las Casas read a version of the *Brevísima relación de la destrucción de las Indias* before the Council of the Indies and other officials at the emperor's request. Alonso de la Santa Cruz records the event in his chronicle of the reign of Charles V, reporting that the councilors gathered "for many days at a certain hour until the friar read in its entirety a certain account, very lengthy, that he brought with him." Santa Cruz summarizes, briefly ("brevísimamente"), he says, the contents of the work we know by that name, adding that because of its great length he will treat it fully elsewhere. *Probanzas,* letters, personal interviews, and some of Las Casas's eyewitness accounts—all written for other purposes—documented, some intentionally and some in spite of themselves, abuses committed against the Indians. In painting the cruel behavior of the king's subjects, Las Casas appealed to the moral conscience and sense of legal obligation of Prince Philip (later King Philip II). As he stated in the prologue of the printed version, with a reference to Solomon: "The king who sits on the canopied throne of justice dissipates all evil."[31]

He also presented his treatise "Entre los remedios," in which he rejected the fundamental idea of a natural, paternal rule in order to advocate for civil dominion: the king's rule over his vassals, being of a more modern type and pertaining to *jus gentium,* "rests on the voluntary consent of his subjects and as such does not carry with it the force of natural law nor absolute necessity."[32] His goal was to remove the Indians from the control of private citizens in order to place them under the direct jurisdiction of the crown, with the proviso that this be carried out only with the free consent of the Indians. The outcome—which all his enemies recognized as being attributable to him—was the promulgation of the New Laws on November 20, 1542, which provided for the prohibition of Indian slavery, revoked the encomiendas of public officials, abolished the perpetuity of encomiendas in private hands, made new rules for conducting expeditions and exacting Indian tribute, and exempted from all personal and royal service the depleted native populations of the islands of Hispaniola, Cuba, and Puerto Rico.[33]

One of Las Casas's major achievements in the New Laws, the abolition of encomienda, was revoked three years later. This led Las Casas to take, in 1546, his final step, subjecting himself thereby to a charge of high treason: he wrote twelve rules for confessors which declared the conquests illegal, denied absolution of sins until the penitent had performed restitution (to the Indians), and defied royal authority.[34] In effect, these rules sought, through the means of the sacrament of confession, to force the enactment of the New Law prohibiting encomienda.

"Approved by four masters of theology," including the Dominican friar Bartolomé Carranza de Miranda and Melchor Cano, Las Casas's confessional guide was aimed at those who had been conquistadores,

those who currently held Indians in *repartimiento* (administrative allot-
ment of Indians made to Spaniards in encomienda), and those who sold
arms and provisions to people who made war against the Indians. The
twelve rules of Las Casas's *confesionario* employed the time-honored doctrine of restitution; the controversial character of his argument was its
specific application to the colonizing inhabitants of the Indies and the
basis on which it was elaborated, namely, that all war and gain by Spaniards in the Indies at the expense of the Indians had been unlawful.[35]

Before being printed in 1552 in Seville by Las Casas and sent abroad to
the mission field, these "rules for confessors" were banned by the king
and gathered up and burned publicly by the viceroy of Mexico, Antonio de
Mendoza. They were one of the causes for which Sepúlveda, in 1552,
denounced Las Casas to the Inquisition, on the charge of heresy and high
treason for denying the rights of the pope in his 1493 acts of papal donation of the Indies.[36] The charge was not only high treason for its denial of
the king's right to dominion; it was also heresy because it denied the
pope's power to donate the Indies to the Spanish kings. Las Casas was
required to submit his manuscript work to the Inquisition but was not
prosecuted. In any case, in 1552 such was the potential threat to Las Casas
for clinging to the principle of *dominium,* the notion that legitimate secular power existed outside the church. These ideas, putting in the hands of
the confessing priests the challenge that the crown had refused to face,
did not die but rather became the heart of a reform movement in the
viceroyalty of Peru in the 1560s and subsequent decades.[37]

The less immediate result of Las Casas's appearances at court in 1542
was his publication of the *Brevísima relación* in 1552 (fig. 14). The object of
this pamphlet had been not to deny the legal right of Spanish dominion
(that would come in the accompanying document, "Twenty reasons
against encomienda"), but to impress upon Prince Philip the cruel and
destructive methods by which his vassals had subjugated the natives of
the New World. This interpretation of Las Casas's intention in writing the
Brevísima relación is borne out by that of one of his most hostile readers of
the subsequent century, Bernardo de Vargas Machuca, who in 1612, in
response to Las Casas's work of a half century earlier, defended not the
Castilian right to dominion in the Indies (which his characterization of
the acts of the Indians as crimes assumed), but rather the "just deeds of
the Spanish soldiers who had been defamed."[38]

FIGURE 14. Frontispiece of *Brevíssima relación de la destruycción de las Indias,* by Bartolomé de las Casas. Seville: S. Trujillo, 1552. The John Carter Brown Library at Brown University.

Las Casas explains his reasons for printing the work in his *argumento*, or plan of the work. First, he writes, he had been asked by certain distinguished colleagues to write down an account of his statement from his appearance at the Council of Castile in 1542. Then, he says, some years having passed, he noticed that certain "insolent men," not content with their previous atrocious deeds, asked the king for authority and license to commit them again, that is, to undertake further conquests. In the work's prologue to Prince Philip, Las Casas writes that he is putting this *suma* and *epítome* (compendium or summary of a larger work) before him for a second time because the prince's many travels and obligations may have prevented him from studying the previously deposited manuscript copy. Las Casas expresses the hope that the work's printing for the court will awaken the consciences of the royal ministers who could advise Philip to resist the importunings of conquistadores for further licenses for conquest. Since he mentions a previous copy he had submitted to the prince earlier, printing the work was his way of drawing attention to a document that the royal household had evidently ignored.[39]

After 1552, the *Brevísima relación* would not be published again in Spanish until 1646. In the meantime, beginning twelve years after Las Casas's death, the work was published abroad in other languages with great frequency. The first translation was into Flemish, in 1578, and it was followed in 1579 by a translation into French by Jacques de Miggrode that was published in Antwerp; both were accompanied by the notice "To serve as example and warning to the seventeen provinces of the Low Countries."[40] Thus the international denigration of Spanish history known as the "Black Legend" to which the publication of *Brevísima relación* contributed, was concerned with Philip's actions in the Low Countries of Europe, more than with the comportment of Castile's soldiers in America as such. A staggering number of translations appeared from that point through the seventeenth century. Pérez Fernández compiles a complete list of them through 1996: by the end of the seventeenth century there had appeared twenty-nine editions in Dutch, thirteen in French, six in English, six in German, three in Italian, and three in Latin. The timing of these translations, Saint-Lu suggests, usually corresponded to the most critical periods in the wars between the Spain of the Hapsburgs and its enemies in Europe.[41] The original watercolor drawings in a manuscript of the Miggrode translation graphically depicted the acts described by Las

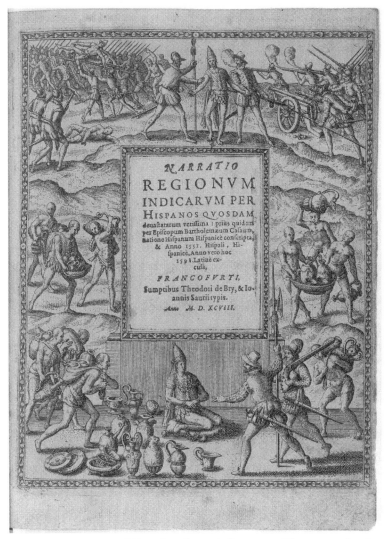

FIGURE 15. Frontispiece of *Narratio regionum Indicarum per Hispanos quosdam devastatarum verissima*, by Bartolomé de las Casas. Frankfurt am Main: Theodor de Bry and Johannes Sauer, 1598. The John Carter Brown Library at Brown University.

Casas, and they became the basis for the copper engravings that appeared in the Latin translation of the *Brevísima relación* published in Frankfurt in 1598 by Theodor de Bry (figs. 15, 16).

A second florescence of the *Brevísima relación* occurred in the late eighteenth century, but this time with specific reference to America,

FIGURE 16. The garroting of Atahualpa Inca by Pizarro's men, in *Narratio regionum Indicarum per Hispanos quosdam devastatarum verissima*, by Bartolomé de las Casas. Frankfurt am Main: Theodor de Bry and Johannes Sauer, 1598. The John Carter Brown Library at Brown University.

during the period of the Wars of Independence of the Latin American republics from Spain. An outstanding example is provided by Fray Servando Teresa de Mier, the Mexican Dominican friar who preached a sermon on December 12, 1794, the day of the Virgin of Guadalupe, in which he argued that the gospel had been preached in Mexico by the apostle Saint Thomas, understood by the ancient Mexicans to have been the man-god Quetzalcoatl, and that all of Mexican mythology could be interpreted in the light of the Christian religion (see chapter 12 on the fictionalization of Fray Servando). In 1812, Mier prologued and published an edition of the *Brevísima relación* in seven hundred copies in London, followed by editions in Philadelphia and Mexico. In his historical and polemical writings, Fray Servando subscribed to Las Casas's fundamental ideas: that the Indians had never offended the Spanish, who therefore had no right to make war against them; that the papal bulls of donation should be rejected in their temporal interpretation; that the famous Requerimiento was deserving of ridicule; and that the only legitimate role of the Spanish monarchy over the Indies was as a universal monarchy compatible with, and recognizing the sovereignty of, the indigenous lords of America.[42]

Mier made Las Casas into the father of the creoles of New Spain as well as the protector of the Indians; he handled this contradictory position of the creoles being the descendants of the wicked conquistadores by asserting that the laws promulgated in the middle of the sixteenth century, that is, the New Laws, were not revoked but in fact honored, protecting the Indians and preventing further conquests; thus he turned the creoles into the true spiritual heirs of the religious defenders of the Indians of the sixteenth century. Simón Bolívar, in his *Carta de Jamaica* of September 6, 1815, cites the *Brevísima relación* as a work founded on the authority of authentic documents and warranted by the most respected sources, and one whose veracity was attested by the best historians of the era. In these claims Bolívar follows Mier's *Historia* almost to the letter, including his praise for Las Casas as "the philanthropic bishop of Chiapas, apostle of America, friend of humanity" [filantrópico obispo de Chiapas, apóstol de la América, amigo de la humanidad].[43]

The Black Legend regarding relations between Spain and America is thus more recent than Las Casas's lifetime in the first half of the sixteenth century, but it is much older than Las Casas with respect to Europe. Sverker Arnoldsson (1960) has studied the earliest versions of anti-Spanish sentiment, found in Italy in the fourteenth and fifteenth centuries, that condemned Castilian militarism, Catalonian mercantilism, and the Spanish heritage of Semitic and Saracen blood, on the basis of motivations and biases that were respectively political, economic, and religious. Anti-Spanish sentiment in northern Europe in the sixteenth century had two periods: the first corresponded to that of Luther; the second, to the last forty years of the century, during which time Europe was engulfed in religious wars in the Low Countries, France, and the British Isles. Spain increasingly distinguished itself as the secular arm of the Catholic church while solidarity among Catholic countries grew and that among Protestant countries was heightened as well. Las Casas's unwitting contribution to the Black Legend of Spanish history would nevertheless become his longest remembered legacy; and it is a legacy remembered not only by Spain and Latin America, but also by Anglo– and Latino–North America as well.

THE GREAT DEBATE IN VALLADOLID (1550–1551)

Convened by the emperor Charles V, the Valladolid debate likewise turned on the question of governance, specifically in relation to Christian indoctrination (see Abril-Castelló). In advance of the debate, the emperor had, by secret instructions to President Pedro de la Gasca in Peru and to the viceroy Antonio de Mendoza in New Spain on April 16 and April 24, 1550, respectively, ordered the suspension of all conquests. Such instructions had been requested by the Council of the Indies on July 3, 1549, and had been the major impetus for the Valladolid debate. The councilors had requested that the emperor convene learned men, theologians, and jurists to gather with others to consider and decide upon the manner in which conquests should be carried out, so that they could be made justly and with the certainty of conscience, and that a formal instruction should be (subsequently) issued for that purpose.[44]

On July 7, 1550, royal letters were sent to the fifteen potential members of the junta who were to judge the merits of the arguments presented for the purpose of setting or modifying royal policy accordingly. The invitees included seven members of the Council of the Indies; four theologians, three of whom were Dominicans (Fray Domingo de Soto, Fray Melchor Cano, and Fray Bartolomé Carranza de Miranda) and the other a Franciscan, Fray Bernardino de Arévalo; two councilors of the Council of Castile (Licenciado Mercado and Dr. Ayala); Licenciado Pedrosa, of the council of religious orders (Consejo de las Órdenes); and the bishop of Ciudad Rodrigo, Pedro Ponce de León. Arévalo was ill, so ultimately the tribunal consisted of fourteen members.[45] The meeting was convened on August 15, 1550. This session lasted about a month; the second session, after numerous delays, was convened in mid-April 1551.

The task before Las Casas and Sepúlveda was to determine, as stated by de Soto in his detailed summary of the proceedings, "whether it is legitimate for His Majesty to make war on those Indians before preaching the faith to them, in order to subject them to his rule, so that, once subjugated, they more easily can be instructed and enlightened by the evangelical doctrine of the knowledge of their errors and Christian truth" [si es lícito a Su Majestad hacer guerra a aquellos indios antes que se les predique la fe, para subjectallos a su Imperio, y que después de subjectados puedan más fácil y cómodamente ser enseñados y alumbrados por la doctrina evangélica del conoscimiento de sus errores y de la verdad cristiana].[46]

Sepúlveda answered in the affirmative, arguing that it was not only legitimate but also expedient to do so. Las Casas responded in the negative, arguing that such a position failed on the criteria of both legitimacy and expediency and that it was contrary to the teachings of the Christian faith. From his canonist outlook, Las Casas maintained the right to sovereignty of the American peoples, both before and after their acceptance of the Christian religion. Sepúlveda introduced the issue of the Indians' rational capacity into the debate, justifying the war against them by pointing to their (theoretical) natural ineptitude. This was not, however, the issue under consideration but rather a claim that Sepúlveda brought into the debate in order to support his side of the question. Las Casas rejected such arguments; his canonist perspective focused not on the innate capabilities or learned conduct of the Indians but on their legal right to freedom and sovereignty.

At the end of the second session in April 1551, each of the fourteen judges was to issue his opinion in writing ("por escripto su parecer"). Military conquests were still officially suspended, except for those directed by missionary priests for the purpose of Christian indoctrination and conversion. In 1552 Las Casas published an account of the debates that included Soto's summary (fig. 17). All formal opinions were submitted except for that of Cano, who delayed until 1557. Under the pressure of constant demands for authorizations and licenses for conquests, specifically that of the viceroy of Peru, Andrés Hurtado de Mendoza, the marquis de Cañete, the emperor authorized new conquests for Peru on December 24, 1555. On May 13, 1556, new formal instructions on how to proceed with conquests were issued.[47]

LAS CASAS AND THE ENCOMENDEROS OF PERU

The third significant moment of Las Casas's political activism occurred when he went back to Spain for the last time and was granted permanent access to the Council of the Indies, where he continued his advocacy for reform. After Charles V abdicated the throne in 1556, Las Casas's influence at court decreased; Philip did not look upon him sympathetically as

FIGURE 17. Frontispiece of *Aquí se contiene una disputa . . . entre el obispo . . . Bartolomé de las Casas . . . y el doctor Ginés de Sepúlveda,* by Bartolomé de las Casas. Seville: S. Trujillo, 1552. The John Carter Brown Library at Brown University.

an advisor. This did not prevent the Dominican, however, from working to block the purchase, by the encomenderos of Peru, of perpetual rights to the labor and tribute of its native inhabitants. Neither did it prevent him from dedicating to Philip II his last two great juridical works, *De thesauris* (*On the Tomb Treasures of Peru*) (1562) and *Tratado de las doce dudas* (*The Treatise of the Twelve Doubts*) (1564).[48] There he expounded the same principles of secular dominion and the rights of all peoples to sovereignty in their own lands on the basis of canon law principles he had espoused most of his activist life.

The events leading up to Las Casas's composition of these treatises can be summarized as follows: In 1554–1555, the encomenderos of Peru presented the prospective king Philip II with a remarkable offer: They would buy the perpetual rights to the use of the lands and services of the native peoples of Peru from the king of Spain. In 1556, after Philip had begun his reign, he was in dire financial straits and accepted the proposal. This provoked Las Casas's renewed attack on the encomienda system. He immediately urged Philip not to accept the encomenderos' offer. Presenting twenty reasons why the new king should reject so inviting an opportunity, Las Casas argued that Philip should release the holdings of the native lords of Peru and make restitution to them, returning them to their dominions and estates. They in turn, as free vassals of the king, would offer the customary tribute that such relationships between sovereign and subject mandated. This would yield far more than the sums which the encomenderos' agent had promised to pay, as it was clear the encomenderos did not have the millions promised but rather would extract them from the labor and lives of the Indians.[49]

Fortunately for Las Casas's cause, it took the Council of the Indies more than two years to appoint a commission to oversee the sale. In the interim, Las Casas and Domingo de Santo Tomás, through their Dominican colleagues in Peru, organized the native lords of Peru (*kurakas*) and received powers of attorney from them.[50] In 1560, on behalf of himself and Santo Tomás, Las Casas presented Philip with an offer more remarkable than that of the encomenderos: The *kurakas* would buy their freedom, paying whatever sum the encomenderos had offered (if said sum could be verified) plus one hundred thousand ducats more. In addition, the native lords offered one-third, retaining for themselves two-thirds, of the wealth of any hidden tomb treasures they might discover. The mines in particular would offer the crown an ongoing source of revenue, in contrast to the encomenderos' offer, by which, Las Casas and Santo Tomás reminded the king, he would lose all claim to sovereignty and effective control over Peru.[51]

The two Dominicans sought to persuade the king of "five great and irreparable losses" the monarchy would incur in selling out to the encomenderos: The loss of great numbers of loyal Indian vassals; the relinquishment of great income; the loss of the rule of justice in the Indies; the loss of control over the encomenderos who would surely rebel against the crown: "They will see to it that you are king or lord of nothing more than the roads, and even those they will take away from you";[52] fifth and finally, the Dominicans argued, Philip would fail in his obligation to ensure the well-being of the Indians so that the sacred charge, given by the popes to the Catholic kings, to bring the Christian gospel to the newfound peoples could be fulfilled (466). In the end, Philip sold some minor posts, but he neither accepted the counteroffer nor sold the encomiendas to private Spanish citizens.

Soon afterward, however, a new and equally disturbing issue surfaced full-blown: the discovery of pre-Hispanic tomb treasures, particularly in the northern coastal areas of Peru. Who owned these magnificent riches? Even the conviction that the wars of conquest had been just did not provide an answer that favored the conquerors. This debate brought the eighty-year-old Las Casas to write his last works, which, as mentioned, proposed the restoration of Inca rule in the Andes. Las Casas referred to his Latin treatise of 1562, *De thesauris,* and its Castilian sequel of 1564, the *Treatise of the Twelve Doubts*—both dedicated to Philip II—as his "last will and codicil," respectively; in other words, he offered them as his enduring and final gift to his sovereign. Apart from the specific Peruvian problems addressed, these works were meant to stand as general and lasting guides to Philip on the management of his empire.[53]

Because they had a common theoretical foundation, the principles organizing the *Twelve Doubts* and the *De thesauris* can be described as follows. First, all peoples had the right to sovereignty over their own lands; second, the only right granted to the Catholic kings by the pope had been the right to evangelize, not to conquer, subdue, or rule the native populations; third, the Spanish conquests in the Indies had been illegal as well as immoral.[54]

In the *Treatise of the Twelve Doubts,* Las Casas spelled out eight specific principles: First, all non-Christians ("infieles"), regardless of sect or religion and by right of natural and divine law as well as that made by men, enjoy dominion over all their own territories and estates; second, among the four basic situations in which non-Christians live, those who had never invaded the lands of Christian princes nor offended any of them in any way could not be deprived of their sovereignty. Thus, the native inhabitants of the Indies should be allowed to exercise "freely and legitimately" sovereignty in their own domains.[55] Third, the only concession regarding the Indies granted by the Holy See to the monarchs of Spain was that of preaching the gospel and spreading the Christian faith and religion. Fourth, in making such concessions the Holy See had intended neither for the kings and rulers of the Indies to be deprived of their states, jurisdictions, honors, or dignities, nor for the kings of Castile and Leon to use the papal license granted to impede the preaching of the faith and the conversion of the peoples. Fifth, the costs of religious conversion were not to be borne by the peoples of the Indies themselves but rather by the kings of Castile and Leon (491). Sixth, the Castilian monarchs' possession of the Indies could be considered legal and just only under the condition that there had been "necessary prior consent by the kings and peoples of the mentioned lands, such that they freely consented to the institutions and donations granted by the Holy See to our King and Queen" (495).[56] Seventh, every military invasion in the Indies by Spain had been evil and tyrannical and the governance subsequently established was the same (496). Eighth, to the present date there had been no man of good faith at work in the Indies (498).

By all these principles, Las Casas argued that the only way the king could save his soul was by making restitution to the Incas and their descendants and restoring the Incas as legitimate lords in their own lands: "The Catholic king of Castile, our lord, is obligated, by the need to save his soul, to make restitution of the kingdoms of Peru to the Inca, grandson of Huayna Capac, that is, to the one who is the heir of the said kingdoms. And he [the king] likewise is obligated to give back to the other lords that which was theirs" (531).

In recommendations made nine years earlier (in 1555), in a letter to Philip's royal confessor, the Dominican friar Bartolomé Carranza de Miranda, Las Casas had also argued that for the king's spiritual well-being he should order that the autochthonous lords be restored to their rule and that Philip serve in a merely symbolic role as "universal lord," being acknowledged for this universal hegemony with an annual token of payment ("paria") from the Inca of a single jewel, such as the king of Tunis gave each year to the emperor.[57] These two final works of Las Casas constituted the fullest expression of his application of the principles of canon law whereby a ruler could not be imposed on a people without their consent. The notion that the king of Spain should give up immediate jurisdiction over the Indies and restore native autonomy was put into practice in the creation of the kurakas' counteroffer of 1560 and their other related efforts from 1559 to 1564 to combat the encomienda system.

Although Las Casas's writings spanning over half a century often seem inconsistent and contradictory to the casual reader, if examined sequentially and systematically, it is clear that he did not operate on contradictory principles but rather strove to apply them in the first half of his career to two different but, to his mind, related goals: service to the crown and the protection of its interests as well as the protection of the Indians as the vassals of the crown. Yet he came to understand that these seemingly complementary goals were impossible to sustain in tandem. Thus we interpret the three signal moments of his political evolution and reformist career: from the 1516 recommendation to increase the number of African slaves imported to the Indies and his first attempts in 1518 to challenge the Indians' subjection to slavery and the encomienda system, to his successful 1542 proposal for the abolition of encomienda and Indian slavery, to his 1562 and 1564 recommendations that Spain abandon its political rule of the Indies altogether. These shifts chart the course of a lifetime of political thought during which Las Casas came to the conclusion that serving both the interests of the crown in Spain and those of the peoples it subordinated abroad was untenable and impossible.

LAS CASAS, HISTORIAN

Las Casas's repentant recognition of the role he had played in 1516 in supporting African slavery reveals that he saw himself as a significant actor or agent in the early history of the Indies. This is a key to understanding his *Historia de las Indias,* in which his focus is always on the actors, including himself (this explains his third-person self-references). Taking a long view of that history, he summed it up as a devastating decline of native Indies populations for which royal governance of more than a half century's duration could not be held blameless before God: "And for these acts of destruction and very grave offenses and arrogance against God and the unheard of diminution of the human race, the Council [of the Indies] has no excuse before God, because these things had not been done in a single day or a year, or even in ten or twenty years, but rather in sixty years and more" [Y destos estragos y ofensas gravísimas de Dios y jactura y diminución tan nunca oída del linaje humano, no tiene ninguna excusa el Consejo ante Dios, porque no se hicieron en un día, ni en un año, ni en diez, ni en veinte, sino en sesenta y más años].[58]

The *Historia de las Indias* is today perhaps the least understood of Las Casas's major works. His plan, though not achieved, was to write the history of the Indies decade by decade for the first sixty years. His extraordinary efforts came to rest somewhere in the fourth decade, not because he lacked further information, but because he ran out of time. The intense scrutiny he applied from the beginning of the Columbian era and in particular the detail with which he examined Columbus's maritime and administrative career and actions take up approximately half of his account, ending with the Admiral's death on May 20, 1506.[59] Because Las Casas's criticism of the deeds of his fellow Spaniards (and also of himself) was harsh, it is assumed he was simply interpreting events according to an ideology that left no room for European heroism or native American malevolence and that can be reduced to the opposition of greedy oppressor versus innocent victim. But Las Casas tells a much more complex story.

Las Casas's *Historia de las Indias* was written over a period of some thirty years. He began it in 1527, a year after leaving the Dominican House of Studies on the island of Hispaniola, where he had spent four years. He worked on it intermittently and continued it after his final return to Spain in 1547. He wrote the prologue in 1552 and probably finished the entire work around 1559. In his last will and testament, he ordered that the autograph manuscript of his *Historia* remain permanently with the rest of his works at the Dominican convent of San Gregorio in Valladolid and that it should on no account leave those confines; even if, God willing, the occasion arose for it to be printed, the originals were to remain in the convent's library. Notations in a manuscript copy suggest that he requested that the *Historia* not be published for at least forty years after

1560.[60] Thus he would assure the *Historia*'s preservation, whether it was ever printed or not. He also saw a predictive value in history, insofar as he requested that the accounts he received daily from many places should be catalogued as to the date of their arrival and from whence they came. He explained, as mentioned earlier, that "if God ever saw fit to destroy Spain, those accounts of all that destruction that we have carried on in the Indies would serve to explain the reason for such an act of [divine] justice" [porque si Dios determinare destruir a España, se vea que es por las destrucciones que habemos hecho en las Indias y parezca la razón de su justicia ("Cláusula," 540)].

The sources Las Casas used to write about matters with which he was not personally familiar, namely, many critical events in the life of Columbus, consisted of printed material and manuscripts as well as oral interviews. According to Consuelo Varela, the premier editor of Columbus's writings, Las Casas copied no fewer than twenty-five of Columbus's letters for use in his *Historia*. Sources at his disposal in Seville included printed versions of Pietro Martire d'Anghiera's *Décadas del Nuevo Mundo* (1530), Gonzalo Fernández de Oviedo's *Historia general de las Indias* (1535) and *Sumario de la natural historia de las Indias* (1526), and the histories of Portugal by João de Barros (1553) and Gomes Eanes de Zurara (1453). Moreover, he had access to the Biblioteca Colombina of Hernando Colón (some fourteen thousand volumes, the largest private collection in Europe), and, thanks to the help of the Admiral's grandson, Don Luis Colón, access to the Columbus family archives at the Convento de la Cartuja.[61]

Furthermore, Las Casas knew personally both sides in the famous Columbus/Pinzón dispute that started around 1537 (and that, through their heirs, would last for some 250 years), thanks to the fact that his father had gone to the Indies on Columbus's second voyage and worked with Columbus's nemesis, Nicolás Bobadilla. As to the influence and circulation of the *Historia de las Indias,* it was used liberally, as mentioned, by Herrera in his *Historia general de los hechos de los Castellanos en las islas y tierra firme del Mar Oceano* (1601–1615).

For Las Casas, the issue was not how to narrate history but rather what history was to be. His prologue to the *Historia de las Indias* is one of the most remarkable texts of the period, and, reviewing the works of Jewish, Greek, Roman, and other historians, it ruminated on the problem of the purpose of written history. The critical history of the Jewish historians, such as Josephus, was Las Casas's preference, and he set about trying to understand how the consequences he saw around him came into being. His view of history was providentialist, and he saw the hand of divine providence in the great challenge placed before Christopher Columbus. From Augustine he took another element in the theory of human history: humanity's "predestination," that is, its "predisposition to do the great work of God," all the while choosing its own path and bearing its full consequences, whether those purposes be for good or ill.

Las Casas's narrative about Columbus in the *Historia de las Indias* reveals that he examined history not in the certitude of his moral harangues but in perplexity at the great conundrums of Columbian history. Although Las Casas describes Columbus as a "good Christian," he shows him to have been caught in a web of conflicting goals and motivations. The following passage illustrates the point:

> But the Admiral, with the great desire he had to offer wealth to the king and queen in order to compensate the great expenses they had incurred, . . . and as a foreigner and alone (as he said, disfavored) . . . together with his great blindness and ignorance of the limited authority he had, believing that merely by having discovered the Indies and by having been sent by the king and queen to propagate the faith and Christian religion, that they, the Indians, were all deprived of their freedom, he was impelled to rush and surpass even the disorder that he already created, or might have created; because certainly he was a Christian and virtuous and of very good intentions [my translation].
>
> [Pero el Almirante, con el gran deseo que tenía de dar provecho a los Reyes de Castilla para recompensar los grandes gastos que hasta entonces habían hecho y hacían, . . . y como hombre extranjero y solo (como él decía, desfavorecido), . . . juntamente con su gran ceguedad e ignorancia del derecho que tuvo, creyendo que por sólo haberlas descubierto y los Reyes de Castilla enviarlo a los traer a la fe y religión cristiana, eran privados de su libertad todos, le causó darse más priesa y exceder en la desorden que tuvo, que quizá tuviera; porque ciertamente él era cristiano y virtuoso y de muy buenos deseos]. (*Historia* 1:418 [bk. 1, chap. 105])

This passage, which consists of fragments of a sentence nearly a page long, demonstrates how Las Casas shifts the reader's attention from one consideration to another. Just as the reader identifies the factor that seems to be Las Casas's target of culpability, another element is brought into play to redirect the reader's consideration. Columbus turns out to be neither Las Casas's hero nor the villain of his history, but rather the exemplary case of a man who, like almost any other, fails to understand the gravity of the stakes of the enterprise in which he is engaged or to anticipate the larger consequences and implications of his most mundane decisions. Columbus was an appropriate subject for reflection because his most casual decisions contributed to chains of events and patterns of behavior that ultimately brought about, in Las Casas's view, the ruin of the Indies and its peoples, that "never-before-heard-of diminution of the human race" [diminución tan nunca oída del linaje humano].[62]

Las Casas wrote the history of Columbus's career to probe the agonizing question: How did things come to turn out as they had after a half century of Spanish rule in the Indies? Given the natural bounty and beauty of the Antilles that Columbus came upon in 1492, and given the generosity and helpfulness with which the lord Caonabo and his people had aided the Spaniards' efforts at permanent settlement on the island of Hispaniola in December of that year, how is it that matters stood as they did at the middle of the sixteenth century, with the twin goals of native evangelization and an economic system benefiting both Spaniard and Indian still not achieved? Las Casas's meditation on the history of the Portuguese in the Canaries and in Africa, in which the Columbus family also had participated, forms part of a globalizing view of history that transcended the particular case and opened a vista onto what the New World meant then, a view with tremendous vitality today. In this regard, there is no single culprit or scapegoat in this masterful history. Las Casas unfolds the narration of events and leaves enough leverage so that readers must decide. In other words, he does not offer a facile interpretation which one may accept or reject, but rather displays the complexity of factors from which readers must determine for themselves the causes and consequences of specific actions and larger patterns of behavior. Conscience and judgment are present to greater or lesser degrees, and although Las Casas describes the Admiral as a "good Christian," he reveals him to have been caught between incompatible priorities and goals.

Ultimately, Las Casas shifts his attention from Columbus to his men, then to the encomenderos, then to the king's ministers, and finally to the monarch himself. To remedy the situation in the Indies, Las Casas declared, all that was needed was a king who had one foot in the grave and who was unoccupied with wars.[63] He does not present this seemingly ironic reflection as a judgment of royal motivations, but he does hint at one of the most potentially powerful interpretations of royal conduct as being driven by youthful princely ambitions for greater territories, thus draining the royal treasury through expensive wars. (The long, costly reign of the recently abdicated Charles V comes to mind.) Unlike almost all of his contemporaries who wrote histories of Spain in America, Las Casas did not accept, in the end, Spain's right to civil and political rule of the Indies. What makes his historical questions different from those of others, therefore, is his assumption that things had gone wrong, not right, in the Indies, and that even the best of intentions had produced the worst of results.

There is a prophetic quality in this history, not because Las Casas intended to make it so (apart from his predictive, priestly warnings about the high cost of evil to its doers), but because it ruminates on the origins of the modern world. Although Las Casas as a historian adhered to spiritual mandates that were biblical and evangelical, applied juridical principles that were medieval and canonical, and followed a philosophy of history that was Augustinian, the disciplines of theology, law, and philosophy provided answers only to questions about what *should* be done. Their perspectives of interpretation and judgment could not explain what *had* been done. The absolute character of the principles Las Casas applied prospectively did not aid in the decipherment of the meaning of past actions. The modernity of Las Casas as a historian resides in his presentation of a broad display of the actions and opinions of the protagonists of Columbian history and leaves it up to the reader to assess, from all the fragments, all the cacophonies, the meaning of the whole. Like the best of modern essayists and historians, Las Casas raises more questions, and of a larger magnitude, than the particular and local ones he answers.

LAS CASAS, THEORIST OF AMERINDIAN CHARACTER AND CUSTOM

Las Casas's treatise on natural and moral history in the *Apologética historia sumaria* began as part of his general history of the Indies. However, at the end of chapter 67 of book 1 of the *Historia de las Indias*, he (1:307) acknowledges that the material he desired to discuss there on the customs of the native peoples was far too voluminous to insert and that by itself it would require "a not so small volume" to recount. This great work of ethnological theory was a landmark in the sixteenth-century development of such inquiries. Nevertheless, it has been largely ignored until quite recently. John Howland Rowe left the work out of consideration altogether in his seminal essays in the 1960s on the Renaissance origins of anthropology. More recently, Anthony Pagden's *Fall of Natural Man* discusses the work, although mainly the four final chapters which had been appended as an epilogue. The most illuminating examination of the significance of Las Casas's *Apologética,* as it pertains specifically to Andean religion, is found in Sabine MacCormack's *Religion in the Andes.*

Rowe excluded the *Apologética* from consideration on the basis that works unpublished in their day would not have been influential. Shortly afterward, in 1967, Henry Raup Wagner and Helen Rand Parish discovered that the bulk of Las Casas's discussions of Caribbean and Mesoamerican societies and customs had been rewritten into Román y Zamora's twice-published *Repúblicas del mundo* (1575, 1595). My own painstaking line-by-line comparison of Las Casas's and Román y Zamora's works has revealed that the same is true of his account of Peru. Thus it seems that Las Casas's work *was* influential. For example, in his *Comentarios reales de los Incas,* El Inca Garcilaso de la Vega quoted Román y Zamora with admiration; he surely did so without knowing that Las Casas had been one of his most important sources. El Inca Garcilaso would have been chagrined to know it was Las Casas he was quoting. As suggested earlier, Garcilaso had a particular loathing for the Dominican because of his career-long opposition to encomienda; the young Peruvian had met Las Casas in person in Seville in 1562. At that moment, Las Casas had just successfully prevented the sale of the rights in perpetuity to the Spanish holders of Peruvian encomiendas (see above), and he surely knew, as I have discovered, that El Inca Garcilaso's father had been one of the *encomenderos* who had given financial support to the plan for the sale.[64]

The essential point of departure of Las Casas's analysis in the *Apologética historia sumaria* is natural history, in which he takes classical and medieval environmental theories and applies them to the Antilles, demonstrating that this area was a most propitious place to favor humanity and foster the development of a benign human nature (Casas, *Apologética*, bk. 1, chaps. 1–22) and that the Indians possessed full rationality, granted them by nature: "humanity considered in its organic dimension," as Edmundo O'Gorman phrased it. Moving on to moral history, "humanity considered in its moral or historical dimension," Las Casas employed the model of the city, derived from Aristotle and Saint Augustine, to theorize civil life and ultimately to show, in hundreds of chapters, that the diverse native societies of the New World had established civil orders.[65] Las Casas follows Aristotle's *Politics* in defining the city as a social unit that was self-sufficient, inasmuch as it provided for the temporal and corporal needs of its inhabitants as well as their moral ones (their protection from internal and external threats of harm and the maintenance of peace) (1:237–38 [chap. 45]). He combined this view with that of Augustine, for whom the city was the life of a community, carried out in concordance and harmony and living in peace (1:239 [chap. 45]).

Las Casas insisted that the inhabitants of the New World satisfied these criteria for social order, even if their cities were constituted by "some number of districts and kinship groups or lineages made up of houses set together, be they made of straw or any other material" [algún número de barrios y de parentelas o linajes que se hacen de casas juntas, puesto que sean de paja o de otra cualquiera material] (1:241 [chap. 45]). Relying on the principles expounded in Aristotle's social philosophy and Augustine's theology, Las Casas argued, against the opinions of Sepúlveda and others, that the natives of the Americas had achieved the creation of civil order. To that he could apply the canon law principle of dominium; although Las Casas rightly called his work a defense or apology, it was also fundamentally theoretical inasmuch as he developed effective means by which to theorize the civility and sovereignty of Amerindian societies.

When in the *Apologética historia sumaria* he discussed America's native societies historically and geographically, Las Casas commanded a broad and extraordinarily detailed knowledge of the differences among them. In the more than forty-five years he spent going back and forth between Spain and America, he came to know Bermuda, Cuba, Jamaica, Hispaniola (the island he knew and loved most), the kingdoms of New Spain (including the environs of the Mexican capital), the provinces of Jalisco and Nicaragua, Tierra Firme, or the Spanish Main, the northern coast of South America to Cumaná, the kingdom of Yucatán, and Chiapas and Guatemala.[66] He explicitly pointed out that he did not know from personal experience the immense territories of Peru, La Florida, or Cíbola, that is, most of South America and the area of North America occupied today by the southeastern and southwestern United States (1:178 [bk. 2, chap. 34]). Altogether, Las Casas gathered his data not only from personal experience, but also and importantly, from the writings of dozens of other persons (works he acknowledged with care), including, he writes admiringly, the friars who knew Indian languages as well as others whose accounts he could take as authoritative (1:355 [bk. 3, chap. 68]). Cabeza de Vaca's *Relación* was one of those important sources.[67]

When Las Casas introduced the subject of the peoples of La Florida, the vast continental territories to the north of New Spain and the Gulf of Mexico which he called a "great and long land" containing "immense nations" [la grande y luenga tierra que llamamos la Florida, donde caben inmensas naciones] (see fig. 23), he made two points: European explorers discovered neither idolatry nor sacrifices there, and "the one who knew most about it was Álvar Núñez Cabeza de Vaca, a gentleman born in Jerez de la Frontera" (1:651 [bk. 3, chap. 124]). Las Casas utilized Cabeza de Vaca's work in two ways, first, as an authority on native customs of the vast area of La Florida and, second, to elucidate the readiness of Amerindian peoples to receive Christianity, thereby supporting his arguments for peaceful colonization. The purpose of his *Apologética*, Las Casas wrote, was to "investigate, conclude, and prove with evidence that all, speaking in general about all peoples, although some more and others a bit less but none excluded, enjoy the benefit of very good subtle and natural intellects and most capable understanding and are likewise all prudent and endowed naturally with the three types of prudence described by Aristotle, as being exercised in relation to oneself, one's family, and society at large [se averigua, concluye y prueba haciendo evidencia, ser todas, hablando *à toto genere*, algunas más y otras muy poco menos, y ningunas expertes (Latin *expers*, having no part in) dello, de muy buenos, sotiles y naturales ingenios y capacísimos entendimientos; ser así mismo prudentes y dotados naturalmente de las tres especies de prudencia que pone el Filósofo: monástica, económica y política] (1:4 [argumento]). In particular, he underscored the precept of natural law whereby humanity "inclines and desires to know all truths, principally to know God" [el hombre, naturalmente, es inclinado y desea saber las verdades, mayormente cognoscer a Dios (1:213 [bk. 3, chap. 40])].

The Dominican's acute reading of Cabeza de Vaca identified, for the first time among Cabeza de Vaca's readers, two types of orientation he and his companions had to the lands and peoples they came to know: considerable knowledge of the groups "close to the coast of the North Sea and those who neighbor them and not very many leagues inland" versus the "diverse and more organized nations, of whose customs he [Cabeza de Vaca] could know very little, due to his hurried passage" through north-central and northwestern Mexico (2:361 [bk. 3, chap. 206]). Las Casas found essential all the information Cabeza de Vaca provided about native groups, both along the coastal region of today's Texas and, from north to south, inland to the west. He used it to create his panorama of cultures that existed in "the great land we call La Florida" since "all this land we call La Florida is continuous with the land of the kingdom of Cíbola."[68] Appreciating Cabeza de Vaca's firsthand experience as an invaluable source, Las Casas was able to make some of his most subtle and potentially most effective arguments in favor of the "foundations and principles and natural inclinations toward the sciences and virtues" that these "very barbarous people" possessed and shared with the rest of humanity.[69]

Las Casas also drew from Cabeza de Vaca an authoritative elucidation of Amerindian readiness to receive Christianity that undergirded his model of peaceful colonization. Las Casas's pragmatic goal of bringing Amerindian peoples into the Christian fold is never far from the surface of his academic study. The argument that the Amerindians were worthy of Christ and capable of leading virtuous lives was essential to the *Apologética,* as it had been the explicit program of Las Casas's first major work, *Del único modo de atraer a la gente a la verdadera religión* (circa 1534), discussed above. On this score, Las Casas cited verbatim long passages from Cabeza de Vaca's account, particularly his invocation of the emperor Charles, urging him to facilitate the conversion of the Floridian peoples, Las Casas writes, quoting Cabeza de Vaca, "because in the two thousand leagues that we traveled by land and through the sea on the rafts and another ten months that we went through the land without stopping once we were no longer captives, we found neither sacrifices nor idolatry."[70]

That Las Casas saw powerful consequences issuing from Cabeza de Vaca's testimony is manifested by the frequency with which he cited that testimony on crucial topics: the absence of such obstacles to the faith as idolatry and sacrifice, the intuitive worship of the Judeo-Christian god under another name and the aptitude for conversion, and the good treatment received by the unarmed Spaniards from the peoples of northwestern Mexico. Las Casas's readings of Cabeza de Vaca on these issues transformed the latter's interpretation of his historical experience into a theoretical argument about the spiritual worth of all peoples; utilizing the empirical in the service of the theoretical, Las Casas constructed the theoretical with pragmatic consequences in view. In sum, the information provided by Cabeza de Vaca's interpretation of his experience with the natives of La Florida became for Las Casas not only eyewitness testimony but also moral authority, which he put to the service of his own far-reaching philosophical arguments.

Las Casas occupies a central position in the polemics of possession not only because of the positions he successively took regarding Spanish colonialism and the role his polemical writings came to play in the works of other writers. The value he placed on his readings in ancient philosophy, patristics, law, history, and the ethnographic accounts of the new-found Amerindian peoples reveals that, where his personal knowledge was lacking or where it failed (as in his ignorance of the origins of African slavery), he relied for authority about historical events on the writings that interpreted them. So much weight did he place on this literary authority that he claimed for it a transcendent role in the consequences that divine justice could rain down upon Spain—and also upon himself. For Las Casas, the written record, to which he devoted his life in reading and writing, was the infallible witness to human frailty and folly—that of others and his own. This was the conviction of the historical Las Casas, and it suggests why other writers on the Indies of his generation and the successive ones, as well as fictionalized versions of them created centuries later, attributed so much importance to their literary endeavors.

CHAPTER 4

Councilors Warring at the Royal Court

IN 1550 THE FIRST VICEROY of New Spain, Antonio de Mendoza, observed the following in his report to his successor, Luis de Velasco: "Some will tell Your Lordship that the Indians are simple[-minded] and humble, that neither arrogance nor malice reigns in them and that they are not greedy. Others, on the contrary, will say that they are very rich and that they are vagabonds and that they do not want to cultivate the land. Do not believe either group, but rather deal with the Indians as you would any other people, without making special rules [by relying] on third-party accounts, because there are few in these regions who are not moved by some form of self-interest, be it for temporal or spiritual gain, or passion or ambition, vice or virtue."[1] Mendoza's advice to his successor was practical, and his consideration, timely, because it was at midcentury that the discussion of the character and comportment of the Amerindian reached its apogee. It had not emerged as a topic in its own right but rather appeared within the context of a larger debate: the right of the Castilian crown to conquer the lands and native inhabitants of the Americas and, in particular, how to govern them.

Mendoza's remarks set forth the two principal arenas in which the question of the Indians was debated: the civil government and the missionary church. In both cases, when the incapacity of the Indian was proposed, it was done in the name either of defending the interests of the crown and the *encomenderos* or of protecting the interests of the church.[2] Colonial policies were closely related to the differences the Spanish encountered among the native peoples. Variations in royal policy from region to region were reflections of the problems created by these regional and cultural differences, and it was in consideration of those circumstances that laws were formulated and ideological positions took root.[3]

There were three basic alternatives with respect to the actions of the Europeans toward the natives.[4] The sedentary groups (mostly agriculturalists) could be employed on the *encomiendas* or in other systems of forced labor. The less sedentary groups, either by individual or by family, were forced to work as domestic servants and slaves. For the native groups that could not be subdued, the options were extermination or dispersion, which were permitted very early by the royal decrees and provisions that were issued against the presumed cannibals of the Caribbean.[5] Thus, when the discussion of the Indian was inaugurated, it did not emerge at the abstract, theoretical level but in response to particular sets of circumstances, be they real and confirmed or merely asserted and believed, as in the case of the laws regarding the inhabitants of the Antilles (Castañeda Delgado, 81–85; Hanke, "Studies," appendix VI).

The disputation regarding the treatment of the Indians culminated in relation to the colonial institution of the encomienda, which had its origins in Spain and became, from the earliest days of the sixteenth century in the Spanish Caribbean, the "chief means of private Spanish control over Indian peoples" (Gibson, *Aztecs,* 58). It consigned groups of Indians to privileged Spanish colonists; these grantees (*encomenderos*) were entitled to receive labor and tribute in goods from the designated Indians. An encomienda grant conferred no landed property or juridical jurisdiction; as Charles Gibson (58) writes, it "was a possession, not a property, and it was per se inalienable and non-inheritable. Save insofar as the terms of particular grants might allow." Its use spread from the Antilles and was imposed on the peoples of the former Mexica federation in New Spain, those of the former Inca empire in Peru, and all Spanish possessions in the Americas. The Indians were regarded as juridically free, yet the legal distinctions between encomienda, slavery, and other forms of servitude did not suffice to render the differences clear in practice.[6]

The high point of this discussion in Spain is commonly identified with the debate in Valladolid in 1550–1551 between Fray Bartolomé de las

Casas and the humanist and chronicler of the emperor, Juan Ginés de Sepúlveda.[7] The Valladolid debates, carried out before a select body of the emperor's councilors, was a signal event in the larger controversy. While the question of the character or comportment of the Indian was not the central issue of that dispute, it was introduced there by Sepúlveda and it cannot be separated from the events of conquest and colonization and the elaboration of royal policy pertaining thereto. The trajectory of the larger debate and pertinent legal actions can be quickly summarized.[8]

LEGISLATIVE EVENTS AND POLEMICAL CONFRONTATIONS

In 1495, because of the shipment of Indians from the island of Hispaniola to Spain to be sold as slaves, Ferdinand and Isabel ordered a meeting of theologians and other learned men to consider whether this could be done according to the requirements of Christian conscience. The conference resolved that the Indians were free and that they could not be sold, with the exception of those captured in a just war. This provision repeated Isabel's formal instruction ("Instrucción") delivered to Columbus at Barcelona on May 29, 1493 (Castañeda Delgado, "La política," 115), which stated that the Indians were free vassals of the crown and that enslaving them was prohibited, except for those who refused to submit themselves; these could be enslaved according to the rights of war, especially the Caribs, who were "cruel and ate human flesh." On June 20, 1500, a royal decree of Ferdinand and Isabel condemned Columbus's taking of Indian slaves in the Caribbean, prohibited their sale in Andalusia, mandated their freedom, and forbade that Indians be taken as slaves in the future (Rumeu de Armas, *La política,* 341–342). In August of 1503, the crown of Castile issued a royal decree permitting the capture and enslavement of Indians reported to be cannibals on the Caribbean islands and at Cartagena (CDI 31:196–200). On November 15, 1505, the authorization was repeated when by royal decree Nicolás de Ovando, as governor of Hispaniola, was permitted to enslave Indian "cannibals" found in the area of the Caribbean (CDU 5:110–113). Another royal provision signed by Doña Juana on June 3, 1511, authorized making just war against the same Indians of the Caribbean and its rim in order to enslave them (CDU 5:258–262). Also in 1511 the activism of the Dominicans of the island of Hispaniola against the ill treatment of the Indians took shape in the form of sermons delivered by Fray Antonio de Montesinos.

In 1512, the Laws of Burgos lightened the burden of the Indians, but without eliminating their distribution to conquistadores and settlers. In 1514, Juan López de Palacios Rubios drafted the Requirement (*requerimiento*). Designed to be used in initial encounters between the Spanish and Amerindian groups, it was a formal proclamation that offered the Indians the choice of accepting peacefully the Castilian king's sovereignty or being subjected to a war that would end in their death or enslavement. (See the section entitled "The Requirement," in chapter 10.)

In 1516, the regent Cardinal Francisco Jiménez de Cisneros sent three Hieronymite friars to Hispaniola to advocate the freedom of the Indians. On drafting a questionnaire concerning the mental capacity of the Indians, the Hieronymites judged them to be lacking in the exercise of sufficient reason so as to be capable of governing themselves. Since the alleged cannibalism of the Caribbean Indians was questioned by antislavery critics, an inquiry was authorized on June 18, 1519, to call witnesses for the purpose of citing direct or hearsay evidence about the practice. Unlike the rulings cited above, this hastily executed investigation broadened the range of legitimate offenses for which Indians could be enslaved beyond anthropophagy to include "infidelity," "idolatry," and "the abominable sin against nature," that is, sodomy. The resultant "cannibal questionnaire" was used to solicit testimony from Castilian ship captains and officers. This 1519 document and the testimony it produced made a case for the enslavement of Caribbean Indians that no longer rested exclusively on charges of anthropophagy; now, idolatry and sodomy seemingly provided equivalent just cause. The next day, June 20, 1519, the licenciate Alonso de Zuazo, chief justice official (*justicia mayor*) of Hispaniola, ruled that it was legitimate to make war on such Indians and to take them to Hispaniola, "where they are greatly needed," and sell them freely.[9]

On December 12, 1519, Las Casas and Fray Juan Quevedo, the first bishop of Darién on Tierra Firme, debated the case of the Indians before Charles V at the royal court, which was in Barcelona at that time.[10] Quevedo argued in favor of the natural slavery of the Indians, which John Mair, a Scottish theologian at the Collège de Montaigu in Paris, had advocated in 1510. Mair was the first to apply the Aristotelian concept of natural slavery to the problems of governance in the Indies. In effect, he established the principle that "the Christians' right claims to sovereignty over certain pagans could be said to rest on the nature of the people being

conquered, instead of on the supposed juridical rights of the conquerors."[11] Arguing against Quevedo (and Mair), Las Casas defended the rationality of the Indians, taking the position that, according to the Christian
religion, all nations of the world were equal and all were by nature free
and that neither their freedom nor their dominions could be taken away,
nor could the Indians be placed in servitude under the pretext or guise
["so color ni achaques"] of calling them "slaves by nature."[12]

In a meeting convened at court in La Coruña in May 1520, Cardinal
Adrian (Florenz, of Utrecht) convinced the assembly that "the Indians
should be free and treated as free and brought to the faith by the means
established by Christ."[13] In a royal letter of May 18, 1520, Charles V proposed the eventual abolition of the encomienda system in the Antilles and
ordered that holdings not be reassigned to the current encomenderos'
heirs but rather revert to the crown when vacated because of death or
other cause. This order was not obeyed, and, as mentioned above, the
encomienda system subsequently was instituted in New Spain and then
throughout the Indies; Charles's official position, echoing that of Ferdinand and Isabel before him, was that the freedom of the Indians was, in
fact, not compromised by their being placed in encomienda.[14] In 1525,
Fray Tomás Ortiz argued against the freedom of the Indians before the
Council of the Indies, citing the "bestial customs" of the native inhabitants of Tierra Firme.

The question of the nature of the Indians emerged forcefully in the
1530s and 1540s. Two significant factors can be cited: First, the number of
encomenderos was increasing rapidly because the encomienda had come
to be a form of rewarding services to the emperor, and it was freely
distributed to individuals whose service may or may not have included
participating in the wars of conquest. In this way, many civil and ecclesiastical officials in the royal service came to be very powerful encomenderos. Second, there were no major new indigenous societies to conquer,
and the number of natives was declining because of illness and epi-
demics. For example, an epidemic in 1520 was followed by one in 1545
that reduced the indigenous population of central Mexico by one third.[15]
Against this background of increasing demands on a declining native
population, in 1530 and 1534 there appeared two royal decrees on the
legitimacy of capturing and enslaving the Indians; the first of these,
signed on August 2, 1530, prohibited the capture and enslavement of

Indians for any reason; the second, dated February 20, 1534, authorized the right to enslave Indians in war and by barter.[16]

In 1537, Pope Paul III announced his famous bull (*Sublimis Deus*) in favor of the freedom of the Indians, in the introduction of which he denounced the thesis of their alleged barbarity and condemned as heretical the opinion that Indians were incapable of receiving the faith:

> The sublime God so loved the human race that He created man in such wise that he might participate, not only in the good that other creatures enjoy, but endowed him with capacity to attain to the inaccessible and invisible Supreme Good and behold it face to face; and since man, according to the testimony of the sacred scriptures, has been created to enjoy eternal life and happiness, which none may obtain save through faith in our Lord Jesus Christ, it is necessary that he should possess the nature and faculties enabling him to receive that faith; and that whoever is thus endowed should be capable of receiving that same faith. Nor is it credible that any one should possess so little understanding as to desire the faith and yet be destitute of the most necessary faculty to enable him to receive it. Hence Christ, who is the Truth itself, that has never failed and can never fail, said to the preachers of the faith whom He chose for that office 'Go ye and teach all nations.' *He said all, without exception, for all are capable of receiving the doctrines of the faith.*"[17]

Taking as a necessary premise the Indians' rationality, the bull's purpose was to assert the Indians' freedom. In the same year of 1537 and through the academic years of 1537–1538 and 1538–1539, Fray Francisco de Vitoria delivered lectures at the University of Salamanca on the right to Spanish conquest in the Indies that became the basis for his famous *relecciones*, or dissertations (*Relectio de Indis*) of 1539 (see below).

In 1542, after Las Casas's fiery appearances at court and persuasive proposals, the New Laws prohibiting Indian slavery and encomienda were promulgated.[18] However, the resistance of colonists in Mexico persuaded the viceroy Antonio de Mendoza to refrain from formally announcing the new legislation, and the rebellion of the conquistadores against the crown in Peru resulted in the assassination of its first viceroy, Blasco Núñez de Vela. In these circumstances, the new legislation was not put into effect.

Recognizing that the New Laws were unenforceable, the crown repealed them in 1545–1546.[19]

In 1549, the Council of the Indies recommended to the emperor that all conquest missions that did not already have prior approval from the crown and council be suspended. On April 16, 1550, Charles ordered the suspension of all conquests until a council of theologians and advisers to the emperor could recommend a just means of carrying them out. As mentioned, with Las Casas and Sepúlveda as the opponents in the debate, the junta was convened in Valladolid before a panel of fourteen judges on August 15, 1550. A second session was convened in April of 1551. Although scholars have tended to conclude that the debate had no formal outcome (Hanke, *Spanish Struggle*, 119; Losada, "Introducción," 19), formal opinions were submitted by at least thirteen of the judges. In the face of this apparent inconclusiveness and under pressure from colonial officials and encomenderos abroad, in 1555 and 1556 the crown reactivated the authorization for further conquests (Manzano y Manzano 187, 201–203) (see the section entitled "The Great Debate in Valladolid (1550–1551)," in chapter 3).

Another junta was convened at the royal court in Valladolid in 1550; although much less well known, its topic was the right to grant encomiendas in perpetuity, and it played a significant role in the origins of Bernal Díaz del Castillo's *Historia verdadera de la conquista de la Nueva España* (see the section entitled "Bernal Díaz's Interactions with Las Casas," in chapter 6).

THE RATIONAL CAPACITY OF THE INDIANS

Judging from this outline of events, it is clear that any question about the nature of the Indians of the New World was generated, from Mair onward, as a way of dealing with the right of military conquest and the imposition of colonial governance. Las Casas (*Historia* 2:455 [bk. 3, chap. 8]), in fact, identified the earliest landholding Spanish residents (*vecinos*) on Hispaniola as people who commonly found it convenient to condemn the Indians as politically incompetent, that is, as incapable of governing themselves and, in an extreme form of the assertion, incapable of receiving the Christian faith: "All these [*vecinos*], or some of them, were the first, as I understand and have always understood it, who at court defamed the Indians as being incapable of governing themselves, and that it was necessary to give them guardians [*tutores*], and that this evil that so belittled them became more widespread, to the point of declaring them incapable of receiving the faith, which is no small heresy, making them the equivalent of beasts." The issue of subjecting the Indians to the rule of the Spanish was thus the motor that generated the opinions against their mental capacity.

From the earliest years of the Spanish presence in the Indies, theologians, jurists, and missionaries did not doubt the humanity of the Indians and never raised the question. That is, although the *level* of the Indians' rational capacity and the character of their customs were debated (and about which cannibalism was legislated, as noted above), no member of the Castilian elite denied the Indians' condition as true human beings. The only exceptions were two Dominican friars, the aforementioned Ortiz and, a decade later, Fray Domingo de Betanzos, who defamed the natives of the New World by declaring that they were incapable of receiving the Christian faith.[20] Ortiz had denounced the Indians as cannibals. On presenting his position at court (sometime after a massacre carried out by the Indians at Chiribichi on the Gulf of Santa Fe on Tierra Firme), he contributed to the creation of the authorization of 1525 to enslave the natives of the Tierra Firme coast. The other Dominican, Betanzos, asserted that God had condemned the Indians and that all laws promulgated for the purpose of protecting them were useless. Betanzos's judgment became the moral authority on whose basis in 1534 the president of the Council of the Indies, Cardinal García Jofre de Loaysa, revoked the law prohibiting Indian slavery and sanctioned the continuation of Indian slaving.[21]

Thus, although it has been asserted that "the utterances in which the Indians are described as beasts in an absolute sense appear on the lips of their defenders attributing the concept to members of the opposite band,"[22] accusations against the Indians had an effect on the laws drawn up to govern them on at least three occasions: the licenciado Zuazo's order of 1519, the royal authorization for enslaving Indians in 1526 (CDU 9: 268–280) and the revocation, on February 20, 1534 (CDU 10: 192–203), of the order of August 2, 1530 (CDU 10: 38–43), that had prohibited Indian slavery.[23]

At the same time, the meaning of all these references to the "bestial" character of the Indians, attributed by Las Casas to those who scorned and mistreated them, forms part of a rhetorical strategy aimed at shaming the encomenderos and proponents of Indian slavery and to provoke them with a call to conscience by insisting that the ill treatment of the Indians was equivalent to considering them lacking in the dignity they possessed as fellow human beings. This is apparent on considering the classic example that Las Casas offers in his *Historia de las Indias* on recounting the sermon preached by the Dominican friar Montesinos in Santo Domingo on the third Sunday of Advent in 1511, as mentioned above.[24] On addressing the encomenderos, Fray Antonio proclaimed, "Tell me, by what right and with what justice do you keep those Indians in such cruel and horrible servitude? By what authority have you made detestable wars on these peoples, who were living tranquilly and peacefully on their lands, where you have consumed such an infinite number of them, with assaults and deaths never heard of?. . . These Indians, are they not human beings? Do they not have rational souls? Are you not obligated to love them as you love yourselves?"[25]

The persuasive strategy that Las Casas attributes to Montesinos in the sermon is the one he employs. That is, the key to Las Casas's argument against the conquistadores is the treatment of the Indians, *not* their nature, character, or customs. As Edmundo O'Gorman ("Estudio preliminar," 305) points out, "Las Casas and the papal bulls *Sublimis Deus* and *Veritas ipsa* specifically . . . declare that the Indians were *treated like* brute animals, and that the relationship was understood to be one of association, *not* identification." Not only Las Casas but also the bishop of Michoacán, Vasco de Quiroga, and the Dominican chroniclers Juan de la Cruz y Moya, Agustín Dávila Padilla, and Antonio Remesal were among those who commonly made reference to colonists as treating the Indians as if they were not human beings; they attributed this judgment, rightly or wrongly (but definitely rhetorically), to common soldiers who participated in the conquests.[26]

Sublimis Deus has also suffered confused interpretations. Decreed in order to establish the freedom of the Indians, the bull came to be interpreted, erroneously, as a (needed) declaration of their humanity. This second interpretation emerged in the early biographies of Las Casas, written by Cruz y Moya and Dávila Padilla.[27] Reviewing the disputes that had occurred in Hispaniola over the capacity of the Indians for self-governance, these biographers read Las Casas incorrectly on the controversy about the irrationality of the Indians; they assumed he had argued *for* their humanity (which for Las Casas was never in dispute and not open to discussion), when in fact he had argued *against* their mistreatment by the colonists. Thus was attributed to *Sublimis Deus* a meaning, the defense of the Indians' humanity, it did not have.[28]

The purpose of the bull was to prevent and condemn the usurpation of the Indians' sovereignty, the confiscation of their property, and their enslavement. The bull presents in its introduction an account of the current mistreatment of the Indians: "The enemy of the human race, who opposes all good deeds in order to bring men to destruction, beholding and envying this, invented a means never before heard of, by which he might hinder the preaching of God's word of Salvation to the people: he inspired his satellites who, to please him, have not hesitated to publish abroad that the Indians of the West and the South, and other people of whom we have recent knowledge, should be treated as dumb brutes created for our service, pretending that they are incapable of receiving the Catholic faith."[29] The core of the document is this declaration: "Desiring to provide ample remedy for these evils, we define and declare by these our letters, or by any translation thereof signed by any notary public and sealed with the seal of any ecclesiastical dignitary, to which the same credit shall be given as to the originals, that, notwithstanding whatever may have been or may be said to the contrary, the said Indians and all other people who may later be discovered by Christians, *are by no means to be deprived of their liberty or the possession of their property*, even though they be outside the faith of Jesus Christ; and that they may and should, freely and legitimately, enjoy their liberty and the possession of their property; nor should they be in any way enslaved. Should the contrary happen, it shall be null and of no effect."[30]

The bull makes clear that the Indians' status as non-Christians could not be used as a pretext to deprive them of those rights. This is also the thrust of the papal brief "Pastorale officium" (1537), in which the pope declared that the inhabitants of the Indies, and whatever other "infidels" that might yet be discovered, possessed the right to their liberty and dominion over their lands and possessions. It bears emphasizing that the position expressed by Las Casas and the bulls *Sublimis Deus* and *Veritas ipsa* was that the treatment of the Indians by the Spanish, not the nature of the Indians, was bestial.[31]

FRAY FRANCISCO DE VITORIA

Essential to the Indies debates were the lectures delivered in 1537–1539 by the theologian and professor (*catedrático*) of the University of Salamanca, the learned Dominican Fray Francisco de Vitoria (c. 1492–1546). More important still were the dissertations, or *relecciones*, that Vitoria delivered in 1539, the second of which has survived in the transcriptions and summaries prepared by his disciples, colleagues, and first editors. The *relección* was an academic literary genre that existed at the University of Bologna and was imported to Salamanca from universities in France. It was not a recapitulation of a topic previously treated but an inquiry into its concrete points that explored its propositions in greater detail. Although the *Relectio de Indis* was not printed until 1557, it "circulated widely in manuscript before that date both inside and outside the university of Salamanca and had a lasting impact on every subsequent discussion of *las cosas de Indias*."[32]

The Spanish university of those years was an influential institution, with its independent prerogatives, exemptions, and rights governed and guaranteed by its internally elected professoriate and rectorship. As a result, the Castilian monarchs frequently called upon its most illustrious thinkers, such as Vitoria and his colleagues Domingo de Soto and Melchor Cano, to offer their counsel on such matters as the justice of the wars of conquest and the pastoral issue of the appropriateness of the mass baptism of adults without prior instruction. However, the influence of these theologian-jurist teachers as judges and arbiters of royal policy came to an end at Salamanca after Vitoria and in general with the Las Casas–Sepúlveda debate of 1550–1551, when it was deemed that the complex, academic consideration of such issues and the counsel provided presented more problems than they resolved.[33]

In his *De templanza* of 1537, Vitoria focused on the practice of anthropophagy and the derivation of principles for justifying intervention and war with respect to cannibalism in the Indies (Urdánoz, "Introducción," 996). He denied the right of the foreign prince to wage war on a people for their crimes against nature (such as consuming or sacrificing human flesh): the sole legitimate motive for war would be the protection of innocent persons from injury.

In his *De Indis* of 1539, Vitoria focused on the right of dominion over the Indies. Here he argued that a prince could exercise dominion over a foreign people because of their natural need to be ruled and governed by others. In response to the question as to whether, before the arrival of the Spanish, the Indians had been legitimate lords of their domains and possessions, Vitoria (*Relectio*, 13–14) answered in the affirmative, although he asserted, "As Aristotle said, learnedly and with elegance, 'There are those who are slaves by nature,' or, rather, there are those for whom 'it is better to serve than to lead.' They are the ones who do not possess sufficient reason even to govern themselves, but only to follow the orders of their masters, and whose strength is more in the body than in the spirit. Truly, if there be peoples of such a nature, these barbarians are it above all others, for they hardly seem to differ from brute animals, and they are completely incapable of governing. And without a doubt it is better for them to be governed by others than to govern themselves. Since, as Aristotle says, it is just and obvious that they are slaves; and, as a result, they cannot be masters."

At the same time, again interpreting Aristotle's thought, Vitoria took the position that limited intellect did not per se deny the Indians of the prerogatives of self-governance or ownership of their possessions. He added, however, that Aristotle had recognized that they had certain needs (*Relectio*, 30–31):

> I answer that Aristotle refused to affirm that those who have limited intellect are by nature slaves or that they do not have dominion over themselves and their possessions. This is civil and legitimate servitude that makes no one a slave by nature. Neither does the Philosopher mean that those who are limited and of little intelligence by nature can be deprived of their goods, reduced to slavery and sold. What he meant was that there is in them a natural *need* to be ruled and governed by others, just as children need to be subjected to their parents and the wife to the husband. And it is clear that this was the intention of the Philosopher, because in the same way he says that there are some who by nature are lords, that is, those who are endowed with powerful intellect. And it is certain that he does not mean here that these such ones can appropriate to themselves the rule over the rest on account of being wiser, but rather on account of their having received from nature the faculties to govern and rule others.

It is, in Vitoria's view, the moral obligation of some to exercise their God-given talents and to rule over others, and for those others, it is their moral responsibility to accept that imposition.

On the subject of dominion Vitoria (*Relectio*, 30–31) states, "And thus, even assuming that these barbarous peoples are as inept and brutish as is said, not on account of that can they be denied dominion [over their own properties and possessions], nor included in the category of civil slaves. It is true, nevertheless, that on account of this reason and motive there is some right by which to subjugate them, as we will later make clear. One sure conclusion, then, results: that before the arrival of the Spaniards, they were, privately and publicly, true lords." After thus concluding his argument to the effect that, before the arrival of the Spanish, the Indians of America were "true lords," and after entertaining the consideration of seven titles to conquest he did not judge as legitimate, Vitoria went on to propose seven that were so. Two of them merit our attention. His second just title was the Christians' right to propagate the Christian faith; he argued that any war that had to be undertaken to achieve that goal was legitimate and just: "It is lawful to occupy their [the Indians'] territories and settlements if there exists no other way to attend to the good of the religion. They may name new governors, destroying the former ones, and do everything that is lawful by the rights of war in any just war" (*Relectio*, 90). He added, however, that this could be done only as long as the interests and well-being of the Indians took priority over that of their Christian aggressors and that, in fact, he feared that excesses that went beyond the limits of the law and Christian morality had already been committed (*Relectio*, 91). Vitoria's fifth legitimate title for conquest was based on the practices of human sacrifice and anthropophagy; they became just causes for foreign rule, not as the right to punish pagans for their sins against nature, but rather as the moral obligation to defend innocent persons against tyranny (*Relectio*, 93).

To these seven legitimate titles of conquest, he added "another title" that "cannot be affirmed with certainty but that merits debate and that seems, to some, to be legitimate" [Hay otro título que no podría afirmarse con seguridad, pero sí discutirse y que parece legítimo para algunos]: "The title is this: 'Those barbarians, although, as has been said, they may not be completely incompetent, are, nevertheless, at such a short remove from the mentally retarded that it seems they are not fit to constitute and administer a legitimate republic within the limits of humaneness and order' " [El título es éste: 'Esos bárbaros, aunque, como se ha dicho, no sean del todo incapaces, distan, sin embargo, tan poco de los retrasados mentales que parece no son idóneos para constituir y administrar una república legítima dentro de límites humanos y políticos' (*Relectio*, 97)].

Here Vitoria sets forth the deficiency of a capacity for rational self-governance as a (possibly) legitimate title by which to subject the Indians to foreign rule. However, reiterating his fundamental caveat, he declares that he cannot accept or reject it definitively: "I accept it, as I said, without affirming it categorically and only on condition that it be done for the good and well-being of the Indians themselves and not as a pretext for profit by the Spanish" [Lo acepto, (como dije) sin afirmarlo absolutamente y aun con la condición de que se haga por el bien y utilidad de los mismos y no como pretexto del lucro de los españoles (*Relectio*, 98)]. He sees as complementary his argument about natural slavery: "Also pertinent to this argumentation is what was previously stated, to the effect that some human beings are slaves by nature. And these barbarians seem to be such, and in part they could for this reason be governed in servitude" (*Relectio*, 98).

Thus the incapacity for self-governance emerged as Vitoria's eighth possible legitimate title authorizing Spanish conquest in the Americas. It has been suggested that Vitoria's position in the eighth "doubtful" title to conquest, delivered in December 1538 or the beginning of 1539, was colored by the pressure put on him, and that this last title, about which he felt uncertain, was elaborated "to mollify the emperor."[34] This might explain the ambiguity and self-contradiction of his position, accepting the principle guardedly, approving its application only if for the good of the Indians, not the gain of the Spaniards. Nevertheless, in the last of his dissertations on the Spanish right to make war against the Indians (*De indis, sive de iure belli hispanorum in barbaros, relectio posterior*) in 1539, Vitoria concluded that the sole just cause for war was to repel injuries received and that the offenses suffered by the Indians had to be very grave in order to justify making war against them, because "everything done in war is of great consequence and heinous, consisting of massacres, conflagrations and devastations, and it is not legitimate to punish trivial offenses by means of war because the harshness of the punishment must be proportionate to the gravity of the injury received" (Vitoria, *Obras*, 823–826).

After this pronouncement by Vitoria, the emperor Charles V decided the time had come for these professor-priests ("maestros religiosos") to keep silent on the questions of "our right to the Indies, the islands and lands of the ocean sea" as well as on the authority of the pope in that regard. On November 10, 1539, the emperor wrote to the prior of Vitoria's Dominican monastery, San Esteban, in Salamanca and ordered that "such teachers and members of the Order" who had discussed these matters in sermons or their university lessons should give sworn statements about their past actions, surrender any writings they had produced on such matters, and refrain from lecturing or preaching or printing anything pertaining thereto, without the express permission of the court.[35]

JUAN GINÉS DE SEPÚLVEDA

In this context, I turn to the theorization offered by the humanist philosopher and imperial chronicler Juan Ginés de Sepúlveda (1490–1573). Sepúlveda's *Demócrates Segundo, o De las Justas Causas de la Guerra contra los Indios,* a defense of the legitimacy of the wars of conquest of the Indians, was a dialogue written in Latin circa 1545 (Losada, "Juan Ginés," xiv–xv). Anthony Pagden (*Fall,* 111) has called it "the most virulent and uncompromising argument for the inferiority of the American Indian ever written," and at the same time acknowledged that "Sepúlveda's reading of Aristotle turns out in the end to be not so very far from Vitoria's own." Vitoria's opinion on natural slavery and the Indians of America clarifies Sepúlveda's interpretation of the concept and its Indies application. There are strong similarities between the principles that Vitoria and Sepúlveda elucidated, and their major difference is the degree of certainty they respectively expressed about their applicability: Vitoria equivocates and qualifies; Sepúlveda is certain. Sepúlveda, in fact, asserted that Vitoria would approve his arguments while Las Casas declared that such an affinity could be explained only by certain erroneous conclusions drawn by the Salamanca theologian, conclusions that were occasioned by the "false information" Vitoria had received from others.[36] Vitoria's reading of Aristotle is confirmed by that of Sepúlveda. For both Vitoria and Sepúlveda, natural slavery consisted of a hierarchical relationship between those with the talent and training to rule and those who were better off being ruled by others.

In the years following the promulgation of the 1542 New Laws, the law that abolished the institution of encomienda was revoked, and increasing pressure was placed on the need to justify Spanish dominion in the Indies. According to Hanke (*Spanish Struggle*, 114), Sepúlveda wrote *Demócrates Segundo* at the request of Cardinal García Jofre de Loaysa, president of the Council of the Indies. Sepúlveda cited four causes that justified the waging of war against the Indians: (1) to impose guardianship, that is, both the right and the need to govern those who were incapable of governing themselves, the "natural slaves" (*siervos a natura*); (2) to do away with the crime of devouring human flesh; (3) to punish those who committed crimes against innocent persons; and (4) to subdue peoples prior to preaching to them the Christian faith. Sepúlveda (*Demócrates Segundo*, 19) set forth as the first argument for the justification of the Spanish conquests in the Indies "the rude nature of those peoples": "Those whose natural condition is such that they should obey others, and if they refuse their dominion and there remains no other recourse, they may be subjugated by force of arms; such a war is considered just in the opinion of the most eminent philosophers." To explain his meaning, Sepúlveda (21) rehearsed the Aristotelian principle of the rule of the less perfect by the more perfect: the soul over the body, reason over passion, the husband over his wife, the adult over the child, the father over his son. To make his argument concrete with respect to the Indians, he gave the example of their cowardice in war and the rude character of their institutions (36–37) (see the section entitled "Sepúlveda as Just War Theorist," in chapter 5).

As is evident, Sepúlveda shared some, though not all, of Vitoria's principles for a just war against the Indians. Vitoria admitted among his just titles to the Indies, that is, the authorization for its native inhabitants to be placed under the governance of the Spanish, the "natural need" that some peoples had to be ruled by others who were more competent: (Vitoria's eighth, uncertain legitimate title). He considered as a just title the right to evangelize the Indies' pagan inhabitants (his second legitimate title). Nevertheless, for Vitoria human sacrifice in and of itself did not legitimate a just war (the second just cause of Sepúlveda); only the need to protect the innocent could do so. This is Vitoria's fifth legitimate title; Sepúlveda takes the protection of the innocent as his third just cause for war. Finally, both Vitoria and Sepúlveda argued in favor of natural slavery with regard to the right of superior persons to govern over their inferiors, and they proposed, consequently, the existence of a natural or paternal dominion. Here the difference between certainty and doubt is patent: The right to make war against, and rule, the intellectually inferior is, as discussed above, Vitoria's eighth doubtful title; it is Sepúlveda's unequivocating first just cause.

In the *Apología* (61), which he published in Latin in Rome (1550) as the summary of his *Demócrates Segundo,* Sepúlveda reduced the previous discussion to a few paragraphs, because there he omitted the theory of natural slavery and replaced it by the Augustinian argument that slavery was a punishment for sin: "Thus, such peoples, by natural law, should obey those who are more civilized ["humanos"], more prudent, and more perfected, in order to be governed by better customs and institutions; if when given this warning they refuse to accept such authority, they can be obligated to accept it by force of arms."[37] Here, as previously, Sepúlveda consistently interprets the inferiority of the Indians as a hierarchical relationship with respect to a superior people, and he employs exactly the same concept: the relationship that, he argues, ought to obtain between those entities when one is more perfected than the other. In this way, there are three problems to resolve: first, the character of the juridical relationship that Sepúlveda proposes for the Indians with the Spanish; second, what he means by the phrase "more human" ("más humano," which I have translated above as "more civilized"); and, third, the question as to whether his concept of inferiority is fixed and immutable or susceptible to improvement.

Sepúlveda did not consider the Indians of America to be deficient in human reason as such. He characterized the barbarity of the Indians not as innate but rather as a product of custom that, with time and contact with Christians, would be improved: "It is more to the benefit of these Indians and more in consonance with natural reason that they be subjected to the rule of princes or nations more civilized (*más humanos*) and virtuous than they are, so that, given the example of their [masters'] virtue and prudence and the fulfillment of their laws, they can abandon their barbarity, embrace a more civilized life, conduct themselves in a more moderate (*morigerada*) manner, and practice virtue."[38] In book 1 of his *Demócrates,* Sepúlveda expressed the belief that the Indians could and would be assimilated to European ways, when "their submission to the rule of those who with their prudence, virtue and religion are to convert them from their state of barbarity and barely men, into humane (*humanos*) and civilized [men] to the degree that they are capable, that is, from delinquents into virtuous men, from being impious and enslaved by demons, into becoming Christians and worshipers of the true God in the true religion."

When Sepúlveda speaks of the progress that had been made in bringing the natives to the practice of European customs, the image of the half-human being that scholars have wanted to impose on him disappears. On insisting that these peoples were "sheep of the Lord but of a different fold," Sepúlveda (76) paraphrased the gospel of John (10:16) that Las Casas also invoked to describe the status of these groups. The biblical passage (King James Version) reads, "And other sheep I have, which are not of this fold: them also I must bring, and they shall hear my voice; and there shall be one fold, and one shepherd." Sepúlveda (76) stated, "It is not true, as you say, that there is nothing in common between us and the pagans. On the contrary, there exist many things in common, for they are, and are called, our companions and fellow human beings and sheep of the same Lord, although not of the same fold. For One alone is the God of all, generous (*rico*) to all who invoke Him, and He wants all to be saved and to arrive at the knowledge of the Truth."

With regard to the meaning of "humano" in relation to the character of the Indians, it should be clear that Sepúlveda was not referring to the condition of humanity as such, in the meaning of "a group of individuals of the human species or race," nor to "human nature" as such, but rather to the constellation of virtues that accompanies the plentitude of the exercise of rationality.[39] Sebastián de Covarrubias Horozco's Castilian dictionary (1611) states it succinctly: "Human: the one who is peaceable, compassionate, benign, and gentle" [Humano: el que es apazible [*sic*], compassible, acariciador, benigno y manso] (*Tesoro*, 704). This is the evaluative sense of *humanitas*, that is, the Renaissance notion of courtesy, kindness, gentleness, and empathy for—and solidarity with—others of one's kind, in other words, the ideal human type.[40] For Sepúlveda, what was natural or innate was not lack of reason or of rational capacity on the part of the Indians but rather the need for them to enter into a relationship of hierarchy, assuming the inferior rank upon coming into contact with a superior (meaning Christian) people.

This concept is set forth even more emphatically in book 2 of the

Demócrates Segundo where Sepúlveda (120) makes analogous the royal rule of a city or nation and the domestic administration of a household and conceptualizes the rule that should apply to the Indians of the Americas as a cross between social relationships based on the imposition of law and force and those based on the mutual recognition of a natural hierarchy. Sepúlveda suggests that just as the household is constituted by the family, including its sons and daughters, and also by its slaves, as well as by its servants, who are free, and just as the father of the family rules over them all, treating each according to his condition and station, so the king should rule:

"An eminently good and just king who wants to imitate such [an ideal] paterfamilias, as is his obligation, should govern the Spaniards with a paternal rule and [treat] those barbarians like servants, who are free, with a certain tempered rule, in which he acts as both a master (*heril*) and a father/king (*paternal*), and treats them according to their [current] state and the demands of circumstances." Sepúlveda here proposes a mixture of two types of servitude, deriving one from (Aristotelian) philosophy and the other from jurisprudence. "Herile" rule, which is likened to the dominion of the mind over the body, is translated into the social relationship of natural slavery in which, according to Aristotle, "the relationship between the [natural] slave and his master is natural, they are friends."[41] "Paternal" rule, analogous to the control of the soul over the passions, implies the social relationship of civil slavery, in which rule relies on law and force.[42]

Sepúlveda (120) concludes that this combination will have positive results: "In this manner, with the passage of time, when they have become more civilized and under our rule the probity of customs and the Christian religion have been reaffirmed in them, they should be given greater freedom and treated with greater liberality." Although almost always overlooked, Sepúlveda's proposal is novel. It is not a direct throwback to Aristotle's theory of natural slavery, but rather a new position that finds inadequate both the philosophical notion of natural slavery and the juridical institution of civil slavery when it comes to defining the hierarchical relationship that, in his view, ought to obtain between the European colonizers and the Amerindians.

Sepúlveda (117, 121–124) again insists that Indian slavery be prohibited, and he (86–87) condemns the abuses of the Indians by those who "torment and annihilate them with intolerable burdens or unjust slavery and with arduous and unbearable labors, as is said some have done with consummate greed and cruelty in certain islands"; he asserts further that the Indians cannot be deprived of their estates or properties on account of being natural slaves. In short, the essence of Sepúlveda's position is not the characterization of the Indians as such, but rather in the hierarchical relationship that emerges from their encounter with other (superior) peoples. The relational character of his theory is evident from the outset, when he announces that his theme will be dominion. Although there are diverse modes of exercising dominion, all of them, he (20) says, have their foundation in "a single principle and natural dogma: the rule and dominion of perfection over imperfection, strength over weakness, virtue over vice." Sepúlveda would reiterate the principle in the Valladolid debates of 1550–1551. As recorded by Soto, Sepúlveda summed up the principal points of his arguments ["refirió de palabra las cabezas de sus argumentos"]. The second of these was that, because of the rudeness of their minds [*ingenios*], and on account of being people "by nature servile and barbarous," the Indians were obligated to serve those more gifted ("de ingenio más elegantes") than themselves, such as the Spanish.[43]

This is the basic presupposition of Sepúlveda's thinking, and it is similar to Vitoria's reasoning on the same subject. For this reason, Sepúlveda places great confidence in Vitoria's implicit support for his position. In the *Apología* Sepúlveda quotes directly the favorable opinion of Fray Diego de Vitoria (the Salamanca professor's brother) regarding the *Demócrates Segundo,* and he infers that it signifies Fray Francisco's approbation as well, because "this author would not have pronounced this judgment so freely and without vacillation against the common opinion of his own confreres [the Dominicans] if he had not felt confirmed by the authority of his brother Francisco, a most learned man, of noble and generous spirit, who was living only two days' distance from him."[44]

Las Casas, however, sees the similarity of the positions of Vitoria and Sepúlveda and attempts to distance them from one another. In the first instance, he declares that, "in order not to be deprived of his own glory," Sepúlveda stated that "that very learned Father had not formulated in any way the principles that he [Sepúlveda] adduces." At the same time, Las Casas (*Apología,* 629), who rejected all of Vitoria's legitimate titles for making war against the Indians, excuses Vitoria on the grounds of having been convinced of "certain very false things . . . which were told him by these aggressors, who, without any consideration, sow destruction throughout the world." Thus, Las Casas (*Apología,* 629) concludes, "Now, since the circumstances which that learned priest presumes are false ones, and given that he affirms certain things with timidity, Sepúlveda certainly should not oppose me on the authority of the judgment of Vitoria, which is based on false information." There is no doubt that the "false information" mentioned by Las Casas has to do with the content of the eighth legitimate title presented by Vitoria, that is, the deficiency of the Indians' rational capacity as reason to justify making war against them.

Sepúlveda (*Demócrates Segundo,* 20) did not confuse natural slavery with civil slavery. He did not consider the former to be a legitimate pretext by which to institute the latter. In his view, the imposition of the punishment of civil slavery on those who have been defeated in a just war, in which the vanquished deliver themselves, along with their possessions, to the victors, could not be admitted in the case of the Indies (*Demócrates Segundo,* 90–92, 117). Sepúlveda lamented that his doctrine was interpreted in that manner; at the beginning of his *Apología* (*Apología de Juan Ginés,* 58), he defended himself from the accusations of being "the advocate of slavery": "Thus, I will begin by not hiding my opinion about which it is necessary to dispute, and I will set forth that I do not affirm that it is necessary to confiscate the goods and possessions of these barbarians nor to reduce them to slavery, but rather to subject them to the government of the Christians, so that they do not create obstacles to the faith and its propagation."

It has been argued that Sepúlveda's offensiveness lay not in his ideas but in his "rhetorical mode," trespassing onto the domain of the theologians and their hold on moral theology and creating, perhaps without intending to do so, "an image of a half-man creature" in which the rhetorical effect was to "thrust the Indian back again among the *similitudines hominis.*"[45] In my view, the greater (and more offensive or dangerous) effect of Sepúlveda's ideas was to affirm with certainty principles already elucidated by Vitoria, to articulate a type of relationship that combined, in the role of the overlord, the attributes of both master and tutor, and to argue, on philosophical grounds, the right of the Spanish conquests in the Indies that could not be justified, as Las Casas always argued, on the basis of the traditionally accepted theories of the just war (see chapter 3).

PRINCIPAL ARGUMENTS IN THE LAS CASAS—
SEPÚLVEDA CONFRONTATION

After Sepúlveda's and Las Casas's disagreement on the question of the Indians' right to self-governance (Sepúlveda arguing from philosophical principles, Las Casas showing the lack of legal foundations), the second great point of contention between them was the relationship between the waging of war and the preaching of the gospel. The maximum contest in this regard was the Valladolid debates. Although there were only two combatants in the royally convened junta, Vitoria's thought must also be considered.

Here is a brief review of pertinent events leading up to the debate: As mentioned in chapter 3, although Las Casas began his intervention in the debate on governance in the Indies very early, in 1516, he was concerned at the time not with the right of Castile to govern the Indies, which he did not question, but rather with the treatment of the Indians. Upon joining these discussions in the 1530s, Vitoria's concern was Castile's right to rule. Following Vitoria's lectures of 1537–1539, the next contribution of importance to the polemic was that of Las Casas in 1542, with his proposals "Entre los remedios," which led to the promulgation of the New Laws to abolish the encomienda system and Indian slavery. Sepúlveda entered the scene with his justification for just war *after* the promulgation of the New Laws and the emergence of the controversy that they immediately created. His *Demócrates Segundo* created a furor: It was refused publication by the faculties of the Universities of Alcalá de Henares and Salamanca, and when its summary, the Latin *Apología,* was published in Rome in 1550, Las Casas, who had been influential in the suppression of the *Demócrates Segundo,* persuaded the court to prohibit its importation into Spain, to seek out and burn all smuggled copies, and to prevent its exportation to the Indies.[46] In short, Sepúlveda's response to the New Laws, the writing and manuscript circulation of his *Demócrates Segundo,* and its suppression with the help of Las Casas are seen as the most immediate provocation for the convening of the royal junta. The theoretical and ideological opposition between Las Casas and Sepúlveda culminated in their personal confrontation.

In 1550, the opposition of Las Casas and Sepúlveda rested on two fundamental points: the character of Spanish dominion over the Indies and the relationship between the use of force and evangelization. The question debated by Las Casas and Sepúlveda was the following: "Is it lawful for the Spanish king to wage war against the Indians before preaching the faith to them?" [¿Es lícito que el rey español haga la Guerra a los indios antes de predicarles la fe?].[47] The issues that resulted in the polarization of their views with respect to the wars of conquest were three in number: the right to intervention in the Indies, the consent of the Indians, and their subjugation to Spanish rule.[48] Sepúlveda incorporated into the first issue the other two, while Las Casas treated the questions in reverse order. That is, political subjugation came first for Sepúlveda and last for Las Casas; what was first for Las Casas (the peaceful acceptance of Christianity by the Indians) was the last step for Sepúlveda. The free consent of the Indians was foregrounded, as Vidal Abril-Castelló (235) concludes, thus becoming "the epicenter of the problem in all its dimensions."

The trajectory of this dispute has been summarized as follows:[49] The initial topic was whether or not the Indians were obligated to obey and submit to the pope and the Spanish king in the ethical, judicial, and political orders, and if they could be obligated to do so through the use of force or warfare. At the beginning of the debate, both Las Casas and Sepúlveda seemed to want to best the other on their respective positions on the role of the spiritual and temporal power of the pope. In the end, Sepúlveda followed the strict traditional interpretation of the papal bulls in favor of the powers, interests, and duties of rule. As mentioned in chapter 3, Las Casas rejected the principle of papal authority over temporal matters and interpreted the papal bulls of donation as granting the right to evangelize only. He favored Indian autonomy to the extent of advocating the full political sovereignty of Indian communities, even following their conversion to the Christian faith. Only after their conversion, and by their free will and consent, should they be placed under Spanish rule. Within this framework the question of the nature of the Indian is introduced.

The fundamental disagreement between Las Casas and Sepúlveda (and Vitoria) pertains to the interpretation of the fifth chapter of the first book of Aristotle's *Politics*. Vitoria (*Relectio,* 31) had insisted that Aristotle "meant to say that there exists in them [the barbarians] a natural need to be ruled and governed by others, this subjection to others being very much in their interest, just as children need to submit to the will of their parents, and the woman to her husband." Sepúlveda (*Demócrates Segundo*, 21–22) writes, "For the same reason a husband has dominion over his wife, the adult over the child, the father over his son, in a word, the superior and more perfect over the inferior and more imperfect. *And it is said that this same reason is valid for the rest of humankind in its mutual relations,* for some men belong to a class in which by nature they are lords and others to another in which they are by nature slaves" (emphasis added).

The core of the conflict between Sepúlveda and Las Casas was the principle of separation versus unity; that is, do the two entities, one more perfect and one less so, refer to different subjects or to the same one? Sepúlveda (*Demócrates Segundo*, 20) considered that "this is in such accordance with nature that in all things that appear in many other things, some continuous, some separate, we observe that one of them, the most important to be sure, has dominion over the rest, just as the philosophers teach, and the other entities are subjected to it." Las Casas did not accept Sepúlveda's principle, but in order to reject it he turned away from Sepúlveda's approach and emphasized uncharacteristically the criterion for rationality. That is, Las Casas allowed "that these people may be as weak in ingenuity as they are in ability and industriousness," but he insisted that "despite this, in truth, they are not obligated to submit to a more civilized people or to adopt their way of life, and, if they are invited but refuse to do so, they are not obligated to do so by means of war and submission into slavery, which, in fact, occurs nowadays" [no por ello, en verdad, está obligado a someterse a un pueblo más civilizado que él y adoptar su manera de vida, de tal manera que si rehusa hacer esto, pueda ser obligado a hacerlo mediante la Guerra y sometido a esclavitud, lo que en realidad hoy ocurre].[50]

Then Las Casas moved on to the argument about the hierarchical relationship and in doing so attempted to reduce it to a secondary element in Sepúlveda's program: "Sepúlveda alleges furthermore, it should be known, that the more imperfect things should cede—by nature—upon encountering more perfect things, such as matter cedes before form, the body before the soul, and sentiment before reason, which is certainly something that I do not deny. However, this is true when the two things are found to be united by nature 'in actu primo,' as when matter and form, which gives 'being' to the thing, occur in one single thing, as for example, when the body and the soul converge in the formation of an 'animal' or when both feelings and reason exist in the same individual. This being said, if the perfect thing and the imperfect thing are found to be separate and refer to different subjects, in this case the imperfect does not give way before the most perfect, for they are not united 'in actu primo.' "[51]

On this basis, Las Casas (*Apología de Juan Ginés,* 139) denies the possibility of a "natural," hierarchical ordering of the relationship between the Spanish and the Indians. Citing Augustine and Giles of Rome, he concludes, "In effect, no free people can be obligated to submit to a more educated people, even if such submission would redound to great advantage of the former." Las Casas ended his refutation of Sepúlveda's position by rejecting categorically the notion of natural inferiority as a criterion to impose Spanish dominion over another people.

Thus the discussion on the nature and treatment of the Amerindians was crystallized in the middle of the sixteenth century. On one hand, there were those who applied philosophical ideas of a natural order among creatures with respect to the relationship among peoples (Vitoria, Sepúlveda) and, on the other, those who relied on legal tradition and conceived the relation among peoples according to a criterion of jurisprudence pertaining to *jus gentium:* the civil order founded on the voluntary consent of its subjects (Las Casas and his collaborators). This formulation of the relation between the crown of Castile and the inhabitants of the Indies suggests that the formal debate and the larger polemic no longer rested solely on the question of submission by force before evangelization (Sepúlveda) or initial, peaceful evangelization followed by political submission by free consent (Las Casas). Neither Vitoria nor Sepúlveda saw the Amerindian polities as civic or political entities. Although Vitoria was of the opinion that the Indians were true owners of their dominions before the arrival of the Spanish, and although Sepúlveda recognized that the Aztecs had institutions and laws, neither of them entertained the idea that the Indians had formed an authentic polis. Here Las Casas's foundation on the discipline of law, instead of on philosophy or theology, stood out and made possible his formulation of the maintenance of the sovereignty of the peoples of the Indies.

Following the juntas at Valladolid, Las Casas went on to write his own *Apología* (1552–1553), already mentioned, in response to the debate and to Sepúlveda's 1550 *Apología.*[52] In his *Apología,* Sepúlveda had accused Las

Casas of provoking "a great scandal and infamy against our kings," and Las Casas now accused Sepúlveda of "defaming these peoples before the entire world."[53] The official suspension of conquests was lifted and conquest activity was resumed. Las Casas and his collaborators continued to defend the rights of indigenous lords before the king, and, as discussed in chapter 3, Las Casas ultimately proposed to the Spanish monarch that Castile abandon its rule over the Indies altogether. In the meantime, the historian Francisco López de Gómara declared in 1552 that those who wished to learn about the justice of the conquests could consult with confidence Sepúlveda's published works in Latin.

When in 1550 the debates over royal policy were coming to a head and the practical-minded Viceroy Mendoza recommended that his successor treat the Indians as he would any other group for whose welfare he was responsible, the controversy, dismissed by Mendoza as being driven by "some form of self-interest, be it for temporal or spiritual gain, or passion or ambition, vice or virtue" and thereby deemed an annoying disturbance, was not ephemeral. The polemics on the Indians' capacity for and right to self-rule and the Spaniards' right to govern them continued throughout the sixteenth century, with regularity though with less intensity, in the corridors of the royal court and in the viceregal capitals and provincial centers of Spain's America. The writers considered here did not resolve the issue of colonialism nor did they defeat it. But they did think about it long and hard and wrote about it, too. Their legacy is not the history of the practice of colonialism but the history and practice of its questioning. That questioning continued, with unmitigated though sometimes veiled intensity, not only in the writings intended to set or influence royal policy on the Indies but also in the works of historical interpretation and poetic imagination considered here.

CHAPTER 5

Historians of War and Princely Warriors

IT SEEMS INESCAPABLE THAT the interpretation of the nature of a war be determined by the characterization that the protagonist makes of the enemy; in turn, the characterization of the enemy is used to justify (or condemn) the war itself. Given the European and particularly Spanish values of Christian militancy, the battlefield and wartime conduct of the Amerindians became the measure of their behavior and the indication of their nature as the Europeans theorized it with regard to their own value system. At one extreme, the manner of the natives' aggression in war, their behavior in victory or defeat, because different from European conduct, was devalued and denigrated. For Juan Ginés de Sepúlveda of the *Demócrates Segundo,* one of the proofs of their inferiority to the Europeans was the behavior of the Amerindians in battle. At the other end of the spectrum, the dignity of the Amerindians was argued, by Las Casas and like-minded individuals, on the basis of their lack of aggression. Thus, whether characterized by ferocious aggression or vigorous self-defense, cowardliness and timorousness or a peaceable character, whether attacked for their presumed cultural inferiority or defended for their potential perfectibility, the Amerindian natives' battlefield conduct was used as evidence in the debates.[1]

The wars of conquest were recast time and time again over the decades following the European invasion not only to put forward favored interpretations of the events of violent war—interpretations that suited the political agendas of their authors or their authors' sponsors—but also to frame, through those narrated actions, arguments about the way the defeated participants should be governed. Sepúlveda was a key figure among prominent humanists who proposed theories of just war and narrated histories of the conquests. As examined in chapter 4, his theory of just war was based on prior theorizing about the state of cultural development of the peoples judged, which had as its consequences, in his view, the failure of the Amerindians to organize proper social institutions and to constitute civil societies, with the result that they did not merit civil and property rights.[2]

SEPÚLVEDA AS JUST WAR THEORIST

Sepúlveda wrote three works on war: a discourse to Charles V urging him to make war against the Turks (1529), which was a response to Luther's denial of the right of Christians to take up arms against that foe; a treatise on the compatibility between waging war and being a Christian (1533); and—the work by which he is best known today—a treatise on the just war in the Indies (1545). He wrote his dialogue on the compatibility of war and religion partly as a response to the radical pacifism of Erasmus and his followers. In Bologna in 1530 for the coronation of Charles I of Spain as Charles V of the Holy Roman Empire, Sepúlveda (*De la compatibilidad*, 134) noted with alarm that many young Spanish gentlemen were torn by scruples over the possible contradiction between waging war and practicing a religion of love, thanks to the "influence of those given over to the desire for the novelty of new ideas." In arguing that military values did not conflict with those of being a Christian, Sepúlveda asserted that waging war was consistent with natural law and that it was a means of seeking peace, as Augustine, Aquinas, and Vitoria had argued. No Erasmist in Spain chose to challenge Sepúlveda, and, after Alonso de Valdés, no Spanish Erasmist contributed to the humanist debate on war.[3]

Since Sepúlveda was a theorist of the just war, not a theorist on the nature of cultural differences, it is hardly surprising that he described Amerindian humanity in terms of its wartime conduct. In his inquiry into the conditions under which a just war might be waged in the Indies and his prescription for the behavior of the antagonists that might justifiably provoke such a war, he presented characterizations that already had outlived the initial wars of conquest that were their referent. In fact, the values of military, chivalric culture were to remain the yardstick by which Europeans and Amerindians alike would evaluate the intentions, conduct, and worth of one another in the narratives of the events of Spanish conquest in the Americas.

Book 1 of his two-part *Demócrates Segundo* (1545) consists of an outline of the problem of just war in general and a lengthy discussion of the four reasons according to which he argued that a just war could be waged against the inhabitants of the Indies. Book 2 consists of a discussion of the juridical status that ought to obtain between the Spaniards and the Amerindian natives. Although book 2 often has been criticized as being irrelevant or contradictory to book 1, it is an essential part of the work, consisting of the application of theory to practice.[4] As such, it can be an aid in the judicious interpretation of book 1, which was at the time, and has continued to be, the object of much controversy.

The first of the four causes by which Sepúlveda argued that war against the Amerindians was justifiable concerned the implications of the "natural condition" of the antagonists in their relationship to the Europeans: "that those whose natural condition is such that they should obey others, if they refuse their dominion and there remains no other recourse, they may be dominated by force, for such a war is just according to the opinions of the most eminent philosophers" (19). This is the argument which has been interpreted—and disputed—to represent Aristotle's theory of natural slavery.[5] Sepúlveda argued that the Spanish rightly exercised their dominion "over those barbarians of the New World and adjacent islands" because the natives "in prudence, ingenuity, and all types of virtue and benevolent sentiment are as inferior to Spaniards as children are to adults, women to men, the cruel and ferocious to the gentle, the excessively intemperate to the continent and moderate" (33). The Amerindians lacked writing, monuments of their history, written laws; their institutions and customs were barbarous: they were subject to abominable passions ("nefandas livindades") and "not a few are given to eating human flesh" (35).

Sepúlveda considered such persons capable of understanding but not of exercising practical wisdom; they could "have no share in virtue except with reference to another 'whole' person, . . . no share in the life of happiness, . . . nor any ability to participate in the civil community"; that is, such individuals could not take any "independent part in the life of any civil society."[6] In *Demócrates Segundo,* "crimes against nature" such as human sacrifice and cannibalism appear as aspects of the characterization of Mexica military institutions, and those of a sexual nature (sodomy) bespeak the lack of institutions and laws regulating marriage and therefore the family, these latter being considered, as Pagden (*Fall,* 53) points out, the origin of civil society. Accordingly, the Amerindians, argued Sepúlveda, were duty bound to submit themselves, their possessions, and their lands to the invading members of a superior culture that constituted a civil society (58, 82–83).

To Sepúlveda, the greatest proof of this lack of civil prerogatives was the barbarous institutions of the Mexica. To illustrate his point, he offered the case of their conduct in the war of conquest (35–37). Although Sepúlveda defined the concept of the barbarous society and the right to make war against it on the basis of infidelity and "crimes against nature" (62), his major attempt to reveal the absence of civil qualities among the Amerindians was through his interpretation of Mexica conduct on the battlefield. Principal among the virtues Sepúlveda considered abundant in the Spanish and lacking in the Amerindians was bravery. He praised Spanish valor in war from Numancia to the wars of Charles V; he extolled the deeds of Spanish soldiers who died in the epidemic following the sack of Rome for acts of restitution performed from their deathbeds (33–34). Likewise, the virtues he found lacking in the Amerindians, including *prudencia,* that is, refined judgment, were normally those exercised in war.[7] He asserted that the Indians' wars in pre-Columbian times were continuous and always accompanied by the devouring of captives. However, when confronting Spanish forces in the conquest, the natives were cowardly, "thousands and thousands of them fleeing like women" when the Spanish troops numbered "not one hundred" (35). The depictions of the Mexica as cannibals in pre-Columbian times and as cowards in the conquest era were manifestations of the same phenomenon: the surrender to appetite instead of the exercise of reason, to violence instead of peace, to savagery instead of restraint.

According to Sepúlveda, it was in the conquest of Mexico that the lack of these virtues showed at its worst, leading Sepúlveda/Demócrates to utter, "And thus Cortés held oppressed and terrorized, at the beginning and over many days, only with the help of such a small number of Spaniards and so few indigenous warriors, a multitude so immense that it gave the impression that they [the Mexica] lacked not only ability and prudence but even common sense. Can there be any greater or clearer testimony of the advantage that some men have over others in ingenuity, ability, fortitude of spirit and virtue?" (36). For one whose values were firmly rooted in the chivalric military code, the ultimate proofs of a people's inferiority rested squarely upon their presumed failure to subscribe to those values and adhere to those practices which the European soldier—at least ideally —exemplified (37; see Caro Baroja, "La milicia cristiana," 438–444).

For Sepúlveda the practices of human sacrifice and cannibalism were taken as definitive of the barbarous status of Amerindian peoples, and their wartime conduct was considered illustrative of that cultural deficiency in or deviance from the norms that were necessary to govern a civil society. According to Sepúlveda, the submission of the lesser to the greater was natural justice, according to which "matter is subject to form, the body to the soul, the passions to reason, brute animals to man, that is to say, the imperfect to the perfect, the worse to the better" (84). This hierarchical relation of the lesser to the greater, that is, the barbarous to the civil, was revealed, in Sepúlveda's view, by the ease with which Cortés had conquered Mexico.

Indian flight in the face of Spanish attack, the captivity of Moctezuma resulting in the stupefaction of his court, and the surrender of México-Tenochtitlán to Cortés and a few hundred men revealed these grave deficiencies, of which the lack of bravery and prudence stood out in particular: "Cortés, for his part, after having taken over the city, so scorned the cowardice, ineptitude, and rudeness of those people that, inspiring terror, he not only obliged the king and his principal subjects to receive the yoke and dominion of the king of Spain but also, because of suspicions that in a certain province the king Moctezuma had ordered the death of some Spaniards, Cortés had him put in chains before his stupefied and immobile subjects, who were indifferent to their situation and concerned about anything except taking up arms to liberate their king" (Demócrates, 84).

In spite of the fact that Sepúlveda used the Mexica loss in the war to demonstrate that they were justly punished for their collective crimes against nature and their failure to create a civil society, he modified the severity of his attacks against the Amerindians as he moved from constructing a theory of just war to writing the history of the conquest of

Mexico. Demetrio Ramos ("Sepúlveda," 120–123) has argued that the low estimation in which Sepúlveda held the Mexica in the *Demócrates Segundo* (lacking "wisdom and judgment and even common sense") had its origin in Pietro Martire d'Anghiera's *De Orbe Novo,* published in Alcalá de Henares in 1530. As he could not account for the apparently apathetic submission of the Mexica, Martire (353) attributed their passivity to lack of spirit and expressed shock at the ease of the conquest victory. Sepúlveda echoed this sentiment, almost verbatim, in his *Demócrates Segundo* (36). However, Sepúlveda's portrait of the Mexica war community in his history of the discovery of the New World and conquest of Mexico is quite different. It is a more generous assessment, and it can be understood in the light of the histories written by his colleagues Francisco López de Gómara and Francisco Cervantes de Salazar.

CORTÉS AND HIS HISTORIANS

Justifying a war retrospectively and colonization currently were related yet distinctive pursuits. Striking is the fact that, again, conduct in war becomes the principal focus of interpretation. In his chronicle of the deeds of the Spanish in the New World and Mexico (*De rebus Hispanorum gestis ad Novum Orbem Mexicumque*), written between 1553 and 1558, in the decade following Cortés's death in 1547, Sepúlveda described the Mexica as a noble, warlike people, noted for their valor and patriotism.[8] He placed this assessment within a framework of optimism about their potential for acquiring the civilized (= European) customs he had extolled in the *Demócrates Segundo:* "Now, upon receiving with our rule our letters, laws, and moral code, and imbued with the Christian religion, those who have accepted peacefully the priests we have sent, as many of them have done, differ from their previous condition as the civilized from the barbarous, those endowed with sight from those who are blind, those who are violent from those who are peaceful, the pious from the impious, in a word, and to say it once and for all, almost like men from beasts" (38; see also 76, 80).

In his chronicle of the Mexican conquest, Sepúlveda rejected the portrait he had painted in book 1 of the *Demócrates* of Mexica cowardice and inertia upon the arrival of the Spanish and replaced it with Moctezuma's courtly welcome—peaceful and prudent—of Cortés's company to México-Tenochtitlán. He based this interpretation on the account, received from Cortés through Gómara, that the Mexica believed Cortés to be the returning lord Quetzalcoatl.[9] From those sources, Sepúlveda produced an eloquent speech of Moctezuma about the ancient prophecy of the return of Quetzalcoatl (see the section entitled "Quetzalcoatl and Santo Tomás," in chapter 12). Moctezuma identified the king of Spain as the heir to that ancient lord, and Cortés acknowledged that such was the case (*Hechos*, 344). This portrait of Moctezuma is not one of timorousness but rather of *prudencia*, with Cortés confirming the wisdom of Moctezuma's reaction.

In the shift from justifying the wars of conquest to celebrating their victory, Sepúlveda described the conduct of the Mexica during the final defense of México-Tenochtitlán during the summer of 1521 in terms that recalled the valor of the ancient Numantian defense against the Romans. He created heroic profiles of the Mexica lords as protagonists (*Hechos*, 432), almost executing an about-face in his characterization of the enemy in battle. In fact, one of the topics to receive greatest attention in his chronicle is the military values of the Mexica.[10] His change in perspective is striking, and it included many other topics. He downplayed the vices he had condemned in the *Demócrates Segundo* and attributed to the Mexica an intuitive knowledge of the immortality of the soul and the aspiration for salvation. The key issue in the debate was the right of the Mexica to govern themselves when in contact with a civil society ruled by a Christian prince (*Demócrates*, 82). Although he never came close to changing his views on this matter, he now described the Aztec federal assemblies and their leaders in terms that recalled the noble state tradition of the ancient Romans. Nevertheless, as mentioned in chapter 4, neither Sepúlveda nor Vitoria entertained the idea that the Indians had formed an authentic polis.

This portrayal of statecraft also marked an important shift from Sepúlveda's account in the *Demócrates Segundo*. There he had called the Indians' public institutions "servile and barbarous" and "the greatest proof that reveals the rudeness, servility and barbarity of those peoples" (37). In his later writings, including the *Apología* published in Rome in 1550, we find a progressive enrichment of content and a decided softening in the most virulent expressions about the "barbarity" of the Amerindians. The result is a relatively positive description of Mexica society. Thus, in his history of the conquest of Mexico, he praised the Mexica for their religiosity, personal valor, customs and institutions, political and administrative capacity, and talent for military logistics.[11]

The greatest change in Sepúlveda's outlook was the substitution of the "Mexica warrior as cowardly as a woman" with the portrait of the Mexica warrior as noble protagonist. This is confirmed by section 26 of book 7 of Sepúlveda's chronicle, which was centered on the argument that it was not the bravery of the American Indians that was inferior but only their manner of fighting. Sepúlveda explained that their initial apparent passivity and cowardice were due primarily to their lack of armaments: those nearly unarmed fighting against those who were armed; novices or apprentices in the military arts struggling against veteran soldiers; those without horses or cannons opposing those who had them. He assured his readers that when the Spanish realized that the Mexica were not "men of feminine spirit but, rather, vigorous, able people" [se trataba no de hombres con espíritu femenino, sino de gente fuerte], the conquistadores realized that they should not act rashly or advance against this enemy with scorn or contempt (Hechos, 442).

The advent of this more dignified view of the Mexica might well lead one to ask how influential Cortés himself was in persuading Sepúlveda and other historians, notably Gómara and Cervantes de Salazar, of the worthiness of his opponents. After all, in the Demócrates Segundo, Sepúlveda was an advocate of the conquest; in his Hechos de los españoles . . . , he (like his colleagues) was an advocate of the conquistador.

The writing of learned histories of the conquest of Mexico came at the behest of Cortés at the time of the New Laws and the rising tide of opinion against the conquistadores.[12] To the accusations and endless litigation fomented by his enemies, Cortés would pose the learned, professional history, and thus both Gómara and Sepúlveda undertook their historical writings. Gómara knew Cortés personally and is said to have lived in Cortés's household for several years while he was writing the Historia.[13] According to his own account and that of others, Cervantes de Salazar was a personal acquaintance of Cortés in Spain and also of several other conquistadores.[14] Sepúlveda met Cortés on at least three occasions, and he utilized Cortés's manuscripts for the preparation of his New World/ Mexican conquest history. Sepúlveda's admiration for Cortés was patent in his works, including the Demócrates Segundo, even though the specific influence of Cortés is absent from that treatise.[15]

In his *Historia general de las Indias* and *La conquista de México* (1552), Gómara emphasized the religious conversion of the Amerindians. He described the native inhabitants of the New World in terms of the greatest barbarity and yet assured the emperor that all the Indians who were his subjects were already Christian, thanks to the mercy and benevolence of God and to the monarch's efforts and those of his parents and grandparents, who had converted the Indians to Christianity.[16]

The enormous contrast between Gómara's projection of the most profound barbarity and his insistence on the thoroughness of Amerindian conversion to Christianity did not strike him as odd, for he confidently assured the emperor: "Toils and dangers your Spaniards take up cheerfully, as much in preaching and converting as in discovering and conquering" [El trabajo y peligro vuestros españoles lo toman alegremente, así en predicar y convertir como en descubrir y conquistar (*Historia*, 70)]. Gómara presented a euphoric vision of a nearly bloodless conquest and subsequent conversion of hundreds of thousands of natives; he attributed all to a nearly single-handed effort on the part of Cortés (see the section entitled "Bernal Díaz Reads Gómara," in chapter 6). The endeavor —converting and conquering—was all of a piece, in Gómara's influential view, not only in the conquest of Mexico but in relation to the reconquest of Spain as well: "The conquests of the Indians began once that of the Moors was finished, because Spain was always meant to struggle against infidels" [Comenzaron las conquistas de indios acabada la de moros, porque siempre guerreasen españoles contra infieles].[17]

That Gómara looked upon this mission as accomplished is evident in his dedication of the *Historia de la conquista de México* to Cortés's son and heir, Don Martín Cortés, marqués del Valle. Reminding Don Martín that "history lasts much longer than one's estate" [la historia dura mucho más que la hacienda], he added the history of the conquest of Mexico to the great feats of human history and portrayed the conquest of many and great kingdoms as a civilizing endeavor with little harm and loss of blood to the natives: Many millions were baptized, he asserted, and currently lived as Christians. The Mexica men had left many wives to marry only one; they had turned away from sodomy, having learned how filthy and unnatural a sin it was; they had thrown out their infinite numbers of idols, believing in the Christian God; they had abandoned human sacrifice and their former custom of killing and eating men every day, now abhorring the consumption of human flesh. They had, in short, abandoned their barbarism and cruelty. Gómara's wish for the legacy of Hernán Cortés was that "the name and memory of the one who conquered so much land, converted so many persons, destroyed so many false gods, eliminated so much human sacrifice and cannibalism, would remain forever alive."[18] Clearly, the portrait of the conqueror and the character and progress of the conquered were integrally related; the celebration of the accomplishments of the conquest hero required the confirmation that his will had been worked on the defeated enemy.

Another Spanish humanist to interpret Cortés's actions and the character of the native in this coordinated manner was Cervantes de Salazar, author of the *Crónica de Nueva España* (1567) and translator and editor of two humanist treatises: Hernán Pérez de Oliva's *Diálogo de la dignidad del hombre* and Juan Luis Vives's *Camino para la sabiduría,* published in 1546. Cervantes de Salazar dedicated the *Diálogo de la dignidad del hombre* to Hernán Cortés.[19] In his dedicatory epistle to the first marqués del Valle, he cited Cortés as a protagonist comparable to Alexander and Caesar, "vanquishing thousands of men and conquering great expanses of land." Accompanied "only by his virtue," Cortés became a religious figure who emulated the vocation of Saint Paul: "Many people admired you as a father and followed you as an apostle" (fol. 4v). Indeed, as Cervantes de Salazar extolled, the land was now entirely Catholic—as Catholic as Spain, he insisted—and governed by as many bishops and holy men. In his glorious vision, the Indians had become Renaissance exemplars too, taking up the pen against the beliefs they had formerly and falsely held and entering into great theological disputations among themselves (fol. 5r).

In Cervantes de Salazar's portrait of his protagonist, Cortés's great virtues are prudence, benevolence, and liberality: He governed with such prudence that nothing ever happened that he had not anticipated; his compassion was such that those who lost their lives in his service felt they were gaining it. Once conquered, the natives never rebelled, but it was impossible to know whether they were more moved by the fear of Cortés's valor in battle or the love of his clemency in peace. Renowned for his liberality, no one ever felt a slight from him that was not remedied (fol. 4r–v). The virtues outlined and attributed to Cortés by Cervantes de Salazar harked back to those of military conquerors and emperors of old, and they were complemented by his view of the dominated peoples. Again, the characterization of the Mexica was determined by the portrait that the historian offered of their conqueror.

The vindication of the conquistadores amidst the conflicts caused by the New Laws and the rebellion of Gonzalo Pizarro in Peru was a difficult task, and the histories of the Indies were created out of that crucible.[20] The depiction of laudable, "civilizable" Amerindians came into being around the middle of the sixteenth century, when the right of Spanish dominance to those actual communities was most seriously challenged. In addition, Cortés's humanist historians saw the New World conquests as sites of spiritual achievement and perpetual glory because of their deep admiration for the past and the ease with which they imposed visions of Roman and gospel glory on the present: Alexander, Caesar, and Saint Paul were often-cited points of comparison for Cortés.

Another echo resonating in the Cortesian/Amerindian apotheosis constructed by these historians was the emperor Carlos V's imperial dream of Spanish hegemony and Christian unity, which captivated Spanish humanists like Antonio de Nebrija and Vives.[21] Most Spanish thought on war and peace during the reign of Charles V was carried out by men marginal or even hostile to Erasmus, and the tenor of Spanish humanist thought was generally imperialistic. Spanish humanism abetted the royal policy of national unification under Ferdinand and Isabel, and, when overseas expansion began, Christian humanism helped to unify Spain in monarchy, faith, and culture.[22]

Under the influence of such ideals, it is hardly surprising that Cortés himself, in the flesh and a living protagonist, should so strongly impress these Spanish humanists. Given their bookish and academic pursuits, the appearance of the marqués del Valle in their lives must have persuaded them powerfully of the simultaneous achievements of conquest and conversion. What unites these humanist writers is that not one of them expressed any doubt about the meaning of the conquest or the success of the conversion process. They were persuaded by Cortés of two things: They shared his conviction that such Christianizing and civilizing processes could and would be carried out successfully; like him, they were persuaded that the Amerindians, under the tutelage of European institutions and laws, were moving toward participation in a civil order, though not as full and equal partners.

Cortés's writings attest to the importance he placed on that mission.

From the first letters he wrote from Vera Cruz, after the fall of México-Tenochtitlán, and on the expedition to Honduras (Hibueras), his requests to the emperor to send missionaries and his own self-proclaimed evangelizing reveal his preoccupation with Christianization.[23] Bernal Díaz del Castillo corroborated that testimony in his account of the conquest of Mexico (although perhaps out of self-interest) (see chapter 6). Cortés apparently convinced Sepúlveda, Gómara, and Cervantes de Salazar of his zeal for Amerindian conversion; Cervantes de Salazar opened his *Crónica* with Cortés giving a speech to his company in which he said that they were on an apostolic mission to liberate the natives from the servitude and captivity of the devil and that those who would die on this mission should die consoled, knowing they would have lost their lives in the service of God and the faith. Gómara attributed to Cortés similar actions and pronouncements, and Sepúlveda's history of the Mexican conquest also contains such lengthy discourses by Cortés to his troops.[24]

These speeches invented for the Cortés of the histories draw attention to the importance his historians placed on the attribution of these sentiments to Cortés personally. Neither the generalized and impersonal ideology of conquest nor the royal prerogatives glossed in their accounts adequately took the measure of the enterprise; it was the individual, Hernán Cortés himself, whose intentions and actions constituted the whole. This view is corroborated by the sixteenth-century theory of written history espoused by Gómara as the story of the lives, or the principal deeds, of great men.[25]

This type of portraiture also reveals the position taken by the historians on the relationship between providence and the historical actions realized by the conqueror. This perspective was adopted by the humanist writers and was exemplified by Sepúlveda in his work as a historian of the Mexican conquest. Three principles guided the writing of Sepúlveda's history: (1) the idea that all acts were the result of a divine decision or permission, (2) that there were certain actions, signaled in the divine design, which were almost miraculous in their realization, and (3) that Providence itself illuminated its chosen leaders, so that they were conscious of fulfilling a divine mission and of valuing the prodigious signs that were sent.[26] In this light, Cortés's pronouncements in the histories not only personalized the action but also related it to divine will. In Sepúlveda, as in Cervantes de Salazar and Gómara, the cultural improvement and spiritual redemption of the Amerindians were accepted without debate. In his *Hechos de los españoles,* Sepúlveda modified his earlier ideas about the supposed cowardliness of the indigenous peoples, their presumed predisposition to submit themselves indiscriminately to any dominion whatsoever, and their surrender to the vices of which he had accused them (Ramos, "Sepúlveda," 165–166). As far as the generally positive assessment of the native Americans contained in all three histories is concerned, Cortés again would have been a principal source (Gurría Lacroix, *Historia* 1:xxii). Sepúlveda and his contemporaries were influenced not only by their classical readings and ancient authorities, but also by the personality and prose of the veteran conquistador himself. These relationships between the humanist scholars and "los caudillos de la conquista," as Sepúlveda called them, provide a useful complement to the scholars' reliance on classical sources and highlight the interaction between scholarly pursuits and political ideologies in the early postconquest period of Spanish American cultural history.

A TEXCOCAN HISTORIAN OF THE MEXICAN CONQUEST

The war community was as central to pre-Hispanic Mexican tradition as Christian militancy was to the European. In his study of Aztec warfare, Ross Hassig explains that, to the Aztecs, "war was not simply the fulfillment of some religious imperative or the defense of what they perceived as vital interests."[27] In his words, "war *was* the empire" (20). The centrality of warfare to Aztec life is evidenced in the fact that no one was exempt from service; nobles as well as commoners received military training from preadolescence onward and learned to face death early. Commoners could achieve noble status through feats of military prowess, which were usually measured by captives taken in battle. Since some enemy groups were considered more difficult to capture than others, social advancement, according to Hassig, depended "on the quality as well as quantity of one's captives" (28). Clearly, war was a chief means by which the peoples of the Central Valley of Mexico took the measure of their own worth and that of others.

Inga Clendinnen's study of Aztec warfare from an ideological point of view suggests the ways in which Aztec society identified its own civil order and differentiated itself from that of other groups. Taking as an example the Feast of the Flaying of Men, she analyzes the warrior/captive relationship on the basis of Fray Bernardino de Sahagún's account as follows: Only captive warriors from tribes fully participant in Mexica understandings of war were chosen; their fate, after four days of participating in mock battles and mock heart excisions, was to be tied to what the Spaniards called the gladiatorial stone, then to be armed and attacked by four warriors. Subsequently, the warrior victim's heart was extracted, his skin flayed, and his body dismembered, the latter action being performed by his original captor. The captor would watch his kin eat the victim's flesh but did not partake himself. A ritual lament, recorded in the Florentine Codex, explains his restraint and reveals the meaning of the occasion: "Shall I perchance eat my very self?"[28]

For twenty days, the captor and his kin would observe a state of penance. As Clendinnen describes it, "For those days he was engaged in a different zone. The young man he had captured had been close to him in age, aspirations, and military prowess. He had tended him through the days before the ceremony, through his unmaking as the warrior, his making as the victim. And he had watched his captive's performance in an agony of identification: it was his own prowess being tested there on the stone" (79). Clendinnen explains that "he could not eat of what was indeed his 'own flesh,' for he too, ideally, would die on the stone, and his flesh be eaten in another city" (74).

Militarism was fundamental to the Mexica way of life. The close relation of trading and warfare and the association of military prowess and nobility were regular features of imperial tradition. Noble status generally required legitimation through feats of bravery in battle, and since armed trading caravans often acted as spies, armed reprisals against them afforded the Mexica further pretext for war and imperial expansion. Correcting earlier characterizations of Mexica warfare as primarily ritual in nature, recent studies emphasize ethnographic sources that reveal that Mexica "ordinary wars" had the typical features of state-level warfare elsewhere: heavy slaughter of combatants, calculated slaughter of noncombatants, seizure of lands, burning of elite structures, and the incorporation of the vanquished as tributaries. Valor on the battlefield was an important means for the ordinary soldier to receive honors and even advance in social status. From the point of view of the Mexica administration, the waging of war met the ever-increasing food tribute demands of the state.[29] This meant that a primary objective was the outright conquest of other groups, not the taking of captives as in the ritualistic Wars of the Flowers.

The native Mexican and *mestizo* authors who took up the pen would have been contemporaries of the native informants of Fray Bernardino de Sahagún and Fray Diego Durán. Principal among those writers known today are Hernando Alvarado Tezozomoc, *Crónica mexicana escrita hacia el año de 1598, Crónica mexicayotl* (1609); Juan Bautista Pomar, *Relación de Texcoco* (1582); Diego Muñoz Camargo, *Historia de Tlaxcala* (between 1576 and 1595); Fernando de Alva Ixtlilxochitl, *Historia de la nación chichimeca* (between 1610 and 1640); and Diego de San Antón Múñoz Chimalpahin, born in 1579, who wrote a dynastic history of his native Amaquemecan Chalco in classical Nahuatl. Although these chroniclers wrote about war and shared the knowledge of the traditions cited above, their own efforts in the postconquest era, like those of the European historians, were designed to serve the needs of the present and future as well as to recall the past.[30] As heirs or claimants to nobility, however, the historians of Mexican birth or heritage did not see their aspirations for recognition fulfilled. Charles Gibson sums up the situation of colonial social organization and the new status of former elites in this manner: "Conquest destroyed Aztec nationalism and fixed adjustments at a local level. Nearly everything that could be called imperial in Aztec affairs came to an end. If Aztec society be thought of as a graduated complex of progressively more inclusive units, from the family and *calpulli* at one end to the total empire at the other, it becomes evident that conquest eliminated all the more comprehensive structures while it permitted the local and less comprehensive ones to survive. . . . Indians were at first divided between those who cooperated and those who resisted, and between the upper class and the *maceguales*. Both lines of division tended to disappear."[31]

In the struggle for a larger share for themselves, those individuals who turned to writing centered their efforts on two crucial points: the interpretation of the wars of conquest and claims about their society's acceptance of the Christian gospel, insisting thereby on native abandonment of traditional beliefs and practices. These narrations, representing a range of native American viewpoints, took into account the values of Christian militancy (*la milicia cristiana*) espoused by the earlier Spanish histories of the American conquests. The conduct of the wars of conquest was a key to historical self-evaluations offered by members of the conquered societies. As discussed in chapter 2, the Andean chronicler Felipe Guaman Poma de Ayala made the war of the Spanish conquest of Peru and the conduct of his Andean forbears central to his arguments in defense of Andean sovereignty. His focus on war denied the military conquest by proclaiming the peaceful reception of the invading army (he cast his father in the role of Huascar Inca's emissary), the deflection of potential Inca resistance by miraculous visions of the saintly warrior Santiago (see figs. 9 and 10), and the capture by Andean lords (again, Guaman Poma's father and his clansmen) of the rebel Francisco Hernández Girón against the king (Guaman Poma, *Nueva corónica*, 377–378, 404–406, 432–437). Alva Ixtlilxochitl likewise fought a war in words that emphasized his dynastic heritage and its role in the Spanish conquest history of his homeland.

The historical writings of Alva Ixtlilxochitl are of interest because his forefathers had collaborated with Cortés and his company in the conquest of Mexico. He was the direct descendant of the last sovereign lord of Texcoco; his noble ancestors included the prince Ixtlilxochitl and the lord Nezahualpilli. His mother, from whom he took his last name, was the great-granddaughter of Ixtlilxochitl, the last lord of Texcoco, and Beatriz Papantzin, daughter of Cuitláhuac, the penultimate lord of Mexico. His father, Juan de Navas Pérez de Peraleda, was Spanish.[32]

Born around 1578 and deceased in 1650, Don Fernando seems to have lived a life that was typical of the colonial Aztec aristocracy. Studying for several years with the Franciscans at the Colegio de Santa Cruz de Santiago Tlatelolco, he spent much of his adult life in short-term occupations of local colonial government. Like Guaman Poma in Peru, Alva Ixtlilxochitl lived during that early colonial period when the intrusion of nonhereditary *gobernadores* and the diminished position of *caciques* and *principales* induced the native aristocracy to take up Hispanic ways and to "Hispanize themselves as actively as circumstances allowed."[33] The available evidence regarding Don Fernando's life and writings corroborates this tendency.

Alva Ixtlilxochitl wrote several historical *relaciones* and the *Historia de la nación chichimeca*, all of which are known only in manuscript copies.[34] In the *Historia de la nación chichimeca*, Don Fernando made two moves: first, to pull Christian warrior culture over to his side, and second, to fill that reorganized space with protagonistic actions and actors that were entirely missing from Spanish accounts of the same episodes of the war of the Mexican conquest. At the same time, he had to reduce to an absence the image of Mexican sacrificial society as nonculture. His historical research was based on sources including the ancient paintings and oral traditions of his people. He declared proudly in his *Historia chichimeca,* "All that I have written and in future I will write is told according to the narrative accounts [*relaciones*] and paintings that the natural lords, who found themselves in the events which occurred then, wrote shortly after the territory was taken over."[35] Yet we know that such was not entirely the case.

Having read Gómara's *Historia general de las Indies y la conquista de México* (1552) and Antonio de Herrera's *Historia general de los hechos de los castellanos en las islas y tierra firme del mar oceano* (1601–1615), Alva Ixtlilxochitl created a Cortés of impressive evangelical accomplishments in the same conventional and glowing terms the Spanish historians had used in decades past. The Texcocan historian compared Cortés with Alexander the Great and Julius Caesar and insisted upon the conversion of the natives to Christianity. Yet Don Fernando saw his own work as a different version of conquest history—that which told the Texcocan version of the story—and suggested that his readers look at Gómara, Herrera, Torquemada, and the letters of Hernán Cortés if they wished to learn about the deeds of "our Spaniards" (*Historia,* 235). For Cortés's biography, Alva Ixtlilxochitl invited his readers to peruse the same sources. His declaration in the *Compendio histórico del reino de Texcoco* reveals his consciousness about the fragmentation of history: "Here I have not treated of conquistadores, as they say, for they are not of my history, besides there are many historians who have occupied themselves with them, which they have not done for Ixtlilxochitl and his vassals" (514).

Lamenting Cortés's failure to include in his writings any mention of the prince Ixtlilxochitl and the thousands of warriors he commanded, Don Fernando registered his awareness of being made invisible, of being erased from history, that is, from the partial history of the powerful, altogether.[36] He parted company with the Spanish humanist historians mentioned earlier when he described the war as "the most difficult conquest that the world had ever seen" (*Historia,* 194). Alva Ixtlilxochitl may have been very pleased with the accounts of mass Christianization and postconquest abandonment of "cruel practices" which he read in Gómara, but he did not accept Gómara's view of a swift and easy conquest. The European historian had neither understood the character of the war (which had been in reality a question of "so many against so many," rather than "so few against so many," as the marveling Spanish historians had written) nor appreciated the qualities of the Mexican allies of Cortés and their warriors. The main thrust of the portion of Alva Ixtlilxochitl's history devoted to the Spanish conquest was to expound the enormous contributions his ancestral namesake and the Texcocan leadership had made to Cortés's war effort. His goal was to put forward the military values that characterized his own culture (including the quintessential traits of prudence and valor) but which had been exclusively associated, in the Spanish historians' works that he read, with the European war protagonist (259).

Alva Ixtlilxochitl narrated how, even before Cortés and his company founded Vera Cruz on the eastern coast of Mexico, the prince Ixtlilxochitl had sent ambassadors to welcome Cortés and to offer him an alliance with Texcoco in order to avenge the death of the prince's father, which had resulted from Moctezuma's treachery (203). At another critical moment during the conquest, the prince Ixtlilxochitl captured the lord Cacama and turned him over to Cortés, by which act "many great obstacles to the designs of Cortés and the entry of the Holy Faith were removed" (223–224). In his descendant's historical account, the prince Ixtlilxochitl "endeavored always to bring to the devotion and friendship of the Christians not only the subjects of the kingdom of Texcoco but also those of even the most remote provinces" (248). In the final victory of the Spanish over Tenochtitlán, it was the Texcocans who provided food and necessary provisions to the conquerors: "for which purpose more than 20,000 carriers came and went, and in the lagoon more than a thousand canoes, and in their defense 32,000 warriors so that the enemies would not be able to attack and destroy the provisions they brought; all this was not the least that Ixtlilxochitl did in the service of His Majesty, providing all that was necessary to supply so powerful an army, and all at his own cost and that of his brothers, subjects, and other lords" (259).

Here, as in the Spanish writers, conduct in war was the hallmark of the society. Bravery, diplomacy, and prudence were the keys to assessing the worth of the culture. Meritorious conduct in war was the basis for seeking royal reward, and to this extent Alva Ixtlilxochitl's account has the

effect of a petition citing the petitioner's noble antecedents and his present services (*relación de méritos y servicios*) written on behalf of himself as a
direct descendant of the indispensable princely ally of Cortés. At the same
time, Alva Ixtlilxochitl's account envisioned the goal of persuasively asserting the historical and contemporary dignity of his people. His denial
of the familiar stereotype of native cowardice and inertia and his assertion
of loyal service to the Spanish crown gave twofold significance to his claim
that the war in Mexico was "the most difficult conquest the world had ever
known."

In this manner, Alva Ixtlilxochitl claimed a historical share in the
dominant values of Christian militancy. Ironically, his efforts point out the
fact that the concept of *la milicia cristiana* itself had no place, thanks to its
Eurocentrism, for the protagonist who was not European. That is, Cortesian historiography gave short shrift to the critical role the Mexican allies
of the conquerors had played in the wars of conquest; as mentioned
earlier, Spanish historians always cited the large numbers of enemies
vanquished, not the multitude of allies mobilized, in order to emphasize
the extraordinary nature of the Spanish victory. In Sepúlveda's *Demócrates
Segundo* the importance of the thousands of native allies who were instru-
mental to Cortés's victory was effectively denied. In fact, one point that the
Bernal Díazes and the Alva Ixtlilxochitls had in common was to stress,
from their diverse perspectives, the role of collective rather than individual valor in war (see chapter 6).

Alva Ixtlilxochitl's emphasis on the collective dimension was nonetheless realized through the construction of individual leadership and
protagonism. Thus, while he made repeated references to the thousands
of troops who intervened on behalf of the Spanish, he took special pains to
foreground the role of his ancestor's leadership, wisdom (*prudencia*), and
bravery. In this respect, too, Alva Ixtlilxochitl was typical of those American chroniclers who responded to a European oversight.[37] In most of the
accounts of Spanish authorship, the figure of the incarcerated lord Moctezuma became the proof of European cultural superiority and the site of
Christian mercy. In the end, the response of writers like Alva Ixtlilxochitl
to the view that deprecated the native populations for being so easily
conquered was to inscribe that collaboration as evidence of the values—
prudencia, ingenio, and valor—they were accused of lacking. Their agenda,
building the historical reputation of their peoples in the postconquest era,

required them to express their values in terms understood and appreciated by the European audience to whom those claims were directed.

Although Alva Ixtlilxochitl, the seventeenth-century historian, descended from one of the houses of the fifteenth-century Triple Alliance formed by the rulers of Tenochtitlán, Texcoco, and Tacuba, he passed over detailed accounts of the ritual aspects of Mexican warfare. Suppressing such ritual practices in general, he acknowledged them in the only way he could in his own time, summarily noting that prisoners of war had been sacrificed to "false gods" (*Historia,* 154). (One wonders if he ever saw the Nuremberg 1524 volume (see fig. 1); the evidence of human sacrifice it displays would have been matched by Don Fernando's chagrin if not horror at its depiction.) The importance of prowess in war in pre-Columbian times rings clear, however, in his account of the origins of his people: Tlotzin, great lord, led his people to be cultivators of fertile lands, hunters of wild beasts, and husbands who were strictly monogamous; they constituted a nation, in short, "the most bellicose that there ever was and has been in this new world, for which reason they ruled over all others" (27).

Military values indeed ranked highest in the society Alva Ixtlilxochtil described: those worthy of serving their lords were those who had proven themselves in military feats. In electing a successor to the deceased Nezahualpilli, the ability to govern and proof of valor in war were taken by Don Fernando to be the principal criteria for selection (179, 190). Nowhere in Alva Ixtlilxochitl's narrative is this bellicose character of Mexican culture more aggressively realized than in his account of the early life of the prince Ixtlilxochitl: After killing his wet nurse for her crime of fornication with a palace guard when he was three years old, forming armies and squadrons with his friends at age seven, executing, with the help of his military arts teachers, two royal advisers who sought his life when he was but ten or twelve, he persuaded his father that his deeds exemplified the values most highly esteemed in his kingdom. By the age of sixteen, he had earned the insignia of a great captain (175–176). In that same year, the prince Ixtlilxochitl opposed his uncle Moctezuma's selection of Cacama as successor to Nezahualpilli, and the prince Ixtlilxochitl overpowered and captured the Mexican captain Xochitl in hand-to-hand combat. The prince had him burned alive, declares the chronicler, so that his enemies would show him greater fear and respect (192). Don Fernando continues his narration by noting that three years later, in 1519, the prince Ixtlilxochitl met and allied himself with Cortés. He captured Cacama and turned him over to Cortés for punishment. Don Fernando assured his readers that Cortés was delighted to have this prince, "the most feared and respected person in all the kingdom," as his friend (223).

In spite of the fact that Alva Ixtlilxochitl celebrated the military values shared by the peoples of the Central Valley of Mexico, it would be misleading to overstate his independence of expression from that of the conqueror. Like Guaman Poma (see chapter 2) and the other members of their generations, Alva Ixtlilxochitl occupied a subject position that is not that of the pure indigenous pre-Hispanic past, but rather that of a colonial subject whose conscious attempts to accommodate himself to new doctrinal and literary historiographic norms bespeak an ethnic ambition and an effort to remake cultural identity. That identity is bound up with an emphasis on the House of Texcoco from which he descends, and the effort, as has been discussed, to place Texcoco centrally with regard to Spanish welfare at the time of the conquest. In this way, the Mexican values of pre-Hispanic origin are compromised by Alva Ixtlilxochitl, who renders them in the language of the conqueror and sets them in the context of European fortunes. Alva Ixtlilxochitl's portrayal of the Mexica as warriors is consonant with his effort to make them intelligible and sympathetic to his potential European reader. From his readings, he was probably aware that during the reign of Charles V enemies in war who were closest to the Spanish in culture and ideology were lauded for their battlefield comportment while those farthest removed were condemned. That is, while chivalry, courage, liberality, and perseverance characterized the French (as Christian and Catholic enemies), the Turks and Muslims (as infidels and "enemies of Christ") were cited contemptuously for cowardice, treachery, and inertia. As Muslim fortunes declined in Spain, the general attitude expressed in literature was "religious hatred and contempt for a foe no longer able to struggle with Spain on something like equal terms." The literary evidence of appreciation of courage on the part of individual Muslims was one vestige of the respect formerly held for Moorish power in general.[38] As traditional autochthonous elites were transformed into "Indians," the protestations of ancient noble valor and individual heroism were, on the battlefield of letters, the best line of defense for historical (and contemporary) human dignity.

Alva Ixtlilxochitl and his peers countered views of their peoples as the defeated collective enemy by emphasizing their wartime conduct in a way that expressed their adherence to the values of a military culture recognizable to a European audience. The writing colonial subject, however, did not assimilate uncritically a battery of alien values. He was engaged instead in an effort to reformulate the values of Texcocan and Spanish imperial cultures into one comprehensive model of war culture. To acknowledge this complicity is not to deny the legitimacy of the position of the colonial subject, but rather to outline its features. This complex and compromised subject position does not fit the neat model of binary opposition; the acknowledgment of a third or intermediate position is closer to historical reality than is any abstract, binary model that in itself is a feature of the reductive outlook imposed by the colonizing culture.

DEFINING CIVILIZATION THROUGH WAR

In its dual purpose of identifying and differentiating itself from all others, the war community became the hallmark of the civilization it represented. The figuration of the Amerindian and the debates surrounding those ideas, plus the challenge to them presented by the literate American native, all centered from the outset on notions about ideal and historical comportment in war. European imperial and Spanish Reconquest concepts of war as well as pre-Columbian and postconquest Amerindian conceptualizations and experiences of war were central to discussions of notions of the civilized order. There is no question that European cultural concepts of warfare played a decisive role. This is borne out by the literary practices of writers such as Alva Ixtlilxochitl and Guaman Poma, who simultaneously dismantled and reconstructed the narratives of the wars of conquest in order to take an effective adversarial position in the battle lines drawn by Spanish imperial history and colonial law. Insofar as one of the mainstays of European writing on the Indies pertained to the exploration and representation of Amerindian ritual and religious practices (see chapter 8), the autochthonous Amerindian versions of the history of the conquest played a virile and "defeminizing" role.

Indigenous American historians writing about the wars of conquest cast aside that degrading, feminizing portrayal (for example, Sepúlveda's passionate Mexica, who fought endless and ferocious wars only to "flee like women" during the Spanish conquest of Mexico) on two counts: first, by denying the characterization of historical behavior as ferocity and feminine cowardice (both being signs of the surrender to appetite and passion), and second, by inscribing their lived experience in the book of dynastic history rather than in that of "false beliefs" (the ecclesiastical inspection report). Rejecting the representation of traditional native experience as superstitious rituals and barbaric customs, the Alva Ixtlilxochitls reinstated native history, which was denied in European accounts, by creating narrative sequences intelligible to Europeans and based on the serialization of dynasties and the narration of the conduct of war. This devotion to letters was a devotion to arms, retrospectively.

In the European/American encounter, the figure of the warrior stands as the reigning symbol of civilized culture. Ironically, this warrior figure was an archaic one, in both its European and native American manifestations. Bernal Díaz's protestations notwithstanding (see chapter 6), the conquistador of the 1520s and 1530s was far removed from the chivalric Castilian caballero of the Reconquest era; by 1600, the native American elites and their warrior classes had already been processed into undifferentiated masses as Indians. The war community, central as it was to both Europeans and Amerindians in conceptualizing civilization, was, in each case, a community more longed for than remembered, and it lingered on long after the plenitude of its existence. Writing about pre-Columbian and Spanish conquest wars, Europeans and native Americans of autochthonous tradition, respectively, took the measure of themselves and one another. Collectively their works constitute an early chapter in the history of Latin American letters. It was written long before it was named —by Domingo Faustino Sarmiento—as a struggle to the death between civilization and barbarity.

CHAPTER 6

The *Encomendero* and His Literary Interlocutors

THE INTERPRETATION OF RECENT EVENTS occupied many minds in New Spain in the decades following the defeat of the Aztec confederation by the Spanish (1519–1521), and it was carried out in the exercise of daily affairs in the palace of the viceroy, the *audiencia* (highest judicial court) of the viceroyalty and its provinces, their city councils, and, as discussed in chapter 5, among the historians gathered at Cortés's Andalusian home in Spain and by elite native graduates of the Colegio de Santacruz de Tlaltelolco in New Spain's capital. The topic, however, was nowhere more passionately taken up than in the petitions and writings of the "old conquistadores": their letters to the king, the civil suits they filed against those who contested their interests, the notarized reports of their merits and services, and, in the case of a few, historical writings such as Bernal Díaz del Castillo's *Historia verdadera de la conquista de la Nueva España* (written 1551–1584, published 1632).[1] Like Alva Ixtlilxochitl in his *Historia de la nación chichimeca* but from a soldierly Castilian perspective, Bernal Díaz is an author who wrote from the position of being excluded from the written narratives of history. He emerges here as a protohistorian who exemplifies a uniquely Spanish American discourse of history, the echoes of which would reverberate well into the next century and beyond.[2]

Like many historical works of his day, Bernal Díaz's chronicle contributed to a broader debate concerning the relationship between Spanish peninsular history and recent events in the Indies. There existed great chronological continuity between the recovery by Spain of its peninsular territories from the Muslims and the Spanish establishment in America; on January 2, 1492, the Muslim kingdom of Granada fell to Ferdinand and Isabel, and by Christmas of that year, thirty-seven members of Columbus's first expedition made preparations to spend the winter in a fortified outpost on the north coast of the Caribbean island of Hispaniola.

The conceptual continuity between these events, however, was challenged from many quarters. The detractors included, on one side, colonial reformers such as Bartolomé de las Casas, other members of the regular clergy, and royal officials who saw night-and-day differences between the defeat of Granada and the fall of the Aztec capital México-Tenochtitlán; on the other side were advocates of conquest—governors and judges—who exercised their authority to enhance the positions of newcomers to the Indies like themselves. Yet the pretensions of men like Bernal Díaz were challenged not only by those who condemned the conquests, but also by those recent arrivals against whose interests the old soldiers now had to compete. In 1543, Charles V reluctantly designated all of those who had accompanied Cortés in the war that ended with the fall of México-Tenochtitlán as "first discoverers" in response to the conquistadores' demands that the priority of their interests be recognized.[3] I take this situation to be crucial for understanding the underlying tensions involved in Bernal Díaz's apprenticeship for becoming the historian of his own deeds. Bernal Díaz's claims to write "plain speech" and the "unvarnished truth" belie a highly mediated and nuanced account that has much to tell us about the blurring of discursive boundaries between history, jurisprudence, and eyewitness testimony in the Spanish Indies of the early modern period.[4] His work is remarkably revealing in this regard, often disguising polemical argumentation as neutral historical narration, and, at the same time, offering an undisguised and candid commentary on the values and craft of the writing of history (see chapter 7). My overarching argument is that the *Historia verdadera* exemplifies the capacity of prose exposition both to contain and conceal the argumentation that drives it.

When Bernal Díaz began to write his history of the conquest of Mexico, Hernán Cortés was already deceased, having died on December 2, 1547. Bernal Díaz mentions that he was already at work when he chanced upon Francisco López de Gómara's *Historia de las Indias y la conquista de*

México (1552). In 1549–1550, Bernal Díaz had been in Spain and had made at least two appearances at the royal court, as advocate (*procurador*) and representative of the city of Santiago de Guatemala. In the last chapters of his work, he writes indirectly about one of these experiences (in chapter 213 he defends his participation in the capture and branding of Indian slaves), and he narrates in detail the events of the second of these occasions (his appearance at court in Valladolid in 1550, in chapter 211). The latter meeting was a junta convened by the Royal Council of the Indies in order to deliberate the right of Spanish settlers to hold encomiendas in perpetuity.[5] In petitions of 1549 and 1550, the interests of Bernal Díaz and his encomendero peers were bested by the arguments of Las Casas and his supporters. After these experiences, Bernal Díaz undertook the writing of his work.[6] His appearances at court had shown him that his heirs would not likely receive rights in perpetuity to his encomienda grants, or he learned, at least, that such long-term rewards for his long-ago efforts in the conquest of Mexico were far from being assured.

Bernal Díaz also understood that the war to be fought and won at court had to be engaged on the battlefield of the documentary record and especially written history. The challenge was to bring alive those forever absent deeds and to do so not in relationship to the conquest events themselves, but rather in hand-to-hand combat with those works "in the field," that is, the library of published works on the subject (see chapters 7 and 11, on Bernal Díaz and El Inca Garcilaso de la Vega, respectively). Thus he remarks, "I wish to return to my story pen in hand as a good pilot carries his lead in hand at sea, looking out for shoals ahead, when he knows that they will be met with, so will I do in speaking of the errors of the historians, but I shall not mention them all, for if one had to follow them item by item, the trouble of discarding the rubbish would be greater than that of gathering in the harvest."[7]

These words long have been considered the motto of Bernal Díaz's historiographic project. Readers have agreed that the contentious nature of the *Historia verdadera de la conquista de la Nueva España* is owed to Bernal Díaz's desire to correct Gómara's *Historia de las Indias y la conquista de México* (1552) and to share a spot in the historical limelight with Cortés. Notable editors of Bernal Díaz's work, Carmelo Sáenz de Santa María and Miguel León-Portilla, answer the question, Why did Bernal Díaz write his history? by emphasizing his polemic against Gómara.

When Sáenz de Santa María introduces Bernal Díaz and talks of polemics, he refers to his references to Gómara and to the historians Gonzalo de Illescas and Paulo Giovio in chapter 18: "From this point onward
the chronicle acquires a certain polemical tension that serves it very well.
. . . a polemic, after all, more apparent than real, since one cannot deny
that neither don Francisco López de Gómara, nor much less the team
Illescas-Giovio, deserve the reprimands of our author."[8] Sáenz mentions
Las Casas only incidentally, although he suggests that Las Casas's *Brevísima relación de la destrucción de las Indias* (1552) was in Bernal Díaz's
library (122).

Choosing to leave polemics aside in his attribution to Bernal Díaz of
reasons for taking up the pen, León-Portilla in his edition of the *Historia
verdadera de la conquista de la Nueva España* (1984) omitted any reference
to Las Casas, even as he discussed Sáenz's arguments. León-Portilla cited
three factors in Bernal Díaz's literary vocation : the great contributions he
and his fellows had made to the war of conquest, the small compensation
he had received for those efforts, and the desire that his account of his
deeds be accepted for all time as valid ("para que su dicho tuviera perenne
validez").[9]

Scholars who have looked into Bernal Díaz's strident and withering
criticism of Gómara on matters of historical content and rhetorical style
have discovered that Bernal Díaz's comments were often either exaggerated or misplaced. Ramón Iglesia's examination of the works of the two
authors revealed that on matters of substance Bernal Díaz and Gómara
often gave virtually identical accounts and that in certain other cases
Bernal Díaz attributed to Gómara statements he in fact had not made.[10]
Iglesia suggested that Bernal Díaz, by criticizing the historian who took
down the account which Cortés had given him, may have used Gómara to
challenge Cortés's account (28). Iglesia also suggested that Bernal Díaz
was jealous or contemptuous of Gómara because his social and literary
status as a cleric and rhetorician ("clérigo," "gran retórico") lent him an
authority Bernal Díaz considered false: it did not depend on eyewitness
participation and yet was capable, thanks to the prestige of the professional historian, of undermining the truer authority of the eyewitness
account (29). Of interest in this regard is Robert Lewis's exploration of
Bernal Díaz's criticism of Gómara's language and style. Lewis writes that
Gómara did not indulge in the obfuscating rhetorical pyrotechnics of

which Bernal Díaz accused him, but adhered to a style of simplicity and clarity that Bernal Díaz presumably could have admired.[11] Gómara's status as a professional historian and his evident literary skill made him, in Bernal Díaz's view, a hard act to follow but a necessary one. Since some of his most strident accusations against Gómara have been revealed to be exaggerated or unfounded, Bernal Díaz's relationship to his other literary interlocutors merits investigation.

Bernal Díaz wrote and revised tirelessly. Having begun his work sometime in 1551, upon his return to Guatemala from his recent trip to Spain, he didn't put down his pen until 1568, and then only provisionally. The juxtaposition of the fullest version of his work, the Guatemala manuscript, with the 1632 published version provides access to Bernal Díaz's ongoing elaboration of his "true history."[12] According to his own testimony, as noted above, Bernal Díaz was already at work when he came upon Gómara's *Conquista de México*.[13] Since Gómara's work was ordered withdrawn from circulation and prohibited from being printed further in 1553,[14] Bernal Díaz's persistence in attacking Gómara suggests he was either unaware of the prohibition or, if he did know about it, had little confidence it would be effective; possibly, he thought the damage already inflicted was irrevocable. (His statement in the Guatemala manuscript that the Council of the Indies should expurgate Gómara's history does not appear in the 1632 imprint.)[15]

Bernal Díaz's complaint that the indispensable and tireless heroism of the conquistadores was eclipsed by Gómara's overglorification of their captain is necessary but insufficient to explain the old foot soldier's ire. His passion on this point is well articulated: he blamed Cortés's (legitimate) son Martín, "the one who now holds the title of marquis" [el marqués que ahora es], as well as Gómara, for this emphasis: "Moreover it appears that Gómara was inspired to write with such laudation of Cortés, for we look upon it as certain that his palms were greased, for he dedicated his history to the present marquis, the son of Cortés, insisting on his right so to dedicate and recommend it before our lord the King" (*True History* 1:68).[16] Bernal Díaz's writings and rewritings were an attempt to keep abreast of the pace of events, which profoundly threatened his economic well-being. The policies and politicking concerning the institution of the encomienda in the 1540s and 1550s can further explain his complaints about Gómara and, at the same time, define his indignation against another, more directly threatening adversary who looms larger in his work but is named many fewer times, Fray Bartolomé de las Casas.

Anticipating Bernal Díaz's literary endeavors were several years of legislation negatively affecting encomienda. Owing to a major epidemic in 1545, which reduced by about one-third the native population and labor supply in New Spain, a substantial portion of all encomienda income was eliminated.[17] In 1549, a number of royal decrees aimed at protecting Indians under encomienda were passed. The crown ruled that encomenderos could continue to receive tribute but no longer demand the personal services of the natives under their jurisdiction; with personal service in encomienda eliminated, the institution lost much of its economic power, which would come to be substituted by a system of forced labor administered publicly, not privately as the encomienda grants had been, under the royal institution of the *corregimiento*.[18] Indians were prohibited from being sent by encomenderos to work in the mines; they were no longer to be used as carriers (*tamemes*). A further legislative blow to the encomenderos was a decree of 1550 ordering that encomiendas automatically revert to the crown when the current encomendero left no heirs.[19] In this setting, Las Casas made himself the greatest enemy of the encomenderos, declaring that there were two types of tyranny imposed by the Spanish over "those so innumerable republics." The first was the war of conquest; the second was encomienda, a "government of tyranny much more unjust than that to which the Hebrews were subjected by the Egyptian Pharaoh."[20]

BERNAL DÍAZ READS SEPÚLVEDA

Bernal Díaz's *Historia verdadera* is unique among histories of the conquest of Mexico because its narration spans events from 1514, when Bernal Díaz accompanied the reconnaissance expedition of Francisco Hernández de Córboba that reached the shores of Mexico for the first time, through the early 1580s, when Bernal Díaz added the last emendations to his manuscript. It is an account that dialogues (ferociously) with the published accounts of that history: the published letters (*cartas de relación*) of Cortés, the histories of the conquest of Mexico by Gómara, Illescas, Giovio, and Gonzalo Fernández de Oviedo, and the "books and paintings" of Nahua tradition, with which he claimed to be familiar. His verbal expressiveness is marked by the poignancy of recollection and loss, the vividness of dramatic personification (see chapter 9, on "Gonzalo Guerrero"), and, most of all, the ability to convey an illusion of what might have been his own flesh-and-blood personality via the image he creates of Bernal Díaz, the writing subject. His narrative buildup to the initial meeting with Moctezuma is appropriately suspenseful, and it includes his account of events at Cholula (the most controversial military action of the conquest march before the arrival at México-Tenochtitlán), in which the events he narrates fulfill each of the four criteria of Juan Ginés de Sepúlveda's program for a just war against the Indians. Bernal Díaz lays them out, one by one, in hair-raising details of the Cholultecans' presumed fearsomeness (Bernal Díaz's chapters 82 and 83; see below). The progression of the narrative from that moment until Moctezuma's death is so carefully plotted that the reader familiar with Sepúlveda's principles by which a war against the Indians might be justly conducted (see chapter 4) will know that all the conditions have been met. The steps in the diplomatic phase of Spanish/Mexica relations, climaxing in Moctezuma's voluntary submission to Cortés and his men as the "returning lords, long awaited" (chapters 88–90), followed by the resistance which qualifies as rebellion after Moctezuma's peaceful submission and culminates in the Mexica lord's imprisonment (chapters 103–105), fulfill the conditions of Sepúlveda's just war theory. This is the subtle dimension of Bernal Díaz's superbly crafted narrative. Less subtle—in fact, not subtle at all—is his head-on engagement with the writings of the elite historians of his day.

BERNAL DÍAZ READS GÓMARA

Bernal Díaz's principal task, as revealed by the points on which he attacked Gómara, was to refute the information (or impression) given by Gómara that the conquistadores killed great numbers of Indians and destroyed many cities and temples. He accuses Gómara of giving a sensational account in order to appeal to the lowest common denominator of his readership and of deliberately ignoring the accounts that the "true conquerors" and all discerning readers knew to be true:

> Then about the great slaughter which they say we committed:—
> As we were only four hundred and fifty soldiers who marched to
> that war, we had enough to do to defend ourselves from being
> killed or defeated and carried off; and even had the Indians been

craven cowards, we could not have committed all the slaughter attributed to us, more particularly as the Indians were very bold warriors who had cotton armour which shielded their bodies, and were armed with bows, arrows, shields, long lances, and two-handled stone-edged swords, which cut better than our swords did. . . . To go back to my story, they say that we destroyed and burnt many cities and temples, that is, their *Cues,* and in saying this, they seem to think that they are giving pleasure to those who read their histories, and they do not understand when they write, that the conquerors themselves, and the inquisitive readers, who know what really took place, could tell them clearly that if they write other histories in the way they have written that of New Spain, such history will be worthless.[21]

Bernal Díaz's comprehensive assertion that the conquistadores were not as destructive as Gómara (and, following him, Illescas) claims is the first hint that the simple correction of factual errors for the sake of the historical record was not the only agenda of the old war veteran: at stake as well was the personal and collective history of the conquistadores.

Among the specific errors of which Bernal Díaz accuses Gómara, one which he added to the Remón manuscript and printed version of chapter 18 but which is not present in the Guatemala manuscript concerned Gómara's account of the treachery of Moctezuma's captain, Quetzalpopoca, and his execution by burning at the stake: "He also tells how Cortés ordered an Indian named Quetzalpopoca, one of Moctezuma's captains, to be burned, along with the settlement that was burned."[22] Nevertheless, in chapters 95 and 141 of both the Guatemala and Remón manuscripts, Bernal Díaz himself tells how his company burned Quetzalpopoca to death, calling it a just punishment ("Quetzalpopoca, que ya habíamos quemado por justicia"); he further remarks that the news spread throughout New Spain, frightening even aggressive coastal natives into serving the Spanish settlers at Vera Cruz.[23] Gómara's account of that episode in chapter 87 ("Quema del señor Cualpopoca y de otros caballeros") of his history exceeds Bernal Díaz's justifications for the event insofar as the Spanish historian presented the burning of Quetzalpopoca as the just punishment of a traitor who had confessed his guilt to Cortés.

In the subsequent chapter ("La causa de quemar a Cualpopoca")

Gómara describes in detail the treachery Quetzalpopoca had carried out at Moctezuma's command.[24] One could not imagine a single reason for Bernal Díaz to be displeased with this extensive account, amply justifying the conquistadores' actions, but for one single element: a casual observation by Gómara that raises the issue of the right of conquest. Gómara concluded his account by noting that the Mexica captain and his collaborators were executed publicly without native protest or incident: "And thus they were burned publicly in the main plaza, before the entire settlement, without there being any scandal; rather, all was silence and horror at the new manner of justice that they saw foreigners and guests execute upon so great a lord and in the kingdom of Moctezuma."[25] Given the scrupulous care that Gómara took in showing that this punishment was executed for just cause, indicating that Quetzalpopoca's treachery was confirmed by letters sent from Pedro de Hircio to Cortés at Cholula, there is only the slightest cause for Bernal Díaz's uneasiness upon reading this passage. It is found in the last line of Gómara's account, cited above: those responsible for killing a captain of the Mexican lord in his own kingdom were foreigners and outsiders.

The comment is an answer to one of the many questions posed in the just war debate: Did the Spanish have the right to invade the realm of a sovereign lord who had not offended any Christian prince and to force him to submit to Spanish rule? Bernal Díaz, like Gómara and Sepúlveda, would say yes, providing that certain conditions, such as the presence of barbarous customs of human sacrifice or idolatry, and therefore the need to protect the innocent, prevailed (see chapter 4). Las Casas would say no, taking the view that it was unlawful under any circumstances to make war against the princes of kingdoms who had never attacked one's own (see chapter 3).[26] By implicitly answering a just war question, Gómara had effectively raised it. At the same time Bernal Díaz felt the need to provide a corrective to the view that the war of conquest was won by Cortés alone in order to secure his place in history, he was also confronted by increasing criticism of the conquest that was being translated into legislation limiting the prerogatives of the old conquistadores, now encomenderos. Because of Gómara's recently published history, Bernal Díaz saw his historical due as a conquistador slipping away and the integrity of the conquest (which he did not doubt) being inadvertently but effectively undermined.

On the first point, Bernal Díaz worked hard to enlarge history's purview to include himself. A decisive experience in this regard had occurred during his trip to Spain with Cortés in 1539–1540. At one of the sessions of the Council of the Indies that Bernal Díaz attended, the prosecuting attorney (*fiscal*) Juan de Villalobos reportedly objected to the privileges requested by Bernal Díaz, "because he had not been such a conquistador, as he claimed, nor had the aforementioned Indian settlements been entrusted to him for services rendered."[27] Bernal Díaz did not dignify the accusation with so much as a reference to Villalobos when he described his visit to Spain (chapter 201). Nevertheless, the accusations of Villalobos, compounded by the silences of Gómara, no doubt gave particular urgency to Bernal Díaz's plan to write his own history of the conquest. Thus, in chapter 212, Bernal Díaz listed all the battles in which he claimed to have fought, and, after railing against Gómara, he declared, referring to the coat of arms granted by the crown to Cortés and the images it bore of the heads of seven vanquished Mexica lords, "I am entitled to a share of the seven kings' heads, and of what is written on the culverin, 'I, second to none in serving you,' for I assisted him in all the conquests and in winning the honor and glory which is well exemplified in his very valiant person. . . . I do not praise myself as much as I ought."[28] (Bernal Díaz got his due indirectly insofar as Cortés's shield, with its encircling garland adorned by the severed heads of the seven Mexica captains, appears in the lower pictorial field of the engraved *Historia verdadera* title page printed in 1632.)

Apart from creating a dialogue with allegorical Fame (chapter 210) and responding to charges that he had praised himself too much, Bernal Díaz replied that the viceroy Don Antonio de Mendoza as well as Cortés had written to the emperor on his behalf and that he, not unlike Julius Caesar, was duty-bound to write his war memoirs (*Historia verdadera* 2: 376–378) (see chapter 7). Yet controlling his self-image was much easier than controlling the damage being done to the historical reputation of the conquest. Bernal Díaz's quarrel with Gómara was in part a product of the conquistador's frustration at the harm that the written histories did to the conquistador/encomendero's cause. Thus, when Bernal Díaz harangued Gómara and others for lacking the authority of the eyewitness, his real complaint was not that they could not get their facts straight, but rather that they could neither share the conquistadores' point of view nor write about them in an appropriately sympathetic manner. This is why, in Bernal Díaz's view, they presented accounts—whether accurate or inaccurate in detail—that missed the mark ("no aciertan") because their narratives did not capture the perspective and therefore did not reflect the interests of the veterans who had fought the war.

BERNAL DÍAZ READS LAS CASAS

The just war debate was not merely a generalized and self-evident background to Bernal Díaz's writing but also the very platform on which it unfolded. Bernal Díaz emerges in his work not only as a "true conquistador"-cum-historian, but also as an encomienda holder and polemicist; this is evident in the few but crucial points in his narrative at which he brings Las Casas into the discussion. The first is the episode of the military encounter and massacre at Cholula (chapter 83). The second is the account of the killings Pedro de Alvarado incited during the fiesta of Toxcatl in the main plaza of México-Tenochtitlán while Cortés and the major portion of his army (including Bernal Díaz) were on the coast confronting Pánfilo de Narváez. (Narváez, under orders from the governor Diego Velázquez, led a force of some nine hundred troops to arrest Cortés and his men and take them back to Cuba) (chapters 125–126). The third is Bernal Díaz's recreation of the 1550 junta held in Valladolid, convened by the Royal Council of the Indies to debate and set policy on the issue of perpetuity in encomienda grants (chapter 211).

The encounter of the Spaniards with the Cholulans and the invaders' attack on the Indians were the subjects of many diverse opinions and much controversy. Opinions ranged from the accusation by the conquistador-turned-Dominican-friar Francisco de Aguilar that Cortés had killed innocent Cholulans while they went about their daily business, carrying water and wood, to the praise rendered by the mestizo historian from Tlascala, Diego Muñoz Camargo, for the triumph of his compatriot Tlascalans, allies of the victorious Spaniards. Apparently the first to accuse Cortés of wrongdoing in the Cholula affair was Bernardo Vázquez de Tapia, a former captain in Cortés's army, whom Bernal Díaz recalled as being "prominent and wealthy, and dying a natural death"; another was Las Casas, who in 1552 published a scathing account of the episode in his *Brevísima relación de la destrucción de las Indias*.[29]

Bernal Díaz defended the Spanish cause at Cholula, and in chapter 82 he prepared the reader to interpret those events according to his point of view by conveying, through his representation of the lords of Cempoal, the claim that the Cholulans, as friends of Moctezuma, were known to be traitors to the Spanish cause. Bernal Díaz narrates the event in chapter 83, whose title makes the point: "How, at the orders of Montezuma, they had planned to kill us in the City of Cholula, and what happened about it."[30] Bernal Díaz recreated in great detail the events that came to be known as the massacre of Cholula and to which he referred as "the affair of Cholula when they wanted to kill us and eat our bodies—I do not count this as a battle."[31] Even including the detail that Cortés warned the treacherous Cholulan enemies before attacking them, all the narrative elements added up to exemplary conditions and causes by which a war could be waged justly, according to the theory of just war against the Indians offered by Sepúlveda and endorsed by Bernal Díaz.[32]

In Bernal Díaz's account, the Spaniards defeated the Cholulans, stopped the allied Tlascalans from carrying out excessive looting, made peace with the Cholulans, and established a lasting friendship with them. The war produced the desired result not only in Cholula but throughout New Spain, for word of the Spanish triumph spread throughout the country: "And if we had a reputation for valour before (for they had heard of the wars at Potonchan and Tabasco, of Cingapacinga and Tlaxcala and they called us Teueles, which is to call us gods or evil things), from now on they took us for sorcerers, and said that no evil that was planned against us could be so hidden from us that it did not come to our knowledge, and on this account they showed us good will."[33] Here Bernal Díaz sought to communicate that the triumph at Cholula had been a strategic psychological victory as well as a crucial military turning point in the conquest campaign; henceforth, he claims, the bearded white strangers would be more respected and feared than ever before.

In addition to telling how and why the attack on the Cholulans was carried out, Bernal Díaz added to this chapter a footnote that had the effect of confirming his position that the conquest had been just. After having told how the Spanish soldiers, if defeated, were to have become sacrificial victims (their thighs and arms and legs to become sacrifices and their entrails and carcasses to be eaten by caged snakes, serpents, and tigers [1:248]), Bernal Díaz closed his case regarding Cholula by describing how the conquistadores broke open the cages containing potential sacrificial victims and how Cortés ordered the Mexican captives to return to their homelands and exhorted their Cholulan captors to cease the barbaric practice of human sacrifice. According to Sepúlveda's point of view as expressed in the *Demócrates Segundo* (62) and in his oral intervention in the 1550 Valladolid debate, "crimes against the innocent" constituted one of four principal causes by which a just war could be waged against those found guilty of such acts. After reporting Cortés's exhortation to the Cholulans that they cease the practice of human sacrifice, Bernal Díaz comments that they promised to do so, "but what use were such promises? as they never kept them."[34] With this remark his portrayal of the Cholulans as marked by savagery and incorrigible barbarism underscores his narration of the episode with an argument for the war's justification, according to Sepúlveda's first cause: to attack those who, inferior by nature, do not accept the authority of those superior to them.

Before Bernal Díaz concludes this chapter, however, he brings Las Casas to center stage and scorns him for being one of those who reports what he has not seen. Bernal Díaz cites the Franciscan panel of inquiry and the opinion of Las Casas's old enemy, Fray Toribio de Benavente ("Motolinía"), to refute the account of the Cholula encounter that the influential Dominican bishop offered in the *Brevísima relación* (107–108). Significantly, the Cholula and Toxcatl episodes were the ones that Las Casas had singled out to characterize and condemn the entire campaign of the conquest of Mexico. Not coincidentally, Bernal Díaz openly disputed Las Casas's accounts in his own narration of them.

Bernal Díaz claimed that Las Casas attributed the Cholulan killings to the conquistadores' lust for violence, "asserting that for no reason whatever, or only for our pastime and because we wanted to, we inflicted that punishment."[35] Bernal Díaz's accusation against the Dominican sounds like one he made against Gómara in the 1632 published edition of *Historia verdadera*, which greatly expands the version of chapter 18 that appears in the autograph Guatemala manuscript: "Because since we returned to conquer the great city of Mexico and we won it, Gómara does not tell about our soldiers who were killed and wounded in the conquests, but rather writes as though we found it all as one going to weddings and enjoying occasions of merriment."[36] What galled Bernal Díaz was the accusation, made, on one hand, by a defender of the conquest, Gómara (see chapter 5), and, on the other, by its principal antagonist, Las Casas—both of whom Bernal Díaz faulted for being unable or unwilling to sym-

pathize with the soldiers' hardships—that the soldiers had acted frivo-
lously, as if enjoying easy times, and wantonly, as if unaffected by the
demands of Christian conscience.

Las Casas did not in fact attribute the massacre at Cholula to the
soldiers' wanton lust for violence, as Bernal Díaz said he had. Rather, the
Dominican criticized the Spanish decision to carry out an exemplary punishment: "The Spaniards resolved among themselves to make a slaughter
there, or a punishment (as they call it), in order to cast and sow fear of
them and of their ferocity throughout every corner of those lands. For this
was always the Spaniards' resolve in all the lands that they have entered, it
is well to note: to wreak cruel and most singular slaughter, so that those
meek lambs might tremble before them."[37] As we have seen, Bernal Díaz
subsequently defended this tactic as necessary and extraordinarily successful. His refutation of Las Casas consisted of an eloquent and dramatic
defense of the preemptive strike as exemplary punishment (which he
presented as being based on receiving prior evidence of the Cholulans'
treachery) while refusing to acknowledge that this was the precise source
of Las Casas's criticism.

Sáenz de Santa María observed that this was one of the chapters that
Bernal Díaz did not submit to extensive rewriting, as was his usual practice, although Fray Alonso Remón, the Mercedarian editor of the work as
published in 1632, suppressed passages he considered too bluntly critical
of Las Casas, such as the following: "And he even says it so artfully in his
book that he would make those believe, who neither saw it themselves,
nor know about it, that these and other cruelties about which he writes
were true (as he states them) while it is altogether the reverse of true."[38]
Although Remón did not wish to seem too contentious with respect to Las
Casas, it is clear that for Bernal Díaz refuting the arguments of the Dominican friar was a matter of great importance.

When Bernal Díaz refuted Gómara, it was by his testimony alone,
pitting the word of the participant and eyewitness against that of someone
who had not been present at the events in question. When he refuted Las
Casas, the stakes shifted from the eyewitness/noneyewitness opposition
to include as well that of secular versus religious authority, and Bernal
Díaz made sure to bring the authority of the religious community to his
side. Relying on the influence and prestige of the Franciscan panel of
inquiry that had been sent, after 1524, to investigate the Cholula massacre

of 1519, Bernal Díaz expressed the conviction that if the Spaniards had
been vanquished at Cholula, the conquest of New Spain would have taken
much longer, with the result that the native peoples would still persist in
their idolatry. To Las Casas's old enemy Motolinía, Bernal Díaz attributes
similar sentiments: It would have been better if the killing could have
been avoided, but even though it had not been, the cause of evangelization had nevertheless been served, by dissuading the Mexicans from following their false idols.[39]

Refuting Las Casas's account of the massacre that took place in
México-Tenochtitlán during the fiesta of Toxcatl was more difficult because Bernal Díaz did not have his own authority as an eyewitness on
which to rely. In Las Casas's *Brevísima relación* account, the Spaniards
attacked this gathering of "the very cream of the nobility of all Moten-
zuma's [*sic*] kingdom" [toda la flor y nata de la nobleza de todo el imperio
de Motenzuma] without provocation: "they called out: 'Santiago, to them!'
and they began with their naked swords to rend those naked, delicate
bodies and to spill that generous blood, and they left not a man alive; and
the others in the other plazas did the same."[40] Las Casas summarized his
account, calling it an event that would fill the people of those kingdoms
with anguish and mourning until the end of time: "And from this day
until the end of the world, or until the Spaniards do away with them all,
they shall never cease lamenting and singing in their *areítos* and dances,
as in the *romances* (as we call them here), that calamity and loss of the
succession of all their nobility, which for so many years past they had
treasured and venerated."[41]

Bernal Díaz's account of this event in chapter 125 includes an internal, that is, an insider's, critique of Alvarado's instigation of the killings by
a stern and outraged Cortés, against whom Alvarado defended himself by
arguing that he had simply made a preemptive strike against the planned
treachery. Two aspects respond to the polemic that would continue to
surround those events long after even Bernal Díaz's death.[42] Both appear
in the Guatemala manuscript but were later (at some indeterminate point
in time) crossed out. The first was not carried forward into the 1632
edition (but appears in subsequent ones that were based on the Guatemala manuscript), while the second excision was, in fact, carried forward
in the 1632 edition. The first affirms the providential character of the
outcome; the published *Historia verdadera* text proclaiming that mirac-

ulous visions of Saint James (Santiago Mayor) and Saint Mary had appeared to the Mexica, causing them to cease their resistance to the Spanish, and that thus many of their lives were spared.[43]

The second refutes Las Casas's interpretation of the event. As in the previous case regarding the massacre at Cholula, Bernal Díaz attributes to Las Casas an accusation he did not in fact make. In the *Brevísima relación* Las Casas condemned the Spaniards for using the opportunity of the fiesta to impose an exemplary punishment to frighten the Mexicans: "These latter Spaniards resolved to do another thing to increase the fear of them in all that land—a stratagem (as I have said) which they have often used."[44] But Bernal Díaz's published history, that is, the first of the two 1632 printings, claims that Las Casas condemned Alvarado for greed. Although the long passage that included this claim was canceled in the Guatemala manuscript (at what point in time and by whom, we cannot be sure) it was brought forward in the 1632 edition and even highlighted there: "The Bishop of Chiapa's Error Regarding This Event" [Error en este suceso del Obispo de Chiapa] appears as a carefully placed announcement of the topic in the margin, and the text reads, uniquely, "and the other things that some persons say, that Pedro de Alvarado, out of greed for the great amount of gold and gems of great value with which the Indians were adorned as they danced, attacked them; I do not believe it nor did I ever hear such a thing, nor is it credible that such a thing occurred, although the bishop of Chiapas, Fray Bartolomé de las Casas, tells this and other things that did not happen."[45]

After this long passage, canceled, as mentioned, in the Guatemala manuscript but reproduced in the 1632 edition, Bernal Díaz goes on to refute the accusation of Alvarado's greed as being untrue, making instead the argument that Alvarado's goal was the preemptive strike and exemplary punishment, which was precisely the argument that Las Casas, in fact, had made. Instead of refuting Las Casas, this passage, carried forward in the 1632 version but canceled in the Guatemala manuscript, corroborates Las Casas's claim.[46] Perhaps Bernal Díaz, rereading the *Brevísima relación*, attempted to correct his own error of attributing to Las Casas an accusation he had not made, thus canceling the passage when it was too late to correct the manuscript already sent to Spain.

While I have long argued the importance of Las Casas as a principal target of Bernal Díaz's polemical posture during their lifetimes, the 1632 imprint extends the argument about the Dominican's influence into the seventeenth century. While Las Casas was Bernal Díaz's most threatening and formidable opponent in the debate centered on the justice of the conquest, his refutation of Las Casas consisted of acknowledging and simultaneously belittling his opposition, or, in the case of his account of the massacre that occurred during the ritual fiesta in the capital, accusing Las Casas of a claim he had not made and heralding as a right-minded and moral action the very one, without acknowledging it, that Las Casas had condemned. Furthermore, the Guatemala manuscript facsimile allows us to see that anti–Las Casas criticism set forth by Bernal Díaz was mitigated, not only in the long canceled passage in chapter 125 just cited, but also previously, in chapter 83, where he had criticized Las Casas for his book ("The bishop of Chiapas writes and never ceases reiterating"), yet adding, then deleting, a few lines later: "may his lordship pardon me for speaking so clearly" [perdóneme su señoría que lo diga tan claro] (*Historia verdadera*, ed. Miguel Ángel Porrúa, 1: fol. 60r; 2:223). This utterance, rendered and then withdrawn, illuminates the complexity of Bernal Díaz's views about and interactions with the Dominican bishop of Chiapas.

BERNAL DÍAZ'S INTERACTIONS WITH LAS CASAS

The substantial weight of Bernal Díaz's concerns for Las Casas and the Lascasian point of view can be demonstrated by the fact that Bernal Díaz, back in Spain and at court, was present at the debate organized by the Council of the Indies to determine whether to continue to grant rights to encomienda holdings in perpetuity. Bernal Díaz devoted chapter 211 in its Guatemala version to the historic meeting, and it also appeared in the subsequent printings of the work under the title, "How in the year 1550 when the Court was at Valladolid there met together in the Royal Council of the Indies certain prelates and gentlemen who came from New Spain and Peru as Proctors, and other noblemen who were present, in order to give the order that the Assignment [of Indians or pueblos] should be in perpetuity, and what was said and done at the meeting is what I shall relate."[47] Interested not in wars of conquest to be carried out in the future but in the rewards rightfully earned by those who had participated in those of the past, Bernal Díaz referred to the topic under discussion as the "assignment of Indians or pueblos in perpetuity," which is not to be confused with the debate at court in Valladolid in 1550 between Las Casas and Sepúlveda (see chapter 4), the topic of which the Dominican friar and theologian Domingo de Soto described at the time as "whether it is lawful and just for His Majesty to make war on the Indians before the Christian gospel is preached to them, in order to subdue them to his imperial rule."[48]

Although the assembled junta decided to leave the final determination of the matter for consultation with the emperor upon his return from Germany, Bernal Díaz returned to New Spain with a series of royal decrees granting him certain privileges and apparently leaving his desire and need for compensation somewhat satisfied.[49] Having met face to face the power of Las Casas and his arguments against the conquests as illegal and scandalous, and therefore against those who would be its principal benefactors, Bernal Díaz discovered that his own interests needed to be protected in every way possible. His appearance at the Valladolid perpetuity debate plus the fact that he took up the writing of his *Historia verdadera* the year after his return from Spain provide strong circumstantial evidence of one of the most weighty motivations for the creation of his work, a motivation which is borne out by the work itself and its refutation of any interpretation of the conquest of Mexico that would undermine— either deliberately or unwittingly—the justice of the Spanish cause and victory and therefore the conquistadores' right to its rewards.

On this point Bernal Díaz had considered Gómara to be guilty of having assumed that the interpretation of the war as just did not need to be defended, and he so stated in the last sentence of the last chapter of his *Historia general de las Indias*. He concluded this chapter 214, "In Praise of the Spaniards" [Loor de españoles], and his book by remarking on those Spaniards who were not praiseworthy and who ended badly, having made the Indians suffer in the mines, pearl diving, and cargo carrying. He suggests that they were punished by God for these very grave sins, and then he reminds the reader that his topic has been exclusively, and briefly, the conquest of the Indies. He adds, "Whoever wants to understand the justification for it should read the work of Dr. Sepúlveda, the emperor's chronicler, who wrote most learnedly about it in Latin; thus the reader will be completely satisfied on this matter."[50] Having assumed that Sepúlveda's views had prevailed and would continue to do so, Gómara left the good name of Cortés, whom he would exalt, and those of all his soldiers, whom he did not, open to the charges that were increasingly made against them.

Prior to the 1550 junta on perpetuity, Bernal Díaz, as *procurador* of

Santiago de Guatemala, petitioned the Council of the Indies to protest the liberation of Indian slaves authorized by Licenciado Juan López Cerrato, the new president of the Audiencia de los Confines. He pronounced the order to free them to be of "great harm to the welfare of the entire republic and province" [un agravio en toda la república y provincia], and he adduced a total of twenty-six objections to the liberation order, citing as the first one the argument that the Indians had been enslaved legally (on the legislation on Indian slavery, see the section entitled "Legislative Events and Polemical Confrontations," in chapter 4). Las Casas, knowing of Bernal Díaz's appearance at court in 1549, answered the petition, addressing it to Philip II. He suggested that such advocates, after the destruction they had wreaked in the conquest of the Indies, should be ashamed to appear before the king or his council with such demands. He underscored that the Indians were at present legally free, and he repeated one of his frequent recommendations, namely, that peasant laborers be sent to the Indies to cultivate the land so that those who disdained manual labor and considered themselves to be "gentlemen and squires" would no longer gain their comfort from the blood and sweat of the Indians.[51]

Bernal Díaz devotes a chapter in the *Historia verdadera* to the issue of Indian enslavement, but it appears only in the editions based on the Guatemala manuscript, on which Bernal Díaz worked until the end of his life. The 1632 imprint prepared by Remón, which today serves as the basis for the canonical version of Bernal Díaz's work, does not include this chapter. This chapter, numbered 213, and the following one clearly were written after the dispatch of the copy intended for publication in Spain.[52] In it Bernal Díaz defended his participation in the taking and branding of Indians as slaves in New Spain. His exposition, entitled "Why many Indian men and women were branded as slaves in New Spain, and the account I give of it,"[53] reveals that the debate on Indian slavery was carried on in the decades following its official suppression, thus compelling Bernal Díaz to justify his personal participation in it.

In recounting the 1550 perpetuity junta in Valladolid in chapter 211, Bernal Díaz recalled how his testimony had no effect, either on Las Casas and his supporters or upon the representatives of the Council of the Indies: "However, we availed nothing with the Lords of the Royal Council of the Indies, and the Bishop Fray Bartolomé de las Casas and Fray Rodrigo his companion, and with the Bishop of Las Charcas, Don Fray Martín [blank space], and they said that as soon as His Majesty came from Augusta it would be adjusted in such a way that the Conquistadores would be very contented, and thus it remained pending."[54] Nothing was resolved, and subsequently Bernal Díaz complained, "And in this manner we proceed, like a lame mule, from bad to worse, and from one Viceroy to another and from Governor to Governor."[55]

Bernal Díaz's and Las Casas's views later coincided on a different issue, and Bernal Díaz sought Las Casas's aid on numerous occasions. In 1552, they wrote parallel letters to the Council of the Indies denouncing the actions of the president of the Audiencia de los Confines, the licenciate Juan López Cerrato, in making grants of Indians to his relatives ["repartimientos de indios . . . y los ha dado a sus parientes y criados y amigos"], and both pleaded for help to impoverished old conquistadores.[56] Bernal Díaz also wrote personally to Las Casas on at least four occasions. In the fourth of these letters, dated February 20, 1558, he referred to three previous letters that were unanswered and suggests that perhaps they had not been delivered. He describes himself as a pious encomendero and a friend of the Dominican friars, and he asks Las Casas, "since your lordship is the father and defender of these poor Indians," to seek redress for some Indians under his charge ("caciques de los pueblos de mi encomienda") who had been cheated out of their lands. He also requests that Las Casas aid him in having his position as official inspector of weights and measures [*fiel ejecutor*] be made permanent, because he is burdened with a large family: "I am old and loaded down by children and grandchildren and with a young wife" [estoy viejo y muy cargado de hijos, y de nietos, y de mujer moza]. He adds that he appeals to Las Casas, rather than to the king, because he knows that wherever Las Casas puts his hand, he gets results, which is as it should be ("sé que donde V.S. pusiere la mano saldrá ello, siendo justo como lo es"). However, he also wrote a letter of petition to Philip II on the same day with the same requests for the Indians of his encomienda and himself. There, too, he declares himself a friend of the Dominican friars who, together with himself, can be credited for preventing the flight of Indians from his domains. He adds that he is the king's faithful servant, having participated with the marquis del Valle in the conquest of Mexico, and that Las Casas, who had been the bishop of Chiapas, could vouch for him ("Lo sabe bien don fray Bartolomé de las Casas, obispo que fue de Chiapa.")[57]

COMMON CAUSE

As an encomendero, Bernal Díaz was not unique. His concerns were typical of those men who, "proud of their achievements and unbothered by moral doubt, were nonetheless greatly perturbed in their old age by a growing governmental reluctance to allow them to pass on their status and wealth undisturbed to the next generation."[58] Yet the encomenderos faced a monarch who was determined to reduce their pretensions. Throughout the sixteenth century, as encomiendas reverted to the crown, a progressively greater share of Indian tribute was directed to the royal treasury, and, as midcentury approached, the institution of encomienda was weakened, not so much by Indian resistance as by the intensified application of royal law.[59] In the face of this decline, encomenderos typically made their complaints known through that common forum of political action in the age of the absolutist monarchy, the letter to the king.

Bernal Díaz's complaints, both in the *Historia verdadera* and in his petitions and letters, are echoed by others. One such case is the letter of Ruy González, *conquistador viejo*, encomendero, and town councilman [*regidor*] of the city of México-Tenochtitlán. His 1553 letter to Charles V has been considered "an excellent example of the genre of correspondence sent by the conquerors and early settlers of the colonies back to Spain,"[60] and it places Bernal Díaz's laments in their most familiar setting. González states his grievances more bluntly than Bernal Díaz in the *Historia verdadera*, but his complaints are instructive in the weight they lend to the importance of the role of advocacy in Bernal Díaz's narrative. They also underscore the proconquest views represented best in Sepúlveda's *Demócrates Segundo* and reveal the influence of Sepúlveda's work.

The main topic of González's several-page missive is the hardship and aggravation caused him by Las Casas's merciless antagonism of the encomenderos. He decries Las Casas's accusations that the conquistadores were tyrants and robbers and that the encomenderos should reject encomienda grants in perpetuity and provide instead immediate restitution of lands and goods to their Indian owners in order to save their own souls. Particularly vexatious, in González's view, is the guide to Christian confession (*confesionario*) that Las Casas prepared for confessing encomenderos and merchants and demanding the full restitution of all lands and properties to their native owners (see chapter 3).[61] Despite the attempts to prohibit the circulation and use of the scandalous "Avisos para confesores," González's complaint reveals that it was abroad and circulating in the capital of New Spain.

González accused Las Casas of overlooking the great good the conquistadores had done in making possible the salvation of the Indians' souls while condemning the conquistadores for having done so. González asserted (incorrectly) that Las Casas had spent little or no time in New Spain and that therefore he neither knew about nor understood what the conquistadores had suffered and what they had achieved, nor anything about the conditions of the land and peoples with which they had to deal.[62]

In any case, in order to establish "the principles and basis of our blamelessness and innocence" [los principios y fundamentos de nuestra disculpa e inocencia],[63] González insisted that the conquest of Mexico had a legal basis, pointing to the capitulations granted to Diego Velázquez in 1518. González conveniently ignored the fact that Cortés had not been authorized to act upon them, a circumstance of which, as one of Cortés's original 450 men (*"primeros descubridores"*), he could hardly claim ignorance. In addition, he asserted that Moctezuma ruled Mexico as a usurper ("he was not a legitimate lord" [no era legítimo señor]), and, he argued, this factor, too, justified the conquest. Furthermore, he reminded the king that the great lords of Mexico had collaborated with Cortés and had given their obedience to him willingly in order to liberate their domains from the Aztecs' tyranny. As a result, Cortés honored their titles and jurisdictions as he had promised (479). Finally, as Bernal Díaz had done implicitly at the end of the account of the massacre at Cholula, González asserted that the customs and sins of the native peoples justified their conquest by the Spanish: "These people were barbarous, idolatrous, sacrificers and murderers of innocent people, eaters of human flesh, most filthy and abominable sodomites" (*True History*, 478) [esta gente era bárbara, ydolátrica, sacrificadora, matadora de inocentes, comedora de carne humana, expurçíssima y nefanda sodomía] (*Historia verdadera*, 485)]. If cannibalism and other crimes against nature commonly practiced were not sufficient cause for them to lose their kingdoms, the abuses and atrocities they committed during the war of conquest were.

Thus González summed up familiar arguments about the causes of the conquest wars as just, and the reward of encomienda as merited: legitimate titles of conquest, the just treatment of the natives, the destruction of an illegitimate and tyrannical rule, the suppression of many sins and the destruction of Satan's hegemony, and the preparation for the natives' conversion to Christianity. How, then, he asked rhetorically, could the conquistadores be vilified and the emperor's rights challenged by an activist, proindigenous clergy: "Your Majesty has no less title [here] than to the patrimony of the kings your ancestors of glorious memory. And may God will that Your Majesty be not deceived by, nor listen favorably to, what is ignorantly being said in the pulpit by discordant voices—things they neither know nor understand" (479) [Vuestra Majestad no tiene menos título que al patrimonio de los reyes vuestros antepasados de gloriosa memoria y no quiera Dios que Vuestra Majestad sea el más engañado ni se dé oído a los que ignorantemente en los púlpitos diciendo con vozes desentonadas lo que ni saben ni entienden (486)]. González ends his letter with the complaints against the colonial administration expressed by Bernal Díaz ("like a lame mule we go forward"): royal officials make and repeal laws at their whim; friars arrange Indian affairs with no regard to the encomenderos' needs; and administrative and bureaucratic confusion reigns (479, 486).

Setting Bernal Díaz's work in relief against the writings of a fellow ex-conquistador and encomendero illustrates the kind of relations in which he was involved. The portrait that emerges responds to the final transformation of the old chivalric formula of the valorous vassal ever loyal to his king: his most dreaded enemies are no longer barbarous princes and warriors but now royal bureaucrats and court councilors. Royal vacillation and bureaucratic chaos, Bernal Díaz claimed, brought only insecurity and hardship to the veteran of the conquest who expected to live out his life being served and supported by the native peoples whose souls through a just war of conquest he had helped to save. Reading Bernal Díaz alongside the writings of his literary interlocutors (Las Casas) and peers (González) adds an essential missing dimension to the overall portrait of this "true conqueror"; it expands the objectives of the *Historia verdadera* and takes account of the high-stakes polemics into which it fed.

The facets of the literary subject Bernal Díaz include, as elaborated at various moments in his narration, the adventurous young soldier mesmerized by the fabulous sight of México-Tenochtitlán, the disgruntled, unappreciated old war veteran, the conquistador who recalls with considerable eloquence and sympathy the person and plight of Moctezuma, and the aging colonial settler (with a young wife) who wants to insure that the grants of Indian labor and the fruits of the land will be passed on to his descendants. Like many Castilians of those first decades who journeyed into never-before-seen lands and colonized its peoples, Bernal Díaz can be characterized by what he hoped to achieve (royal recognition of his efforts, a comfortable life) and, at the same time, by a set of attitudes and series of insights that confounded and conflicted with those goals and required him to rationalize and justify his right to gain. He did so not only at court but in his own "library," creating the scenes of his hardships and his glory so as to serve his interests in portraying the conquest as just and his rewards merited.

Bernal Díaz's truest and most far-reaching achievement is his rhetorical persuasiveness. Although he did not persuade the members of the Council of the Indies or those of the emperor's royal juntas of his right to permanent recognition and reward, he succeeded in convincing his many generations of readers of the literary if not political merits of his case. As a literary subject, he did so by setting up David-and-Goliath-like narrative and argumentative oppositions: Bernal Díaz the worthy soldier versus the self-serving captain (Cortés), Bernal Díaz the eyewitness participant versus the ill-informed professional historians (Gómara, Illescas, Giovio). Another opposition present in his work but not emphasized (at least not by most of his readers) is that of the petitioning advocate and encomendero contra the court councilor (Las Casas), royal prosecutor (Villalobos), and colonial official (Cerrato). These oppositions and Bernal Díaz's acknowledgment of his role as encomendero and insistence that it was unappreciated and unrewarded by the authorities make it possible to overcome the simple, dichotomous distinctions (foot soldier versus captain, eyewitness versus armchair historian) that Bernal Díaz repeatedly emphasized. Yet the consideration of Bernal Díaz's polemical *Historia verdadera* response to the equally polemical writings of Las Casas brings up directly and explicitly the problem of the relationship of the Castilian conquistador and encomendero to the conquered peoples of Mexico and to the Spanish colonial administration. The attentive reading of Bernal Díaz's work demonstrates that he never forgot it, and it accounts, at least in part, for the passions that stimulated him to write his true history.

CHAPTER 7

The Conquistador-Chronicler and His Literary Authority

IF BERNAL DÍAZ WAS MOTIVATED to vanquish his anonymity in the histories that celebrated the conquest of Mexico, it could only come from his own writing of history. By what authority would he do so? His eyewitness testimony was a start, and it was necessary but not sufficient; he had to seek and rely on other credentials. He turned to the arena he knew best: witnessed legal petitioning. His chronicle reveals the pressure of particular social, economic, and historical imperatives and combines distinct sources of authority to justify the conquest in a kind of test case for the emerging modern discipline of history, particularly that of the Indies. As is by now apparent, the interpretation of law and that of history converged in dramatic and urgent ways in the writings on the Spanish conquests in the New World, and Bernal Díaz's *Historia verdadera de la conquista de la Nueva España* makes it possible to focus more sharply on the point at which the quest for royal reward met the writing of history. Here I want to explore the relationship between sixteenth-century judicial practice, the Castilian legal tradition, and Bernal Díaz's establishment of literary authority. His metacritical commentary is the focal point of this discussion, and the explanatory power it wields foregrounds the importance of the nexus of law and history in his prototypical "true history."[1]

Bernal Díaz's ruminations on the writing of history reveal the dilemma he had faced as a soldier-cum-*encomendero* who entered a field of

activity customarily occupied only by the learned. Two types of authority—
one of humanist learning, the other of Castilian law—were called up;
Bernal Díaz acknowledged that he could not meet the demands of the
former, but he strove mightily to master those of the latter. For expressing
his views in the debate on authority in history he casts his argument in the
form of a conversation he presumably had with two learned gentlemen.

As Bernal Díaz told the tale, two gentlemen with university degrees
asked to read his just-finished account of the conquest of Mexico in order
to determine if and how his version differed from the *Historia de la conquista de México* (1552) of Francisco López de Gómara and the account
given in the *Historia pontifical y católica* (1565) of Gonzalo de Illescas.[2]
Bernal Díaz loaned his two local interlocutors his manuscript and warned
that they were not to change anything in it because its contents were all
true: "And I told them not to alter a single thing, for all that I write is quite
true" (*True History* 5:286) [y les dije que no enmendasen cosa ninguna,
porque todo lo que escribo es muy verdadero (*Historia verdadera* 2:375)].
After having read Bernal Díaz's account, one of these readers rebuked
him for writing about his own deeds: The old conquistador should have
relied on the historians who had written about them, because a man could
not serve as a witness on his own behalf (*Historia verdadera* 2:375–376).[3]
In a single stroke, Bernal Díaz's sole claim to authority—that of the eyewitness—was dismissed and his monumental efforts brushed aside. He
reports that he replied that if he told the truth, and if this was supported by
what the emperor, the marquis, and eyewitnesses affirmed and his account related, why could he *not* write about his own deeds? He continues:
"It even should be written in letters of gold! Did they expect that clouds in
the sky or birds on the wing in those times could have told it?" [si digo la
verdad y lo atestigua Su Majestad y su virrey, y marqués y testigos y
probanza, y más la relación da testimonio de ello, ¿por qué no lo diré? Y
aun con letras de oro había de estar escrito. ¿Quisieran que lo digan las
nubes o los pájaros que en aquellos tiempos pasaron por alto? (*Historia
verdadera* 2:377)].

Bernal Díaz thus responded to the challenge placed before him from
within his own frame of reference by proclaiming the authority of the
mundane documents that certified his achievements. He remarked that
the marqués del Valle, Hernán Cortés, had made a report to the emperor
in 1540 commending Bernal Díaz's deeds and services; the viceroy An-

tonio de Mendoza had done the same.[4] Alongside these witnesses, Bernal Díaz declared, stood the *probanzas* (the certified testimony of witnesses to his deeds) that had been presented on his behalf at the Council of the Indies in Spain in 1540.[5] If the marquis and the viceroy and the captains (the latter as witnesses in his probanzas) and the probanzas themselves were not enough, he would call as his witness the emperor, whose "royal letter, sealed with his royal seal" ("sus cartas selladas") had been sent to the viceroys and presidents on Bernal Díaz's behalf.[6] For Bernal Díaz, historical authority rested on sworn testimony of the type taken in a legal proceeding and relying on eyewitness validation and, importantly, on the resultant actions of the emperor favoring his petitions.

Bernal Díaz's tactic in the face of his opponents was a clever one. Used as part of his argument, his probanzas of 1539 and the royal decrees they generated in 1540 authenticated his military service in the conquest. His participation as a witness in some ten or more probanzas, dating from 1557 to 1576, attested to the importance and prestige he would have considered them to hold.[7] Bringing them to the attention of his erudite interlocutors, Bernal Díaz used the documented confirmation of his deeds as a soldier to speak for his credibility as a witness and therefore his appropriateness as a reliable source for his own history.

The probanzas also guided him in setting his own standards for truth in history. Bernal Díaz spelled out the reasons for the inadequacy of the historians' works: they had not been present at the conquest, and they had failed to overcome this shortcoming in the appropriate manner, that is, by employing witnessed, certified testimony ("verdadera relación") on which to rely (on these historians, see chapter 5). Bernal could only explain their unforgivable omissions of the deeds of the captains and soldiers of Cortés by the fact that they had taken their accounts from conversations with the marquis: "and not hearing a true account, how can they write it down without going wrong, only from the flavour of their palates—unless it were through the conversations they held with the Marquis himself?"[8] With this complaint Bernal Díaz distributed blame between the historical distortions rendered by Cortés and the carelessness of his supposedly prestigious historians; Bernal Díaz effectively chastised them for relying on gossip and hearsay when they should have sought out certified legal testimony that would have given them a broader (and presumably more balanced) pool of sources from which to elaborate their accounts. Cortés's social soirees were a far cry from the protocols governing judicial juntas, and his casual conversation did not have the weight of law because it was not testimony taken under oath. As to Bernal Díaz's own writing of history, how could his critics be so obtuse as to not understand that he had met these criteria of responsible reporting? Did his presumptuous interlocutor not understand that the letters of Cortés and the viceroy and Bernal Díaz's own probanzas were the very witnesses his interlocutor demanded?[9]

PROBANZAS AND THE WRITING OF CONQUEST HISTORY

As an "old conquistador" of Mexico, Bernal Díaz belonged to a generation whose claims to royal reward and influence in local affairs depended on testimony and credentials whose referents were the events that constituted major episodes in the history of New Spain.[10] The historical actor gained an authority as witness from the juridical means used to assess the conquests and reward their protagonists. Paradoxically, the need to verify those services to the crown appeared, as mentioned earlier, just as the rights to reward of the claimants met their most serious challenge: the New Laws of 1542–1543, which sought to abolish *encomienda,* the most highly prized reward a "first discoverer" could receive.[11] The granting of such concessions from king to vassal had its origins in the Christian reconquest of Muslim Spain, and men like Bernal Díaz sought to exploit the connection by emphasizing the fulfillment of their own obligation to provide the indigenous polities under their jurisdiction with Christian religious instruction (see below).

In order to calm the fears of the encomenderos of New Spain after news of the New Laws of November 20, 1542, reached them in 1543, the viceroy Antonio de Mendoza sought to postpone their publication and enforcement in 1544, and he made promises to the encomenderos of appropriate recognition and possibly further rewards. On Mendoza's request for information about current encomienda holdings under these circumstances, there was not a single settler, rich or poor, who did not register, hoping for greater rewards or the confirmation of those already possessed. A total of 1,385 persons inscribed themselves in the register; only 15 or 20 did not plead extreme poverty.[12]

Mendoza's request has been interpreted as merely a "pretext of making certain that deserving persons who took part in the conquest, or were among the early settlers, were adequately rewarded, while in reality [he was] taking inventory of individual holdings as a step toward satisfying royal desires to dissolve the *encomienda* system."[13] Whatever Mendoza's motives, antecedents for gathering information about the military service of vassals had included King Ferdinand's request for an inventory of persons and property after the 1490 siege and capture of Málaga; the Second Audiencia of New Spain's invitation to settlers to disclose their holdings in 1531 likewise required that the claimants reiterate the services they had originally performed on behalf of the emperor (315).

By the time Bernal Díaz began writing, therefore, being a self-interested historian of the conquest generated a double challenge: to prove one's honorable and valorous participation in order to earn the right to tell the "true story" and to demonstrate the justice and honorable conduct of the war in order to lay claim to reward and earn a place in history. The complementary goals of immediate economic reward and eternal fame and glory stand in uneasy tension in the *Historia verdadera.* The abundant evidence of both attests to their simultaneity, and it would be misguided to suggest that the long-term goal of fame overtook the quest for immediate reward.[14]

As is apparent from the remarks of Bernal Díaz cited above, the juridical forms provided the standard against which novice historians such as himself wrote. The writers of eyewitness *relaciones* were simultaneously stimulated and frustrated by the criterion against which their first-person writings could not compete: the collective and corroborative model of assertion, claim, and proof found in the *probanza* or *información de méritos y servicios.* This realization must have troubled Bernal Díaz as he wrote a monumental history whose ultimate and humble origin had been the first-person *relación de méritos y servicios,* the account of his inherited merits and personal deeds accomplished in service to a higher authority.[15] Although writers like Bernal could not duplicate the probanza-as-standard-of-truth in their own writings, his example shows that they often sought to over-come it.

The probanza was a written document consisting of the plaintiff's statement of his case, along with the testimony of friendly witnesses who corroborated his petition. As a form of legal testimony, a probanza or información was an ex parte proceeding (that is, representing one side of the case only) taken under oath. Witnesses were called and presented with an interrogatory, on which they affirmed the points the party sought to prove. Designed to clarify facts that the plaintiff wished to set forth in perpetuity, the probanza was the means by which lawyers or advocates informed the judges about the claims of the parties they represented.[16] The interrogatorio was "a highly formalized and obviously highly important step in the procedure and the skill employed in framing it might affect the result considerably."[17] It consisted of three parts: a series of general questions prescribed by law and designed to discover the character of the witness being interrogated, his interest in the case, and the degree of credence to be given to his statements; a series of particular questions relating to the case, drawn up by the litigant or his advocate; and a general question concerning hearsay evidence about the litigant, under the heading de pública voz y fama, "that which is widely and publicly known" (157). There was a tendency to call the largest possible number of witnesses on one's behalf to testify to the same set of facts or assertions.

The probanza would be presented to a judge in the absence of the interested party and his representatives; the law required merely that they be summoned to hear the final judgment. The relator, an official of the court, presented the case for its first hearing, and only the advocates (abogados, qualified lawyers) were always present but spoke only when and if invited to do so. Witnesses were normally not examined in person. The danger of the privacy of these proceedings, leading to the sale of justice, was self-evident in the admonitions against irregularities (158).

The surviving 1539 probanza on Bernal Díaz's behalf contains an interrogatorio of twenty-one questions probably drawn up by Bernal Díaz himself. There he sought favorable testimony as to (1) his participation in the expedition of Francisco Hernández de Córdoba to Mexico in 1517; (2) his service to Cortés from the time of their arrival in Mexico to the death of Moctezuma's successor, Cuauhtémoc (1519–1525); (3) his participation in the conquest of Coatzacoalcos (1522) as well as in the expedition to Tabasco and Chiapas (1525); and (4) the (injustice of the) withdrawal in 1528 of encomienda grants he had received in those areas.[18] The character of the probanza and its effective legal validation or rejection of claims in court underscore why Bernal Díaz would have insisted on the importance of such documents when in chapter 212 he answered his interlocutors' challenge to his authority.

The sworn probanza and the grants and decrees that resulted from their royal acceptance were the very basis—and the highest possible legal ground—on which Bernal Díaz could stake his claim to write the history of the events in which he had participated. When he declared he would introduce as a witness on his behalf the emperor himself, he meant that Carlos V's royal seal was the ultimate proof of his services and his truthfulness in reporting them.

Once again, legal practices reveal the shortcomings of the professional historians from Bernal Díaz's perspective. Not only had they used inadequate sources of information under inappropriate circumstances, but they had failed to obtain information from Cortés as a witness to the deeds of others (see chapter 6). It was bad enough that when Cortés wrote to the king, "pearls and gold always dripped from his pen instead of ink." These "pearls" were lavished in his own praise, but he was silent regarding his men's deeds ["siempre por tinta le salían perlas y oro de la pluma, y todo en su loor, y no de nuestros valerosos soldados"] (*Historia verdadera* 2:378 [chap. 212]). Worse still, Bernal Díaz lamented, was the fact that neither Gómara nor Illescas had written about the deeds of the soldiers, having failed to interrogate properly their principal informant, Cortés. In contrast to this irresponsible mode of history writing, Bernal Díaz conscientiously had written of the others as well as of himself. How could his critics, he asked rhetorically, thus fail to understand that he, in contrast to Cortés, was writing not merely on his own behalf, but for all the captains and soldiers of the conquest and Cortés, too? He was, in other words, taking the broader standard set by the probanza as a witness for many others, whereas his learned predecessors had contented themselves with the narrow limits of a single source (akin, in Bernal Díaz's view, to the model of the *relación de méritos y servicios*).

Here, in the final chapters of his work, Bernal Díaz sought to evoke the collective ethos of the conquistadores and to assume the proper role of witness to his fellow soldiers. He made a revealing textual emendation in the Guatemala manuscript, changing an earlier statement about retelling his own deeds ("the battles in which I fought and all that happened") to one emphasizing those of the entire company ("the heroic deeds of the valorous Cortés as well as my own and those of my companions").[19] Furthermore, he devoted chapters 204 through 206 to the great achievements of his fellow conquistadores.

Why, in the last chapters of his chronicle, did Bernal Díaz attempt to evoke the probanza that testified to the services performed by all the "first discoverers" of Mexico? His effort to move from the autobiographical and self-referential *relación* to the illusion of the extrareferential probanza reveals that the stakes involved were higher than his own self-interest. In conducting the affairs of his daily life, he was accustomed to such collaborative effort. As mentioned earlier (see chapter 6), he was sent to Spain as an advocate representing the city of Santiago de Guatemala, seeking before the Council of the Indies the repeal of the order of the president of the Audiencia de los Confines to liberate Indian slaves, and in 1550 at the royal junta in Valladolid he testified in favor of granting encomiendas in perpetuity. In both instances, he represented the larger group. Such efforts corroborate and complement his efforts in the *Historia verdadera*. His objective to save the glory of the conquests for posterity was an ever more pressing need as the 1550s and 1560s passed; his conceptualization of this pursuit historiographically relied on the spirit of the collective probanza.

THE *SIETE PARTIDAS* AND THE CONQUEST OF MEXICO

One of the most effective ways to counter the condemnation of the conquest was to link recent events to a more distant past. Like Cortés at the time of the invasion of Mexico, Bernal Díaz appealed to hallowed Castilian traditions. Whereas Cortés had done so to legitimize at the time his unauthorized and illegal conquest of Mexico, Bernal Díaz now used that Castilian heritage to counter the disrepute into which the conquests had fallen more than three decades after the fact. The great thirteenth-century body of Castilian law, the *Siete partidas* (1256–1263) of Alfonso X, codified those traditions, and their role as ideological underpinnings of the writings of Cortés has been amply demonstrated.[20] They were also fundamental to Bernal Díaz's historiographic efforts.

The *Siete partidas* effectively regulated the institutions of civil and criminal law in the juridical life of the Indies in Bernal Díaz's day. Most relevant were the principles concerning the relationship of vassal to sovereign, combining the absolutism of Roman imperial law with the sociofeudalist mandates of medieval doctrine according to which the king should live in organic unity with his subjects, and they with him.[21] With respect to the rule of law, four principles were significant. The first was that the will of some ought not to override the good of the many. Second, the right to rescind unjust laws required appropriate consultation and consensus. Third, the exercise of *jus gentium,* derived from natural law, was necessary to keep the peace. Finally, the *caballero* should be a selfless vassal who always honored his lord by speaking only the truth ("palabras verdaderas") to him.[22] With respect to the notion of the just war, Alphonsine tradition, echoed in the sixteenth century as previously mentioned, named three causes: to enlarge the faith and destroy those who opposed it; to serve, honor, and protect one's lord; to defend, enlarge, and honor one's homeland.[23]

On balance, the Alphonsine principles most prominent in Cortés's writings had been the recognition of the need to abolish and change laws in conformity to new situations and the requirement to serve the greater good of king and commonweal over private interests. The same may be said for Bernal Díaz.[24] Like Cortés, he was a highly subtle and astute interpreter of the conquest, and he took an active, not a passive, role in crafting (at least retrospectively) Cortesian politics vis-à-vis the crown.

Bernal Díaz's reliance on Alphonsine precepts to legitimize past actions and ensure their continued reward in the future is evident in the later chapters of his work. He approached the task by creating a series of reflections on the conquistadores, their good works, and the hard times they endured because of the vicissitudes of local colonial government. He framed these arguments-by-narration with a contrastive chapter, 204, recounting Cortés's life and ascent to the aristocracy once back in Spain. He then went on to discuss, among other things, the "valorous captains and brave soldiers" who accompanied Cortés from Cuba to conquer Mexico (chaps. 205 and 206) and the merits of the "true conquistadores" (chap. 207). He aspired to privileges such as those enjoyed by medieval warriors in the reconquest of Spain.[25]

Making an argument for their inherited merits and performed services, Bernal Díaz asserted that the conquistadores of New Spain distinguished themselves much more than soldiers of earlier times. However, having read the old histories, he said, he had learned that many knights had been elevated to great estate in Spain and other places, either for serving in war or in other ways. Indeed, some knights would not go to war without first being paid, and beyond being salaried for their services, some also received titles of nobility, towns, castles, estates, and lands in perpetuity. Furthermore, those privileges were now enjoyed by their heirs. "Yet we," he declared, "won New Spain without the king even knowing about it!"[26] Bernal Díaz made his judgment very clear: Like the warriors who fought for Don Jaime of Aragon against the Muslims and those who won Granada and Naples, the true conquistadores too should be remunerated and rewarded.[27] Here he followed the argument elaborated earlier (in chapter 36) about Cortés's establishment of authority independent of that of the governor Diego Velázquez; he expressed implicitly that same argument in chapter 1 of the Guatemala manuscript, namely, that they had conquered, pacified, and settled Mexico as good and loyal servants of the king, whom they were obliged to obey, and then advised Charles of what they had done. In other words, he intimated, they disobeyed direct orders only in order to comply with a higher mandate, serving their king with their conquest and their faith with new souls to convert (*Historia verdadera* 1:39 [chap. 1]).

Before resting his case, and by way of conclusion, he proclaimed himself among the most valiant of soldiers and the oldest of them all: "And I say again that I, I, I,—I say it so many times—that I am the oldest and I have served His Majesty as a very good soldier. And I say it with sadness in my heart, because I find myself poor and very old, a daughter to marry, and sons now grown and with beards, and others to raise, and I cannot go to Castile before His Majesty to inform him of things I have done in the fulfillment of his royal service in order that he make me rewards, as they are owed to me, well deserved" [y digo otra vez que yo, yo, yo, dígolo tantas veces, que yo soy el más antiguo, y lo he servido como muy buen soldado a Su Majestad, y diré con tristeza de mi corazón, porque me veo pobre y muy viejo y una hija para casar y los hijos varones ya grandes y con barbas y otros por criar, y no puedo ir a Castilla ante Su Majestad para representarle cosas cunplideras a su real servicio, y también para que me haga mercedes, pues se me deben bien debidas (2:365 [chap. 210])].

Underneath the apparent self-promotion lie the traditional precepts of the reciprocal relation of king and vassal, the communication from one to the other and the king's obligation to honor the *hidalgo*. Bernal Díaz understood that the vassal was honored by his lord "according to his rank and the services performed by him," that is, according to his merits and services.[28] Bernal Díaz increasingly joined his claims to service as a soldier to his presumed merits as an *hidalgo*. To make his point, Bernal Díaz invented a dialogue in which his interlocutor was the allegorical figure of "the fair and illustrious Fame." She asks, he writes, "Where are our palaces and mansions, and what coats of arms are there on them distinguishing us from the others?" and "Are our heroic deeds and arms carved on them and placed as a memorial in the manner that gentlemen have them in Spain?" Upon hearing his sad reply followed by an account of the conquistadores' great deeds and accusations against the historians who ignored them, he tells how "Good Fame promises me besides that, on her part, wherever she may be, she will proclaim it in a clear and ringing voice, and in addition to this, that she will explain so that, as soon as my history (if it is printed) is seen and heard, all will give it true belief and will cast doubt on the flatteries which the former [historians] have written" (*True History* 5:274–277; *Historia verdadera* 2:366–368 [chap. 210]).

In this and successive chapters he took advantage of the invented conversation. The technique he used—reminiscent of the probanza—was to create an authoritative interlocutor to whom he could respond as a witness on behalf of his comrades; in these exchanges his readers become the *oidores*, or judges. In these dramatized encounters, he cleverly presented the illusion of escaping the bonds of first-person narration and participating in a judicial proceeding, that is, moving from the role of the petitioner in the *relación* to that of witness in the probanza. By illusion at least, Bernal Díaz succeeded in becoming a witness for himself.

After writing the episode about his encounter with the allegorical figure of Fame, he passed on to a more mundane but important interlocutor: a judge of the Audiencia of Guatemala. The judge asked why, if Bernal Díaz and others had done so much, the now-titled Cortés had not sought reward for them. Bernal Díaz offered several reasons. First, Cortés thought that he would be an absolute lord and that it would be in his hands to give Indians to his faithful soldiers or take them away. But then the king refused him the governorship and gave him instead a title and huge private estates. Second, although Cortés could have divided the territories at the time of the conquest, he had not done so, and the soldiers, says Bernal, did not know what it meant to demand justice, or to whom to appeal, except to Cortés, for reward for their services (2:368–369 [chap. 210]). (Here he reveals, with some pain, the awkward circumstances produced by the unauthorized conquest.)

Later, he continues, he and his companions discovered that those who had gone before the king had been rewarded, and so they sent an agent to Spain to request that properties vacated be granted to them in perpetuity. The king responded by sending Nuño de Guzmán as president of the first Audiencia of New Spain; he was instructed to make the grants. But Guzmán, Bernal Díaz remarks, was persuaded that to do so would make the conquistadores impossible to rule, so he refrained from carrying out the royal order to the full extent. However, he and the judges did distribute some lands, not badly says Bernal Díaz, before being removed from office because of conflicts with Cortés and the scandal over the branding of free Indians as slaves (2:369–370 [chap. 210]).

Bernal offered as his next piece of evidence an account of the royal junta on perpetuity and the impasse with which it ended (chap. 211) (see chapter 6). Finally, he closed his book (chap. 212) with his conversation with the licentiates, on the problem of self-praise in the writing of history. He reiterated the absence of the soldiers' deeds in the histories of Gómara and Illescas, insisted that he deserved part of the credit given to Cortés, and concluded, "And besides this I want to set forth another matter so that it be evident that I do not praise myself as much as I should" [y además de esto quiero poner aquí otra plática, porque vean que no me alabo tanto como debo] (2:378 [chap. 212]). He ended the chapter (and the first version of his book) with the battles and encounters in which he had served (2:379–383 [chap. 212]).

Closely scrutinized, these final chapters constitute an advocacy almost parodic in its self-portrait of the questing petitioner and yet systematically argued with the persuasiveness of a lawyer who transformed himself from plaintiff into witness. The dialogue with allegorical Fame allowed him to make continual comparisons between the conquistadores of Mexico and the medieval warriors who became the grandees of Spain; the question from the judge of the Audiencia of Guatemala allowed him to reiterate the history of how the conquistadores missed out, time after time, in obtaining their due. Particularly poignant is Bernal Díaz's revelation of what the unauthorized conquest of Mexico meant; after the fact, the soldiers could turn only to Cortés for reward, and the latter's efforts on his own behalf to take the best lands of New Spain were patent.

By the time the issue of appropriate reward was considered by the court and the Council of the Indies in 1550, action on making encomienda grants in perpetuity, as discussed earlier, had been effectively blocked by

Las Casas and his allies. Thus it is not surprising that in his chronicle Bernal Díaz staked his ultimate claim to reward on having brought the Christian gospel to the Indians. Once again, the intimate relation between the shape of the narration and legal precept comes into view. On the matter of the religious indoctrination of the Indians, he expressed a theme common to other conquistadores who found themselves similarly vexed and unsatisfied with their rewards and reputation. One, Ruy González, a veteran of the conquest of Mexico, encomendero, and city councilman of México-Tenochtitlán whose complaints were examined in chapter 6, also laid claim to effecting conversion and the salvation of countless souls that had been in danger of being lost to the power of the devil.[29] With this argument, the conquistadores appealed ultimately to the papal bulls of donation of 1493, which constituted the fundamental legal claim to the Spanish presence in the New World. In asserting these claims, they took a position opposite to that of Las Casas, against whom they complained bitterly for his attacks on the historical reputation of the conquest and the right to enjoy its rewards.

The three papal documents—the bulls of donation, demarcation, and extension of donation—were widely debated in the period: Did the Catholic kings hope to achieve a juridical title that would allow them to justify their dominion over those islands and lands? or did they seek merely the confirmation of the right acquired through the discovery itself? Had the pope conceded political dominion or only the authority to propagate the gospel?[30] (See chapter 4.) Whatever the original intent had been, the pontifical decrees were used to produce the *requerimiento*, the judicial tool that offered the indigenous peoples of America the option of accepting the gospel and Spanish rule or facing a war of conquest (see the section entitled "The Requirement," in chapter 10). The jurists who devised it rested their claim on one of the means (the fourth justification) proposed by Alfonso el Sabio to establish kingship. (Again the Reconquest heritage is implicitly taken as precedent for Castilian conduct in the Indies.) The first was by inheritance, the second by election, the third by marriage, and the fourth, by the pope or emperor when either appointed kings to those lands over which they had right and dominion.[31]

This is the resolution Bernal Díaz appealed to in his petition of 1549 to rescind the prohibition of slavery as well as in the *Historia verdadera*. In his chronicle he paraphrased the requerimiento in Cortés's speeches to local caciques en route to Mexico as well as prior to the decisive battle at Cholula, the latter of which, as has been discussed (chapter 6), had been interpreted by Las Casas and others as an unprovoked massacre.[32] These had been crucial moments in the conquest and responded to the current critical debates taken up in Bernal Díaz's conquest history. By breaking the law of Velázquez, Bernal Díaz thus argued, Cortés and his army had served the greater good by conquering Mexico, to honor not only their king but their god. They did so by executing a juridical protocol instituted for New World conquests by the Roman Catholic pope. The papal decrees, Bernal Díaz argued, constituted the highest authority by which to justify the (officially unauthorized) conquest of Mexico.

In this manner, he probed and refined—through his "plain talking" narrative—the relationship between legal tradition, juridical practice, and the interpretation of the Mexican conquest. Modernity (or the lack of it) was conceived in terms of medieval legal principles, and historical authority was sanctioned by everyday judicial practices. The remarkable resilience and deeper implications of this approach as exemplified by Bernal Díaz are borne out well into the seventeenth century.

THE BATTLES OF CONQUEST HISTORY RENEWED

Seventeenth-century writings shed considerable light on the particular irritations of Bernal Díaz and his peers and on the urgency with which they had reconstructed conquest history. These commentaries include those of heirs to the conquistadores (Bernal Díaz's, regarding the conquest of Mexico, Francisco Pizarro's, concerning the conquest of Peru) and the sentiments that attended the first publication of Bernal Díaz's chronicle in 1632, forty-eight years after his death. The posthumous publication of the *Historia verdadera* was involved in a propaganda war of international proportions—one much broader than the Castilian Indies debate with which Bernal Díaz had been concerned.

This international forum emerges into view with the remarks of the seventeenth-century authorities who prefaced Bernal Díaz's published work. The official chronicler of the king and *cronista mayor de las Indias*, Luis Tribaldos de Toledo, lauded the history of "the captain" Bernal Díaz for being that of an eyewitness of everything that had occurred in its course.[33] Such exaggerated claims, of which Bernal Díaz himself had been innocent, allowed Tribaldos to underscore the virtues of this work over against those written from secondhand sources and to find in the *Historia verdadera* what had been lacking in many others, namely, the "exact truth" of all the important events. Fray Diego Serrano, master general of the Mercedarian order, also lauded the work for being an eyewitness account and for protecting "with holy zeal the reputation of our Spain, [which has been] defamed in the histories by foreign envy." The author of the unsigned prologue to the reader ("Al lector") (Remón had edited Bernal Díaz's 1568 manuscript but died before the edition appeared) praised "el capitán" Bernal Díaz and declared: "If Spain owes him a share of conquest glory for the good done for the nation, it also owes him entire credit for saving the reputation of Spain in the eyes of foreign nations," adding that without embellishments he had told the truth that had been absent from previous histories.[34] This criticism of secondhand accounts once again suggests the deleterious role played by Las Casas's *Brevísima relación de la destrucción de las Indias* and his advocacy of the 1542 New Laws to abolish encomienda.

Just a few years after Bernal Díaz's *Historia verdadera* was published, one of the heirs of Francisco Pizarro, Fernando Pizarro y Orellana, brought out his *Varones ilustres del Nuevo Mundo* (1639) to support the pretensions of his cousin Juan Fernando de Pizarro for royal recognition and reward. This catalogue of Castilian heroes of the New World conquests further reveals the juridical role assigned to historical treatments of the conquests of a century earlier. Pizarro y Orellana cited Fray Prudencio de Sandoval, the imperial chronicler of Charles V, on the point that the tracts written by Las Casas in 1542 in support of the New Laws had done great harm to the conquistadores, giving foreigners in their histories the means to speak ill of the Spanish nation, for which they had a "natural hatred."[35] Pizarro y Orellana argued that now at all costs Pizarro's heirs should be rewarded in order to avoid the condemnation of foreign nations who would take the crown's indifference toward the marquis's heirs as confirmation that the conquests had been unjust.[36] Thus he argued that the lack of royal reward would have the effect of publicly undermining the veracity and value of efforts made in the king's service a century earlier. In the same way, Bernal Díaz's and his fellows' unsuccessful bids for grants of encomienda in perpetuity in 1550 would be interpreted as deepening the plight of their descendants, depriving them of material wealth and the royal recognition and attendant social status to which Bernal Díaz and his fellows had aspired, as his own dialogue with "Good Fame" (chap. 210) and modern studies (Durand, Himmerich y Valencia) have attested.

In 1672, forty years after the publication of the *Historia verdadera,* Bernal Díaz's great-great-grandson, Francisco Antonio Fuentes y Guzmán, discovered the manuscript of the *Historia verdadera* that had remained in Guatemala. Don Francisco was able to "follow its accredited truth" in his own *Historia de Guatemala o recordación florida.*[37] Relying directly on the accounts of his ancestor, to whom he refers as "mi verídico Castillo,"[38] Fuentes y Guzmán's goal was to celebrate (and defend) Pedro de Alvarado's great deeds. With a clever sleight of hand, Fuentes y Guzmán suppressed the 1520 massacre of Mexica nobility in Tenochtitlán for which Alvarado had been responsible.[39] He manipulated it in order to avoid rehearsing once more an event that had long since remained notorious. He focused instead on Cortés's simultaneous and successful defeat of Pánfilo de Narváez's forces on the coast, lauding Cortés's victory over Narváez's army as "a cause of silence and confusion for those Spaniards who say that the conquistadores of these kingdoms did nothing of great valor, fighting only against naked Indians."[40] Fuentes y Guzmán thus rebutted Las Casas's account in the *Brevísima relación,* in which the Dominican friar had described the scene of unsheathed Spanish swords attacking naked Indians, and he explicitly refuted Las Casas on the point that the Spaniards had allowed their Indian allies to butcher and eat captive Indian enemies because the Spanish could not feed their multitudinous armies.[41]

Fuentes y Guzmán's account reveals the ongoing need in the seventeenth century to defend the sixteenth-century conquests from the persistent influence of Las Casas's work. In this regard, a notable omission in Bernal Díaz's *Historia verdadera* is any discussion of the New Laws, promulgated in 1542 but never enforced in Mexico and rescinded three years later (see chapter 4). Their relatively rapid repeal had given hope that encomienda grants might yet be made in perpetuity. The failure of the 1550 junta to produce them, duly recorded by Bernal Díaz, helped bring him to the decision to write the history of the conquest of Mexico. That this is so is evident from the importance he attached to written history as a weapon by which to promote his interests and those of his remaining peers and their heirs.

BERNAL DÍAZ AND THE ETHOS OF
THE HISTORICAL PROTAGONIST

There is no doubt about the significance Bernal Díaz attributed to written history as the second battleground, the one on which to defend territories and wealth already taken and to seek the right to more. Writing his history of the conquest was not an idle pastime but rather the ground on which to defend and expand the encomenderos' diminishing opportunities for perpetual rewards. This much may be clear from studying him in a head-to-head confrontation with Las Casas (see chapter 6); but what about his disgruntlement with Gómara, whose history he had read, he says, after having already started his own? How do Gómara and his colleagues fit into this picture of history as advocacy? What is the ultimate source of Bernal Díaz's complaints against him and his fellow historians?

The standard (and generally accepted) answer has been that Gómara and the others emphasized the achievements of Cortés to the exclusion of his several hundred soldiers. This is so, but as an explanation it does not go far enough. Another answer has been Bernal's complaints about Gómara's factual errors and high style, but this has now been demonstrated to be a hollow charge.[42] Bernal Díaz's criticism of Gómara has an additional if not different target. Bernal Díaz's quibbles over historical fact and rhetorical style reflect neither his disinterested devotion to historical accuracy nor a preference for simplicity of prose expression. They speak to a deeper type of truth in history: the capacity to recreate not only the specific outline of events but also the ethos of the culture of its protagonists, in this case, the conquistadores. The unnamed author of the prologue to the 1632 edition of the *Historia verdadera* gave a clue to this assessment by signaling two chapters, 18 and 34, that would reveal Bernal Díaz's search for particular kinds of historical truth.

The first instance puts it most bluntly: about Gómara, Illescas, and Giovio, Bernal Díaz stated simply, "[At] beginning and middle and end they do not address what actually happened in New Spain" [y desde el prinçipio y medio ni cabo no hablan lo que pasó en la Nueva España] (1:79 [chap. 18]). He was chagrined because the learned historians exaggerated the violence of the conquistadores' deeds. Such remarks are centrally relevant to his position once one understands that it had been an embattled one. He stated clearly, "The chroniclers mentioned by me write that we were responsible for more deaths and cruelties than Athalric, the most bloodthirsty king, and Attila, bellicose warrior" [Y escriven los coronistas por mí memorados, que hazíamos tantas muertes y crueldades, que Atalarico, muy brabosísimo rey, y Atila, muy soberbio guerrero] (1:79). His other accusation against the historians concerns the participation of the soldiers and the arbitrariness with which the historians wrote about them, raising some and lowering others, inserting into the conquests men who had not been there, and, even worse, declaring that Cortés's decision to scuttle the ships had been made secretly when it had been done with the counsel of most of his companions (1:79–80). Gómara's history, Bernal Díaz argued, comprehended neither the dynamics of the conquistadores' collective efforts nor the standards of conduct they observed.

In chapter 34, his complaint took a different twist: the spotlight that should have fallen upon the soldiers' valor in Gómara's account was cast instead on miraculous appearances of Santiago Mayor (St. James Major), or Saint Peter. All Bernal Díaz saw at the time, he said, was Francisco de Morla on a chestnut horse! Until he read Gómara on this point, he said, he had never heard of such visions. Indeed, if such had occurred, the soldiers, who always attributed their victories to God, would have taken testimony of the event, built a church upon the spot, and named the settlement Santiago or San Pedro de la Victoria (1:115–116 [chap. 34]). Gómara, Bernal Díaz implies, obviously knew nothing about the way conquistadores conducted themselves; had he had such knowledge, he would have questioned the account he had received and avoided the mistake of making the conquistadores guilty of failing to observe traditional religious protocols.

Overall, Bernal Díaz's arguments against Gómara were not that he did not get the facts straight but rather that he represented an external perspective that was incapable of understanding the conquistadores' actions or outlook, that is, of understanding the conquest from the inside. For this reason, the ironic conclusion must be drawn that, for Bernal Díaz and his fellows, not only Las Casas but also the proconquest historians were perceived as damaging to the cause of the conquistadores. Fundamental to the misapprehension of conquistador culture by the historians, argues Bernal Díaz, was their failure to appreciate the juridical and ethical code to which he and his fellow veteran soldiers had always subscribed.

Still, there is no question that the anticonquest writers had a more protracted negative effect on the encomenderos' plight. That this crisis was real for Bernal Díaz and members of his generation is borne out by those seventeenth-century advocates of the conquistadores' heirs considered here. Pizarro y Orellana dramatically concluded that Francisco Pizarro's assassination could be appropriately attributed not to tyrannical soldiers but rather to interested historians and malevolent writers of history.[43]

More than half a century earlier, Bernal Díaz would have agreed. Cortés's self-serving, published letters to Charles V and Las Casas's sensational tract and legislative efforts had served as a catalyst to Bernal Díaz as he initiated his historical project; the learned histories of Gómara, Illescas, and Gonzalo Fernández de Oviedo confirmed for him the necessity of the decision he had made. For the conquistadores as well as their heirs in the following century, the writing of history took up where the filing of probanzas, petitions, and relaciones left off. With its origins in the mundane documents of historical testimony, the historiography of the Indies bore in its development the juridical principles of legal testimony and the values and traditions of Alphonsine law. The "plain talk" of the curmudgeonly Bernal Díaz, who wrote, according to his interlocutor, in the manner "common to men of Castile," leads one to contemplate again the peculiar powers of prose and the presumably "plain speaking" narratives of sixteenth-century Castile and Spanish America.

The great lesson that the reading of Bernal Díaz's chronicle teaches is that he did not derive his literary authority from the truth of historical events or from having been an eyewitness to them. He sought the source of his credibility instead in the juridical tradition that, on the basis of medieval legal principles and the legacy of the Reconquest of Castile, took shape in his day with regard to the Spanish conquests in the Indies. Bernal Díaz did not defer to the writings of Cortés or Gómara on many points because he was polemicizing against them on many others (and sometimes he polemicized against Gómara and others when, in fact, his and their accounts agreed). The search for authority in the writing of Indies history continued into the seventeenth century, and its sources were found increasingly in Castilian law and the writings of earlier historians. The model that Bernal Díaz's work provides invites consideration of other ways, outside the events of history, in which writers of his day and afterward staked their claims to literary authority.

CHAPTER 8

The Amerindian, Studied, Interpreted, and Imagined

GRACING THE FRONTISPIECE OF Fray Fernando de Valverde's *Santuario de Nuestra Señora de Copacabana en el Perú* (1641) is an Inca prince, Yupanqui Toca, who sits with his chin resting upon his interlaced fingers, lost in thought. Before him is the image of the Andean sacred, a boulder, or *huaca,* interpreted in Christian perspective by the figure of a small devil standing atop it (fig. 18). Yupanqui Toca appears in Valverde's poem of seventeen strophic *silvas* and laments the loss of his kingdom "to a frail woman" [una hembra flaca], who was so poor that she gave birth to her son in a stable. So humble was she, he intones, that in all matters she obeyed her husband, a simple carpenter. Her last hardship was watching her son expire, nailed to a timber ["quien en fin, por último regalo, espirar a su hijo vio en un palo"]. This proud Inca, vanquished and still disturbed at his defeat by a humble woman and with his own sacred beings (*huaca*) still before him, stares ahead in an attitude of perpetual perplexity.[1]

"Yupanqui Toca" is assigned an uncharacteristically nuanced role in the sixteenth- and seventeenth-century literary depictions of the Amerindian. His attitude of thoughtful and bewildered contemplation is exceeded only by El Inca Garcilaso's brilliant portrait of Atahualpa, struggling to make sense of the news of the Christian gospel as presented to him, under the most trying circumstances, by another friar by the name of Valverde, Fray Vicente de Valverde, who accompanied Pizarro's con-

FIGURE 18. Frontispiece engraving by Francisco de Bejarano, in Fernando de Valverde, *Santuario de Nuestra Señora de Copacabana en el Perú: poema sacro*. Lima: Luis de
Lyra, 1641. The John Carter Brown Library at Brown University.

quest expedition to Peru.[2] I have invoked Fray Fernando de Valverde's Inca, Yupanqui Toca, to draw attention to the problem of reading and writing about Indians in colonial Spanish America.[3] The Inca prince dramatizes the paradox of high and low forms, the sacred and all-powerful Inca defeated by an ordinary and humble woman, inverting the relationship that the poet Valverde presents in his poem. As if echoing the perplexity of the prince, but righting the Inca's upside-down opposition of values, the Augustinian writer confesses his dilemma to the readers of his *Santuario de Nuestra Señora:* how to write about the miracles performed by Our Lady of Copacabana and, in the same poem, narrate the deeds of the humble Colla Indians who were the witnesses and beneficiaries of those miraculous events. Fray Fernando de Valverde's sublime subject was the founding of the Christian faith near the site of the famed Inca shrine, the Temple of the Sun, on an island in Lake Titicaca.[4] His problem was that its protagonists were "not emperors and princes in Rome, Madrid, or even Lima," but rather, as he put it none too kindly, a "forlorn settlement of Collas who are among the most barbarous and dull-witted Indians in all Peru."[5]

The author Valverde's perplexity in dealing with high and low poetic subjects was resolved by alternating the epic meter and mode with the pastoral in order to narrate the miracles of Saint Mary and the actions of the rustic Colla shepherds, respectively. In doing so, Valverde addressed a problem that was not only literary but also cultural and political. His preoccupation about how to introduce the figure of the Amerindian into his poem was part of a general phenomenon that appeared frequently in the writings on America of the sixteenth and seventeenth centuries. The justification writers offered for their study of Amerindian subjects and the strategies they used to appeal to their readers' interest bear investigation, as they shed light on the literary production of the period and offer indirect evidence about that elusive problem of colonial literary culture: censorship and suppression.[6]

When the Amerindian became the focus of colonial writing, both religious and lay authors expressed an unusual self-consciousness in bringing forth this new subject. Accounts ethnographic, philosophical, and fictional were commonly introduced with justifications or disclaimers indicating how it should be taken by the reader that the author was writing about Indians. Although European writers used European concepts of culture and languages of representation to describe the new-found humanity, they did so with self-conscious self-justifications when-ever they introduced their novel subject matter. The writers' basic move was a double and contradictory one: to exploit aspects of their subjects the European reader would find fabulous and sensational and, simultane-ously, to shy away from any association with the kinds of writing which were condemned by Christian moralists and censors. These efforts by authors to position themselves and their subject matter reveal why eth-nographic history and epic poetry enjoyed such different editorial fates during the second half of the sixteenth century and how the literary por-trayal of the figure and myriad cultures of the Amerindian was a signifi-cant determinant in the publication and suppression of writings in that period. A further problem to be examined is the way in which other types of works and topics—romances of chivalry, books and codices in Amerin-dian languages, and books on magic and superstition—were implicated in the ways that Europeans wrote and read books about Indians. The books of chivalric adventure play a significant role; the relationship between chivalric fiction and writings about Amerindian cultures challenges one of the commonplaces of colonial Latin American literary history. Through such juxtapositions it will be possible to see why attempts at ethnographic representations of Amerindian experience were often considered too dan-gerous to disseminate. Bernal Díaz here provides insight into a literary authority negatively defined: Poets, chroniclers, and ethnographic writers cited the chivalric romance to make the paradoxical point that, like the chivalric romance, what they wrote about might seem to the reader un-believable, but was, unlike the tales of chivalry, nevertheless true.

THE HISTORIOGRAPHIC PRESENTATION OF
INDIAN RITE AND CUSTOM

Since the Amerindian came, before the end of the sixteenth century, to be the topic of ethnographic histories, it would seem that historiography would handle quite deftly the introduction of the new subject matter.[7] Yet the authors writing these histories took very particular measures to justify their historiographic practice, the development of which often surprised them, exceeding their original expectations. When Fray Bartolomé de las Casas set forth his agenda for his *Historia de las Indias*, in which he made his topic the chronological narration of the deeds of the Spanish in the

Indies, he declared that his goals were to recount the secular and profane events as well as the ecclesiastical ones of his own times, occasionally putting in some "decisive summaries" [mortales apuntamientos] and "making some mixture of the quality, nature, and properties of these regions, kingdoms, and lands and that which they contain, with the customs, religion, rituals, ceremonies, and condition of their native peoples."[8] It turned out, however, that the ethnography and cosmography of the Indies to which he referred, initially planned to highlight and complement his account of secular and ecclesiastical Spanish Indies history, became such a comprehensive and demanding subject that he ultimately separated it out from his *Historia de las Indias,* creating his *Apologética historia sumaria* (see the section entitled "Las Casas, Theorist of Amerindian Character and Custom," in chapter 3).

Francisco López de Gómara provides another glimpse at the problem of incorporating discussions about Amerindian culture into Spanish history. In the first three editions of his *Historia general de las Indias y la conquista de México* (Zaragosa 1552, 1553; Medina del Campo 1553), an introductory note describes the contents of the work and states that the history of the Indies, with regard to the conquests, will be treated summarily but that the conquest of Mexico will be treated in detail, and that therefore it is set apart. The two-part composition of the work, which Gómara defended, pertains not only to his panoramic/particular (Indias/México), dual subject matter but also to the fact that his topic was alternately the deeds of the Spaniards and the customs of the Indians. He described his book as being "very notable for [its depiction of] the very strange religion and cruel customs of the Indians of Mexico."[9]

The fundamental reason for writing about Indians was the need to know the Amerindian peoples in order to convert them to Christianity. Thus Fray Bernardino de Sahagún justified the creation of his monumental work on Nahua culture, the *Historia general de las cosas de Nueva España* (1569), and so, too, José de Acosta defended his investigations of native Mexican beliefs in the *Historia natural y moral de las Indias* (1590).[10] For the Spanish or *criollo* reader who had nothing to do with evangelization efforts in America, Acosta declared that his accounts would lead to the "edifying and grateful contemplation of the true God who gave to the Christians His holy law."[11] In this way, Acosta effectively added the history of the Amerindians to the list of sanctioned topics of history: Europeans should read about Amerindians—and his work was written for an audience far wider than the Peruvian missionary establishment, as his statement above indicates—because of the same reasons they should read any history: to learn how to live a moral life ("aprender a vivir bien") and to turn from evil ways to good by reading about appropriate examples. Although Acosta put the matter of history about Amerindians forthrightly, his widely read and influential work did not settle the issue. Midway through the seventeenth century, the claim to write history about Amerindians was still a problematical one.

In 1646, the Jesuit Alonso de Ovalle published his *Histórica relación del reyno de Chile*. In the terms that Ovalle understood, his work was *not* a history, for it was about natives of the Indies. Apologizing to his readers for discussing matters "not entirely fitting for a work of history" ("no tan propias de historia") such as native customs and religion, and "extraordinary things so common to that land" ("cosas extraordinarias y tan proprias de aquella tierra"), he explained that he would accommodate those readers fond of history by offering a brief account of the discovery of the Indies and the conquests of its kingdoms, according to their order of occurrence and with regard to the persons who took part in them.[12] History, in Ovalle's terms, was to take as its proper subject the great deeds of Europeans, carefully articulated in a chronological narrative framework; thus he defined history both by its form and its subject, with characteristically narrow limits on the latter.

Ovalle devoted the final book of his work to the "progress of the faith" in Chile, and it concludes with the engraving pictured here: Our Lady of Arauco being worshiped by two recently converted Araucanians (fig. 19).[13] In contrast to the cautious attitude this Jesuit author expresses in his prose text about the success of evangelization, the accompanying engraving narrates pictorially the triumph of the Christian faith. Its Latin inscription tells how the sacred image, found in a cave formed like a chapel, was sculpted not by any human hand (in contrast to Our Lady of Copacabana, engraved by a rustic Andean artist) but by the Author of nature Himself. Made of precious stones, the image's face was white, its hair very black, its red cape embossed with roses and featuring a lining of azure blue.[14] The devout, prayerful Araucanian couple worshiping Our Lady communicates the success of evangelization and, at the same time, their adolescent faces underscore the principle of the relative position that

Vera effigies alterius, quæ in rupis cauitate in modum capellæ concameratæ, non ab
opifice aliquo delineata, sed ab auctore naturæ ex Iaspide varij coloris costruc
ta candido vultu, sub nigro capillo, palio iteri cæruleo exteri rubro veste rosis contexta cospicitur.

FIGURE 19. The adoration of Our Lady of Arauco. Alonso de Ovalle, *Histórica relación
del reyno de Chile y de las misiones*. Rome: Francisco Cavallo, 1646, 393. The John Carter
Brown Library at Brown University.

these idealized neophytes are to occupy in the Christian community: the rule of the less perfect by the more perfect, that is, reason over passion, the adult over the child (see chapter 4).

Most of the writers of the time considered the native peoples of the Americas to be lacking in history, which generally meant that their European observers lacked the tools (native languages, most of all) to apprehend it. The idea of the preservation of a history was causally linked to the notion that a human community had experienced a process of cultural and societal development; thus many writers excluded Amerindian peoples from historiographic consideration, assuming they lacked the development of a civilization to historicize.[15]

Besides this blindness, which was overcome by the great ethnographic historians such as Sahagún and by the Andean and Nahua authors of their own histories, such as Felipe Guaman Poma de Ayala and Fernando de Alva Ixtlilxochitl (see chapters 2 and 5), there existed other, more specific factors which suggest why writing about Amerindians was problematical. Overall, the accommodation of Amerindians in historiography was not a historiographic problem as such but rather a cultural and, even more immediately, a political one. When in the 1570s, for example, the viceroy of Peru, Francisco de Toledo, wanted to convince Philip II of the legitimacy of Spanish rule in the Andes, he used the vehicle of historiography as a political tool to do so (see the section entitled "Old Models and New Monarchies," in chapter 2). By exploiting the viewpoint of ethnic groups conquered by the Incas, Toledo and his colleagues, such as Pedro Sarmiento de Gamboa, wrote the history of the Incas as usurpers and tyrants, thus assuring Philip that the imposition of Spanish imperial rule was a legitimate liberation from native tyranny.[16] The historiography of the Indies in large measure was shaped not by formal considerations of genre but by such factors as the imperial demand for information (the *Relaciones geográficas de Indias*), political motivations (Toledo, Las Casas), and the ethnographic and philosophical examination of native cultures (Sahagún, Las Casas, Acosta).

THE POETIC PRODUCTION OF THE EXOTIC

The way historians discussed the dilemmas of writing about Amerindian culture can be put into relief by considering the strategies that poets employed to introduce the figure of the Amerindian into their writings, just as the Augustinian friar Valverde managed to put humble Colla Indians where he thought lords and princes ought to be. Not surprisingly, the incorporation of the Amerindian into epic poems was accompanied by a variety of self-conscious gestures by their authors. Alonso de Ercilla's justification for celebrating the valor of the Araucanians is well known: He would spare the Araucanians no praise because they deserved even more admiration and acclaim than he was capable of expressing.[17]

Other poets resolved the issue of subject matter in various ways. In the southern province of Río de la Plata, Martín del Barco Centenera, in his *Argentina y conquista del Río de la Plata* (1602), announced that his history of the Spaniards, distributed in his poem's cantos, would also treat of the setting in which they found themselves, "so that the world might have complete information and a true account of the Río de la Plata."[18] He projected his treatment of the Amerindian as just one among many of the delightful and exotic subjects which would move the emotions of the reader. He would tell of "provinces so large, people so extremely greedy for war, animals and wild beasts so fierce, birds so different, serpents and snakes that have had combat with man, fishes in human form, and things so unique that they leave in ecstasy the minds and spirits of those who consider them closely."[19]

In New Spain the criollo poet Antonio Saavedra Guzmán, author of *El peregrino indiano* (1599), claimed as his goal the preservation of the memory of the deeds of Hernán Cortés and the other conquistadores.[20] At the same time, he offered such detailed descriptions of Nahua customs that he felt the need to explain his exuberance on the subject: He had been born in New Spain, and his knowledge of native Mexican society was due to having been municipal civil administrator (*corregidor*) of Zacatecas, "where no historian has been" [donde ningún historiador ha auido]. Thus, he found it difficult to omit the discussion of matters with which he was so familiar. At the same time, he stopped short of relating in detail the Indians' rites and laws because, he said, being infinite in number, they would tire the reader.[21] The reasons for his silence and that of others on native rituals will become apparent in the following section. All these efforts to explain or explain away what the epic authors had done in writing about Amerindian actions and customs reveal that the prescriptions about the choice of subject matter and the tone adopted to treat it were challenged by the presence of the new topic, even though the literary response was to cast the new actors into familiar molds of representation.

In his *Philosophia antigua poética* (1596), Alonso López Pinciano prescribed for the successful epic poem the requirement of verisimilitude, which mandated that the customs and usages of the lands being portrayed be preserved. However, in the case of portraying characters the likes of which European readers had never seen, artistic verisimilitude corresponded not to the relationship between the world represented and the artistic representation, but rather to that between the artistic representation and the anticipated expectations of the reader. (This principle pervades this study; see the section, "Chivalric Fiction and the Narratives of the Conquest of America," below, and chapter II.) Thus, when the criollo writer Pedro de Oña attempted to maintain linguistic verisimilitude in his *Arauco domado* (1596) through the use of certain lexical items of the indigenous language, he took special precautions to clarify his intentions. In his prologue, he stated that his reader should look upon the incorporation of Amerindian terms into his poetic narration not as "simple barbarisms" that might shock the reader, but rather as the result of his desire to be true to his subject matter, seeking artistic correspondence between thematic substance and its formal expression.[22] As he pointed to the congruence of theme and artistic form in the linguistic portrayal of the Araucanian warrior, he appealed to the epic requirement for verisimilitude, although he feared that in this case, honoring the principle of verisimilitude could likely be misunderstood by the European reader, who would see it as an unwarranted display of offensive barbarism.

Although both poets and historians took considerable care to explain and justify their presentation of the Amerindian, the history of colonial publication and suppression shows that their efforts met different results. Poetry did not triumph over history from the viewpoint of intellectual production, for the missionary ethnographers were at work on descriptions of various Amerindian cultural groups, starting with Fray Román Pané's report on the Antillian natives from the second voyage of Columbus,[23] and picking up momentum with the establishment of the Franciscan mission in New Spain early in the sixteenth century. Nevertheless, the most frequently published and widely circulating works on America over the entire century were the epic poems of conquest. The impressive number of editions of Ercilla's epic of the Araucanian wars, the writings of others on the same subject, and the epic poems of the Mexican conquest (seldom read today) attest to this importance.[24] From the standpoint of publication and circulation, the abundance of poetic idealizations of Indians is sharply contrasted by the dearth of ethnographic descriptions.

Why did the fictionalization of the Amerindian produce a more acceptable, less controversial figure than did the attempts at documentary description? First, because the formulaic prescriptions for epic characterization allowed for only a limited number of attributes, the reader's interpretation of indigenous characters and events was easily controlled in advance. As López Pinciano had observed, the poet constructed the epic imitation through the creation of literary personae other than and including himself.[25] In the epic, the characterization was controlled not only through the constructed characters themselves but also through the interpretation of characters and events offered by the author's interventions as narrator or protagonist (or both) in his own poetic composition.

In relation to poetry, the discourse of the ethnographic historian was not bound by narrow formulae of characterization; as a result, the readers' interpretation was virtually impossible to anticipate, if not to control. Acosta, for example, was concerned that reading accounts of Amerindian customs would be condemned as being a waste of time equivalent to that spent reading the *libros de caballerías.*[26] Acosta's claim that the reader might be bored or discard the information as frivolous hid a contrary concern: that the reader would find these exotic descriptions all too fascinating. Barco Centenera had remarked, after all, about the ecstatic state of mind ["éxtasi"] that the reader might experience on learning about these ferociously belligerent peoples ["gentes belicosíssimas"].

Furthermore, poetic teleology served the purpose of the colonialist outlook that favored the hierarchical relationship of domination of the conquered peoples (see chapter 4).[27] That is, the epic formulations showed the Amerindian as victim, either vanquished and destroyed on the battlefield or Christianized and executed in the public plaza. The celebration of these autochthonous lords and warriors' heroic values was never threatening because they always ended up either docile or dead; even in the case of the poems on Araucania the wars raged on long after the poems had ended them.[28] On the other hand, the ethnographic histories wrote about Amerindian survival: the persistent presence of Amerindian societies and, explicitly, their tabu customs. The documentary or ethnographic accounts, from Pané and Oviedo onward, contained reports of unsanctioned sexual activity and rites and customs that gave themselves over to excesses often described as diabolical. Such reports would have been highly undesirable from the viewpoint of state and church, which judged the veneer of civilization in Europe to be a very thin one. European readers had to be protected from these accounts which, unlike the "fables and fictions" of the books of chivalry, told of things that were fantastic *and also (presumably) true*.[29]

For the period in question, that is, from the 1540s through the first decades of the seventeenth century, the Inquisition's attention was turned away from its first-phase preoccupation with formal heresy and the racial minorities; nearly two-thirds of those detained by the Holy Office were ordinary Catholic Spaniards. The largest and most important category of offenses tried by the Inquisition in this period was that of "propositions," verbal assaults which were of concern for the intentions behind them and their implicit danger to faith and morals. The most common charges included blasphemous oaths, sexual advances made to young girls during religious processions, obscene references to Saint Mary, and anticlerical sentiments or actions.[30]

A major sphere of inquisitorial activity concerned sexual behavior. From the punishment for "simple fornication" (voluntary intercourse between two unmarried adults) to the regulation of matrimony and celibacy, from the control over the lay population to that of the clergy, sexual behavior was a matter of considerable concern. Sodomy (*pecado contra natura*) was the most significant prosecutorial charge in the area of sexual practices; from the beginning of the sixteenth century, the tribunal of Aragon punished it, irrespective of the absence of heresy, whereas in Castile it was punishable in the civil courts.[31] Sodomy was the sexual practice most consistently attributed to the Amerindians. The first editions of Cieza de León's *Primera parte de la crónica del Perú* (Seville, 1553) vividly illustrate the controversial, sensational content of the chronicles of the Indies. This repertory of woodcuts presents two pictorial themes: foundations of Spanish cities in the Indies and the "diabolical" customs of South American coastal and Andean peoples, which included the sacrifice of war prisoners, wrenching the heart from the body (a Mexican theme), the veneration of an emerald globe, natives depicted in conversation with the devil (repeated eight times throughout Cieza's *Primera parte*), and the

FIGURE 20. Ancient giants caught in the act of sodomy by an avenging, sword-wielding angel. Pedro de Cieza de León, *Primera parte de la chrónica del Perú*. Seville: M. de Montesdoca, 1553. The John Carter Brown Library at Brown University.

image reproduced here: A divine punishment being meted out against the ancients of this land (supposedly giants) caught in the act of sodomy (fig. 20).[32] All in all, the fact that blasphemy, or disrespect for sacred things, and "simple fornication" were dominant preoccupations of the Inquisition at this time suggests that books on Amerindian customs would come under fire for their potential threat to faith and morals. At the same time, editions like Cieza's exploited the sensationalizing, exoticizing themes designed to appeal to readers' interests.

Finally, the ethnographic histories were the most authentic forum of the debates on the rights of Spanish conquest and evangelization in the

Indies insofar as they took seriously the classification of the Amerindians in the hierarchy of cultural typology. José de Acosta's *Historia natural y moral de las Indias* stands out for its attempt to "crush the common and ignorant contempt in which the Indians are held by Europeans who think that these people lack the qualities of rational and prudent men."[33] In a very real sense, Las Casas's *Apologética historia sumaria* (1559) was a much more radical work than his *Brevísima relación de la destrucción de las Indias* (see chapter 3). In the *Brevísima relación*, Las Casas simply condemned Spanish conquering practices; in the *Apologética*, he explored the ways in which Western humanity could (and should) come to understand other cultures and societies in light of itself and its own ancient pagan legacies.[34] In contrast, the epic poems, however much they celebrated and defended the honor of the conquered and therefore glorified them, did so within a typology of behavior that was their own. The epic poets did not really entertain notions of cultural variation; differences were fictionally dissolved in displays of chivalric exotica or in representations of a conventional savagery. In contrast, ironically, while Las Casas, Acosta, Sahagún, and others sought to find in the Amerindian the evidence of universal human reason in which they believed, they could not do so without bringing to mind that condition of cultural strangeness, even as those differences were understood to be, in terms of Scholastic philosophy, accidental variants, that is, not substantive and therefore not deviating from the traits essential to the quality of being human.[35]

The self-conscious efforts of historians to justify the inclusion of the Amerindian as a historical topic and of epic poets to generate interest in their accounts of Amerindian customs point to a number of accommodations that had to be made between genre and subject matter. Historiographic practice was broadened, while epic poetry retained its narrow limits, molding the new subject matter to the requirements of its generic conventions. In both cases, literary practices were supported or suppressed insofar as they served or subverted political and ideological programs. The dangers of the ethnographic history consisted of its freedom from producing formulaic portrayals of its objects. The suppression during this period of some of the greatest works of this type underscores the point. Meanwhile, the overdetermination of the Amerindians' characterization in poetry and the frequent publication of such works assured that the sanctioned discussion of American humanity would be noncontroversial, that it would be fictionalized before it was described.[36]

AMERINDIAN CULTURE AND CENSORSHIP IN SAHAGÚN AND ACOSTA

The contrasts cited between the poetic and historiographic formulations of Amerindian culture suggest a literary paradox: The representation of the Amerindian as new subject matter reversed the accepted wisdom of the period that historical truth was to be valued over fiction, when fiction, that is, was defined not as the purveyor of edifying, universal truths but as the vehicle for improbable and impossible fantasies. Historical truth served the faith and protected morals, and fancy served only vanity and offered useless tales that were harmful because, at worst, they actively corrupted morals and, at best, they turned the idle away from good reading.[37] Yet where the Amerindian was the historical subject, truth was dangerous, as the review of works censured and suppressed and of those approved and published will make clear.

Censorship and its specific rationales are difficult to deal with because the documentation on works denied publication is almost impossible to uncover. Sahagún's case, in which the reasoning behind the Council of the Indies' confiscation of his work was never stated officially, is typical.[38] In addition, the royal decrees on books suppressed or withdrawn from circulation are equally unenlightening; they state the ordinance, not the reasons for its enactment.[39] Expurgated works offer better clues, if the original versions can be located and identified, as in the discovery in the 1980s of the original manuscript of Acosta's *De procuranda indorum salute* (1588). In fact, expurgated works offer the best information (if the expurgations can be read) as to the criteria employed in specific instances of censorship, as in the case of Fray Jerónimo Román y Zamora's *Repúblicas del mundo* (1575, 1595) or Fray Martín de Murúa's *Historia general del Perú* (1613).[40]

The comparison of contemporaneous works dealing with the same topic, when one is suppressed and the other published, can suggest internal, textual reasons for the difference in their editorial fates. Although this approach takes into account only one type of factor involved in censorship, it is nevertheless revealing. Sahagún's *Historia general de las cosas de*

Nueva España and Acosta's *Historia natural y moral de las Indias* provide an illuminating contrast in this respect. Although they differ in length and in the detail of their discussions, both write about Nahua ritual practices and religion, and both present native Nahua accounts of the conquest of Mexico. Each represents an extraordinary intellectual achievement: linguistic and ethnographic in the case of Sahagún, philosophical and theoretical in that of Acosta. Both experienced rigorous censorship of their writings, though with opposite results. Sahagún's major work went unpublished until the nineteenth century, while Acosta's enjoyed many printings in Spanish and translations into European languages in the decades following its completion.[41]

Obviously, the accounts of Amerindian ritual life were the most controversial, and both authors used the same strategy to justify their discussions of these topics. Sahagún and Acosta engaged in a double move: they suggested terms of comparison—*libros de caballerías* and *fábulas y ficciones*—against which the reader might be tempted to measure their accounts, and then told them not to do so. In other words, anticipating that their descriptions might seem fantastic and interpreting for their readers the content of native Mexican beliefs as false, both authors suggested and then dismissed terms of comparison which the reader should *not* use to interpret their writings.

Sahagún referred to the beliefs of the Mexicans as "fables and fictions" as he began his book 3, "On the origin of the gods" [Del principio que tuvieron los Dioses], by citing Saint Augustine on the true value of reading false tales: "The divine Augustine did not consider it useless or vain to consider the fabulous theology of the pagans, in the sixth book of *The City of God,* because, as he says, by knowing the vain fables and fictions that the gentiles had regarding their false gods, they [the Christians] could easily make them understand that they were not gods, and that they [the false gods] could not provide anything of value to the rational being. For this purpose, this third book presents the fables and fictions that these people had concerning their gods, because, upon understanding the vanity that they took for faith regarding their lying gods, they will come more easily, by means of the doctrine of the gospel, to know the true god."[42]

Acosta made reference, in a similar context, to the romances of chivalry: "That which has been said is sufficient to understand the care which the Indians exercised in serving and honoring their idols and the devil, which is one and the same thing. Because to tell everything that is contained in this business is an infinite task and of little use, and even the material that has been presented may seem to some to be of little or no use, that is, that it seems like wasting time in reading the nonsense that the books of chivalry pretend. But if these [skeptics] reflect carefully upon it, they will find it to be a very different matter, and that it can be beneficial, for very many reasons, to be informed about the rites and ceremonies that the Indians performed."[43] Exploiting the effective safety zone drawn around one of the more notorious types of fiction, the chivalric—frivolous and useless perhaps but passing censors and enjoying wide circulation[44] —Acosta here downplayed the "satanic" and pagan aspects of the practices he described in a double move, first, by equating them to fiction-as-chivalric-nonsense, thus rendering them harmless, and then by insisting that knowledge of them was nevertheless useful.

As if to defuse and avoid any conflict over the volatile potential of the subjects about which they were writing, both Acosta and Sahagún associated them with the lack of value often attributed to fiction (as fantastic tales or popular lore), which suppressed their danger and rendered them innocent. By initially scoffing at these "fables and fictions," they denied their potency. (Cabeza de Vaca recreates a similar strategy in his account of the fabled being Mala Cosa in his *Naufragios* [see chapter 10]). What Sahagún and Acosta offered is a justification that goes something like this: For the missionary readership, there is genuine, positive value in writing true accounts about false beliefs because it is a fundamental step in finding effective ways to evangelize the native peoples of America. For the lay readership, there is genuine, positive value in reading true accounts about false beliefs because thus the Christian reader is reminded to be grateful for the invitation, already received, to his own salvation.

The contrast between Sahagún and Acosta with regard to their success at publication is pertinent to understanding the dynamics of colonial writing practices. Some external factors should be noted first. In the dedication of his work to Fray Rodrigo de Sequera and, more completely, in the prologue to book 2, Sahagún described his problems with censorship and confiscation within the Franciscan order. He told about the prohibition against receiving further assistance from his native scribes and collaborators, the subsequent confiscation and reading of his writings by prominent members of the Franciscan order in New Spain, the eventual return of his manuscripts to him, and the preparation of the Spanish translation to accompany the original Nahuatl text to be sent to the Council of the Indies at the request of its president, Juan de Ovando. Subsequently, in 1577, all of Sahagún's papers were confiscated by royal decree.[45]

Acosta's encounter with ecclesiastical and state censorship, not with regard to his *Historia natural y moral de las Indias,* but in reference to his controversial treatise on evangelization in America, *De procuranda indo- rum salute,* is also pertinent.[46] Acosta's work, which was written in light of a collective effort by a commission of priests and theologians to revise missionary methods in Peru, was intended to present a program of mis- sionary action based on the evaluation of specific historical experience in the Peruvian viceroyalty. Acosta's description and interpretation of the violent conquest of Peru as well as his treatment of the native population at the hands of European colonialists provoked the Jesuit general Claudio Aquaviva to demand careful and repeated reviews of the original manu- script. The process, begun in 1577 and not concluded until 1588, reduced the work from a treatise on colonial ethics rooted in a historical perspec- tive into a merely prescriptive guide to missionary pedagogy. Removed was every single reference or critical judgment that could harm, in the opinion of the censors, the prestige of Spain in Europe. Aquaviva's sub- mission of the work to Castilian state censorship, done out of prudence and political expediency, meant that the work was ultimately molded to the exigencies of Spanish politics in its European context. Subsequently and in contrast, Acosta's *Historia natural y moral de las Indias,* which shared with Sahagún's work the effort to present the viewpoint of Nahua informants on the Spanish conquest, survived the perils of censorship intact a year after the publication of the *De procuranda.* The *Historia* was reprinted several times during the following decades.[47]

The question arises as to whether censorship, state and ecclesiastical, was primarily concerned with the portrayal of Spanish actions in relation to Amerindian societies, or whether it was also occupied with the presen- tation of Indian societies and cultures in their own right. Both Juan Friede, in his 1959 study of censorship of books on America, and the editors of the original version of Acosta's *De procuranda* in 1984, demon- strate persuasively that state and ecclesiastical censorship, despite its avowed goal of protecting faith and morals, was concerned, in practice, with emphatically political issues. However, a comparison of Acosta's published *Historia* with the sequestered and suppressed Sahagún treatise reveals that the discussion and analysis of Amerindian culture were in and of themselves problematic.

Striking at the outset is the fact that Sahagún let the Amerindian voices speak for themselves, while Acosta presented a carefully framed account in which Indian testimony was presented only occasionally and always indirectly. Although Sahagún's invisible presence in the Nahuatl accounts cannot be overlooked, the subtlety of the interpenetration of the voices of Sahagún and his Amerindian informants has been the object of ongoing attention.[48] Nevertheless, the *illusion* of the bald, unembellished Nahuatl account prevails, even in its Spanish translation, in which the controlling voice of Sahagún must also be acknowledged. Another difference in approach between Acosta and Sahagún concerns their assumptions about their readers. Sahagún assumed his readers would understand that reading about Amerindian culture was a valid and even important pursuit. Acosta assumed nothing, and he was not only explicit but emphatic and occasionally strident on the reasons the "Christian reader" would find his work edifying.

Sahagún and Acosta were men of different generations and different experiences. Sahagún was active in the Franciscan mission in New Spain from the 1530s, when optimism about evangelization ran high and the pro-Amerindian position in state and church establishments was common.[49] This was the period in which Las Casas exercised enormous influence, at court and abroad, published his treatises in 1552–1553 in Seville, and obstructed the publication of works by those he considered prejudicial to the Indians' cause.[50] The Jesuit Acosta, however, came to the mission field when the evangelization of the native populations was acknowledged to be a much more elusive goal, when European and colonial attitudes had hardened against the Amerindians and when the writings of Las Casas and others on America and its inhabitants were ordered sequestered by royal decree (see chapters 3 and 4). Within this context, the first chapter of Acosta's book 7, entitled "That it is important to be informed about the deeds of the Indians, especially the Mexicans" [Que importa tener noticia de los hechos de los indios, mayormente de los mexicanos], begins with an elaborate defense of the utility and merit of reading about these peoples, acknowledging the low opinion of them generally held abroad. As a Jesuit and key figure in the Peruvian missionary church, Acosta was involved in local, provincial, and papal affairs. In the same decade, the indefatigable Franciscan Sahagún was devotedly continuing his research and writing on native Nahua culture, even as his previous works were taken from him. Living under the Franciscan Rule, his official obligations were confined mostly to managing affairs internal to the order.[51] The difference in their perspectives, evident in the examples of their work that follow, should reveal why, in the 1580s, their works represented, respectively, exemplary cases of publication and prohibition.

The treatment of the subject of human sacrifice is illustrative. In book 2 of the *Historia general de las cosas de Nueva España,* Sahagún devoted some twenty chapters and fourteen separate accounts to the topic. These three dozen accounts he gave are all narratives that seemingly have been recorded just as given in the oral reporting of his informants. Such an unembellished presentation would perhaps be acceptable, if Sahagún had framed the accounts carefully. The prologues to each of his twelve books were the opportunity he often took to do so, as in book 3, cited above, when he introduced the fables and fictions that the Indians believed about their own origins. On the odious topic of human sacrifice and ritual cannibalism, however, Sahagún's fatal flaw was in making no such disclaimers; as discussed earlier, he chose the prologue to book 2 as the very place to describe in detail the obstacles that the Franciscan order had presented in the writing and confiscation of his work; the short text ("Al sincero lector") simply outlined some technical details of the Mexican calendar.

Sahagún assumed that the human sacrifices he described were so obviously diabolical that they needed no editorial comment: "There is no need, in this second book, to present any refutation of the idolatrous ceremonies that are told here, because in their own expression they are so cruel and so inhuman that anyone hearing about them will be filled with horror and dread; and thus I do no more than simply transcribe the account to the letter."[52] The problem here is not only Sahagún's failure to present a moral commentary, but also his assumption that the "horror y espanto" produced in the reader would be automatically a moral reaction and not only an esthetic response. As already discussed, several poets and historians exploited that potential. Gómara called his readers' attention to the "very strange religion and cruel customs of the Mexicans," and Ovalle promised to tell of "extraordinary things unique" to the land of Chile. In any case, the accounts that immediately follow Sahagún's statement coolly describe the sacrifice of children, their mutilated bodies being cooked and consumed, and the sacrifice of adult war captives, whose bodies are subsequently dismembered and their flesh cooked and devoured.[53] Only at this point in a long series of such gruesome chapters does the author intervene with another commentary, "Exclamación del autor," in which he cautions that the reader should attribute to Satan, not to the parents who sacrificed their children, the greatest blame for these inhuman practices.[54] Acosta gave similar accounts of Mexican ritual life: chapter 20 of his book 5 details the practices described above, and the narration ends with the bodies of war captives, hearts removed, rolling down the steps of the temple, to be caught, carried away, and eaten by their warrior captors.[55]

The significant difference between Sahagún and Acosta is not what is said but how it is presented. First of all, Acosta devoted three short chapters to the description of Mexican sacrifice, whereas Sahagún had devoted about three dozen. Second, the accounts Acosta presented were carefully couched in a series of scriptural texts and cultural comparisons (chapter 19), vigorous arguments to the effect that the Indians were now repulsed by these traditional practices (chapter 22), and a lengthy sermon on the spiritual good the reader would reap from reading about Amerindian superstitions and practices (chapter 31).

On the particularly sensitive topic of the conquest of Mexico, Acosta and Sahagún prepared for their readers' potential reactions in strikingly different ways. Acosta opened his book 7, fifteen chapters of which narrated native versions of the conquest of Mexico, with an emphatic defense of the value of studying the history of the Amerindians and an attack on the foolish scorn ("necio desprecio") in which Europeans held them (see above). Acosta deliberately exploited the prospect of intellectual and esthetic pleasure as well as moral edification that the reader could experience on reading about the origins, ways of being, and prosperous and adverse times of non-European peoples.[56]

In spite of the immense bulk of Sahagún's native accounts in contrast to the relative brevity of those of Acosta, the most pronounced difference between them is the continual interweaving by Acosta of his own providentialist interpretation of conquest history with the indirectly presented native testimony. Besides such commentary, he carefully points out that while the Spanish could be faulted for cruelty during the conquest, the Amerindians were also to be criticized for the commission of atrocities. In doing so, he deliberately distanced himself from polemicists such as Las Casas, whom he does not name.[57] In contrast, Sahagún's masterful and monumental orchestration of native accounts of the Mexican conquest provides the reader no such filter through which to view its particular contours. The result is the poignant account of the death of a civilization and a blinding summary of devastation and destruction. If Sahagún's work was censured for political reasons by the Council of the Indies, it was surely for his Nahua rendition of the history of the conquest, which lacked Acosta's elaborate and thorough providentialist framing.

Sahagún's approach resulted in the "burial" of his writing labors "underneath the earth and even under ashes" [debajo de tierra y aún debajo de la ceniza], as he had described the situation in 1575.[58] The suppression of his work is the clearest evidence of the crisis that bringing Amerindian culture into the forum of public discourse provoked. Apart from presenting apparently unmediated accounts about "barbaric" peoples and narrations prejudicial to the self-interest of the Castilian state, the portrayal of native customs, not only in Spanish but also in Nahuatl, would constitute, if disseminated, a danger in keeping alive and fomenting pagan ways.

Sahagún's, Acosta's, and by extension all ethnographic historians' writings constituted a challenge not to the genre of historiography itself but rather to the cultural and political uses of historiography. This becomes particularly obvious in Sahagún's case because of his use of the Nahuatl language as the medium of literary expression. Taking the testimony of his native informants and collaborators, his *Historia*, as has been mentioned, was originally set down in Nahuatl with a Spanish translation added later. Placing his use of Nahuatl in the context of the controversy about the use of "infidel" languages reveals the cultural and political stakes involved in his efforts.

In Sahagún's time, the native Mexican codices had been systematically destroyed by the first archbishop of Mexico, Fray Juan de Zumárraga, and, according to period sources, the native Mexican lords took it upon themselves to voluntarily destroy codices they owned, out of fear of being charged with idolatry for possessing them.[59] These acts of effacement occurred at the same time the use of the Arabic language was outlawed in

Spain in order to control, politically and spiritually, the Morisco population and books in Arabic were sought out and destroyed for the same
reason.[60] There was a growing official tendency against the practice of
writing about non-Christian, non-European cultures in their original languages. The fatal connection seen between such spiritual traditions and
the languages in which they were conceptualized and practiced would
lead ultimately, in 1596, to the formulation of a legal project, presented to
the Council of the Indies, which would abolish the use of the native
languages of the Americas. Juan de Solórzano Pereira, in his *Política
indiana* (1629), forcefully pressed the argument for a linguistic politics
that would ban the use of Amerindian languages, and he took exception to
the "dangerous" plan adopted by Acosta and his colleagues at the church's
Third Provincial Council of Lima of 1583–1584, which published doctrinal
Christian texts in Quechua and Aymara.[61] No doubt benefiting from an
appreciation of the difficulties and debates entailed in producing religious
works in Amerindian languages, Acosta stayed safely away from their use
in his *Historia natural y moral de las Indias*.

Acosta's editorial triumph is registered in the dedication of his *Historia natural y moral de las Indias* to the infanta, Doña Isabel Clara Eugenia.
In a bold and revealing statement about the necessity and pleasure of
studying barbarous peoples ("gentes bárbaras"), he deftly linked the desire for indulgent entertainment with the need for responsible instruction. His statement suggests the delicate balance that (published) authors
achieved between serving state prerogatives and appealing to individual
proclivities in the context of the stringent royal policy of monitoring and
censoring works written about America and on Amerindian topics.[62] His
use of the literary commonplace ("utilidad y provecho") has the special
resonance of an authorial coup in combining moral function with the
esthetic excitement produced by the exotic: "But because the knowledge
and speculation about natural things, especially if they are noteworthy
and rare, creates a natural pleasure and delight in refined temperaments,
and the information about strange customs and deeds also provides pleasure with their novelty, I consider that for Your Highness it will serve as a
chaste and useful entertainment, providing the opportunity to contemplate the works that the Almighty has created in the machine of this
world, especially in those regions that we call the Indies, which, because
of being newly found lands, they offer much upon which to reflect, and

because of being about new vassals that the most high God gave to the crown of Spain, their knowledge is neither extraneous nor irrelevant."[63] But, against this background, what of the still unsettling term of comparison Acosta used for reading about Indian customs: the impossible tales of the romances of chivalry?

CHIVALRIC FICTION AND THE NARRATIVES OF THE CONQUEST OF AMERICA

Since Irving A. Leonard published his *Books of the Brave* in 1949, the subject of the relationship between the Spanish conquistador and his possible literary inspiration in the books of chivalric romance has been a seductive topic.[64] With the Spanish translation of *Books of the Brave* in 1953, the reprinting of the original English-language text in 1964 and more recently in 1992, and the reissue of the Spanish translation in 2006, the circulation of this highly attractive idea has been universal. Unfortunately, the notion that popular fiction inspired the deeds of the conquistadores has been as undemonstrable as it has been appealing. So Leonard himself admitted, and so other readers have observed.[65] The idea has survived as an intriguing piece of intuition, although many generations of readers seem to have accepted it as an established cultural historical fact.

The single statement by Bernal Díaz del Castillo that inspired the notion that popular literature influenced the attitudes and actions of sixteenth-century Spaniards makes it possible to reorient its significance. Here Bernal Díaz appears to us not only as a soldier, but also as a writer and reader, as we saw in chapters 6 and 7. Recalling his first sight of Tenochtitlán some thirty to forty years after the fact, Bernal remarks,

> The next day, in the morning, we arrived at a broad causeway, and continued our march toward Iztapalapa, and when we saw so many cities and villages built in the water and other great towns on dry land and that straight and level causeway going towards Mexico, we were amazed and said that it was like the enchantments they tell of in the legend of Amadís, on account of the great towers and *cues* [temples] and buildings rising from the water, and all built of masonry. And some of our soldiers even asked whether some of the things we saw were not a dream? It is

not to be wondered at that I here write it down in this manner, for there is so much to think over that I do not know how to describe it, seeing things as we did that have never been heard of or seen before, not even dreamed about.[66]

The evidence suggests that chivalric fiction inspired neither Bernal Díaz's actions of soldiering nor his act of narrating. Instead, they become a solution to his search for a way to communicate the magnificence and splendor of his first sight of Tenochtitlán. His statement reveals that the books of chivalry stood as a common reference point by which the sixteenth-century Spanish reader could make meaning of the account of a place unseen (America) as given to him by another reader (the reader-cum-writer, Bernal Díaz) who shared similar literary cultural experiences.

Bernal Díaz's strategic use of chivalric fiction is confirmed by his additional references to the *Amadises*. On more than one occasion, he complains about the seemingly infinite number of battles he had to describe to account for the ninety-three-day siege of Tenochtitlán. Although his readers were surely tired of reading about them, he says, it was nevertheless necessary to rehearse how and when those battles had occurred. In this aside to his readers on the problems of writing history, he mentions that he had considered organizing the narration so that each encounter would occupy a separate chapter. But this, it seemed to him, would be an endless task and, even worse, would make his work seem like an *Amadís*.[67] Here the reference to chivalric tales is clearly negative. Is Bernal Díaz saying that a narration à la Amadís would produce an overlong account, putting the reader to sleep with the tiresome description of battle after battle? or, even worse, that the reader might thus suspend belief in this true account, sentencing it to guilt by association, if it followed the narrative model of chivalric fiction? Both questions can be answered in the affirmative, as the testimony of other chroniclers confirms.

Pedro de Castañeda Nájera, for example, who wrote some twenty years after the fact about the Coronado expedition of 1540–1542, in which he had participated as a soldier, remarked in reference to the exploits of Captain Juan Gallego and the twenty companions who went with him, "We shall tell them in this chapter in order that those who, in the future, may read and talk about them may have a reliable author on whom to depend, an author who does not write fables, like some things we read nowadays in books of chivalry. Were it not for the fables of enchantments with which they are laden, there are events that have happened recently in these parts to our Spaniards in conquests and clashes with the natives that surpass, as deeds of amazement, not only the aforesaid books but even the ones written about the twelve peers of France."[68]

The phrase "fables of enchantments with which they are laden" suggests an a posteriori gloss of the fantastic onto the narration, which would prevent the reader from appreciating the historical event. In his *Historia general y natural de las Indias*, Gonzalo Fernández de Oviedo voiced the same uneasiness: "After all, I do not recount the nonsense of the books of chivalry, nor such matters as are dependent upon them."[69] Oviedo, himself the author of a chivalric romance, *Don Claribalte*, was genuinely concerned lest his readers impose the expectations of fantasy on reading the narration of history.[70]

Bernal Díaz and the others faced a common problem, one that their references to the novels of chivalry bring into sharper focus. They were writing about events and topics that seemed fantastic: great numbers of battles, horrifying evidence of human sacrifice, landscapes never before seen, and even real-life "enchanters" (shamans) (see chapter 10). They wished to articulate that hitherto-unseen dimension accurately in order to be truthful to their understanding of their experience. At the same time, they (Bernal Díaz in particular) wanted to exploit the unique elements of what they saw in order to engage their readers' interest. Hence, they were caught in the dilemma of producing faithful accounts that would be appealing, but for which they and their readers had no common points of reference. Bernal Díaz summed it up best in reflecting on his description of Tenochtitlán, quoted above: "It is not to be wondered at that I here write it down in this manner, for there is so much to think over that I do not know how to describe it, seeing things as we did that had never been heard of or seen before, not even dreamed about." Bernal Díaz, Castañeda, and Oviedo all suggest that the comparison of their writings with the books of chivalry was inevitable. Their point, however, was that fiction paled by comparison with what they themselves had witnessed, that the historical deeds and experiences they described *exceeded* the only possible model for comparison that existed in their readers' imaginations.

In contrast, the epic poets accepted the chivalric representation, using it to dramatize the actions of both conquistadores and Amerindians. Alonso de Ercilla, among others, superimposed the world of medieval chivalry on that of the Araucanian warriors even as he described them in terms of unheard-of, animal-like ferocity in battle. He resorted to the chivalric formulation not because he saw the Araucanians as chivalric heroes but because he needed a language of common reference with his readers to communicate his admiration of the Araucanian cultural values of liberty, courage, and the refusal to be conquered.

The question that remains is why the books of chivalry were chosen by some chroniclers as the common (negative) reference in writing about the New World, and why chivalry in general was emulated by the epic poets in the creation of the figure of the Amerindian. First, thanks to the enormous popularity of the books of chivalry throughout the sixteenth century,[71] as well as the fact that they were defended as exemplary works by some and condemned as frivolous and harmful by others,[72] the chroniclers could have it both ways with regard to this cultural reference point. That is, they had at their disposal a double code: Like advocates of the chivalric tale, they could celebrate the military values of medieval *caballería* and extol things unheard of and unseen; like the moralists, they could reject the idea of the fictional tale, not because their own representations were immoral but because, unlike the books of chivalry, they were true. This is the point at which the *libros de caballerías* served more as a trap than as a useful cultural and literary reference. The subjects of magic, sorcery, and superstition, which were the stock ingredients of the chivalric fiction that gave the moralists reasons to decry their pernicious influence, had their counterpart, or so it could seem to the reader, in the ethnographic descriptions of Amerindian ritual practice.

One of the reasons for the popular appeal of chivalric fiction was its fascination with magic. Recent studies have attributed the editorial success of the romances of chivalry in the sixteenth century to the attraction that their chivalric ideals held for an increasingly urban, courtly aristocratic male readership.[73] At the same time and apart from that factor, the other major engaging element was magic. It was the enchanted atmosphere of the lands visited by the Amadises and Palmerines and the enchanters and magicians who inhabited them that held readers under their spell.[74] Furthermore, the acts and feats of wizardry and magic in the books of chivalry were often regarded by readers as faithful records of actual fact.[75]

Magic was a vast topic in literature, the arts, theology, the sciences, and medicine of the period, and it could be held to be "good or bad, or white or black, that is, beneficent or evil in its effects"; its positive manifestations could be regarded as an aspect of the supernatural.[76] At the same time, magic and witchcraft were considered extremely dangerous when presented in published treatises on the subject. Indexed by the Inquisition were all erudite treatises and popular works on magic and witchcraft; practice of the same was widely punished in sixteenth-century Spain.[77]

Within this cultural context, the ethnographic works on Amerindian cultures were no doubt considered dangerous precisely for the description of native customs and their potential assault, therefore, on faith and morals. Divinations and other practices attributed to sorcery and superstition were commonly regarded as inspired by the devil. Against the European background of cultural referents, it is not surprising that works such as Sahagún's were not merely never granted license to be printed but were in fact confiscated from their author's possession. The expression of the period attitude that best summarizes the implicit connection between the ethnographic account and "lying and immoral fictions" is found in Fray Luis de León's *De los nombres de Cristo* (1591). Without referring explicitly to the books of chivalry, he complained about the pernicious effect of reading vain and harmful books "at all hours, at all times": they contributed to the contemporary degeneration of customs and morals, the root and cause of which were to be found in deceitful fictions, which smacked of heathenism and disbelief in Christianity.[78]

At the same time, the epic poets took advantage of the appeal that chivalric formulations held for readers as they dissolved into fiction the dangerous specter of Amerindian humanity. Although it did not conceal the spectacle of sometimes horrific military conquest, the epic dramatization of the Amerindian offered an alternate interpretation. The escape into fantasy and the reaffirmation of chivalric values addressed the readers' simultaneous and contradictory desires to flee from harsher realities and at the same time come to grips with them. The Christian caballeros of the medieval chronicles and the knights errant of popular fiction served the interpretative effort of bringing under a single purview of control the historical past and the uncertain future. It was at once a political and linguistic phenomenon: to make the European (Spanish Reconquest) past rule the European-in-America (Spanish colonial) present and to establish a language of external reference which could communicate the natural and human wonders of the New World. In this light, the celebration of the heroic Age of Reconquest becomes the strategy by which to read and interpret the present, rather than to reproduce the past as such. (Bernal Díaz's engagement with chivalric fiction is resonant here.) The epic poets who wrote about America, and the ethnographic writers too, deliberately exploited the chivalric tale in creating and presenting their own literary efforts. While moralists condemned the books of chivalry, the writers who focused on the Americas took advantage of the very features—novelty, exoticism, adventure—that made those tales appealing. This was the site of the influence of chivalric fiction on the writings about the New World. Not a filter through which participants interpreted their own historical experience, popular fiction instead made possible a strategy that employed a common and attractive cultural referent; through this means, author and reader could take new sightings that facilitated the literary exchanges of writer and reader contemplating the vastness of the New World and its myriad peoples.

Fray Fernando de Valverde and his literary dilemma of how to bring the Colla Indians into the poetic composition that was to celebrate the triumphs of the Christian faith serves as the literary expression of the moral challenges faced by the royal court and the viceregal audiencias at the time. After a century and a half of European colonization in the Americas, Valverde acknowledged the fundamental and insurmountable problem that stood at the heart of colonial-era writings: The introduction of the Amerindian, not only as a new literary topic but also as a cultural and human entity, confounded not only the prescriptions of poetics, but also the existing philosophical formulations and juridical theories. A full century after the conquest of Peru, Valverde's Inca prince, Yupanqui Toca, is lost in contemplation and bewilderment. Writing about Amerindians, their cultures, and their experience under Spanish rule was a problem that brought the poets and historians of the period up short. But Spanish colonial-era literary production was concerned not simply with finding the appropriate language to describe the New World's peoples; it was constituted by the complex and contradictory impulses that stood inside and outside the writings themselves and that sought to address and answer the questions produced by the polemics of political (and literary) possession.

CHAPTER 9

The Narrative Invention of Gonzalo the Warrior

THE TALE OF GONZALO GUERRERO, or Gonzalo the Warrior, is commonly acclaimed as the first notable mainland instance of "going native" in the Spanish conquest of America. Yet what sort of a case it is remains open to debate since the historical evidence of Gonzalo's experience is all hearsay, and even the name by which this figure is known was a posthumous christening done two decades after last notice was given of him. Gonzalo Guerrero is mostly the collection of tales told and written about him, so it is not as a historical figure but as a dramatization of varied and shifting preoccupations about Spain's role and its settlers in America in the sixteenth and seventeenth centuries that his tale is considered here. The case combines some of the tantalizing, sensationalizing, and dangerous features that were applied to imagining the figure of the Indian (see chapter 8), and it pertains to the larger-than-life, self-perpetuating narrative legacy of a little known figure about whom the historical record contains evidence that is slim, contradictory, and, as noted, entirely based on hearsay. Along with Francisco López de Gómara, Bernal Díaz del Castillo was responsible for the plenitude of fame enjoyed by the shadowy shipwreck victim in the historical writings of the time. The narrative accounts of the story of Gonzalo Guerrero reveal how literary authority can overpower and erase, paradoxically, the lack of historical evidence.

The name of Gonzalo Guerrero was applied to a sailor of uncertain identity, probably from Palos de Moguer in the province of Huelva on the southwestern coast of Spain, who arrived in Yucatán in 1511 as a survivor of shipwreck. He reportedly became a great warrior among the Maya, created the first mestizo family in Yucatán, and refused, when offered, to be rescued when Hernán Cortés's expedition arrived in 1519 en route to its illegal conquest of Mexico. Because of the interpretations that grew up around the case in the 1540s through the 1560s, Gonzalo Guerrero plays a unique role in the polemics of possession. Here the possession is of a new identity and a new life; the polemics appear in the controversial and contradictory representations of what constituted that new life.

Two great questions plagued the minds of the historians and moralists who would retell and reinterpret the tale: Why did this shipwreck survivor refuse to rejoin his countrymen? And what did it mean that he painted and tattooed his body in the style of the Maya, particularly in relation to his refusal to return? An alternative to the second question for some writers was: How did his domestic life among the Maya affect his decision? In all likelihood this former sailor and alleged Maya captain never made *any* decision about returning because he was never found by any Spanish party, but this has proved to be no obstacle to speculation on the matter. The further likelihood is that the failed Spanish attempts to conquer Yucatán were the most significant factor in the arousal of interest in "those who did not come back" and stimulated the recollection and reinvention of such a figure as this Gonzalo.

News of the presumed shipwreck survivor comes from Cortés's expedition of conquest to Mexico in 1519 and the written accounts it generated. Although there was no direct evidence from this sailor to verify his story during his lifetime, in the last thirty years of the twentieth century two contradictory sets of Gonzalo's "memoirs" have been published in Mexico, the second as recently as 1994 by two anthropologists at the Universidad Autónoma de Yucatán under the imprimatur of that university. The stakes of the Gonzalo Guerrero example in identity politics escalated significantly after Tzvetan Todorov brought the tale to an international readership in 1982 in *The Conquest of America*. Indeed, since the mid-1970s, when at least two castings of a statue of Gonzalo Guerrero, his Maya wife, and their mestizo children were erected in Mexico (in Mérida, Yucatán, and Akumal, Quintana Roo) (fig. 21), the debates about today's meanings of the Gonzalo Guerrero experience have proliferated.[1]

If the issue is whether he was a traitor to Castile or a first white-skinned patriot of Mexico is obviously resolved in favor of the latter. The local, essentialist definitions give way to broader themes which are perhaps best expressed in Fernando Savater's presentation of a popular account called "The Disappearance of Gonzalo Guerrero," published by the National Fifth Centenary Commission of Spain in 1992: "Are those who abandon their culture or nation of origin impelled to do it because of historical or personal circumstances? Or do they simply take the opportunity to deny what would have seemed to be their probable destiny? Don't we all have a secret and repressed—sometimes badly repressed—desire to deny our own condition, to elect other ways of being and landscapes that don't seem to correspond to us, to demonstrate that we can better be *who* we are by renouncing *what* we are?"[2] My point in introducing Gonzalo Guerrero in this manner is to emphasize that nothing is known directly about him, that he is as much a source of speculation today (1970s and 1990s memoirs included) as he was in the sixteenth century, and that he is kept alive in no small measure by the tantalizing notion of having seemed to make daring, even thrilling choices about his future.

The imagined existence of this social type hung as a low, dark cloud on the horizon of the ethical and exemplary values of Castilian history and the Spanish version of Roman Catholic orthodoxy, and it is evidenced by the persistence with which the case was treated in histories of the conquest of Mexico from the 1540s through the mid–eighteenth century. On one hand, the tale of Gonzalo Guerrero retold in Spain and New Spain revealed the controversies regarding racial and cultural hybridization in Spanish America's new mestizo societies.[3] At home in Spain (and in America, especially New Spain at the time), Gonzalo's appearance also coincided with the height of the obsession about the relationship of religion and race, exemplified by the statutes of purity of blood [*limpieza de sangre*], which meant "freedom from any taint of semitic blood."[4] Christian honor depended on the unity of belief and blood, and deviation on either score brought punishment and infamy. Against the practices of the Inquisition in Spain and New Spain as backdrop, the exemplary tale of Gonzalo Guerrero becomes more intelligible. It was not a curiosity or an eccentric case but exactly the type of cultural boundary crossing that concerned the royal and ecclesiastical guardians of the faith and customs of the kingdoms of Spain in Europe and America.

FIGURE 21. Statue of Gonzalo Guerrero (detail), in sculptural ensemble by Raúl
Ayala Arellano, Club de Yates Akumal Caribe, Akumal, Quintana Roo, Mexico. Photo-
graph by Rolena Adorno.

BELIEF, BLOOD, AND CUSTOM

The state of affairs surrounding the relationship of belief, blood, and custom in sixteenth-century Spain is a necessary primer for the consideration of the Gonzalo Guerrero case. Historians tend to trace the limpieza de sangre doctrine not to such statutes' initial implementation in the late fifteenth and early sixteenth centuries but rather a little earlier, to the riots of 1449 in Toledo, which are cited as "the first serious effort in Castile to discriminate between Christians on the basis of race alone."[5] On that occasion, anti-Semitism, fanned by social antagonisms, came violently to the surface when converso tax collectors (heirs to the tradition of Jewish tax gatherers and fiscal officials to the crown and aristocracy of the preceding century) employed by the royal minister Álvaro de Luna were murdered; their properties were sacked by angry Christian mobs. After 1480, however, it was the Spanish Inquisition that gave major impetus to the spread of racial discrimination in favor of purity of blood, and limpieza statutes were independently adopted by the Colegios Mayores of Castile, the universities of Salamanca and Valladolid, the military-religious orders of Santiago, Calatrava, and Alcántara, the religious orders of the Jeronymites, Dominicans, and Franciscans, and some cathedral chapters.[6] Historians do not tend to blame the Inquisition for generating this preoccupation, but rather see it as its institutional defender in the wake of a Castilian drive from the aspiring lower ranks of society to acquire for themselves a dignity enjoyed by the aristocrats of noble ancestry.

The archbishop of Toledo, Juan Martínez Siliceo (appointed in 1546), provides the paradigmatic example. After an unsuccessful attempt was made in 1539 by his predecessor to impose a limpieza de sangre statute on the cathedral of Toledo, Siliceo succeeded in doing so over the objections of the cathedral's aristocratic canons, thus providing himself (and many aspirants to rank from the popular classes) with a way of ensuring status in the intensely hierarchical society of sixteenth-century Spain. In 1556, Siliceo obtained royal ratification of the statute from Philip II, who justified it on the basis of his conviction that all the "heresies" that had occurred in Germany and France had been sown by descendants of Jews. Although the pressure for limpieza statutes came not from the top of Spanish society but from the bottom, the royal sanction and the application of the statutes in certain conspicuous religious and learned institutions had the effect of confirming in the popular mind the "correlation between heresy and a non-Christian background."[7] As J. H. Elliott put it, "Indeed, alongside the obsessive concern with purity of the faith there flourished a no less obsessive concern with purity of blood; both obsessions were at their most violent in the middle decades of the sixteenth century; both employed the same techniques of informing and delation; and both had the effect of narrowing the extraordinarily wide range of Spanish life, and of forcing a rich and vital society into a strait-jacket of conformity" (217).

The need to provide genealogical proofs that the limpieza statutes demanded generated, in turn, fraud, perjury, extortion, and blackmail: "In an age when written evidence was rare, the reputation of applicants lay wholly at the mercy of local gossip and hostile neighbors" and, as the cases documented by Henry Charles Lea revealed, " 'common rumour' was generally allowed as evidence."[8] One's observed or alleged social practices were then easily made the source of denunciation. Any hint or evidence of the practice of ritual customs was most suspect; even learned, literary descriptions of Jewish marriage and burial customs were expurgated and torn from Spanish books that documented and displayed the cultures and customs of the world's peoples.[9]

Spain's empire was tainted by the same atmosphere of accusation. If 1539 marked the unsuccessful attempt by Siliceo's predecessor to prohibit all conversos from holding office in the cathedral of Toledo,[10] it was also the year that saw two acculturated Indians of México-Tenochtitlán charged by the Mexican Inquisition with dogmatizing against the Christian faith and banished from Mexico. In that same fateful year, a baptized Texcocan lord, Don Carlos Ometochtzin, was burned at the stake for heresy.[11] The first act of the Mexican Inquisition in 1523 (a mere two years after the fall of Tenochtitlán to Cortés) had been to enact statutes against Jews and heretics. In 1528, two conversos were the first to be burned at the stake, while a third was reconciled to the church and escaped sentencing (108–109). Like Don Carlos in 1539, the conversos Hernando Alonso and Gonzalo de Morales, prosecuted in 1528, were processed in the customary sanbenito costume (saco bendito, the penitential garments consisting of a short, broad cape or tunic and tall pointed hat) and then burned to death in the presence of the representatives of Cortés and other government officials (110). In 1536 Archbishop Zumárraga severely fined one Gonzalo Gómez and exiled him to the seclusion of a monastery, obliging him to perform public prayers on his knees in the cathedral for the sin of performing Jewish rites. Also in 1539 the archbishop sentenced the converso Francisco Millán to the perpetual wearing of the sanbenito and banishment from New Spain upon conviction of charges of practicing Jewish rituals.[12]

In all these cases, heresy was associated with a non-Christian background, and the punishment for heresy always included the wearing of the sanbenito, which in Spain would be preserved, hanging in the churches as "perpetual memory of the infamy of the heretics and their descendants."[13] Decaying sanbenitos were replaced by new ones bearing the names of the offenders, the goal of the tribunals being to keep them on public display (this was done throughout Spain until the end of the eighteenth century) so that genealogical proofs could easily be either contradicted or confirmed against the evidence of the infamous, displayed garments. In criminal courts, humiliating punishments that brought public shame [vergüenza] were greatly feared because they tended to ruin one's reputation; in the Inquisition "the gravest of all punishments was the sanbenito since its duration was perpetual, bringing shame both on family and local community" (123). Since the declared aim of the sanbenito's use was to publish and perpetuate the infamy of condemned persons by being perpetually displayed in a local church, it did not matter whether the victim had been burned to death or merely forced to do penance; his or her descendants would labor under "civil disability and public infamy" in either case (123, 303). I have emphasized this point about the body becoming the site of the evidence of transgression punished by the Inquisition because, from the inquisitorial perspective, the body, by virtue of the ritual mutilation practiced by some Amerindian groups, was already the site of transgression itself.[14] Bodily mutilation was the defining feature of Gonzalo Guerrero's transgression in the eyes of its sixteenth-century interpreters.

FIRST SIGHTINGS OF AN INDIVIDUAL OF UNCERTAIN NAME

The first printed account of the shipwreck that left its survivors (Jerónimo de Aguilar and, presumably, the still-unnamed Gonzalo) in Yucatán was Pietro Martire d'Anghiera's *Second Decade* of *De orbe novo*, written in Latin in 1514 and published for the first time in 1516. In Anghiera's account a caravel under the command of a captain Valdivia under orders of Vasco Núñez de Balboa set out from Darién in 1511; bound for Spain, it was carrying the royal fifth (twenty thousand ducats) to the king, and it was to deliver news en route to the Admiral and governor of Santo Domingo, Diego Colón, about the difficulties Balboa was having with his rival, Diego de Nicuesa. At Jamaica the ship ran aground on the shoals, and some twenty men boarded a rowboat and rowed for thirteen or fourteen days until being carried by a strong current to the shores of Yucatán. After coming ashore, the surviving crew members were captured and enslaved by the Maya of the area.[15]

These events of 1511, and the next mention of possible shipwreck survivors (not twenty, but three), are found in Diego Velázquez's 1518 instructions to Hernán Cortés to reconnoiter (not conquer) the lands of Mexico. Having heard of the shipwreck and the survivors' arrival in Yucatán, Velázquez ordered Cortés to recover any such captives, "by any means not harmful to the Spaniards or the Indians."[16] A few months later, in February 1519, Cortés succeeded in rescuing one of these lost Spaniards, Jerónimo de Aguilar, who had been living in Yucatán for the previous eight years. With Doña Marina, one of the twenty young native women who had been captured by Cortés and his men at Tabasco on the southern gulf coast of Mexico, Aguilar would serve as Cortés's interpreter. Together, because of their role as communicators and facilitators with friendly and hostile native groups in the Spanish conquest of Mexico, Doña Marina, also known throughout history as La Malinche, and Aguilar became the most famous (or infamous) team of interpreters [lenguas] in the history of Latin America.[17]

But what about Gonzalo? When Cortés reported the acquisition of Aguilar in the town council's letter [carta del cabildo] sent to the emperor from the newly elected town council of the newly established Spanish municipality of Veracruz on July 10, 1519, he did not mention any captives other than Aguilar, and, in fact, he emphasized Aguilar's failure to have made contact with any other presumed shipwreck survivors: "The others who were shipwrecked with him were scattered throughout the land, which, he told us, was very large, and it would be impossible to rescue them without spending [or wasting] much time there" [los otros españoles que con él se perdieron en aquella carabela que dio al través estaban muy desparramados por la tierra, la cual nos dijo que era muy grande y que era imposible poderlos recoger sin estar ni gastar mucho tiempo en ello].[18] Aguilar's failure to communicate with the other shipwreck victims is also registered in the conquistador Andrés de Tapia's account of his deeds and services [*información de méritos y servicios*] in the conquest of Mexico ("Relación" [1561]) and in Fray Diego de Landa's *Relación*. Though not a firsthand witness, Landa, who lived in Yucatán, knew the local history well.

The first mentions of any other captive—and the first references to the Gonzalo figure—would not appear until 1534 and 1536, a full twenty-three to twenty-five years after the shipwrecked Jerónimo de Aguilar and his fellow sailors arrived at Yucatán in 1511. There are two sources: The first is Cortés, in a questionnaire (*interrogatorio*) of 1534 to be answered by witnesses on his behalf for the purpose of testifying to his achievements as military and civil ruler of New Spain.[19] Thus the "debut" of the figure eventually called Gonzalo Guerrero is owed to Cortés's preparation for defending himself in the official investigation [*residencia*] of his governorship of New Spain.[20] The second source is the civil and military governor of Honduras-Higueras, Andrés de Cereceda, reporting in 1536 on Pedro de Alvarado's attempted conquest of Yucatán in 1534, in which Cereceda participated.[21]

Why does the shipwrecked sailor who refused to return not appear in the documentary record before the 1530s? In the preceding years of 1527 and 1528, as well as during 1530–1534, Francisco de Montejo repeatedly had attempted and failed to conquer Yucatán. There was reluctance at the time to blame Montejo's failure on the Mayas' expertise in war or on Montejo's inability to conduct jungle and guerrilla warfare. To explain the difficulty of achieving a conquest, another explanation was sought. The remaining 1511 Spanish captive or captives, it was argued, must have had a hand in thwarting Montejo's repeatedly unsuccessful efforts. The 1534 and 1536 accounts were in some measure responses to that state of affairs.[22]

In his questionnaire of 1534 Cortés claims that Jerónimo de Aguilar had told him that there had been only two survivors of the 1511 shipwreck. One was Aguilar himself, and the other one, who "had not wanted to come back," was identified by Cortés as a certain Morales. According to Cortés quoting Aguilar, this Morales refused to join the Cortés party because he "had his ears pierced and he was painted like an Indian and married to an Indian woman, and he had children by her."[23] This is the first account and the complete, basic narrative outline of the story but for one essential element. Only a participant in the Spanish war of conquest in Yucatán was likely to have provided it, and that man was Cereceda, in his 1536 account of a white man's role as a warrior alongside the Maya against the Spanish.

Cereceda reported not his own experience with the captive but rather a secondhand account that he said the Maya cacique Cizumba had given to him about a "Christian Spaniard named Gonzalo Aroça" (or Azora, depending on the transcription). This Gonzalo Aroça (Aroza) was "the one who lived among the Indians of the province of Yucatán for twenty years or more." He was "the one who they say brought the military commander (*adelantado*) Montejo to ruin" and who, two years earlier, in 1534, had "been killed by a shot from an arquebus." This Gonzalo, added Cereceda, had "gone about naked, his body tattooed and in the garb of an Indian."[24] These two slim accounts from the 1530s, in fact, these few sentences—mostly if not entirely secondhand—are the closest in time to the events and the nearest to firsthand sources by which Gonzalo (so named by Cereceda) is known. Cortés and Cereceda provide the origins of the tale: Gonzalo had lived for two decades as a warrior among the Maya; his body was tattooed in their fashion. He did not return to the Spanish because of his corporal mutilation and his marriage and family (Cortés), and he had successfully prevented Montejo's repeated attempts at conquest and settlement in Yucatán (Cereceda). Hence, Cortés gives us the domestic Gonzalo, and Cereceda, the warrior.

GONZALO, THE MARINER APOSTATE (OVIEDO)

Matters became more complicated when historians began to interpret the bare-bones, vague account. Gonzalo Fernández de Oviedo was the first. In his *Historia general y natural de las Indias,* drafted in 1542, he consolidated the twin roles of Gonzalo's acculturation to Maya domestic and warrior life.[25] When in 1542 he wrote his version of the history of the conquest of Yucatán, he presented the first, full-blown story of Gonzalo as warrior, although he called him Gonzalo, the sailor [Gonzalo, el marinero]. Oviedo located the activity of the former Spanish captive in the province of Chetumal along the southeast coast of the Yucatán Peninsula in today's state of Quintana Roo. He condemned Gonzalo's military prowess on behalf of the Mayas as treasonous, and he assigned heresy as the cause. Oviedo's

Gonzalo was not, in a word, an Old Christian; his cultural transformation to Maya ways could be attributed only to a spiritual legacy tainted by a Semitic (converso or morisco) heritage.

Oviedo attributed to Gonzalo a second opportunity (perhaps it was the first, in fact) to rejoin his countrymen: Not in 1519 but in 1528, when, according to Oviedo, Francisco de Montejo communicated with Gonzalo and offered to make him, if he rejoined the Spanish, "one of the principal men, one of the most favored and best loved that there may be in all these regions."[26] In Oviedo's dramatic account, Gonzalo responded by writing with charcoal on the back of the letter: "Señor, I kiss the hands of your mercy, but as I am a slave I have no liberty, although I am married and I have a wife and children, and I remember God. You, sir, and the Spaniards have a good friend in me." Oviedo writes that Gonzalo went on not only to fight the Spanish but also to trick both Montejo's party and his lieutenant captain Alonso Dávila's forces into thinking that the other had perished, thus compelling both forces to abandon the campaign of conquest until, to their utter surprise, they were reunited sometime later.[27] Oviedo described Dávila's second expedition to Chetumal in 1531 for the purpose of "punishing that infidel sailor and the rebellion and uprising of the Indians";[28] according to Oviedo, Gonzalo was killed by the Spanish on the field of battle at that time. Of the many lives that the Gonzalo figure lived, this was chronologically the first of his deaths (1531), the second being attributed, as we saw, to the year 1534, by Cereceda. In the hands of the historians many stories emerged about Gonzalo's life as a leader of native warriors, and in the next decades Bernal Díaz del Castillo (1:54, 55; [chaps. 29, 30]) would retrospectively attribute to Gonzalo attacks on the expedition of Francisco Hernández de Córdoba in 1517 at Cotoche and on that of Juan de Grijalva in Champoton in 1518. (These are most unlikely since they were so distant from the province of Chetumal where the alleged Gonzalo lived.)[29]

Oviedo's 1540s explanation of Gonzalo's behavior is a harsh condemnation, and he attributed it, as noted, to spiritual infidelity: "And this Gonzalo, a sailor, . . . was converted into an Indian and much worse than an Indian, and married to an Indian and with his ears and tongue pierced and his body worked and painted like an Indian, and with a wife and children. . . . Well it is to be believed that such people could not be but of vile caste, vile heretics" [Y este Gonzalo, marinero, . . . estaba ya convertido en indio, e muy peor que en indio, y casado con una India, e sacrificadas las orejas e la lengua, e labrado la persona, pintado como indio, e con mujer e hijos. . . . Bien es de creer que los tales no podían ser sino de vil casta e viles heréticos].[30] Oviedo speculated that either Gonzalo "was raised among vile and low people" who failed to instruct him in the Christian faith, or else he was, "as one might suspect," to be of an abhorrent caste that was "suspicious of the Christian religion itself" [e por ventura (como se debe sospechar) él sería de ruin casta y sospechosa a la mesma religión cristiana (3:233)]. Thus Oviedo calls him a "bad Christian," "traitor and apostate sailor," "that infidel mariner," and "that bad Christian Gonzalo, sailor, transformed into an Indian" (3:234, 244, 245, 246).

Oviedo's inquisitorial wrath can be understood if it is situated within the context of two relevant events taking place in Spain and New Spain while the unsuccessful war of conquest in Yucatán was still going on. Oviedo was convinced of the key role Gonzalo (and perhaps other former captives) played in the Mayas' successful repulsion of Spanish attempts at conquest. The limpieza statutes meant that the lower classes could challenge the code of the aristocracy: "Pure ancestry thus became for the lower ranks of Spanish society the equivalent of noble ancestry for the upper ranks"; orthodoxy meant to mid–sixteenth century Spain "not only the profession of a strictly orthodox faith, but also the possession of a strictly orthodox ancestry."[31] In Oviedo's view, if Gonzalo could turn himself into an "Indian, and worse than an Indian," renouncing the Christian culture that a New World Indian had never known, then it must have been because he was not of Old Christian ancestry in the first place. Cult and culture, or rather cult and customs, went hand in hand. The reprehensible acculturation of Gonzalo to Maya ways and the threat this posed to the imposition of the Christian religion and Castilian governance in Yucatán could be attributed only to heretical (and treasonous) leanings. Gonzalo's choice, in Oviedo's view, was conditioned at best by an imperfect Christian upbringing and at worst by the heretical proclivities of his forefathers. So much for the "infidel sailor."

GONZALO BECOMES GONZALO GUERRERO (GÓMARA)

Oviedo's account of "Gonzalo the sailor" was transformed into Francisco López de Gómara's tale of "Gonzalo the warrior"; that is, it was Gómara's *Historia de las Indias y la conquista de México* that bestowed on the shipwreck survivor the alliterative name of Gonzalo Guerrero, by which this shadowy figure has been known ever since. The name appeared in the initial publication of Gómara's work in 1552, almost twenty years after the shipwrecked sailor to whom he refers had first been identified (but not by the name of Guerrero) in the documentary record.

Gómara placed the burden of Gonzalo's decision to remain with the Mayas not, like Oviedo, on spiritual infidelity but instead on lasciviousness and shame. Gómara's Gonzalo was carried away by carnal desire (and perhaps greed, since the object of his affections was a rich Maya noblewoman) and had undergone a corporal mutilation that made him too ashamed to return to his countrymen. In Gómara's account, Aguilar refers to Gonzalo's failure to rejoin the Spaniards in the following manner: "I think because of shame, on account of having his nose pierced, his ears perforated, his face and hands painted in the manner of that land and people, or on account of his lust for a woman and the love of his children."[32] Here either shame or sexual passion and the disinterested love of his children explain Gonzalo's decision. Although Gómara reports in Aguilar's voice Gonzalo's success as a military leader under the lord of Chetumal, Nachancán ("he is highly esteemed for the victories he wins in the wars they have with their enemies"), he does not emphasize the role of political treason, as Oviedo did, and he omits altogether Oviedo's ringing condemnation of Gonzalo as an infidel. Gómara sees Gonzalo as an instance of predictable behavior, but not as a threat to Castile's paradigmatic Christian values. On the other hand, it is possibly because of Oviedo's familiarity with the existence of mestizo communities on the island of Hispaniola that he attached such threatening importance to the notion of a European "going native."[33]

In giving Gonzalo his surname, Guerrero, Gómara contributed much more to this obscure figure than an explanation of his behavior; he confirmed him in his identity as a warrior. Why the iconic name Guerrero and why in the 1550s? The continued failure of the war of conquest of Yucatán until 1547, when Spanish control over settled areas was finally assured, helped immeasurably to make the specter of the Spaniard who became a great military leader of the Maya a narrative staple in the accounts of the conquest of Mexico.[34] This tendency, initiated by Cereceda in his 1536 testimony and vividly elaborated by Oviedo in 1542, is now consolidated (and in fact christened) by Gómara in 1552. In the most complete version of the story to that date, Gómara introduced other vivid new elements that would be repeated and varied in subsequent accounts.[35] Gómara's lively, detailed narration concludes with his justification for lingering over it: the providential return to Cozumel of Alvarado's leaky ship provided the Spanish with Aguilar as interpreter and, ultimately, assured them of the conquest of Mexico. Focusing on Aguilar, Gómara ends the chapter by telling how, on contemplating the captivity of her son in a barbaric land where he had lived "under the control of people who devoured human flesh," Aguilar's long-suffering mother regularly exclaimed, upon seeing roasted or skewered meat, "Miserable me! This is my son and my pride and joy!"[36]

BERNAL DÍAZ AND THE BEAUTY OF MESTIZO CHILDREN

Gómara's evocation of Aguilar's anguished mother may be read today as humorous because of its boldness in projecting fears that were, however peculiar to modern eyes, alive and well in 1519 (see the mention in chapter 4 of the "cannibal questionnaire"). As Gómara had done before him, Bernal Díaz adds further humanizing touches, but it is Bernal Díaz who brings the story to its most vivid realization. He is often erroneously credited with being the primary source of the tale, yet his writing on the subject comes relatively late in the generative sequence: Because he uses the surname Guerrero for Gonzalo, contradicting the earlier names Morales (Cortés's 1534 recollection) and Aroza/Azora (Cereceda's, of 1536), it is evident that Bernal Díaz followed Gómara, whom he often criticizes even as he uses him as a source (see chapter 6). If Oviedo did not look approvingly at Gonzalo's heresy and creation of a mestizo family (as mentioned, Oviedo had scorned the creation of mixed-blood communities on Hispaniola from the early years of the sixteenth century), and Gómara was seemingly indifferent to it, Bernal Díaz, by contrast, as a longtime settler, offers the interpretation of one for whom mestizaje was a fact of life (and its reproduction).

Although Bernal Díaz placed on Gonzalo's lips the announcement that "they have me as lord and captain when there are wars" and claimed that Gonzalo Guerrero had fought against the Spanish, he balanced Gonzalo's betrayal of, and opposition to, his countrymen against a sympathetic portrait of the creation of a domestic and occupational life in which cultural and biological mestizaje were the predominant themes. Bernal Díaz puts these words in Gonzalo's mouth:[37] "Brother Aguilar, I am married and have three children, and they have me as a lord and captain when there are wars; go yourself with God, for my face is tattooed and my ears are pierced. What will those Spaniards say of me if they see me like this?" [Hermano Aguilar, yo soy casado y tengo tres hijos, y tiénenme por cacique y capitán cuando hay guerras; idos con Dios, que yo tengo labrada la cara y horadadas las orejas. ¡Qué dirán de mí desde que me vean esos españoles ir de esta manera!].[38]

Bernal Díaz adds a crucial new element to the tale, one that accounts in great measure for Gonzalo's popularity today: This is Gonzalo's affective, even sentimental attachment to his mestizo children, which Bernal Díaz dramatizes in a most empathetic manner: "And you now see these my children, how handsome they are" [Y ya veis estos mis hijitos quán bonitos son]. He quickly adds, "Give me these green glass beads for them, and I will tell them that my brothers send them to me from my homeland" [Por vida vuestra que me deis de esas cuentas verdes que traéis, para ellos, y diré que mis hermanos me las envían de mi tierra].[39] Such sentiments come as no surprise, given Bernal Díaz's long life spent in Mexico and Guatemala, where he was surely surrounded by mestizo children, some of whom were likely to be his own progeny.

Another new element that Bernal Díaz adds to the story is the place that mestizaje will occupy in the new society. This was a dimension that Gómara did not bring into focus for lack of Indies experience, and that the older Oviedo placed under a highly negative (and heretical) sign. Instead of fearing that those who adopted or kept to indigenous customs and ways could only be false Christians, the old Indies-hand Bernal Díaz is ready to welcome the mestizo family into the fold of Spanish creole society. He paints it vividly, right down to the detail of the furious, haranguing female. Gonzalo's Maya wife tells Aguilar, "Look at the promises with which this slave appeals to my husband! Go away and don't bother us with more speeches!" [¡Mira con qué viene este esclavo a llamar a mi marido; idos vos y no curéis de más pláticas! (*Historia verdadera* 1:98 [chap. 27]). Although he creates a speech in which the pious Aguilar reminds Gonzalo that he is a Christian and cautions him "not to lose his soul over an Indian woman," he urges him at the same time to bring his native wife and mestizo children along with him if he does not want to leave them behind [que por una india no se perdiese el ánima, y si por mujer e hijos lo hacía, que la llevase consigo si no los quería dejar (1:98)].

Furthermore, Gonzalo's change of dress and corporal mutilation apparently did not signify, for Bernal or for Gómara, the spiritual transgression that was postulated by the stern Oviedo. Bernal Díaz described Aguilar as being, in appearance, "neither more nor less than an Indian" [Aguilar ni más ni menos era que indio].[40] His acceptance of Aguilar's and Gonzalo's acculturation and his portrayal of Gonzalo's tenderness toward his mestizo family bespeak Bernal's appreciation and understanding of such social and familial phenomena, seeing the mixed society (in which he himself lived), as unthreatening.

For both Gómara and Bernal Díaz, the salient feature of Gonzalo's status as warrior was not his betrayal of his countrymen but his attainment of high social status. In his *Historia del Nuevo Mundo* (1562) Juan Ginés de Sepúlveda likewise emphasized the high regard in which Gonzalo was held because of the wars he had successfully conducted as a captain leading troops against his people's neighbors. Like Gómara and Bernal Díaz, Sepúlveda added, in this case in the voice of Aguilar, "Gonzalo Guerrero, who has adopted the life of the Indians, pierced his ears and perforated his nose, according to their customs. Owing to the shame that this produced, he refused to accompany me when I informed him about the emissary and the letter."[41] The explanation once again is shame and embarrassment—what kind of shame?

In Covarrubias's *Tesoro de la lengua española, o castellana* of 1611, the one who experienced shame was "he who in his own opinion has failed to do something with the decency required; he turns red and we call him ashamed, which is a sign of virtue and modesty" [el que de qualquiera cosa que a su parecer no aya hecho con la decencia devida se pone colorado y le llamamos vergonçoso, indicio de virtud y de modestia (1002)]. The subject has violated the standards of conformity to what is considered honorable or socially acceptable. But in sixteenth-century Spain, the embarrassment produced by shame was also related to or signified transgression of a far greater sort. In order to understand how important *vergüenza* was, Covarrubias (1002) advised the reader to refer to the (now familiar) *Siete partidas*, the Castilian king Alfonso the Wise's great thirteenth-century legal compendium that continued to be an essential guide to life and law throughout the early modern period. It admonishes: "Vergüenza, as the wise have declared, is the sign of fear that is born of true love," that is, the desire to do things right, in accordance with that which is honorable and therefore socially acceptable. "Vergüenza," the Alfonsine text continues, "does two things in the way that vassals relate to their kings. The first is that it removes them from impudence (*atrevimiento,* which is to do or say what one ought not to, in the place where it is not proper), and the second is that it makes them obey the things they should. Impudence brings many ills because after men lose their shame and become emboldened, they enter on the path of disobeying what they should obey and become immune to the conduct that should shame them."[42]

Because of shame Gonzalo did not return, the chroniclers said. It was not merely the social embarrassment ("What would his fellow Spaniards say?") but the awareness of having committed the transgression of bodily mutilation that so severely challenged Christian propriety and the external signs of Christian obedience that Gonzalo simply could not go back.

Apart from Sepúlveda's, two other accounts of the 1560s, offered by writers who lived in New Spain at and after midcentury, deepened the significance of the corporal mutilation or, at the very least, made explicit what these other commentators might have silently assumed.

The role of Gonzalo as warrior and captain among the Maya is his primordial characteristic in the 1561 account by the Franciscan priest and second bishop of Yucatán, Fray Diego de Landa. Landa (*Relación,* 44 [chap. 2]) followed Gómara (*Historia* 26 [chap. 12]) word for word on the chain of events that led to the shipwreck, but he took the events in Yucatán outlined by Gómara and gave them a logical causality that in Gómara had been merely a string of associations.[43] Landa claimed that Gonzalo never tried to leave the Mayas because, in the first place, he was made a military leader under the Maya lord, Nachancán, in matters of war: "Gonzalo went to Chectemal, . . . and there he was received by a lord named Nachancán, who placed him in command of the affairs of war. He was very skilled at this and many times defeated his master's enemies; he also showed the Indians how to fight, teaching them how to build fortresses and bastions. In this manner, and by behaving like an Indian, he built up a great reputation for himself and they married him to a very high-ranking lady by whom he had children. For this reason he, unlike Aguilar, never made any attempt to escape. On the contrary, he tattooed his body, grew his hair long, and pierced his ears so as to wear earrings like the Indians: and it is possible that he also became an idolater like them."[44] In contrast to Gómara's, Landa's recreation of Gonzalo's cultural mestizaje was grounded not in private and intimate actions but in his public and political deeds; this political and cultural conversion probably produces, in Landa's view, his renunciation of Christian beliefs and adoption of those of the Mayas.

In addition to Gómara and Sepúlveda, another historian of the conquest of Mexico who formed part of Cortés's social circle in Spain, Francisco Cervantes de Salazar (see chapter 4), included an observation that his colleagues and peers had not made about Gonzalo but that would be repeated by chroniclers who subsequently used Cervantes de Salazar as a direct or indirect source. Unlike Gómara and Sepúlveda, Cervantes de Salazar went to New Spain. He was appointed the first master of rhetoric at the university, newly founded in 1552 in the viceregal capital, as well as the city's first official chronicler. In his *Crónica de la Nueva España,* of 1566 (116 [bk. 2, chap. 27]) (unpublished in its day), he, like Landa, followed Gómara's (*Historia* 26 [chap. 12]) remarks almost to the letter, citing as Gonzalo's reasons for refusing to join the Spanish in 1519 his shame at his bodily mutilation and his lust for his wife and love of his children.[45] On two points he diverged: Cervantes de Salazar emphasized further Gonzalo's status among the Maya, writing that he was highly esteemed and well loved for having won many victories from the enemies of his lord Nachancán. Upon giving the reasons for Gonzalo's refusal to rejoin the Spanish, he sharpened Gómara's focus on Gonzalo's bodily mutilations and made them the mark of Maya military prestige: "according to the custom of that country, in which only the brave are allowed to wear their hands tattooed" [por tener . . . labradas las manos al uso de aquella tierra, en la cual los valientes solos pueden traer labradas las manos (116)]. This remark was incorporated almost verbatim from Cervantes de Salazar's unpublished manuscript into Antonio de Herrera y Tordesilla's *Historia de los hechos de los castellanos,* published in 1601, and from there to Juan de Torquemada's *Monarquía indiana* of 1615.[46] Both, however, attribute only to shame (*vergüenza*) Gonzalo's refusal to return to his countrymen; they omit the motives of love and lust that Cervantes de Salazar had taken from Gómara. Only the Franciscan friar, Bishop Landa, suggests that Gonzalo has abandoned Christianity for pagan idolatry. By speculating that Gonzalo turned away from his identity as a Christian, Landa stands as a complement to Oviedo, who had asserted that Gonzalo had never really been an adherent to the Christian faith.

SIGNIFICANT OMISSIONS AND NEW ADAPTATIONS
(MUÑOZ CAMARGO AND ALVA IXTLILXOCHITL)

The potency of Gonzalo the warrior as a dangerous symbol of cultural mestizaje is best demonstrated by the fact of its absence, and this is found in the Mexican mestizo writers of the late sixteenth and early seventeenth centuries. There are two kinds of omissions. If for Bernal Díaz the wonder of mestizaje was the very beautiful children born to Gonzalo and his Maya wife, as described in Bernal Díaz's imaginative account by Gonzalo himself, the mestizo chroniclers suppressed altogether any mention of mestizo offspring (which they themselves were). Second, they effectively erased the figure of the acculturated warrior Gonzalo Guerrero.

Diego de Muñoz Camargo's *Historia de Tlaxcala*, of 1576, as well as Fernando de Alva Ixtlilxochitl's *Historia de la nación chichimeca*, of circa 1625, make the point (on Alva Ixtlilxochitl see chapter 5). Both authors suppress the figure of Gonzalo Guerrero. In Muñoz Camargo he is identified by the name of García del Pilar. The historical García del Pilar was an interpreter in Nuño de Guzmán's 1530–1531 conquest of northwestern Mexico, known afterward as Nueva Galicia, where he had infamously participated in the torture of the native lord (Cazonci) of Michoacán. He was known as a man without scruples who went about dressed like an Indian ("naked, wearing a cloak and carrying a staff as the Indians do") and having an Indian concubine with whom he had several children. The correspondence of the attributes and comportment of the historical García del Pilar and the historiographic Gonzalo Guerrero is too close to be coincidental; Muñoz Camargo's substitution of the name of one for the other adds historical resonance to the figure of the traitor.[47]

In Alva Ixtlilxochitl's work Gonzalo Guerrero is dispatched in a single, subordinate sentence: "There remained only him [Aguilar] and one Gonzalo Guerrero, who married in that land, who was very rich and refused to come with him, because he was ashamed that they [the Spaniards] would see him, with his nose pierced in the manner of that land" [Y no había quedado más que él y un Gonzalo Guerrero, que se casó en aquella tierra, quien estaba muy rico y no quiso venir con él, porque tuvo vergüenza de que le viesen las narices horadadas al uso de la tierra"].[48]

With regard to Jerónimo de Aguilar, Muñoz Camargo and Alva Ixtlilxochitl emphasized his firmness of Christian belief in spite of whatever native customs he might have adopted. This was the case put forth decisively by Bernal Díaz for Jerónimo de Aguilar, and with the mestizo chroniclers it gains special prominence. Muñoz Camargo's portrait of Aguilar daringly conflates the bodily mutilations of previous Gonzalo Guerreros with the traditional Christian piety of Aguilar, declaring that Aguilar's ears and nose were pierced and his face and body tattooed "in the style of the Indians." He added, "Compelled by pure necessity, he did everything [demanded of him], although he always and continuously observed the Christian faith and was a Christian and kept the knowledge and observance of the law of God" [Compelido a la pura necesidad se puso a todo, aunque siempre y a la continua observó su cristianidad y fue cristiano y guardó el conocimiento y observancia de la ley de Dios].[49]

Muñoz Camargo's recreation of Aguilar takes to an extreme the convergence of pagan costume and customs, on one hand, and Christianity and its rituals, on the other. Gómara had inaugurated this tendency when he materialized for Aguilar a prayer book [tenía unas horas en que rezaba cada día], and Bernal Díaz developed it further: "He had on a ragged old cloak, and a worse loincloth with which he covered his nakedness, and he had tied up, in a bundle in his cloak, a Book of Hours, old and worn" [y una manta vieja muy ruin, y un braguero peor, con que cubría sus vergüenzas, y traía atada en la manta un bulto que eran Horas muy viejas].[50] By giving Aguilar the bodily markings of the tattooed Gonzalo, Muñoz Camargo pushes forward the argument about the compatibility of Christian cult and non-Christian custom. From his dual-heritage perspective situated somewhere between the poles of Spanish and native Nahua cultural traditions, this was a provocative gesture. But this is where Muñoz Camargo's speculation about such compatibilities ended, because the tattooed, prayer-book-carrying Aguilar was, after all, an Old Christian, not a neophyte mestizo. There will be no such mixed-blood New Christians in his work or in Alva Ixtlilxochitl's.

On the other issue that was troublesome for men and women of mestizo birth, namely, mestizo children, their books describe none. Both authors suppress Doña Marina's (La Malinche's) concubinage to Cortés by marrying her off, not to Juan Jaramillo (her historical husband), but to Jerónimo de Aguilar.[51] By virtually removing from the scene the specter of the Spanish Gonzalo figure taking as a concubine a pagan Maya woman (a pattern all too common in mestizo genealogies), these mestizo authors instead marry the chaste and pious Aguilar to the most prominent mem-

ber of the first group of native women to be baptized in Mexico (at Potonchán in 1519). A cultural mestizaje is thus established on the doubly
solid Christian foundation of a marital bond between a Christian Spaniard, whose time among the natives of Yucatán had not swayed him from
his Christian beliefs, and a baptized Indian woman.

This was a fully Christian marriage, but it is a marriage, significantly,
without children. The threat posed to religious orthodoxy by cultural (and
biological) mestizaje was present in the Gonzalo Guerrero tale right from
its beginning, in the fourth decade of the sixteenth century. Its potency is
confirmed in its suppression by mestizo authors who, near the end of that
century and afterward, craft their narrative accounts in such a way as to
avoid repeating the accounts of the writers that preceded them and produce instead a "safe" marriage (were they thinking of their own mothers?): Jerónimo de Aguilar will not be tempted into concubinage with
native women, and Doña Marina, being married to the pious and chaste
Aguilar, will be spared the depredations of multiple forced sexual al-
liances and abandonment.

CYNICISM AND SLOTH (SOLÍS Y RIVADENEIRA)

Finally, on the theme of love and mestizaje, Antonio de Solís y Rivadeneira, the Spanish author of the *Historia de la conquista de México* (1684)
in the last years of the Hapsburg monarchy under the reign of Charles II,
took a critical approach to the familiar sources and told how Aguilar
showed Cortés's letter to Gonzalo, but that Gonzalo refused to come
along because "he was married to a rich Indian woman and he had with
her three or four children, to whose love was attributed his blindness" [Se
hallaba casado con una India bien acomodada, y tenía en ella tres o cuatro
hijos, a cuyo amor atribuía su ceguedad]. For Solís (56 [bk. 1, chap. 16]),
this cynical Gonzalo's refusal to return was based on his dissimulation "of
those natural affections in order to not leave that pitiful comfort of few
obligations" in which he lived and which mattered more to him than
religion and honor [fingiendo estos afectos naturales para no dejar aquella
lastimosa comodida que en sus cortas obligaciones pesaba más que la
honra y que la religión].[52] Solís would gladly have struck this case from the
historical record; he claimed it was the only such instance in the entire
history of the Spanish conquests [No hallamos que se refiera de otro
español en estas conquistas semejante maldad], but he had to content

himself with the hope that there was a lesson to be learned from contemplating the depths of baseness to which man could descend if God permitted him to do so [No podemos borrar lo que escribieron otros, ni dejan de tener su enseñanza estas miserias a que está sujeta nuestra naturaleza, pues se conoce por ellas a lo que puede llegar el hombre, si le deja Dios (56)].

Solís y Rivadeneira's desire in the last quarter of the seventeenth century to expunge Gonzalo Guerrero's name from the record of Spain's history in America constitutes the last and merely the most blatant entrant in the debate on racial and cultural mixture of the period. The tale of Gonzalo Guerrero defied even its own condemnation as historians from Oviedo to Solís attempted to explain the phenomenon and condemn it. Sensitive to the social stigma attached to mestizaje, Muñoz Camargo and Alva Ixtlilxochitl came closest to the resolution that the orthodox Solís could only hope for: they allowed former shipwreck victims to marry only those who were clearly bona fide Christians (in this case, the ubiquitous Doña Marina). Cortés, Gómara, and Bernal Díaz presented cultural and biological mestizaje as a (not so) simple social fact. Oviedo and Bishop Landa argued that the relationship of cult and custom was a close one, indeed, a single consideration; the treachery and treason of Oviedo's Gonzalo the Infidel Mariner could be explained only on the basis of tainted caste and blood; for Landa, Gonzalo's initiation into the warrior world of the Maya was accompanied by a rejection of Christianity and immersion in pagan rites. For Solís y Rivadeneira, the cultural mestizaje lived daily by Gonzalo led necessarily to slothful self-indulgence in the appetites of the barbarian. Even the love that bound relationships of mestizaje—from Bernal Díaz's admiration for the beauty of mestizo children to Muñoz Camargo's account of how Maya (a language foreign to both Aguilar and Doña Marina, in his account) became the lingua franca on which this marriage of Christian communication was based—is denied by Solís. If for Gómara it may have been, among other possible explanations, lasciviousness to which Gonzalo Guerrero succumbed, for Solís it was clearly the deadly sin of sloth.

The tale of Gonzalo Guerrero, as early as it appeared, already lagged decades behind the experiences it encapsulated and the traditions it challenged. As mentioned earlier, the emergent pattern of racial mixture was well established by the time Cortés arrived at Cozumel in 1519. At the time of the conquest of Mexico there was already a healthy representation of men of mixed race among the troops, to whom Fray Pedro de Aguado would refer as "Indianized soldiers."[53] When in 1519 Cortés and his soldiers had the surprise of their lives in meeting someone who looked, in every aspect but for the presence of a beard, like an Indian of Yucatán, Aguilar and his fellows had already spent approximately eight years living a Maya life, facing a Maya future. (An eight-year captivity was also the major fact of Cabeza de Vaca's historical experience a decade after that of Aguilar; see chapter 10.)

The fictional invention of the figure of a captive-who-did-not-return, based on a historical individual who had not even been in contact with his fellow shipwreck survivor at the time of the arrival of Cortés and whose very name was a matter of uncertainty (Morales? Aroza? Azora?) is one of the remarkable (but perhaps not uncommon) phenomena of Spanish-conquest-era historiography. "Gonzalo Guerrero" is a haunting, tantalizing tale, marked by its tellers with transgression in every conceivable variant: sexual, religious, cultural, and political; Gonzalo Guerrero variously embodies lasciviousness, miscegenation, apostasy, heresy, military valor, and treason. Even the positive trait of love of family, or building a family, had two sides: Bernal Díaz's Gonzalo admires his children; Muñoz Camargo's and Alva Ixtlilxochitl's Aguilar and Doña Marina remain childless.

TWENTIETH-CENTURY SEQUELS

Gonzalo Guerrero has been a malleable figure in the history of Spanish American colonial-era narrative, and his personification has given rise to twentieth-century sequels.[54] Separated in their appearance by some twenty years, two recently found "documents" purport to contain his true (if mutually contradictory) memoirs. In the mid-1970s, there appeared the first publication of Gonzalo Guerrero's alleged memoirs, *Gonzalo de Guerrero, padre del mestizaje iberoamericano* (Mexico City, 1975). The text is presented as a paraphrase of a supposedly autobiographical account written by Gonzalo Guerrero that the editor claims comes from a manuscript in a private collection in Mexico City and consists of some thirty folios, including some sheets of deerskin vellum. This Gonzalo claims to have been born not in maritime Andalusia but in Extremadura, and he is of humble origin; he is presented as a firm ally of the Maya, although at one point he expresses the hope that Spanish arms will prevail.[55]

In 1994, another set of Gonzalo's memoirs appeared, published by the Facultad de Ciencias Antropológicas of the Universidad Autónoma de Yucatán. Under the title *Historia de la conquista del Mayab, 1511–1697*, Gonzalo's supposed memoirs are part of a longer manuscript. In this case, it is not the original text by Gonzalo that is presumably preserved but rather the account of a Franciscan friar who came upon it two centuries later, in 1725. This Fray Joseph de San Buenaventura y Cartagena, or Fray Ventura, as the editors call him, is not to be found in the Franciscan records of New Spain for this period, the editors admit, and they likewise acknowledge the curious similarity of the glyphic representations in Fray Ventura's manuscript with those found in modern studies today. They additionally note that Fray Ventura made many observations which resemble those found only in modern historiography and ethnohistorical studies. The editors nevertheless vouch for the work's authenticity as a true reflection of the historical Gonzalo.[56]

Fray Ventura does not seem to have offered a literal transcription of Gonzalo's words; rather he paraphrases his source and allegedly supplements it with information from the oral tradition. In addition to the friar's paraphrase, the editors have modernized the orthography and introduced thematic chapter or section divisions into the text, so that the current version is one step further removed from the supposed original source.[57]

Like the 1975 memoir, this one from 1994 also claims that Gonzalo was from Extremadura, yet this one is not of humble but rather of higher origins, being a "man of arms and letters." This latest Gonzalo is pro-Spanish and pro-empire, maintains his Christian faith, and takes pride in having taught the Spanish language to his mestizo children. This Gonzalo, like the earlier one, expresses the hope that Spanish arms will prevail, only more forcefully. He suggests that Spanish victory would readily turn the Maya out of their barbarous, idolatrous ways because they are "by nature peaceful, free from wars of their own, and untainted by the vices and filthy habits that characterize other native groups."[58] (Again, "sins against nature" and the presence or absence of warfare define civilization and barbarity; see chapters 4 and 5).

This Gonzalo laments the ferocious resistance of the Maya to the Spanish, and he includes his own son among the militants. A very dramatic tale of generational conflict ensues. Captured by Francisco de Montejo, the younger, Gonzalo's mestizo son is saved by his father, who promises Montejo, on behalf of his son, that he will never take up arms against the Spanish in the future (89, 91). Here the memoir ends, with Gonzalo's militant mestizo son rejecting the Spaniards and his own father, and the Spanish father seeking to protect the life of his son by making Montejo a promise the son cannot keep (92). With this very contemporary dilemma the memoir ends in its own irreconcilability.

The implausibility of both of these allegedly autobiographical accounts is patent. The authenticity of either manuscript is far from being proven, and the contents of both are enough steps removed from any potentially original account by Gonzalo as to inspire skepticism rather than confidence. Contrary to the claims made in both accounts, Cortés would not have sent "paper and other supplies" to this Gonzalo in 1519 after his refusal to join the Spanish. (The 1519 *carta del cabildo* from Veracruz stated that Cortés and his men had been unable even to make contact with any captives apart from Aguilar.) Additionally, these modern claims that Gonzalo was from landlocked Extremadura rather than coastal Andalusia contradicts the early histories of Anghiera, Oviedo, Gómara, and Bernal Díaz on this fundamental and (probably sole) unembellished point. Although the 1975 account coincides with the 1536 Cereceda and subsequent sources on Gonzalo's alliance with the Maya and his military service on their behalf against the Spanish, Fray Ventura contradicts the period sources by making Gonzalo a pacifist and a Spanish loyalist. Yet all of the above considerations—not to mention the claim of Gonzalo's literacy—are conditions contrary to fact, since there are no facts on which to anchor them.

The implausibility of these accounts (not so very different from their sixteenth- and seventeenth-century predecessors in interpretation, if not in intent) is not as captivating as their very creation. The two great elements of the story are patriotism (Maya or Spanish) and mestizaje (biological and cultural). Gonzalo is cast more as a Maya patriot than as a traitor to Castile, and he is celebrated as the creator of postconquest mestizaje. Gonzalo, after all, is not Doña Marina / La Malinche betraying her people, but a new man making a new life in a new land. Gonzalo's tale is an appeal to the sentiments of personal, affective attachment to one's progeny. Bernal Díaz stated it most memorably: "Y ya veis estos mis hijitos quán bonitos son." This same attachment in Fray Ventura's account is suffered as loss. Bernal Díaz never ventures to speculate on whether those small children lived to grow up, or if they grew up to be warriors. Fray Ventura claims that one did.

Thus this latest incarnation of Gonzalo Guerrero replays not the drama of conquest but rather, taking Bernal Díaz's cue, the story of the family, ultimately transformed into the war of the family, that is, the civil war. The drama is that of the father facing the son in mutual incomprehension. It is a wrenching tale of familial and filial politics of confrontation and contestation, rendered as dramatic as the opposition of Maya versus Spaniard in jungle warfare. If the 1970s version of Gonzalo's autobiography, with its racial blending and societal harmony, seems out-of-date and old-fashioned, the 1990s version revives the issue in a more up-to-the-minute sense of irreconcilable hopes and values that divide one generation (and one race) from another. Whereas the 1970s narrative espoused the old ideal of creole patriotism for the new land and the notion of mestizaje as a happy ending, the 1990s account exchanges patriotism for contested political commitment and mestizaje for the contested ground of cultural identities. These latest versions reiterate and transform Gonzalo's story, which began in the sixteenth century, with the hotly polemical issue of mestizaje. As these latest versions reveal, mestizaje, or rather its current figuration as "cultural identity," constitutes the ground of a polemic that is as much political as it is cultural.

Is this the final transformation of the Gonzalo Guerrero phenomenon? Not likely: The retelling of the tale will continue to be a greater part of modern cultural history than the historicity of the shipwrecked sailor from Palos de Moguer could ever be. A very few lines written down in 1534 and 1536 provided the seeds for the evolving interpretations of one of the most arresting tales told in the Spanish conquest era. Gonzalo Guerrero is nothing more or less than a collection of tales, told and retold over the centuries. The fact that he is presented insistently as a historical figure, and that there is no basis on which to postulate with certainty even the name of such a person, is no obstacle to his vitality and perseverance. The boundary that Gonzalo Guerrero ultimately transgresses is not only cultural and religious: that is, the one that divides Maya from Spaniard (Cortés), native warrior from Spanish conquistador (Cereceda, Bernal Díaz), or Christian from heretic (Oviedo). It is, instead, the low wall that, mostly by illusion, separates the realm of history from that of literature.

CHAPTER 10

The Narrative Reinvention of
the Conqueror-Captive

IF GONZALO GUERRERO WAS an idea that played a role in the polemics of possession from the mid–sixteenth century into the eighteenth,
with new versions being written up to the present day, Álvar Núñez
Cabeza de Vaca was his real-life counterpart: He was a native of south-
ernmost Andalusia; he arrived at the site of his captivity not in a Spanish
galleon but in a small, makeshift craft; and he and his fellow survivors
spent eight years in captivity (1528–1536), just as Jerónimo de Aguilar in
Yucatán had (1511–1519) when Aguilar was rescued. When the Gonzalo
Guerrero story appeared full-blown in Gómara's 1552 history of the conquest of Mexico (see chapter 9), Cabeza de Vaca's account had been in
print for a full decade. In 1552 also, Cabeza de Vaca's criminal sentence,
resulting from his conviction by the Council of the Indies for misconduct
in office while serving as governor of the province of Río de la Plata, was
drastically reduced. Gómara's fresh and fully minted tale of Gonzalo
Guerrero must have sparked renewed interest in Cabeza de Vaca's experience. One can only imagine what Cabeza de Vaca might have replied
when queried by interlocutors who must have had Gonzalo's story in
mind. This would have been the opportunity for him to emphasize his
valorous and devout conduct as a Christian caballero in the service of his
king, just as he had done in his 1542 *Relación,* soon to be republished in

1555 under the heading, "Naufragios," along with Pero Hernández's apologia of Cabeza de Vaca's South American governorship.

THE LIFE AND TRIALS OF CABEZA DE VACA

If there was a dearth of information about the uncertainly named sailor and shipwreck victim in Yucatán, there is an abundance of documented information about Cabeza de Vaca. Cabeza de Vaca's life story is cartographically projected onto the map that traces his journeys in Europe and to the Americas (fig. 22). Like many Andalusians of his regional and familial traditions and other men of his generation, the maritime perspective of this native of Jerez de la Frontera was oriented first to the Mediterranean and then to the Atlantic. While his forebears had occupied themselves on the frontiers of Muslim Spain in Andalusia and on the seacoasts of southern Spain and northern Africa, Cabeza de Vaca and his contemporaries were involved in broader, international domains. National and international conflicts during the reigns of King Ferdinand of Aragon and his grandson, Charles I of Spain (Charles V of the Holy Roman Empire), were part of Cabeza de Vaca's military experience before he set sail, for the first time, to the Indies.

Cabeza de Vaca was born in Jerez de la Frontera sometime between 1485 and 1492, and he died after 1559.[1] He prided himself on his noble lineage. At the end of the *Relación/Naufragios* he honored his paternal grandfather, Pedro de Vera Mendoza, as the conqueror of the island of Gran Canaria in the Canary Islands. His maternal lineage, whose surname, Cabeza de Vaca, he bore, dated back at least to the early thirteenth century. Members of the untitled, middle-ranking nobility (*caballeros*) of the Cabeza de Vaca line had participated in the conquest of Spain from the Muslims. Fernán Ruiz Cabeza de Vaca's chronicled participation in the Christian conquest of Córdoba in 1236, which took place under the leadership of one of the most celebrated Christian monarchs of medieval Spain —Fernando III of Castile and León, later sainted—links the Cabeza de Vaca name to one of the major military offensives of that era. (The popular legend that the Cabeza de Vaca name was created when bestowed upon a humble shepherd for his role in the battle of Las Navas de Tolosa in 1212 is apocryphal.)[2]

Serving the house of the dukes of Medina Sidonia from his youth until

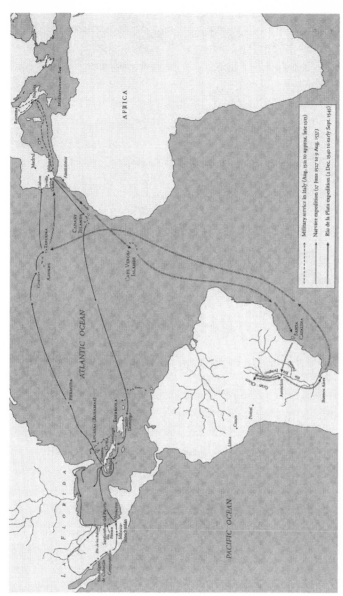

FIGURE 22. Travels of Álvar Núñez Cabeza de Vaca (1511–1545). Reprinted from *Álvar Núñez Cabeza de Vaca: His Account, His Life and the Expedition of Pánfilo de Narváez* by Rolena Adorno and Patrick Charles Pautz by permission of the University of Nebraska Press. Copyright © 1999 by the University of Nebraska Press. 1:xxviii–xxix.

his departure for America (1503–1527), Cabeza de Vaca saw his career at arms span the period of King Ferdinand's North African campaigns and the defense and expansion of his Aragonese territories in Italy (1511–1513). In Italy, under Ferdinand's banner, Cabeza de Vaca participated in the battles of Ravenna and Bologna in 1512 and in the siege of the lands of the duke of Ferrara. As a reward, he was appointed royal standard-bearer (*alférez*) of the city of Gaeta, near Naples.[3] Cabeza de Vaca's *Relación* contains an occasional fleeting reference to these earlier military experiences. Upon recalling the warlike character of the natives of eastern coastal Texas, he remarked, "They have as much cunning to protect themselves from their enemies as they would have if they had been raised in Italy and in continuous war."[4]

During the early years of the reign of Charles V, Cabeza de Vaca again supported the crown while in the employ of the dukes of Medina Sidonia. In Spain in 1521 Cabeza de Vaca participated in the final defeat of the year-long Comunero revolution that had threatened the stability of the Castilian state by reasserting local interests against Charles's centralized royal power and the threat of treasury-draining wars abroad. In the same year Cabeza de Vaca participated in the battle of Puente de la Reina, in Navarre, in which Charles's forces repelled those of Francis I of France in the first of the series of wars between those monarchs.[5]

Cabeza de Vaca's easy familiarity with European and Mediterranean reference points reveals the breadth of his personal horizons. His Indies career was remarkable for its geographical range over North and South America, first to North America (La Florida) as royal treasurer and later to Río de la Plata as governor of the province centered at Asunción, in today's Paraguay (see fig. 22). His governorship lasted from March 1541 until April 1544, when he was arrested and imprisoned for eleven months before being sent home in chains, arriving in Spain in September 1545. He was tried by the Royal Council of the Indies on criminal charges that accused him of misconduct in office, indicting him for mistreating the Indians and for raising his own heraldic standard, the charges read, when he should have raised the king's. In 1551 he was found guilty and sentenced to be stripped of all titles conferred on him, banned in perpetuity from the Indies, and banished to the penal colony of Oran on the North African coast for five years of service to the emperor at his own expense. Cabeza de Vaca appealed the sentence, and in 1552, as noted, it was reduced: his banishment from the Indies henceforth pertained only to Río de la Plata, and he was relieved from the obligation of service in Oran.[6] The perpetual loss of his titles was still apparently in effect, as was his liability for court costs and any civil suits that might be brought against him.[7]

Cabeza de Vaca's triumphant vindication is patently in evidence in the 1555 publication, which includes the accounts of his North and South American sojourns, in the dedication of his work to Philip II's son, the Infante Don Carlos (1545–1568). This short composition offers a vivid demonstration of Cabeza de Vaca's intimate relationship with the life of the royal court during the previous decade. Since 1546, when he spent a year as a prisoner of the court, and through the mid-1550s, the caballero from Jerez de la Frontera and former military commander (*adelantado*) and governor of Río de la Plata found the court an amenable residence. He presents himself as friend and admirer of its most learned men, particularly the Infante Don Carlos's tutor and majordomo, Don Antonio de Rojas y Velasco, and the young Don Carlos's teacher, Honorato Juan. Cabeza de Vaca extols the nobility and virtue of Rojas y Velasco and lauds the lineage and learning of Honorato Juan, later bishop of Osma (1564–1566). Honorato Juan had taught Prince Philip mathematics and architecture, while Juan Ginés de Sepúlveda instructed the future Philip II in geography and history. (The reader of chapters 4 and 5 can appreciate what the tenor of those lessons might have been.) Honorato Juan and Sepúlveda shared two deep interests: classical learning and a historical interest in the Indies. Honorato Juan's fascination with the Indies is revealed by his possession of the papers of Francisco López de Gómara, which he acquired after the historian's death in 1559; Don Carlos, as Honorato Juan's universal heir, may have been responsible for depositing them in his father's library at the monastery of San Lorenzo del Escorial.[8] If Honorato Juan was interested in Gómara's historical writings about the Indies, there is no doubt he and Cabeza de Vaca would have conversed at length on the topic, which the latter knew, both north and south. The Indies must have been the spark that ignited their amicable relationship.

Cabeza de Vaca's greatest cause for the expression of pride and pleasure in 1555, however, was the release from the main obligations of his sentence. Despite the enmity of Cabeza de Vaca's accusers and detractors, the good offices of the emperor through his ministers had restored to Cabeza de Vaca his good name. He writes in the proem, "And even when envy should seek to impede and obstruct this necessary work, the clear virtue and merits of such princes will defend us, God giving us the peace, calm, and tranquility that is abundantly granted in times of good kings."[9]

Even in his last days, back home in Jerez de la Frontera, Andalusia, where he had reestablished his official residence in the district of San Salvador, Cabeza de Vaca looked outward: the last known, documented public act of his life was his 1559 ransom of a young distant relative, Hernán Ruiz Cabeza de Vaca, who was being held captive by the king of Algiers after being captured in an expedition against the Ottoman Turk. As a member of the caballero class of the Jerez de la Frontera house of Cabeza de Vaca, Álvar Núñez (often synonymously referred to as an hidalgo) almost certainly ended his days in Jerez de la Frontera, and he was probably interred in the Dominican convent of Santo Domingo el Real, where his paternal grandfather, Pedro de Vera Mendoza, had been buried.[10] (The popular notion that Cabeza de Vaca died "penniless, old, and broken-hearted," in Valladolid, as Morris Bishop [*Odyssey*, 290] wrote, is another bit of oft-repeated apocrypha.) If he ended his days as a person at his ease at home and at court, fulfilling the demands and expectations placed upon him as a Christian caballero, he had presented himself in the same manner in the *Relación/Naufragios*. It was the perspective that Cabeza de Vaca offered on his North American experience, which is the focus of our interest here, that generated the interest of its many generations of readers over the centuries.

The Pánfilo de Narváez expedition of which Cabeza de Vaca was the king's representative as royal treasurer was a failure of epic proportions. Of this major settlement expedition, which began with nearly six hundred persons, including ten Castilian women and an unknown number of black African slaves, no settlement was achieved, and only about one hundred persons survived: Approximately ninety men and the ten women survived by staying with the ships, and only four of the three hundred men who disembarked on mainland Florida—Álvar Núñez Cabeza de Vaca and his fellow *hidalgos* Andrés Dorantes and Alonso del Castillo Maldonado, along with Dorantes's black slave from northwest coastal Africa, Estevan (Estevanico in Cabeza de Vaca's *Relación*)—lived to tell the tale.

The basic outline of the expedition is visually summarized in figure 23, which traces its course and aftermath by location and chronology. The expedition set sail in June 1527 to conquer La Florida, that is, the vast territory to the north of New Spain that included the rim of the Gulf of Mexico and the unexplored regions along the Atlantic seaboard and as far north and west as the Spaniards imagined the continent to extend (see fig. 23). The series of misfortunes that debilitated the expedition and brought it to a disastrous end included a devastating hurricane on the southern shore of Cuba (November 1527), the loss of the expedition in the storm-tossed gulf for a month before landing on the gulf coast of present-day Florida (March–April 1528), the confusion as to what point along the arc of the Gulf of Mexico the expedition had actually landed, and Pánfilo de Narváez's pie-in-the-sky idea of abandoning the ships on the coast to undertake a three-hundred-man overland expedition into the Florida pan-handle to locate the presumed land of wealth called Apalache. The men commanding the remaining ships of the expedition, instructed to later pick up the overland party, never found the three hundred men, and, after a year or so, the ships sailed back to Cuba in 1529. Back at the Florida shoreline in 1528 Narváez and his desperate overland company lost some fifty men to Indian attacks and illness while building makeshift rafts. For a month and a half the survivors coasted along the northern shore of the gulf, hoping to reach the northernmost Spanish outpost at Pánuco in present-day Tamaulipas. Of the five rafts carrying a total of approximately two hundred and fifty men that embarked from the Bay of Horses and headed for Pánuco, Cabeza de Vaca and his three companions were ul-timately the only survivors. They endured enslavement and hardship among the Indians of the Texas coastal region for more than six and a half years; during four of those years Cabeza de Vaca was separated from the other three men. After their reunion and escape in the summer of 1535, they were guided by native groups through the high country and deep valleys of southwestern Texas and northwestern Mexico during ten months in 1535–1536. They emerged in 1536 at the Sinaloa River, where they encountered slave-hunting Spanish soldiers attached to the north-ernmost outpost of San Miguel de Culiacán in Sinaloa in northwestern Mexico. The drama of the episodes he recounts about that reunion and its aftermath have proven over time to be memorable as subsequent writers over the centuries have recounted it for their own varied purposes (see below).

Despite the failure of the expedition, as royal treasurer Cabeza de Vaca owed the emperor a full report. He presented it, both in fulfillment

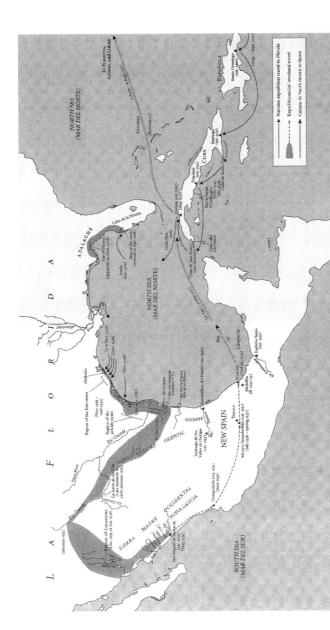

FIGURE 23. Areas traversed by the Narváez expedition (1527–1528) and Cabeza de Vaca and his three companions (1528–1536). Reprinted from *Álvar Núñez Cabeza de Vaca: His Account, His Life and the Expedition of Pánfilo de Narváez* by Rolena Adorno and Patrick Charles Pautz by permission of the University of Nebraska Press. Copyright © 1999 by the University of Nebraska Press. 1:xxvi–xxvii.

of the obligations of his royal commission and in hopes of receiving another one, in the form of his published *Relación*, which he called the only positive result of the many years he "walked lost and naked through many and very strange lands."[11] Of all he recounted, the healing episodes became legendary. At the heart of their presentation Cabeza de Vaca told the tale of Mala Cosa.

MIRACLE CURES AND MALA COSA

The most dramatic portion of Cabeza de Vaca's account begins when the raft that was carrying him was pitched by a wave onto land off the eastern coast of Texas. Although knowing they were near land, the men turned the stern of their craft toward the sea. Still near land (Cabeza de Vaca implies but does not state), it was as if the "hand of divine providence" intervened, because, he writes, "a wave took us that pitched the raft out of the water the distance of a horseshoe's throw, and with the great blow that its fall occasioned, almost all the people who were nearly dead upon it regained consciousness. And since they saw themselves near land, they began to leave the raft, half walking, half crawling" (93). Near Galveston Island at Galveston Bay, Texas, they discovered that they were on an island; Cabeza de Vaca dubbed it "Malhado," the "Island of Ill Fate" (107).

He later reports that it was on that island that the natives "tried to make us physicians without examining us or asking us for our titles, because they cure illnesses by blowing on the sick person, and with that breath of air and their hands they expel the disease from him. And they demanded that we do the same and make ourselves useful" (113). He explains that the natives' methods included making surgical incisions and performing cauterizations with fire, "and after this, they blow upon the area that hurts, and with this they believe that they have removed the malady." He adds: "The manner in which we performed cures was by making the sign of the cross over them and blowing on them, and praying a Pater Noster and an Ave Maria, and as best we could, beseeching our Lord God that he grant them health and move them to treat us well. Our Lord God in His mercy willed that all those on whose behalf we made supplication, after we had made the sign of the cross over them, said to the others that they were restored and healthy, and on account of this they treated us well" (115).

The Spanish-language term that Cabeza de Vaca used is "físico." The thirteenth-century *Siete partidas* describes the *físico* as one who possesses the "knowledge of the nature of things and their interactions; knowing such things, one can do much good and remove evil, particularly preserving the life and health of men and preventing them from falling ill." According to the early seventeenth-century dictionary of Sebastián de Covarrubias Horozco, the *físico* is, similarly, "he who professes the science of the nature of things and knows their qualities and properties." Gonzalo Fernández de Oviedo, who wrote an account of the Narváez expedition based on the now-lost official report prepared by the three Castilians, likened the Narváez men's manner of curing to that of *saludadores,* or curers, in Castile, who cured by blessing and breathing upon the patient. Covarrubias defines this type of healer as one who by grace, *gratis data,* cured men of madness and restored livestock to health, and he adds, tongue-in-cheek (no pun intended), that such individuals should be called "salivadores" instead of "saludadores" because they used their saliva as an agent in curing.[12]

Although both Cabeza de Vaca and Oviedo give accounts of the curings performed by the men, Oviedo identifies the commencement of this practice not in 1528 but in 1535, that is, after the four Narváez survivors have been reunited (for the second time) just prior to their escape from their masters to undertake the overland journey that led them to northwestern Mexico. That is, Oviedo, relying on the men's collective report of their experience, marked the inauguration of the healing episodes as occurring at a late point in the narrative.[13] Cabeza de Vaca, however, claimed that the healing rituals began on the island of Malhado, which would have been some six years earlier, at the end of 1528 or the beginning of 1529. Cabeza de Vaca no doubt made a belated interpolation into the early portion of his narrative in order to anticipate and reinforce his later accounts of healing.[14] This seems plausible because of the discrepancies in Cabeza de Vaca's account between his claims of good treatment received from the Indians for curing and, at the same time, the terrible hardships that he said they endured in forced labor during six and a half years of captivity by various native groups.[15] In this regard, there is more consistency between the specific content of Cabeza de Vaca's and Oviedo's accounts than between Cabeza de Vaca's account and his claim about beginning the curing on Malhado.

Cabeza de Vaca's shift backward in time, claiming that the healing episodes began on Malhado in November 1528 rather than in south-ernmost Texas, just before the men crossed the Rio Grande for the first time in late summer 1535, enhances the providential quality of the entire narration. Nevertheless, Cabeza de Vaca makes his most dramatic claim about the healing practices at this very point in the narration, when they were among the Avavares. Cabeza de Vaca writes that he seemingly brought a dead man back to life and cured many others. The natives reported that he had been successful: "At nighttime they returned to their houses and said that that one who had been dead and whom I had cured in their presence had arisen revived and walked about and eaten and spoken with them, and that as many as I had cured had become well and were without fever and very happy" (163). And while they were in that same location for some eight months, "people came from many areas looking for us and they said that truly we were children of the sun." Now, Cabeza de Vaca asserts, Dorantes and Estevan also began to practice heal-ing, "although in boldness and daring to perform any cure I was the most notable among them" (165).

Also at this precise point in the narration, in which he had just given an account of the increasing and near-complete reverence in which the four men were held during their eight-month stay among the Avavares (in southeastern-most Texas),[16] Cabeza de Vaca asserts, "They believed that as long as we were there, none of them would die" (165). He tells how these Indians, as well as others whom they had encountered, reported the exis-tence of a man who some fifteen or sixteen years earlier had terrorized the people of the area. This strange being, who performed acts of bodily dismemberment and remarkable cures, was called, says Cabeza de Vaca, Mala Cosa, literally, "bad thing."[17] This Mala Cosa was described as bearded and short. Occasionally dressed as a woman, other times as a man, he sometimes presented himself among them when they were dancing. He could send a hut flying through the air and ride it to the ground. Many times, the Indians said, they had given him food, but he never consumed it. When the Indians asked him where he came from, he pointed to a cleft in the earth and said that his home "was there below."

The account Cabeza de Vaca gives of Mala Cosa's deeds is strikingly vivid: Appearing at the door of a house with a burning firebrand, Mala Cosa would enter the dwelling, select a man, and perform two surgical operations, giving his victim three large incisions in his sides with a very sharp flint, a hand wide and two spans long. He would place his hand into the wounds and pull out the entrails, cut off a piece more or less a span long, and throw it into the fire. Afterward he would make three cuts in the arm, the second at the crook, and dislocate it. Mala Cosa then would reset the dislocated limb and place his hands over the wounds. Cabeza de Vaca reports, "They told us that later they were healed" (167). When the Narváez survivors dismissed the tale with a laugh, the Indians brought forward many of their number who said they had been taken by Mala Cosa. Cabeza de Vaca confesses, "We saw the scars of the cuts that he had made in the places and in the manner they had said" (169).

In its own right, the story of Mala Cosa can be identified with one of humanity's oldest inventions, the trickster figure. With a nearly universal distribution that included the ancient Greeks, the Chinese, the Japanese, and the Semitic world, the figure had its earliest and most archaic forms among the Indians of North America, and its patterns have apparently changed little over time, according to Paul Radin's classic study.[18] In its North American Amerindian manifestations, Radin described the trickster as "at one and the same time creator and destroyer, giver and negator, he who dupes others and who is always duped himself. . . . He knows neither good nor evil yet he is responsible for both. He possesses no values, moral or social, is at the mercy of his passions and appetites, yet through his actions all values come into being" (xxiii). Lacking a well-defined or fixed form, the trickster figure was characterized as looking something like a man whose specific features were never seen (xxiv). He remained isolated from the company of society and had the ability to transform himself sexually (133, 137). If divinity was attached to him, it always seemed to be a secondary (not an original) attribution (164). The significance of the trickster theme consisted of its embodiment of "the vague memories of an archaic and primordial past, where there as yet existed no clear-cut differentiation between the divine and the non-divine:" "For this period Trickster is the symbol. His hunger, his sex, his wandering, these appertain neither to the gods nor to man. They belong to another realm, materially and spiritually, and that is why neither the gods nor man know precisely what to do with them" (168–169).

Cabeza de Vaca's Mala Cosa fits this paradigm. The indiscernible facial features of this short, bearded man, his habitation in a cleft in the earth, and his sudden appearances among the Indians, variously dressed in male or female garb as an indication of his sexual transformability, all correspond to the traits of this ancient mythical figure. Whether or not the Indians considered Mala Cosa to be divine, they certainly considered him powerful, setting forth his magical qualities and the fear they experienced upon his appearance: "When he came to the house where they were, their hair stood on end and they trembled."[19]

Other Tricksters

Although neither Oviedo nor Las Casas repeated the Mala Cosa tale reported by Cabeza de Vaca, and other reader-writers who cited the *Relación* were likewise silent about it, the Mala Cosa account bears resemblance to other myths collected in Mesoamerica in the sixteenth and subsequent centuries. Accounts of magical bodily dismemberment and restoration are recorded by other Spanish reporters, such as Cabeza de Vaca's contemporary, the Franciscan friar Bernardino de Sahagún (1499–1590), and, a century and a half later, the Dominican friar Francisco Jiménez (1666–c. 1730), who transcribed and preserved the *Popol Vuh*, the sacred book of the highland Quiché Maya.

In the 1570s Sahagún collected materials about magicians and mountebanks that he mentioned in passing but did not integrate into his *Historia general de las cosas de la Nueva España*.[20] In this constellation of conjurers, Sahagún included seers, diviners, and curers as well as those who terrorized people in order to rob them of their wealth and possessions. Among such charlatans and fakers, the one he described as "the destroyer" (*el destrozador*) is perhaps the most relevant. Always and only performed in the sanctuaries of lordly elites, the legerdemain practiced by the destroyer consisted of a daring stunt of cutting off hands, feet, and other body parts and placing them in various locations. Then he would cover all with a red mantle, and the parts would grow back together as if they had never been cut asunder. At this point, he would reveal the restored body of the victim. In a different register of magical experience, Fray Francisco Jiménez collected the sacred traditions of the *Popol Vuh* in 1701–1703, and he also recorded a myth of corporeal dismemberment.[21] Despite the fact that the mythical and magical content of these tales held meanings specific to Mexica (Nahua) and Quiché Maya cultural settings, the general principle of bodily dismemberment and restoration is shared

with the Indians of coastal Texas and northern Mexico in the tale preserved by Cabeza de Vaca.

With respect to North American Plains Indians, in the lands that the
Spanish from the 1540s onward had called Cíbola, Woodbury Lowery
found cultural resonance between Cabeza de Vaca's account of Mala Cosa
and the Pawnee Indians "of our own day," that is, 1901, in a tale collected by
George Bird Grinnell in 1893 on the basis of the testimony of a friend,
Captain L. H. North, about the deeds carried out by the "masters of mystery" of the Pawnee nation. (Grinnell speculated that the Pawnee had come
from the south, from Mexico along the Río Grande and in Texas, later
migrating as far north as southern Kansas.) The physicians of the Pawnee
were curers, not priests, and their trade was healing sicknesses caused by
evil spirits by expelling them from the victim's body. Among various
descriptions Lowery singled out as being similar to the story of Mala Cosa,
he recounted the tale of a boy of six or eight years of age who was laid down
naked in the middle of a circle of men. Two men sat on him and opened his
abdomen with a knife and pulled out what appeared to be part of his liver.
One cut out the organ and gave it to the other, who ate it. The rest of the
organ was put back in place, and the child carried away. Afterward, he was
seen again, apparently recovered and restored.[22] Whether or not a common cultural origin accounts for the similarity of these Meso- and North
American beliefs, it is clear, following Radin's thesis, that there was a wide
cultural range and time span over which phenomena like that of the
trickster figure occurred and that such accounts of bodily dismemberment
and radical recovery were not uncommon.

The Good Healer Versus the Evil Enchanter

How Cabeza de Vaca and his companions would have understood this
phenomenon in the sixteenth century is another matter. He indicated, by
the laughter that signified his and his companions' dismissal of the Mala
Cosa tale, that the Indians' senses had deceived them. Deception by the
senses was the way that learned men at the time explained such phenomena. In the *Apologética historia sumaria,* Las Casas explained that such
deceptions subverted the external senses (sight, hearing, etc.) or the internal senses (imagination, fantasy, and common sense) and were produced
by three means: (1) the "art and industry of men," without diabolical

intervention; (2) natural causes that lacked both diabolic and human intervention; (3) demons, "when God allows them to use the virtues and powers over certain inferior things that He had given them in their apprenticeship as good angels."[23] These diabolical deceits occurred always with divine consent and often also with the express collaboration of magicians and charlatans working in concert with the devil by means of "the pact and partnership between them" (495).

Mala Cosa's transformations were likely to be considered diabolical by Cabeza de Vaca and his fellows, and the Indians who bore scars as evidence of their wounds from his surgical rituals could be considered innocent victims or themselves sorcerers in concert with the devil. Consistent with his position that human sacrifice and idolatry were absent among all the Indian groups he encountered, Cabeza de Vaca implicitly suggests the Indians' innocence by observing that he and his fellows attempted to comfort them in their fears of Mala Cosa. At the same time, he assessed Mala Cosa and his actions as diabolical when he remarked that he assured the Indians that if they believed in the Christians' god they would need not fear Mala Cosa, as well as when he claims he had promised that, as long as he and his companions (as Christians) were in the land, Mala Cosa would not dare reappear.[24]

Cabeza de Vaca did not have to attribute the visits of Mala Cosa explicitly to satanic intervention in order for his readers to understand that such was his implicit and obvious interpretation of the deed. In this light, the sort of myth that would have interested Cabeza de Vaca and his readers did not pertain to Amerindian but rather to Christian mythology, that is, those tales by which Christian culture represented and reproduced itself from medieval times onward. In this respect, Cabeza de Vaca and his fellows played the role of the good angel, the Christian proselytizer, engaged in a struggle for men's souls against the bad angel, the pagan sorcerer.

In Cabeza de Vaca's story, the tale of Mala Cosa takes on meaning according to the model of comportment of the Christian warrior that came from a chivalric tradition of which the thirteenth-century Ramón Llull (c. 1235–1316) was an early exemplar. To Llull, the first duty of the Christian knight was to defend the faith and convert infidels to it. The tradition was brought to the Indies in the sixteenth century in a later transformation by which Hernán Cortés became the model of the *dux populi* in his own writings and in those of others, most notably Fray Gerónimo de Mendieta's (1525–1604) *Historia eclesiástica Indiana,* in which he is characterized as the "Moses of the New World."[25] Gómara's dedication of his *Historia general de las Indias* to Charles V emphasized the point: "The conquest of the Indians [of the Americas] began when that of the Muslims was completed, because the Spanish have always warred against infidels" [Comenzaron las conquistas de indios acabada la de moros, por que siempre guerreasen españoles contra infieles].[26]

The Christian caballero as defender and promoter of the faith with the capacity to lead great numbers of people is the implicit model presented by Cabeza de Vaca for the men's experience in the Texas-Tamaulipas area, and it anticipates his fully realized *dux populi* interpretation of the final portion of the men's journey, through the area of Sinaloa in Nueva Galicia (see fig. 23). Representing the triumph of the Christian cavalier over the pagan necromancer, the myth of Mala Cosa is a key insertion into Cabeza de Vaca's account; it reproduces the paradigmatic episode from the history of the evangelization of the pagans as bringing the Christian gospel to the Amerindians. This is the first of only two occasions in Cabeza de Vaca's account in which he indicates that he and his companions tried to teach the natives about the Christian religion. The second occurs later at Culiacán, when the men call down to the floodplain the people who had fled to the sierras to persuade them to worship the Christian god (see below). Only in the case of Mala Cosa does a contest between the good healer and the evil enchanter appear, and the four men's apparent triumph over his influence represents a triumph over the devil.

The Mala Cosa episode brings to a conclusion a narrative cycle that began with Cabeza de Vaca's (probably apocryphal) account of his experience as a healer on the island of Malhado and ends in the last moments before the men put into action their plan to leave the Avavares and make a concerted, collective effort to push forward to Pánuco. The presentation of this story-within-a-story is teleologically effective, claiming the triumph of the Narváez survivors' faith over the Indians' superstition. The Mala Cosa story narrates the confrontation between Christianity and superstitious or diabolical paganism that occurred only indirectly; the protagonists were the four Christians and Mala Cosa's victims (not Mala Cosa himself), since Mala Cosa had allegedly been in the area a decade and a half earlier. As a result, the tale stands as a bold emblem not of the four men's actual experience in coastal Texas, but rather of the dramatic *dux populi* interpretation Cabeza de Vaca made of it.

Within the larger narrative, the Mala Cosa episode serves to focus and define the providential character of the mission Cabeza de Vaca implicitly assigned to himself and his companions as physicians and healers in the lands to the north of New Spain. In the sequence of the account it not only concludes one thematic cycle (from Cabeza de Vaca's first curings to the men's first attempt to teach their hosts about Christianity), but also begins another: the men's liberation from native captivity, the doubt that they had achieved liberation when they fell into the hands of Spanish slave hunters, and the denouement, that is, their resettlement of native peoples in northwestern Mexico, the baptism of the children of their lords, and the sworn promise (the *requerimiento*) to accept the lordship of the Castilian monarch and his Christian religion.

PARADISE LOST

After Cabeza de Vaca's account of the four men's departure from Texas and Tamaulipas in the summer of 1535, they arrive at the Río Yaqui around Christmastime that year (see fig, 23). From this point on in the narration, and from the Río Yaqui to Compostela, the capital of Nueva Galicia in the present-day state of Jalisco, Cabeza de Vaca's narrative is concerned with the devastating effects of the conquest of Nueva Galicia, which had been undertaken by Nuño Beltrán de Guzmán in 1530–1531, when he was president of the first Audiencia of New Spain.[27] Cabeza de Vaca's account of the trip south from the Río Yaqui is a description of depopulated lands and ill and starving people worn down by the hardships caused by their flight from Spanish slave hunters. He does not mince words: "We traveled through much land and we found all of it deserted, because the inhabitants of it went fleeing through the sierras without daring to keep houses or work the land for fear of the Christians. It was a thing that gave us great sorrow, seeing the land very fertile and very beautiful and very full of waterways and rivers, and seeing the places deserted and burned and the people so emaciated and sick, all of them having fled and in hiding. And since they did not sow, with so much hunger they maintained themselves on the bark of trees and roots. This hunger affected us in part along this entire road, because only poorly could they provide for us, being so displaced from their natural homeland that it seemed that they wished to die."[28]

Reiterating that the Indians "were determined to let themselves die" rather than "waiting to be treated with as much cruelty as they had been up to that point" by the Spanish slave hunters, Cabeza de Vaca states that he and his party anticipated with fear their eventual encounter with the Indians "who held the frontier against the Christians and were at war with them," anticipating that "they would treat us cruelly and make us pay for what the Christians were doing to them." So stating, he prepares the moment for a strategic pronouncement: "But since God our Lord was served to bring us to them, they began to fear and respect us as the previous ones had done, and even somewhat more, about which we were not a little amazed, by which it is clearly seen that all these peoples, to be drawn to become Christians and to obedience to the Imperial Majesty, must be given good treatment, and this is the path most certain and no other" (241).

Here there are no accounts of healings. Instead, the work described by Cabeza de Vaca in the last few chapters of his narration is that of pacifying or resettling abandoned lands. After they had crossed the Río Yaqui in Sonora and continued to head south the challenge would come not from hostile natives but from the Spaniards' hostile countrymen: "And we always found traces and signs of where Christians had slept," and he reported that the Indians "went hidden through the mountains, fleeing to avoid being killed or made slaves by the Christians, and that the previous night while they were behind some trees watching what they were doing, they had seen the Christians and saw how they were bringing many Indians in chains" (243).

Now, for the first time since leaving Cuba in the spring of 1528, Cabeza de Vaca and his companions met fellow countrymen, led by Diego de Alcaraz, a magistrate (alcalde) in northern Nueva Galicia. The site was the Río Petatlán in Sinaloa. Alcaraz's men's actions had driven away their native suppliers of food and labor, so at Alcaraz's request Cabeza de Vaca and his men managed to persuade the natives to come forth and bring their hidden supplies of food from the hills. When some six hundred natives appeared with an abundance of foodstuffs, the Alcaraz party expected to be able to enslave the natives who had succored them. Cabeza de

Vaca's trial by fire occurred when he and his men bribed the slave hunters, with the native goods they carried, to desist in their plan (249). However, while the Cabeza de Vaca party was led over a torturous inland route on which they would have no further contact with the natives of the area, Alcaraz and his men went off into the hills to capture more slaves (253).

This is a tale of paradise lost, and Cabeza de Vaca attempts to turn it into a spectacle of paradise regained. Some twenty-five leagues farther south, at the native settlement of Culiacán, Cabeza de Vaca explains, his party met the chief justice and civil official (*alcalde mayor*) of the province, Melchor Díaz, who persuaded Cabeza de Vaca to help resettle the natives of the area. The accounts of Nuño de Guzmán's incursions had shown this region to be one of the most well-populated and well-developed in the Indies. Cabeza de Vaca feared they would not be able to accomplish the feat of resettlement because, he remarked, "we did not bring any Indian of ours or any of those who usually accompanied us and were skilled in these matters" (255). So they entrusted the task to two of the local Spaniards' Indian captives, who had "been with the Christians when we first arrived to them, and they saw the people who accompanied us and learned from them about the great authority and influence that through all those lands we had possessed and exercised, and the wonders that we had worked and the sick people we had cured and many other things" (255–257).

RESETTLEMENT AND *REQUERIMIENTO*

This major resettlement follows a pattern Cabeza de Vaca had established much earlier in his account; that is, he implies (but does not assert) that the authority he and his fellows enjoyed with the natives was granted by the natives themselves.[29] Long before he and his three companions had come upon areas where Europeans had had previous contact, he suggests, their skills at negotiating between groups and working with native strategies of contact and movement had prepared them well for the challenge later to be placed upon them by the Spanish colonizers of Nueva Galicia. And he takes advantage of his earlier assertion about the ten months of overland travel to the effect that news of the four men anticipated their arrival, and so they were accordingly always well received by each successive new group encountered. (This will be significant in El Inca Garcilaso's reading of Cabeza de Vaca's *Naufragios;* see chapter 11.)

The event that Cabeza de Vaca next reports constituted a legal act of conquest. Cabeza de Vaca stated that, in seven days, three native lords came down from their mountain refuge, bringing all their people. Melchor Díaz recited to them the *requerimiento*, the legal ultimatum imposed in 1526 as a requisite feature of all Spanish conquests, by which its hearers were given the option to accept either Spanish dominion or war, slavery, and death (257, 259). If they chose to be Christian, the newcomers would be their friends; if not, they would be treated badly and taken as slaves to other lands.[30] Cabeza de Vaca's careful reiteration of Melchor Díaz's reading of the requerimiento was deliberate and pointed because Pánfilo de Narváez's expedition was the first that was legally bound to employ it.[31] The Requirement was an infamous document. Although it and related laws have been interpreted by Lewis Hanke and others as the means to protect the Indians, the requerimiento in particular served the purpose of legalizing Indian slavery and facilitating its execution.

The Requirement

The Requirement had been espoused, formulated, and imposed by a junta of jurists and theologians who met at the Dominican monastery of San Pablo in Valladolid in 1513. It was reasoned that man had been created by God as a rational being with the knowledge of good and evil; if the Indians did not worship the single god who had created them but rather many gods (and hence, were idolaters), this was sufficient cause to conquer them and take away their lands.[32] The argument formulated at the junta was based on an interpretation of how the ancient Israelites rightfully gained the Promised Land ("la tierra de Promisión," the land of Canaan) from gentiles and idolaters. After Moses' death, Joshua led the Israelites across the River Jordan and presented an ultimatum to the people of Jericho, demanding that they abandon the city to the Israelites, to whom God had promised it (see Josh. 3.7–13, 6.16–21). When the Canaanites refused, Joshua took the land by force, "killing an infinite number of them, capturing many; the ones he captured he took as slaves and used them as such. And all this was done by the will of God, because they were idolaters" (CDI 1: 443–444). By this logic, the pope, surrogate for God on earth, gave the Indies, possessed by idolaters, to the Castilian king, who likewise could rightfully demand (*requerir*) that the Indians, as idolaters, relinquish their lands to the Christian monarch to whom the pope had assigned it. If the Indians failed to give up the land, the king could take it by force, killing and capturing and granting as slaves those who were prisoners, "as Joshua had done to those who inhabited the Promised Land" (CDI 1: 444). This proposition was to be contained in the proclamation to be read to the Indians.

The requerimiento was subject to criticism by both proponents and opponents of the Spanish conquests in the Indies. Oviedo rejected it as ridiculous. He suggested that it best be read to some Indian confined in a cage, "so that he could learn it slowly and the lord bishop could teach him its contents." Meeting the author of the document, the jurist Juan López de Palacios Rubios, in 1516, Oviedo inquired if Christian conscience was satisfied by the use of the requerimiento, and Palacios Rubios replied that it was, if the conquest was carried out as the document dictated. Oviedo was not convinced because it was clear to him that the Indians had no way of understanding the ultimatum without "the discourse of years and time."[33]

Unlike Oviedo, who rejected the requerimiento because it could not be understood by the Indians, Las Casas repudiated it because Palacios Rubios based it on what Las Casas considered to be grave errors in the theological doctrine of the thirteenth-century canonist Enrique de Susa (El Ostiense, Hostiensis). This doctrine effectively granted the pope temporal dominion on earth not only over Christians but also over infidels and idolaters, against whom war could be justly waged because, according to Susa, Christ's coming denied to those who did not accept the gospel the ownership of their properties and possessions.[34] Cabeza de Vaca's detailed reference to the requerimiento is well placed.

MELCHOR DÍAZ, GÓMARA, AND LAS CASAS

After Melchor Díaz's declaration, which includes, in Cabeza de Vaca's account, Díaz's extemporized remarks about the nine-year peregrination of the four Narváez men, the assembled lords accept Melchor Díaz's invitation to submit peacefully, giving assurances that they would "be very good Christians and serve God."[35] At this climactic moment of the acceptance of the requerimiento, Cabeza de Vaca again interrupts the narrative action to present a discussion of native beliefs: "And when asked to what they gave reverence and made sacrifices and whom they asked for water for their maize fields and health for themselves, they responded that it was to a man who was in the sky. We asked them what his name was. And they said it was Aguar, and that they believed that he had created the whole world and all the things in it. . . . We told them that the one to whom they referred we called God, and that thus they should call him and serve and adore him as we commanded and they would be well served by it" (259). As in accounts of the conquest of New Spain, the next ritual action is baptism; Cabeza de Vaca tells that they now baptized the children of the principal lords: "And we had them bring the children of the most important lords and baptize them" [E hizimos traer los hijos de los prinçipales señores y bautizarlos] (261).[36]

Cabeza de Vaca goes on to tell how they then instructed the Indians, who represented those from the Río Petatlán (Sinaloa River) and the sierras, to resettle and place crosses at the entrances to their homes. When Christians came, they were to go out and receive them, "with the crosses in their hands, without their bows and other weapons," and offer them food from their own provisions. If they did this, the Christians would not harm them but would be their friends. According to Cabeza de Vaca, Melchor Díaz gave these people animal-skin robes and treated them well. All then returned to their homes, including the two captives who had served as intermediaries (257, 259). Cabeza de Vaca underscores the formal character of this negotiation by noting that the lords' agreement to these conditions was given in the presence of many witnesses, and the notary (escribano) certified its occurrence.

Cabeza de Vaca thus gives assurances regarding the most pressing issue of his time, that of renewing the productivity of lands left uncultivated and people dislocated and starving because of conquest. In these episodes, Cabeza de Vaca anticipates Gómara's dictum: "Whoever fails to populate the land does not make a good conquest; without conquering the land, the people will not be converted. Thus, the maxim of conquerer must be to people the land" [Quien no poblare, no hará buena conquista, y no conquistando la tierra, no se convertirá la gente; así que la máxima del conquistar ha de ser poblar].[37] Gómara expresses here a conviction he shared with Sepúlveda: conquer first, convert second. Las Casas's opposing view—namely, that only after voluntary and peaceful conversion should neophytes decide, of their own free will, to accept (or not) the sovereignty of the king of Castile—explains why he does not reiterate Melchor Díaz's ultimatum when he reports Cabeza de Vaca's commentary on the scene. (As mentioned earlier, the requerimiento was rejected by Oviedo because of its unrealistic demand and by Las Casas because of its flawed theology that held that the pope possessed temporal as well as spiritual dominion over the world and that the practice of idolatry was cause for just war and enslavement.)

Moving on to the Spanish *villa* of San Miguel de Culiacán (see fig. 23), and after being there two weeks, Cabeza de Vaca relates that Diego de Alcaraz arrived to report that the desired resettlement had taken place and that the Indians "came out to receive them with crosses in their hands and took them to their houses and shared with them what they had" (263). In other words, according to Cabeza de Vaca, the conditions of Melchor Díaz's requirement have been carried out to the letter. At this climactic moment, Cabeza de Vaca addresses the emperor directly: "May God our Lord in his infinite mercy grant, in all the days of Your Majesty and under your authority and dominion, that these people come and be truly and with complete devotion subject to the true Lord who created and redeemed them. And we hold it for certain that it will be so, and that Your Majesty will be the one who is to put this into effect, that it will not be so difficult to do, because in the two thousand leagues that we traveled by land and through the sea on the rafts and another ten months that we went through the land without stopping once we were no longer captives, we found neither sacrifices nor idolatry" (263).

These are the very words Las Casas takes up in his *Apologética historia sumaria,* citing them in full when he introduces Cabeza de Vaca and his discussion of the Indians of La Florida (see the section, "Las Casas, Theorist of Amerindian Character and Custom," in chapter 3). Las Casas introduces the citation by stating, "This [caballero], having lived and walked through those lands nine continuous years, in the report that he gave to the emperor about them, says these words, nearly at the end."[38] Las Casas also repeats the account, in the post-requerimiento phase of Melchor Díaz's and Cabeza de Vaca's exchange with the natives, of how Cabeza de Vaca, once united with Spaniards in the territory of "the kingdoms of Jalisco," discovered that the Indians worshiped "a man who was in the sky" whom they called Aguar and to whom they attributed the "creation of the world and everything in it" (652). Thus Las Casas uses Cabeza de Vaca's testimony in making one of his central arguments about the Indians' possession of an ancient, intuitive but vague notion about the Judeo-Christian god, which therefore predisposed them to accept the

Christian faith: "Great and very great is the propinquity, aptitude, and disposition that those peoples have to come to the knowledge of their and our true Lord." He adds that every true lover of God would relish the opportunity to serve in the evangelization of those "starving and ignorant and well-disposed peoples."[39] He was also no doubt heartened by Cabeza de Vaca's claim that Melchor Díaz "made a solemn oath to God to neither make nor consent to making any incursion nor to take slaves in that land or among people whom we had secured, and that this he would uphold and fulfill until His Majesty and the governor Nuño de Guzmán or the viceroy in his name acted to comply with what would best serve God our Lord and His Majesty" (261).

The scene portrayed by Cabeza de Vaca and repeated by El Inca Garcilaso (see chapter 11) of the natives coming forth with crosses in their hands, intended to be spiritually edifying, was criticized by Las Casas in his *Historia de las Indias* as an ill-thought-out practice that would promote native belief in material objects (the wooden cross rather than the invisible, all-powerful deity for which it stood).[40] Nevertheless, Cabeza de Vaca's emphasis on the theme was read with profit by his readers in successive centuries. The resettlement of native peoples in their homeland laid the groundwork for what would become one of the themes regularly taken up in the readings and rereadings of Cabeza de Vaca's account. Resettlement is the first realization of the theme, and it is followed by that of new settlement and new foundations. Inasmuch as this topic, the notion of a traditional native paradise lost and recovered, led to the creation (and loss) of new foundations in the novels of the twentieth century, the sixteenth-century *Relación/Naufragios* of Cabeza de Vaca emerges as one of the founding works of the Latin American literary tradition. This claim can be made because of the persistence of the theme in the works of successive centuries.

MYTHS OF FOUNDATION

This importance of place, as Cabeza de Vaca portrays it in his party's resettlement of native peoples in Culiacán, initiated a series of writings by readers who recorded the establishment of new foundations and new settlements in such a way that the Cabeza de Vaca account gave way to, or became, their foundational myth.[41] Whereas northwestern Mexico was inhabited by the Spanish since 1530–1531 following Nuño de Guzmán's conquest of the vast area that was named Nueva Galicia (not Mayor España, as he would have preferred it to be designated, in order to best Cortés's Nueva España), the areas of today's Nuevo León and Coahuila would not be visited by Europeans until several decades after Cabeza de Vaca and his party had passed through the region (see fig. 23). Still, in one of the earliest works written about the area Cabeza de Vaca and his fellows became its founding figures. In 1649, Captain Alonso de León finished his *Historia de Nuevo León,* in which he sought to study "this land, its discoverers and wars, the temperament and condition of its native inhabitants."[42] He incorporated the Cabeza de Vaca sojourn into his history, employing it in the first part of his tripartite work, in which he concluded that the Indians of "the New Kingdom of León" (which he defined as bordered by the limits of New Spain, La Florida, Nueva Vizcaya, and the North Sea [Atlantic] coast) had "neither a true nor false but rather confused knowledge of God" and that their barbarism was such that they had "left the nature although not the form of men and become savages, forgetting the purpose for which they were created, recognizing neither God nor king" (24–25).

After painting this grim picture, which combines Las Casas's emphasis on the lost knowledge of the Judeo-Christian god and Sepúlveda's focus on savage customs, and in order to mitigate it, León wrote the succeeding chapter on the topic of how "no nation has lacked teachers to teach the knowledge of the true God, and there have been signs of the same in this kingdom" (26). Searching for appropriate antecedents in pre-Columbian times, he suggested that the Mexican god Quetzalcoatl, described by Torquemada, Gómara, and others, might in fact have been such an apostolic visitor, Saint Thomas (see chapter 12). Likewise, the people of Nuevo León could not have failed to be visited by "some man or, by the will of God, some angel," who would have given them the light of truth. As evidence of such a visit, he pointed to a mysterious rock painting in a certain settlement, the subject of which seemed to be persons "dressed in Spanish garb" with hens or other barnyard fowl of Castile placed alongside them (28).

Against the background of such tentative evidence regarding the announcement of the Christian gospel in the region, León concluded his chapter with reference to the "account that Cabeza de Vaca gives" of his journey. It stood to reason, León argued, that to have emerged from their captivity and wandering where they did (in Sinaloa), the four men would have had to have traveled very near the spot of the present-day *villa* of Cerralvo as they went about teaching the people, performing miracles, and resuscitating the dead. The Cabeza de Vaca example bolstered his argument to the effect that no territory—not even Nuevo León—was so remote as to not have been visited at some point by bearers of the "good news" (30). León's account makes two pertinent points. Not only did Cabeza de Vaca and his companions pass through *here*, that is, Nuevo León, but in doing so they removed the taint of remoteness, or the indifference of providence, that characterized those isolated frontier lands. This is similar to the argument that El Inca Garcilaso makes a few decades earlier about La Florida (see chapter 11), and it is one that readers of Cabeza de Vaca carry forward in increasingly secularized versions into the twentieth century.

Another tendency was to identify Cabeza de Vaca and his companions as the founding figures of the area not only by their passage through it, but particularly by claiming that they resettled native peoples of the area. Thus, the Jesuit Andrés Pérez de Ribas, in his *Historia de los triumphos de nuestra santa fee entre gentes las más Bárbaras y fieras del Nuevo Orbe* (1645), attributed a spiritual evangelizing role to the Cabeza de Vaca party.[43] He added, however, something more: the "transmigration," as he called it, of the natives. Like Padre Vicente del Águila shortly before him, Pérez de Ribas referred to the establishment of the Christian faith in Sinaloa through the settlement of peoples from the north (north of New Spain, that is) accompanying the Cabeza de Vaca party: "Those who came with them remained to settle in this land."[44] He called the settlement Bamoa and said it "still exists today [that is, 1645], and it is of the language and nation of a people [Nebomes] from more than a hundred leagues away."[45] He could not be more emphatic about the meaning of the sojourn of the Narváez survivors and this migration: "Thus it may be seen that the great pilgrimage of these four companions was the medium of Divine Providence for bringing the first notice of these faraway peoples, who inhabit places so distant that their limits are not yet known."[46] Pérez de Ribas later compared this to the Exodus of the Israelites from Egypt, telling of a migration of three hundred and fifty Nebomes who, despite endless obstacles over the eighty-league journey, came to live at Bamoa. When he declared that the means by which divine providence was thus served had been Cabeza de

Vaca's settlement of their kinsmen in 1536, and when he called this migration and settlement the "miraculous exodus from Egypt,"[47] Pérez de Ribas cast Cabeza de Vaca implicitly in the role of Moses. Another seventeenth-century religious author, the Franciscan friar Antonio Tello in his *Crónica miscelánea de la Sancta Provincia de Xalisco* (1650–1653), also presented Cabeza de Vaca and his companions as larger-than-life figures in the "spiritual conquest" of the north; Tello's signal contribution had been his attempt to write their story into the conquest history of the area undertaken by Nuño de Guzmán a century earlier.

The eighteenth century marked the beginning of a "new era" of the reception of the Cabeza de Vaca account.[48] In addition to the bibliographic foundation provided by Andrés González de Barcia Carballido y Zúñiga's edition of the *Naufragios,* its interest lay in the fact that it was accompanied by a polemical treatise by Antonio Ardoino, a member of an aristocratic ruling family of northeastern Sicily who served the Spanish crown as governor of Tarragona, Catalonia, as well as in other positions in the early to mid–eighteenth century. Ardoino's goal in his *Examen apologético de la histórica narración de los Naufragios, peregrinaciones i milagros de Alvar Núñez Cabeza de Vaca en las tierras de la Florida i del Nuevo México* was to refute the claims made a century earlier, in 1621,[49] by a Benedictine monk in Austria (one Caspar Plautius, also known as Honorio Philopono) to the effect that Cabeza de Vaca's *Relación* was incredible as a history and false with respect to the performance of miracle cures. Whereas Plautius's contemporary the Jesuit José de Acosta used the lay status of the men to enhance the prospect of Amerindian conversion, the Benedictine considered that their vocation (the "mean and vulgar" pursuits of soldiering) denied the possibility altogether.[50] Plautius argued against the principle of the unity of cross and conquest inaugurated by Constantine ("In hoc signo vinces") and concluded that "it is agreed that these works [of conversion] have been performed by those friars and priests who are holy and not by evil soldiers."[51]

In addition insisting on the veracity of the events and the miracle cures, Ardoino attempted to plot those deeds in the geographic locations and political contexts of La Florida and Nuevo México, that is, Spain's lands beyond the borders of New Spain. Ardoino thus continued the trend of making regional identifications, and his work was taken up by regionalist writers of the subsequent decades, in particular, Matías de la

Mota Padilla and Fray Pablo Beaumont.[52] Mota Padilla's *Historia del reino de Nueva Galicia en la América septentrional* was published in 1742; Beaumont's *Crónica de la provincia de San Pedro y San Pablo de Michoacán* was written circa 1777 but went unpublished until the nineteenth century. Both reproduced the now-familiar themes associated with Cabeza de Vaca of the "spiritual conquest" of the area of northwestern Mexico, Jalisco, and Michoacán (Spanish Nueva Galicia).

PLACE AS *PATRIA*

To trace these trends in the readings of Cabeza de Vaca, we need a map. These writers were mapping their territories politically as well as spiritually, and Cabeza de Vaca and his fellows became the earliest European (and African) surveyors of areas they barely knew (or, more likely, did not know at all). The seventeenth- and eighteenth-century writers told a very old tale about the Americas; they were versions of the visits of Christ's disciples in apostolic times.[53] The pertinent feature of the application of the tradition of evangelizing, miracle-performing tales to the Cabeza de Vaca experience is that the focus is not on the performance of miracles in the abstract, but rather on the fact that those miracles were performed *here*. The pilgrim figure consecrates the place.

Through the occurrence of several historical transformations, other principles applied to the readings of Cabeza de Vaca in the nineteenth century and well into the twentieth. Now the phenomenon of travel, rather than settlement and resettlement or the performance of miracles, became the dominant theme. The passion for locating the sites of the Cabeza de Vaca sojourn and passage became an abiding interest in the United States from the middle of the nineteenth century when Buckingham Smith translated Cabeza de Vaca's account into English for the first time. By the 1930s and 1940s, the obsession with finding Cabeza de Vaca's route across North America acquired a fever pitch as geographers, historians, and amateur archaeologists sought to make Cabeza de Vaca part of Anglo-American history by projecting his party's route across Texas and into New Mexico and maybe even Arizona before slipping, somewhat reluctantly, southward into Mexico.[54] Among the many U.S. scholars of the Cabeza de Vaca route, the Berkeley geographer Carl O. Sauer, following the lead of the Swiss-born anthropologist/archaeologist Adolph Bandelier, who was one of the first to study native Amerindian cultures of the U.S. Southwest, worked hard to know the country. With respect to discovering not the Cabeza de Vaca route per se but rather the "great arterial highway" that "led by way of the coastal lowlands of the Mexican Northwest to the northern land of the Pueblo Indians, and at the last, to California," the Indian road that became the path of European exploration, which Sauer called "the Road to Cíbola," Sauer stated: "I had the occasion to cover, by car, on horseback, and afoot, virtually all the country between the Gila River on the north and the Río Grande de Santiago at the south. I have seen all but a very few miles of the route herein examined, and have been over a good deal of it a number of times and at different seasons of the year."[55] Apart from such historical and geographical study, there was considerable interest from state historical societies and other regional patrimonies in making the Cabeza de Vaca route part of local history. "Cabeza de Vaca slept here" hallowed the historical ground in a secular way in the twentieth century in contrast to the sacred histories elaborated from the mid–seventeenth century onward.

Cabeza de Vaca (and now Estevan) becomes the vehicle to connect people to a place. It was so in the seventeenth and eighteenth centuries, and it seems to be clearly so now. *Patria*, homeland, is not a place but a relationship, and the Cabeza de Vaca phenomenon has served as a catalyst to create relationships between peoples and places. The constellation (probably a universe) of ideas identified by the name Cabeza de Vaca seems to do that, and also—and maybe most of all—to connect people with their imaginations.[56] In this sense, it is as difficult to account objectively for the passion for Cabeza de Vaca the phenomenon today as it is to try to understand the passionate ambitions of Cabeza de Vaca the man four and a half centuries ago. While the healing miracles as such give but one dimension of the interpretive history of the Cabeza de Vaca story, its significance can be configured more broadly. The casting of the four men as founders and civilizers in the northwest (and in one instance, the northeast) of New Spain became a prominent theme that identified them as the Adam of the Spanish presence on the northern frontier and the Moses of the native peoples to the north. In this manner, readers, beginning in the seventeenth century, grafted the civic and patrimonial impulse onto the religious initiative and subtly transformed the realization of the universal goals of Spanish territorial expansion and Christian religious conversion in the eighteenth century into the harbingers—even in the word's archaic sense as "people sent ahead to provide lodgings"—of regional identity.

More recently, the Cabeza de Vaca account has been appropriated to identity politics. This has been the largest and most perceptible trend in interpretation since the 1960s. Cabeza de Vaca's account of the experience of a handful of survivors of a huge and failed seagoing expedition has provided a nearly inexhaustible body of material to the literary and cultural domains that include Spanish, Spanish-speaking Latin American, and U.S.-based, that is, Anglo-American, Mexican American, Latino-American, and African American constituencies.[57] The figure of Estevan specifically has called the attention of U.S. African American cultural interests, which find Cabeza de Vaca's account notable for its unique portrayal of the black African historical presence and protagonism in the prehistory of the United States.

Estevan, Andrés Dorantes's slave, was an Arabic-speaking black man (*negro alárabe*) from Azemmour, a city and fortified outpost of Portugal from 1508 to 1540, located in the Doukkala province of the kingdom of Morocco.[58] The figure of Estevan has become a staple in Latin American cultural studies, and it has also been the subject of interpretation in historical novels and academic compendia.[59] In 1997, *The Norton Anthology of African American Literature* made a significant but indirect reference to the Narváez expedition and Cabeza de Vaca's account in its chronology, "African American Literature in Context," by citing 1526 (1527 is the correct date) as the year when the first African slaves were "brought to what is now the United States by the Spanish."[60] (For the record, it should be noted that African slaves had been brought to the Caribbean Islands, including Puerto Rico, since at least 1501; see chapter 3.)

HISTORY'S SECRETS, NARRATIVE'S POTENTIAL

History's secrets are hinted at, but not told, in narrative accounts like Cabeza de Vaca's. This is what keeps alive the potential for rereading, retelling, and reinventing the tale over the centuries. The historical protagonist as narrator is not a well-rounded figure; he conceals more than he reveals, in part intentionally and in part despite himself. His profile, even his portrait, is therefore susceptible to reinvention. Ironically, fictional characters, if exquisitely crafted, are harder to reform and reinvent; their contours and outlines may be too well chiseled for us, as readers, to be convinced by a look-alike simulacrum. The slim notice of the possible shipwreck survivor whose life was created in books and who became known as Gonzalo Guerrero, and the one who was christened Álvar Núñez and took the distinguished maternal surname of Cabeza de Vaca were both, ultimately, historical. The shipwreck victim thought to have survived in Yucatán was almost entirely unknown; the information about him can be summed up in two items: he was a sailor, probably from Palos de Moguer, and he was shipwrecked in Yucatán. His identity and actions were a mystery, and both dimensions have been invented and reinvented, right up through the end of the twentieth century. Cabeza de Vaca, meanwhile, was less known in his person than in the vividly articulated deeds he narrated with clarity and apparent conviction. His historical actions have become stylized and narrowed as those of the Christian caballero devoted to settling and civilizing Indians and serving a demanding but grateful monarch.

The lesson learned from these readings of the narratives written about Gonzalo Guerrero as well as the one written by Cabeza de Vaca and the retellings they have generated is that, contrary to common expectations, history, by keeping its secrets, lends itself to fictionalization. The best meditations on this phenomenon come from writers of fiction. If the historian is caught up in the lust for data, the novelist reveals the folly of such a craving. Juan José Saer, in his novel *El entenado* (1983), translated as *The Witness*, and Abel Posse, in his novel *El largo atardecer del caminante* (1992), which I translate loosely as "The Long Twilight of the Wanderer," have taken up the theme of the quintessential, mythic experience of the European lost in the wilderness of the Americas and living among its native peoples. Both Saer and Posse wrote their novels from the perspective of the protagonist writing his memoirs decades later.[61] Saer's inspiration for his protagonist, a former cabin boy (*grumete*), was not Cabeza de Vaca's account, but Posse's protagonist is Cabeza de Vaca himself. Their choices suggest that history's secrets pertain, respectively, to the events narrated and to the subject who is their protagonist. That is, by creating an anonymous protagonist, Saer focuses on the challenge that his witness/ survivor/narrator faces in attempting to describe the customs and contradictions of the native group with whom he had lived long ago and for whom he felt both compassion and repugnance. His inability to recapture their essence, if he ever understood it, is further confounded by the theatrical representation that he had produced about them. In the end, his attempts at writing about them reveal only himself.[62] In contrast, by giving his protagonist the name and identity of the historical figure, Posse focuses on the events. His Cabeza de Vaca dispatches the desire of others for certainty in his recollections as well as the old conquistador's illusions about the possibility of reproducing them. One of the protagonist's interlocutors remarks, "They say that you have a secret version, a third version of your travels or journey." Reflecting on this assertion some time (and pages) later, the aged Cabeza de Vaca replies, to himself, "I have no patience for the prestigious lie of exactitude."[63] In this way he assures himself that he does not need to give an accounting, even to himself. His gesture conceals the problem not only of what he *did not* or *would not* say, but what he *could not* utter. The issue is twofold: possessing knowledge and communicating it.

With characteristic economy and elegance, Jorge Luis Borges offers the most convincing dramatization of these matters in his story "The Ethnographer." The leanness of his narrative account and the simplicity of his protagonist's remarks, uttered in direct dialogue, evoke the significant silences of any Cabeza de Vaca; this one is named Fred Murdock. Borges begins, "I was told about the case in Texas, but it had happened in another state."[64] Murdock, a university student, followed the recommendation of his professors and devoted himself to the study of Amerindian languages. To do so, he spent two years on an Indian reservation in some U.S. state in prairie country. Upon returning to the university, he announces to his mentor that he will not be writing the anticipated doctoral dissertation because, he says, "I learned something out there that I can't express."[65] When he's asked if perhaps the English language is incapable of communicating what he has learned, Murdock answers, "That's not it, sir. Now that I possess the secret, I could tell it in a hundred different and even contradictory ways. I don't know how to tell you this, but the secret is beautiful, and science, *our* science, seems mere frivolity to me now." After a pause he adds, "And anyway, the secret is not as important as the paths that led me to it. Each person has to walk those paths himself." Upon coldly being asked by his former academic mentor if he plans to live with the Indians, Murdock replies, again in the negative: "No. I may not even go back to the prairie. What the men of the prairie taught me is good anywhere and for any circumstances" (335).

Borges thus sets forth in a few succinct sentences the conundrum: his possession of the knowledge has changed him, and the fact that he is now possessed by it. Unlike the aging protagonists of Saer and Posse, Borges's has been less confounded than enlightened by his experience. The key to keeping the new knowledge is not to write about it (neither dissertation nor memoirs) but rather to live it, and to live with it. Borges's fictional response via Fred Murdock postulates the timelessness that emanates from the unuttered experience that can be understood only through the unmediated experience itself, not through any (contradictory) interpretive utterance. Murdock keeps his significant silences. After the conversation and cacophony of marriage, he opts for divorce and the silence of solitude. Silence, too, characterizes his workaday world: Borges's Fred Murdock "is now one of the librarians at Yale" (335). We imagine Mr. Murdock there (here), spending his days and years classifying an endless miscellany of books, all of them full of incertitudes aimed at giving testimony to what Posse would later call prestigious lies of exactitude.

In the "pursuit of exactitudes" from the sixteenth century through the twentieth, the link between Cabeza de Vaca's narrative and the identification and affect of place is a constant. It seems that one must always entertain Cabeza de Vaca, as has been done here, with a map in hand, and then look for the road where there may be none. Assessing this difficulty centuries ago, El Inca Garcilaso eliminated it for his *Historia de la Florida* by claiming that news of the four men influenced native peoples even in areas they had *not* traversed.

CHAPTER 11

From Guancane to Macondo

LITERARY PLACES AND THEIR PREDECESSORS

THE ARGUMENT I MAKE in this chapter concerns the mutual enrichment of colonial- and contemporary-era writings that comes from reading
backwards and forwards, that is, from one to the other and back again.
There are two sets of propositions, and one follows upon the other.
The first involves El Inca Garcilaso de la Vega reading back to the mid-
sixteenth-century *Naufragios* of Álvar Núñez Cabeza de Vaca. Here I argue
that Garcilaso took as one of the most important sources for his narration
of the Hernando de Soto expedition to La Florida not the accounts of the
oral testimony from participants that he received in writing or viva voce,
but rather his (chosen) literary predecessor, the *Naufragios* of Cabeza de
Vaca. It is my contention that Garcilaso sought the confirmation of the
deeds he memorialized not in the supposed veracity of historical testimony but in the plausibility consecrated in the narrative tradition by the
chronicles and accounts of conquest; I take the position that he sought his
authorization, and hence his truth, not with respect to the world of military deeds and exploits but rather according to the content and configuration of the narrative system itself. (As I argued in previous chapters, Las
Casas, Bernal Díaz, and Guaman Poma have done the same.) This phenomenon is revealed because of Garcilaso's location of a crucial series of
actions at a site, "Guancane," that does not appear in any of the testimonial accounts of the De Soto expedition. It comes, Garcilaso declared,

from an eyewitness source whom he did not name. More important than a mysterious place identified by an unnamed source are the actions carried out there, and for this purpose Garcilaso invokes and relies on the literary authority of Cabeza de Vaca.

My second set of arguments depends on reading forward, and there the emphasis is not upon the narrative actions but rather on the identification and characterization of place. In chapter 10 I traced the narrative legacy of Cabeza de Vaca's account and the importance of the identification of place within it. Here I continue from El Inca Garcilaso and his "Guancane" to Juan Rulfo's *Pedro Páramo* and Gabriel García Márquez's *Cien años de soledad,* that is, to Comala and Macondo. Reading from Guancane to Comala and Macondo, and then back again, these literary geographies lend depth and resonance to one another (Borges will be cited later). If in the case of the Cabeza de Vaca/Garcilaso duo I speak of literary sources and their transformation from one author to the other, I want to make clear that in constructing the triad Garcilaso/Rulfo/García Márquez I do not present an argument that pertains to actions on the part of these authors (following sources, seeking precursors) but rather to the actions of us as readers who enrich our understanding of the persistence of great literary ideas and themes over time by doing the productive work of reading, both backward and forward.

Near the beginning of *La Florida del Inca,* El Inca Garcilaso de la Vega makes note of the expeditions that had preceded that of Hernando de Soto (1539–1543) to La Florida. After that of Lucas Vázquez de Ayllón, he cites the expedition of Pánfilo de Narváez in 1527. He briefly mentions Narváez and his pilot, Miruelo, but he foregrounds the experience of Álvar Núñez Cabeza de Vaca and his fellow overland survivors, thanks to his careful reading of the *Naufragios:*[1]

> After Judge Lucas Vázquez de Ayllón, the next explorer in Florida was Pámphilo de Narváez, who went there in the year 1537. As Álvar Núñez Cabeza de Vaca, who accompanied him as Treasurer of the Royal Purse, tells us in his *Naufragios,* this captain and all of his men except Cabeza de Vaca himself, three other Spaniards and one Negro, were miserably lost. Our Lord God was so merciful to the five [sic] who escaped that they succeeded

in performing miracles in His name and thus gained such a reputation and esteem among the Indians that they were worshiped as deities. Nevertheless they did not want to remain in this land, and as soon as they were able to do so, left very hastily and came to Spain to solicit new governorships. [Después del oidor Lucas Vázquez de Ayllón, fue a la Florida Pánfilo de Narváez, año de mil y quinientos y cincuenta y siete, donde con todos los españoles que llevó se perdió tan miserablemente, como lo cuenta en sus *Naufragios* Álvar Núñez Cabeza de Vaca que fue con él por tesorero de la Hacienda Real. El cual escapó con otros tres españoles y un negro y, habiéndoles hecho Dios Nuestro Señor tanta merced que llegaron a hacer milagros en su nombre, con los cuales habían cobrado tanta reputación y crédito con los indios que les adoraban por dioses, no quisieron quedarse entre ellos, antes, en pudiendo, se salieron a toda priesa de aquella tierra y se vinieron a España a pretender nuevas gobernaciones].[2]

Despite the prominence Garcilaso accords to Cabeza de Vaca and his "miraculous" experience of curing and survival, scholars reviewing Garcilaso's sources have tended to overlook the role of Cabeza de Vaca's text, emphasizing Garcilaso's (admittedly central) oral and manuscript sources as well as his classical and Renaissance references. Four works—those of Francisco López de Gómara, Juan de Castellanos, José de Acosta, and Álvar Núñez Cabeza de Vaca—have been considered "sources of general reference" and have been attributed a "minimal presence" in Garcilaso's account of the De Soto expedition. Others have made some observations pertinent to my pursuit, noting points of convergence where Garcilaso has cited Cabeza de Vaca.[3]

Garcilaso not only privileges Cabeza de Vaca's testimony regarding Spanish interactions with the Amerindians of La Florida but also models key episodes of his own narration on scenes of spiritual edification he found in Cabeza de Vaca's work.[4] At certain epiphanic points in his narration Garcilaso articulates Cabeza de Vaca's work with one of those of De Soto's chroniclers, who, in turn, had relied not only on Cabeza de Vaca's account but also on earlier ones: the paradigmatic episodes of Columbus's encounter with the Taínos of the Caribbean islands and Cortés's account of his encounter with Moctezuma. Such textual density is not uncommon; expedition reports and chroniclers' accounts written retrospectively tend to echo well-known, previously published and circulating reports.[5] Yet this is a special case because it involves not merely empirical information about events but, more important, the exegetical twists and assignment of authority that the "second author," Garcilaso, gives to his readings in light of his own narrative agenda.[6]

In attributing authority to the works he has read, Garcilaso performs exegetical transformations of very high valence. In the first place, the author-reader (Garcilaso) selects the predecessor who will increase the weight or value of his own work, and this election enriches our estimation of the work of the author chosen (Cabeza de Vaca). Beyond that—here the Borgesian principle becomes more complex—our author-reader (Garcilaso) creates the illusion that he provides a trustworthy historical plausibility with respect to the deeds he narrates, but, in fact, this plausibility exists only within the domain of the narrative: the credibility Garcilaso claims does not belong to the world of the referent, that is, the deeds narrated, but rather to the narrative tradition that shapes them. This textual "prestidigitation," or sleight of hand, is one of the crucial elements, even though he conceals it, of Garcilaso's conceptualization of his *Historia del adelantado Hernando de Soto, governador y capitán general del Reyno de la Florida, y de otros heroicos cavalleros españoles e indios* (1605), as the title of his work announces. In this case, as Borges wrote, the labor of each author "modifies our conception of the past, just as it must modify the future" [modifica nuestra concepción del pasado, como ha de modificar el futuro (89–90)]. Garcilaso enhances the accounts of the "civilizing" actions told by Cabeza de Vaca not so much to glorify the historical past as to affirm the importance of the narrative tradition that will keep it vibrant and alive in the future.

The early sixteenth-century Spanish concept of La Florida is central to this discussion for its pertinence to Garcilaso's reading of Cabeza de Vaca. As mentioned earlier, La Florida was the vast northern territory, the most precisely defined portion of which is described in the 1526 contract (*capitulaciones*) that Pánfilo de Narváez received from the crown for its conquest.[7] This area was the rim of the Gulf of Mexico, running all the way from northern Mexico (roughly, from today's Soto la Marina River in Tamaulipas, known as the Río de las Palmas in 1526), around the arc of the gulf to the Florida Cape. Up until the time of Francisco Vázquez de Coronado's expedition in the early 1540s, which resulted in today's southwestern United States being designated by the Spanish as Cíbola, La Florida spread at the time of the Narváez expedition, as mentioned, as far north and west as the Spanish imagined the North American continent to extend (see fig. 23). The *Carta universal*, of 1527, known as the Hernando Colón map (fig. 24), identifies the area that Lucas Vázquez de Ayllón had encountered (and failed to settle) in 1526[8] and that Pánfilo de Narváez was to conquer and settle in 1527. The "land of the Licenciate Ayllón" [Tierra del licenciado Ayllón] is located on the southeastern seaboard of today's United States, and "the land that Pánfilo de Narváez is now to settle" [Tierra que agora va a poblar Pánfilo de Narváez] was to include and extend beyond the territory first encountered by Francisco de Garay [Diende (*sic*) aquí descubrió Francisco de Garay] in 1518–1519.[9]

For Garcilaso, writing in the 1580s, La Florida was almost as vast as it had been in Cabeza de Vaca's day. He described its confines as "still a mystery." Although "to the south of it lie the ocean sea and the great island of Cuba," he continued: "We are still ignorant as to whether or not it is limited on the north by more lands or by the sea itself." To the east, he said, it was bound by the Tierra de los Bacallaos although "a certain French cosmographer states that between Florida and this land there lies another which he even calls New France." To the west, he understood La Florida to be bordered, as mentioned above, by Cíbola, or "the Provinces of the Seven Cities."[10]

In *La Florida del Inca* points of territorial correspondence between the trajectories of the Narváez and De Soto expeditions are of interest to Garcilaso because of his desire to link the De Soto experience to that of Narváez. Although Cabeza de Vaca mentioned the differences among the native groups that he and his companions came upon in the course of their North American captivity and odyssey, Garcilaso preferred to ignore them. He could not have avoided noticing these distinctions in the course of his reading of Cabeza de Vaca's work; Cabeza de Vaca declares in his proem to the emperor that he will offer an account of "the diverse customs of many and very barbarous peoples with whom I conversed and lived," and he identifies and comments upon them, region by region, in the course of his narration.[11] Additionally, Cabeza de Vaca's references to his arrival at the South Sea as well as his calculation of the distance from

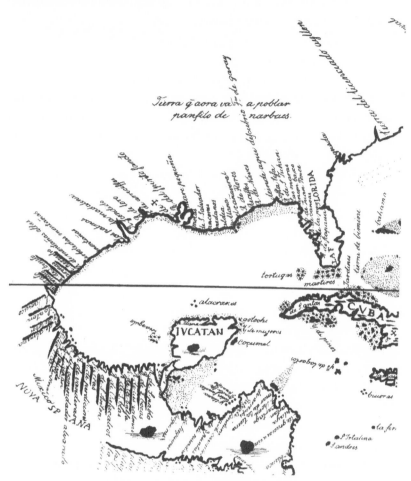

FIGURE 24. Detail of Mexico, the Gulf of Mexico, and Caribbean section of the world map titled *Carta universal* (1527), known as the Hernando Colón map. USLC, Geography and Map Division, Johann Georg Kohn Collection, no. 38.

the North Sea to the South Sea, "from one coast to the other," could clarify for Garcilaso how far Cabeza de Vaca and his companions had gone.[12] Garcilaso's deliberate geographical "indifference" is central to the argument I present here. The immensity of the Floridian territories as well as the European reader's ignorance of them served Garcilaso as a central element for the claims he made with respect to the geographical areas traversed by the De Soto expedition and the accounts of the Spaniards about the native groups found in them.

TEXTUAL GENEALOGIES

Like earlier accounts by other explorers, conquistadores, and settlers, Garcilaso's sought to enhance the significance of the failed De Soto expedition. It is not surprising that his work would come to be considered a wholesale apology for Hernando de Soto, especially given that De Soto had been one of Garcilaso's father's most illustrious companions and compatriots in the conquest of Peru. Ennobling De Soto would serve, albeit indirectly, Garcilaso's aspirations for recognition as the son of one of Peru's conquerors and also enhance the historical reputation not only of De Soto but also of his peers. Garcilaso declared that his goal was to present an account "of what Spaniards have discovered so near to their own land" so that "they may not permit themselves to lose what their predecessors struggled for, and instead may strive and become inspired to conquer and populate *a kingdom as extensive and fertile as Florida is.*"[13] Indeed, his effort to promote the colonization and evangelization of La Florida and thus to save the lost efforts and imperiled historical reputation of De Soto and his companions was, as Sylvia Hilton (37) emphasizes, Garcilaso's expressed goal. His view of the vastness of La Florida is crucial to the assertions he makes about shared or reiterated experiences of the Narváez and De Soto expeditions regarding the areas they traversed and the peoples they encountered.

At the same time, Garcilaso takes into account his own identity as a person of mixed, Spanish-Inca blood. In his proem he announced his lineage, making it relevant to his contemplation of "the numerous very illustrious deeds that both Spaniards and Indians performed in the process of the conquest of La Florida." He remarked that he felt obligated to bring forth the great deeds of both groups precisely because of his own background: "Feeling myself therefore under obligation to two races, since I am the son of a Spanish father and an Indian mother, I many times urged this cavalier [Garcilaso's unnamed conquistador informant] to record the details of the expedition, using me as his amanuensis."[14] He goes on to state: "This man was so anxious to be accurate that he corrected each chapter as it was written, adding what was lacking or deleting what he himself had not said, for he would not consent to any word other than his own. I, therefore, as the author contributed no more than the pen."[15] In making reference to this labor, Garcilaso rehearses the scenes of his youth as the literate Indian son of the Spanish captain Garcilaso de la Vega, serving his father as amanuensis.[16]

With his own dual patrimony in mind, Garcilaso emphasizes afresh, in the fourteenth chapter of the fourth book, the need to praise the great deeds of the Indians as well as those of the Spaniards: "The facts of history demand that we narrate the brave deeds of the Indians as well as those of the Spaniards, and that we not do injury to either race by recounting the valiant achievements of one while omitting those of the other, but instead tell all things as they occurred and in their proper time and place."[17] À la Borges, Garcilaso elected the *Naufragios* as the precursor he needed in order to posit the Floridian Amerindians' potential for Christian civilization. He did so to support the propagandistic purpose of fomenting Spanish settlement in La Florida and to enhance, however indirectly, his own status as a "native-born son" of Spanish America. In this light, his identification of Cabeza de Vaca as an eyewitness authority on La Florida and its peoples was central. There was no written authority more unequivocally in favor of the Indians of La Florida and their potential for Christian civilization than Cabeza de Vaca.[18]

The heart of Garcilaso's reading of *Naufragios* is found in the following affirmation with regard to Cabeza de Vaca's encounter with the natives of northwestern Mexico, between the Río Yaqui and the Río Petatlán (today's Río Sinaloa) (see fig. 23):

> And they showed very great pleasure with us, although we
> feared that when we arrived at the ones who held the frontier
> against the Christians and were at war with them, they would
> treat us cruelly and make us pay for what the Christians were
> doing to them. But since God our Lord was served to bring us to
> them, they began to fear and respect us as the previous ones had
> done, and even somewhat more, about which we were not a little
> amazed, by which it is clearly seen that all these peoples, to be
> drawn to become Christians and to obedience to the Imperial
> Majesty, must be given good treatment, and that this is the path
> most certain and no other. (Cabeza de Vaca in Adorno and
> Pautz, *Álvar Núñez* 1:240–241)

Before coming upon the dramatic scenes that Garcilaso offers with regard to this declaration, certain earlier episodes in the narrative sequence of *La Florida del Inca* must be set forth.

As part of his discussion of Floridian customs, Garcilaso readjusted and then repeated Cabeza de Vaca's sweeping affirmation about there being neither idolatry nor human sacrifice in La Florida. Garcilaso did so in his customary fashion of making an assertion in order to qualify and ultimately neutralize it: "The Indians are a race of pagans and idolaters; they worship the sun and the moon as their principal deities, but, unlike the rest of heathendom, without any ceremony of images, sacrifices, prayers, or other superstitions."[19] Idolaters yes; but practitioners of human sacrifice, no. Cabeza de Vaca had been unequivocal: "In the two thousand leagues that we traveled by land and through the sea on the rafts and another ten months that we went through the land without stopping once we were no longer captives, we found neither sacrifices nor idolatry."[20]

Along with this highly developed sense of spirituality, Garcilaso postulated an absence of sinful customs and crimes against nature. Here Cabeza de Vaca's account again proved authoritative. Garcilaso lauded the Floridian Indians' rejection of adultery and the sanctity of their laws against it as well as their abomination of cannibalism: "People who say that the Indians eat human flesh attribute this practice to them falsely, at least to those of the provinces our Governor [Hernando de Soto] discovered. They, on the contrary, abominate this practice, as Álvar Núñez Cabeza de Vaca notes in his *Naufragios*, chapters fourteen and seventeen."[21] Nevertheless, on cannibalism Garcilaso takes a more cautious stand; he does not rule out altogether the possibility of the existence of cannibalism in La Florida, noting that "it may be, however, that the Indians do eat human flesh in places where our men did not penetrate, for Florida is so broad and long that there is space enough within it for anything to happen."[22] As an aristocratic Inca, Garcilaso is less emphatically categorical about the common Floridian Indians' customs than Cabeza de Vaca was, and he leaves open the possibility for behaviors that fall into the domain of unmistakable barbarity.

In his chapter fourteen, Cabeza de Vaca had written about five Narváez expeditionaries who "came to such dire need that they ate one another until only one remained, who because he was alone, had no one to eat him." After naming these five men, Cabeza de Vaca adds: "The Indians became very upset because of this and it produced such a great scandal among them that without a doubt, if at the start they had seen it, they would have killed them, and all of us would have been in grave danger."[23]

Garcilaso cited Cabeza de Vaca as an authority not only on the benign and well-disposed character of the Florida Indians but also, from time to time, on their resistance to the Spaniards. Garcilaso's insistence on the Indians' willingness to mislead the armed soldiers of De Soto in order to discourage the Spaniards from advancing farther, for example, derived valuable support from Cabeza de Vaca. In the Indians' effort to thwart the invaders' penetration of their homeland, Garcilaso concludes, "our story does not give the lie to the cavalier, Álvar Núñez."[24] Here the adversarial relationship denotes the Indians' fierce and uncompromising loyalty to their homeland, which was a value that in the *Comentarios reales de los Incas* Garcilaso dramatized to great effect with regard to the Incas. There as here, the only value to override that of patriotism, that is, a natural love of homeland and the will to defend it, was the desire to receive the "greater truth" of the revelation of the Christian gospel.

The worthy deeds of Garcilaso's Indians of the Florida Cape are significantly not those of military heroism as warring adversaries to the Spanish settlement enterprise but rather, in strong contrast to the ferocity of Cabeza de Vaca's Indians of the same area, as its faithful guides and willing adjuncts. This contrast is seen in Garcilaso's account of the Indians at the Bay of Horses. This is the site on the northwestern coast of present-day Florida at which the Narváez overland expedition had built, between early August and late September of 1528, the five rafts that would carry some 250 men along the northern coast of the gulf to the Galveston Bay area (see fig. 23).[25] In Cabeza de Vaca's account, the hostility of the Indians resulted in ten members of the expedition being killed within sight of their camp, "shot through and through with arrows."[26] At the same site in Garcilaso's narration of the De Soto expedition, these Indians, some ten years later, are no longer adversaries but rather serve the Spanish, remarkably, as able guides and are, even more remarkably, speakers of Castilian:

> The guides now pointed out the spot where the Indians had
> killed ten of those Christians (as Álvar Núñez Cabeza de Vaca

tells us in his history), and they led their captors step by step
through all of the places where Pánfilo de Narváez had traveled,
pointing out where such and such a thing occurred and eventually giving by signs and words, some well and some poorly understood, an account of all the remarkable things that worthy
cavalier had done at the bay. Some spoke in Castilian, for the
people along that entire coast prided themselves on their knowledge of that language and made every effort possible to learn
even isolated words, which they repeated again and again. (Garcilaso, *The Florida*, 192; idem, *La Florida*, 135–136 [bk. 2, pt. 2,
ch. 6])

Whether Garcilaso imagines them as the Florida Indians who had murdered Narváez's men or their peers or immediate successors, they become in his narration the Castilian-speaking friends and guides to De
Soto's company. Garcilaso's reference to Cabeza de Vaca's account makes
visible his fanciful argument that an important historical transformation
has occurred in the time elapsed (approximately a decade) between Narváez's sojourn and that of De Soto: the Floridians have gone from being
foe to friend; they were desirous of learning the Castilian language and
well along on the road to Christian civilization. How they became, im-
plausibly, speakers of Castilian is implied through their presumed contact
with the Narváez men as they built their rafts at the Bay of Horses. Garcilaso introduces here a principle that will have ever-greater relevance in
the course of his narration: he postulates that the Narváez expedition,
even after its departure from the area some ten or so years earlier, had left
its mark—in this as in successive instances, a positive one—on the natives
of this corner of vast La Florida.

IN THE PROVINCE OF PACAHA

To narrate a particularly edifying episode about native beliefs, Garcilaso
devotes an entire chapter to "a solemn procession of Indians and Spaniards for the purpose of adoring the cross" (bk. 4, chap. 6). Here Cabeza
de Vaca is conspicuous by his absence; Garcilaso does not cite him at all.
Presenting a spectacular tableau of multitudes of people gathered together, Garcilaso narrates an encounter that harks back to the writings of
Columbus and Cortés but clearly got its Floridian antecedents from the

series of episodes in the last section of Cabeza de Vaca's *Naufragios*. In fact, Garcilaso suggests that his principal source had been Juan Coles, a De Soto expeditionary whose manuscript account Garcilaso said he found in the shop of a printer in Córdoba. Garcilaso describes Coles as a native of the Andalusian town of Zafra who wrote a "brief and disorganized account of the expedition" at the request of the provincial of the Franciscan province of Santa Fe, Fray Pedro Aguado, and that the friar had gathered "many diverse accounts from trustworthy people concerning the discoveries they had seen accomplished in the New World" and left them in the hands of the Cordoban printer. Garcilaso laments that Coles observed no chronology or sequence of events, that he named only a few of the provinces visited (again, not in any order), and that he related "some things with greater awe and exaggeration than I, as will be seen in the passages quoted."[27]

Garcilaso gives the impression that Coles was the principal source of this narration. In the proem he declares that he had finished writing his history when he came upon Coles's work. Because the Coles manuscript is lost, the account of Luis Hernández de Biedma, the De Soto expedition's accountant (*factor*), can serve to place in relief Garcilaso's elaborate narration. Writing his official account of the expedition in 1544, when he presented it to the Council of the Indies, Biedma would have seen or known about the first edition of Cabeza de Vaca's work, published in Zamora in 1542.

It is evident that even Biedma's firsthand but retrospective formulation of his experience on the De Soto expedition was neither entirely original nor unmediated. Like the other De Soto narrators after him, Biedma was informed by the narratives (oral and written) of Cabeza de Vaca and, before him, of Hernán Cortés. An episode in Biedma's account suggests how the narrative legacy left by Cabeza de Vaca became part of the De Soto reporters' own. The signal encounter occurs in the "province of Pacaha," which is generally acknowledged to have been located along the Mississippi River in a maize-growing area of present-day Arkansas bordering western Tennessee (fig. 25).[28] Biedma explained that in going upstream on the river toward Pacaha, his party came first to the province of a lord called Icasqui. (He is referred to as Casqui in the accounts of the Gentleman of Elvas, Rodrigo Ranjel, and El Inca Garcilaso.) In a passage whose elements recall Columbus and Cortés as well as Cabeza de Vaca,

Biedma declared, "This cacique came forth in peace, telling us that he had been hearing of us for a long time, and that he knew that we were men from heaven and that their arrows could not do us harm, and that therefore they wanted no war with us, but rather wanted to serve us."[29]

He adds that later "the cacique spoke with the Governor [Hernando de Soto], telling him that he knew that he was a man from heaven, and since he had to continue onward, he should leave a sign indicating whom he could ask for help for his wars, and whom his people could ask for water for their fields, because they were in great need of it, since their children were dying of hunger." Biedma further tells how De Soto ordered that a cross be set up on the summit of one of the "very high mounds, made by hand" [cerros muy altos hechos a mano] and how sometime later Icasqui gave De Soto many thanks "for the cross that he had left him, saying that it had rained a great deal in his land the day before, and that all his people were so content that they did not wish to leave us but rather to go away with us."[30]

There is no doubt that the first portion of this scene resonates with and was probably inspired by the popular Spanish lore that had been set down in print in Columbus's letter of February 15, 1493, to Luis de Santángel and in Hernán Cortés's second letter, of October 20, 1520. Columbus's reference, "gente [que] venía del cielo," was generally interpreted as meaning that the natives (in this case, the Taínos of the Caribbean) understood the Europeans to have come from heaven and that they were therefore taken to be gods or the representatives of gods.[31] The act of a ruler submitting in obeisance to foreign but "rightful" lords came from Cortés's account of Moctezuma's "donation" of the Mexica empire to Cortés as the representative of Charles V.[32] In Cortés's speech, Moctezuma accepted Charles V as the Mexicas' "natural lord," that is, in the tradition of the Hispano-Christian states of medieval times, the ruler autochthonous to the land and people, also native to the land, over whom he rules:[33] "So because of the place from which you claim to come, namely, from where the sun rises, and the things you tell us of the great lord or king who sent you here, we believe and are certain that he is our natural lord, especially as you say that he has known of us for some time. So be assured that we shall obey you and hold you as our lord in place of that great sovereign of whom you speak."[34] Biedma's account records Icasqui's recognition of the superiority of the Christians' god in a synthetic version of the Columbian and Cortesian ideas.

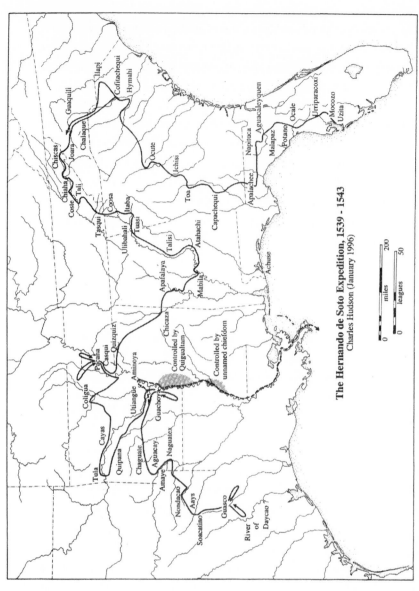

FIGURE 25. The route of the Hernando de Soto expedition through sixteenth-century La Florida. Map by Charles Hudson. Courtesy of Charles Hudson, Franklin Professor of History and Anthropology Emeritus, University of Georgia.

The second portion of Biedma's report, pertaining to the erection of the Christian cross on the summit of an artificial mound, harks back to Cabeza de Vaca's account, in which, in Nueva Galicia in northwestern Mexico, Cabeza de Vaca and his companions instructed the natives to "put up their houses and in the midst of them make one for God and put a cross at the entrance, like the one we had there, and that when Christians came there, to come out and receive them with the crosses in their hands." Cabeza de Vaca subsequently reported that after arriving at the Spanish *villa* of San Miguel de Culiacán, "Indians came who told us how many people were coming down from the sierras and populating the plain and making churches and crosses and doing everything we had commanded them."[35] There is no question that the patterns of Spanish–Indian interaction reported by Cabeza de Vaca were given powerful resonance in the De Soto expedition accounts and that, in some implicit fashion, such as certain episodes of peaceful encounter in Cortés's second letter, Cabeza de Vaca's *Relación/Naufragios* was being read as a model by which to elaborate accounts of the successful negotiations between the conquerors and the conquered.

Garcilaso's account of the events at Pacaha can now be examined in the light of Biedma's. As mentioned earlier, in another instance Garcilaso claimed that Cabeza de Vaca's use of the symbol of the cross had spread among Floridian peoples in lands that the Narváez survivor and his companions had not even reached. Garcilaso continues to give prominence, in fact, paramount importance, to the symbolism of the cross in the epiphanic chapter in which he does not cite Cabeza de Vaca but for which Cabeza de Vaca's final chapters in *Naufragios* provided the precedent.

Garcilaso narrates that the lord Casquin and his nobles came forth to meet De Soto and his men, and on the fourth day after the army had bivouacked in the settlement he has Casquin make this declaration to De Soto: "My Lord, since you have the advantage over us in strength and arms, we are of the opinion that yours is a better god than ours. Therefore these nobles of my land whom you see assembled here (and who because of their low estate and little merit have not dared appear before you) and I with them do now beseech that you deign to request your god to grant us rain, for our crops are very much in need of water."[36] De Soto replied that he and his men, although they "were but sinners," would pray for God's mercy. Then De Soto ordered that a cross be built, and Garcilaso makes this the focal point of his exposition. To be fashioned "from the highest and thickest pine to be found in the whole of that region," the cross, once constructed, required one hundred men to lift it from the ground. It was "a perfect cross in the proportion of five and three, which, because of its great height, turned out to be magnificent." It was then placed "at the summit of a lofty mound which had been built on a cliff overlooking the river, and which served the Indians as a lookout, since it was higher than all the other hills of that vicinity."[37]

Garcilaso then creates an extraordinary scene: A few days later, a procession of a thousand people (with many of the native lords scattered among the Christians) came forth, kneeled down, and kissed the cross. The grandeur of Garcilaso's tableau is completed by the fifteen to twenty thousand souls of both sexes and all ages on the other side of the river who "with arms outstretched and hands uplifted . . . stood watching the Christians. From time to time they raised their eyes to the heavens and made gestures with their hands and faces as if they too were beseeching God to give ear to the request of these strangers." He concludes,

> Thus on both sides of the river all of this ceremony and ostentation was being rendered for the purpose of adoring the cross, and the Governor and many of his men were moved to much tenderness on perceiving that in such strange lands and among people so far separated from the Christian doctrine, the symbol of our redemption should be adored with such an abundance of tears and great manifestations of humility. When all had worshipped, in the manner we have described, they returned as they had come, observing the same order of procession while the priests chanted the *Te Deum Laudamus* to the close of that canticle. Only after four long hours was the ceremony of the day concluded. (Garcilaso, *The Florida*, 433; idem, *La Florida*, 303 [bk. 4, ch. 6])

Garcilaso's stunning account echoes and heightens Cabeza de Vaca's paradigmatic one, in which he had told of the general success of his and his companions' passage through northwestern Mexico in 1536:

> Throughout all these lands those who were at war with one another later made friends in order to come to receive us and bring

us everything they had. And in this manner we left the entire land and we told them by signs, because they understood us, that in heaven there was a man whom we called God, who had created the heaven and the earth, and that we adored him and served him as Lord, and that we did whatever he commanded us, . . . And henceforth when the sun rose, with very great shouting they opened their joined hands to the sky and afterward passed them over their entire bodies. And they did the same when the sun set. (Cabeza de Vaca in Adorno and Pautz, *Álvar Núñez* 1:232–235)

In sum, the edifying scenes of the natives' requests that the strange white men bring the rains, the throngs of Indians stretching their hands to the heavens and coming forth to receive the Christians with crosses in their hands, all first set out in Cabeza de Vaca's *Relación/Naufragios*, were given new, more vivid, and more enduring life in Garcilaso's *La Florida del Inca*. Garcilaso stopped short, however, of making any claim about the identity of Amerindian and Christian deities, such as Cabeza de Vaca had done regarding the Indians of Sinaloa, when he boldly proclaimed "the one to whom they referred we called God."

IN GUANCANE

Garcilaso pursues this line more emphatically and directly when he claims that the natives of La Florida are now engaged in carrying out exemplary customs, thanks to the visible spiritual legacy that the Narváez survivors had inspired in lands they had not even reached. Garcilaso claims that there were wooden crosses adorning the dwellings in the province of Guancane[38] and that these could be explained by the

news of the benefits and marvels Álvar Núñez Cabeza de Vaca and Andrés Dorantes and their companions had performed in virtue of Jesus Christ Our Lord within the provinces of Florida through which they had traveled during the years they were held in bondage by the Indians, as Álvar Núñez himself has recorded in his *Comentarios* [sic]. And even though it is true that Álvar Núñez and his companions did not come to this particular province or to a number of others which lie between it and the lands where they traveled, still the fame of the deeds performed by

God through these men eventually, by passing from hand to hand and from land to land, reached the province of Guancane. And since the Indians here had learned of these things and had heard it said that the Christians had brought the cross in their hands as a device, and that all benefits performed by them in curing the sick were accomplished by making above them the sign of the cross, there arose the pious practice of putting this symbol over their houses, for they believed that just as it had cured those sick, so it would also deliver everyone from all evil and danger. (Garcilaso, *The Florida*, 482–83; idem, *La Florida*, 336 [bk. 5, pt. 1, ch. 2])

Garcilaso's account echoes one found in Cabeza de Vaca (cited above), in which the Indians were instructed to receive the Christians by offering them food and provisions and by carrying crosses, but no weapons.[39] Nevertheless, the episode told by Garcilaso is literally utopian: It recreates a practice described by Cabeza de Vaca in a province that not only was not reached by Narváez, as Garcilaso indicates, but—something he does not mention—that is a place not cited in any of the accounts of the De Soto expedition.

These matters were irrelevant to Garcilaso, however. The "greater truth" to be heralded by Garcilaso on Cabeza de Vaca's authority concerned the "readiness which the Indians in general had, and these in particular do have, for receiving the Catholic Faith if there were only someone to cultivate it, especially by good example, which commands their attention more than anything else."[40] This statement is directly reminiscent of Cabeza de Vaca's pronouncement about the Indians encountered very far west in La Florida in the Sonora River area of northwestern Mexico: "by which it is clearly seen that all these peoples, to be drawn to become Christians and to obedience to the Imperial Majesty, must be given good treatment, and that this is the path most certain and no other."[41]

Overall, Garcilaso's reading of Cabeza de Vaca and the De Soto accounts, which, in turn, had taken Cabeza de Vaca and others among their precursors, provided the means by which to posit and vouchsafe the dignity of the Floridian Indians and to echo the heroic sentiments of Spanish militarism in the service of the Castilian monarchy. It is not surprising that Garcilaso used the account of the unarmed Cabeza de Vaca—who, as has been discussed, had much to say about the merits and potential of Amerindian peoples—to serve the purpose of attributing dignity to the Amerindians of Florida. It is not without irony that, in order to celebrate the values of militant Christian overseas expansion, Garcilaso used as the subject of his study the failed De Soto expedition and, as one of his authoritative sources, the only available firsthand account of the disastrous Narváez expedition. What is at stake, though, in these cases is not, in the long view, the specificity of these choices of precursors but rather the general mythologizing of the Spanish experience that comes out of these sequential instances. This is the larger, popular Spanish story of the good will between conqueror and conquered, between the valiant Spaniard and the worthy Indian (precursor of the noble savage), between the merciful victor and the assimilating vanquished.

The supreme moments of these narrations, whose historical events were constituted by expeditionary bad judgment, violent conquest, and, at best, varying degrees of native cooperation, could be realized only in triumph as spiritual epiphany, not military conquest. Cabeza de Vaca's raising of crosses in natives' hands, on native huts, and atop native-built makeshift churches in northwestern Mexico became Garcilaso's magnificent "perfect cross in the proportion of five and three" raised somewhere in present-day Arkansas. In its perfect proportions and in the silence of the intermingled Spanish soldiers and Floridian lords at its base and across the river, it represented a perfectly balanced Renaissance image of the encounter of the Old World with the New. Its realization is uniquely El Inca Garcilaso's, but for its creation he made Cabeza de Vaca one of his most authoritative predecessors.

THE INVENTION OF GUANCANE

The most intriguing feature of Garcilaso's narration stands apart from, and yet is consonant with, his reliance on written and oral antecedents. Guancane is the case par excellence of an authorial sleight of hand that seeks to lend historical credence to an account that is entirely fictional. Guancane is an elaboration whose geographical location does not exist but whose reality is no less certain. It refers, in Garcilaso's account, to a province of La Florida that, as noted, is absent from all three testimonial sources on the expedition (Gentleman of Elvas, Biedma, and Ranjel).

In Garcilaso its source is Gonzalo Silvestre. John R. Swanton, the author of the *Final Report of the United States De Soto Expedition Commission*, which was issued in 1939 and reissued in 1985, considered that upon writing "Guancane" Garcilaso's informant could have corrupted the name of "Aguacay," mentioned by Ranjel, or "Lacane," cited by the Gentleman of Elvas.[42] But if "Guancane" was the historical Aguacay or Lacane, as Knight points out,[43] both of them would have to be situated, like Naguatex, very far to the east, yet in fact the provinces of Aguacay and Lacane pertain to the portion of the expedition carried out toward the west by Luis de Moscoso Alvarado after the death of De Soto in 1542 (see fig. 25). The portion of Garcilaso's narrative that corresponds to that year is of little use to historians because Garcilaso situates events that occurred after the death of De Soto under the subsequent leadership of Moscoso too early, that is, during the final months of De Soto's life.[44] Thus, for example, Garcilaso writes that in the winter of 1541–1542 De Soto made an incursion into the province of Naguatex and that the following spring, upon departing for Utiangue, the governor entered once more the Naguatex province before passing through Guancane and seven other provinces to arrive at Anilco. The three testimonial accounts of the expedition all agree that Naguatex was not visited by the Spanish until the late summer of 1542, after De Soto's death.

In narrating the passage of the Spanish force through this province of "Guancane," Garcilaso claims that De Soto "set forth from Guancane in search of the Rio Grande." As if Garcilaso were anticipating that it would be necessary for him to "respond to an objection" as he had done earlier (bk. 2, pt. 1, chap. 27), he points out that "even though in this stage of my history as in others I have given the route that the army traveled when it left some one province for the purpose of going to another, I have not shown the latitude of each province or pointed out strictly the course that our men took. For, as I have already stated elsewhere, in spite of the fact that I have endeavored to learn these details, it has not been possible for me to do so because he who gave me the account was neither cosmographer nor mariner and as a result did not know them." He adds that the army carried no instruments to take land elevations nor was there anyone capable of looking into it; because of their anger and disappointment at finding neither gold nor silver, he writes, they were little disposed to query such matters.[45]

In the face of this geographical uncertainty, it is necessary to add a linguistic datum. In the provinces of the area in question, to the west of the Mississippi River and along it, the language spoken was Caddo.[46] "Guancane" is not a lexical item in that language, but we do find variants of the toponym in Quechua, one of the languages of the South American Andes and El Inca Garcilaso's mother tongue. Garcilaso makes reference to a "people and nation" called Huancani in his *Comentarios reales* upon narrating the conquests carried out by the second Inca, Sinche Roca: "But others say he went far beyond and won many towns and tribes on the Umasuyu road, such as Cancalla, Cacha Rurucachi, Assillu, Asancatu, Huancani, as far as the town called Pucara."[47] (Huancané, Asillo, and Pucará are Andean towns that exist in Peru to the present day, in the respective provinces of Huancané, Azángaro, and Lampa in the Department of Puno.)[48] Upon expressing doubt whether these territories had been conquered by the second or the third Inca, Garcilaso emphasizes that it was a "peaceful conquest," carried out without the force of arms: "The fact remains that they were won, and won not by force of arms, but by persuasion, promises, and proofs of what was promised." He adds that the Inca carried out this successful conquest with great patience, "like a good gardener who, having planted a tree, tends it in every necessary way so that it may bear the desired fruit. This is what this Inca did with all care and diligence, and he saw and enjoyed, in great peace and quietness, the harvest of his toil."[49]

For the reader of Garcilaso's era, however, the apparently familiar resonances of "Guancane" would be Caribbean, that is, seemingly corresponding to the language of the Taínos of the Antilles. Although the juxtaposition of two consonants (the "nc" in "Guancane") is not found in the Taíno language, its words could seem more familiar to the reader than those of the Quechua language, because of the wider publication and circulation of materials about the Caribbean than about the Andes in the sixteenth century. Although "Guancane" in itself is not found in known writings, similar words appear from the letters of Columbus and the *De orbe novo* of Pietro Martire d'Anghiera onward. In fact, the island of Guanahaní, the site of Columbus's landing on October 12, 1492, is a first example, and in the Taíno lexicon, there are similar names that were cited by Columbus and his chroniclers: the inlet of Guanaba, the islands of the Guanajas, or Guanajos, the settlement of Guanica on the island of San Juan (Puerto Rico), the island of Guanín, and so forth.[50]

In light of these considerations, the strange occurrences in Garcilaso's province of Guancane merit another look. In Guancane, in spite
of the field of crosses that greet the passing Spanish army, as Garcilaso
spelled out in the lengthy passage cited at the beginning of the previous
section, "In Guancane," De Soto and his soldiers dare not pause in their
advance. The reason was the hostility of the inhabitants of this province:
"Here the natives differed from those in the past, for whereas the others
had been affable, these proved to be hostile and showed no desire for
friendship. Instead, they demonstrated their hatred in every way possible,
many times presenting themselves for battle." Garcilaso concludes, "The
Spaniards took eight days to cross this province, not resting a single day
within its confines because of their desire to avoid a conflict with these
people who were so eager to fight."[51]

The province of Guancane presents a unique case in *La Florida del
Inca:* its Indians showed evidence of being influenced, somehow schooled
in Christian customs, by the hearsay reports of certain Christians (the
Cabeza de Vaca party) whom they had never seen, while at the same time
manifesting a hostile attitude toward the armed Christians who passed
through their territory. Fearing this hostility and finding themselves weakened because of the lack of horses, the Spaniards did not dare stop to rest a
single day but continued their march, trying to pass through undetected or
at least without provoking the Guancanians, who knew well how to defend
their land and people from soldiers who traveled on foot. Although he does
not announce it as such (nor would he have dared to do so), Garcilaso has
created a postconquest Amerindian utopia. That this is the case becomes
apparent by a comparison of this episode with the one that concludes
the work.

El Inca Garcilaso makes special reference at the conclusion of *La
Florida* to an Indian, a lord of vassals, who returns to his Floridian province after having been taken to Castile. The lord organizes an attack
against the Christians while at the same time promising to assist in the
task of the conversion of his people: "He went forward four or five leagues
to prepare the Indians of that province to listen to the Christian doctrine."[52] Once again, Garcilaso echoes Cabeza de Vaca in the gesture of the
native lord calling forth his people, as Cabeza de Vaca so dramatically
portrayed for the province of Culiacán in northwestern Mexico; but in
Garcilaso this happens *à la inversa:* Here it is a ruse created to trap and

ambush the Christians. The Indians appear, but they assassinate the priests and friars who await them. After the massacre, the Indians seize a chest filled with breviaries, missals, books of scripture, and sacred vestments worn for saying mass. Leaping gleefully about, wearing the vestments and ridiculing them, three Indians seize a crucifix from the chest. Then something miraculous occurs. As they look upon the cross they suddenly fall dead. In this tableau created by Garcilaso to draw to a close his narration of the De Soto expedition, "Spaniards and Indians lie dead, one next to the other, in a land soaked with the blood of both races."[53]

Seen in relation to this conclusion to the work, the Guancane episode seems to be a minor event: it did not involve a violent encounter between Spaniards and Indians, of either positive or negative valence, that is, there is no spiritual apotheosis either in the style of the episodes related by Cabeza de Vaca or in Garcilaso's Pacaha, nor is there a violent conquest. Notable for its absence is submission to the Spanish, voluntary or forced, on the part of the Guancanians. The absence of such narrative elements calls our attention. The (secret) signature of Garcilaso to his work will be the nonencounter at Guancane, whose inhabitants know how to defend themselves on account of their natural love of homeland ("amor natural a la tierra"), as Garcilaso will write about the Incas in his *Comentarios reales*, and where the natives ostentatiously display the cross, the maximum symbol of Christianity: in Guancane Indians appear with crosses in their hands, but they never submit either themselves or their will to the Spanish. (There are echoes here of the 1560s proposal for the restoration of Inca sovereignty by Las Casas as well as variants on Guaman Poma's theme of an autonomous Indies under the spiritual monarchy of the Castilian king; see chapters 2 and 3.)

In the nonexistent province of Guancane, the scene of the silent march of the Spanish soldiers who cross a landscape populated by potential enemies whose homes, nevertheless, display the Christian cross is utopian in two senses. In the literal one of his account, it is a "no place." In the symbolic sense it is utopian because the natives of the province, the lords of vassals as well as the vassals themselves, reside tranquilly in their homes and work peacefully in their fields but are poised to defend their lands and themselves from invaders. In Guancane the equilibrium is not that of harmony, but of tension, a tension that is grave and ominous. The stability that reigns can be broken at any moment. At any moment the weakened, horseless Spanish army can become the victim of the wrath of the Guancanians, just as happens in the episode that concludes the work, when the Indians kill the unarmed priests.

FROM GUANCANE TO COMALA AND MACONDO

Guancane anticipates the creation of the preeminent fictional towns and communities that populate the history of Latin American literature. Guancane is the "seed" out of which will grow the plants that produce the novelistic pueblos in now-canonical narrative works of the 1950s and 1960s. Garcilaso's Guancane captures a moment of unstable and threatening equilibrium in the history of a community. Empirically, this place does not exist, but its reality is coherent and powerful. Memorable instances of Guancane's successors are found in Comala and Macondo, the town-scenarios of Juan Rulfo and Gabriel García Márquez, respectively, in *Pedro Páramo* (1955) and *Cien años de soledad* (1967).

My argument here is not that Garcilaso was a source for Rulfo or García Márquez. The operative principle is not causality but continuity and consistency in the transformative life of a literary culture. Here appears a twist of the phenomenon I attribute to Garcilaso, who, I assert, in reading and citing Cabeza de Vaca seeks not the authority of history but that of the Castilian narrative tradition, nearly a century old, devoted to the Indies. I intend to show at this point that colonial-era narratives do not stand apart from, but rather constitute an integral (not eccentric or irrelevant) dimension of, the Spanish American literary heritage. Guancane is as real, and as Latin American, as Comala and Macondo. And, à la Borges, we can thank Rulfo and García Márquez as much as Garcilaso, although in different ways, for giving us Guancane.

In *Pedro Páramo*, Juan Preciado arrives in Comala in search of the father whom he does not know and about whom he created "a world around a hope centered on the man called Pedro Páramo, the man who had been my mother's husband" [un mundo alrededor de la esperanza que era aquel señor llamado Pedro Páramo, el marido de mi madre],[54] because he wants to avenge himself for what Páramo did to his mother.

Upon approaching Comala he remarks that he began to be filled with illusion and anticipation, imagining seeing it all through his mother's memories, who always lived pining for the Comala to which she never returned [Siempre vivió ella suspirando por Comala, por el retorno; pero jamás volvió]. But soon the asphyxiating air he breathes distracts him from the pleasant memories of his mother. After crossing the hills, Juan Preciado and Abundio, the muleteer who is taking him to Comala, descend to the plain: "We had left the hot wind behind and were sinking into pure airless heat" [Habíamos dejado el aire caliente allá arriba y nos íbamos hundiendo en el puro calor sin aire]. The heat of Comala grows more fierce. Abundio assures Preciado that he will feel it even more keenly upon arriving in Comala: "The town sits on the coals of the earth, at the very mouth of hell" [Aquello está sobre las brasas de la tierra, en la mera boca del infierno].[55] Sound follows sight and the sensation of heat on his skin and in his lungs: "Now here I was in this hushed town. I could hear my footsteps on the cobbled paving stones. My hollow footsteps, echoing against walls stained red by the setting sun" [Ahora estaba aquí, en este pueblo sin ruidos. Oía caer mis pisadas sobre las piedras redondas con que estaban empedradas las calles. Mis pisadas huecas, repitiendo su sonido en el eco de las paredes teñidas por el sol del atardecer]. The houses were empty, and the doors, splayed open, are invaded by weeds, and although there were no children playing or doves cooing or roofs tiled in blue, he felt that the pueblo was alive [sentí que el pueblo vivía].[56] With all his senses sharpened, and in spite of the silence and the evidence of abandoned houses, Juan Preciado feels the life that surrounds him. (Think of the Spanish foot soldiers, in the tense silence of Guancane.) Comala: land of the living dead, the land destroyed by the rancor of Pedro Páramo, who allowed Comala to die of hunger.

Comala's priest, Padre Rentería, offers a further meditation. Reflecting on how he had served Pedro Páramo as an accomplice in his crimes and abuses against the townspeople, Father Rentería goes to the town of Contla to make a general confession with its priest. Rentería makes his confession but upon hearing it the priest denies him absolution. Rentería objects, but with the greater fear that he is in danger of being removed from his parish, he resigns himself to continuing to carry his now-acknowledged guilt. When amicability is restored, the two men sit down together under an arbor loaded with ripening grapes: "They're bitter, Father," the priest says, anticipating Father Rentería's question. "We live in a land in which everything grows, thanks to God's providence, but everything that grows is bitter. That is our curse." "You are right, Father. I've tried to grow grapes over in Comala. They don't bear. Only guavas and oranges: bitter oranges and bitter guavas. I've forgotten the taste of sweet fruit" [Son ácidas, padre — se adelantó el señor cura a la pregunta que le iba a hacer —. Vivimos en una tierra en que todo se da, gracias a la Providencia; pero todo se da con acidez. Estamos condenados a eso.—Tiene usted razón, señor cura. Allá en Comala he intentado sembrar uvas. No se dan. Sólo crecen arrayanes y naranjos; naranjos agrios y arrayanes agrias. A mí se me ha olvidado el sabor de las cosas dulces].[57]

Within the world ruled by Pedro Páramo with the collusion—out of fear or indifference—of the residents of Comala, the ruined pueblo functions as the setting from the beginning of the novel. It is the reign of silence, in this case, achieved by Pedro Páramo's destruction of the town and its infernal, suffocating, "airless heat." In fact, two days after his arrival in Comala, Juan Preciado dies of asphyxiation. The novel recreates the death of Pedro Páramo, who sees that "the ruined, sterile earth lay before him" [la tierra en ruinas estaba frente a él, vacía].[58] The land is in ruins and the paradise lost, thanks not to the violence of nature but to that of man.

If the world of Comala is presented to the reader after its destruction, the Macondo of García Márquez appears before us from prior to its foundation until the moment when it disappears, enveloped in a great wind, for all time. If the heat and silence and consequences of Pedro Páramo's rape of the town produce in Comala a static, asphyxiating environment, without movement and without air, Macondo brings with it a vibrant and organic dynamism. If Comala is a corpse, Macondo is a tender infant, then an adolescent, and, later, an adult who breathes air that is life-giving until that air is transformed into a biblical, destructive force that carries itself and Macondo away, off the face of the earth.

If Comala is a cadaver abandoned by the violence that destroyed it, Macondo is a creature whose conception and birth were produced in the same crucible. That is, its foundation was provoked by the consequences of an act of remembered violence: the return of the ghost of Prudencio Aguilar, assassinated by José Arcadio Buendía, inspires in Buendía the idea of founding a new town where it will be possible to live in peace.[59] The trajectory of its history is characterized by a double violence. Political violence is created by a municipal government that is alternately arbitrary and benign, by twenty years of civil war at the level of the nation, and by a government external to the town that is ever more powerful and arbitrary, ever more distant yet ever more intrusive. Economic violence is constituted by foreigners' discovery of the sweetness of the Macondo region's nature (the banana groves) and its conversion into an exploitative industry that is, in the last instance, the source of the destruction of all the resources—natural and human—of Macondo. Like Comala in its bitter fertility and living death, Macondo is the site of the ruin of nature and the destruction of humanity. Together they provide the novelistic transformations of the narrative literary monuments that dominated the predawn of Latin American literature: the natural and moral histories of the Indies (Oviedo, Las Casas, Acosta, Sahagún), all of which told versions of the story of the New World's natural and human bounty and the Old World entrepreneurs and institutions that transformed them.

FORWARD TO THE PAST

Reading contemporary Latin American novels' variations on the theme of the expulsion from Paradise, and focusing on the narrative role of space and place, I identify in the novelistic worlds of Rulfo and García Márquez narratives that carry us back to the narrative traditions of the colonial period. There are elements in the novels of the twentieth century that refine our readings of colonial-era writings and place them on a new path ("perfecting [afinar] and perceptibly altering [desviar]" them, in Borges's words). Turning back to them, we discover that even the royal treasurer Cabeza de Vaca's report to the emperor told of the expulsion from Paradise, without, no doubt, meaning to do so: "We traveled through much land and we found all of it deserted, because the inhabitants of it went fleeing through the sierras without daring to keep houses or work the land for fear of the Christians. It was a thing that gave us great sorrow, seeing the land very fertile and very beautiful and very full of waterways and rivers, and seeing the places deserted and burned and the people so emaciated and sick, all of them having fled and in hiding."[60] (The death of Comala and the disappearance of Macondo are here foreshadowed.) On reading forward from Cabeza de Vaca to El Inca Garcilaso, narrative scenes of the effects of devastation and destruction like the one just cited are presented in order to be erased later and replaced by the edifying episodes of spiritual density of the multitudes adoring the Christian cross in Garcilaso's Pacaha. The resistance on the part of the natives and their submission are parts of a single narrative sequence, consisting of two actions: conquest erased by conversion.

Reading backward, not, as in chapter 2, from Guaman Poma's reading of Las Casas's political philosophy to the Andean's formulation of
Spanish conquest history in Peru, but rather from our own readings of
Rulfo and García Márquez to Cabeza de Vaca and Garcilaso, reveals other
things. In particular, the Latin American literary tradition whose nuclei
are acts of violence and destruction are not novelties of the twentieth
century but rather elements at home and "indigenous" in the sixteenth.
The difference is that in the sixteenth century the narrative that defends
European invasion and colonization must conceal destruction (the flight
of the natives to the highlands) with the achievement of a "greater good"
(their ultimate submission to the Spanish). In the narrative of the twentieth century, there is no need for such camouflage: violence and destruction are told starkly; there is no regeneration, as Richard Slotkin has put it
in studying the North American frontier, through acts of systematic (or
casual) violence.

In sum, the frequency and manner with which Garcilaso cited the
Cabeza de Vaca of *Naufragios* reveal that the authority Garcilaso sought
was not that which he would achieve by gaining a consensus among the
surviving conquistadores as to what happened in La Florida between 1539
and 1543. Nor was it the authority of the testimony uniquely given by his
privileged but anonymous conquistador-informant. The authority Garcilaso pursued was, instead, the correspondence of his account with the
narrative tradition in which were consecrated, from 1493 onward, a series
of paradigmatic episodes that would create, in effect, a typology (and a
mythology) of the basic elements that constitute these writings from and
about the Indies. Garcilaso preferred, in short, the ethereal airiness of
myth to the cold antechamber of the archive.

La Florida del Inca and the *Naufragios* may surprise the reader with
their pertinence to the longer Latin American literary tradition. The characteristics of potential conflict and threatened violence held in suspension
that Garcilaso locates in his nonexistent Guancane find their most powerful legacy in the novels of the twentieth century. Their place in the roll call
of the "polemics of possession" is compelling, as they answer in the
negative the question posed in sixteenth-century Castile (most notably by
Juan Ginés de Sepúlveda) as to whether regeneration is, in fact, possible
through violence. About Comala and Macondo much more might be said.
It has nevertheless been possible to glimpse how the narrative nuclei of

the enduring works of the Spanish colonial era provide the long Spanish American narrative tradition with great novelistic and humanistic reach. The consciousness of space and domain cannot be greater than for those who inhabit it, or for those who consider themselves heirs to the world that, since Pietro Martire d'Anghiera, was called new, but which José de Acosta insisted was old ("the New World is no longer new, but old" [el Mundo Nuevo ya no es nuevo sino viejo].[61] The expression "New World," like "Guancane," finds its full value within the expressive literary system where it resides. It is the labor of the creators of Comala and Macondo, to paraphrase Borges, that has modified our conception of Guancane and of ancient La Florida, not to mention the New World. At the same time, the labor of the narrators who bequeathed to posterity the provinces of Nueva Galicia and Guancane give weight and depth to the human geographies of Comala and Macondo.

CHAPTER 12

Seeing Ghosts

THE LONGEVITY OF "SERPENTS IN SANDALS"

"SILENCE FELL. And the friar saw the figure of the woman multiplying through all the mirrors, parceling itself out into innumerable figures, until it was no more than a whirlwind of women every second gesturing to him, beckoning him to a mysterious ritual."[1] With these words, Reinaldo Arenas (1943–1990) evoked the dizzying, disorienting pursuit undertaken by his Fray Servando, the fictional Dominican friar whose real-life prototype was Fray Servando Teresa de Mier y Noriega (1763–1827). Mier was an admirer of the work of Bartolomé de las Casas, and a fictional Las Casas appears in a devastatingly effective cameo role in the final scenes of the last novel of Alejo Carpentier (1904–1980). Many Latin American novels on Spanish-colonial-era themes have been written in the past few decades. Arenas inaugurated the series in 1966 with his *El mundo alucinante,* and its culmination (though not its chronological terminus) is marked by Carpentier in 1979 with *El arpa y la sombra.* The stylistic virtuosity and the complexity of plot and reference in these works simultaneously move backward and forward in time, and they are of interest not because of their historical themes but because of the vitality and the currency with which these elements are charged. Arenas's figure of the woman "multiplying through all the mirrors" and "beckoning him to a mysterious ritual" is like the appeal of the past's narratives: mysterious, fragmented, beckoning, and, most of all, demanding that we look at, and see, ourselves.[2]

One of the achievements of Arenas's and Carpentier's novels, integrated with their ribald good humor, their satirical verve, and their biting burlesque, is their deep reflection on Latin American cultural and literary traditions and their contemporary legacies. These reflections can be summed up under the rubric "Bartolomé de las Casas."[3] Born in 1484, deceased in 1566, the historical Las Casas was both writer and fighter on the subject of the Spanish in the Indies, that is, Spain's right (or not) to rule in the Indies and its treatment of America's indigenous peoples and enslaved black Africans (see chapter 3). Arenas and Carpentier do not take the historical Las Casas's writings as a source as such; "Las Casas" is an idea that permeates them metaphorically, as in the utterance in Ricardo Güiraldes's *Don Segundo Sombra* (1926): "I thought I had seen a phantom, a shadow, something that passes and is more an idea than a being" [Me pareció haber visto un fantasma, una sombra, algo que pasa y es más una idea que un ser].[4] "Las Casas," however, is not the only shadow-phantom-whirlwind that inhabits the novels in question; each evokes other narratives of the past, Carlos de Sigüenza y Góngora and Cabeza de Vaca most prominently among them. Arenas's feminized whirlwind and the presence and passing of Güiraldes's disembodied phantom are apt descriptions of a narrative effect that enriches, deepens, and transforms the literary legacy of the Latin American past.

What is the magnitude of the Lascasian shadows in these works, and which of the several possible Las Casases do they appeal to? There are at least two: the saintly so-called "apostle to the Indians,"[5] or, from the opposite perspective, the vilified, demonized servant of Satan. Running a close second to this version there is the thesis that Las Casas deliberately ruined Spain's international reputation (as the single-handed author of the Black Legend) because of having been a double agent for the British(!). All of these are extreme, Manichean views that in their radical forms reflect the controversial subjects that Arenas and Carpentier chose to novelize: Fray Servando Teresa de Mier and Cristóbal Colón, aka Christopher Columbus (c. 1451–1506), respectively. Arenas and Carpentier do not permit facile Manichean perspectives to prevail in the case of either of the literary characters of Fray Servando or Colón, and they challenge it with equal vigor in the case of Las Casas. Both authors avoid taking one or the other polarized positions regarding their principal subjects, and they do so by humanizing them. Arenas creates around Fray Servando a world populated by types more eccentric than even the historical Fray Servando was considered by some to be. Carpentier does so by resting his case on Colón as a fabulator, that is, as a writer carrying out, in the final moments of his life, the evaluation of what he has achieved in life (and what not) and the value of his work. In the same way, Carpentier also contemplated, through his Colón and thus at a remove of a certain esthetic distance, his own imminent end. (When he finished the novel it was known he was suffering from cancer.)

ARENAS'S FRAY SERVANDO

So where does this Lascasian specter or shadow appear in the novels in question? To put it simply: in the episodes that take into account the themes of wanton violence and slavery, that is, black African slavery in Arenas's novel, Indian slavery in Carpentier's. The historical Las Casas weighed in heavily on both of these fundamental issues, although there exists a general and popular misunderstanding about one of them, namely, on African slavery in the Americas (see chapter 3). On the topic of violence, subjugation, and slavery, Arenas's narration of Fray Servando's sea voyage on the "Nueva Empresa" and, ultimately, on the back of a whale from Veracruz, Mexico, to Cádiz, Spain, is pertinent. This was the journey of transit from Fray Servando's inquisitorial imprisonment at San Juan de Ulúa near Veracruz to the prison of Las Caldas, in Cádiz. In the novel, Fray Servando's ship, the "New Enterprise," was attacked by pirate ships, and these in turn were attacked by a flotilla of slaving ships. In the manner of Arenas throughout *El mundo alucinante,* the perspective fictionalized is that of the narrative subject enduring, in his own flesh, the outrageous offenses and humiliating abuses of his countrymen: "Thus I was here in this packet of slave ships, held as but one slave the more. . . . I thought I had been loosed from my captivity by the soldiers, so that I attempted, in a hundred ways, to pass unnoticed in that sea of blackness."[6] Fray Servando passed unnoticed because his skin had so darkened by long exposure to the sun that "not for a single moment did the men of the crew believe me one of their own kind" (46; 57).

Fray Servando describes the pitious plight of these future slaves, "so crowded and huddled up against one another that hardly could they move, and many had to sleep upright." Death by starvation, observes our peripatetic friar, was common. Suffering the plight of the black slaves, he nevertheless mocks his countrymen. Knowing both the "miseries of the species and its weakness for fawning and puffery," he "pretended great and abject devotion" to these "superior beings" (46; 57). Knowing "the little learning possessed by the sailors, especially if they were Spaniards," he spoke to them in Latin so that they might think it was an African dialect: "And then they would mock and jeer me while I, in the chastest Latin, would curse their mothers to endless lives in seaside whorehouses kept by Arab brothel keepers" (47; 57–58). Arenas irresistibly carries the satire further, as the sailors shout at the mocha-colored Fray Servando, "Black savage, you need to learn human ways!" and threaten him with death if he dare to open his mouth to speak a language apart from the sacred one, that is, Spanish. "Black savage, mouthing your bestial African talk," you must learn "the holy Spanish language" (46–47; 57–58).

Arenas rounds out this display of human cruelty and degradation with the arrival of a ship loaded with Negresses, destined to be enslaved. The sailors, comporting themselves "like so many Mediterranean monkeys," made their way to the other boat and had their way with the women, who, sadly, had long since been raped for the first time and finally, on this occasion, did not resist their attackers. The horror was the gang rape of one young woman, who was "always revealed to be little more than a girl" [resultaba ser siempre una niña] (46–47; 57–58). Since Fray Servando's attempts, when forced to serve as interpreter between the white sailors and the future black female slaves, met with failure, he was thrown into the brig. As he gradually lost his dark color and grew whiter—whiter, of course, than the perpetually sun-bronzed sailors—he was decried by them as being "the very devil himself" and was thrown overboard (48; 59).

This episode has certain resonances with the pirate captivity in Sigüenza y Góngora's *Los infortunios de Alonso Ramírez* (1690), which itself harks back to Cabeza de Vaca's *Naufragios* in the encounter of pirate and slaving ships. Sigüenza y Góngora's tale recounts the adventures of Alonso Ramírez as he travels from Puerto Rico to Havana to Mexico and finally to the Philippines via Acapulco.[7] Devoting himself to maritime mercantilism, he and twenty-five other men are captured by English pirates, led by "maestre Bel" and captain "Donkin." They undergo countless hardships and cruelties at the hands of their captors, and, in the Indian Ocean, they are carried to Madagascar, where Donkin and Bel decide to leave the captives. Begging them not to do so, fearful of being left in the hands of the heretical "black Moors" of Madagascar, Ramírez and his men are finally taken along on the condition that they agree to become pirates. From there to Africa and across the Atlantic they go, to the mouth of the Amazon River in Brazil. Instead of leaving the captives on land, in the Amazonian jungle, the pirates give them a small frigate obtained in Singapore, on which, now liberated, they coast the shores of Brazil and head toward Trinidad. Sighting an English flotilla, they turn back north and head toward Barbados. They are finally cast ashore on the coast of Yucatán, where they suffer no less ill fortune. Fearful that they have landed on the shore of La Florida, known for its savage and cannibalistic inhabitants(!), they are relieved to discover they are in Yucatán.

There are strong echoes here of the tale of the 1511 shipwreck victims, Jerónimo de Aguilar and the phantom-made-flesh Gonzalo Guerrero among them, about whom Sigüenza y Góngora surely read in Gómara's *La conquista de México* (1552) or in Bernal Díaz del Castillo's *Historia verdadera de la conquista de la Nueva España* (1632). Sigüenza's account of the fear of Floridians recalls Cabeza de Vaca's *Naufragios* and his many years of captivity in La Florida, specifically his description of Indians of the Florida Peninsula: "As they are of large build and go about naked, from a distance they appear to be giants."[8] As for the maritime resonances of Cabeza de Vaca in *El mundo alucinante,* in both cases the encounter with pirates resulted in a serious threat, but not capture. In Cabeza de Vaca's 1542 account, French privateers, who operated at the strategic site of the Azores as well as in the Caribbean, played an intricate game of deception on the Spanish treasure ship, loaded with gold and silver, on which Cabeza de Vaca was traveling back to Spain.[9]

FRAY SERVANDO, MIER, AND LAS CASAS

This Fray Servando episode is one of many that in seriated fashion harks back to the litany of atrocities in Las Casas's *Brevísima relación de la destrucción de las Indias* (1542, pub. 1552). While the structure of *El mundo alucinante* has been described as that of a Byzantine novel or the picaresque, it is more to the point to observe that Arenas has marked its discrete units exactly as Las Casas did in the *Brevísima relación.* Just as Las Casas proceeds via narrative sections entitled "the island of Hispaniola," "San Juan (Puerto Rico) and Jamaica," "Cuba," "Tierra Firme," "Nicaragua," "Nueva España," and so forth, so Arenas divides his work into major narrative segments (each of which consists of several numbered and titled short chapters). Arenas gets to Las Casas via Mier. The narrative divisions' titles of geographical designation—"México," "España," "Francia," "Italia," "España," "Portugal," "Inglaterra," "Estados Unidos," "México," "Havana," "Estados Unidos," and finally, again, "México"—mimic those of the historical Fray Servando's *Memorias,* which in turn paid homage to Las Casas's tract. As a kind of *Brevísima relación à la inversa,* Arenas reads out a litany of outrages and atrocities committed against the Indians of Mexico and blacks in the United States—for example, both being used as kindling for fires (Arenas, *El mundo alucinante,* 24, 191)—on repeated occasions, more than half of which occur not in Latin America or the Caribbean but in Europe and the United States.

In identifying the countries where the atrocities against the innocent were committed as well as the sites of the corruption of the powerful, including Roman Catholic priests, Arenas pays his respects to the historical Fray Servando for having edited the *Brevísima relación de la destrucción de las Indias.* Mier managed to get the work published in various locations: London (1812), Philadelphia (1821), Mexico City (1822), and possibly in Puebla, Mexico (also 1822) (Mier y Noriega, *Historia,* cxviii). These were, in fact, the first publications of the tract in the Spanish language since Las Casas published it in 1552 in Seville and its subsequent, posthumous publication eighty years after his death, in Barcelona in 1646. Mier's publications of Las Casas's exposé are also the objects of Arenas's homage.

Arenas creates a Fray Servando who lacks all guile and seeks the truth at all costs. Mier's *Apología* is the source: "My innocence excludes all cunning."[10] The old, cynical priest with whom Arenas's Fray Servando is conversing denies such a possibility: "A friar that has no taint of guile is a mythical beast" (59) [Un fraile que no haga fraude es cosa increíble (67)]. After Fray Servando is trapped by his archenemy, the evil Francisco Antonio León, he is chided for the same fault, being told by the woman into whom León has transformed himself, "Thou shalt learn that what most must be hidden is the truth, reason, right, for rare is the time it is worth its salt. It is a weapon for losers, *friar,* for the conquered and vanquished and stepped upon" (102; 113). If reason is the weapon of the vanquished and the victor never depends on it, Fray Servando's antagonist and mortal enemy seems to be saying, then the defender of right, not might, is unlikely ever to come out the winner.

Yet this viewpoint, however true Arenas's Fray Servando may have found it to be, did not defeat him. Imprisoned in Madrid, nearly perishing of cold and covered with lice, the fictional friar echoes his historical antecedent in the *Memorias:* "And I marveled at thinking how, the worse luckless circumstances grew, and the harder life got, the more determined a man became to overcome it, and how, the meaner and pettier our fellow men were, and the more intolerable our lots, the stronger and more potent the ideas that came and allowed us to combat them" (151; 161).

Las Casas was not "a winner" either, but that did not stop him from developing to their full potency his ideas for reform, which ended (one regent and two monarchs later) with his recommendation that Spain withdraw its rule from the Indies. The long struggle for justice in the Americas that he advocated over the course of a half century spanned the period from the regency of Cardinal Francisco Ximénez de Cisneros through the first decade of the reign of Philip II. Except for the hiatus of the years he spent at the Dominican House of Studies, the royal court was never free of Las Casas's dogged pursuit of colonial reform, and his thinking advanced from his early advocacy of lightening the burden on the declining indigenous population (which produced, retrospectively, the erroneous claim that Las Casas was responsible for the institution of African slavery in the Indies), through his promotion of the 1542 New Laws, which sought to abolish the encomienda and Indian slavery, to his final proposal to return sovereignty in the Americas to its native princes or their heirs (see chapter 3).

The historical Fray Servando's admiration for Las Casas was unequivocal. In the face of the accusations made against the Dominican for authoring African slavery in the Americas, Mier discovered that the accusation was a false attribution. He demonstrated in his *Historia de la revolución de Nueva España* (1813) that it was the Englishman William Robertson, in his influential *History of America* (1776), who had popularized the idea by attributing to Las Casas the origin of African slavery in America in 1516 or 1517. It was in fact Mier who discovered the historical records showing that as far back as 1501 Ferdinand and Isabel had mandated that black African slaves be allowed passage to the Indies (provided they had been born in the power of Christians).[11] Mier's investigations on the matter led him to the *Historia general de los hechos de los castellanos en las islas y tierra firme del mar océano* (1601–1615) of the royal chronicler Antonio de Herrera y Tordesillas. In Herrera's account he discovered slavery's earlier origins, for Herrera, in turn, had taken his information directly from the royal instructions issued to Nicolás de Ovando as governor of Hispaniola on September 16, 1501.[12]

If the historical Fray Servando carried in his memory the record of the false accusations against Las Casas, in his *Apología* he lamented the false accusations that had been made against himself. It is therefore not surprising that in his *Historia de la revolución de la Nueva España* he tried to correct the misunderstanding about Las Casas's intervention in slavery policy and to lift the charge wrongly placed on his shoulders. All these matters are bound together in the episode in which Arenas has his Fray Servando defend himself against the sailors who shout, "Black savage, you need to learn human ways!" or, more literally, "Black savage, you need to get used to living like a human being."[13] Arenas's Fray Servando suffers in his own flesh Mier's and Las Casas's persecutions by their enemies and the horrors (both physical and psychological) to which the enslaved Africans were themselves subjected.

LAS CASAS IN CARPENTIER

Alejo Carpentier's engagement with the legacy of Las Casas in *El arpa y la sombra* is more apparent than in Arenas's novel because in Carpentier's Vatican chambers Las Casas appears, literally a Lascasian shade, as a witness before the pontifical tribunal that is considering the canonization of the Admiral. There are two grave charges being made against Colón. The first is his unsanctioned liaison with Beatriz Enríquez, the mother of the Admiral's illegitimate son, Hernando Colón (1488–1539). The second charge, described as being "no less grave" (but also "no more grave," which is Carpentier's tongue-in-cheek way of letting us know that his pontifical protagonists did not necessarily consider it any more serious), was the institution of slavery—Indian slavery—in the New World. Las Casas is called to the witness stand to testify, and, upon seeing him, Colón, no longer incarnate but represented by the Invisible One, shrinks down to near deflation. " 'I'm screwed,' moaned the Invisible One, 'now I'm really screwed' " ['Me jodí,' gime el Invisible, 'ahora sí me jodí'].[14] When Las Casas appears, looking like "one of Zurburán's monks," in reference to the austere depictions of friars and priests by the Spanish baroque painter Francisco Zurburán (1598–1662), he is greeted by all those who hold him responsible for the Black Legend of Spanish history with cries of "Hypochondriac! Opportunist! Falsifier! Calumniator! Big bag of bile!" and, my personal favorite, "Serpent in sandals!" [¡Hipocondriaco! ¡Oportunista! ¡Falsario! ¡Calumniador! ¡Saco de bilis! ¡Serpiente con sandalias!] (144–145; 208).

Las Casas testifies, and Carpentier, as he did in his accounts of Columbus's voyages in the same novel, cites Las Casas's own words as testimony. He paraphrases the *Apologética historia sumaria,* which affirms that the indigenous peoples of the Americas fulfilled Aristotle's six criteria for prudence and therefore showed themselves capable and fit for self-governance.[15] Carpentier does the same regarding the historical Las Casas's *Apologética*'s arguments on cannibalism; namely, he cites Las Casas's words to the effect that cannibalism had existed in parts of the Old World long ago and that therefore it should not be a surprise (or a source of condemnation) that it was now found in parts of the New.[16] Carpentier has his Las Casas declare, as the historical Fray Bartolomé had done, that Columbus would have brought about the extinction of all the indigenous inhabitants of the islands if his fortunes had not gone awry and if Isabel had not ordered that the sale of Indian slaves in Seville and Granada be halted (146–147; 211, 212).

Carpentier's Las Casas is the ephemeral but substantive "more an idea than a being" that Güiraldes evoked, and it is, at the same time, something still greater. Carpentier brilliantly weaves Las Casas's own writings into the drama of his narrative and brings them to life, personifying them in the voice of his fictional protagonist and giving new meaning to old ideas. Las Casas's *Apologética historia sumaria* was not published until the nineteenth century, and then only partially. Recent studies, such as those of Anthony Pagden, and especially Sabine MacCormack, suggest that the work's "real life" can begin only now. Carpentier's exquisite reading of Las Casas's *Apologética* stands as the literary inaugural of these new explorations.

ARENAS'S INVISIBLE ONE: THE IMPLICIT LAS CASAS

In the writings of the historical Fray Servando Teresa de Mier y Noriega, two main tendencies can be isolated: his political ideology regarding colonial oppression and the independence of America from Spain, on one hand, and, on the other, the apologetic and autobiographical writings, in which he denounced colonialism, dodged the Inquisition, made propositions to the Spanish Cortes, and suffered his final conflicts with the newly independent but not exactly liberated regime in Mexico. Of these two tendencies, Arenas emphasizes the latter: the struggle for personal freedom of movement and ideas against institutional, inquisitorial persecution, fueled by institutional foes who had become personal enemies. This is a compelling choice, particularly for Arenas, whose autobiographical affinity for the figure of Fray Servando has been remarked upon by others and acknowledged by himself: "What has helped me most to 'apprehend' you," writes Arenas to Fray Servando in the epistolary prologue to *El mundo alucinante,* "has been my discovery that you and I are the same person."[17] Arenas's short novelistic epistle demonstrates with poignancy, better than any professorial exposition can, the novelist's understanding of, and common cause with, the lost agents (actors) of history.

The picaresque and cruel character of the historical Fray Servando's misfortunes was registered when he introduced his *Apología* with the statement, "Although with twenty-four years of persecution I have acquired a talent for painting monsters, my exposition will make clear that I do no more than copy originals."[18] In this protestation of his truthfulness, Mier provides Arenas with—Arenas elects—the key to the novel's liveliness: painting monsters. Las Casas, too, had "painted monsters" in the *Brevísima relación,* but in displaying them on his canvas he did no more than "copy originals," the originals being the reams of archival documentation that were his sources. Although in a different key and register, the fantastic, hallucinating adventures that Arenas gives Fray Servando are no less dizzying and disorienting than Las Casas's narrative recreation of the atrocities of Spanish conquest in the Indies. But the seemingly outlandish is often in fact true, just as truly horrific events are dismissed as outlandish and exaggerated but in fact turn out to be more than true (the synecdoche standing for the whole).

Arenas creates in his Fray Servando the attacks on their credibility that Mier and Las Casas suffered.[19] Yet even Mier's Sevillan jailor had to acknowledge that his prisoner's ideas and expectations, though perhaps unbelievable, were real. Although the veracity of the episodes the historical Fray Servando narrated in his *Apología* and his *Memorias* has often been questioned, the historical Fray Servando's jailor, José María Rodríguez, the administrator of Los Toribios, the prison for clerics in Seville where Mier was incarcerated in 1804–1805, documented the pertinent events. He also complained of the mad jocularity [la jocundidad algo loco] of his prisoner: "I think that there's something wrong with him in the head, because by no other means would he . . . believe such nonsense, while being at this low point, that he would leave here to be named a dean or a bishop."[20] After numerous failed attempts, Mier managed to escape from Los Toribios; at that point, the jailer Rodríguez asked to be relieved of his duties, "not having the strength to do battle" with such prisoners as Mier, adding that "every effort is useless with this type of monster, not to say man."[21] Sometimes truth is stranger (and stronger) than fiction.

In spite of the fact that the figure and writings of Las Casas are present in the historical Fray Servando's works, Arenas does not mention the Dominican from Seville in any passage of *El mundo alucinante*. Arenas's homage to the tireless Dominican friar who would not give up his ideas, even under duress, is as profound as it is implicit. Regarding persecution, Mier wrote that Las Casas's had lasted for three hundred years.[22] It is the tenacity with which he holds on to his ideas in spite of personal persecution that Arenas saw and silently admired in Las Casas. What Arenas could not share was Mier's vision of Las Casas as an inspirer of any political liberation from the religious perspective, where the viewpoints of Mier and Las Casas converged. Here Mier's epithets for Las Casas are revealing. Calling him frequently "the holy bishop Las Casas" [el santo obispo Las Casas] and even simultaneously "our father Las Casas" [nuestro padre Casas] and "the father of the Indians" [el padre de los indios], Mier sums up his apology by proclaiming Las Casas to be "the originary genius of the Americas, the bishop of Cuzco and Chiapas" [el genio titular de las Américas, Obispo del Cuzco y de Chiapa].[23] This is the Las Casas-via-Mier that Arenas leaves to one side. In doing so, he shows how literary tradition is transformed over time, that is, not by wholesale appropriation, but by careful processes of reevaluation and selection. It is the "making new" that assures the continuity of literary and cultural tradition.

QUETZALCOATL AND SANTO TOMÁS: THE PLUMED SERPENT IN SANDALS?

One of the ways of making new a time-honored cultural tradition was carried out by Mier, and it is one of the fundamental ideas of Mier on which Arenas anchors his novel. This is Mier's thesis that the arrival in America of the miracle of the gospel occurred in the time of the apostles and that the god/man Quetzalcoatl ("the plumed serpent," here in sandals) had been none other than Jesus' disciple Saint Thomas. Arenas puts in the mouth of José Ignacio Borunda the declaration, "The Virgin of Guadalupe did not make her appearance in that filthy cape of the Indian called Juan. Who could imagine such nonsense! Our Lady to appear in that disgusting poncho? No, she came in the coat of Quetzalcoatl, his very own raiment, and when I speak of Quetzalcoatl I am speaking of Saint Thomas, who could never under any circumstances have disobeyed the orders of Christ Himself."[24] Borunda's evidence is, first, Mesoamerican and hieroglyphic: "Look at these Yucatecan codices! Observe these Zapotecan inscriptions! And these markings of the Zacatecans, the direct descendants of the Toltecs! Here, now look'st thee at this thousand-odd lot of Chichimec stones and tell me that the proof is not irrefutable!" Second, it is biblical and scriptural: "Did not Jesus say to his apostles, 'Take the Word to all the world?'" And here is the thesis, hidden behind all the others, of which Arenas makes the point: In the mouth of Borunda he puts the words, "And America, by which of course I mean all the lands of the Americas, even those which we may not know but yet believe in, all the lands of the Americas, of course, are a great part of this world, a very great and excellent principal part" [y la América, desde luego, forma parte muy principalísima del mundo] (29; 39).

While the notion of the Quetzalcoatl/Santo Tomás visitation to the Indies can be attributed to Sigüenza y Góngora, it was the Las Casas of the *Apologética historia sumaria* who was the first thinker to dare to associate indigenous American beliefs with Christian notions of the Trinity, the Flood, and so forth.[25] He also accepted the view, not uncommon among the Indies-oriented theologians of his day, that the New World's native inhabitants had lost the original, ancient, and imperfect knowledge of the divine they once had.[26] There was, nevertheless, one great difference between the historical Las Casas and the historical and novelistic Fray Servandos: Las Casas was never persecuted by the Inquisition (although a list of charges against him was sent to the Holy Office; see chapter 3). If he had been charged, it would have been for his heretical political ideas, not for his radical views on the possible forgotten knowledge in the New World of Old World religious beliefs.[27] In any case, as established by Las

Casas and confirmed and consolidated by Fray Servando, this long Lasca-sian shadow of the indefatigable and intrepid Dominican friar became a permanent figure in the Latin American cultural pantheon. Arenas's nov-elistic homage, explicit to Fray Servando, implicit to Las Casas, is of a cultural valence greater than the lost historical figures of Fray Servando and Las Casas individually or both of them together.

THE LONGEVITY OF SERPENTS IN SANDALS

Carpentier's case, interestingly, is different insofar as his sixteenth-century figures are placed in their century and then are also seen from the perspec-tive of the nineteenth. By means of the canonization tribunal, Carpentier achieves the postindependence-era dimension that temporally formed part of Fray Servando's life in Arenas's account. Las Casas is vilified by his nineteenth-century detractors in the third section of Carpentier's novel, but only, as Carpentier's playing of this scene makes explicit, because the Dominican's figure—his specter, his shadow, his ideas—has not been for-gotten by time or erased from history. Reflecting the Cuban novelist's careful readings of the most important of Las Casas's voluminous works, the gravity of the words Carpentier chooses to represent Las Casas carries considerable weight and resonance. This selection, combined and con-trasted with the crazed attack on the Dominican by the cacophony of tribunal voices ("Hypochondriac! . . . Serpent in sandals!"), places the Lascasian presence at the center of a nineteenth-century debate.

Although Las Casas's role in the novel is not extensive, it is substan-tive, and it appears at a decisive moment. This is the moment of truth, Columbus's last judgment, his living inferno, that is, the discovery that he is condemned to take his place in history: "There are many like us, who, because of their fame, because people keep talking about them, cannot disappear into their transparency, removed from this screwed-up world where they put up statues of us, where new historians knock themselves out trying to bring to light the worst secrets of our private lives."[28] It turns out that there is a system of classification of historical Invisibles, depend-ing on the degree of demand: Class A Invisibles, such as Charlemagne and Philip II; Class B, the Princess of Eboli and so forth (156; 223–224). For Carpentier's Colón, this is the worst news of all: he will be judged once again! In this hilariously funny scene, the reader cannot refrain from imagining the protagonist, anxiously trying to figure out if, and how, he can manage to improve his ranking.

On balance, these novels attest to the power of certain fundamental, enduring ideas that constitute Latin America's abiding legacies to itself and to the world. The deftness of Arenas and Carpentier is in evidence in that such ideas as sovereignty, slavery, and freedom never overwhelm their novelistic creations but rather are woven in and out, never occupying for long the foreground or attempting to take it over. With respect to America from 1493 onward, there have always been those who struggled for justice so vigorously that, in the eyes of others, their views were judged either as sheer madness or as genuine insight, one being separated from the other by the finest of lines, merely a whisper apart. Arenas's Fray Servando and Carpentier's Las Casas walk that fine line. Neither angelical martyr nor hero would Arenas allow Fray Servando to be, but rather, as Arenas writes, simply what he was: "one of the most important figures in the literary and political history of the Americas."[29] The same can be said for the Las Casas and Colón of Carpentier, in which the specter, "more an idea than a being," ends up having greater volume and weight than men of flesh and blood and bone.

Bones, relics, and tradition draw together the themes of both novels.[30] The failed process of beatification of Colón in Carpentier's novel (and in pontifical history) augments and underlines the failed effort in Arenas's novel (and in Mexican history) of Fray Servando's intended replacement of Juan Diego by Quetzalcoatl/Santo Tomás as the bearer of Our Lady of Guadalupe. In the way that only reality itself can outdistance fiction, the themes of Carpentier's and Arenas's novels converged some two and three decades, respectively, after their publication and during the months I was contemplating writing about them. I am referring to the canonization not of Columbus but of Juan Diego, "the first indigenous saint on the American continents."[31] Carpentier's Las Casas surely would have been pleased, and his Colón no doubt would have been chagrined to find himself thereby dropping a category or two in the Rankings of the Invisibles. The new saint proclaimed in Mexico on July 31, 2002, speaks eloquently, as do the novels under consideration here, about the legacy of Latin America to the world and the peculiar union between the materiality of history and the force of tradition. The ceremonial act carried out at the basilica of

Guadalupe proves once more that these "merely historical" themes are still today the object of passionate and ongoing debate and that their import is related not only to the past but also, and always, to the future.

COLOPHON

The energy of the protagonists who have filled this book was driven by the claims they made to historical truth. The majority were authors of works they signed, and even those who theorized cultural hierarchies and political relationships when not historicizing them claimed that their formulations were based on the truthful knowledge of historical experience, be it their own or that of others. Some of these historical figures who were writers (Las Casas and Cabeza de Vaca), and a few others considered here but not as authors (Christopher Columbus and Fray Servando Teresa de Mier), have appeared as fictional characters recreated in twentieth-century fiction. Abel Posse, and especially Reinaldo Arenas and Alejo Carpentier have provided these novelistic ruminations. Then there is Fred Murdock, the fictional (I think!) bibliographer at Yale, not to mention the unnamed protagonist of *El entenado*, rendered, respectively, by Jorge Luis Borges and Juan José Saer.

The liminal figure that ties together the personalities who occupy this spectrum from history to fiction is the shipwreck victim whose historical survival was never verified but whose presumably historical existence as Gonzalo Guerrero was crafted and imposed by the narratives written about him. Gonzalo Guerrero is the binding agent that holds this corpus together. The phenomenon that goes by that name has made it possible to argue that narrative interpretation, not historical truth, provides the energy needed to materialize as historical and geographical the personalities (Gonzalo Guerrero) and the places (Guancane) that, in fact, were not so.

The other binding agent of this corpus is its principal referent: the Amerindian. This fact raises the stakes of every encounter between each protagonist and the words he wrote, whether it was the historical writer or the fictional character representing him who did so. The dilemma raised by the presence of the Amerindians is twofold: the ethical issue of their treatment by the invading Europeans and the rhetorical issue of their literary representation. And when those of Amerindian heritage took up the pen, the debates were renewed and the tropes reconfigured. At the heart of this cacophonous conversation is the claim to authority: Whose voice speaks the greatest truth? Which voice speaks the loudest? Which voices have the right to be heard?

The polemics of possession of the rights to conquest and those of sovereignty were carried out by court councilors, royally appointed expeditionary officials, learned historians, and theorists of cultural difference and social hierarchy. When their voices were joined (and countered and corrected) by the nonelite of Castilian tradition and the elite of autochthonous Amerindian tradition not recognized as such in Castile, the question became the third one cited above: Who had the right to speak? Bernal Díaz championed the quest for literary authority and achieved it by relying on juridical traditions and legal protocols he knew well. Guaman Poma, Alva Ixtlilxochitl, and El Inca Garcilaso did so, heroically, by citing and manipulating some learned printed authorities and by refuting others (the latter tendency was Bernal Díaz's strong suit). As to whose voices spoke the loudest, the ethnographic writers and theorists were bested by the epic poets: The Amerindian warrior and prince always ended up, in the dark perfection that only teleology can provide, either docile in captivity or dead on the battlefield. These paper lives, nevertheless, are a living legacy.

If the most prominent Indies thinkers of the sixteenth century relied on ancient learned authorities, they augmented them with materials from their own times. But, as argued here, these sources of authority were not history's lost referents but rather the narratives that interpreted them. I stated at the outset that today's reader must always have in hand a map, and now I add a point that has become clear over the course of this inquiry: the writer of the period in question always needed a library, whether it was a large collection of printed vellum-bound volumes, a few indispensable tomes with soft parchment covers, or a single tattered, well-worn and well-read manuscript. And always, no matter the size or prestige of the written works at their disposal, these reader-writers shared a single aim: to persuade the reader that what they wrote, though unbelievable, was also always true—be it about Spanish feats of conquest, Amerindian acts of peaceful submission, the strange and savage customs of the Amerindians, or their exemplary Christian ways. These writers' common approach boils down to this rhetorical stance: "Although you may find it impossible to believe what I am about to tell you—what you are about to read—it is altogether true." How they worked to achieve that goal of credibility has filled their many pages (and my own).

The twentieth-century writers who have created this book's colophon (the word is Latin, from Greek: *summit, finishing touch*) offer testimony to the enduring interest of the themes of conquest, colonization, and encounters with the unknown as well as to the conundrums of history's secrets and the potential of narrative to reinterpret the phenomena that it simultaneously conceals and reveals. The meditations produced in contemporary fiction reaffirm the vitality of Spanish America's sixteenth-century polemics of possession and its capacity to be transformed and become pertinent in our own day.

The bridge between past and present in this regard has been the figure of Las Casas: the historical Las Casas, as author and commentator of his own actions as well as those of countless others, and the fictional Las Casas, who raises an equally strong and strident voice, even though as a shade in Carpentier's fictionalization of the nineteenth-century tribunal considering the canonization of Christopher Columbus. Carpentier's brilliant meditation on Las Casas brings to life the final point I would make about the polemics of possession: Although no longer present in flesh and blood and bone but visible only in the words he wrote and uttered, Las Casas (but it could as well be Sepúlveda, Cabeza de Vaca, Bernal Díaz, Guaman Poma, or El Inca Garcilaso) hovers, like a cloud or like a conscience, over Old and New World landscapes and peoples to this day. So we find him (or them) when we sit and read—whenever, in fleeting moments, the house is quiet and the world calm enough for us to discover, to our surprise and consternation, that the Invisible Ones have never departed.

NOTES

CHAPTER 1. OVERVIEW

1. I have in mind Alejo Carpentier's *El arpa y la sombra* (1979) and Washington Irving's *A History of the Life and Voyages of Christopher Columbus* (1828). The early North American writers include Irving, William Hickling Prescott, and Herman Melville, to name those who are most prominently identified by their literary and historical interests in the Hispanic world (see Williams, *The Spanish Background*). The roll call of Latin American novelists writing on conquest- and colonial-era themes includes, to name a few, in addition to Carpentier, Reinaldo Arenas, Gabriel García Márquez, José Juan Saer, Antonio Benítez Rojo, and Abel Posse. See note 7, below.

2. Andrés González de Barcia Carballido y Zúñiga (1673–1743) inaugurated the modern study of sixteenth- and early seventeenth-century Spanish writings on the exploration, conquest, and settlement of the Americas by publishing a representative corpus of them in the 1720s through the 1740s; his three-volume *Historiadores primitivos de Indias* was published posthumously in 1749; see Carlyon, *Andrés González*, 201–206, for a complete listing. Barcia was one of the founders of the Spanish Royal Academy (Real Academia Española) and a prominent royal counselor during Spain's early Bourbon era.

3. The term *New World* appeared in print for the first time in 1511 in the pirated edition of the First Decade of Pietro Martire d'Anghiera's *De orbe novo Decades* [*Decades of the New World*]. Along with the Second and Third Decades, it was published with his authorization in Alcalá de Henares in 1516. The 1511 imprint covered Columbus's proposal to Ferdinand and Isabel, his first voyage, and his preparations for the second; it also included brief notices of the lands discovered between 1500 and 1510.

4. Carpentier, "Conciencia e identidad," 133. All English translations of Spanish-language texts throughout this book are my own, unless otherwise credited.

5. The most notable examples are Mariano Picón-Salas's *De la conquista a la Independencia: tres siglos de historia cultural hispanoamericana* (1944) and Pedro Henríquez Ureña's *Literary Currents in Hispanic America* (1945). Picón-Salas wrote his work after teaching at Columbia University, Smith College, and Middlebury College in 1942 and 1943; Henríquez Ureña's critical survey of the Spanish American literary tradition was first presented as the 1940–1941 Charles Eliot Norton lectures at Harvard University, and it later appeared in Spanish as *Las corrientes literarias en la América Hispánica* (1969).

6. González Echevarría, "A brief history," 23–24.

7. Carpentier's already mentioned *El arpa y la sombra* (1979), Reinaldo Arenas's *El mundo alucinante* (1966), Antonio Benítez Rojo's *El mar de las lentejas* (1979), Abel Posse's *Daimón* (1989 [c1978]) and *El largo atardecer del caminante* (1992), José Juan Saer's *El entenado* (1983), and Gabriel García Márquez's *El general en su laberinto* (1989) are outstanding examples. English translations of these novels appeared as follows: Carpentier, *The Harp and the Shadow* (1990), Arenas, *Hallucinations* (1971), idem, *The Ill-Fated Peregrinations of Fray Servando* (1987), Benítez Rojo, *The Sea of Lentils* (1991), Posse, *Daimón* (1992), Saer, *The Witness* (1990), and García Márquez, *The General in His Labyrinth* (1990). Chapter 12, "Seeing Ghosts: The Longevity of 'Serpents in Sandals,'" examines the novels of Arenas and Carpentier.

8. Irving A. Leonard's *Books of the Brave* and Lewis Hanke's *The Spanish Struggle for Justice in the Conquest of America,* both published in 1949, set the standard. Arturo Torres Ríoseco's *The Epic of Latin American Literature* (1942), later published in Spanish as *La gran literatura iberoamericana* (1945), inaugurated the trend.

9. I have elsewhere examined the development and transformation of Latin Americanist studies in the U.S. academy from the pre–World War II years through the end of the twentieth century, taking into account the respective roles of private foundations, the U.S. federal government, and the universities in fomenting these studies (Adorno, "Havana and Macondo"; idem, "Sur y norte").

10. My "Comentarios: Creadores de historia y progreso" and "Early Anglo-American Hispanism," both 1997, and "Washington Irving's Romantic Hispanism," 2002, address this triangulation of interests.

11. Adorno, "Warrior and War Community," 225.

12. Adorno, "New Perspectives," 181.

13. Sepúlveda, *Demócrates Segundo,* 76. Sepúlveda (80), that is, "Demócrates," makes explicit the "all mankind is one" theme by asserting that "all are united among themselves by proximity and kingship." See chapter 4, "Councilors Warring at the Royal Court."

14. Adorno, "Arms, Letters," 218.

15. See chapter 6, "The *Encomendero* and His Literary Interlocutors."
16. See Vološinov's study "Reported Speech" (1930).
17. I review the work of sixteenth-century preceptists on the goals and functions of writing history in Adorno, *Guaman Poma: Writing*, 36–39. If the ultimate goal of written history was to serve the public good ("El fin de la Historia es la utilidad pública," Luis Cabrera de Córdoba wrote in *De historia*, fol. 83r–v), the historian's mission was closely related to the task of governing. It was thus the prince's responsibility to choose the best historians possible and, Las Casas would add, to heed the lessons of history they provided. In this regard, his prologue to the *Historia de las Indias*, which reviews the aims of written history as expressed by ancient classical and Jewish historians, all of whom were authors of historical apologias, reveals the profound moral imperative that writing history entailed. I acknowledge here with gratitude José Cárdenas Bunsen's observation that each and every one of the examples studied by Las Casas were the prefaces of historical works that explained or defended the positions taken by their authors.
18. See chapter 7, "The Conquistador-Chronicler and His Literary Authority."
19. See González Echevarría, "José Arrom."
20. Oviedo, *Historia general* 3:615 [bk. 35, chap. 7]. See chapter 10, "The Narrative Reinvention of the Conqueror-Captive."
21. Cortés, *Cartas de relación*, 309; Elliott, "Cortés, Velázquez, and Charles V," xxvi–xxvii.
22. Ercilla spent seven and a half years (1555–1563) in South America; from April 1557 to December 1558, he participated in the war against the Araucanians. After his return to Spain in 1563, he published part 1 of *La araucana* in 1569; it was followed by parts 2 and 3, in 1578 and 1589, respectively. See Moríngo and Lerner, "Introducción biográfica y crítica," 10–11, 25.
23. See chapter 4, "Councilors Warring at the Royal Court."
24. See chapter 11, "From Guancane to Macondo: Literary Places and Their Predecessors." In contrast to Florida, the state of the U.S. union, "La Florida" refers throughout this study to the vast territories, so identified by the Spanish in the 1520s and 1530s, lying to the north of New Spain. See figure 23.
25. Esteve Barba, *Historiografía Indiana*, 19.
26. The long chain of narrative reports (letters, *probanzas,* and individual and collective accounts) of the Pánfilo de Nárvaez expedition that antedates the canonized 1555 *Naufragios* of Cabeza de Vaca is a salient example. Patrick Pautz and I reconstructed this series and sequence of writings in Adorno and Pautz, *Álvar Núñez* 3:8–84.
27. See chapter 9, "The Narrative Invention of Gonzalo the Warrior."
28. "Cuando vino [el emperador] de Alemania, [Las Casas] le propuso su causa con mucha erudición y prudencia, hablando como santo, informando como jurista, decidiendo como teólogo y testificando como testigo de vista" (Fernández, *Historia eclesiástica*, 30 [bk. 1, chap. 6]). Book 1 "treats the conversion of the New World, or Occidental Indies, and its surrounding islands" [trata

de la conversión del Nuevo Mundo, o Indias Occidentales, con sus islas cir-
cunvecinas]. My earlier quotation of Fernández's remark was misprinted so
that Las Casas was cited as "informing like a tourist" [informando como
turista] (!) (Adorno, "Nuevas Perspectivas," 14).

29. "Vivían en sus casas pacíficos y seguros" (Casas, *Historia* 1:133–134 [bk. 1,
chap. 25]; see also 3:177, 275 [bk. 3, chaps. 102, 129]). He argues that "of one
hundred thousand [black Africans], not ten had been legitimately enslaved"
as captives taken in war against the Muslim enemies of the Christian faith
(*Historia* 1:144 [bk. 1, chap. 26]. See chapter 3, "Bartolomé de las Casas, Polemicist and Author."

30. William Robertson's *History of America* (1776) was the first English-language
publication to make this false assertion; see the section entitled "Las Casas
on African Slavery," in chapter 3.

31. The state inspection and approval of books to be printed was mandated in
1554, making the Council of Castile (instead of local authorities, as was previously the case) the licensing body. This law was augmented in 1556 by the
specific order that books "dealing with matters pertaining to these our Indies" be permitted to be printed only upon receiving the Council of Castile's
approval plus an additionally mandated inspection and approval by the
Council of the Indies. See Adorno and Pautz, *Álvar Núñez* 3:73–74, 87–88,
for a review of the pertinent legislation.

32. Patricia Meyers Spack probes this question in "Reality—Our Subject and Discipline."

33. These reflections were presented in the keynote address I delivered at the international symposium "Mapping the Worlds of Sixteenth-Century Mexico,"
Beinecke Rare Book and Manuscript Library, Yale University, September 15,
2006. I thank my distinguished colleague Mary E. Miller, Vincent Scully Professor of the History of Art, who organized the conference, for the privilege
of participating in this pathbreaking event.

34. Stevens, *Collected Poetry,* 311.

CHAPTER 2. FELIPE GUAMAN POMA DE AYALA AND THE POLEMICS OF POSSESSION

1. It has long been understood that the manuscript had been obtained by a former Danish diplomat in Madrid, as Sir Clements Markham announced in
his introduction of Richard Pietschmann at the 1912 International Congress
of Americanists in London (*Proceedings,* xxxii–xxxiv). The Danish research librarian, Harald Ilsøe, has determined that the manuscript had probably entered the royal collections by 1663 and that the probable donor, as also
mentioned by the Peruvian historian Raúl Porras Barrenechea (*El cronista,*
79), had been Cornelius Pedersen Lerche. Cornelius Lerche (1615–1681)
served as Danish ambassador to Spain from 1650 to 1655 and again from
1658 to 1662. He owned manuscripts acquired from the library of Don Gas-
par de Guzmán (1587–1645), the count-duke of Olivares, which made his

Spanish collection unequaled in Denmark at the time; after being knighted
by Frederick III in 1660, he likely presented the manuscript to the monarch
upon his return to Copenhagen in 1662 (Adorno, "Witness," 16–23). My
2001–2002 codicological examination of the manuscript, GkS, 2232, 4to,
completes and updates my 1977 analysis (Adorno, "Witness," idem, "La redacción").

2. "Es precisamente esta diferencia la que hace de la obra de Waman Poma una
apertura casi única para reconstruir la experiencia del *indio ladino*—el indígena que sabía español y vivía en la zona de contacto directo entre la tem-
prana sociedad colonial española y la nativa—durante el primer siglo colonial
en Hispanoamérica" (Adorno, "Waman Puma," xviii). Mary Louise Pratt later
(1992) popularized the term in the introductory chapter of her *Imperial Eyes,*
which features Guaman Poma, where she announced, "I have manufactured
some terms and concepts along the way. One coinage that recurs through the
book is the term 'contact zone.' " She adds, "By using the term 'contact,' I
aim to foreground the interactive, improvisational dimensions of colonial encounters so easily ignored or suppressed by diffusionist accounts of conquest
and domination." I had earlier (1988, 1990) emphasized this interactive and
relational quality of colonial encounters, postulating "the model of discourse
in the colonial setting as the study of interactive, relational, dialogic and synchronic cultural practices. With this emphasis on the dialogic, the objects of
analysis are changing so that the subject category is pushed open to include
. . . those subjects whose ethnic or gender identifications do not reproduce
those of the dominant partriarchal and imperial ideology" (Adorno,"Nuevas
perspectivas," 11; idem, "New Perspectives," 173–174).

3. *Ladino* originally referred to the common Romance vernacular language of
Spain, excluding Catalunia. Roger Wright ("Early Medieval Spanish," idem,
"Latin and ladino") explains how the relationship of the concepts *latín* and
"ladino" in medieval Spain resulted in the latter term's subsequent meaning
with reference to the Sephardic Jewish cultural tradition. Manuel Alvar
("Aceptaciones") surveys the many usages of the term *ladino* and its expressive connotations.

4. Alvar, "Aceptaciones," 28–29.

5. Oviedo, *Historia general* 1:140 [bk. 5, chap. 4]; Alvar, "Aceptaciones," 30.

6. Guaman Poma, *Nueva corónica,* 796, 838; see also 733, 738. I use the con-
secutive pagination of the original manuscript as corrected from Guaman
Poma's original numbering. This is the standard system, used since the 1980
editions of the *Nueva corónica* by Murra and Adorno, and Pease, respectively,
and appearing in the Murra-Adorno edition of 1987 as well as in the updated
digital Murra-Adorno edition of the complete manuscript, prepared with the
collaboration of Ivan Boserup, Keeper of Manuscripts and Rare Books at the
Royal Library, on the website of the Royal Library of Copenhagen:
http://www .kb.dk/permalink/2006/poma/info/en/frontpage.htm.

7. I have surveyed the range of social roles of "indios ladinos" as described in

sixteenth- and seventeenth-century sources (Adorno, "Images of Indios Ladinos"; idem, "The Indigenous Ethnographer"). John Charles, "Indios ladinos," investigates the evidence of the presence of these individuals in the documentary record. Juan Carlos Estenssoro, *Del paganismo,* and Kenneth Mills, *Idolatry,* use such testimony to examine the relations between native peoples, as agents of their own history, and the church, from the early to mid colonial period. All three focus their work on colonial Peru.

8. Solano, "El intérprete," 267–268; Hemming, *Conquest,* 281.

9. Guaman Poma's reiteration of the Albornoz report's information is documented in Adorno, "Introduction to the Second Edition," xlv–xlvi.

10. Guaman Poma, *Nueva corónica,* 1089–1090.

11. Guaman Poma's participation in proceedings confirming land titles in 1594 and 1595 is documented in Pereyra Chávez, "Un documento," 261–270; Salazar, "Pieza," in Varallanos, *Guaman Poma,* 210–211; Stern, "Algunas consideraciones," 226; and Zorrilla, "La posesión," 50n1. His signature, "Don Phelipe Guaman Poma," indicates the elite social status by which he was recognized (Varallanos, *Guaman Poma,* 31, 38n9).

12. I have reconstructed the course of events as contained in these documents (Adorno, "Genesis"), and the present discussion reiterates my principal findings.

13. Monica Barnes, "La Nueva corónica," makes this well-informed observation.

14. Guaman Poma, *Nueva corónica,* 886, 918.

15. Lohmann Villena, "Una carta," 325–327. I have newly transcribed and translated the letter (Adorno, *Guaman Poma and His Illustrated Chronicle,* 79–86). Guaman Poma (*Nueva corónica,* 7, 11) requests that his work be printed as "a great service to His Majesty."

16. Housed in the private collection of Seán Galvin in Ireland, Murúa's *Historia del origen y genealogía* was published in December 2004 by Testimonio Compañía Editorial, Madrid, in a printed color facsimile that reproduces all the characteristics of the original except for the manuscript's basic construction of its sheets into quires.

17. Adorno and Boserup, "Guaman Poma," 191–198, 234–235; "The Making of Fray Martín de Murúa's *Historia general del Peru,*" section 10.

18. Ossio ("Introducción," 18, 50, 191n175) has shown 1606 to be the latest documented date for Murúa's additions to his *Historia del origen* manuscript: on fol. 106r, Murúa recounts his punishment of three Indian "idolaters" in the province of Aymaraes, carried out when he was serving there. Ossio has deduced that Murúa held this assignment between 1604 and 1606.

19. This discussion of the Murúa/Guaman Poma collaboration relies on my study, coauthored with Ivan Boserup, "Guaman Poma and the Manuscripts of Fray Martín de Murúa." Our detailed arguments about their distant working relationship were presented at the 52nd International Congress of Americanists, Seville, Spain, July 18, 2006, in our two-part paper, "Illuminating

Working Relationships through Manuscript Studies: Fray Martín de Murúa and Felipe Guaman Poma de Ayala."

20. Adorno and Boserup, "Guaman Poma," 193–199; idem, "The Making," section 10.

21. "Of these kingdoms of Peru the first great lord over the other three was the powerful lord Guaman Chaua, Yarovilca, Allauca Hánuco, from the settlement of Huánco el viejo" [Destos rreynos del Pirú el primero gran señor sobre los tres fue Apo Guaman Chaua, Yarobilca, Allauca Guanoco, del pueblo de Guanoco el biejo (Murúa, *Historia general*, fol. 307r)].

22. Murúa took two depictions of "generic" Incas in procession drawn by Guaman Poma in the earlier *Historia del origen* manuscript and recycled them in his later *Historia general* manuscript, renaming them as the twelfth Inca, Huascar Inca, and his royal consort, Chuqui Llantu.

23. Adorno and Boserup, "Guaman Poma," 234–235.

24. "Y ancí no multiplica y se acaua y se acauará los yndios en este reyno"; "se [*sic*] se acaua quedará la tierra yermo y solitario la tierra" (Guaman Poma, *Nueva corónica*, 616, 988). Guaman Poma's warnings are legion in number, and they echo the customary warnings issued decades earlier by Las Casas to the king: "Your Majesty can take it for certain that the Indians will perish and the land remain useless and empty, as is the island of Hispaniola and the other kingdoms and provinces" [Vuestra Alteza tenga por cierto que los indios han todos de perecer y la tierra quedar perdida y malaventurada, como lo está la isla Española y los reinos y provincias demás]" (Casas, "Respuesta," 425).

25. There are some nineteen "prologues" throughout the work, coming at the end, not the beginning, of the chapters they accompany and combining sermonlike admonitions with specific recommendations for colonial reform. See Adorno, *Guaman Poma*, 48–49, 75–77.

26. The organization of major portions of the *Nueva corónica*, especially the chapters devoted to the inspection tour of Tupac Inca Yupanqui and the description of the age-grades of Andean society, reproduce the specific format of the inspection tour report (*Guaman Poma*, 184–236). All the chapters that deal with ancient Andean religious and ritual practices are materials at least in part gathered, as Guaman Poma (285) himself declares, on the tour(s) of inspection on which he accompanied Cristóbal de Albornoz.

27. He utilizes the precepts of the provincial church councils as the authority by which to advocate his program of goals, which include fomenting literacy among the Andean people, examining and reforming the conduct of the Christian missionary clergy, achieving and maintaining the segregation of Andean communities from those of the colonizing groups, prohibiting mestizos and mulattoes from residing in native Andean communities, and removing the practitioners of Andean cults from their local communities so that "the things that the ministers of God devote a year to building cannot be destroyed in a single day" (Bartra, ed., *Tercer concilio*, 80, 153, 154, 168).

28. Guaman Poma, *Nueva corónica*, 1104–1139; see Adorno, "Witness," 76–80, on the late composition of this chapter.

29. "Otros quieren decir que los yndios salieron de la casta de judíos; parecieran como ellos y barbudos, zarcos y rubios como español, tubieran la ley de Muyzén y supieran la letra, leer y escriuir y serimonias. Y ci fuera de la casta de turcos o moros, tanbién fueran barbudos y tuviera la ley de Mazoma. Y otros dixeron que los yndios eran saluages animales; no tubieron la ley ni oración ni áuito de Adán, y fuera como caballo y bestia, y no conocieran al Criador ni tubieran sementeras y casas y arma, fortaleza y leys y ordenanzas y conosemiento de Dios y tan santa entrada" (Guaman Poma, *Nueva corónica*, 60–61).

30. In this passage Guaman Poma (*Nueva corónica*, 52) uses "español" to refer generically to all non-Indian peoples, including those of Semitic traditions and backgrounds. See also pp. 50, 58, 62, 73, 201, 925 regarding his insistence on the ancient knowledge of God by the Andeans. His source was likely Fray Luis de Granada, as, for example, his *Introducción del símbolo de la fe* ([1582], 400 [parte 3, tratado 1, chap. 1]), in which he describes the ways of knowing God: by the light of natural reason ("la lumbre de la razón") and the light of revelation. Las Casas argued specifically for the knowledge of the true God by the inhabitants of the Americas, as an ancient though imperfect phenomenon (*Apologética historia sumaria* 2:369–370 [bk. 3, chap. 71]: "tanto quiso y amó Dios a las criaturas racionales, que son los hombres, que a su imagen y semejanza quiso criar, y con su visión propia determinó graciosamente beatificar, lo cual ser no podía sin que los hombres, mientras en la vida corporal duraban, cognoscieran y amasen a Dios. De aquí fue poner la benignidad divina en cada ánima de los hombres al instante de su creación una lumbre natural intelectual y cognoscimiento por ella puesto, que confuso y juntamente [es] un ímpetu, por otro nombre apetitu, e inclinación natural de cognoscer que hay Dios y criador, y que se debe buscar para le servir e adorar como a Dios y señor."

31. "And thus we Indians are Christian, by the redemption of Jesus Christ and his holy mother, Saint Mary, patroness of this kingdom, and by the apostles of Jesus Christ, Saint Bartholomew, Saint James the Major, and by the holy cross of Jesus Christ, all of whom arrived in this kingdom long before the Spaniards. Because of them [not the Spaniards] we are Christian and we believe in one God of the Holy Trinity" [Y ací los yndios somos cristianos por la rredimción de Jesucristo y de su madre bendita Santa María, patrona de este rreyno y por los apóstoles de Jesucristo, San Bartolomé, Santiago Mayor y por la santa crus de Jesucristo que llegaron a este rreyno más primero que los españoles. De ello somos cristianos y creemos un solo Dios de la Sanctícima Trinidad] (Guaman Poma, *Nueva corónica*, 1090).

32. "And thus we have no encomendero or conquistador [over us], but rather only the royal crown of His Majesty, for the service of God and king" [Y ací no tenemos encomendero ni conquistador, sino que somos de la corona rreal de

su Magestad, seruicio de Dios y de su corona] (Guaman Poma, *Nueva coró-nica*, 564).

33. Adorno, "Andean View," 129–130; idem, *Guaman Poma: Writing*, 24–27; Lohmann Villena, "La restitución," 67; see the section entitled "Las Casas and the *Encomenderos* of Peru," in chapter 3.

34. Wagner and Parish, *Life and Writings*, 234.

35. Casas, *Tratado de doce dudas*, 535.

36. Guaman Poma's (929) text reads as follows: "Que uien puede ser esta ley porque un español al otro español, aunque sea judío o moro, son españoles, que no se entremete a otra nación sino que son españoles de Castilla. La ley de Castilla, que no es de otra generación que a razón de los yndios que se qüenta y le dize por la ley y la de llamar estrangeros, y en la lengua de los yn-dios, *mitmac*, Castilla *manta samoc*, que uiniera de Castilla."

37. Höffner, *La ética*, 331–343.

38. Wagner and Parish, *Life and Writings*, 234.

39. Casas, *Tratado de doce dudas*, 505.

40. Casas, "Memorial-sumario," 459.

41. Casas, *Tratado de doce dudas*, 531.

42. "A de ser monarca el rrey don Phelipe el terzero que Dios le acresente su uida, estado para el gobierno del mundo y defensa de nuestra santa fe católica, servicio de Dios. El primero: Ofresco un hijo mío, príncipe deste rreyno, nieto y bisnieto de Topa Ynga Yupanqui, el décimo rrey, gran sauio, el que puso ordenansas; a de tener en esa corte el príncipe para memoria y grandesa del mundo. El segundo, un príncipe del rrey de Guinea, negro; el terzero, del rrey de los cristianos de Roma o de otro rrey del mundo; el quarto, el rrey de los moros de Gran Turco, los quatro coronados con su septro y tuzones. En medio destos quatro partes del mundo estará la magestad y monarca del mundo rrey don Phelipe que Dios le guarde de la alta corona. Representa monarca del mundo y los dichos quatro rreys, sus coronas bajas yguales. . . . Porque el rrey es rrey de su juridición, el en-perador es enperador de su juridición, monarca no tiene juridición; tiene de-bajo de su mano mundo estos rreys coronados" (Guaman Poma, *Nueva corónica*, 963).

43. Ossio, "Guaman Poma," 170–181; Wachtel, *Los vencidos*, 251–261. This sec-tion incorporates material from my "Colonial Reform or Utopia?"

44. Milhou, *Colón*, 406–407; Bettex, *Discovery*, 30–31.

45. Milhou, *Colón*, 405, 412–426.

46. Wagner and Parish, *Life and Writings*, 213–215; Casas, "Carta al maestro," 430–450.

47. It was to be "like the single jewel the King of Tunis gave the emperor [Charles]" [como el rey de Tánez (*sic*) quedó por vasallo del Emperador con servirle con ciertos caballos o ciertas joyas, que llaman parias, con que cada año como a superior le servía], or like the salary the natives paid "to Moc-tezuma or another lord" [el rey de Castilla ha de ser reconocido por supremo

señor de todas las Indias descubiertas, para fundar y conserver la religión cristiana, y para esto y por ello le han de dar su salario, como lo daban a Montezuma o a otro señor] (Casas, "Carta al maestro," 444–445).

48. Domingo de Santo Tomás's creation of these linguistic codifications was itself a highly political act, favoring not only the dignity of the Andean language but also its use in the affairs of the colonial church and state.

49. Murra, "Waman Puma," xviii–xix.

50. Ugarte y Ugarte, "Los caciques."

51. In her introduction to *The Only Way*, Helen Rand Parish makes this important point in contrast to earlier characterizations of Toledo's project as proving the right to Spanish rule (see, for example, Hanke, *History of Latin American Civilization* 1:87–89). Like Parish, Hemming (*Conquest*, 421) sees the debate as hinging on the Incas' moral, historical, and legal right to rule Peru, with Toledo's being convinced by the inquiries he had commissioned that they had none.

52. See Hanke, ed., *History of Latin American Civilization* 1:89–93 for the summary of these testimonies.

53. Hemming, *Conquest*, 412.

54. Levillier, *Gobernantes* 4:442, 462; idem, 5:312, 405.

55. See chapter 1, note 31.

56. Zimmerman, *Francisco de Toledo*, 105; Levillier, *Gobernantes* 4:462.

57. Cook, "Introducción," ix; Guaman Poma, *Nueva corónica*, 454, 455. In addition, Guaman Poma's (411, 454) references to the 1557 *visita* of Huamanga by Damián de la Bandera, of whom he drew a portrait, suggests his early acquaintance with these systematic efforts at census taking (see Jiménez de la Espada, *Relaciones geográficas*, 176–180).

58. These recollections are registered on the following pages of the *Nueva corónica:* Toledo's arrival in Cuzco (447), the laws promulgated by the viceroy (287, 302, 448, 449, 598, 951, 966, 967, 989), his execution of Tupac Amaru (452, 461, 950, 951), and the forced resettlements (*reducciones*) of native communities (965); see also pp. 450, 1044, 1056, 1058, 1076.

59. Guaman Poma, *Nueva corónica*, 753, 754, 948. The Inca heirs of Sayri Tupac and Paullu Inca, who had collaborated with the Spanish, prospered, in contrast to the heirs of Manco Inca (Hemming, *Conquest*, 472–473). However, Melchor Carlos Inca's penchant for high living and trouble led the viceroy Luis de Velasco to want to send him to Spain. Melchor Carlos obliged, by making his own request to go to Spain; it was readily granted when his father-in-law was arrested in Cuzco on charges of conspiracy. A coconspirator, García de Solís Portocarrero, was arrested and beheaded in Cuzco (Hemming, *Conquest*, 462–463).

60. Morrall, *Political Thought*, 102.

61. Ibid., 118, 120–121, 133.

62. According to Morrall (ibid., 136), "The explicitly accepted religious fragmen-

tation of western Christiandom in the sixteenth century was the final proclamation that the old ideal was dead and with it the medieval world."

63. Frankl, "Imperio," 459, 461. To be sure, the notion of the universal dominion of the Spanish monarch had its antecedents in the writings of Pedro
López de Ayala in the fourteenth century and in Juan de Mena, among others. However, only one treatise, that of the Spanish theologian Juan de Torquemada of 1467–1468, gives it the Aristotelian-Thomist foundation
expressed by Cortés that there be nothing "superfluous on earth" (Frankl,
"Imperio," 463).

64. Elliott, "Mental World," 39–40.

65. Morrall, *Political Thought*, 102.

66. Milhou, *Colón*, 423.

67. Guaman Poma, *Nueva corónica*, 377, 378, 564.

68. The second Inca uprising of 1538–1539, which was the "last effort on a national scale to dislodge the invaders," was not recorded by any single chronicler at the time; Hemming reconstructed the events of this insurrection only
some thirty to forty years ago on the basis of dispersed public records (*Conquest*, 255, 584).

69. The accounts of Cristóbal de Mena and Francisco de Xerex, published in 1534
after their return to Spain at the end of 1533, became best-sellers and were
translated into other European languages (Hemming, *Conquest*, 90). "Post-
Renaissance Europe," writes Hemming (90), "was dazzled by the discovery
and sudden conquest of an unimagined empire of such brilliance."

70. Hemming, *Conquest*, 140. Among eyewitness accounts, Pedro Pizarro provides the only exception; he continued his narrative well beyond the events of
1535 (Hemming, *Conquest*, 140).

71. Casas, *Tratado de doce dudas*, 531; Guaman Poma, *Nueva corónica*, 388.

72. On the first count, Guaman Poma described the uprising as occurring during a time when "there was neither the God of the Christians, the king of
Spain, nor justice" (391). The Spaniards, the Chancas, Chachapoyas, and
Huancas were robbing and looting (391, 397). He next described the murder
of the Inca captain Quizu Yupanqui by Luis de Ávalos de Ayala in Lima: "And
thus the Inca who had not defended himself in any city was conquered"
(395). As it happened, however, Quizu Yupanqui's army, marching north
from Cuzco, had succeeded in annihilating almost all of the Spanish between Cuzco and the sea. Quizu Yupanqui was killed by the Spaniards during his attack on Lima (Hemming, *Conquest*, 206–207, 212).

73. Casas, *Tratado de doce dudas*, 507, 508, 531.

74. Cf. Adorno, "Andean View," 130; idem, *Cronista*, 94–95.

75. Hanke, *History of Latin American Civilization* 1:87–88.

76. Casas, "Cláusula del testamento," 540.

77. Guaman Poma, *Nueva corónica*, 751, 991: "Lo tendrá en el archibo del mundo
como del cielo, en el catretral [*sic*: catedral] de Roma para memoria y en la

cauesa de nuestra cristiandad de nuestra España, adonde rrecide Sacra Católica Real Magestad, que Dios le guarde en España, cauesa del mundo"; "y ací escribo esta historia para que sea memoria y que se ponga en el archibo para uer la justicia."

CHAPTER 3. BARTOLOMÉ DE LAS CASAS, POLEMICIST AND AUTHOR

1. This portrait of Las Casas was drawn by Juan López Enguídanos and engraved by Tomás López Enguídanos (*Retratos de los españoles ilustres con el epítome de sus vidas* [Madrid: Imprenta Real, 1791]), no. 82 (Madrid, Biblioteca Nacional, Gabinete de Estampas, ER-303).

2. This chapter updates my "Intellectual Life of Bartolomé de las Casas" and incorporates material from my "The Discursive Encounter of Spain and America."

3. In "Censorship and its Evasion," I have studied Román's debt to Las Casas, the inquisitorial expurgation of Román's 1575 work, and the publication in 1595 of his expanded account.

4. Parish and Weidman, "Correct Birthdate," 394–403; cf. Pérez Fernández, *Cronología documentada,* 96–97.

5. Casas, *Historia de las Indias* 2:533–541 [bk. 3, chap. 20].

6. Pérez Fernández, *Inventario documentado,* 48–67, and Wagner and Parish, *Life and Writings,* 17–24, 259–262, document and analyze these early writings.

7. Four of these documents, "Memorial de remedios para las Indias" (1516), "Memorial de remedios para las Indias" (1518), "Entre los remedios" (1542), and the *Tratado de las doce dudas* (1564), are reproduced in Las Casas, *Obras escogidas,* 5–27, 31–35, 69–120, 477–536; the other, "De thesauris qui reperiuntur in sepulchris indorum" (1562–1563), is transcribed and translated into Spanish in Casas, *Los tesoros.*

8. Pérez Fernández, *Cronología documentada,* 318, 340.

9. Casas, "Cláusula," 540.

10. Ovando's 1503 request, made a year after his arrival in Hispaniola, is recorded in Herrera y Tordesillas, *Hechos* 2:457–458 [dec. 1, bk. 5, chap. 12].

11. Casas, "Memorial" (1516), 9, 17.

12. The following paragraphs summarize Parish's account in Casas, *The Only Way,* 201–208.

13. Casas, *Historia* 1:134–35 [bk. 1, chap. 25]; Sepúlveda, *Demócrates Segundo,* 16–17.

14. Philips, *Slavery,* 107, 155.

15. Casas, *Historia* 3:177 [bk. 3, chap. 102]; Casas, *The Only Way,* 202. Parish's translation modified.

16. The passage appears in Herrera's decade 2, book 2, chapter 2, and it quotes the statement found in Las Casas's 1516 memorandum, mentioned above (Llorente, *Colección* 2:335, 375–76, 440; Casas, "Memorial" [1516], 17).

17. Robertson, *History* 1:320–321 [bk. 3, year 1517].
18. Casas, *Historia* 1:134 [bk. 1, chap. 25].
19. Llorente, *Colección* 2:577–578.
20. See Losada, "Introducción," 38–42; Parish and Weidman, *Las Casas*, 133–145, 372; and especially Pennington, "Bartolomé." José Cárdenas Bunsen is analyzing the evidence of Las Casas's use of canon law precepts in his historical and theoretical writings.
21. Pérez Fernández, *El anónimo*, 115. Polo de Ondegardo was the principal proponent of the viceroy Toledo's inquiries into the recent advent of Inca dominion over the Andes, which led to the conviction that their rule had been tyrannical and illegitimate; see the section entitled "Old Models and New Monarchies," in chapter 2. Although these ideas circulated in viceregal circles before Toledo's arrival in Peru in 1569, Polo provided the impetus to make this the official view. He was Toledo's official defender of Spain's right to rule Peru and the major opponent of Las Casas's views on Inca sovereignty (Porras, *Los cronistas*, 335–336).
22. Pérez Fernández, *El anónimo*, 95, 114–138.
23. Ibid., 117, 121.
24. Hanke, *Bartolomé*, 42, quoted in Pennington, "Bartolomé," 160.
25. Pennington, "Bartolomé," 151.
26. Ibid., 155, 156.
27. Casas, "Memorial" (1518), 33–39.
28. Parry and Keith, eds., *The Conquerors*, 271.
29. Casas, *De unico vocationis modo*, 162–163, 573–575 [bk. 1, chap. 5, sec. 15]; idem, *The Only Way*, 70–71.
30. Matthew 10:11–13, King James Bible. The versions in the books of Mark and Luke add menacing notes to the account. Mark 6:10–11: "And he said to them, 'If you enter a house anywhere, stay there until you leave the district. And if any place does not welcome you and people refuse to listen to you, as you walk away shake off the dust from under your feet as a sign to them"; Luke 10:10–11: "But whenever you enter a town and they do not make you welcome, go out into its streets and say, 'We wipe off the very dust of your town that clings to our feet, and leave it with you. Yet be sure of this: the kingdom of God is very near.'"
31. Casas, *Brevísima relación*, ed. Saint-Lu, 71 [prologue].
32. Casas, "Entre los remedios," 95.
33. The New Laws are transcribed in Alonso de Santa Cruz's *Crónica del emperador Carlos V* 4:222–236 [pt. 6, chap. 43]; Wagner and Parish, *Life and Writings*, 114–115. Regarding the role of Las Casas in the creation and passing of the New Laws, see Manzano Manzano, *La incorporación*, 90–136; Wagner and Parish, *Life and Writings*, 108–120; Parish, "Introduction," 40–41; Pérez Fernández, "Apéndices," 968–971.
34. Casas, "Aquí se contienen unos avisos," 235–249; Parish, "Introduction," 45–47; Parish and Weidman, *Las Casas*, 63–66, 109–110.

35. Casas, "Aquí se contienen unos avisos," 235, 241–242; Wagner and Parish, *Life and Writings*, 167–168.

36. The accusation of Las Casas before the Inquisition is recorded in the nineteenth-century critical history of the Inquisition by Juan Antonio Llorente, who wrote that the cause was Las Casas's attempts "to prove that the kings had no power to dispose of the persons and liberty of their subjects, to make them vassals of another lord, by way of fiefs, encomienda, or in any other way." He was denounced to the Inquisition, according to Llorente, for advocating policies "contrary to the doctrine of Saint Peter and Saint Paul about the subjection of serfs and vassals to their lords and kings" (Wagner and Parish, *Life and Writings*, 187; Llorente, *Historia*, 5:172–173).

   Sepúlveda's accusations against Las Casas appear in a document entitled "Reckless, troublemaking, and heretical propositions, noted by Doctor Sepúlveda in the book about the conquest of the Indies, which Fray Bartolomé de las Casas, former Bishop of Chiapas, had printed 'without license' in Seville, the year of 1552" (Wagner and Parish, *Life and Writings*, 189) [Proposiciones temerarias, escandalosas y heréticas que notó el doctor Sepúlveda en el libro de la conquista de Indias, que fray Bartolomé de las Casas, Obispo que fue de Chiapa, hizo imprimir "sin licencia" en Sevilla, año de 1552 (Fabié, *Vida y escritos*, 2:543)]. Although the book Sepúlveda condemned was Las Casas's published account of the 1550–1551 disputation in Valladolid ("Aquí se contiene una disputa"), he also denounced Las Casas's confessional guide and declared how it was judged to be inflammatory and irresponsible by the royal council, which reprimanded Las Casas for it and had it withdrawn from the monasteries of Castile and the Indies (Sepúlveda in Fabié, *Vida y escritos* 2:557–558).

37. Parish and Weidmann, *Las Casas*, 63–65, 109–110; Lohmann Villena, "La restitución," 66–74; see the section entitled "Old Models and New Monarchies," in chapter 2.

38. Vargas Machuca in Fabié, *Vida y escritos* 2:413; see Parish, "Introduction," 41. Vargas Machuca, ex-soldier and conquistador, governor and captain general of the island of Margarita in the second decade of the seventeenth century, wrote in 1612 a work entitled *Apologías y discursos de las conquistas occidentales* in which he argued that the conquests were carried out not with cruelty but with the "juridical" or legal punishments the Indians deserved for crimes committed (Fabié, *Vida y escritos* 2:409–517). He (413) declared, "In the year [15]52, under that unworthy title *Destruction of the Indies*, [Las Casas] attempted to characterize as wanton acts of cruelty the juridical punishments that the conquistadores executed—and execute—in all the Indies upon the Indians for the enormous crimes they committed—and still commit—every day." His harangue also reveals that it was the foreign, not domestic, publication of the work that brought national shame: "And it [the *Brevísima*] has had such an effect among the Huguenots, following their ancient malice and scorning the great Christianity of Spain, that they have made engravings in

which they describe the Indies with several forms of cruelty, citing the Bishop of Chiapas by the chapters of his treatise, some which he truly wrote, others which they completely invented" (413). Vargas Machuca refers to the edition with copper engravings published by DeBry (see figs. 15 and 16). By the time Vargas Machuca was writing in 1612, the anti-Spanish sentiment that, centuries later, in 1914, would be given the name Black Legend by the Spanish apologist Julián Juderías was in full swing. Isacio Pérez Fernández ("Apéndices," 917–938) has catalogued the series and sequence of Las Casas's detractors, specifically those who protested against the *Brevísima relación* from the sixteenth through the twentieth centuries, beginning with the conquistadores of Mexico, Bernal Díaz among them, and ending with Ramón Menéndez Pidal.

39. Casas, *Brevísima relación*, ed. Saint-Lu, 72–73.
40. Saint-Lu, "Introducción," 44.
41. Pérez Fernández, "Estudio crítico preliminar," 357–365; Saint-Lu, "Introducción,"45.
42. Mier, *Historia*, xx, lxvii, cxviii. On the Requerimiento, see in chapter 10 the section entitled "Resettlement and *Requerimiento*." On arguments regarding the return to indigenous rule in America, see the section, "Old Models and New Monarchies," in chapter 2.
43. Mier, *Historia*, lxvi–lxvii, 471–628 [bk. 14]; idem, *Historia*, xcix–c.
44. The text of the conciliar request is recorded in Manzano Manzano, *La incorporación*, 168–169: "Mandase juntar letrados, theólogos y juristas con las personas que fuesse servido que tratasen y platicasen sobre la manera como se hiziesen estas conquistas, porque justamente y con seguridad de conçiençia se hiziesen, y que ordenase una ynstrucción para ello."
45. Manzano Manzano, *La incorporación*, 171–173.
46. Casas, "Aquí se tiene una disputa," 295.
47. Manzano Manzano (*La incorporación*, 187–189, 201–203) outlines and documents these events.
48. Pérez Fernández, *Inventario documentado*, 714–715, 728. See the section entitled "Las Casas' *Doce dudas* in Guaman Poma's *Buen gobierno*," in chapter 2.
49. Las Casas, "Memorial-sumario," 453–460; Wagner and Parish, *Life and Writings*, 212, 217, 284.
50. The document is published in Hanke, "Un festón," 204–208.
51. Casas, "Memorial del obispo," 465–468; Wagner and Parish, *Life and Writings*, 216–219, 287, 291.
52. Casas, "Memorial del obispo," 466.
53. Lohmann Villena, "La restitución," 66; Pérez Fernández, *Inventario documentado*, 715; Wagner and Parish, *Life and Writings*, 231–233; Parish and Weidman ("Correct Birthdate," 385) correct Lohmann Villena's ("La restitución," 66) calculation of Las Casas's age at the time.
54. Wagner and Parish, *Life and Writings*, 234, 295.
55. Casas, *Tratado*, 489.

56. Translation from the Latin by Patrick Charles Pautz.
57. Casas, "Carta al Maestro," 444–445. For Guaman Poma's use of these principles, see in chapter 2 the section entitled "Old Models and New Monarchies."
58. Casas, *Historia* 3:179 [bk. 3, chap. 102].
59. *Historia* 2:329 [bk. 2, chap. 38].
60. Casas, "Cláusula," 538–541; Pérez Fernández, *Inventario documentado,* 694.
61. Parish, "Introduction," 48.
62. Casas, *Historia* 3:179 [bk. 3, chap. 102].
63. "Para remediar las Indias no era menester sino un rey de viejo, el pie en la huesa y de guerras desocupado" (Casas, *Historia* 3:111 [bk. 3, chap. 85]).
64. Rowe, "Ethnography," 2–3; Wagner and Parish, *Life and Writings,* 287–289; Adorno, "Censorship"; Garcilaso, *Comentarios* 2:173–174 [pt. 1, bk. 5, chap. 18]); idem, *Comentarios* 3:227 [pt. 2, bk. 4, chap. 3]; USLC, *Harkness Collection,* 190–92, 206.
65. For natural history, see O'Gorman, "Estudio preliminar," liii–lv; Casas, *Apologética,* bk. 2, chaps. 22–39; see 1:178–79, 190–91 [bk. 2, chaps. 34, 36]; on moral history, O'Gorman, "Estudio preliminar," liv–lv; Casas, *Apologética,* bk. 3, chaps. 40–263.
66. Tierra Firme was the stretch of Caribbean coastline and adjacent inland territories of southern Central America and northwestern South America that in 1513 was designated Castilla de Oro; tradition kept the name alive well into the sixteenth century (Adorno and Pautz, *Álvar Núñez* 2:29).
67. The relevant materials are Cabeza de Vaca's chapters 32–36 (although Las Casas read the 1542 edition, which had no chapter divisions; Adorno and Pautz, *Álvar Núñez* 3:137–139) and Las Casas's *Apologética,* bk. 3, chaps. 124, 168, 205–207.
68. Casas, *Apologética* 2:357–361, 366, 375–376 [bk. 3, chaps. 206, 208, 210).
69. "Son hombres racionales como los otros y les fueron conferidas en sus ánimas, en su creación, las simientes y principios e inclinaciones naturales de las ciencias y de las virtudes, y no les falta sino sólo el ejercicio dellas" (*Apologética* 2:362 [bk. 3, chap. 207]).
70. Casas, *Apologética* 1:651 [bk. 3, chap. 124]; Cabeza de Vaca, "Transcription," 1:262–263.

CHAPTER 4. COUNCILORS WARRING AT THE ROYAL COURT
1. Mendoza, "Relación," 499. This chapter updates and expands my "Los debates sobre la naturaleza del indio."
2. Gómez Canedo, "¿Hombres?," 51.
3. Service, "Indian-European Relations," 411.
4. This paragraph summarizes ibid., 412–414.
5. Castañeda Delgado, "La política," 114–122.
6. In a fundamental study of the encomienda of New Spain Lesley Byrd Simpson (*Encomienda,* xiii), characterizes the institution as follows: "As developed in the Antilles, the encomienda was at first (up to the passage of the New

Laws of 1542) the delegation of the royal power to collect the tribute from, and to use the personal services of, the King's vassals (the Indians). The encomendero undertook to look after the welfare of his charges and to educate them in proper (Spanish) norms of conduct, as well as to discharge the usual feudal obligation of bearing arms in the King's defense. In reality the encomienda, at least in the first fifty years of its existence, was looked upon by its beneficiaries as a subterfuge for slavery, and it was only after half a century of furious agitation on the part of Las Casas and the reformers, and the active interest of the Crown in suppressing it, that it was shorn of its most profitable and harmful feature, the privilege of using the services of the Indians, and was reduced to some semblance of a social system. Indeed, the metamorphosis of the encomienda, which achieved lasting notoriety for its shocking wastage of labor, into a kind of benevolent paternalism is one of the most curious phenomena of colonial history."

7. The classic account of the Valladolid debate is Hanke's *Aristotle and the American Indians*. See the section entitled, "The Great Debate in Valladolid (1550–1551)," in chapter 3.

8. This account of legislative events follows Zavala, *Instituciones*, 45–53.

9. Castañeda Delgado, "La política," 81. The questionnaire (*interrogatorio*) was transcribed by Hanke ("Studies," 388–93) and discussed in context and fully identified as "A.G.I. *Justicia*, 47, fols. 69–72" by Castañeda Delgado (84). It was drawn up by Zuazo, chief justice (*justicia mayor*) of the island of Hispaniola, and several witnesses were quickly called and swore to their observation or knowledge of one or more of the named offenses among the Indians of the Caribbean.

10. Giménez Fernández, *Bartolomé*, 246.

11. Pagden, *Fall*, 39; Zavala, *Filosofía*, 46. Pagden (*Fall*, 38–40), comments in detail on the importance of Mair's formulations.

12. Casas, *Historia* 3:343 [bk. 3, chap. 149].

13. Casas, *Historia* 3:361 [bk. 3, chap. 155]. Adrian of Utrecht (1459–1523), formerly dean of the College of Canonists of Saint Peter of Louvain and tutor to Prince Charles until 1515, became, with the cardinal of Spain, Fray Francisco Jiménez de Cisneros, Charles's surrogate Castilian ruler of Spain in January 1516. He was named bishop of Tortosa in July 1516 and cardinal in July 1517, and he was elected pope, as Hadrian VI, on January 9, 1522 (Millares Carlo, "Indice analítico," 411).

14. Gibson, *Spain*, 54–55.

15. Gibson, *Spain*, 56; idem, *Aztecs*, 62.

16. CDU 10:38–43, 192–203.

17. MacNutt, *Bartholomew*, 427, rpt. Parry and Keith, *The Conquerors*, 386–388, my emphasis. See also Zavala, *Instituciones*, 48.

18. Las Casas's role in the promulgation of this legislation has long been acknowledged. The 1999 biography by Álvaro Huerga disputes this (and many other critical points about Las Casas's life); Huerga's claims are laid to rest by

Isacio Pérez Fernández (in Las Casas, *Brevísima relación* [2000]), who corrects these assertions with considerable data, including the recently published document (Mss 22605) in the Biblioteca Nacional of Madrid, which adds new evidence reconfirming Las Casas's role in the establishment of the New Laws (Casas, *Conclusiones*).

19. Gibson, *Spain*, 59.

20. Wagner and Parish (*Life and Writings*, 23, 106, 205) and Parish ("Introducción," 31–32) have studied these actions and their consequences.

21. Fray García de Loaysa (1478–1546), master general of the Dominican order, the emperor Charles's confessor, bishop of Osma and subsequently of Sigüenza, was later archbishop of Seville and a member of the College of Cardinals. He served as president of the Council of the Indies for more than twenty years (1524–1546), and was named inquisitor general (Millares Carlo, "Indice," 472; Schäfer, *El consejo real*, 351).

22. O'Gorman, "Sobre la naturaleza," 305.

23. Francisco López de Gómara attributed the 1526 authorization for Indian enslavement to Ortiz's appearance before the Council of the Indies in 1525 (Gómara, *Historia*, 309–11 [chap. 217, "De la libertad de los indios"]; Wagner and Parish, *Life and Writings*, 106). Ortiz's speech on Indian bestiality was recorded in 1524 by Anghiera, *De orbe novo*, 609–610 [dec. 7, bk. 4]), and Gómara (310) reproduced it from that source. In the case of Betanzos, plentiful documentation confirms the friar's influence (see Parish and Weidmann, *Las Casas*, 85nn9, 10).

24. This sermon has been identified as the first cry of protest against the ill treatment of the Indians (Hanke, *Spanish Struggle*, 17; Losada, "Introducción," 13–14); Hanke (17) called it "a turning point in the history of America" and, quoting Pedro Henríquez Ureña, "one of the great events in the spiritual history of mankind." It has become famous, in any case, as the first known recorded event of its type.

25. "Decid, ¿con qué derecho y con qué justicia tenéis en tan cruel y horrible servidumbre aquestos indios? ¿Con que autoridad habéis hecho tan detestables guerras a estas gentes que estaban en sus tierras mansas y pacíficas, donde tan infinitas dellas, con muertes y estragos nunca oídos, habéis consumido? . . . Estos, ¿no son hombres? ¿No tienen ánimas racionales? ¿No sois obligados a amallos como a vosotros mismos?" (Casas, *Historia* 2:441–42 [bk. 3, chap. 4]).

26. Hanke, *Aristotle*, 79; Gómez Canedo, "¿Hombres?," 35–37.

27. Gómez Canedo, "¿Hombres?," 50–51. Pérez Fernández ("Apéndices," 946) names them among the first three biographers, all Dominicans, of Las Casas. Cruz y Moya was the only one to write during Las Casas's lifetime, as he points out.

28. Gómez Canedo, "¿Hombres?," 42.

29. Translated by MacNutt, *Bartholomew*, 429; rpt. Parry and Keith, *The Conquerors*, 387.

30. MacNutt, *Bartholomew*, 429; my emphasis.

31. Gómez Canedo, "¿Hombres?," 42–44.

32. Pagden, *Fall*, 66. Pagden's 1982 monograph is essential reading on the complexity of Vitoria's thought and its role in the Castilian debates on the right to rule in the Indies. Equally indispensable is the multiauthored introduction to the 1967 edition of the *Relectio de Indis* (in Vitoria, *Relectio*, xiii–cxcii).

33. Losada, "Introducción," 14–15.

34. Wagner and Parish, *Life and Writings*, 106.

35. This royal letter of prohibition is reprinted in Vitoria, *Relectio*, 152–153.

36. Sepúlveda, in Casas, *Apología*, 79; Las Casas, in Casas, *Apología*, 627–629.

37. Pagden, *Fall*, 112–113.

38. *Demócrates Segundo*, 22; see also 27, 38, 63.

39. O'Gorman, "Sobre la naturaleza," 306.

40. Gómez Robledo, *Humanismo*, 232–233. Sepúlveda had particularly occupied himself with the concept of the perfect caballero in the *Demócrates Primero*, where he contemplated the compatibility between war and Christianity, opposing the arguments of pacifists such as Erasmus and Luther, who considered war and religious faith to be antithetical; Sepúlveda insisted upon the traditional harmony between the military vocation and the militant Christian faith.

41. Pagden, *Fall*, 115–116.

42. Ibid.

43. Soto, in Casas, "Aquí se contiene una disputa," 295–296.

44. Sepúlveda, in Casas, *Apología*, 79.

45. Pagden, *Fall*, 117–118.

46. Losada, "Introducción," 18; Wagner and Parish, *Life and Writings*, 174–176.

47. Soto, in Casas, "Aquí se tiene una disputa," 295.

48. Abril-Castelló, "La bipolarización," 235.

49. Ibid., 248. The principal arguments and the points of conflict among its protagonists are also summarized by Losada ("Introducción," 19–26).

50. Casas, *Apología de Juan Ginés*, 137.

51. Ibid., 139.

52. Losada, "Introducción," 30.

53. Sepúlveda, *Apología de Juan Ginés*, 78; Casas, *Apología de Juan Ginés*, 134.

CHAPTER 5. HISTORIANS OF WAR AND PRINCELY WARRIORS

1. An earlier version of this chapter appeared as my "The Warrior and the War Community."

2. See Pagden, *Fall*, 41–44.

3. Bataillon, *Erasmo*, 632; Pagden, *Fall*, 114; García-Pelayo, "Juan Ginés," 16–17. According to Bataillon (633, 641) only one Spanish Erasmist, Lázaro Bejarano, a Sevillan who migrated to Santo Domingo in 1535, wrote a *Diálogo apologético* against Sepúlveda.

4. Hanke, *Aristotle*, 67–68.

5. See Hanke, *The Spanish Struggle*, 121–128; Hanke, *Aristotle*, 22–24; Pagden,

Fall, 109–118. For opposing interpretations, see Marcos, "Ideología," xxxvi–xxxvii; Queraltó Moreno, *El pensamiento*, 140–141; Quirk, "Some notes," 357–364. As mentioned in chapter 4, Sepúlveda's second, third, and fourth arguments in favor of waging war were, respectively, to banish cannibalism and the worship of the devil, to protect the innocent from injury, and to preach the gospel (83–84). In the summary of the *Demócrates Segundo*, which he succeeded in publishing in Rome in 1550 under the title *Apología*, Sepúlveda listed as his four just causes the right of Christians to conquer peoples of barbarous customs and vices ("todos bárbaros en sus costumbres y la mayor parte por naturaleza sin letras ni prudencia y contaminados con muchos vicios bárbaros" [61]; the prerogative to banish sins against nature committed by such peoples; the need to protect the innocent; and the right to evangelize (61–70).

6. Pagden, *Fall*, 43–44.

7. Covarrubias (*Tesoro*, 885) defined the prudent person: "Prudente, el hombre sabio y reportado, que pesa todas las cosas con mucho acuerdo" [the wise and moderate man, who weighs all things with much consideration].

8. Ramos, "Sepúlveda," 142, 145.

9. Ibid., 123, 146.

10. See ibid., 166–167.

11. Abril-Castelló, "La bipolarización," 274–276.

12. Ramos, "El movimiento," 195–202; idem, "Sepúlveda," 126–127, 136–137; see chapter 4.

13. Gómara was present during the imperial campaign to Algiers in which Cortés participated in 1541, and the historian registers his shock at the emperor's failure to include Cortés in the war council: "y yo, que me hallé allí, me maravillé" (*Conquista*, 373 [chap. 251]). It was then that Gómara served as Cortés's chaplain and went to live at his home (Gurría Lacroix, "Prólogo," xii). Another source for Gómara's stay in Cortés's household is Las Casas (*Historia* 2:528–529 [bk. 3, chap. 27]). According to existing documentation, Gómara was paid five hundred ducats by Don Martín, the second marqués del Valle, in 1553, presumably for having written the history of his father's conquest of Mexico (Wagner, "Francisco López," 269).

14. Magallón, "Prólogo," ix, xxiii; Ramos, "Sepúlveda," 113. The scholarly gatherings in Cortés's home are described in Navarra, *Diálogos*.

15. Losada, "Hernán Cortés," 132–133; Ramos, "Sepúlveda," 123.

16. "Y como no conocen al verdadero Dios y Señor, están en grandísimos pecados de idolatría, sacrificios de hombres vivos, comida de carne humana, habla con el diablo, sodomía, muchedumbre de mujeres y otros así. Aunque todos los indios que son vuestros subjectos son ya cristianos por la misericordia y bondad de Dios, y por la vuestra merced y de vuestros padres y abuelos, que habéis procurado su conversión y cristiandad" (Gómara, *Historia*, 7 [dedication to Charles V]).

17. Gómara, *Historia*, 8 [dedication to Charles V]. Charles Gibson ("Reconquista

y conquista," 20–21) explains that, philologically, *reconquistar* and *Reconquista* are neologisms, inventions of the eighteenth century, but that the concept, if not the word, was used by Hernán Cortés in his letters and, as seen here, by Gómara in his history.

18. Gómara, *Conquista,* 4 [dedication to Don Martín Cortés]. This interpretation of a single-handed effort on the part of Cortés is exactly what angered Bernal Díaz del Castillo about Gómara's history. However, as a veteran of the conquest of Mexico and *encomendero* whose self-interest he sought to protect, Bernal Díaz was already busy refuting the positions of Las Casas on the conquest when Gómara's work fell into his hands (see chapter 6).

19. Francisco Cervantes de Salazar, "Epístola al muy ilustre señor don Hernando Cortés, marqués del Valle, descubridor y conquistador de la Nueva España" (*Obras,* fol. 3v).

20. Ramos, "Sepúlveda," 128; Ramos, "El movimiento," 202–203.

21. Charles V's hegemonic vision was shared by Erasmists as well as by the most orthodox, and it extended to linguistic matters; the use of the vernacular and the spread of Castilian were essential. Language was always the companion of empire, as Nebrija had proclaimed, and a good part of *prudencia* consisted of knowing well and using with great skill the language into which one was born, according to Ambrosio de Morales (fol. 14r) in his prologue to the works of Cervantes de Salazar; see also Green, "A Critical Survey," 242–243.

22. Green, "A Critical Survey," 242; Bataillon, *Erasmo,* 631; Liss, *Mexico,* 15, 17.

23. Velasco, "El alma," 109–112; Liss, *Mexico,* 23–24.

24. Cervantes de Salazar, *Crónica,* ed. Miralles Ostos, 433–434 [bk. 4, chap. 81]; Sepúlveda, *Hechos,* 322–326; idem, *Historia,* 111.

25. "There are two ways, illustrious Sir, of writing histories: one consists of writing the life, the other, the deeds of an emperor or valiant captain. . . . More common is writing of that other type, in which, to satisfy the reader, it is sufficient to narrate only the great deeds, wars, victories, and misfortunes of the captain; in the first category, all the vices of the person about whom one is writing are to be told" (Gómara, *Crónica,* 331–332. My translation).

26. Ramos, "Sepúlveda," 165–166.

27. Hassig, *Aztec Warfare,* 20; see pp. 26–62.

28. Clendinnen, "Cost of Courage," 72; Sahagún, *Historia,* 103.

29. Ingham, "Human Sacrifice," 380–382; Isaac, "Aztec Warfare," 128.

30. See Adorno, "Cultures in Contact"; idem, "The Indigenous Ethnographer." Frank Salomon's words regarding the indigenous chroniclers of the Andes are pertinent to the historians of Mesoamerican background and the discussion of Alva Ixtlilxochitl's works: "In both the realms of diachronic explanation and religious expression, the Andean writers were bound at once to highlight the qualitative differences between American and European voices, and at the same time to envision some higher-order system or image spanning them" ("Chronicles," 12).

31. Gibson, *The Aztecs,* 403–404.

32. O'Gorman, "Estudio introductorio," 27; Martínez, *Nezahualcóyotl*, 139.

33. Gibson, "Aztec Aristocracy," 180–181. Regarding the colonial appointment of native officials lacking inherited ethnic rank, Alva Ixtlilxochitl (*Sumaria relación*, 287) complained that it was common to select an individual who was "*muy ladino*," that is, well versed in European ways and language, and raised by clerics, even though he might be of low birth.

34. O'Gorman, "Estudio introductorio," xiii. In November of 1608, Don Fernando presented his *Compendio histórico del reino de Texcoco* and other documents to the native authorities of Otumba and San Salvador Cuatlazinco. His goal was to obtain their approval and ratification of his accounts of Toltec and Chichimec history, the eighty laws and ordinances of Nezahualcoyotzin, and the kind and quantity of tribute paid by the provinces of New Spain to the Spanish monarchy. All were approved and ordered to be translated from Nahuatl to Spanish by the interpreter Francisco Rodríguez (O'Gorman, "Estudio introductorio," 23; the document is reproduced in Alva Ixtlilxochitl, *Obras* 1:521).

35. Alva Ixtlilxochitl, *Historia*, 235; see also 215. He makes a similar commentary on sources in his *Sumaria relación*, 285–288.

36. Here Alva Ixtlilxochitl performs his own sleight of hand, because no one was more aware than he that there were conflicting native versions of the history of the conquest or of the credit that one or another group received: "No one remembers about the Acolhuas-Texcocans and their lords and captains, although it is all the same house, but rather the Tlascaltecas, who, according to all the historians, say that most often they came to rob and plunder rather than help" (*Compendio*, 468).

37. Epic poems of the conquest in this period echo the content of these histories (see chapter 8). In the published epic poems on the conquest of Mexico, the importance of native allies is minimized, and autochthonous heroic figures are seldom created. The Cacique de Tabasco in Gabriel Lobo Lasso de la Vega's *Mexicana* (1594) and the personage of Guatemozin (Cuautémoc) in Antonio Saavedra Guzmán's *El peregrino indiano* (1599) are notable exceptions (Van Horne, "Attitude," 360). The most striking exception to the general practice is, of course, Ercilla's *La Araucana* (1569–1589). Ercilla responded to anticipated criticism that he had emphasized Araucanian affairs and their bravery more extensively than was warranted for "barbarians" by defending his choices in the prologue to his work (1:121–122). See chapter 8, note 17, for the transcription and translation of Ercilla's statement.

38. Van Horne, "Attitude," 349.

CHAPTER 6. THE *ENCOMENDERO* AND HIS LITERARY INTERLOCUTORS

1. I cite Joaquín Ramírez Cabañas's two-volume edition of the *Historia verdadera*, which utilizes Genaro García's 1904 transcription of the partially autograph Guatemala manuscript that Bernal Díaz completed in 1568 and

emended until near the time of his death in early 1584. In English I cite, unless otherwise noted, Alfred Percival Maudslay's *True History,* which translates García's transcription. I have opted for the Guatemala manuscript version over that published in Madrid in 1632 by the Mercedarian historian Fray Alonso Remón, with its additions, prepared by himself or Fray Gabriel Adarzo y Santander. Ramírez Cabañas's edition is also preferable to the more recent one prepared by Carmelo Sáenz de Santa because Sáenz's attempted reconstitution of Bernal Díaz's "intended text" integrates the text published in Madrid in 1632 with material from the Guatemala and "Alegría" manuscripts. The Alegría manuscript is a copy made in Guatemala in 1605 at the order of Bernal Díaz's son, Francisco Díaz del Castillo, most recently located in Murcia in the possession of the bibliophile José María Alegría, whose heirs presented it to the Biblioteca Nacional in Madrid (Sáenz de Santa María, "Plan de la edición," xi, xxxvi, xxxvii). Sáenz's discussion of the relationship among the manuscripts and the 1632 publication is, overall, very helpful. Regarding the 1632 edition, there were two printings; one bears a plain title page and the other an elaborate engraving. Sáenz reproduces both title pages (Díaz del Castillo, *Suplemento,* 5; idem, *Historia verdadera,* ed. Sáenz de Santa María, vii), and assumes that the printing with the engraving is the initial one. It is, however, more likely to be the reverse because it was common editorial practice to issue a printing with a simple, printed title page before going to the time-consuming expense of producing an elaborate engraving. As we will see below, an editorial insertion regarding an "error of the bishop of Chiapa" appeared in the first printing but was withdrawn in the second.

    The full title of the first of the two 1632 printings, as it appears on the title page is "*Historia verdadera de la conquista de la Nueva-España,* Escrita por el Capitán Bernal Díaz del Castillo, uno de sus Conquistadores. Sacada a luz por el P. M. Fr. Alonso Remón, Predicador y Coronista General del Orden de Nuestra Señora de la Merced, Redempción de Cautivos. A la Catholica Magestad del mayor monarca, Don Felipe Quarto, Rey de las Españas y Nuevo Mundo, N. Señor. Con privilegio. En Madrid en la Imprenta del Reyno. Año de 1632."

2. This chapter updates the arguments presented in my "Discourses on Colonialism."

3. According to J. H. Elliott ("The Spanish Conquest," 191), "the 607 men who first accompanied Cortés jealously guarded their pre-eminence against the 534 men who only joined him later. But they banded together in a common front against all later arrivals and finally, in 1543, extracted from a reluctant Charles V a statement declaring that the first 'discoverers' (*descubridores*) of New Spain—he avoided using the word *conquistadores*—were those who 'first entered that province on its discovery and those who were there for the winning and conquering of the city of Mexico.'" The expression "primeros conquistadores" was also used in official documentation (CDI 16:398–399).

4. Díaz del Castillo, *Historia verdadera* 2:375, thus identified his plain-talking

Castilian manner ("común hablar de Castilla la Vieja"), the characterization of which he attributed to one of his interlocutors, who remarked that "as to the style, it followed the customary speech of Old Castile, and that in these times it is accounted the more agreeable because there are no elaborate arguments nor gilded elegance such as some writers are wont [to display], but all is in plain simple language, and that all really good narration is comprised in this true statement" (Díaz del Castillo, *True History* 5:287).

5. Díaz del Castillo, *Historia verdadera* 2:370–374 [chap. 211]. This was not the junta convened on August 15, 1550, for the debate between Las Casas and Sepúlveda, but rather an earlier one. This corrects Adorno, "Discourses on Colonialism," 239, 250, 251, and Sáenz de Santa María, *Historia de una historia,* 97. Wagner and Parish (*Life and Writings,* 211–212) describe the junta on perpetuity and its circumstances.

6. Based on the available evidence, Bernal Díaz must have begun writing (at the latest) between 1553 and 1557 and completed his work in 1568, when he had two copies made; he continued modifying both until dispatching one to Spain in 1575 (this is the manuscript, edited in Madrid by Remón and now lost, that was the basis for the 1632 edition), while continuing to work on the other (the Guatemala manuscript) till near the end of his life (Barbón Rodríguez, *Bernal Díaz,* 17–19; Sáenz de Santa María, *Historia de una historia,* 98).

7. Díaz del Castillo, *True History* 1:68. "Quiero volver con la pluma en la mano, como el buen piloto lleva la sonda por la mar, descubriendo bajos por la mar adelante, cuando siente que los hay; así haré yo en decir los borrones de los coronistas; mas no será todo, porque si parte por parte se hubiesen de escribir sería más la costa de recoger la rebusca que en las verdaderas vendimias" (Díaz del Castillo, *Historia verdadera,* ed. Ramírez Cabañas, 1:80).

8. Sáenz de Santa María, *Historia de una historia,* 54. Illescas, the learned doctor from Palencia, was chronicler to Charles V and a prominent historian of the Roman Catholic papacy; Giovio was the papal diplomat and bishop from Lombardy who frequented the court of Charles V and wrote extensively about Spanish deeds and men (Ballesteros Gaibrois, "Estudio preliminar," xv–xxv).

9. León-Portilla, "Introducción," 47.

10. Iglesia, *Dos estudios,* 30.

11. Lewis, "Retórica," 37–47.

12. Sáenz de Santa María, "Plan de la edición," xxxvii.

13. On beginning his chapter 18, Bernal Díaz clarifies the sequence of literary events: "While I was writing this story, I saw by chance, what had been written by Gómara, Yllescas and Jovio, about the conquest of Mexico and New Spain, and when I had read their accounts and saw and appreciated their polished style, and thought how rudely and lamely my story was told, I stopped writing it, seeing that such good histories already existed" (*True History* 1: 66) [Estando escribiendo en esta mi corónica [por] acaso vi lo que escriben Gómara, e Illescas y Jovio en las conquistas de México y Nueva España, y de-

sde que las leí y entendí y vi de su policía y estas mis palabras tan groseras y sin primor, dejé de escribir en ella (*Historia verdadera* 1:79)].

14. The royal decree of November 17, 1553, is reproduced in Torre Revello, *El libro*, x.

15. Bernal Díaz concluded chapter 18 in the Guatemala version of his manuscript with the recommendation that Gómara's work be reviewed and expurgated by the Council of the Indies: "And the members of the Royal Council of the Indies ought to have had the mistakes erased that are written down in his books" (*True History* 1:68) [Y habían de mandar borrar los señores del Real Consejo de Indias los borrones que en sus libros van escritos (*Historia verdadera* 1:80)].

16. "Más bien se parece que Gómara fue aficionado a hablar tan loablemente del valeroso Cortés, y tenemos por cierto que le untaron las manos, pues que a su hijo, el marqués que ahora es, le eligió su corónica, teniendo a nuestro rey y señor, que con derecho se le había de elegir y recomendar" (*Historia verdadera* 1:80).

17. Gibson, *Aztecs*, 62.

18. Simpson (*The Encomienda*, 85–87) characterizes the corregimiento as a crown-controlled system of Indian government, aimed at checking incipient feudalism in New Spain by placing Indian towns under royally appointed authorities (corregidores) who were to see to the Indians' instruction, aided by a priest, and monitor the demands of neighboring encomenderos, reducing excessive tribute. The corregidores' salaries were to come, however, from the Indians' tribute as well as remittance to the crown. Ousted encomenderos were sometimes compensated for the loss of encomiendas by being appointed as corregidores.

19. Simpson, *The Encomienda*, 140–141; Zavala, *La encomienda indiana*, 101.

20. Casas, "Entre los remedios," 74.

21. *True History* 1:66–67. "Pues de aquellas matanzas que dicen que hacíamos, siendo nosotros cuatrocientos y cincuenta soldados los que andábamos en la guerra, que harto teníamos que defendernos [que] no nos matasen y nos llevasen de vencida, que aunque estuvieran los indios atados, no hiciéramos tantas muertes, en especial que tenían sus armas de algodón, que les cubrían el cuerpo, y arcos, saetas, rodelas, lanzas grandes, espadas de navajas como de a dos manos, que cortan más que nuestras espadas, y muy denodados guerreros. . . . Pues tornando a nuestra plática, dicen que derrotamos y abrasamos muchas ciudades y templos, que son *cues*, y en aquello les parece que placen mucho a los oyentes que leen sus historias y no lo vieron ni entendieron cuando lo escribían; los verdaderos conquistadores y curiosos lectores que saben lo que pasó claramente les dirán que si todo lo que escriben de otras historias va como lo de la Nueva España, irá todo errado" (*Historia verdadera* 1:79).

22. My translation. "También [Gómara] dice cómo Cortés mandó quemar un indio que se decía Quetzalpopoca, capitán de Moctezuma, sobre la población

que se quemó" (Díaz del Castillo, *Historia verdadera*, ed. Sáenz de Santa María, 34).

23. I return to the citation of the Ramírez Cabañas edition: *Historia verdadera* 1:296–297, 461.

24. Gómara, *Conquista*, 140.

25. My translation. Gómara, *Historia de la conquista*, 140: "Y así, se quemaron públicamente en la plaza mayor, delante todo el pueblo, sin haber ningún escándalo, sino todo silencio y espanto de la nueva manera de justicia que veían ejecutar en señor tan principal y en reino de Moteczuma, a hombres extranjeros y huéspedes."

26. "All of these have their own kingdoms, dominions, rulers, high and low jurisdictions, judges, magistrates, and territories, within which they may freely and legitimately exercise their authority and within which no other king in the world—without breaking natural law—may enter or exercise authority there without the permission of their kings or republics and much less use or exercise any jurisdiction or power" (Casas, *Tratado de doce dudas*, 489. Translation by Andrew M. Shapiro).

27. Bernal Díaz's *probanza de méritos y servicios*, which is reproduced in Ramírez Cabañas's edition of the *Historia verdadera* (2:407–431), includes Villalobos's accusation ("No había sido tal conquistador como decía, ni le habían sido encomendados los dichos pueblos por servicios que hubiese hecho" [408]), as well as the royal decree that earlier had granted Bernal Díaz certain privileges.

28. *True History* 5:290. "Parte me cabe de las siete cabezas de reyes [que Cortés tiene por armas y blasón] y de lo que dice en la culebrina 'yo, en serviros, sin segundo,' pues yo le ayudé en todas las conquistas y a ganar aquella prez y honra y estado, y es muy bien empleado en su muy valerosa persona. . . . No me alabo tanto como debo" (*Historia verdadera* 2:378).

29. "Y pasó un Bernaldino Vázquez de Tapia, persona muy prominente y rico; murió de su muerte" (*Historia verdadera* 2:337). Vázquez de Tapia's criticism of the Cholula massacre is found in CDI 26:417–418; see Sáenz de Santa María, *Introducción crítica*, 56–58. Casas, *Brevísima relación*, 107–108.

30. *True History* 2:4. "Cómo tenían concertado en esta ciudad de Cholula de matarnos por mandado de Moctezuma, y lo que sobre ello pasó" (*Historia verdadera* 1:238). The earlier mention of Cholulan treachery is found in chapter 62 (1:185).

31. *True History* 5:292. "La de Cholula, cuando nos quisieron matar y comer nuestros cuerpos, y no la cuento por batalla" (*Historia verdadera* 2:379).

32. Sepúlveda's just causes for war against the Indians were realized in Bernal Díaz's narrative as follows: (1) Sepúlveda: the rejection of the authority of those more prudent by those who were by nature slaves: Bernal Díaz: "they wanted to kill us by eating our flesh"; (2) the practice of anthropophagy: "to eat our flesh they had the cauldrons prepared with salt, hot peppers, and tomatoes"; (3) the need to protect the innocent: "three nights earlier they had

sacrificed seven Indians to assure their victory"; and (4) to propagate the Christian faith. On this point, it was recognized at the time of the conquest that Cholula was a major religious ceremonial center (Sepúlveda, *Demócrates Segundo*, 83–84; Díaz del Castillo, *Historia verdadera* 1:189–192 [chap. 83]); on the importance of Cholula, see Thomas, *Cortés*, 258–259).

33. *True History* 2:20. "Si de antes teníamos fama de esforzados y habían sabido de las guerras de Potochan y Tabasco y de Cingapacinga y lo de Tlaxcala, y nos llamaban *teules*, que es nombre como de sus dioses, o cosas malas, desde ahí adelante nos tenían por adivinos, y decían que no se nos podría encubrir cosa ninguna mala que contra nosotros tratasen que no lo supiésemos, y a esta causa nos mostraban buena voluntad" (*Historia verdadera* 1:248; see 1:238–249 for the complete narrative sequence).

34. *True History* 2:20. "Mas, ¿qué aprovechaban aquellos prometimientos que no lo cumplían?" (*Historia verdadera* 1:248).

35. *True History* 2:20. "Porque afirma que sin causa ninguna, sino por nuestro pasatiempo, y porque se nos antojó, se hizo aquel castigo" (*Historia verdadera* 1:248).

36. My translation. I cite here, exceptionally, Sáenz de Santa María's edition: "Pues desque tornamos a conquistar la gran ciudad de México e la ganamos, tampoco dice [Gómara] los soldados que nos mataron e hirieron en las conquistas, sino que todo lo hallábamos como quien va a bodas y regocijos" (*Historia verdadera*, ed. Sáenz de Santa María, 35). See Díaz del Castillo, *Historia verdadera*, ed. Miguel Ángel Porrúa, 2:46.

37. Casas, *An Account*, 30. "Acordaron los españoles de hacer allí una matanza o castigo (como ellos dicen) para poner y sembrar su temor y braveza en todos los rincones de aquellas tierras. Porque siempre fue ésta su determinación en todas las tierras que los españoles han entrado, conviene a saber, hacer una cruel y señalada matanza, porque tiemblen dellos aquellas ovejas mansas" (Casas, *Brevísima relación*, 107).

38. *True History* 2:20. "Y [Las Casas] aun dícelo de arte en su libro [la *Brevísima*] a quien no lo vio ni lo sabe, que les hará creer que es ansí aquello y otras crueldades que escribe, siendo todo al revés que no pasó como lo escribe" (*Historia verdadera* 1:248). See Díaz del Castillo, *Historia verdadera*, ed. Miguel Ángel Porrúa, 1: fol. 69r; 2:46. Sáenz de Santa María (*Introducción crítica*, 58) observed that this sentence was omitted from the 1632 edition.

39. "I have heard a Franciscan Friar called Fray Toribio Motolinea [*sic*], who led a good life, say that it would have been better if that punishment could have been prevented, and they had not given cause for its being carried out; but, as it had been carried out, it was a good thing that all the Indians of the provinces of New Spain should see and understand that those Idols and all the rest of them were evil and lying" (*True History* 2:21) [Yo he oído decir a un fraile francisco de buena vida, que se decía fray Toribio Motolinía, que si se pudiera excusar aquel castigo y ellos no dieran causa a que se hiciese, que mejor fuera; mas ya que se hizo, que fue bueno para que todos los indios de

las provincias de la Nueva España viesen y conociesen que aquellos ídolos y todos los demás son malos y mentirosos (*Historia verdadera* 1:248–249)].

40. Casas, *An Account*, 33. "Dicen: '¡Santiago y a ellos!,' y comienzan con las espadas desnudas a abrir aquellos cuerpos desnudos y delicados y a derramar aquella generosa sangre, que uno no dejaron a vida; lo mesmo hicieron los otros en las otras plazas" (Casas, *Brevísima relación*, 110).

41. Casas, *An Account*, 34. "Y de aquí a que se acabe el mundo, o ellos del todo se acaben, no dejarán de lamentar y cantar en sus areítos y bailes, como en romances (que acá decimos), aquella calamidad e pérdida de la sucesión de toda su nobleza, de que se preciaban de tantos años atrás" (Casas, *Brevísima relación*, 110).

42. These are additions that do not appear in the Guatemala manuscript but were introduced in the 1632 edition, evidently on the basis of one of the versions, prepared or supervised, respectively, by Don Francisco Díaz del Castillo, Bernal Díaz's son, or Fray Alonso Remón, the 1632 editor. (See Sáenz de Santa María, "Plan de la edición," xxviii–xxx; *Historia verdadera*, ed. Sáenz de Santa María, 272.)

43. "I also want to say that Pedro de Alvarado said that, when the Mexican Indians were fighting with him, that many of them said that a great *tecleciguata*, which is a great lady, very similar to the one in the great temple, threw dirt into their eyes and blinded them, and that a great lord, who was mounted on a white horse, did them much more harm, and that, if it had not been for them, all would have been massacred; and that all that they say was told to the great Moctezuma by his lords: and if that was the case, they are very great miracles and we must continually give thanks to God and the Virgin Saint Mary, Our Lady, his blessed mother, who aids us in all things, and to the blessed lord Saint James" (my translation) [También yo quiero decir que decía Pedro de Alvarado que, cuando peleaban los indios mexicanos con él, que dijeron muchos de ellos que una gran *tecleciguata*, que es gran señora, que era otra como la que estaba en su gran *cu*, les echaba tierra en los ojos y les cegaba, y que un gran *teule* que andaba en un caballo blanco, les hacía mucho más daño, y que, si por ellos no fuera, que les mataran a todos; e que aquello diz que se lo dijeron al gran Montezuma sus principales: y si aquello fue así grandísimos milagros son y de continuo hemos de dar gracias a Dios y a la virgen Santa María nuestra Señora, su bendita madre, que en todo nos socorre y al bienaventurado señor Santiago (*Historia verdadera*, ed. Sáenz de Santa María, 272)]. See Díaz del Castillo, *Historia verdadera*, ed. Miguel Ángel Porrúa, 1: fol. 110v; 2:365.

44. Casas, *An Account*, 33. "Acordaron aquellos españoles de cometer otra cosa señalada, para acrecentar su miedo en toda la tierra: industria (como dije) de que muchas veces han usado" (Casas, *Brevísima relación*, 109).

45. "Que lo demás que dicen algunas personas, que el Pedro de Albarado, por codicia de haber mucho oro y joyas de gran valor con que bailaban los indios, les fue a dar guerra, yo no lo creo ni nunca tal oí, ni es de creer que tal

hiciese, puesto que lo dice el obispo fray Bartolomé de las Casas, aquello, y otras cossas que nunca pasaron" (*Historia verdadera*, ed. Remón, fol. 102r; my translation). See Díaz del Castillo, *Historia verdadera*, ed. Miguel Ángel Porrúa, 1: fols. 110v–111r; 2:365–366.

46. "Verdaderamente dio en ellos por meterles temor, e que con aquellos males que les hizo tuviesen harto que curar y llorar en ellos, porque no le viniesen a dar guerra; y como dicen que quien comete vence" (*Historia verdadera*, ed. Remón, fol. 102r) [Truly he attacked them to inspire fear in them, and . . . with those bad things he gave them much to ponder and lament, in order that they not come to make war on him; and as they say, he who attacks, wins" (my translation)].

47. *True History* 5:280. "Cómo en el año 1550, estando en la corte de Valladolid, se juntaron en el Real Consejo de Indias ciertos prelados y caballeros que vinieron a [*sic*] la Nueva España y del Perú por procuradores, y otros hidalgos que se hallaron presentes para dar orden que se hiciese el repartimiento perpetuo. Y lo que en la junta se hizo y platicó es lo que diré" (*Historia verdadera* 2:370 [chapter 211 title]). For a discussion of the perpetuity junta, see Wagner and Parish, *Life and Writings*, 209–212, 220.

48. Soto, "Prólogo del maestro Soto," 295.

49. Wagner and Parish, *Life and Writings*, 212. On July 2, 1540, the emperor commanded the viceroy Antonio de Mendoza to provide Bernal Díaz with a post as corregidor (municipal administrator) if no vacated encomiendas could be found for him in compensation for his lost encomienda holdings; this decree is reproduced in Díaz del Castillo, *Historia verdadera* 2:410–411.

50. "Yo escribo sola y brevemente la conquista de Indias. Quien quisiere ver la justificación de ella, lea al doctor Sepúlveda, cronista del emperador, que la escribió en latín doctísimamente; y así quedará satisfecho del todo" (Gómara, *Historia general*, 320 [chap. 214]; my translation).

51. This "Petition of Bernal Díaz del Castillo, *procurador* [advocate] of the City of Guatemala, to the Council of the Indies against the liberation of the Indian slaves, February 1, 1549," is reprinted in Simpson, *Studies*, 32–36. Las Casas answered Bernal Díaz's petition point by point, in "Representación al Consejo de Indias, contra las pretensiones de un procurador enviado por la provincia de Guatemala, 1549" (Casas, "Representación," 290–292).

52. This chapter, numbered 213 (*Historia verdadera* 2:384–390), and the following and final one (chapter 214) are found exclusively in the Guatemala manuscript. Because they are absent from the Alegría manuscript as well as from the 1632 publication prepared by Remón, Ramírez Cabañas (in *Historia verdadera* 2:384n88) and others have concluded that the two chapters must have been written subsequent to the dispatch of the copy intended for publication. Bernal Díaz begins the chapter by remarking, "Certain monks have asked me to tell them and explain why so many Indian men and women were branded for slaves throughout New Spain, and whether we branded them without reporting it to His Majesty. To this I replied, and repeat it now, that His Majesty

sent twice to order it, and, that this may be clearly understood, interested readers should know that this was the way of it" (*True History* 5:301) [Hanme rogado ciertos religiosos que les dijese y declarase por qué causa se herraron muchos indios e indias por esclavos en toda la Nueva España, si los herramos sin hacer relación a Su Majestad. A esto dije, y aun digo ahora, que Su Majestad lo envió a mandar dos veces, y para que esto bien se entienda sepan los curiosos lectores que fue de esta manera (*Historia verdadera* 2:384)]. He sums up at the end by stating, "I wish to leave this subject which has been very long and prolix, but in it can be seen the permission we had from His Majesty and the Lords of his Royal Council to brand slaves" (*True History* 5:311) [Quiero dejar esta materia, aunque ha sido muy larga y prolija, en la cual por ella verán las licencias de Su Majestad que para herrar esclavos teníamos y de los señores de su Real Consejo (*Historia verdadera* 2:390)].

53. My translation. "Por qué causa en esta Nueva España se herraron muchos indios e indias por esclavos, y la relación que sobre ello doy" (*Historia verdadera* 2:384).

54. *True History* 5:285. "Y no aprovechamos cosa ninguna con los señores del Real Consejo de Indias, y con el obispo fray Bartolomé de las Casas, y fray Rodrigo, su compañero, y con el obispo de las Charcas, don fray Martín [en blanco], y dijeron que en viniendo Su Majestad de Augusta se proveería de manera que los conquistadores serían muy contentos; y así se quedó por hacer" (*Historia verdadera* 2:373). Maudslay (in Díaz del Castillo, *True History* 5:283, 285) notes that the blank space left in the original should be completed with the name of the Dominican friar Tomás de San Martín.

55. *True History* 5:285. "De esta manera andamos de mula coja, y de mal en peor, y de un visorrey en otro, y de gobernador en gobernador" (*Historia verdadera* 2:374).

56. See Casas, "Informe al Consejo"; Díaz del Castillo, "Carta de Bernal Díaz del Castillo al emperador don Carlos."

57. Díaz del Castillo, "Carta de Bernal Díaz del Castillo, dirigida a fray Bartolomé de las Casas"; idem, "Carta de Bernal Díaz del Castillo al rey don Felipe II."

58. Stabler and Kicza, "Ruy González's 1553 Letter," 473.

59. Gibson, *The Aztecs,* 61–62.

60. Stabler and Kicza, "Ruy González's 1553 Letter," 473.

61. Stabler and Kicza, "Ruy González's 1553 Letter," 476. Las Casas's controversial confessor's guide was one of the tracts he had published in Seville in 1552–1553 for distribution to the Spanish missionary community in America. See the section entitled "Las Casas, the New Laws, and the Black Legend," in chapter 3.

62. Stabler and Kicza, "Ruy González's 1553 Letter,"476. Las Casas's career in Mexico, comprising four stays between 1535 and 1546, is the subject of Parish and Weidman's, *Las Casas en México.*

63. I have modernized the orthography of Stabler and Kicza's transcription of the letter.

CHAPTER 7. THE CONQUISTADOR-CHRONICLER AND
HIS LITERARY AUTHORITY

1. An earlier version of this chapter appeared as my "History, Law, and the Eye-witness."

2. Barbón Rodríguez ("La conquista," 207–218), studied the reliance of Illescas on Gómara's work and pointed out that parts 1 and 2 of the *Historia pontifical*, first published in 1565, appeared again in 1569, 1573, 1574, and 1583. Illescas's papal history was influential in Spain and was also a popular item on the Spanish colonial book trade (Leonard, *Books of the Brave*, 163–64, 208).

3. "And also that in order to give greater credibility to what I write I should cite witnesses, as the chroniclers are accustomed to insert and quote proofs from other books dealing with past events, for I am not a witness for myself" (*True History* 5:287) [Y también que para dar más crédito a lo que escribo diese testigos, como suelen poner y alegar los coronistas, que aprueban con otros libros de cosas pasadas lo que de ello han dicho otras personas que lo vieron, y no decir secamente esto hice y tal me acaeció, porque yo no soy testigo de mí mismo (*Historia verdadera* 2:375–376)].

4. Both letters are dated February 28, 1539, and are reproduced in González Obregón, *Bernal Díaz del Castillo*, 73–75, and in Ramírez Cabañas's edition of the *Historia verdadera* 2:413–414.

5. The *probanza de méritos y servicios*, dated September 7, 1539, is reproduced in Ramírez Cabañas (*Historia verdadera*, by Bernal Díaz, ed. Ramírez Cabañas) 2:407–431.

6. *Historia verdadera* 2:377. The royal decrees, dated June 2, 1540, June 19, 1540, and July 2, 1540, are reproduced in *Historia verdadera* 2:407–413.

7. Sáenz de Santa María, *Introducción crítica*, 130, lists the probanzas in which Bernal Díaz participated on behalf of others.

8. *True History* 5:289. "Y sin tener verdadera relación, ¿cómo lo podían escribir, sino al sabor de su paladar, sin ir errados, salvo que en las pláticas que tomaron del mismo marqués?" (*Historia verdadera* 2:377).

9. "I offer these letters as evidence—two of them were placed before His Majesty and the originals are preserved" (*True History* 5:287) [Estas cartas doy por testigo y los traslados de ellas están presentadas ante Su Majestad y los originales están guardados (*Historia verdadera* 2:377)].

10. Bernal Díaz's reference to himself as "one of the oldest conquistadores" of New Spain [uno de los más antiguos conquistadores] repeats the phrase used in the emperor's order of July 2, 1540, to Don Antonio de Mendoza to reward Bernal Díaz with a position as administrator (*corregidor*) of a municipal Indian district (*corregimiento*). The document is reproduced in *Historia verdadera* 2:410.

11. Simpson, *The Encomienda*, 140–141; Wagner and Parish, *Life and Writings*, 108–116.

12. Aiton, *Antonio de Mendoza*, 97–98; Icaza, *Diccionario autobiográfico* 1:xxvi, xxxiii; Ramírez Cabañas, "Introducción," 13.

13. Himmerich y Valencia, *The Encomenderos*, 301.

14. Indeed, the two final chapters Bernal Díaz added to the Guatemala manu-
    script (but which do not appear in the version he completed in 1568 and sent
    to Madrid in 1575) consist of a defense of Indian slavery in New Spain (chap-
    ter 213) and a survey of its governors which is, in effect, a recital of Bernal
    Díaz's dismal views on how the encomenderos' interests had fared in the de-
    cades since the conquest (chapter 214).

15. See González Echevarría, *Relecturas*, 28–29; idem, "Life and Adventures of
    Cipión," 20–21; idem, "Law of the Letter"; the latter is reproduced in *Myth
    and Archive*. Murdo J. MacLeod's "Self-Promotion: The *Relaciones de Méritos y
    Servicios*" has also been a helpful source.

16. Parry, *Audiencia*, 156; Wagner, "Three Studies," 26; Covarrubias, *Tesoro*, 604.

17. Parry, *Audiencia*, 156.

18. The probanza is reproduced in Fuentes y Guzmán, *Historia de Guatemala*
    1:369–381 as well as in *Historia verdadera* 2:407–431.

19. His statement ("Así que no es mucho que yo ahora en esta relación declare
    en las batallas que me hallé peleando") from the published version of 1632,
    finished in 1568, is contrasted by the Guatemala manuscript: "Y así que no es
    mucho que yo escriba los heroicos hechos del valeroso Cortés, y los míos, y
    los de mis compañeros que se hallaron juntamente peleando" (*Historia ver-
    dadera* 2:378 [chap. 212]). These texts are displayed side by side in *Historia ver-
    dadera*, ed. Miguel Ángel Porrúa, 2:903.

20. Frankl, "Hernán Cortés," 9–74. Elliott ("The Mental World," 30) has de-
    scribed the *Siete partidas* as "a code of military and legal conduct, capable of
    providing the Castilian *hidalgo* with an admirably coherent framework of
    ideas."

21. Frankl, "Hernán Cortés," 33–41; Lobingier, "Introduction," liii; Alfonso X, *Si-
    ete partidas*, part. 2, tit. 10, prol.; part. 2, tit. 21, law 23.

22. Alfonso X, *Siete partidas*, part. 3, tit. 28, law 8; part. 1, tit. 1, law 18; part. 1, tit.
    1, law 2; part. 2, tit. 21, law 12; part. 2, tit. 13, laws 5 and 7.

23. Alfonso X, *Siete partidas*, part. 2, tit. 23, law 2 [vol. 1, fol. 79r, fol. 83v]: "E este
    derecho según mostraron los sabios antiguos, sobre que la guerra se deuía
    fazer, es sobre tres razones. La primera, por acrescentar el pueblo su fe, e
    para destruyr los que la quisiesen contrallar. La segunda, por su señor,
    queriéndole seruir, e honrrar, e guarde lealmente. La tercerca, para amparar
    asímismos, e acrescentar, e honrrar la tierra donde son. E aquesta guerra se
    deue fazer, en dos maneras. La una manera es, de los enemigos que son den-
    tro del reyno, que fazen mal en la tierra, robando, esforzando a los omes lo
    suyo sin derercho. . . . Mas la segunda manera de guerra, de que agora
    queremos fablar, es de aquella que deuen fazer contra los enemigos, que son
    fuera del reyno, que les quieren tomar por fuerza su tierra, e amparalles lo
    que con derecho deuen auer."

24. Frankl, "Hernán Cortés," 29–33, 69, 73; see *Historia verdadera* 1:119–122
    [chap. 36].

25. Durand (*La transformación*, 79–87) took Bernal Díaz as a typical example of the conquistadores' ambitions to aristocracy.

26. *Historia verdadera*, ed. Sáenz 1:645 [chap. 207]; this is chapter 206 in the facsimile of the Remón edition of 1632 (*Historia verdadera*, ed. Miguel Ángel Porrúa, 2:880). This statement does not appear at the same point in the Guatemala manuscript; it makes its debut, instead, in its very first chapter, in reference to New Spain: "and that it is one of the best countries yet discovered in the New World, we found out by our own efforts without His Majesty knowing anything about it" (*True History* 1:5) [que es una de las buenas partes descubiertas del Nuevo Mundo, lo cual descubrimos a nuestra costa sin ser sabidor de ello Su Majestad (*Historia verdadera*, ed. Ramírez Cabañas, 1:39, idem, ed. Miguel Ángel Porrúa, 2:4)].

27. *Historia verdadera*, ed. Ramírez Cabañas, 2:357 [chap. 207]. Bernal Díaz echoes the principles of the *Siete partidas*, part. 2, tit. 27, law 6: "There is a noble reason for rewards which are bestowed upon men for signal services rendered to their lords in time of war, as we have already stated. But no one but an emperor, king, or other lord, for whom it is proper, and who has authority over everything in his dominions, has the right to give other rewards, as, for instance, to transfer landed property absolutely, or raise men from one condition to another, as he may think best" (Scott, trans., *Siete partidas*, 502). Part. 4, tit. 25, law 1 is also pertinent: "Vassals are those who receive honor or reward given by their lords, such as *caballerías*, or land, or money, for distinguished services that they have performed" (fol. 61v; my translation).

28. Alfonso X, *Siete partidas*, part. 2, tit. 10, prol.: "Comunaleza deue el rey auer a todos los del su Señorío, para amar, e honrrar, e guardar a ca [*sic*] uno dellos, segun qual es, o el seruicio que del recibe" (fol. 27r).

29. Stabler and Kicza, "Ruy González's 1553 Letter," 476.

30. Manzano Manzano, *La incorporación*, 26–27.

31. Ibid., 30; Alfonso X, *Siete partidas*, part. 2, tit. 1, law 9, f6r: "La iiii es, por otorgamiento del Papa, o del Emperador, quando alguno dellos faze reyes en aquellas tierras, en que han derecho de lo fazer."

32. See Marcus, "La Conquête de Cholula: Conflit d'Interprétations."

33. Bernal Díaz served in the conquest of Mexico as a foot soldier in Pedro de Alvarado's company; although he claimed to have held the rank of captain on Cortés's Honduras expedition, it had been at best only a temporary appointment (Wagner, "Three Studies," 6).

34. Tribaldos, in *Historia verdadera*, ed. Remón, fol. 2v; Serrano, in *Historia verdadera*, ed. Remón, fol. 3v: "con santo zelo de la reputación de nuestra España (menoscabada en las historias por la embidia extranjera)"; unsigned prologue to the reader, in *Historia verdadera*, ed. Remón, fol. 4v: "a quien [Bernal Díaz] si deve España parte de la conquista para el util doméstico, también le deve el todo de su lustre para con los estraños."

35. Pizarro y Orellana, *Varones ilustres*, 363: "Y de aquí tuvieron los Estrangeros motivo, por ser tan natural el odio que tienen a esta Nación, para hablar mal en las Historias de los Españoles."

36. Pizarro y Orellana, *Varones ilustres,* 47, 71.

37. Fuentes y Guzmán, *Recordación florida* 1:8 [al lector].

38. Ibid., 1:113 [bk. 4, chap. 1].

39. Fuentes y Guzmán (*Recordación florida* 1:116–119 [bk. 4, chap. 1]) followed Bernal Díaz's (chaps. 125–126) defensive account of Alvarado's massacre of Mexica nobles in 1520 during the fiesta of Toxcatl celebrated in the Mexican capital.

40. "Siendo este combate, y victoria que Cortés y los suyos alcanzaron de Narváez, confusión y silencio para los españoles que dicen que los conquistadores de estos reignos no hicieron cosa de valor peleando con indios desnudos" (ibid., 1:119 [bk. 4, chap. 1]).

41. Casas, *Brevísima relación,* 49, 153 ("De la Nueva España," "De Guatemala").

42. See Iglesia, *Dos estudios,* 23–35; Lewis, "Retórica," 37–47.

43. "Dexaremos a los tiranos soberbiosos y poderosos con la tiranía que su día se les vendrá, por referir y notar algo de lo que dizen los Historiadores de nuestro Marqués, a quien no creo que dieron la muerte los soldados tiranos, sino los Historiadores conjurados" (Pizarro y Orellana, *Varones ilustres,* 186).

CHAPTER 8. THE AMERINDIAN, STUDIED, INTERPRETED, AND IMAGINED

1. Valverde, *Santuario,* fol. 236r–v. The title-page engraving is by Francisco de Bejarano, an Augustinian born in Ecuador (d. 1659). The figure seated in the lower right-hand corner of the drawing has sometimes been identified as a female, but it is clearly a male figure and an Inca, given the decorated headdress (*llautu*) and the haircut; it is clearly meant to represent the Inca featured in the work, "Yupanqui Toca."

2. Garcilaso, *Comentarios reales,* 3:50–51 [part 2, bk. 1, chap. 24].]

3. The Valverde frontispiece and the images appearing in the works of Alonso de Ovalle and Cieza de León (see figs. 18, 19) are discussed in my 1990 article on the contribution of visual images to Spanish colonial-era polemics (see Adorno, "Retórica," 46, 65). An earlier version of this chapter appeared as my "Literary Production and Suppression."

4. See Fray Alonso Ramos Gavilán's 1621 *Historia,* and the studies of MacCormack, "From the Sun," and Salles-Reese, *From Viracocha,* on the transformation of the site and its Andean and Christian meanings.

5. Valverde, *Santuario,* fol. 8r.

6. For a discussion of how censorship on the topic of the Indies functioned as well as case studies on how it operated for political motives, see Friede, "La censura," and Adorno, "Censorship," idem, "Globalism," idem, "Sobre la censura," idem, "Censorship and Approbation."

7. "Ethnographic history" was a designation created by Eduard Fueter, in *Geschichte der neueren Historiographie* (1911), to describe one of the four major types of history written in the seventeenth century. The histories called eth-

nographic were those written by missionaries or students of the territories
newly discovered in the fifteenth and sixteenth centuries.

8. His words, "haciendo alguna mixtura *de* la cualidad, naturaleza y pro-
piedades destas regiones, reinos y tierras y lo que en sí contienen, *con* las costumbres, religión, ritos, ceremonias y condición de las gentes naturales de
ellas," make clear that he refers not to the opposition between diachronic and
synchronic perspectives (Spanish events, Amerindian practices), which has
been the usual interpretation, but rather that he will mix two types of synchronic description of the Indies, that is, cultural or ethnographic with geographic considerations (Casas, *Historia*, 1:22 [prologue]; my emphasis).

9. "Es muy notable por la estraníssima religión y crueles costumbres de Mexicanos" (Gómara, *Historia* (1552), fol. 1v). This note is written in the first person and was presumably authored by Gómara. See the section entitled
"Cortés and His Historians," in chapter 5.

10. On the lifework of Sahagún, see Ballesteros, *Vida y obra*, Klor de Alva et al.,
The Work, and León-Portilla, *Bernardino de Sahagún*. For that of Acosta, see
the studies by the intellectual historians Anthony Pagden, *The Fall of Natural
Man*, and especially Sabine MacCormack, *Religion in the Andes*.

11. Acosta, *Historia*, 279 [bk. 5, chap. 31].

12. Ovalle, *Histórica relación*, 4–5.

13. Ovalle's work was richly illustrated with some fourteen engravings, for the
execution of which he gave detailed instructions; these are printed in his
work (fols. 3v–4r). Admonishing the printer to place the images in their appropriate places, he remarked that their purpose was to "give more light,"
that is, more illumination, to his work ["Dase alguna razón de las mesmas
Imágenes para dar más luz a la obra"].

14. Ovalle, *Histórica relación*, 393; Adorno, "Retórica," 45–46, 63.

15. The title of Eric Wolf's study of European expansion around the globe in
Asia, Africa, and the Americas is resonant: *Europe and the People without History*. González Echevarría ("José Arrom," 21) argued three decades ago that
decolonization meant not only the recovery of territorial space but also of
time, "that is, history." My conviction in this regard came from my study of
Guaman Poma's work, and so I cited his remark in *Guaman Poma: Writing*
(3, 145n2).

16. Hemming, *Conquest*, 412–416, 451–452.

17. "And if anyone should think that I am partial to the Araucanians, dealing
with their affairs and brave deeds more extensively than is required for barbarians, if we look at their upbringing, customs, manners of conducting war
and their exercise of it, we will see that many peoples have not surpassed
them and there are few who with such great tenacity and determination have
defended their lands against such fierce enemies as are the Spaniards. . . . I
have wanted to express this as proof and guarantee of the worth of these peoples, meritorious of greater praise than I am able to give them with my

verses" (my translation) [Y si a alguno le pareciere que me muestro algo inclinado a la parte de los araucanos, tratando sus cosas y valentías más exten-
didamente de lo que para bárbaros se requiere, si queremos mirar su
crianza, costumbres, modos de guerra y ejercicio della, veremos que muchos
no les han hecho ventaja y que son pocos los que con tan gran constancia y
firmeza han defendido su tierra contra tan fieros enemigos como son los españoles. . . . Todo esto he querido traer para prueba y en abono del valor destas gentes, digno de mayor loor del que yo lo podré dar con mis versos
(Ercilla, *La araucana* 1:121–122 [prologue])].

18. "Porque el mundo tenga entera noticia, y verdadera relación del Río de la
Plata" (Barco Centenera, *Argentina*, fol. 2v).

19. Barco Centenera (ibid.) writes of "provincias tan grandes, gentes tan be-
licosísimas, animales y fieras tan bravas, aves tan diferentes, víboras y ser-
pientes que han tenido con hombres conflicto y pelea, peces de humana
forma y cosas tan exquisitas que dexan en éxtasi los ánimos de los que con alguna atención las consideran."

20. Saavedra Guzmán, *El peregrino*, fol. 9r.

21. Ibid., 298: "No quiero, señor sacro, relataros / Los ritos, y las leyes que ob-
seruauan, / Por entender, sin duda, he de cansaros, / Porque eran infinitas
las que vsauan: / Otros estan dispuestos a informaros, / Que solo este principio desseauan, / Y que yo la vergüenza les quitasse, / Y con lo que padezco
me quedasse.//Pero daros, señor, disculpa desto, / Y de mi loco y grande
atrevimiento / En arrojarme a tanto contrapuesto / Conociendo tan claro el
poco aliento: / Anímame señor a echar el resto, / No con poco temor y senti-
miento, / El ver que soy en Mexico nacido, / Donde ningún historiador ha
auido."

22. De Oña, *Arauco*, n.p.: "Van mexclados algunos términos Indios, no por cometer barbarismo, sino porque, siendo tan propia dellos la materia, me pareció
congruencia que en este también le correspondiesse la forma."

23. See Fray Ramón Pané, *Relación*, and González Echevarría, "José Arrom."

24. Pierce, *La poesía*, and Chevalier, *Lectura*, offer detailed information about the
extent of epic production between 1550 and 1650. Ercilla's *La araucana* was
enormously successful, with twenty-three editions published between 1569
and 1632; it served as the inspiration for many popular ballads (*romances*)
and a number of *comedias* on the Spanish stage (Chevalier, *Lectura*, 106–
108). Medina, *Los romances*, collects the ballads based on *La araucana*.

25. Describing the first of the essential differences between epic and tragedy,
López Pinciano (*Filosofía* 3:149) declares, "Lo primero, en el medio de la im-
itación, porque la trágica imita con personas agenas del poeta, y la épica, con
propias y agenas, por lo qual éste se dize poema común, y aquél, activo."

26. Acosta, *Historia natural*, 278 [bk. 5, chap. 31].

27. On the relationship of Spanish epic poetry to imperial ideology, see Pierce,
La poesía, 214–216, 321–324.

28. El Inca Garcilaso de la Vega praises the elegant verses [*galanos versos*] of

Alonso de Ercilla in *La araucana* and later devotes several chapters to the ongoing Araucanian war against the Spanish in Chile (*Comentarios reales* 2:40, 275–283 [bk. 1, chap. 26; bk. 7, chaps. 20–25]).

29. See in chapter 4 the section entitled "Legislative Events and Polemical Confrontations" for the relationship between hearsay evidence about the natives and the promulgation of colonial policy (the 1519 "cannibal questionnaire").

30. This discussion of inquisitorial charges is based on Kamen, *Inquisition*, 201–02; see also Kamen, *Spanish Inquisition*.

31. Kamen, *Inquisition*, 205–8; idem, *Spanish Inquisition*, 177, 180, 261, 265.

32. This woodcut, which accompanies chapter 52, as well as others from the 1553 Seville edition, are reproduced in the 1984 edition of Cieza de León, *Crónica del Perú. Primera Parte*. This series, redrawn for the 1554 Antwerp edition, reproduces the compositions created for the earlier Seville edition.

33. Acosta, *Historia natural*, 319 [bk., 7, chap. 1]): "Y aun quitan mucho del común y necio desprecio en que los de Europa los tienen, no juzgando de estas gentes tengan cosas de hombres de razón y prudencia."

34. See Pagden, *Fall*, 119–145, on Las Casas's major historical works in relation to the development of comparative ethnology, and especially MacCormack, *Religion*, chap. 5.

35. As noted in chapter 4, Sepúlveda and Las Casas cited the same gospel text on this principle: "And other sheep I have, which are not of this fold: them also I must bring, and they shall hear my voice; and there shall be one fold, and one shepherd" (John 10:16).

36. Here, a small homage to Octavio Paz ("Literatura," 13): "El continente americano aún no había sido enteramente descubierto y ya había sido bautizado." Lysander Kemp ("Literature," 174–175) translates: "The American continent had not yet been wholly discovered when it had already been baptized."

37. This standard period formula on the virtues of historical truth and the vanities of fiction can be found in literary prologues as well as in countless official approbations by state and ecclesiastical censors. For a review of such statements, see, for example, Rodríguez Prampolini, *Amadises*; Leonard, *Books*; Pierce, *La poesía*.

38. See Ballesteros Gaibrois, *Vida y obra*; León-Portilla, *Bernardino de Sahagún*.

39. Antonio Márquez (*Literatura*, 230ff) remarks on these problems in his study of inquisitorial expurgation and censorship of literature in Spain. Torre Revello, *El libro*, published a series of the royal decrees prohibiting works on America, which are illustrative because of what they fail to state.

40. I have studied the case of Fray Jerónimo Román y Zamora, whose *Repúblicas del mundo* (1575) was expurgated. Contrary to the supposition that it had been his material on the Indies that was censored, it turned out that the descriptions of the sacred ceremonial rites of ancient Hebrew culture and the very "naughty" pagan rites of the ancient Romans were the accounts excised. Undaunted, Román y Zamora published an expanded version of his encyclopedic work in 1595 (see Adorno, "Censorship," idem, "Sobre la censura").

In contrast, in Fray Martín de Murúa's *Historia general del Perú* manuscript the description of native Andean customs as well as Murúa's Lascasian critique of the conquest of Peru were canceled by authorities of the Mercedarian order and the royal council who then recommended the manuscript for printing; the license to print the manuscript was signed by Philip III on May 26, 1616 (see Adorno, "Censorship and Approbation").

41. O'Gorman ("Prólogo," lxiii–lxiv) summarizes the bibliographic history of Acosta's *Historia natural y moral de las Indias;* Pagden (*Fall,* 197–98) assesses the intellectual impact of the work. The only work of Sahagún's to be published during the sixteenth century was his *Psalmodía cristiana* (Mexico: Pedro Ocharte, 1583).

42. "No tuvo por cosa superflua, ni vana el divino Agustino tratar de la Teología fabulosa de los gentiles, en el sexto libro de *La ciudad de Dios,* porque, como él dice, conocidas las fábulas y ficciones vanas que los gentiles tenían acerca de sus dioses fingidos, pudiesen fácilmente darles a entender que aquéllos no eran dioses, ni podían dar cosa ninguna que fuese provechosa a la criatura racional. A este propósito en este tercero libro se ponen las fábulas y ficciones que estos naturales tenían acerca de sus dioses, porque entendidas las vanidades que ellos tenían por fe cerca de sus mentirosos dioses, vengan más fácilmente por la doctrina evangélica a conocer al verdadero dios" (Sahagún, *Historia general,* 189 [prologue]; my translation).

43. "Baste lo referido para entender el cuidado que los indios ponían en servir y honrar a sus ídolos y al demonio, que es lo mismo. Porque contar por entero lo que en esto hay, es cosa infinita y de poco provecho, y aún de lo referido podrá parecer a algunos que lo hay muy poco o ninguno, y que es como gastar tiempo en leer las patrañas que fingen los libros de caballerías. Pero éstos si lo consideran bien, hallarán ser muy diferente negocio, y que puede ser útil para muchas cosas tener noticia de los ritos y ceremonias que usaron los indios" (Acosta, *Historia natural y moral,* 278 [bk. 5, chap. 31]).

44. See Leonard, *Books;* Chevalier, *Lectura.*

45. Sahagún, *Historia general,* 74–75 [prologue]; Ballesteros Gaibrois, *Vida y obra,* 76; León-Portilla, *Bernardino de Sahagún,* 214–222.

46. This description summarizes the account given by Luciano Pereña ("Estudio preliminar," 18–24) of the censorial procedures to which the *De procuranda* was submitted from the time of its completion to its publication.

47. As he began his account of the conquest of Mexico, Acosta declared, "And with respect to that which is stated henceforth, I will carefully write only that which the books and accounts of the Indians tell, of which our Spanish authors do not make mention, on account of not having so much understood the secrets of that land, and they are things worthy of being pondered, as will now be evident" [Y en lo que de aquí adelante se dijere, sólo terné cuidado de escrebir lo que los libros y relaciones de los indios cuentan, de que nuestros escritores españoles no hacen mención, por no haber tanto entendido los secretos de aquella tierra, y son cosas muy dignas de ponderar, como agora se

verá (*Historia*, 350 [bk. 7, chap. 22])]. The official procedures of review and approval were repeated prior to each republication of the *Historia* (Friede, "La censura," 50–51).

48. See Klor de Alva et al., *The Work*.

49. See Ricard, *Spiritual Conquest*; Gibson, *Tlascala*.

50. Las Casas's editorial fate reflects the shift in the official outlook on writings on America. During the reign of Carlos V, Las Casas exercised enormous influence, preventing the publication of Sepúlveda's *Demócrates Segundo* and, according to López de Gómara, obstructing the publication of the 1547 version of Fernández de Oviedo's *Historia general de las Indias*. In 1552–1553 he published his series of treatises and pamphlets in Seville for private circulation. After the ascent of Philip II to the throne, however, Las Casas's works, and those of many other writers on America, were ordered sequestered by royal decree (Friede, "La censura," 58). Philip's ascent to the throne occasioned the stricter laws, the first of which, in 1556, explicitly prohibited the publication of books on America without special permission from the Council of the Indies (see chapter 1, note 31).

51. For the activities of Sahagún, see Ballesteros Gaibrois, *Vida y obra*.

52. "No hay necesidad en este segundo libro de poner confutación de las ceremonias idolátricas que en ellos cuentan, porque ellas de suyo son tan crueles y tan inhumanas, que a cualquiera que las oyere le pondrán horror y espanto; y así no haré más de poner la relación simplemente a la letra" (Sahagún, *Historia general*, 98 [bk. 2, chap. 20]).

53. Ibid., 99–100 [bk. 2, chap. 20].

54. Ibid., 100 [bk. 2, chap. 20].

55. Acosta, *Historia natural*, 252 [bk. 5, chap. 20].

56. Ibid., 319 [bk. 7, chap. 1].

57. "It is right that all the things the first conquerors of the Indies did be not condemned absolutely, as some laywers and friars have done with good intentions, no doubt, but in too exaggerated a manner. . . . Neither can it be denied that, on the part of the pagans, there were many evils done against God and our people, which obliged them to use stern force and punishment" [Es bien que no se condenen tan absolutamente todas las cosas de los primeros conquistadores de las Indias, como algunos letrados y religiosos han hecho, con buen celo sin duda, pero demasiado. . . . Tampoco se puede negar que de parte de los infieles hubo muchas maldades contra Dios y contra los nuestros, que les obligaron a usar de rigor y castigo (Acosta, *Historia natural*, 373 [bk. 7, chap. 27])]. Acosta's effort to balance his account has been seen as his desire to cope with the lessons of his past experience, when his condemnations of the conquistadores were expurgated from the *De procuranda indorum salute* (see Pereña, "Estudio preliminar," 34).

58. Sahagún, *Historia general*, 15 [dedication to Fray Rodrigo Sequera]. See León-Portilla, *Bernardino de Sahagún*, 214–222.

59. Juan Bautista de Pomar (4) began his *Relación de Texcoco* (1582) by citing the

1539 inquisitorial execution of Don Carlos Ometochtzin, grandson of the sage and poet Nezahualcoyotl and son of the lord Nezahualpilli, as the reason why the few lords who still possessed any codices burned them for fear of being accused of idolatry and prosecuted if such artifacts were found in their possession.

60. García-Arenal, *Los moriscos*, 29; Bennassar, *Spanish Character*, 93.

61. Solórzano Pereyra, *Política Indiana*, 386. Jákfalvi-Leiva, *Traducción*, 86; see pp. 79–88 for a review of the linguistic politics of the Spanish empire at the end of the sixteenth century and the positions of its major protagonists and critics. See especially Mannheim, *The Language of the Inka*, part 1.

62. A royal decree of September 7, 1558, reveals that neither the Isabeline edict of 1502 (requiring state licensing of all books printed), nor the censorship carried out by the Holy Office through its Index of prohibited books, was considered sufficient to deal with writings on America. Outlawed explicitly were the printing and sale of books in three categories: (1) those listed on the Index; (2) heretical works; and (3) frivolous, lascivious accounts, offering bad moral examples [materias vanas, deshonestas y de mal ejemplo] (Friede, "La censura," 49). In this context, the elaborate arguments of Acosta as to why it was acceptable, even important, to read about the Amerindians, particularly the ancient Mexicans, becomes especially significant.

63. Acosta, *Historia natural*, 9 [dedication to the princess Clara Eugenia]: "Mas porque el conocimiento y especulación de cosas naturales, mayormente si son notables y raras, causa natural gusto y deleite en entendimientos delicados, y la noticia de costumbres y hechos extraños también con su novedad aplace, tengo para mí, que para V. A. podrá servir de un honesto y útil entretenimiento, darle ocasión de considerar en obras que el Altísimo ha fabricado en la máquina de este mundo, especialmente en aquellas partes que llamamos Indias, que por ser nuevas tierras, dan más que considerar, y por ser de nuevos vasallos que el sumo Dios dio a la Corona de España, no es del todo ajeno ni extraño su conocimiento."

64. On the idea of the connection between chivalric romance and the conquest of America, the observations of William Hickling Prescott, Alfonso Reyes, José Torre Revello, Leonard in his *Romances of Chivalry,* and Rodríguez Prampolini, *Amadises*, are also pertinent.

65. Leonard, *Books*, 25, 31, 53, 65; Pastor, *Discurso*, 154–156, 191–192, 238–239; Adorno, "Introduction," xxii–xxiv. This section recapitulates the relevant section of my "Discourses on Colonialism" and appears in my introduction to the 1992 (English) and 2006 (Spanish) editions of Leonard's *Books of the Brave*.

66. Díaz del Castillo, *True History* 2:37 [chap. 87]. "Y otro día por la mañana llegamos a la calzada ancha y vamos camino de Estapalapa. Y desde que vimos tantas ciudades y villas pobladas en el agua, y en tierra firme otras grandes poblazones, y aquella calzada tan derecha y por nivel cómo iba a México, nos quedamos admirados, y decíamos que parecía a las cosas de encantamiento que cuentan en el libro de *Amadís*, por las grandes torres y *cúes*

y edificios que tenían dentro en el agua, y todos de calicanto, y aun algunos de nuestros soldados decían que si aquello que veían si era entre sueños, y no es de maravillar que yo escriba aquí de esta manera, porque hay mucho que ponderar en ello que no sé como lo cuente: ver cosas nunca oídas, ni aun soñadas, como veíamos" (*Historia verdadera* 1:260 [chap. 87]).

67. Díaz del Castillo, *Historia verdadera* 2:30, 49; idem, *True History* 4:136, 163 [chaps. 151, 153].

68. Castañeda Nájera, "Castañeda's History," 276.

69. Oviedo, *Historia general* 1:179: "pues no cuento los disparates de los libros de Amadís ni los que dellos dependen."

70. Oviedo's *Libro del muy esforçado e invencible Caballero de Fortuna, propiamente llamado* don *Claribalte* was published in Valencia in 1519.

71. See Chevalier, *Lectura*.

72. Rodríguez Prampolini, *Amadises*, 12–15; Batallion, *Erasmo*, 210ff.

73. Chevalier, *Lectura*; Eisenberg, "Who Reads."

74. Chevalier, "La Diana," 47; see Pierce (*La poesía*, 111–135) for an analysis of the role magic played in the novels of chivalry.

75. Leonard, *Romances*, 253.

76. Pierce, *La poesía*, 111, 165.

77. Caro Baroja, *Las formas*, 57; see idem, *World*.

78. León, *Los nombres de Cristo*, 404 [dedication to Don Pedro Portocarrero].

CHAPTER 9. THE NARRATIVE INVENTION OF
GONZALO THE WARRIOR

1. The sculptural ensemble was created by the artist Raúl Ayala Arellano between March and August 1974 in his studio in Ciudad Juárez, Chihuahua. One casting is located in Akumal, next to the Akumal Caribe Yacht Club, and the other, on a glorieta, or traffic circle, on the extension of the Paseo Montejo in Mérida, Yucatán. A third is reported in Mexico City, although I have not been able to verify it. The standing Gonzalo is accompanied by his Maya wife, who, seated at his feet, gazes up at him and nurses the smallest of their three children. Their firstborn child, a son, clings to his father's side, and a little girl, seated, is absorbed at play with the Spanish military helmet once used by her father. The brochure prepared in 1975 for the opening of the Club de Exploraciones y Deportes Acuáticos de México describes the ensemble as follows: "Gonzalo contemplates the sea; the wind of the Caribbean rustles his hair. He is a sailor, and his gaze is a mixture of melancholy and challenge. . . . He is no longer alone but is bound by amorous ties to the children of the union with the noble Maya woman who calmly and serenely lifts her gaze to him while she nurses the youngest of their children. . . . A small boy embraces his father, and he, too, scrutinizes the distance, innocent of the imminent fall of his people before the foreign faith imposed with his people's blood. . . . Completing the scene is the small girl who, without knowing its origin, plays with the old helmet of her father. . . . She is open to the sun,

the air, and the water. She was born free and happy" (my translation). The sculpture and its verbal description summarize the two principal dimensions of the Gonzalo Guerrero tale in its sixteenth-century plenitude: the new domestic configuration of the mestizo family and the warrior Gonzalo's heroic defense of his new homeland. This chapter rewrites and augments my "La estatua de Gonzalo Guerrero."

2. Savater, "Presentación," 4 (my translation).

3. Magnus Mörner's *Race Mixture in the History of Latin America* and Alejandro Lipschutz's *El problema racial en la conquista de América*, which includes five pages on Gonzalo Guerrero, are classics in this field. Discriminatory prohibitions against persons of mixed race started appearing in the last quarter of the sixteenth century in the form of royal decrees as well as ordinances from viceroys, judges of the Audiencias, and local governmental officials (*corregidores, gobernadores*) (Lipschutz, *El problema*, 250). Guaman Poma de Ayala harangues about the proliferation of mestizos and the decline of the Andean race, and El Inca Garcilaso proclaims pride in being a mestizo: "I call myself by that name in public and am proud of it, though in the Indies, if a person is told: 'You're a mestizo,' or 'He's a mestizo,' it is taken as an insult" [Me lo llamo yo a boca llena, y me honro con él. Aunque en Indias si a uno de ellos le dicen sois un mestizo o es un mestizo, lo toman por menosprecio (El Inca Garcilaso, *Obras* 2:373; *Royal Commentaries* 1:607 [bk. 9, chap. 31]). Both perspectives reveal, in the persons of these exact contemporaries, the tensions attendant on the larger political and cultural controversy.

4. Elliott, *Imperial Spain*, 217; see also Kamen, *Inquisition*, 122, 302.

5. Kamen, *Inquisition*, 115; see also Elliott, *Imperial Spain*, 104, 216–17.

6. Elliott, *Imperial Spain*, 104; Kamen, *Inquisition*, 8, 116–119.

7. Elliott, *Imperial Spain*, 218–221; see also Kamen, *Inquisition*, 120, 121. The limpieza statutes would come under serious attack from the Inquisition by 1580, and this opposition was led at every stage by inquisitors general and officials of the Inquisition as well as by influential ministers of state, such as the duke of Lerma and the count-duke of Olivares. The official apparatus of limpieza, however, was in place until a law of May 16, 1865, abolished "proofs of purity for marriages and for certain government posts." Limpieza thus outlasted the definitive abolition of the Inquisition in 1834, revealing that it formed part of a discriminatory social system rather than a requirement imposed by strictly religious or ecclesiastical criteria (Kamen, *Inquisition*, 131–32, idem, *Spanish Inquisition*, 304).

8. Kamen, *Inquisition*, 121–22, 285n22.

9. I have in mind Fray Jerónimo de Román y Zamora's *Repúblicas del mundo* (1575). See Adorno, "Censorship," 813–815, idem, "Sobre la censura," 17–26.

10. Kamen, *Inquisition*, 118–19.

11. Greenleaf, *Zumárraga*, 85–86. Although the burning of a lord of Texcoco resulted in exempting the natives from the jurisdiction of the Holy Office, they would be under some form of inquisitorial jurisdiction until 1571, when Phi-

lip II put them under the direct control of the bishops in all matters of faith and customs (93).

12. Greenleaf, *Zumárraga*, 114–115, 117.

13. Kamen, *Inquisition*, 122.

14. On the subject of circumcision, Archbishop Zumárraga prosecuted Juan de Baeza in 1540 on charges of observing Jewish rites and prosyletizing, allegedly circumcising Indian boys by using his fingernails as the cutting instrument (Greenleaf, *Zumárraga*, 119).

15. Anghiera, *Décadas*, 238, 417–18 [dec. 2, bk. 43; dec. 4, bk. 6]; Gómara, *Historia* 26 [chap. 12]; Martínez, ed., *Documentos*, 47–48. Anghiera gave this account of the ship's fate not only in his second "Decade," published in 1516, but also in his fourth, published in 1520.

16. Martínez, ed., *Documentos*, 48, 53.

17. Cortés refers to Doña Marina briefly on just two occasions, in his second and fifth letters: "my interpreter, who is an Indian woman from Potonchán," and "the interpreter with whom he was speaking, Marina, who traveled always in my company after she had been given to me as a present with twenty other women" [la lengua que yo tengo, que es una india de esta tierra que hobe en Putunchán; aquella lengua que con él hablaba, que es Marina, la que yo conmigo siempre he traído, porque allí me la habían dado con otras veinte mujeres] (Cortés, *Letters*, 73, 376, 464–465; idem, *Cartas*, 192, 575). Bernal Díaz (*Historia verdadera* 1:123–124 [chap. 37]) devotes a whole chapter to her. Sandra Cypess's *La Malinche* analyzes the historical figure and the creation of the myth about her, from the colonial period to present times.

18. Cortés, *Cartas*, 124; idem, *Letters*, 17.

19. See chapter 7 for Bernal Díaz's use of such documents of collective testimony. It was Thomas (*Conquest*, 678n34) who identified Cortés's questionnaire as the ultimate source for the history of the shipwreck victim. Most other scholarly and literary critical accounts of Gonzalo Guerrero (Lipschutz, "En defensa"; idem, *El problema*; Martínez Marín, "La aculturación"; Torres Ramírez, "La odisea"; and Rico, "Gonzalo") fail to take into account this earliest, revealing testimony by Hernán Cortés in 1534.

20. The investigation of Cortés's governorship had been initiated eight years earlier, in 1526, by the judge [*oidor*] Luis Ponce de León (Martínez, *Hernán Cortés*, 898). According to Martínez (*Hernán Cortés*, 574–575), Cortés himself must have elaborated this and another interrogatorio with the help of some of his captains and soldiers whose memories about events that occurred a decade and a half earlier were still somewhat fresh. Cortés's aim was to provide public testimony to his deeds from the 1518 departure from Cuba through 1526. These documents are transcribed in *Colección de documentos inéditos* (CDI 27:301–569, 28:388–429).

21. Tozzer, ed., *Landa's Relación*, 8n38.

22. As discussed in chapters 4 and 5, this popular hypothesis pits Spanish "superiority" against Maya "inferiority" insofar as the Mayas' successful resistance

of conquest, so goes the argument, must have been a Spanish, not Maya, achievement, because of the Mayas' "natural inferiority" as warriors. This is Sepúlveda's interpretation of Aristotle's natural slavery concept as the Spanish humanist applied it to the conduct of Amerindians in the war of conquest in his *Demócrates Segundo*.

23. CDI 27:322–23.

24. Tozzer ed., *Landa's Relación*, 8n38; Torres Ramírez, "La odisea," 386.

25. Oviedo, *Historia general* 3:255 [bk. 32, chap. 8].

26. Ibid., 3:233 [bk. 32, chap. 3].

27. Ibid., 2:233–34 [bk. 32, chap. 3].

28. Ibid., 3:244, 246 [bk. 32, chap. 6].

29. Tozzer, ed., *Landa's Relación*, 8n38; Thomas, *Cortés*, 678n34.

30. Oviedo, *Historia general* 3:232–33, 259 [bk. 32, chap. 3, bk. 33, chap. 1].

31. Elliott, *Imperial Spain*, 220, 221.

32. Gómara, *Conquista*, 26 [chap. 12].

33. Ibid.; idem, *Historia* 77 [chap. 53]. The creation of mestizo communities began early. One notable occurrence was the 1499 rebellion of the magistrate (*alcalde mayor*) Francisco Roldán against the governorship of Diego Colón in Santo Domingo. Roldán and his men settled in the province of Xaraguá. Hernando Colón reported that "they chose to settle in this province because it was the pleasantest and most fertile part of the island [Hispaniola], with the most civilized natives and especially the best-looking and best-natured women in the country: This last was their strongest motive for going there" (my translation) [Con resolución de ir a la provincia de Xaraguá, de donde hacía poco que había llegado el Adelantado, con ánimo de quedarse allí, por ser la tierra más abundante y deliciosa de la isla, y por tener la gente más discreta y avisada, en comparación con los otros pueblos de la Española; y especialmente por ser allí las mujeres más hermosas y de agradable trato que en otra parte; y esto era lo que más les animaba para irse allí] (Colón, *Life*, 194–195; idem, *Vida*, 234–235 [chap. 75]). Roldán created his own enemies when he refused to permit Alonso de Hojeda to take as his wife a daughter of Anacaona, "the principal queen of Xaraguá" [que era la principal reina de Xaraguá] (Colón, *Life*, 218; idem, *Vida*, 258 [chap. 84]). My colleague Stuart B. Schwartz ("Spaniards," 7) cites Las Casas's report that "seventy Spaniards, most of them hidalgos," married native women in the newly settled Spanish villa of Vera Paz, also in the Xaraguá province of Hispaniola. See Mörner, *Race*; Lipschutz, *El problema*; Schwartz, "Spaniards"; and Álvarez, "Mestizos," on these early communities.

34. Gerhard, *Southeast Frontier*, 56. See Chamberlain, *The Conquest*.

35. These new elements consist of (1) the text of the letter Cortés wrote to the shipwreck victims, (2) the transport of the letter in the hair of one of the Indian messengers so that it "would not be seen by Indian spies," (3) the name of the captain (Juan de Escalante) who commanded the rescue vessel, (4) the fact that Pedro de Alvarado's ship, after leaving Cozumel, had trouble and

was forced to return to the island, (5) the presence of only Cortés and fifty men when the captive (Jerónimo de Aguilar) arrived in a canoe, (6) the assignment of Andrés de Tapia to the task of awaiting and receiving the arrival of the captive (Aguilar), (7) Aguilar's conversation with Tapia's company: "Sirs, are you Christians?," (8) the explanation of the shipwreck as being ultimately due to "the passions and misfortunes of Diego de Nicuesa and Vasco Núñez Balboa" in Darién (Gómara, *Conquista*, 24–26 [chaps. 11–12]).

36. "¡Desventurada de mí! Éste es mi hijo y mi bien" (Gómara, *Conquista*, 27 [chap. 11]).

37. The issue of having a family to support and protect was a familiar concern for Bernal Díaz. As mentioned earlier, he made the point at the end of the *Historia verdadera* that he was poor and old and that he had a daughter of marrying age, sons who'd sprouted beards, and younger children for whom he needed to provide ["una hija para casar y los hijos varones ya grandes y con barbas y otros por criar"] (Bernal Díaz, *Historia verdadera* 2:365 [chap. 210]).

38. Díaz del Castillo, *Historia verdadera* 1:98 [chap. 27]; my translation.

39. Ibid., my translation. Fray Diego López de Cogollado repeats Bernal Díaz's memorable speech in his *Historia de Yucatán* (1688) (23 [bk. 1, chap. 7]).

40. Díaz del Castillo, *Historia verdadera* 1:102 [chap. 29].

41. Sepúlveda, *Historia*, 97 [bk. 3, par. 6].

42. Alfonso X, *Siete partidas*, part. 2, tit.13, law 16 (1: fols. 38v–39r).

43. Landa, *Relación*, 44 [chap. 2]); Gómara, *Conquista*, 26 [chap. 12].

44. Landa, *The Maya*, 33 [chap. 2].

45. Cervantes de Salazar, *Crónica*, 116 [bk. 2, chap. 27]); Gómara, *Conquista*, 26 [chap. 12].

46. Herrera y Tordesilla, *Historia* 4:324 [dec. 2, bk. 4, chap. 7]); Torquemada, *Monarquía indiana*, 370 [bk. 4, chap. 9]).

47. AGI, Justicia 229, fols. 4r–14v. After participating in the torture and execution of the Cazonci of Michoacán, García del Pilar gave sworn testimony against Nuño de Guzmán in the investigations carried out later (García Icazbalceta, *Colección*, xlii–xliv). Guzmán, the first president of the Audiencia de Nueva España, governor of Pánuco, and later governor of Nueva Galicia, replied to García del Pilar's charges in the *probanza* [sworn oral testimony, written down and certified] cited above. In that testimony Guzmán also claimed that García del Pilar was known for performing native rituals and dancing in the flayed skin of war captives. As governor of Nueva Galicia, Guzmán received Cabeza de Vaca and his companions upon their return to Spanish territory in 1536 (see chapter 10). Nuño de Guzmán's life and career and García del Pilar's role in its major events are examined in Adorno and Pautz, *Alvar Núñez* 3:325–381.

48. Alva Ixtlilxochitl, *Historia*, 196 [chap. 78].

49. Muñoz Camargo, *Historia*, 189 [bk. 2, chap. 2].

50. Gómara, *Conquista*, 25 [chap. 12]); Díaz del Castillo, *Historia verdadera* 1:103; idem, *True History* 1:101 [chap. 29].

51. Muñoz Camargo, *Historia*, 189 [bk. 2, chap. 2]), and Alva Ixtlilxochitl, *Historia*, 198 [chap. 79].

52. Solís y Rivadeneira, *Historia*, 56 [bk. 1, chap. 16].

53. Olaechea Labayen, *El mestizaje*, 266–267.

54. Publications worthy of mention include *Gonzalo de Guerrero, padre del mestizaje iberoamericano*, edited by Mario Aguirre Rosas (Mexico City, 1975); *Gonzalo Guerrero, novela histórica* by Eugenio Aguirre (Mexico City, 1980), which won a silver medal in 1981 from the International Academy of Lutece in Paris; *Gonzalo Guerrero, el primer aliado de los mayas* by Salomón González-Blanco Garrido (Mexico City, 1991); *Conquistadores de Yucatán: La desaparición de Gonzalo Guerrero*, in the series "Relatos del Nuevo Mundo," by the Sociedad Estatal Quinto Centenario (Madrid, 1992); *Historias de la conquista del Mayab, 1511–1697* by Fray Joseph de San Buenaventura, edited by Gabriela Solís Robleda and Pedro Bracamonte y Sosa (Mérida, 1994); and *Gonzalo Guerrero, memoria olvidada* by Carlos Villa Royz (Mexico City, 1995). The books edited by Aguirre Rosas and by Solís Robleda and Bracamonte y Sosa are presented as autobiographical accounts by Gonzalo Guerrero himself, written, according to the editors, on European paper and deerskin, respectively (Aguirre Rosas, *Gonzalo*, 66; San Buenaventura, *Historias*, 9; Solís and Bracamonte, "Introducción," xiv). The others are fictionalizations based on the presumably historical person; in this category, González-Blanco Garrido's book and the picture book *Conquistadores de Yucatán* are aimed at a juvenile audience. As previously mentioned, Gonzalo appears in Tzvetan Todorov's essay, *La conquista de América* (1982) as well as in Hugh Thomas's history of the conquest of Mexico, *Conquest: Montezuma, Cortés, and the Fall of Old Mexico* (1993).

55. Aguirre Rosas, *Gonzalo*, 59, 66, 69, 78, 86, 87.

56. Solís Robleda and Bracamonte y Sosa, "Introducción," xii, xv, xix. Hanns J. Prem, Berthold Riege, and Antje Gunsenheimer ("En torno," 4), anthropologists at the University of Bonn, argue on the basis of the account's contents, cited above, that there is no evidence to support its identification as the memoirs of the sixteenth-century shipwreck victim; Gabriela Solís Robledo, an anthropologist and coeditor of the San Buenaventura manuscript, claims it is authentic ("En torno," 5).

57. Solís Robleda and Bracamonte y Sosa, "Introducción," xii–xiii, xv. They report that a copy of the 1725 Fray Ventura manuscript is housed in CONDUMEX, the Centro de Estudios de Historia de México (xi).

58. San Buenaventura, *Historia*, 50, 52, 54, 55.

CHAPTER 10. THE NARRATIVE REINVENTION OF THE CONQUEROR-CAPTIVE

1. On deducing Cabeza de Vaca's date of birth, see Adorno and Pautz, *Álvar Núñez* 1:343–350; regarding his death, ibid., 1:407–410.

2. The Cabeza de Vaca lineage is traced back fifteen generations to circa 1200,

and the Vera genealogy has been traced back six generations. See the genealogical tables in ibid., 1:306, 314, 324, and see ibid., 1:298–308 for the narrative account of Cabeza de Vaca's life on which this summary is based.

3. See ibid., 1:350–366.

4. Cabeza de Vaca in ibid., 1:181. All quotations of Cabeza de Vaca's *Relación* are from our English translation (ibid., 1:14–279), which accompanies the facing-page transcription of the original 1542 Spanish language text. Ours is the first transcription of the 1542 version; all Spanish-language editions from Barcia's in the 1730s onward are based on the 1555 version. The substantive differences between the 1542 and 1555 versions are analyzed in ibid., 3:84–97.

5. See ibid., 1:366–369.

6. See ibid., 1:382–402.

7. Nevertheless, the royal license to print the 1555 edition of his work, which was signed by the Infanta Juana (daughter of Charles V and Isabel of Portugal) on behalf of her brother, Prince Philip (the future Philip II), identified Cabeza de Vaca by his Río de la Plata title of governor. Ironically, by apparent bureaucratic error the phrase that appeared in the royal license, "el governador Álvar Núñez Cabeza de Vaca," mistakenly referred to the Narváez expedition to North America (ibid., 1:283, 382–402). In the body of Cabeza de Vaca's published *Relación*, he is erroneously referred to as the chief law enforcement official (*alguacil mayor*), which was a royally appointed office held by the captain of the expedition, Pánfilo de Narváez (ibid., 1:22–23; 2:21).

8. Wagner, "The First Lost Letter," 672.

9. "Y aunque la inuidia trabaje de impedir y estoruar esta tan deuida y necessaria obra, la clara virtud y merescimientos de tales príncipes nos defenderá, dándonos Dios la paz, sossiego y tranquilidad que en tiempo de los buenos reyes abundantíssimamente suele dar" (Cabeza de Vaca, *Relación*, ed. Serrano y Sanz, 1:152–153 [proem]; my translation).

10. Adorno and Pautz, *Álvar Núñez* 1:407–412.

11. Cabeza de Vaca in ibid., 1:19.

12. Covarrubias, *Tesoro*, 597, 923; Castile 1:f24r–v [pt. 2, tit. 9, law 10]; Oviedo, *Historia* 3:603; Adorno and Pautz, *Álvar Núñez*, 1:177.

13. Adorno and Pautz, *Álvar Núñez*, 2:253–257.

14. Cabeza de Vaca in ibid., 1:112–115; ibid., 2:281.

15. Cabeza de Vaca in ibid., 1:118–173; ibid., 2:281–284.

16. Ibid., 2:16, 2:249–253.

17. This section is based on my essay "Cómo leer Mala Cosa."

18. Radin, *The Trickster*, xxiii, 132.

19. Cabeza de Vaca in Adorno and Pautz, *Álvar Núñez*, 1:167.

20. These extraneous materials are included as an appendix (Sahagún, *Historia*, 904–909). On Sahagún's work, see the section entitled "Amerindian Culture and Censorship in Sahagún and Acosta," in chapter 8.

21. This tradition involved the principal protagonists of two hero cycles who de-

feated their enemies by failing to restore them after heart sacrifice and bodily dismemberment (Tedlock, ed. and trans., *Popol Vuh*, 153–155).

22. Lowery, *Spanish Settlements*, 202; Grinnell, *Pawnee Hero Stories*, 227–229, 374.

23. Casas, *Apologética* 1:483, see 1:481–485 [bk. 3, chap. 93].

24. Cabeza de Vaca in Adorno and Pautz, *Álvar Núñez* 1:169.

25. Phelan, *Millennial Kingdom*, 30; see 29–38.

26. Gómara, *Historia*, 8 [dedication].

27. See Adorno and Pautz, *Álvar Núñez* 2:344–346, 386.

28. Cabeza de Vaca in ibid., 1:239.

29. In "The Negotiation of Fear in Cabeza de Vaca's 'Naufragios,'" I argued that Cabeza de Vaca reveals, probably inadvertently, that the native lords, not he and his companions, were the protagonists of the series of actions that led the four men forward on their ten-month overland journey (1535–36), all the way from eastern Mexico to its western shore (see fig. 23).

30. As a component of the first important body of law explicitly concerned with the protocols for conducting conquests, the *requerimiento* provided the mechanism whereby Spanish military captains were to inform the Indians whose submission they sought that the Christians had been "sent to teach them good customs, to dissuade them from vices such as the practice of eating human flesh, and to instruct them in the holy faith and preach it to them for their salvation" (Hanke, "Development" 75, 78).

31. Promulgated in Granada on November 17, 1526, the legal criteria for waging a just war against the Indians were as follows: (1) the natives' refusal of obedience to the crown as offered to them by the reading of the *requerimiento,* and/or (2) their armed resistance or defense against the Spaniards' attempts to look for mines or to remove gold or other precious metals (CDU 9:276–77). This body of law was included in the *capitulaciones* signed by Pánfilo de Narváez on December 11, 1526 (CDI 22:224–45; Vas Mingo, *Las capitulaciones de Indias*, 236).

32. Hanke, "Studies," 147–149; Manzano Manzano, *La incorporación*, 37. The account of the junta that formulated the requerimiento is transcribed in CDI 1:441–450. See Adorno and Pautz, *Álvar Núñez* 2:12–15.

33. Oviedo, *Historia* 3:27–29, 31–32 [bk. 29, chap. 7].

34. Casas, *Historia* 3:28 [bk. 3, chap. 57]; see Wagner and Parish, *Life and Writings*, 190n17; Zavala, *La filosofía*, 25–26.

35. Cabeza de Vaca in Adorno and Pautz, *Álvar Núñez* 1:259.

36. The baptism of all Indians held in encomienda had been mandated in the Laws of Burgos of December 27, 1512 (reproduced in Rumeu de Armas, *La política indigenista*, 435–453). In circumstances where clergy were unavailable to do so, a Christian layman in charge of the settlement was required to perform the ceremony. Such was evidently the case here. The provision for the Christian education of the sons of native lords was also made in the Burgos legislation of 1512; thus the selection of these particular children conformed to the standard practice (Rumeu de Armas, *La política indigenista*, 443, 445).

37. Gómara, *Historia general*, 67 [chap. 46].

38. Casas, *Apologética* 1:651 [bk. 3, chap. 124].

39. "Grande y grandísima es la propincuidad, aptitud y propinquísima disposición que aquellas gentes tienen para venir en cognoscimiento de nuestro y suyo verdadero Dios. Plega al mismo Dios que les envíe sus siervos y verdaderos predicadores, pues las crió y redimió. No sé cuál es el ánima que questo leyere y oyere, si tiene sincero amor de Dios, que no gima y sospire por ser tan dichoso que para vaso en que vaya y llegue a aquellas hambrientas y ignorantes y tan dispuestas gentes, su nombre y lumbre, le elija y mueva Dios" (Casas, *Apologética* 2:181–182 [bk, 3, chap. 168]).

40. Among the "final blunders" of conversion by force that Las Casas identified was the imposition of crosses because, without proper instruction regarding their symbolic meaning, the natives, he suggested, would simply adore the cross as a new idol, "mistaking that stick for the Christian's god": "y así los harán idolatrar, adorando por Dios aquel palo" (Casas, *Historia* 3:232 [bk. 3, chap. 117]).

41. This tendency contrasts the interest in geographical location of Cabeza de Vaca's earliest readers, who were sixteenth-century explorers and conquistadores seeking sources of information about peoples to colonize and mines to exploit. For those early readings, see Adorno and Pautz, *Álvar Núñez* 3:132–135, 141–150.

42. León, *Historia de Nuevo León*, 14 [proem]. He had arrived in the province in 1636, and he had been among the early settlers who followed Luis de Carbajal, whom Philip II had commissioned in 1583 to carry out the conquest of the vast territory that ultimately extended two hundred leagues north from the banks of the Pánuco River (in today's Tamaulipas) and again as many leagues inland from the coast of the Gulf of Mexico.

43. See Reff, Ahern, and Danford, eds., *History of the Triumphs;* Ahern, "The Cross and the Gourd"; idem, "Dichosas muertes."

44. Pérez de Ribas, *Historia*, 24 [bk. 1, chap. 7]; Sauer, "The Road," 51.

45. Pérez de Ribas, *Historia*, 25–26, 120 [bk. 1, chap. 7, bk. 2, chap. 33].

46. Robertson, ed. and trans., *My Life*, 8 [bk. 1, chap. 7].

47. Pérez de Ribas, *Historia*, 120, 121 [bk. 2, chap. 33].

48. Andrés González de Barcia's publication of the *Naufragios* in Madrid in the early 1730s and his republication of it in 1749 were the first editions published since 1555; see Adorno and Pautz, *Álvar Núñez* 3:177–179. When Barcia's edition was reedited by Enrique de Vedia in 1852 and appeared as volume 22 of the collection Biblioteca de Autores Españoles, also in Madrid, it secured a canonical place in Spanish literature and history as a work in the two-volume series *Historiadores primitivos de Indias*, which modeled itself on Barcia's three-volume *Historiadores primitivos de las Indias Occidentales* of 1749.

49. It was 1621, not 1728, as Pupo-Walker, *Los naufragios*, 157, claims.

50. Acosta described Cabeza de Vaca and his fellows as being "favored by God with the gift of making cures and performing apostolic works," and he refers

to "some miracles that God has worked in the Indies for the benefit of the faith, without regard to the merits of those who performed them," calling Cabeza de Vaca and his companions "evangelical physicians" (Acosta, *De procuranda*, 314–315 [bk. 2, chap. 9]; idem, *Historia natural y moral*, 371–372 [bk. 7, chap. 27]).

51. Ardoino, *Examen apologético*, 1.

52. Mota Padilla was a layman and viceregal official from Guadalajara; Beaumont was a Franciscan friar; each wrote a political and spiritual history of Nueva Galicia and Michoacán.

53. The legendary hagiographic traditions attributed to Cabeza de Vaca's *Relación* by some literary historians and critics applies in fact to the later readings and appropriations of Cabeza de Vaca's text but is not a feature of the *Relación* itself; this distinction is of some importance in understanding the ebb and flow of the interpretation of the tale over time.

54. Buckingham Smith (1851, 1871), Brownie Ponton and Bates McFarland (1898), O. W. Williams (1899), James Baskett (1907), and Harbert Davenport and Joseph K. Wells (1918–1919), whose study of Cabeza de Vaca's route was entitled "The First Europeans in Texas," were the notable students and exponents of this trend. See volume 2 of Adorno and Pautz, *Álvar Núñez*, where the work of these route interpreters, along with that of their successors Carl O. Sauer (1932), Cleve Hallenbeck (1940), Alex Krieger (1955, 1961, [rpt. 2005]) and T. J. and T. N. Campbell (1981) are discussed. Adorno and Pautz (1999) are among the most recent students of the Cabeza de Vaca route.

55. Sauer, "The Road," 1–2.

56. When the writer Sharman Apt Russell wrote to me from her home in Mimbres, New Mexico, several years ago to contact me about citing my scholarly work in a work of her own, she ended her letter by stating, "I'd also like some sense of why you chose to write about Cabeza de Vaca and of how this research fits into your larger field of work (or your life). I enclose a self-addressed stamped envelope for your reply." I have corresponded with her over the years, but I have never answered that particular query, and I still have the self-addressed stamped envelope—with its now-outdated postage— to prove it. Yet I am obviously persuaded that the question is a serious one and that scholarly passions are as obscure to explain as any other kind.

57. See Adorno and Pautz, "Introduction," 33–36; Adorno, "The Cabeza de Vaca Phenomenon," 14–18, for an overview of these readings.

58. Adorno and Pautz, *Álvar Núñez* 2:414; see ibid., 414–422.

59. His character has been fictionalized at least twice in novels written in the first person, first in juvenile literature in Helen Rand Parish's *Estebanico* (1974), and then in Daniel Panger's novel *Black Ulysses* (1982). In the world of academic reference, the 1994 volume *Historic World Leaders* includes a short essay on "Estevan (d. 1539)," as a "black explorer, who helped open what would become the southwestern United States to Spanish settlement" (Alves, "Estevan," 256).

60. Gates and McKay, eds., *The Norton Anthology*, 2612.

61. The debt of Saer and Posse to Alejo Carpentier's last novel, *El arpa y la sombra* (1979), must be acknowledged. Carpentier's Christopher Columbus on his deathbed has a similar but opposite objective: not how to reveal, but rather how to hide the secrets of his maritime career, already made public in his writings, from his last confessor. The burden of history lies heavily on all three fictional memorialists.

62. See Díaz Quiñones, "Las palabras de la tribu," on Saer's *El entenado*.

63. My translations of "Dicen que ud. tiene una versión secreta, una tercera versión de su viaje o su caminata de ocho años desde la Florida hasta Mexico" and "No tengo paciencia con la prestigiosa mentira de la exactitud" (Posse, *El largo atardecer*, 30, 35).

64. Borges, "The Ethnographer," trans. Hurley, 334.

65. Ibid., 335.

CHAPTER 11. FROM GUANCANE TO MACONDO:
LITERARY PLACES AND THEIR PREDECESSORS

1. Garcilaso's references to the work's title as *Naufragios* reveal that he read the second edition of the work, published in 1555 in Valladolid.

2. Garcilaso, *The Florida*, 11–12; idem, *La Florida*, 16–17 [bk. 1, chap. 3]. The year was 1527, not 1557; the English translation repeats the error of 1537, which had appeared in the second Spanish-language edition. There were only two other Spaniards, Andrés Dorantes and Alonso del Castillo Maldonado, in addition to Dorantes's black Moroccan slave Estevan (Estevanico in the *Relación*), who survived; hence the reference to "five" should instead be "four."

3. Scholars have cited the oral testimony of Gonzalo Silvestre and the written accounts of Alonso de Carmona and Juan Coles, among expeditionaries, and the works of Spanish and Italian authors among his learned sources (Miró Quesada, *El Inca Garcilaso*, 145–163). Hilton ("Introducción," 52) asserts the "minimal presence" of Cabeza de Vaca and others. Lafaye ("Los milagros," 77) observed that Garcilaso elevated Cabeza de Vaca's account by affirming outright (something that Cabeza de Vaca himself never did) that Cabeza de Vaca and his companions had performed miracles; he also noted that Garcilaso changed Cabeza de Vaca's report of the Indians' reference to his companions and himself from "children of the sun" [hijos del sol] to the more bold and unequivocal "deities" [dioses]. Pupo-Walker (*Historia*, 78) rightly intuited but did not develop the observation that Cabeza de Vaca's *Naufragios* "apparently inspire some of the most dramatic and spectacular passages" of the work.

4. An earlier version of this chapter was published in Spanish under the title "De Guancane a Macondo."

5. The resonance of the writings of Columbus and Cortés are found in Cabeza de Vaca's accounts of Amerindian responses to the presence of Europeans as well as in his notions about the South Sea. In turn, Spanish, *criollo*, Euro-

pean, and American readings of Cabeza de Vaca's *Relación* or *Naufragios* over the centuries constitute a literary tradition of considerable variety and longevity (Adorno, "Negotiation," 173–196; Adorno and Pautz, *Álvar Núñez* 3:119–173; Adorno and Pautz in Cabeza de Vaca, *Narrative,* 29–36; see chapter 10).

6. This is the phenomenon that Borges described when he observed that Robert Browning's poem "Fears and Scruples" prophesies the work of Kafka, but that our reading of Kafka perfects and perceptibly alters our reading of Browning's poem [El poema *Fears and Scruples* de Robert Browning profetiza la obra de Kafka, pero nuestra lectura de Kafka afina y desvía sensiblemente nuestra lectura del poema]. Borges's reflection continues: "Browning did not read it as we do today. In the critical vocabulary the word 'precursor' is indispensable, but one would need to purify it from all connotations of polemic or rivalry. The fact is that every writer creates his own precursors" [Browning no lo leía como ahora nosotros lo leemos. En el vocabulario crítico, la palabra precursor es indispensable, pero habría que tratar de purificarla de toda connotación de polémica o rivalidad. El hecho es que cada escritor crea a sus precursores (Borges, "Kafka," 89; my translation)].

7. Vas Mingo, *Las capitulaciones,* 234.

8. On Ayllón's activities and explorations in the gulf area and La Florida (1520–1526), see Adorno and Pautz, *Álvar Núñez* 2:271–278, 280–281.

9. See Adorno and Pautz (ibid., 2:227–245) for a synthesis and overview of Garay's activities in the northern Gulf of Mexico, based on primary sources. He initiated and supervised the earliest Spanish explorations of the gulf.

10. Garcilaso, *The Florida,* 6–7; idem, *La Florida,* 13 [bk. 1, chap. 2].

11. These included, as listed according to volume and page numbers in Cabeza de Vaca in Adorno y Pautz, *Álvar Núñez,* the Indians of the peninsular area of present-day Florida (1:62); those of the island of Malhado in Galveston Bay, off the Texas coast (1:106–110); the groups of the Texas coast (1:136–146); and the groups of the interior of the North American continent from Galveston Bay to the Rio Grande (1:176–190); those who inhabited the area along the coast of Texas and the inland area adjacent to it (1:200–201); the groups of the east coast of Mexico plus those of the adjacent inland areas (1:198–199); those of the northern interior of Mexico (1:234–237); those groups of the coastal area of western Mexico (1:234–237); and, finally, the groups of the Mexican northwest (1:250–251).

12. Cabeza de Vaca in Adorno and Pautz, *Álvar Núñez* 1:262–263.

13. Garcilaso, *The Florida,* 593; idem, *La Florida,* 412 [bk. 6, chap. 9]; my emphasis.

14. Garcilaso, *The Florida,* xxxvii; Garcilaso, *La Florida,* 5 [prologue]. In the chapter "An objection, or counter-view is answered," Garcilaso mentions the author of the oral account that he follows as a source but without naming him: "I have simply recorded the words of another who witnessed and supervised the writing personally" (Garcilaso, *The Florida,* 158; idem, *La Florida,* 112 [bk. 2, pt. 1, chap. 27]) (Miró Quesada, *El Inca Garcilaso,* 148–149).

15. Garcilaso, *The Florida*, 158; idem, *La Florida*, 112 [lib. 2, pt. 1, chap. 27].

16. Upon citing some of the letters received by his father in his office as civil administrador (*corregidor*) of the municipality of Cuzco, Garcilaso declared that he had in his hands all the letters his father wrote to the many parts of the empire ("Yo tuve ambas las cartas en mis manos, que entonces yo servía a mi padre de escribiente en todas las cartas que escribía a diversas partes de aquel imperio") (Garcilaso, *Obras* 4:137 [pt. 1, lib. 8, cap. 6]). He also proudly claims that he had been able to decipher the *quipus*, or Andean record-keeping system of knotted cords, that contained the accounts of the tribute paid by the Indians, and that the native lords asked that he verify the accounts because, "as suspicious people, they did not trust the Spaniards to tell them the truth on those particulars until I verified it for them, reading to them the written calculations of the tribute that they brought and comparing it with their cords; and in this manner I know as much about them [the quipus] as the Indians" [porque como gente sospechosa, no se fiaban de los españoles que les tratasen verdad en aquel particular hasta que yo les certificaba de ella, leyéndoles los traslados que de sus tributos me traían y cotejándolos con sus ñudos; y de esta manera supe de ellos tanto como los indios] (Garcilaso, *Obras* 2:206 [pt. 1, lib. 6, cap. 9]).

17. Garcilaso, *The Florida*, 460; idem, *La Florida*, 322 [bk. 4, chap. 14].

18. As demonstrated earlier, Bartolomé de las Casas read and relied on Cabeza de Vaca's testimony, citing the 1542 version of his work under the title *Relación*. See chapters 3 and 10; also Adorno, "The Discursive Encounter," 220–27; Adorno and Pautz, *Álvar Núñez* 3:137–139.

19. Garcilaso, *The Florida*, 13; idem, *La Florida*, 18 [bk. 1, chap. 4].

20. Cabeza de Vaca in Adorno and Pautz, *Álvar Núñez* 1:262–263.

21. Garcilaso, *The Florida*, 15, 449; idem, *La Florida*, 19, 314 [bk. 1, chap. 4; bk. 4, chap. 10].

22. Garcilaso, *The Florida*, 16; idem, *La Florida*, 19 [bk. 1, chap. 4].

23. Cabeza de Vaca in Adorno and Pautz, *Álvar Núñez* 1:104–107. Later, in chapter 17 of the *Naufragios*, Cabeza de Vaca (in Adorno and Pautz, *Álvar Núñez* 1:134–135 [fol. 31r]) had written about how the men who left Malhado (the Galveston Island area of eastern coastal Texas) in the spring of 1529 to pursue a path southward to Pánuco eventually began to die and of how "the flesh of those who died was jerked by the others." This episode, however, lacks any expression of the Indians' horror that Cabeza de Vaca described in the earlier case.

24. Garcilaso, *The Florida*, 186; idem, *La Florida* 131 [bk. 2, pt. 2, chap. 4].

25. For an analysis of the last fifty days of the overland expedition and the raft voyage along the gulf, see Adorno and Pautz, *Álvar Núñez* 2:134–135, 142–163.

26. Cabeza de Vaca, in ibid., 1:72–73.

27. Garcilaso, *The Florida*, xli, 434; idem, *La Florida*, 7, 304 [prologue; bk. 4, chap. 6].

28. Clayton et al., *DeSoto Chronicles* 2:310.

29. Hernández de Biedma in ibid., 1:239; Hernández de Biedma in Smith, *Colección*, 58.

30. Hernández de Biedma in Clayton et al., *DeSoto Chronicles*, 1:239–40; Hernández de Biedma in Smith, *Colección*, 58–59.

31. Columbus (*Textos*, 142) wrote, "Y no conocían ninguna seta ni idolatría, salvo que todos creen que las fuerças y el bien es en el cielo, y creían muy firme que yo con estos navíos y gente venía del cielo y en tal catamiento me recibían en todo cabo después de haver perdido el miedo." Although most translators render "cielo" as "heaven," Samuel Eliot Morison (*English Translation*, 10) resisted the temptation: "And they know neither sect nor idolatry, with the exception that all believe that the source of all power and goodness is in the sky, and they believe very firmly that I, with these ships and people, came from the sky, and in this belief they everywhere received me, after they had overcome their fear." See Adorno and Pautz (*Álvar Núñez* 2:352–358) for a survey of the tradition of "men come down from heaven" in the foundational texts of Columbus, Las Casas, Hernando Colón, Fray Ramón Pané, Pietro Martire d'Anghiera, Cabeza de Vaca, and Oviedo.

32. Pagden ("Con título," 13) shows how the fictitious episode narrated by Cortés provided a parallel to the "equally fictitious Donation of Constantine, whereby Constantine the Great, the first Roman emperor to convert to Christianity, had supposedly transferred the Imperial capital to . . . Constantinople, so as to leave the Pope and his successors sovereignty over Italy and the countries of the West."

33. Valdeavillano, *Curso*, 429.

34. Cortés, *Cartas*, 211; idem, *Letters*, 86 [second letter].

35. Cabeza de Vaca in Adorno and Pautz, *Álvar Núñez*, 1:258–261.

36. Garcilaso, *The Florida*, 431–432; idem, *La Florida*, 302 [bk. 4, chap. 6].

37. Garcilaso, *The Florida*, 432; idem, *La Florida*, 302 [bk. 4, chap. 6].

38. Clayton et al. (*DeSoto Chronicles*, 2:434n) point out that a province called Guancane is not mentioned by any of the other Soto chroniclers. The questions raised by Garcilaso's naming of this province as a site of Spanish/ Amerindian interaction (or, better said, lack thereof) is examined below.

39. Cabeza de Vaca in Adorno y Pautz, *Álvar Núñez* 1:258–261. In the long passage quoted above, Garcilaso (*La Florida*, 336 [bk. 5, pt. 1, chap. 2]) wrote in error "Comentarios," which refers to the 1555 Valladolid publication's companion account of Cabeza de Vaca's governorship of Río de la Plata, written by his secretary, Pero Hernández. See Adorno and Pautz, *Álvar Núñez* 1:88–116, for the content and scope of the *Comentarios* in relation to the polemics surrounding Cabeza de Vaca's conduct of his governorship in Río de la Plata.

40. Garcilaso, *The Florida*, 483; idem, *La Florida*, 337 [bk. 5, pt. 1, chap. 2].

41. Cabeza de Vaca in Adorno and Pautz, *Álvar Núñez* 1:240.

42. Swanton, *Final Report*, 279.

43. Clayton et al., *DeSoto Chronicles* 1:434n34.
44. Swanton, *Final Report*, 278.
45. Garcilaso, *The Florida*, 484; idem, *La Florida*, 338 [lib. 5, pt. 1., chap. 3].
46. Swanton, *Final Report*, 53.
47. "Empero otros dicen que pasó mucho más adelante y ganó otros muchos pueblos y naciones que van por el camino de *Umasuyu*, que son *Cancalla, Cacha Rurucachi, Assillu, Asancatu, Huancani*, hasta el pueblo llamado *Pucara*" (Garcilaso, *Obras* 2:65; idem, *Royal Commentaries* 1:105; [pt. 1, bk. 2, chap. 16]).
48. Espinoza Galarza, *Toponimia*, 189, 244, 318.
49. Garcilaso, *The Florida*, 1:105; idem, *La Florida*, 2:66 [pt. 1, bk. 2, chap. 16].
50. The prefix *gua-*, common in the Taíno language, has been identified with the pronominal prefix *wa*, which is equivalent to "our" (Arrom, "Notas," 77n122).
51. Garcilaso, *The Florida*, 482; idem, *La Florida*, 336 [bk. 5, pt. 1, chap. 2].
52. Garcilaso, *The Florida*, 642; idem, *La Florida*, 447 [bk. 6, chap. 22].
53. Vaccarella, "Echoes," 114; Garcilaso, *The Florida*, 642; idem, *La Florida*, 448 [bk. 6, chap. 22].
54. Rulfo, *Pedro Páramo*, trans. Peden, 3; ibid., 7.
55. Ibid., 5–6; ibid., 9.
56. Ibid., 7–8; ibid., 11–12.
57. Ibid., 71; ibid., 76.
58. Ibid., 122; ibid., 128.
59. García Márquez, *Cien años*, 108–112.
60. Cabeza de Vaca in Adorno and Pautz, *Álvar Núñez* 1:238–239.
61. Acosta, *Historia*, 13 [proem].

CHAPTER 12. SEEING GHOSTS: THE LONGEVITY OF "SERPENTS IN SANDALS"

1. Arenas, *Ill-Fated Peregrinations*, 101; idem, *El mundo alucinante*, 113.
2. An earlier version of this chapter was published in Spanish under the title "Sombras y fantasmas: El pasado colonial en 'El mundo alucinante' de Reinaldo Arenas y en 'El arpa y la sombra' de Alejo Carpentier."
3. Las Casas is the object of Carpentier's memorable alliterative phrase "serpiente con sandalias," translated by Thomas and Carol Christenson, as might be expected, as "serpent in sandals," to which this chapter's title refers. (See Carpentier, *Harp*, 144–145; idem, *El arpa*, 208.) Quetzalcoatl, the object of the historical Mier's and the fictional Fray Servando's interest, provides "the plumed serpent," as the god portion of that ancient Mexican man/god was known. Accepting hypothetically Mier's argument about the identity of Quetzalcoatl/Santo Tomás, we could derive a "plumed serpent in sandals." This makes two of them, one ancient (Santo Tomás/Quetzalcoatl) and one modern ("Las Casas"), and hence "Serpents in Sandals."

4. Güiraldes, *Don Segundo,* 79. I thank my former student Benjamin Edmunds for bringing this quotation to my attention.

5. The popular terms "Apostle of the Indies" and "Apostle to the Indians" originated in the nineteenth century. Sir Arthur Helps's biography of Las Casas, *Life of Las Casas, the Apostle of the Indies* (1868), started a trend that continued throughout the nineteenth and twentieth centuries among Las Casas's biographers, those writing in Spanish as well as those in English (Wagner and Parish, *Life and Writings,* 241). Las Casas's official title, granted on September 17, 1516, by the Cardinal Adrian, acting as coregent of Spain, was "procurador general de los indios," that is, he was commissioned as "protector general" of all the Indians in the Antilles (the conquests of Mexico and Peru, the mainland phases of Spain's actions, would begin in 1519 and 1528, respectively). As protector general of the Indians, the thirty-three-year-old Las Casas was responsible for seeing to their welfare and giving full reports on their needs and progress to the royal court (MacNutt, *Bartholomew,* 86–87).

6. Arenas, *Ill-Fated Peregrinations,* 45; idem, *El mundo alucinante,* 56.

7. Sigüenza y Góngora, *Infortunios.* This brief description summarizes Leonard, *Don Carlos de Sigüenza,* 44–49.

8. "Como son crescidos de cuerpo y andan desnudos, desde lexos paresçen gigantes" (Cabeza de Vaca in Adorno and Pautz, *Álvar Núñez* 1:62–63.)

9. Ibid., 1:268–269; 2:397–398.

10. "Mi candor excluye todo fraude." This is apparently a direct citation from the historical Fray Servando's *Apología,* for so Arenas annotated it in the novel (Arenas, *Ill-Fated Peregrinations,* 59; idem, *El mundo alucinante,* 67). I have not located this quotation, but a similar one exists: "How am I to be [thought of as] arrogant, if I have never known neither ambition nor envy, the inseparable companions of pride? What characterizes me, in spite of my apparent perspicacity, is an immense candor, which is the source of my life's woes" [¿Cómo he de ser soberbio, si nunca he conocido ni la ambición, ni la envidia, compañeros inseparables del orgullo? Lo que tengo, a pesar de mi viveza aparente, es un candor inmenso, fuente de las desgracias de mi vida] (Mier y Noriega, *Apología,* 182).

11. Mier y Noriega, *Historia,* 147–148; see the section entitled "Las Casas, the New Laws, and the Black Legend," in chapter 3.

12. Herrera, *Historia general* 2:389 [dec. 1, bk. 4, chap. 12]; CDI 31:13–25. With regard to Las Casas's 1516 advocacy of sending more black (and white) slaves from North Africa to the Caribbean, he shared the general understanding at the time that these subjects had been captives taken from the enemy in the war against Islam, and that consequently such persons were enslaved as legitimate war booty (see the section entitled "Las Casas on African Slavery," in chapter 3). Though not responsible for introducing African slavery, he felt responsible for fomenting it. His acknowledgment of this in the *Historia de las Indias* reveals his sense of guilt and, indeed, fear or expectation of divine punishment for it (see chapter 3). This sense of Las Casas's judgment (and

self-judgment) has been brilliantly set forth by Antonio Benítez-Rojo in his essay "Presencia del texto lascasiano" (1987).

13. Arenas, *El mundo alucinante*, 57; my translation.

14. Carpentier, *Harp*, 144–145; idem, *El arpa*, 208.

15. Casas, *Apologética* 1:4 [argumento]; Carpentier, *Harp*, 145; idem, *El arpa*, 208.

16. Carpentier, *Harp*, 145; *El arpa*, 209. Carpentier's Las Casas responds to the question of the tribunal's president about the existence of anthropophagy among the Indians of the Americas as follows: "Not everywhere, although it is true that one will find instances in Mexico, but more for religious reasons than for other causes. But Herodotus, Pomponius Mela, and even Saint Jerome tell us that there were anthropophagi among the Scythians, Masagetas, and Scots" (Carpentier, *Harp*, 145; idem, *El arpa*, 209). Thus Carpentier summarizes the contents of a fragment of the *Apologética historia sumaria*, chapter 205, which offers Las Casas's survey of cannibalism in ancient and modern times, including Cabeza de Vaca's account of cannibalism among starving, stranded Spanish expeditionaries in coastal Texas (Casas, *Apologética* 2:354–355 [bk. 3, chap. 205]; Cabeza de Vaca in Adorno and Pautz, *Álvar Núñez* 1:106–107). In defense of the idea of cannibalism as an isolated or limited phenomenon in the Americas, Las Casas had earlier cited Cabeza de Vaca to the effect that in all his long sojourn, from the Caribbean through Mexico, he and his companions had found no instances of human sacrifice or cannibalism among the Indians of those areas (Casas, *Apologética* 1:651 [bk. 3, chap. 124]; Cabeza de Vaca in Adorno and Pautz, *Álvar Núñez* 1:262–263; see the section entitled "Las Casas, Theorist of American Character and Custom," in chapter 3).

17. "Lo más útil fue descubrir que tú y yo somos la misma persona" (Arenas, *Ill-Fated Peregrinations*, xix; *El mundo alucinante*, 11).

18. "Aunque con veinte y cuatro años de persecución he adquirido el talento de pintar monstruos, el discurso hará ver que no hago aquí sino copiar los originales" (Mier, *Apología*, 54).

19. Mier (*Historia*, 482, 622 [bk. 14]) vigorously attacked the notion that Las Casas's accounts of conquest atrocities were inventions, revealing that the "three hundred year" persecution that Mier insisted that Las Casas had suffered was still in effect in 1813.

20. Rodríguez is cited in Brading, "Prefacio," iv.

21. "No tiene ya fuerza para lidiar con semejantes criaturas, añadiendo que 'todo es inútil con esta clase de monstruos por no decir hombres'" (Brading, "Prefacio," iv).

22. Mier, *Historia*, 622, 646 [bk. 14; appendix].

23. Mier, *Historia*, 314 [bk. 9], 404 [bk. 12], 586, 622, 623, 638 [bk. 14]). Las Casas turned down the appointment of bishop of Cuzco, but Mier likely mentions it to underscore the church's recognition of Las Casas's merits.

24. Arenas, *Ill-Fated Peregrinations*, 29; idem, *El mundo alucinante*, 39.

25. Casas, *Apologética* 1:648, 650 [bk. 3, chaps. 123, 124].

26. Ibid., 1:381 [bk. 3, chap. 74].

27. The charges are contained in a document entitled "Proposiciones temerarias, escandalosas y heréticas que notó el Doctor Sepúlveda en el libro de la conquista de Indias, que fray Bartolomé de las Casas, obispo que fue de Chiapa, hizo imprimir 'sin licencia' en Sevilla, año de 1552." It is transcribed in Fabié, *Vida y escritos* 2:543–569. The ideas considered heretical and treasonous by Sepúlveda—or by an unnamed author of the document who shared his views—were that kings did not possess absolute, unlimited power but rather were servants of the nations whose well-being they were charged to rule. This is a virtual denial of the king's authority to grant encomiendas (Wagner and Parish, *Life and Writings,* 188). See the section entitled "Las Casas, the New Laws, and the Black Legend," in chapter 3.

28. "Somos los Transparentes. Y como nosotros hay muchos que, por su fama, porque se sigue hablando de ellos, no pueden perderse en el infinito de su propia transparencia alejándose de este mundo cabrón donde se les levanta estatuas y los historiadores de nuevo cuño se encarnizan en resolver los peores trasfondos de sus vidas personales" (Carpentier, *Harp,* 156; idem, *El arpa,* 223).

29. Arenas, *Ill-Fated Peregrinations,* xx; idem, *El mundo alucinante,* 12.

30. See González Echevarría's brief but brilliant analysis of *El arpa y la sombra* in the second edition of *Alejo Carpentier: The Pilgrim at Home* (1990), 288–297.

31. These were the words, cited in the *New York Times* (Bruni and Thompson, A10), of Pope John Paul II upon canonizing Juan Diego Cuauhtlahtoatzin in the basilica of Guadalupe.

BIBLIOGRAPHY

Abril-Castelló, Vidal. "La bipolarización Sepúlveda–Las Casas y sus consecuencias: La revolución de la duodécima duda." In *La ética en la conquista de América: Francisco de Vitoria y la Escuela de Salamanca,* edited by Demetrio Ramos et al., 229–288. Corpus Hispanorum de Pace 25. Madrid: Consejo Superior de Investigaciones Científicas, 1984.

Acosta, José de. *De procuranda indorum salute: Pacificación y colonización.* 1588. Edited by Luciano Pereña et al. Corpus Hispanorum de Pace 23. Madrid: Consejo Superior de Investigaciones Científicas, 1984.

——. *Historia natural y moral de las Indias.* 1590. Edited by Edmundo O'Gorman. 2d ed. Mexico City: Fondo de Cultura Económica, 1962.

Adorno, Rolena. "Arms, Letters, and the Native Historian in Early Colonial Mexico." In *1492–1992: Re/discovering Colonial Writing,* edited by René Jara and Nicholas Spadaccini, 201–224. Hispanic Issues 4. Minneapolis: Prisma Institute, 1989.

——. "The Cabeza de Vaca Phenomenon: Confounding the Prestigious Lie of Exactitude." In *Repensando el pasado, recuperando el futuro/Remembering the Past, Retrieving the Future,* edited by Verónica Salles-Reese, 4–23. Bogotá and Washington, D.C.: Editorial Pontificia Universidad Javeriana and Georgetown University, 2005.

——. "Un caso de hispanismo anglonorteamericano temprano: el 'encuentro colombino' de Washington Irving y Martín Fernández de Navarrete." In *El hispanismo anglonorteamericano: aportaciones, problemas y perspectivas sobre Historia, Arte y Literatura españolas (siglos XVI–XVIII),* edited by José Manuel de Bernardo Ares, 1:87–106. 2 vols. Córdoba, Spain: Publicaciones Obra Social y Cultural Cajasur, 2001.

———. "Censorship and Approbation in Fray Martín de Murúa's *Historia general del Perú*." In *Fray Martín de Murúa's* Historia general del Perú*: Essays on the Making of a Manuscript,* edited by Thomas B. F. Cummins and Barbara Anderson, 95–124. Los Angeles: J. Paul Getty Trust, 2008.

———. "Censorship and Its Evasion: Jerónimo Román and Bartolomé de las Casas." *Hispania* 75 (1992): 812–827.

———. "Colonial Reform or Utopia? Guaman Poma's Empire of the Four Parts of the World." In *Amerindian Images,* edited by René Jara and Nicholas Spadaccini, 346–374. Hispanic Issues 9. Minneapolis: Prisma Institute, 1992.

———. "Comentarios: Creadores de historia y progreso: el escritor hispanófilo del siglo 19 y las Antillas de habla hispana." *Op. Cit.: Revista del Centro de Investigaciones Históricas* (Universidad de Puerto Rico) 9 (1997): 109–127.

———. "Cómo leer *Mala Cosa:* Mitos caballerescos y amerindios en los *Naufragios* de Cabeza de Vaca." In *Crítica y descolonización: el sujeto colonial en la cultura latinoamericana,* edited by Beatriz González Stephan and Lúcia Helena Costigan, 89–107. Caracas: Biblioteca de la Academia Nacional de la Historia de Venezuela, 1992.

———. *Cronista y príncipe: La obra de Don Felipe Guaman Poma de Ayala.* Lima: Pontificia Universidad Católica del Perú, 1989; rpt. 1992.

———. "Cultures in Contact: Mesoamerica, the Andes and the European Written Tradition." In *The Cambridge History of Latin American Literature,* edited by Roberto González Echevarría and Enrique Pupo-Walker, 1:33–57, 3:437–452. Cambridge: Cambridge University Press, 1996.

———. "Discourses on Colonialism: Bernal Díaz, Las Casas, and the Twentieth-Century Reader." *MLN* 103, no. 2 (1988): 239–258.

———. "The Discursive Encounter of Spain and America: The Authority of Eyewitness Testimony in the Writing of History." *William and Mary Quarterly,* 3d ser., 49, no. 2 (1992): 210–228.

———. "Early Anglo-American Hispanism in the 'Columbian Encounter' of Washington Irving and Martín Fernández de Navarrete." In *Preactas de la I Conferencia Internacional 'Hacia un Nuevo Humanismo,'* volume 1, edited by José Manuel de Bernardo Ares, 1:5–40. 2 vols. Córdoba, Spain: Universidad de Córdoba, 1997.

———. "La estatua de Gonzalo Guerrero en Akumal: Iconos culturales y la reactualización del pasado colonial." *Revista Iberoamericana,* nos. 176–177 (1996): 905–923.

———. "Felipe Guaman Poma de Ayala: An Andean View of the Peruvian Viceroyalty, 1565–1615." *Journal de la Société des Américanistes* 65 (1978): 121–143. http://www.kb.dk/permalink/2006/poma/info/en/frontpage.htm.

———. "The Friar and the Native Lord: What Manuscript Artifacts Can Tell Us about the Collaboration of Their Makers." A lecture presented at the international symposium "Mapping the Worlds of Sixteenth-Century Mexico," Beinecke Rare Book and Manuscript Library, Yale University, New Haven, Conn., September 15, 2006.

———. "The Genesis of Felipe Guaman Poma de Ayala's 'Nueva corónica y buen

gobierno.' " *Colonial Latin American Review* 2 (1993): 53–91. http://www.kb.dk/
permalink/2006/poma/info/en/frontpage.htm.

———. "La génesis de la 'Nueva crónica y buen gobierno' de Felipe Guaman Poma
de Ayala." *Taller de letras* (Santiago de Chile) 23 (1995): 9–45.

———. "Globalism and Censorship in the Intellectual World of Early Modern
Spain." In *Proceedings of the 23rd Louisiana Conference on Hispanic Languages and
Literatures,* edited by Alejandro Cortázar and Christián Fernández, 1–23. Baton
Rouge: Department of Foreign Languages and Literatures, Louisiana State Uni-
versity, 2003.

———. *Guaman Poma and His Illustrated Chronicle from Colonial Peru: From a Century of
Scholarship to a New Era of Reading/Guaman Poma y su crónica ilustrada del Perú
colonial: un siglo de investigaciones hacia una nueva era de lectura.* Copenhagen: Museum Tusculanum Press, University of Copenhagen, and The Royal Library, 2001.

———. *Guaman Poma: Writing and Resistance in Colonial Peru.* 1986. 2d ed., with a
new introduction. Austin: University of Texas Press, 2000.

———. "De Guancane a Macondo: 'La Florida del Inca' y los albores de la literatura
latinoamericana." In *Franqueando Fronteras: Garcilaso de la Vega y "La Florida del
Inca,"* edited by Raquel Chang-Rodríguez, 149–179. Lima: Pontificia Universidad Católica del Perú, 2006.

———. "Havana and Macondo: The Humanities in U.S. Latin American Studies,
1940–2000." In *The Humanities and the Dynamics of Inclusion since World War
II,* edited by David A. Hollinger, 372–404. Baltimore: Johns Hopkins University
Press for the American Academy of Arts and Sciences, 2006.

———. "History, Law, and the Eyewitness: Protocols of Authority in Bernal Díaz del
Castillo's *Historia verdadera de la conquista de la Nueva España.*" In *The Project of
Prose in the Early Modern West,* edited by Roland Greene and Elizabeth Fowler,
154–175. Cambridge: Cambridge University Press, 1997.

———. "Images of *Indios Ladinos* in Early Colonial Peru." In *Transatlantic Encounters:
Europeans and Andeans in the Sixteenth Century,* edited by Kenneth J. Andrien
and Rolena Adorno, 232–270. Berkeley and Los Angeles: University of California Press, 1991.

———. "El Inca Garcilaso: Writer of Hernando de Soto, Reader of Cabeza de Vaca."
In *Beyond Books and Borders: Garcilaso de la Vega and "La Florida del Inca,"* edited
by Raquel Chang-Rodríguez, 119–133. Lewisburg, Penn.: Bucknell University
Press, 2006.

———. "The Indigenous Ethnographer: The *Indio Ladino* and Cultural Mediation."
In *Implicit Understandings: Observing, Reporting, and Reflecting on the Encounters
between Europeans and Other Peoples in the Early Modern Era,* edited by Stuart B.
Schwartz, 378–402. Cambridge: Cambridge University Press, 1994.

———. *The Intellectual Life of Bartolomé de las Casas.* New Orleans: Graduate School,
Tulane University, 1992. http://www.kb.dk/permalink/2006/poma/info/en/
frontpage.htm.

———, and Patrick Charles Pautz. "Introduction." In *The Narrative of Cabeza de Vaca
by Álvar Núñez Cabeza de Vaca,* edited and translated by Rolena Adorno and Patrick Charles Pautz, 1–37. Lincoln: University of Nebraska Press, 2003.

——. "Introduction to the Second Edition." In Adorno, *Guaman Poma*, xi–lxi.

——. "Literary Production and Suppression: Reading and Writing about Amerindians in Colonial Spanish America." *Dispositio* 10, nos. 28–29 (1986): 1–25.

——. "La negociación del miedo en los 'Naufragios' de Cabeza de Vaca." In *Notas y comentarios sobre Álvar Núñez Cabeza de Vaca*, compiled by Margo Glantz, 309–350. Mexico City: Grijalbo, 1993.

——. "The Negotiation of Fear in Cabeza de Vaca's 'Naufragios.' " *Representations* 33 (Winter 1991): 163–199.

——. "New Perspectives in Colonial Spanish American Literary Studies." *Journal of the Southwest* 32 (1990): 173–191.

——. "Nuevas perspectivas en los estudios literarios coloniales hispanoamericanos." *Revista de Crítica Literaria Latinoamericana*, no. 28 (1988): 11–28.

——. "La prole de Cabeza de Vaca: El legado multicentenario de una de las primeras jornadas europeas en América del Norte." *Revista de Crítica Literaria Latinoamericana*, no. 60 (2004): 251–268.

——. "La redacción y enmendación del autógrafo de la *Nueva corónica y buen gobierno*." In Felipe Guaman Poma de Ayala, *El primer nueva corónica*, edited by John V. Murra and Rolena Adorno, 1: xxxii–xlvi. Mexico City: Siglo Veintiuno, 1980. http://www.kb.dk/permalink/2006/poma/info/en/frontpage.htm.

——. "Retórica y resistencia pictóricas: El grabado y la polémica en los escritos sobre el Perú en los siglos XVI y XVII." In *Imágenes de la resistencia indígena y esclava*, edited by Roger Zapata, 33–77. Lima: Editorial Wari, 1990.

——."Sobre la censura y su evasión: Un caso transatlántico del siglo XVI." In *Grafías del imaginario: Representaciones culturales en España y América (siglos xvi–xviii)*, edited by Carlos Alberto González Sánchez and Enriqueta Vila Vilar, 13–52. Mexico City: Fondo de Cultura Económica, 2003.

——. "Sombras y fantasmas: El pasado colonial en 'El numdo alucinante', de Reinaldo Arenas, y en 'El arpa y la sombra', de Alejo Carpentier." In *Cuba: Un siglo de literatura (1902–2002)*, edited by Anke Birkenmaier and Roberto González Echevarría, 207–219. Madrid: Colibri, 2004.

——. "Sur y norte: El diálogo crítico literario latinoamericanista en la segunda mitad del siglo XX." *Hofstra Hispanic Review* 1, no. 1 (2005): 5–14. Originally published in *Memorias de JALLA 2004 Lima, Sextas Jornadas Andinas de Literatura Latinoamericana*, compiled by Carlos García-Bedoya, 1:17–30. Lima: Universidad Nacional Mayor de San Marcos, 2005.

——. "Waman Puma: El autor y su obra." In Felipe Guaman Poma de Ayala, *Nueva corónica y buen gobierno*, edited by John V. Murra, Rolena Adorno, and Jorge L. Urioste, 1: xvii–xlvii. Madrid: Historia 16, 1987.

——. "The Warrior and the War Community: Constructions of the Civil Order in Mexican Conquest History." *Dispositio* 14, nos. 36–38 (1989): 225–246.

——. "Washington Irving's Romantic Hispanism and Its Columbian Legacies." In *Spain in America: The Origins of Hispanism in the United States*, edited by Richard L. Kagan, 49–105. Urbana: University of Illinois Press, 2002.

——. "A Witness unto Itself: The Integrity of the Autograph Manuscript of Felipe

Guaman Poma de Ayala's 'El primer nueva corónica y buen gobierno' (1615/1616)." *Fund og forskning i Det Kongelige Biblioteks samlinger* (Copenhagen) 41 (2002): 7–106, http://www.kb.dk/permalink/2006/poma/info/en/frontpage.htm.

Adorno, Rolena, and Ivan Boserup. "Guaman Poma and the Manuscripts of Fray Martín de Murúa: Prolegomena to a Critical Edition of the 'Historia del Perú.' " *Fund og forskning i Det Kongelige Biblioteks samlinger* (Copenhagen) 44 (2005): 107–258.

———. "Illuminating Working Relationships through Manuscript Studies: Fray Martín de Murúa and Felipe Guaman Poma de Ayala." Paper presented at the 52nd International Congress of Americanists, University of Seville, Seville, Spain, July 18, 2006.

———. "The Making of Fray Martín de Murúa's 'Historia general del Perú.' " In *Fray Martín de Murúa's* Historia general del Perú: *Essays on the Making of a Manuscript*, edited by Thomas B. F. Cummins and Barbara Anderson 7–75. Los Angeles: J. Paul Getty Trust, 2008.

Adorno, Rolena, and Patrick Charles Pautz. *Álvar Núñez Cabeza de Vaca: His Account, His Life, and the Expedition of Pánfilo de Narváez.* 3 vols. Lincoln: University of Nebraska Press, 1999.

Aguirre, Eugenio. *Gonzalo Guerrero, novela histórica.* Mexico City, 1980.

Aguirre Rosas, Mario. *Gonzalo de Guerrero, padre del mestizaje iberoamericano.* Introduction by Alfonso Taracena. Mexico City: Editorial Jus, 1975.

Ahern, Maureen. "The Cross and the Gourd: The Appropriation of Ritual Signs in the *Relaciones* of Álvar Núñez Cabeza de Vaca and Fray Marcos de Niza." In *Early Images of the Americas,* edited by Jerry M. Williams and Robert E. Lewis, 215–244. Tucson: University of Arizona Press, 1993.

———. "Dichosas muertes": Jesuit Martyrdom on the Northern Frontier of La Florida." *Romance Philology* 53, Special Issue, Part 1 (Fall 1999): 1–21.

Aiton, Arthur. *Antonio de Mendoza: First Viceroy of New Spain.* Durham: Duke University Press, 1927.

Alfonso X of Castile ("the Wise"). *See* Castile.

Alva Ixtlilxochitl, Fernando de. *Compendio histórico del reino de Texcoco.* 1608. In Alva Ixtlilxochitl, *Obras históricas* 1:415–521.

———. *Historia de la nación chichimeca.* c. 1625. In Alva Ixtlilxochitl, *Obras históricas* 2:7–263.

———. *Obras históricas.* 1610–1640. Edited by Edmundo O'Gorman. 2 vols. Serie de historiadores y cronistas de Indias 4. Mexico City: Universidad Nacional Autónoma de México, 1985.

———. *Sumaria relación de las cosas de la Nueva España.* c. 1625. In Alva Ixtlilxochitl, *Obras históricas* 1:261–393.

Alvar, Manuel. "Aceptaciones de *ladino* en español." In *Homenaje a Pedro Sainz Rodríguez: Estudios de lengua y literatura* 2:25–34. Madrid: Fundación Universitaria Española, 1986.

Álvarez M., Víctor M. "Mestizos y mestizaje en la colonia." *Fronteras* (Bogotá) 1, no. 1 (1997): 57–91.

Alves, Abel A. "Estevan." In *Historic World Leaders,* edited by Anne Commire and Deborah Klegner, 256–261. Detroit: Gale Research, 1994.

Andrien, Kenneth J., and Rolena Adorno, eds. *Transatlantic Encounters: Europeans and Andeans in the Sixteenth Century.* Berkeley and Los Angeles: University of California Press, 1991.

Anghiera, Pietro Martire d.' *Décadas del Nuevo Mundo.* Edited by Edmundo O'Gorman. Translated by Agustín Millares Carlo. 2 vols. Santo Domingo, Dominican Republic: Sociedad Dominicana de Bibliófilos, 1989. Translation of *De orbe novo,* 1530.

Archivo General de Indias (AGI). Justicia 229: fols. 1r–16r. "Probanza . . . hecha . . . por parte . . . de Nuño de Guzmán . . . sobre lo que Pilar dispuso contra el dicho señor governador . . . 1532."

Ardoino, Antonio. *Examen apologético de la histórica narración de los naufragios, peregrinaciones i milagros de Álvar Núñez Cabeza de Baca en las tierras de la Florida, i del Nuevo México. Contra la incierta y mal reparada censura del P. Honorio Filipino [sic] . . . 1731.* Madrid: Juan de Zúñiga, 1736.

Arenas, Reinaldo. *Hallucinations: Being an Account of the Life and Adventures of Friar Servando Teresa de Mier.* Translated by Gordon Brotherston. New York: Harper and Row, 1971.

———. *The Ill-Fated Peregrinations of Fray Servando.* 1966. Translated by Andrew Hurley. New York: Penguin, 1987.

———. *El mundo alucinante.* 1966. Barcelona: Montesinos, 1992.

Arias, Santa. *Retórica, historia y polémica: Bartolomé de las Casas y la tradición intelectual renacentista.* Lanham, Md.: University Press of America, 2001.

Aristotle. *Política.* Edited and translated by Carlos García Gual and Aurelio Pérez Jiménez. Madrid: Alianza, 1986.

Arnoldsson, Sverker. *La leyenda negra: Estudios sobre sus orígenes.* Göteborg, Sweden: Göteborgs Universitets Arsskrift, 1960.

Arrom, José Juan. *Aportaciones lingüísticas al conocimiento de la cosmovisión taína.* Santo Domingo, Dominican Republic: Fundación García Arévalo, 1974.

———. "Notas al texto." In *Relación acerca de las antigüedades de los indios,* by Fray Ramón Pané, 57–82. Mexico City: Siglo Veintiuno, 1978.

Augustine. *The City of God.* ca. 412. In *Basic Writings of Saint Augustine,* edited by Whitney J. Oates, translated by M. Dods, with the assistance of G. Wilson and J. J. Smith, 2–663. Vol. 2. New York: Random House, 1948.

Ballesteros Gaibrois, Manuel. "Estudio preliminar." In *El Antijovio,* by Gonzalo Jiménez de Quesada, edited by Rafael Torres Quintero, xiii–cxxii. Publicaciones del Instituto Caro y Cuervo 10. Bogotá: Instituto Caro y Cuervo, 1952.

———. *Vida y obra de Fray Bernardino de Sahagún.* León, Spain: Institución "Fr. Bernardino de Sahagún," 1973.

Barbón Rodríguez, José A. *Bernal Díaz del Castillo.* Enciclopedia Literaria 36. Buenos Aires: Centro Editor de América Latina, 1968.

———. "La conquista de América en la 'Historia Pontifical' de Gonzalo de Illescas." In *Estudios de literatura española y francesa, siglos XVI y XVII: Homenaje a Horst Baader,* edited by Frauke Gewecke, 207–218. Frankfurt: K. D. Vervuert, 1984.

Barcia Carballido y Zúñiga, Andrés González de. *Historiadores primitivos de las Indias Occidentales, que juntó, traduxo en parte y sacó a luz, ilustradas con eruditas notas y copiosas índices, el ilustrísimo señor D. Andrés González Barcia, del consejo, y cámara de S[u] M[agestad].* 3 vols. Madrid, 1749.

Barco Centenera, Martín de. *Argentina y conquista del Río de la Plata, con otros acaecimientos de los reynos del Perú, Tucuman, y estado del Brasil.* Lisbon: Pedro Crasbeeck, 1602.

Barnes, Monica. "La *Nueva corónica y buen gobierno* fue escrita por un residente de Lucanas." Paper presented at Istituto Italo-Latinoamericano, Rome, Italy, September 29, 1999.

Barros, João de. *Asia de João de Barros: dos fectos que os Portugueses fizeram no descobrimento e conquista dos mares e terras do Oriente.* Lisbon: G. Galharde, 1552.

Bartra, Enrique T., ed. *Tercer concilio limense, 1582–1583.* Lima: Facultad Pontificia y Civil de Teología, 1982.

Bataillon, Marcel. *Erasmo y España: Estudios sobre la historia espiritual del siglo XVI.* Translated by Antonio Alatorre. Mexico City: Fondo de Cultura Económica, 1966.

Beaumont, Pablo. *Crónica de la provincia de San Pedro y San Pablo de Michoacán.* 1777. 3 vols. Publicaciones del Archivo General de la Nación 18. Mexico City: Talleres Gráficos de la Nación, 1932.

Benítez-Rojo, Antonio. *El mar de las lentejas.* 1979. Rpt. Barcelona: Plaza y Janés, 1985.

——. "Presencia del texto lascasiano en la obra de García Márquez." In *Selected Proceedings of the Thirty-Fifth Annual Mountain Interstate Foreign Language Conference*, edited by Ramón Fernández-Rubio, 37–44. Greenville, S.C.: Furman University, 1987.

——. *Sea of Lentils.* Translated by James Maraniss. Amherst: University of Massachusetts Press, 1991.

Bennassar, Bartolomé. *The Spanish Character: Attitudes and Mentalities from the Sixteenth to the Nineteenth Centuries.* Translated by Benjamin Keen. 1975. Rpt. Berkeley and Los Angeles: University of California Press, 1979.

Bettex, Albert. *The Discovery of the World: The Great Explorers and the Worlds They Found.* New York: Simon and Schuster, 1960.

Bishop, Morris. *The Odyssey of Cabeza de Vaca.* New York: Century Co., 1933.

Borges, Jorge Luis. "The Ethnographer." In *Collected Fictions*, translated by Andrew Hurley, 334–335. New York: Viking Press, 1998.

——. "El etnógrafo." In *Obras completas* 2:367–368. 4 vols. Buenos Aires: Emecé Editores, 1996.

——. "Kafka y sus precursores." In *Obras completas* 2:88–90. 4 vols. Buenos Aires: Emecé, 1996.

Boserup, Ivan. "A New Interpretation of Guaman Poma's Calculations on the Title Page of the *Nueva corónica y buen gobierno.*" *Fund og forskning i Det Kongelige Biblioteks samlinger* (Copenhagen) 43 (2004): 88–115, http://www.kb.dk/permalink/2006/poma/info/en/frontpage.htm.

Bourne, Edward Gaylord. "Editor's Introduction." In *Narratives of the Career of Hernando de Soto,* edited by Edward Gaylord Bourne, 1:v–xx. New York: A. S. Barnes, 1904.

Boyer, Patricio Edgardo. "Empire and American Visions of the Humane." Ph.D. diss., Yale University, 2006.

Brading, David. "Prefacio." In Mier y Noriega, *Historia,* iii–v.

Bruni, Frank, and Ginger Thompson. "Bolstering Faith of Indians, Pope Gives Mexico a Saint." *New York Times,* August 1, 2002, national edition, sec. 1.

Cabeza de Vaca, Álvar Núñez. *See* Núñez Cabeza de Vaca, Álvar.

Cabrera de Córdoba, Luis. *De historia, para entenderla y escrivirla.* Madrid: Luis Sánchez, 1611.

Carlyon, Jonathan Earl. *Andrés González de Barcia and the Creation of the Colonial Spanish American Library.* Toronto: University of Toronto Press, 2005.

Caro Baroja, Julio. *Las formas complejas de la vida religiosa (religión, sociedad y carácter en la España de los siglos XVI y XVII).* Madrid: Akal Editor, 1978.

———. "La milicia cristiana y la moral del guerrero." In *Las formas complejas de la vida religiosa (religión, sociedad y carácter en la España de los siglos XVI y XVII),* by Julio Caro Baroja, 415–444. Madrid: Akal, 1978.

———. *The World of the Witches.* Translated by Nigel Glendinning. 1961. Rpt. London: Weidenfeld and Nicolson, 1964.

Carpentier, Alejo. *El arpa y la sombra.* 1979. Rpt. Mexico City: Siglo Veintiuno, 1997.

———. "Conciencia e identidad de América." In *Obras completas de Alejo Carpentier: Ensayos* 13:131–140. Mexico City: Siglo Veintiuno, 1990.

———. *The Harp and the Shadow.* Translated by Thomas Christensen and Carol Christensen. San Francisco: Mercury House, 1990.

Carrasco Urgoiti, María Soledad. *El moro de Granada en la literatura del siglo XV al XX.* Madrid: Revista de Occidente, 1956.

Casas, Bartolomé de las. *An Account, Much Abbreviated, of the Destruction of the Indies.* Edited and introduced by Franklin W. Knight. Translated by Andrew Hurley. Indianapolis: Hackett, 2003.

———. *Apologética historia sumaria.* 1527–1560. Edited by Edmundo O'Gorman. 2 vols. Mexico City: Universidad Nacional Autónoma de México, Instituto de Investigaciones Históricas, 1967.

———. *Apología.* Obras completas de Bartolomé de las Casas 9. Edited and translated by Ángel Losada. Madrid: Alianza, 1988.

———. *Apología de Juan Ginés de Sepúlveda contra fray Bartolomé de las Casas y de fray Bartolomé de las Casas contra Juan Ginés de Sepúlveda.* Edited and translated by Ángel Losada. Madrid: Editora Nacional, 1975.

———. "Aquí se contienen unos avisos y reglas para los confesores." 1552. In Casas, *Obras escogidas,* 235–249.

———. "Aquí se tiene una disputa o controversia." 1552. In Casas, *Obras escogidas,* 293–348.

——. *Brevísima relación de la destruición de las Indias*. 1552. Edited by André Saint-Lu. 2d ed. Letras Hispánicas 158. Madrid: Cátedra, 1984.

——. *Brevísima relación de la destruición de las Indias*. 1552. In Casas, *Tratados*, 1:14–199.

——. *Brevísima relación de la destruición de las Indias: primera edición crítica*. Edited by Isacio Pérez Fernández. Estudios monográficos 3. Bayamón, Puerto Rico: Universidad Central de Bayamón, Centro de Estudios de los Dominicos del Caribe, and Instituto de Estudios Históricos Juan Alejo de Arizmendi, 2000.

——. "Carta al maestro fray Bartolomé Carranza de Miranda." 1555. In Casas, *Obras escogidas*, 430–450.

——. "Cláusula del testamento que hizo el obispo de Chiapa, don Fray Bartolomé de las Casas." 1564. In Casas, *Obras escogidas*, 538–541.

——. *Conclusiones sumarias sobre el remedio de las Indias*. 1542. Commentaries by Isacio Pérez Fernández and Helen Rand Parish. Madrid: Ministerio de Cultura, Biblioteca Nacional, 1992.

——. *De unico vocationis modo*. Edited by Paulino Castañeda Delgado and Antonio García Moral. Obras completas de Bartolomé de las Casas 2. Madrid: Alianza, 1990.

——. *Del único modo de atraer a todos los pueblos a la verdadera religión*. Edited by Agustín Millares Carlo. Introduction by Lewis Hanke. Translated by Atenógenes Santamaría. Mexico City: Fondo de Cultura Económica, 1942.

——. "Entre los remedios." 1542. In Casas, *Obras escogidas*, 69–119.

——. *Historia de las Indias*. 1527–1559. Edited by Agustín Millares Carlo. Introduction by Lewis Hanke. 3 vols. Mexico City: Fondo de Cultura Económica, 1951.

——. "Informe al Consejo de Indias sobre el licenciado Cerrato y las encomiendas de Guatemala." ca. 1552. In Casas, *Obras escogidas*, 424–425.

——. "Memorial de remedios para las Indias." 1516. In Casas, *Obras escogidas*, 5–27.

——. "Memorial de remedios para las Indias." 1518. In Casas, *Obras escogidas*, 31–35.

——. "Memorial de remedios para las Indias." 1518. In Casas, *Obras escogidas*, 35–39.

——. "Memorial del obispo fray Bartolomé de las Casas y fray Domingo de Santo Tomás." 1560. In Casas, *Obras escogidas*, 465–469.

——. "Memorial-sumario a Felipe II." 1556. In Casas, *Obras escogidas*, 453–460.

——. *Narratio regionum Indicarum per Hispanos quosdam devastatarum verissima*. Frankfurt am Main: Theodor de Bry and Johannes Sauer, 1598.

——. *Obras escogidas de Fray Bartolomé de las Casas*. Edited by Juan Pérez de Tudela Bueso. Vol. 5. Biblioteca de autores españoles 110. Madrid: Atlas, 1958.

——. *The Only Way to Draw All People to a Living Faith*. Translated by Francis Patrick Sullivan. Introduction by Helen Rand Parish. Mahwah, N.J.: Paulist Press, 1992.

——. "Representación al Consejo de Indias, contra las pretensiones de un procurador enviado por la provincia de Guatemala, 1549." In Casas, *Obras escogidas,* 290–292.

——. "Respuesta al obispo de los Charcas sobre un dictamen de éste acerca de los bienes ganados por conquistadores y encomenderos." ca. 1553. In Casas, *Obras escogidas,* 425–429.

——. *Los tesoros del Perú.* 1562. Translated by Ángel Losada. Madrid: Consejo Superior de Investigaciones Científicas, 1958. Spanish translation of *De thesauris.*

——. *De thesauris.* 1562. Edited by Ángel Losada and Martín Lassègue. Obras completas de Bartolomé de las Casas 11.1. Madrid: Alianza, 1992.

——. *Tratado de las doce dudas.* 1564. In Casas, *Obras escogidas,* 478–536.

——. *Tratados de Fray Bartolomé de las Casas.* Introduction by Lewis Hanke and Manuel Giménez Fernández. Transcription by Juan Pérez de Tudela Bueso. Translated by Agustín Millares Carlo. 2 vols. Mexico City: Fondo de Cultura Económica, 1965.

Castañeda Delgado, Paulino. "La política española con los caribes durante el siglo XVI." In *Homenaje a D. Ciriaco Pérez-Bustamante,* introduction by Carlos Seco Serrano, 73–130. Vol. 2. Madrid: Instituto "Gonzalo Fernández de Oviedo," Consejo Superior de Investigaciones Científicas, 1970.

Castañeda Nájera, Pedro. "Castañeda's History of the Expedition." In *Narratives of the Coronado Expedition, 1540–42,* edited by George P. Hammond and Agapito Rey, 2:191–283. Albuquerque: University of New Mexico Press, 1940.

Castile. Laws, statutes, etc. 1252–1284 (Alfonso X). *Las siete partidas,* by Alfonso X, King of Castile and León. 1256–1263. Introduction by Charles Sumner Lobingier. Translated by Samuel Parsons Scott. Bibliography by John Vance. Washington, D.C.: Commerce Clearing House for the Comparative Law Bureau of the American Bar Association, 1931.

——. *Las siete partidas del sabio rey, don Alfonso el nono, nuevamente glosadas por el licenciado Gregorio López, del Consejo Real de Indias de Su Majestad.* Laws, statutes, etc. 1555. 7 vols. Valladolid, Spain: Diego Fernández de Córdoba, 1587. 4 vols.

Certeau, Michel de. *Heterologies: Discourses on the Other.* Translated by Brian Massumi. Foreword by Wlad Godzich. Theory and History of Literature 17. Minneapolis: University of Minnesota Press, 1986.

——. *The Writing of History.* Translated by Tom Conley. New York: Columbia University Press, 1988.

Cervantes de Salazar, Francisco. *Crónica de la Nueva España.* 1566. Introduction by Juan Miralles Ostos. Mexico City: Porrúa, 1985.

——. *Obras: un diálogo de la dignidad del hombre . . . comenzado por el maestro Oliva acabada por Francisco Cervantes de Salazar, el apólogo de la ociosidad del trabajo . . . por el protonotario Luis Mexia, glosado y moralizado por Francisco Cervantes de Salazar; la introducción y camino para la sabiduría . . . por Luis Vives, buelta en castellano . . . por Francisco Cervantes de Salazar.* Alcalá de Henares: Juan de Brocar, 1546.

Chamberlain, Robert S. *The Conquest and Colonization of Yucatán, 1517–1550.* Washington, D.C.: Carnegie Institution of Washington, 1948.

Charles, John Duffy. "Indios Ladinos: Colonial Andean Testimony and Ecclesiastical Institutions (1583–1650)." Ph.D. diss., Yale University, 2003.

Charlevoix, Pierre-François-Xavier de. *Histoire de l'Isle Espagnole ou de S. Dominque.* 2 vols. Paris: F. Didot, 1730–1731.

Chevalier, Maxime. " 'La Diana' de Montemayor y su público en la España del siglo XVI." In *Creación y público en la literatura española,* edited by Jean François Botrel and Serge Salaün, 40–55. Madrid: Castalia, 1974.

———. *Lectura y lectores de la España del siglo XVI y XVII.* Madrid: Turner, 1976.

Cieza de León, Pedro de. *Crónica del Perú. Primera parte.* 1553. Introduction by Franklin Pease G.Y. Note by Miguel Maticorena. Lima: Pontificia Universidad Católica del Perú, 1984.

Clayton, Lawrence A.,Vernon James Knight, Jr., and Edward C. Moore, eds. *The DeSoto Chronicles: The Expedition of Hernando de Soto to North America in 1539–43.* 2 vols. Tuscaloosa: University of Alabama Press, 1993.

Clendinnen, Inga. "The Cost of Courage in Aztec Society." *Past and Present,* no. 107 (May 1985): 44–89.

Colección de documentos inéditos relativos al descubrimiento, conquista y organización de las antiguas posesiones españolas de América y Oceanía. 42 vols. Madrid: Manuel G. Hernández, 1864–1884. (CDI)

Colección de documentos inéditos relativos al descubrimiento, conquista y organización de las antiguas posesiones españolas de Ultramar. 25 vols. Madrid, 1885–1932. (CDU)

Colón, Cristóbal. *Textos y documentos completos.* 1982. Edited and introduced by Consuelo Varela. Madrid: Alianza, 1989.

Colón, Hernando. *The Life of the Admiral Christopher Columbus by His Son Ferdinand.* c. 1538. Edited and translated by Benjamin Keen. New Brunswick, N.J.: Rutgers University Press, 1992.

———. *Vida del almirante don Cristóbal Colón, escrita por su hijo don Hernando.* c. 1538. Edited by Ramón Iglesia. Mexico City: Fondo de Cultura Económica, 1984.

Cook, Noble David. "Introducción." In *Tasa de la visita general de Francisco de Toledo,* edited by Noble David Cook, ix–xxvii. Lima: Universidad Nacional de San Marcos, 1975.

Cortés, Hernán. *Cartas de relación.* 1519–1526. Edited by Ángel Delgado Gómez. Clásicos Castalia 198. Madrid: Castalia, 1993.

———. *Letters from Mexico.* 1519–1526. Translated and edited by Anthony Pagden. Introduction by J. H. Elliott. New Haven: Yale University Press, 1986.

———. *Praeclara de Nova Maris oceani Hyspania narratio.* Nuremberg: F. Peypus, 1524.

Cortínez, Verónica. *Memoria original de Bernal Díaz del Castillo.* Huixquilucan, Mexico: Oak Editorial, 2000.

Covarrubias Horozco, Sebastián de. *Tesoro de la Lengua Castellana o Española.* 1611. Edited by Martín de Riquer. Barcelona: S. A. Horta, 1943.

Cypess, Sandra. *La Malinche in Mexican Literature: From History to Myth.* Austin: University of Texas Press, 1991.

Davies, Nigel. "The Mexica Military Hierarchy as Described by Sahagún." In *The

Work of Bernardino de Sahagún: Pioneer Ethnographer of Sixteenth-Century Aztec Mexico, edited by J. Jorge Klor de Alva, H. B. Nicholson, and Eloise Quiñones Keber, 161–168. Albany: Institute for Mesoamerican Studies, State University of New York, 1988.

Díaz del Castillo, Bernal. "Carta de Bernal Díaz del Castillo al emperador don Carlos dando cuenta de los abusos que se cometían en la gobernación de las provincias del Nuevo Mundo, Santiago de Guatemala, 22 de febrero de 1552." In Díaz del Castillo, *Historia verdadera*, edited by Ramírez Cabañas, 2:441–446.

———. "Carta de Bernal Díaz del Castillo al rey don Felipe II, en la que denuncia algunos abusos cometidos con los indios, y pide se le nombre fiel-ejecutor de Guatemala en atención a los servicios que expone." 1558. In Díaz del Castillo, *Historia verdadera*, edited by Ramírez Cabañas, 2: 447–449.

———. "Carta de Bernal Díaz del Castillo, dirigida a fray Bartolomé de las Casas, 20 de febrero de 1558." In Díaz del Castillo, *Historia verdadera*, edited by Ramírez Cabañas, 2:451–453.

———. *Historia verdadera de la conquista de la Nueva España*. 3 vols. Mexico City: Miguel-Ángel Porrúa, 1992–2001. Vol. 1 is a facsimile of the autograph codex of 1568.

———. *Historia verdadera de la conquista de la Nueva España*. Edited by Joaquín Ramírez Cabañas. 2 vols. Mexico City: Porrúa, 1977.

———. *Historia verdadera de la conquista de la Nueva España*. Edited by Carmelo Sáenz de Santa María. 2 vols. Monumenta Hispano Indiana, V Centenario del Descubrimiento de América 1. Madrid: Consejo Superior de Investigaciones Científicas, 1982.

———. *Historia verdadera de la conquista de la Nueva España, escrita por el Capitán Bernal Díaz del Castillo, uno de sus conquistadores. Sacada a luz por el P.M. Fr. Alonso Remón*. Madrid: Imprenta Real, 1632.

———. *Suplemento*. In Bernal Díaz del Castillo, *Historia verdadera de la conquista de la Nueva España*, edited by Carmelo Sáenz de Santa María, vol. 2. 2 vols. Madrid: Consejo Superior de Investigaciones Científicas, 1982.

———. *The True History of the Conquest of New Spain*. Edited by Genaro García. Translated by Alfred Percival Maudslay, 5 vols. 2d ser., nos. 23–25, 30, 40. London: Hakluyt Society, 1908.

Díaz Quiñones, Arcadio. "Las palabras de la tribu." In *El arte de bregar: ensayos*, by Arcadio Díaz Quiñones, 105–123. San Juan: Callejón, 2000.

Durand, José. "Los dos autores de 'La Florida.'" *Letras*, no. 64 (1960): 19–27.

———. "Las enigmáticas fuentes de 'La Florida del Inca'." *Cuadernos hispanoamericanos*, no. 168 (1963): 597–609.

———. *La transformación social del conquistador*. 2 vols. Mexico y lo mexicano 15 and 16. Mexico City: Porrúa y Obregón, 1953.

Eanes de Zurara, Gomes. 1453. *Chronica do descobrimento e conquista de Guiné*. Paris: J.P. Aillaud, 1841.

Eisenberg, Daniel. "Who Read the Novels of Chivalry?" *Kentucky Romance Quarterly* 20 (1973): 209–233.

Elliott, J. H. "Cortés, Velázquez, and Charles V." In *Letters from Mexico*, by Hernán

Cortés. Edited and translated by Anthony Pagden, xi–xxxvii. New Haven: Yale University Press, 1986.

———. *Imperial Spain, 1469–1716.* 1963. New York: New American Library, 1966.

———. "The Mental World of Hernán Cortés." In *Spain and Its World (1500–1700): Selected Essays,* 27–41. New Haven: Yale University Press, 1989.

———. "The Spanish Conquest and Settlement of America." In *The Cambridge History of Latin America,* edited by Leslie Bethell, 1:149–206. Cambridge: Cambridge University Press, 1984.

Ercilla y Zúñiga, Alonso de. *La araucana.* 1569–1589. Edited by Marcos A. Moríñigo and Isaías Lerner. 2 vols. Clásicos Castalia 91, 92. Madrid: Castalia, 1983.

Espinoza Galarza, Max. *Toponimia quechua del Perú.* Lima: COSESA, 1973.

Estenssoro Fuchs, Juan Carlos. *Del paganismo a la santidad: La incorporación de los indios del Perú al catolicismo, 1532–1750.* Lima, Instituto Francés de Estudios Andinos and Pontificia Universidad Católica del Perú, 2003.

Esteve Barba, Francisco. *Historiografía indiana.* 1964. 2d ed. Madrid: Gredos, 1992.

Fabié, Antonio María. *Vida y escritos de Don Fray Bartolomé de las Casas, obispo de Chiapa.* 2 vols. Madrid: Miguel Ginesta, 1879.

Fernández, Alonso. *Historia eclesiástica de nuestros tiempos.* Toledo: Viuda de Pedro Rodríguez, 1611.

Fernández de Oviedo y Valdés, Gonzalo. *Historia general y natural de las Indias, Islas y Tierra Firme del Mar Océano.* 1525–1548. Edited by José Amador de los Ríos. 4 vols. Madrid: Real Academia de la Historia, 1881–1885.

———. *Libro del muy esforçado e invencible Caballero de Fortuna, propiamente llamado don Claribalte.* Valencia: Juan Henao, 1519.

Frankl, Víctor. "Hernán Cortés y la tradición de las 'Siete Partidas.'" *Revista de Historia de América,* nos. 53–54 (1962): 9–74.

———. "Imperio particular e Imperio universal en las 'Cartas de Relación' de Hernán Cortés." *Cuadernos Hispanoamericanos,* no. 165 (1963): 443–482.

Friede, Juan. "La censura española del siglo XVI y los libros de historia de América." *Revista de historia de América* (Mexico City) 47 (1959): 45–94.

Fuentes y Guzmán, Francisco Antonio. *Historia de Guatemala o Recordación florida.* Edited by Justo Zaragosa. 2 vols. Madrid: Luis Navarro, 1882–1883.

Fueter, Eduard. *Geschichte der neueren Historiographie.* Munich: Oldenbourg, 1911.

García-Arenal, Mercedes. *Los moriscos.* Madrid: Editora Nacional, 1975.

García Icazbalceta, Joaquín, ed. *Colección de documentos para la historia de México.* 1858–1866. Vol. 2. Biblioteca Porrúa 48. Mexico City: Porrúa, 1980.

———, ed. *Nueva colección de documentos para la historia de México.* 1886–1892. Mexico City: Editorial Salvador Chávez Hayhoe, 1941.

García Márquez, Gabriel. *Cien años de soledad.* 1967. Edited by Jacques Joset. Madrid: Cátedra, 2004.

———. *El general en su laberinto.* Buenos Aires: Editorial Sudamericana, 1989.

———. *The General in His Labyrinth.* Translated by Edith Grossman. New York: Alfred A. Knopf, 1990.

García-Pelayo, Manuel. "Juan Ginés de Sepúlveda y los problemas jurídicos de la conquista de América." In *Tratado sobre las justas causas de la guerra contra los indios,* by Juan Ginés de Sepúlveda, with a foreword by Marcelino Menéndez y Pelayo, 1–42. 1892. Mexico City: Fondo de Cultura Económica, 1941.

Garcilaso de la Vega. *See* Vega, El Inca Garcilaso de.

Gates, Henry Louis, Jr., and Nellie Y. McKay, eds. *The Norton Anthology of African American Literature.* New York: W. W. Norton, 1997.

Gerhard, Peter. *The Southeast Frontier of New Spain.* Princeton: Princeton University Press, 1979.

Gibson, Charles. *The Aztecs Under Spanish Rule: A History of the Indians of the Valley of Mexico, 1519–1810.* Stanford: Stanford University Press, 1964.

———. "Reconquista and conquista." In *Homage to Irving A. Leonard,* edited by Raquel Chang-Rodríguez and Donald A. Yates, 19–28. East Lansing: Latin American Studies Center, Michigan State University, 1977.

———. *Spain in America.* New York: Harper and Row, 1966.

———. *Tlascala in the Sixteenth Century.* New Haven: Yale University Press, 1952.

Gilman, Stephen. "Bernal Díaz del Castillo and Amadís de Gaula." In *Studia philologica: Homenaje ofrecido a Dámaso Alonso por sus amigos y discípulos,* introduction by A. Zamora Vicente, 2:99–114. Madrid: Gredos, 1961.

Giménez Fernández, Manuel. *Bartolomé de las Casas.* 2 vols. Seville: Escuela de Estudios Hispano-Americanos de Sevilla, 1960.

Ginés de Sepúlveda, Juan. *See* Sepúlveda, Juan Ginés de.

Gómara, Francisco López de. *See* López de Gómara, Francisco.

Gómez Canedo, Lino. "¿Hombres o bestias? (Nuevo examen crítico de un viejo tópico)." *Estudios de historia novohispana* 1 (1966): 29–51.

Gómez Robledo, Xavier. *Humanismo en México en el siglo XVI.* Mexico City: Editorial Jus, 1954.

González-Blanco Garrido, Salomón. *Gonzalo Guerrero, el primer aliado de los mayas.* Mexico City, 1991.

González de Barcia, Andrés. *See* Barcia Carballido y Zúñiga, Andrés González de.

González Echevarría, Roberto. *Alejo Carpentier: The Pilgrim at Home.* 1977. 2d ed. Austin: University of Texas Press, 1990.

———. "A Brief History of Spanish American Literature." In *The Cambridge History of Latin American Literature,* edited by Roberto González Echevarría and Enrique Pupo-Walker, 1:7–32. Cambridge: Cambridge University Press, 1996.

———. "José Arrom, autor de la *Relación acerca de las antigüedades de los Indios* (picaresca e historia)." In *Relecturas: estudios de literatura cubana,* by Roberto González Echevarría, 17–35. Caracas: Monte Ávila, 1976.

———. "The Law of the Letter: Garcilaso's *Commentaries* and the Origins of the Latin American Narrative." *Yale Journal of Criticism* 1, no. 1 (1987): 107–132.

———. "The Life and Adventures of Cipión: Cervantes and the Picaresque." *Diacritics* (September 1980): 15–26.

———. *Myth and Archive: A Theory of Latin American Narrative.* 1990. Rpt. Durham: Duke University Press, 1998.

———. "El reino de este mundo alucinante: era imaginaria de fray Servando." In *Isla a su vuelo fugitiva: ensayos críticos sobre literatura hispanoamericana,* by Roberto González Echevarría, 253–257. Madrid: Porrúa Turanzas, 1983.

———. *Relecturas: estudios de literatura cubana.* Caracas: Monte Ávila, 1976.

———. "Semejante a la noche, de Alejo Carpentier: historia/ficción." *MLN* 87 (1972): 272–285.

González Obregón, Luis. *Bernal Díaz del Castillo: Notas biográficas y bibliográficas.* Mexico City: Ministerio de Fomento, 1894.

Granada, Luis de. *Introducción del símbolo de la fe.* 1582. In *Obras de fray Luis de Granada,* edited by Buenaventura Carlos Aribau, 1:181–733. Biblioteca de autores españoles 6. Madrid: Atlas, 1944.

Green, Otis H. "A Critical Survey of Scholarship in the Field of Spanish Renaissance Literature, 1914–1944." *Studies in Philology* 44 (1947): 228–264.

Greenleaf, Richard E. *Zumárraga y la Inquisición mexicana, 1536–1543.* 1962. Rpt. Mexico City: Fondo de Cultura Económica, 1988.

Grinnell, George Bird. *Pawnee Hero Stories and Folk-Tales.* 1889. Introduction by Maurice Frink. Rpt. Lincoln: University of Nebraska Press, 1990.

Guaman Poma de Ayala, Felipe. *Nueva corónica y buen gobierno.* 1615. Edited by John V. Murra, Rolena Adorno, and Jorge L. Urioste. Crónicas de América 29. 3 vols. Madrid: Historia 16, 1987.

———. *El primer nueva corónica y buen gobierno.* Edited by John V. Murra and Rolena Adorno. Quechua translations by Jorge L. Urioste. 3 vols. Colección América Nuestra 31. Mexico City: Siglo Veintiuno, 1980. http://www.kb.dk/permalink/2006/poma/info/en/frontpage.htm.

Güiraldes, Ricardo. *Don Segundo Sombra.* 1926. Rpt. Madrid: Cátedra, 1995.

Gurría Lacroix, Jorge. "Prólogo." In Cortés, *Historia de las Indias,* ix–xxxi.

Hanke, Lewis. *Aristotle and the American Indians.* Bloomington: Indiana University Press, 1959.

———. *Bartolomé de las Casas: An Interpretation of His Life and Writings.* The Hague: Martinus Nijhoff, 1951.

———. "The Development of Regulations for Conquistadores." In *Contribuciones para el estudio de la historia de América: Homenaje al doctor Emilio Ravignani,* foreword by Mario Belgrano et al., 71–87. Buenos Aires: Peuser, 1941.

———. "Un festón de documentos lascasianos." *Revista Cubana* 16 (July–December 1941): 150–211.

———, ed. *History of Latin American Civilization: Sources and Interpretations.* 2 vols. Boston: Little, Brown, 1967.

———. *The Spanish Struggle for Justice in the Conquest of America.* 1949. Rpt. Boston: Little, Brown, 1965.

———. "Studies in the Theoretical Aspects of the Spanish Conquest of America." Ph.D. diss., Harvard University, 1935.

Hassig, Ross. *Aztec Warfare: Imperial Expansion and Political Control.* Norman: University of Oklahoma Press, 1988.

Hemming, John. *The Conquest of the Incas.* San Diego: Harcourt Brace Jovanovich, 1970.

Henríquez Ureña, Pedro. *Las corrientes literarias en la América Hispánica.* 1945. Translated by Joaquín Díez-Canedo. Mexico City: Fondo de Cultura Económica, 1969.

———. *Literary Currents in Hispanic America.* Cambridge: Harvard University Press, 1945.

Hernández, Pero. *Commentarios de Álvar Núñez Cabeca de Vaça [sic], adelantado y governador de la provincia del Río de la Plata.* In *La relación y comentarios del governador Álvar Núñez Cabeça de Vaca, de lo acaescido en las dos jornadas que hizo a las Indias,* by Álvar Núñez Cabeza de Vaca, fols. 58r–139r. Valladolid: Francisco Fernández de Córdova, 1555.

Herrera y Tordesillas, Antonio de. *Historia general de los hechos de los castellanos en las islas y tierra firme del Mar Océano.* 5 vols. Madrid, 1601–1615.

———. *Historia general de los hechos de los castellanos en las islas y tierra firme del mar océano.* 1601–1615. Edited by Ángel de Altolaguirre y Duvale and Miguel Gómez del Campillo. 17 vols. Madrid: Real Academia de la Historia, 1934–1957.

Hilton, Sylvia L. "Introducción." In Vega, *La Florida del Inca,* edited by Sylvia L. Hilton, 7–57.

Himmerich y Valencia, Robert. *The Encomenderos of New Spain (1521–1555).* Austin: University of Texas Press, 1991.

Höffner, Joseph. *La ética colonial española del Siglo de Oro: Cristianismo y dignidad humana.* 1947. Introduction by Antonio Truyol Serra. Translated by Francisco de Asís Caballero. Madrid: Cultura Hispánica, 1957.

Huerga, Álvaro. *Vida y obras.* Obras completas de Bartolomé de las Casas 1. Madrid: Alianza, 1998.

Icaza, Francisco A. de. *Diccionario autobiográfico de conquistadores y pobladores de Nueva España.* 2 vols. Guadalajara, Mexico: Biblioteca de Facsímiles Mexicanos, 1969.

Iglesia, Ramón. *Dos estudios sobre el mismo tema: Bernal Díaz del Castillo y el Popularismo en la Historiografía Española; Las críticas de Bernal Díaz del Castillo a la "Historia de la Conquista de México" de Francisco López de Gómara.* Mexico City: Revista Tiempo, 1940.

Ingham, John M. "Human Sacrifice at Tenochtitlán." *Comparative Studies in Society and History* 26, no. 3 (1984): 379–400.

Irving, Washington. *A History of the Life and Voyages of Christopher Columbus.* 4 vols. London: John Murray, 1828.

Isaac, Barry. "Aztec Warfare: Goals and Battlefield Comportment." *Ethnology* 22 (1983): 121–131.

Jákfalvi-Leiva, Susana. *Traducción, escritura y violencia colonizadora: Un estudio de la obra del Inca Garcilaso.* Foreign and Comparative Studies Publications, Latin American Series, no. 7. Syracuse: Maxwell School of Citizenship and Public Affairs, Syracuse University, 1984.

Jiménez de la Espada, Marcos, comp. *Relaciones geográficas de Indias: Perú.* Vol. 1. Biblioteca de autores españoles 183. Madrid: Atlas, 1965.

Juderías, Julián. *La leyenda negra: Estudios acerca del concepto de España en el extranjero.* 1914. Rpt. Madrid: Editora Nacional, 1974.

Kamen, Henry. *Inquisition and Society in Spain in the Sixteenth and Seventeenth Centuries.* Bloomington: Indiana University Press, 1985.

——. *The Spanish Inquisition: A Historical Revision.* New Haven: Yale University Press, 1998.

Lafaye, Jacques. "Los 'milagros' de Álvar Núñez Cabeza de Vaca (1527–1536)." In *Mesías, cruzadas, utopías: El judeo-cristianismo en las sociedades ibéricas,* by Jacques Lafaye, translated by Juan José Utrilla, 65–84. Mexico City: Fondo de Cultura Económica, 1984.

Landa, Fr. Diego de. *The Maya: Diego de Landa's Account of the Affairs of Yucatán.* Edited and translated by Anthony R. Pagden. Chicago: J. Philip O'Hara, 1975.

——. *Relación de las cosas de Yucatán.* 1566. Edited by Miguel Rivera. Crónicas de América 7. Madrid: Historia 16, 1985.

Lea, Henry Charles. *The Inquisition in the Spanish Dependencies.* New York: Macmillan, 1908.

León, Alonso de. *Historia de Nuevo León con noticias sobre Coahuila, Tejas, Nuevo México.* 1649. Documentos inéditos o muy raros para la historia de México 25. Mexico City: Librería de la Viuda de Charles Bouret, 1909.

León, Fray Luis de. *De los nombres de Cristo.* 1591. In *Obras completas castellanas,* by Luis de León, edited by Félix García, 1:397–825. 4th ed. Biblioteca de autores cristianos 3. Madrid: Editorial Católica, 1957.

Leonard, Irving A. *Books of the Brave: Being an Account of Books and of Men in the Spanish Conquest and Settlement of the Sixteenth-Century New World.* 1949. Edited and with a new critical introduction by Rolena Adorno. Berkeley and Los Angeles: University of California Press, 1992.

——. *Don Carlos de Sigüenza y Góngora: Un sabio mexicano del siglo XVII.* 1929. Translated by Juan José Utrilla. Mexico City: Fondo de Cultura Económica, 1984.

——. *Los Libros del conquistador.* 1953. Introduction by Rolena Adorno. Translated by Mario Monteforte Toledo, Gonzalo Velorio Morayta, and Martí Soler. Translation revised by Julián Calvo and Rolena Adorno. Colección conmemorativa 70 aniversario. Rpt. Mexico City: Fondo de Cultura Económica, 2006.

——. *Romances of Chivalry in the Spanish Indies.* University of California Publications in Modern Philology, vol. 16, no. 3, pp. 217–371. Berkeley: University of California Press, 1933.

León-Portilla, Miguel. *Bernardino de Sahagún: First Anthropologist.* Translated by Mauricio J. Mixto. Norman: University of Oklahoma Press, 2002.

——. "Introducción." In *Historia verdadera de la conquista de la Nueva España,* by Bernal Díaz del Castillo, edited by Miguel León-Portilla, 1:7–58. Crónicas de América 2. Madrid: Historia 16, 1984.

Levillier, Roberto. *Gobernantes del Perú: cartas y papeles, siglo XVI.* 14 vols. Madrid: Juan Pueyo, 1921–26.

Lewis, Robert. "Retórica y verdad: los cargos de Bernal Díaz a López de Gómara." In *De la crónica a la nueva narrativa mexicana,* edited by Merlin H. Forster and Julio Ortega, 37–47. Oaxaca, Mexico: Oasis, 1986.

Lipschutz, Alejandro. "En defensa de Gonzalo Guerrero, marinero de Palos." In

Miscelánea de estudios dedicados a Fernando Ortiz, por sus discípulos, colegas y amigos, con ocasión de cumplirse sesenta años de la publicación de su primer impreso en Menorca en 1895, foreword by José María Chacón y Calvo et al., 2:929–942. Havana: Sociedad Económica de Amigos del País, 1956.

———. *El problema racial en la conquista de América.* 1963. 3d ed. Mexico City: Siglo Veintiuno, 1975.

Liss, Peggy. *Mexico under Spain, 1521–1556: Society and the Origins of Nationality.* Chicago: University of Chicago Press, 1975.

Llorente, Juan Antonio. *Colección de las obras del venerable obispo de Chiapa, don Bartolomé de las Casas.* 2 vols. Paris: Rosa, 1822.

———. *Historia crítica de la Inquisición de España.* 1817–18. 10 vols. Madrid: Imprenta del Censor, 1822–25.

Lobingier, Charles Sumner. "Introduction." In *Las siete partidas,* by Alfonso X, King of Castile and León, translated by Samuel Parsons Scott, xlix–lxxvii.

Lohmann Villena, Guillermo. "Una carta inédita de Huamán Poma de Ayala." *Revista de Indias* 20 (1945): 325–327.

———. "La restitución por conquistadores y encomenderos: Un aspecto de la incidencia lascasiana en el Perú." In *Estudios lascasianos: IV centenario de la muerte de Fray Bartolomé de las Casas (1566–1966),* introduction by Francisco Morales Padrón, 21–89. Seville: Facultad de Filosofía y Letras de la Universidad de Sevilla y Escuela de Estudios Hispanoamericanos, 1966.

López de Cogolludo, Diego. *Historia de Yucatán.* 1688. Introduction by J. Ignacio Rubio Mañé. 5th ed. Mexico City: Academia Literaria, 1957.

López de Gómara, Francisco. *La conquista de México.* 1552. Edited by Jorge Gurría Lacroix. Biblioteca Ayacucho 65. Caracas: Biblioteca Ayacucho, 1979.

———. *Crónica de los Barbarrojas.* 1545. Memorial histórico español, no. 6, pp. 327–539. Madrid: Real Academia de la Historia, 1853.

———. *Hispania victrix: 1 y 2 parte de la Historia general de las Indias.* Edited by Enrique de Vedia. Biblioteca de autores españoles 22. Madrid, 1852.

———. *Historia general de las Indias.* Edited by Franklin Pease. Introduction by Aurelio Miró Quesada. Lima: Comisión Nacional del V Centenario del Descubrimiento de América-Encuentro de Dos Mundos, 1993. Facsímile of 1555 edition, annotated by El Inca Garcilaso de la Vega.

———. *Historia general de las Indias y la conquista de México.* Zaragoza: P. Bernuz and A. Milán, 1552.

———. *Historia general de las Indias.* 1552. Edited by Jorge Gurría Lacroix. Biblioteca Ayacucho 64. Caracas: Biblioteca Ayacucho, 1979.

López Pinciano, Alonso. *Philosophia antigua poética.* 1596. Edited by Alfredo Carballo Picazo. 3 vols. Madrid: Instituto "Miguel de Cervantes," Consejo Superior de Investigaciones Científicas, 1953.

Losada, Ángel. "Hernán Cortés en la obra del cronista Sepúlveda." *Revista de Indias* 8, nos. 31–32 (1976): 127–169.

———. "Introducción." In Casas, *Apología,* 11–42. Madrid, 1988.

——. "Juan Ginés de Sepúlveda y su 'Demócrates Secundus.'" In Sepúlveda, *Demócrates Segundo*, vii–xxxii.

Lowery, Woodbury. *The Spanish Settlements within the Present Limits of the United States, 1513–1561*. New York: G. P. Putnam's Sons, 1901.

Macchi, María Fernanda. "Imágenes de los Incas en el siglo XVIII." Ph.D. diss., Yale University, 2003.

MacCormack, Sabine. "From the Sun of the Incas to the Virgin of Copacabana." *Representations* 8 (Fall 1984): 30–60.

——. *Religion in the Andes: Vision and Imagination in Early Colonial Peru*. Princeton: Princeton University Press, 1991.

MacLeod, Murdo J. "Self-Promotion: The 'Relaciones de méritos y servicios' and Their Historical and Political Interpretations." Lecture at John Carter Brown Library, Providence, Rhode Island, June 20, 1987.

MacNutt, Francis Augustus. *Bartholomew de las Casas, His Life, Apostolate, and Writings*. Cleveland: Arthur H. Clark, 1909.

Magallón, M. "Prólogo." In *Crónica de la Nueva España*, by Francisco Cervantes de Salazar, v–xxiv. Madrid: Hispanic Society of America, 1914.

Mannheim, Bruce. *The Language of the Inka since the European Invasion*. Austin: University of Texas Press, 1991.

Manzano Manzano, Juan. *La incorporación de las Indias en la corona de Castilla*. Madrid: Ediciones Cultura Hispánica, 1948.

Marcos, Teodoro Andrés. "Ideología del *Demócrates secundus*." In Sepúlveda, *Demócrates Segundo*, xxxv–xliv.

Marcus, Raymond. "La Conquête de Cholula: Conflit d'Interprétations." *Ibero-Amerikanisches Archiv*, year 3, vol. 2 (1977): 193–213.

Márquez, Antonio. *Literatura e Inquisición en España, 1478–1834*. Madrid: Taurus, 1980.

Martínez, José Luis, ed. *Documentos cortesianos, 1518–1528*. Mexico City: Universidad Nacional Autónoma de México and Fondo de Cultura Económica, 1990.

——. *Hernán Cortés*. Mexico City: Universidad Nacional Autónoma de México and Fondo de Cultura Económica, 1990.

——. *Nezahualcóyotl: vida y obra*. Mexico City: Fondo de Cultura Económica, 1972.

Martínez Marín, Carlos. "La aculturación indoespañola en la época del descubrimiento de México." In *Homenaje a Pablo Martínez del Río en el vigésimoquinto aniversario de la primera edición de "Los orígenes americanos,"* foreword by Ignacio Bernal et al., 401–410. Mexico City: Instituto Nacional de Antropología e Historia, 1961.

Medina, José Toribio. *Los romances basados en "La Araucana" con su texto y anotaciones*. Santiago de Chile: Elzeviriana, 1918.

Mendoza, Antonio de. "Carta al emperador del 10 de diciembre de 1537." In *Colección de documentos inéditos . . . América y Oceanía* (CDI), 2:179–211.

——. "Relación, apuntamientos y avisos, que por mandado de S.M. dio D. Antonio de Mendoza, virrey de Nueva España a D. Luis de Velasco, nombrado para sucederle en este cargo." In *Colección de documentos . . . América y Oceanía* (CDI), 6:484–515.

Merediz, Eyda. *Refracted Images: The Canary Islands through a New World Lens.* Tempe: Arizona Center for Medieval and Renaissance Studies, 2004.

Mier y Noriega, Servando Teresa de. *Apología.* 1818. Edited by Guadalupe Fernández Ariza. Rome: Bulzoni Editore, 1998.

——. *Historia de la revolución de Nueva España, antiguamente Anáhuac.* 1813. Edited by André Saint-Lu, Marie-Cécile Bénassy-Berling, Jeanne Chenu, Jean-Pierre Clément, André Pons, Marie-Laure Rieu-Millan, and Paul Roche. Preface by David Brading. Série Langues et Langages 20. Paris: Université de Paris III, La Sorbonne, 1990.

Mignolo, Walter. "Cartas, crónicas, y relaciones del descubrimiento y la conquista." In *Historia de la literatura hispanoamericana: I. Época colonial,* edited by Luis Iñigo Madrigal, 57–116. Madrid: Cátedra, 1982.

Milhou, Alain. *Colón y su mentalidad mesiánica en el ambiente franciscanista español.* Cuadernos Colombinos 11. Valladolid: La Casa-Museo de Colón y Seminario Americanista de la Universidad de Valladolid, 1983.

Millares Carlo, Agustín. "Indice analítico." In *Historia de las Indias,* by Bartolomé de las Casas, 3:411–520.

Mills, Kenneth. *Idolatry and Its Enemies: Colonial Andean Religion and Extirpation, 1640–1750.* Princeton: Princeton University Press, 1997.

Miró Quesada, Aurelio. *El Inca Garcilaso y otros estudios garcilasistas.* Madrid: Ediciones Cultura Hispánica, 1971.

——. "Prólogo." In *La Florida del Inca,* by El Inca Garcilaso de la Vega, edited by Emma Susana Speratti Piñero, ix–lxxvi. Mexico City: Fondo de Cultura Económica, 1956.

Moríñigo, Marcos A., and Isaías Lerner. "Introducción biográfica y crítica." In Ercilla, *La araucana,* 1:7–112.

Morison, Samuel Eliot. *A New and Fresh English Translation of the Letter of Columbus.* Madrid: Yagues, 1959.

Mörner, Magnus. *Race Mixture in the History of Latin America.* Boston: Little, Brown, 1967.

Morrall, John B. *Political Thought in Medieval Times.* Medieval Academy Reprints for Teaching 7. Toronto: University of Toronto Press and Medieval Academy of America, 1980.

Mota Padilla, Matías Ángel de la. *Historia del reino de Nueva Galicia en la América septentrional.* 1742. Colección histórica de obras facsimilares 3. Guadalajara, Mexico: Instituto Jalisciense de Antropología e Historia, Universidad de Guadalajara, 1973.

Mundy, Barbara. "Mapping the Aztec Capital: The 1524 Nuremberg Map of Tenochtitlán, Its Sources and Meanings." *Imago Mundi* 50 (1998): 11–33.

Muñoz Camargo, Diego. *Historia de Tlaxcala.* 1576. Edited by Germán Vázquez. Crónicas de América 26. Madrid: Historia 16, 1986.

Murra, John V. "Waman Puma, etnógrafo del mundo andino." In Guaman Poma, *El primer nueva corónica,* 1:xiii–xix.

Murúa, Fray Martín de. *Historia del origen y genealogía real de los reyes Ingas del Pirú. De sus hechos, costumbres, trajes, y manera de gobierno.* 1590.

———. *Historia del origen y genealogía real de los reyes Ingas del Pirú de sus hechos, costumbres, trajes, y manera de gobierno.* 1590. In *Códice Murúa. Historia y genealogía de los reyes Incas del Perú del padre mercenario [sic] fray Martín de Murúa. Códice Galvin.* 2 vols. Testimonio Editorial, Madrid. 2004. Vol. 1, facsimile of manuscript.

———. *Historia del origen y genealogía real de los reyes Ingas del Pirú de sus hechos, costumbres, trajes, y manera de gobierno.* 1590. In *Códice Murúa. Historia y genealogía, de los reyes Incas del Perú del padre mercenario [sic] fray Martín de Murúa. Códice Galvin.* 2 vols. Testimonio Editorial, Madrid. 2004. Vol. 2, 73–258, transcription by Juan M. Ossio.

———. *Historia general del Pirú. Origen y descendencia de los Yncas. Donde se trata, así de las guerras civiles suyas, como de la entrada de los españoles, descripción de las ciudades y lugares del, con otras cosas notables.* 1611–1613. Los Angeles, J. Paul Getty Museum, Ms. Ludwig XIII 16.

Navarra, Pedro de. *Diálogos de la preparación de la muerte, dictados por el ilustrísimo y reverendísimo señor don Pedro de Navarra, Obispo de Comenge.* Tolosa, 1565.

Núñez Cabeza de Vaca, Álvar. *The Narrative of Álvar Núñez Cabeza de Vaca.* Translated by Buckingham Smith. Washington, D.C., 1851.

———. *The Narrative of Cabeza de Vaca.* Edited and translated by Rolena Adorno and Patrick Charles Pautz. Lincoln: University of Nebraska Press, 2003.

———. "Prohemio." In Hernández, *Comentarios de Álvar Núñez Cabeza de Vaca, adelantado y governador de la provincia del Río de la Plata.* In Núñez Cabeza de Vaca, *Relación de los naufragios y comentarios,* edited by Serrano and Sanz, 1:147–155.

———. *Relación de los naufragios y comentarios de Álvar Núñez Cabeza de Vaca, adelantado y governador del Río de la Plata,* edited by Manuel Serrano y Sanz. 2 vols. Colección de libros y documentos referentes a la historia de América 5 and 6. Madrid: Victoriano Suárez, 1906.

———. *La relación que dio Álvar Núñez Cabeça de Vaca de lo acaescido en las Indias en la armada donde iva por governador Pánfilo de Narbáez, desde el año de veinte y siete hasta el año de treinta y seis que bolvió a Sevilla con tres de su compañía.* Zamora: Printed by Augustín de Paz y Juan Picardo for Juan Pedro Musetti, 1542.

———. *La relación y comentarios del governador Álvar Núñez Cabeça de Vaca, de lo acaescido en las dos jornadas que hizo a las Indias.* Valladolid: Francisco Fernández de Córdova, 1555.

———. "Transcription and English Translation of the 1542 'Relación.'" In Adorno and Pautz, *Álvar Núñez Cabeza de Vaca* 1:14–279.

O'Gorman, Edmundo. "Estudio introductorio: Alva Ixtlilxochitl." In Alva Ixtlilxochitl, *Obras históricas* 1:5–257.

———. "Estudio preliminar." In Casas, *Apologética historia sumaria,* 1:vii–clxxiv.

———. "Prólogo." In Acosta, *Historia natural y moral,* xi–lxiv.

———. "Sobre la naturaleza bestial del indio americano." *Filosofía y letras,* 1, no. 1 (1941): 141–158; 1, no. 2 (1941): 305–314.

Olaechea Labayen, Juan Bautista. *El mestizaje como gesta.* Colección Realidades Americanas 16. Madrid: Editorial MAPFRE, 1992.

Oña, Pedro de. *Arauco domado.* 1596. In *Colección de incunables americanos, siglo XVI.* Vol. 11. Madrid: Instituto de Cultura Hispánica, 1944.

Ossio A., Juan M. "Guaman Poma: Nueva corónica o carta al rey. Un intento de aproximación a las categorías del pensamiento del mundo andino." In *Ideología mesiánica del mundo andino,* edited by Juan M. Ossio, 155–213. Lima: Biblioteca de Antropología, 1973.

——. "Introducción." In Murúa, *Códice Murúa* 2:7–72.

Ovalle, Alonso de. *Histórica relación del reyno de Chile.* 1646. Santiago de Chile: Instituto de Literatura Chilena, 1969.

Oviedo y Valdés, Gonzalo Fernández de. *See* Fernández de Oviedo y Valdés, Gonzalo.

Pagden, Anthony. " 'Con título y con no menos mérito que el de Alemania, que vuestra sacra majestad posee': Rethinking the Conquest of Mexico." In *The Uncertainties of Empire: Essays in Iberian and Spanish-American Intellectual History,* by Anthony Pagden, 1–16. London: Variorum, 1994.

——. *The Fall of Natural Man: The American Indian and the Origins of Comparative Ethnology.* Cambridge: Cambridge University Press, 1982.

Pané, Ramón. *Relación acerca de las antigüedades de los Indios.* Edited by José Juan Arrom. 3d ed. Mexico City: Siglo Veintiuno, 1978.

Pardo, Osvaldo. *The Origins of Mexican Catholicism: Nahua Rituals and Christian Sacraments in Sixteenth-Century Mexico.* Ann Arbor: University of Michigan Press, 2004.

Parish, Helen Rand. "Introduction. Las Casas's Spirituality—the Three Crises." In Casas, *The Only Way,* 9–58.

——, and Harold E. Weidman. *Las Casas en México: Historia y obra desconocidas.* Mexico City: Fondo de Cultura Económica, 1992.

——, with Harold E. Weidman. "The Correct Birthdate of Bartolomé de las Casas." *Hispanic American Historical Review* 56:3 (1976): 385–403.

Parry, John H. *The Audiencia of New Galicia in the Sixteenth Century.* Cambridge: Cambridge University Press, 1948.

——, and Robert G. Keith, eds. *The Conquerors and the Conquered.* Volume 1, *New Iberian World: A Documentary History of the Discovery and Settlement of Latin America to the Early 17th Century.* New York: Times Books and Hector and Rose, 1984.

Pastor, Beatriz. *Discurso narrativo de la conquista de América.* Havana: Casa de las Américas, 1983.

Paz, Octavio. "Literatura de fundación." In *Puertas al campo,* by Octavio Paz, 11–19. Mexico City: Universidad Nacional Autónoma de México, 1966.

——. "A Literature of Foundations." In *The Siren and the Seashell and Other Essays on Poets and Poetry,* by Octavio Paz, translated by Lysander Kemp and Margaret Sayers Peden, 173–179. Austin: University of Texas Press, 1976.

Pennington, Kenneth J., Jr. "Bartolomé de las Casas and the Tradition of Medieval Law." *Church History* 39, no. 2 (1970): 149–161.

Pereña, Luciano. "Estudio preliminar." In Acosta, *De procuranda indorum salute*, 3–46.

Pereyra Chávez, Nelson. "Un documento sobre Guaman Poma de Ayala existente en el Archivo Departamental de Ayacucho." *Histórica* 21, no. 2 (1997): 261–270.

Pérez de Ribas, Andrés. *Historia de los triumphos de nuestra santa fee entre gentes las más bárbaras y fieras del Nuevo Orbe*. Madrid: Alonso de Paredes, 1645.

——. *History of the Triumphs of Our Holy Faith Amongst the Most Barbarous and Fierce Peoples of the New World*. Edited and translated by Daniel T. Reff, Maureen Ahern, and Richard K. Danford. Tucson: University of Arizona Press, 1999.

Pérez Fernández, Isacio, ed. *El anónimo de Yucay frente a Bartolomé de las Casas: Edición crítica del Parecer de Yucay*. 1571. Cuzco: Centro de Estudios Regionales Andinos Bartolomé de las Casas, 1995.

——, ed. "Apéndices." In Casas, *Brevísima relación . . . primera edición crítica*, 917–986.

——. *Cronología documentada de los viajes, estancias y actuaciones de Fray Bartolomé de las Casas*. Bayamón, Puerto Rico: Centro de Estudios de los Dominicos del Caribe and Universidad Central de Bayamón, 1984.

——." Estudio crítico preliminar." In Casas, *Brevísima relación . . . primera edición crítica*, 23–368.

——, ed. *Inventario documentado de los escritos de fray Bartolomé de las Casas*. Revised by Helen Rand Parish. Estudios monográficos 1. Bayamón, Puerto Rico: Centro de Estudios de los Dominicos del Caribe, 1981.

Phelan, John Leddy. *The Millennial Kingdom of the Franciscans in the New World*. 2d ed. Berkeley and Los Angeles: University of California Press, 1970.

Philips, William D., Jr. *Slavery from Roman Times to the Early Transatlantic Trade*. Minneapolis: University of Minnesota Press, 1985.

Picón-Salas, Mariano. *De la conquista a la Independencia: tres siglos de historia cultural hispanoamericana*. Mexico City: Fondo de Cultura Económica, 1944.

Pierce, Francis William. *Amadís de Gaula*. Boston: Twayne, 1976.

——. *La poesía épica del Siglo de Oro*. Madrid: Gredos, 1961.

Pizarro y Orellana, Fernando. *Varones ilustres del Nuevo Mundo*. Madrid: Diego Díaz de la Carrera, 1639.

Polo de Ondegardo, Juan. "Traslado de un cartapacio a manera de borrador que quedó en los papeles del licenciado Polo de Ondegardo cerca del linaje de los Ingas y como conquistaron." In *Informaciones acerca de la religión y gobierno de los Incas por el licenciado Polo de Ondegardo*, edited by Horacio H. Urteaga, 95–151. Colección de libros y documentos referentes a la historia del Perú 4. Lima: Librería Sanmartí, 1917.

Pomar, Juan Bautista de. *Relacion de Texcoco*. 1582. In García Icazbalceta, ed., *Nueva colección* 3:1–64.

Porras Barrenechea, Raúl. *El cronista indio Felipe Huamán Poma de Ayala*. Lima: Editorial Lumen, 1948.

——. *Los cronistas del Perú, 1528–1650, y otros ensayos*. Edited by Franklin Pease G. Y. Biblioteca Clásicos del Perú 2. Lima: Banco de Crédito del Perú, 1986.

Posse, Abel. *Daimón*. Buenos Aires: Emecé, 1989.

——. *Daimón*. Translated by Sarah Arvio. New York: Atheneum, 1992.

——. *El largo atardecer del caminante*. Buenos Aires: Emecé, 1992.

Pratt, Mary Louise. *Imperial Eyes: Travel Writing and Transculturation*. New York: Routledge, 1992.

Prem, Hanns, and Berthold Riege, Antje Gunsenheimer, and Gabriela Solís. "En torno a Gonzalo Guerrero." *Arqueología Mexicana* 3, no. 18 (1996): 4–5.

Proceedings of the XVIII International Congress of Americanists. London: Harrison and Sons, 1913.

Pupo-Walker, Enrique. *Historia, creación y profecía en los textos del Inca Garcilaso de la Vega*. Madrid: José Porrúa Turanzas, 1982.

——, ed. *Los Naufragios* by Álvar Núñez Cabeza de Vaca. Nueva Biblioteca de Erudición y Crítica 5. Madrid: Castalia, 1992.

Queraltó Moreno, Ramón-Jesús. *El pensamiento filosófico-político de Bartolomé de las Casas*. Sevilla: Escuela de Estudios Hispano-Americanos, 1976.

Quirk, Robert E. "Some Notes on a Controversial Controversy: Juan Ginés de Sepúlveda and Natural Servitude." *Hispanic American Historical Review* 34, no. 3 (1954): 357–364.

Radin, Paul. *The Trickster: A Study in American Indian Mythology*. 1956. Introduction by Stanley Diamond. Commentaries by Kart Kerényi and C. G. Jung. Rpt. New York: Schocken Books, 1972.

Ramírez Cabañas, Joaquín. "Introducción." In *Historia verdadera de la conquista de la Nueva España,* by Bernal Díaz del Castillo, edited by Joaquín Ramírez Cabañas, 1:7–36.

Ramos, Demetrio, et al., eds. *Francisco de Vitoria y la Escuela de Salamanca: La ética en la conquista de América*. Corpus Hispanorum de Pace 25. Madrid: Consejo Superior de Investigaciones Científicas, 1984.

——. "El movimiento historial coincidente: La literatura testimonial de las historias verdaderas de la conquista." In *Ximénez de Quesada en su relación con los cronistas y el epítome de la conquista del Nuevo Reino de Granada*, by Demetrio Ramos, 195–213. Sevilla: Escuela de Estudios Hispano-Americanos, 1972.

——. "Sepúlveda, cronista indiano, y los problemas de su crónica." In Sepúlveda, *Hechos,* 101–167.

Ramos Gavilán, Alonso. *Historia de Nuestra Señora de Copacabana*. 1621. La Paz, Bolivia: Academia Boliviana de la Historia, 1976.

Retratos de los españoles ilustres con el epítome de sus vidas. Madrid: Imprenta Real, 1791.

Revello, José Torre. *El libro, la imprenta y el periodismo en América durante la dominación española*. Buenos Aires: Facultad de Filosofía y Letras, 1940.

Ricard, Robert. *The Spiritual Conquest of Mexico*. 1933. Translated by Leslie Byrd Simpson. Berkeley and Los Angeles: University of California Press, 1966.

Rico, José. "Gonzalo Guerrero: La frontera del imaginario español." *Latin American Literary Review* 28, no. 55 (2000): 87–109.

Riva-Agüero, José de la. *La historia en el Perú*. Lima: Editorial Nacional de Federico Barrionuevo, 1910.

Roa-de-la-Carrera, Cristián. *Histories of Infamy: Francisco López de Gómara and the Ethics of Spanish Imperialism*. Translated by Scott Sessions. Foreword by David Carrasco. Boulder: University Press of Colorado, 2005.

Robertson, Tomás Antonio, trans. *My Life among the Savage Nations of New Spain*, by Andrés Pérez de Ribas. Los Angeles: Ward Ritchie Press, 1968.

Robertson, William. *The History of America*. 1776. 5th ed. 3 vols. London, 1788.

Rodríguez de Prampolini, Ida. *Amadises de América: la hazaña de Indias como empresa caballeresca*. Mexico City: Junta Mexicana de Investigaciones Históricas, 1948.

Román y Zamora, Jerónimo. *Repúblicas de Indias: idolatría y gobierno en México y Perú antes de la conquista*. 2 vols. Colección de libros raros y curiosos que tratan de América 14, 15. Madrid: Vitoriano Suárez, 1897.

——. *Repúblicas del mundo, divididas en tres partes*. Salamanca: Juan Fernández, 1595.

——. *Repúblicas del mundo, divididas en XXVII libros*. Medina del Campo: Francisco del Canto, 1575.

Ross, Kathleen. *A New World Paradise: The Baroque Narrative of Carlos de Sigüenza y Góngora*. Cambridge: Cambridge University Press, 1994.

Rowe, John H. "Ethnography and Ethnology in the Sixteenth Century." *Kroeber Anthropological Society Papers*, no. 30 (Spring 1964): 1–19.

——. "The Renaissance Foundations of Anthropology." *American Anthropologist* 67, no. 1 (1965): 1–20.

Rulfo, Juan. *Pedro Páramo*. 1955. Rpt. Mexico City: Fondo de Cultura Económica, 1971.

——. *Pedro Páramo*. 1955. Translated by Margaret Sayers Peden. Foreword by Susan Sontag. Rpt. London: Serpent's Tail, 1994.

Rumeu de Armas, Antonio. *La política indigenista de Isabel la Católica*. Documentos 2. Valladolid: Instituto "Isabel la Católica" de Historia Eclesiástica, 1969.

Saavedra Guzmán, Antonio. *El peregrino indiano*. 1599. Edited by Joaquín García Icazbalceta. Mexico City: Editorial 'El sistema postal,' 1880.

Sáenz de Santa María, Carmelo. *Historia de una historia: la crónica de Bernal Díaz del Castillo*. Madrid: Consejo Superior de Investigaciones Científicas, 1984.

——. *Introducción crítica a la "Historia verdadera" de Bernal Díaz del Castillo*. Madrid: Instituto "Gonzalo Fernández de Oviedo," Consejo Superior de Investigaciones Científicas, 1967.

——. "Plan de la edición." In Díaz del Castillo, *Historia verdadera*, edited by Sáenz de Santa María, 1:xi–xxxxvii.

——, ed. *Suplemento*. Supplement to Díaz del Castillo, *Historia verdadera*, edited by Carmelo Sáenz de Santa María. Madrid, 1982.

Saer, Juan José. *El entenado*. Mexico City: Folios Ediciones, 1983.

——. *The Witness*. Translated by Margaret Jull Costa. London: Serpent's Tail, 1990.

Sahagún, Fray Bernardino de. *Historia general de las cosas de Nueva España*. Edited by Ángel Garibay. Sepan cuántos 300. Mexico City: Porrúa, 1979.

——. *Psalmodía cristiana y sermonario de los Santos del año, en lengua mexicana, ordenadas en cantares o psalmos para que canten los indios en los areytos que hacen en las iglesias*. Mexico City: Pedro Ocharte, 1583.

Saint-Lu, André. "Introducción." In Casas, *Brevísima relación*, 11–62.

Saint-Lu, André, Marie-Cécile Bénassy-Berling, Jeanne Chenu, Jean-Pierre Clément, André Pons, Marie-Laure Rieu-Millan, and Paul Roche. "Introducción." In Mier y Noriega, *Historia*, xi–cxxxii.

Salazar, Rodolfo. "Pieza de un expediente de la comunidad de indígenas de Quinua." In Varallanos, *Guaman Poma*, 210–211.

Salles-Reese, Verónica. *From Viracocha to the Virgin of Copacabana: Representation of the Sacred at Lake Titicaca*. Austin: University of Texas Press, 1997.

Salomon, Frank. "Chronicles of the Impossible: Notes on Three Peruvian Indigenous Historians." In *From Oral to Written Expression: Native Andean Chronicles of the Early Colonial Period*, edited by Rolena Adorno, 9–39. Foreign and Comparative Studies Publications, Latin American Series, no. 4. Syracuse: Maxwell School of Citizenship and Public Affairs, Syracuse University, 1982.

San Buenaventura, Joseph de. *Historias de la conquista del Mayab, 1511–1697*. Edited by Gabriela Solís Robleda and Pedro Bracamonte y Sosa. Mérida, Yucatán: Universidad Autónoma de Yucatán, 1994.

Santa Cruz, Alonso de. *Crónica del emperador Carlos V*. c. 1551. Edited by Francisco de Laiglesia y Auser. 5 vols. Madrid: Real Academia de la Historia, 1920–1925.

Sauer, Carl Ortwin. *The Early Spanish Main*. 1966. Foreword by Anthony Pagden. Rpt. Berkeley and Los Angeles: University of California Press, 1992.

——. "The Road to Cíbola." *Ibero-Americana* 3 (1932): 1–58.

Savater, Fernando. "Presentación." In *Conquistadores de Yucatán: La desaparición de Gonzalo Guerrero*, 4–5. Madrid: Planeta-De Agostini and Sociedad Estatal Quinto Centenario, 1992.

Schwartz, Stuart B. "Spaniards, *Pardos*, and the Missing Mestizos: Identities and Racial Categories in the Early Hispanic Caribbean." *NWIG: New West Indian Guide* 71, nos. 1–2 (1997): 5–19.

Scott, Samuel Parsons, trans. and ed. *Las siete partidas* by Alfonso X, King of Castile and León. 1256–1263. Introduction by Charles Sumner Lobingier. Bibliography by John Vance. Washington, D.C.: Commerce Clearing House for the Comparative Law Bureau of the American Bar Association, 1931.

Sepúlveda, Juan Ginés de. *Apología de Juan Ginés de Sepúlveda contra Fray Bartolomé de las Casas y de Fray Bartolomé de las Casas contra Juan Ginés de Sepúlveda*. Edited and translated by Ángel Losada. Madrid: Editora Nacional, 1975.

——. *De la compatibilidad entre la milicia y la religión*. In *Tratados políticos de Juan Ginés de Sepúlveda*, by Juan Ginés de Sepúlveda, edited and translated by Ángel Losada, 127–304. Madrid: Instituto de Estudios Políticos, 1963.

——. *Demócrates Segundo o de las justas causas de la guerra contra los indios.* Edited and translated by Ángel Losada. Madrid: Consejo Superior de Investigaciones Científicas, 1984. Reproduction of the 1951 edition.

——. "Exhortación a la Guerra contra los Turcos." 1529. In *Tratados políticos de Juan Ginés de Sepúlveda,* by Juan Ginés de Sepúlveda, edited by Ángel Losada, 1–27. Madrid: Instituto de Estudios Políticos, 1963.

——. *Hechos de los Españoles en el Nuevo Mundo y México.* c. 1562. In *Juan Ginés de Sepúlveda y su crónica indiana en el IV centenario de su muerte, 1573–1973,* edited and translated by Demetrio Ramos, Lucio Mijares Pérez, and Jonás Castro Toledo, 187–462. Valladolid: Seminario Americanista de la Universidad de Valladolid and Excmo. Ayuntamiento de Pozoblanco, 1976. Translation of Sepúlveda's *De orbe novo.*

——. *Historia del Nuevo Mundo.* c. 1562. Introduction and translation by Antonio Ramírez de Verger. Madrid: Alianza, 1987. Translation of Sepúlveda's *De orbe novo.*

——. "Proposiciones temerarias, escandalosas y heréticas que notó el doctor Sepúlveda en el libro de la Conquista de Indias, que Fray Bartolomé de las Casas, obispo que fue de Chiapa, hizo imprimir 'sin licencia' en Sevilla, año de 1552." In Fabié, *Vida y escritos,* 2:543–569.

Service, Elman R. "Indian–European Relations in Colonial Latin America." *American Anthropologist* 57 (1955): 411–425.

Sigüenza y Góngora, Carlos de. *Infortunios de Alonso Ramírez.* In *Seis obras,* by Carlos de Sigüenza y Góngora, introduction by Irving A. Leonard, edited by William C. Bryant, 3–47. Caracas: Biblioteca Ayacucho, 1984.

Simpson, Lesley Byrd. *The Encomienda in New Spain: The Beginning of Spanish Mexico.* Berkeley and Los Angeles: University of California Press, 1950.

——. *Studies in the Administration of the Indians in New Spain. IV. The Emancipation of the Indian Slaves and the Resettlement of the Freedmen, 1548–1553.* Berkeley and Los Angeles: University of California Press, 1940.

Slotkin, Richard. *Regeneration through Violence: The Mythology of the American Frontier, 1600–1860.* Middletown, Conn.: Wesleyan University Press, 1973.

Smith, Buckingham, ed. *Colección de documentos para la historia de la Florida y tierras adyacentes.* London: Trübner, 1857.

Solano, Francisco. "El intérprete: Uno de los ejes de la aculturación." *Terceras jornadas americanistas de la Universidad de Valladolid: Estudios sobre política indigenista española en América* 1:265–278. Valladolid: Universidad de Valladolid, 1975.

Solís Robleda, Gabriela, and Pedro Bracamonte y Sosa. "Introducción." In San Buenaventura, *Historias de la conquista del Mayab,* ix–xl.

Solís y Rivadeneira, Antonio. *Historia de la conquista de México, población y progresos de la América Septentrional, conocida por el nombre de Nueva España.* 1684. Edited by Edmundo O'Gorman. Notes by José Valero Silva. 4th ed. Mexico City: Porrúa, 1985.

Solórzano Pereira, Juan de. *Política indiana*. 1629. Biblioteca de autores españoles 252. Madrid: Atlas, 1972.

Soto, Domingo de. "Prólogo del maestro Soto." In Casas, "Aquí se contiene una disputa o controversia," *Obras escogidas*, 295–308.

Spack, Patricia Meyers. "Reality—Our Subject and Discipline." *PMLA* 110, no. 3 (1995): 350–357.

Stabler, Arthur P., and John E. Kicza. "Ruy González's 1553 Letter to Emperor Charles V: An Annotated Translation." *The Americas* 42, no. 4 (1986): 473–487.

Stern, Steve J. "Algunas consideraciones sobre la personalidad histórica de don Felipe Guaman Poma de Ayala." *Histórica* 2:2 (1978): 225–228.

Stevens, Wallace. *Collected Poetry and Prose*. Edited by Frank Kermode and Joan Richards. New York: Library of America, 1997.

Stone, Cynthia L. *In Place of Gods and Kings: Authorship and Identity in the Relación de Michoacán*. Norman: University of Oklahoma Press, 2004.

Swanton, John R. *Final Report of the United States De Soto Expedition Commission*. 1939. Introduction by Jeffrey P. Brain. Foreword by William C. Sturtevant. Washington, D.C.: Smithsonian Institution Press, 1985.

Tapia, Andrés de. "Relación hecha por el señor Andrés de Tapia, sobre la conquista de México." In García Icazbalceta, ed., *Colección* 2:554–594.

Tedlock, Dennis, ed. and trans. *Popol Vuh: The Mayan Book of the Dawn of Life*. New York: Simon and Schuster, 1985.

Tello, Antonio. *Crónica miscelánea de la sancta provincia de Jalisco. Libro Segundo.* 1650–1653. Instituto Jalisciense de Antropología e Historia, Serie de Historia 9. Guadalajara, Mexico: Gobierno del Estado de Jalisco and Universidad de Guadalajara, 1968.

Thiesen, Gerald, trans. "The Joint Report Recorded by Gonzalo Fernández de Oviedo y Valdés." In *The Narrative of Álvar Núñez Cabeza de Vaca*, by Álvar Núñez Cabeza de Vaca, translated by Fanny Bandelier, introduction by John Francis Bannon, 159–271. Barre, Mass.: Imprint Society, 1972.

Thomas, Hugh. *Conquest: Montezuma, Cortés, and the Fall of Old Mexico*. New York: Simon and Schuster, 1993.

Thompson, John B. *Studies in the Theory of Ideology*. Berkeley and Los Angeles: University of California Press, 1985.

Todorov, Tzvetan. *The Conquest of America: The Question of the Other*. Translated by Richard Howard. 1982. New York: Harper and Row, 1984.

Torquemada, Juan de. *Monarquía indiana*. 1615. Introduction by Miguel León-Portilla. 3 vols. Mexico City: Porrúa, 1969.

Torre Revello, José. *El libro, la imprenta y el periodismo en América durante la dominación española*. Buenos Aires: Facultad de Filosofía y Letras, 1940.

Torres Ramírez, Bibiano. "La odisea de Gonzalo Guerrero en México." In *Actas del Congreso de historia del descubrimiento, 1492–1556*, 2:369–386. Madrid: Real Academia de la Historia y Confederación Española de Cajas de Ahorros, 1992.

Torres Ríoseco, Arturo. *The Epic of Latin American Literature*. New York: Oxford University Press, 1942.

———. *La gran literatura iberoamericana*. Buenos Aires: Emecé, 1945.

Tozzer, Alfred M., ed. *Landa's 'Relación de la cosas de Yucatán,' a Translation*. Papers of the Peabody Museum of Archaeology and Ethnology, Harvard University, no. 18. Cambridge: Peabody Museum, 1941.

Ugarte y Ugarte, Eduardo L. "Los caciques de Chucuito y Arequipa contra la perpetuidad de la encomienda, 1562." *Hombre y mundo*, no. 1 (1966): 30–50.

United States Library of Congress. Johann Georg Kohl Collection, no. 38. 1527. "Carta universal en que se contiene todo lo que descubrieron del mundo sea fasta ahora."

United States Library of Congress. Manuscript Division. *The Harkness Collection in the Library of Congress. Manuscripts Concerning Mexico: A Guide*. Transcriptions and translations by J. Benedict Warren. Washington, D.C.: Library of Congress, 1974.

Urdánoz, Teófilo. "Introducción a *De templanza*." In Vitoria, *Obras de Francisco de Vitoria*, 995–1003.

Vaccarella, Eric. "Echoes of Resistance: Testimonial Narrative and Pro-Indian Discourse in El Inca Garcilaso de la Vega's 'La Florida del Inca.'" *Latin American Literary Review* 32, no. 64 (2004): 100–119.

Valdeavellano, Luis G. de. *Curso de historia de las instituciones españolas de los orígenes al final de la Edad Media*. 1968. Rpt. Madrid: Alianza, 1998.

Valverde, Fernando. *Santuario de Nuestra Señora de Copacabana en el Perú: Poema sacro*. Lima: Luis de Lyra, 1641.

Van Horne, John. "The Attitude toward the Enemy in Sixteenth-Century Spanish Narrative Poetry." *Romanic Review* 16 (1925): 341–361.

Varallanos, José. *Guaman Poma de Ayala: Cronista precursor y libertario*. Lima: G. Herrera, 1979.

Vargas Machuca, Bernardo. "Apologías y discursos de las Conquistas Occidentales." In Fabié, *Vida y escritos* 2:409–517.

Vas Mingo, Milagros del. *Las capitulaciones de Indias en el siglo XVI*. Madrid: Instituto de Cooperación Iberoamericana, 1986.

Vázquez de Tapia, Bernardino. *Relación de méritos y servicios del conquistador Bernardino Vázquez de Tapia, vecino y regidor de esta gran ciudad de Tenustitlán, México*. Edited by Jorge Gurría Lacroix. Mexico City: Universidad Nacional Autónoma de México, 1973.

Vega, El Inca Garcilaso de la. *Comentarios reales de los Incas*. 1609, 1617. In *Obras completas del Inca Garcilaso de la Vega*. Edited by Carmelo Sáenz de Santa María. 3 vols. Biblioteca de autores españoles 133–135. Madrid: Atlas, 1960–1965.

———. *La Florida del Inca*. 1605. Introduction by Aurelio Miró Quesada. Edited by Emma Susana Speratti Piñero. Bibliographic study by José Durand. Mexico City: Fondo de Cultura Económica, 1956.

———. *La Florida del Inca*. Edited by Sylvia L. Hilton. Crónicas de América 22. Madrid: Historia 16, 1986.

———. *La Florida del Ynca*. 1605. Edited by Sylvia-Lyn Hilton. Madrid: Fundación Universitaria Española, 1982. Facsimile of 1605 edition.

———. *The Florida of the Inca.* Edited and translated by John Grier Varner and Jeanette Johnson Varner. Austin: University of Texas Press, 1988.

Velasco, B. "El alma cristiana del conquistador de América." *Missionalia Hispánica* 28, no. 82 (1971): 107–131.

Villa Royz, Carlos. *Gonzalo Guerrero, memoria olvidada.* Mexico City, 1995.

Vitoria, Francisco de. *De los indios, o del derecho de guerra de los españoles sobre los bárbaros (De indis, sive de iure belli hispanorum in barbaros, relectio posterior).* 1539. In *Obras de Francisco de Vitoria,* 811–858.

———. *De templanza.* 1537. In *Obras de Francisco de Vitoria,* 1004–1069.

———. *Obras de Francisco de Vitoria: Relecciones teológicas.* Edited and translated by Teófilo Urdánoz. Biblioteca de Autores Cristianos 198. Madrid: Editorial Católica, 1960.

———. *Relectio de Indis o libertad de los indios.* 1539. Edited and translated by Luciano Pereña and José María Pérez Prendes. Corpus Hispanorum de Pace 5. Madrid: Consejo Superior de Investigaciones Científicas, 1967.

Vološinov, V. N. "Reported Speech." 1930. In *Readings in Russian Poetics,* edited by Ladislav Matejka and Krystyna Pomorska, 149–175. Ann Arbor: University of Michigan Press, 1978.

Wachtel, Nathan. *Los vencidos: los indios del Perú frente a la conquista española, 1530–1570.* 1971. Translated by Antonio Escohotado. Madrid: Alianza, 1976.

Wagner, Henry Raup. "The First Lost Letter of Cortés." *Hispanic American Historical Review* 21, no. 4 (1941): 669–672.

———. "Francisco López de Gómara and His Works." *Proceedings of the American Antiquarian Society* 58, pt. 2: 263–282. Worcester, Mass.: American Antiquarian Society, 1949.

———. "Three Studies on the Same Subject": "Bernal Díaz del Castillo," "The Family of Bernal Díaz del Castillo," and "Notes on Writings by and about Bernal Díaz del Castillo." *Hispanic American Historical Review* 25, no. 2 (1945): 1–57.

———, with Helen Rand Parish. *The Life and Writings of Bartolomé de las Casas.* Albuquerque: University of New Mexico Press, 1967.

Williams, Stanley T. *The Spanish Background of American Literature.* 2 vols. Hamden, Conn.: Archon Books, 1968 [c. 1955].

Wright, Roger. "Early Medieval Spanish, Latin and Ladino." In *Circa 1492: Proceedings of the Jerusalem Colloquium: Litterae Judaeorum in Terra Hispanica,* edited by Isaac Benabu, 36–45. Jerusalem: Hebrew University and Misgav Yerushalayim Institute for Research on Sephardi and Oriental Jewish Heritage, 1992.

———. "Latin and 'ladino' (in the Eleventh and Twelfth Centuries)." In *Early Ibero-Romance: Twenty-One Studies on Language and Texts from the Iberian Peninsula between the Roman Empire and the Thirteenth Century,* by Roger Wright, 265–276. Newark, Del.: Juan de la Cuesta, 1994.

Zavala, Silvio. *La encomienda indiana.* 2d ed. Mexico City: Porrúa, 1973.

———. *La filosofía política en la conquista de América.* 2d ed. Mexico City: Fondo de Cultura Económica, 1972.

——. "Las Casas ante la doctrina de la servidumbre natural." *Revista de la Universidad de Buenos Aires,* 3d ser., 2 (1944): 45–58.

——. *Las instituciones jurídicas en la conquista de América.* 2d ed. Mexico City: Porrúa, 1971.

Zimmerman, Arthur Franklin. *Francisco de Toledo: Fifth Viceroy of Peru, 1569–1581.* Caldwell, Idaho: Caxton Printers, 1938.

Zorrilla, Juan C. "La posesión de Chiara por los indios Chachapoyas." *Wari* (Instituto Nacional de Cultura, Filial en Ayacucho), no. 1: 49–64.

INDEX

Made in the USA
Columbia, SC
25 January 2018